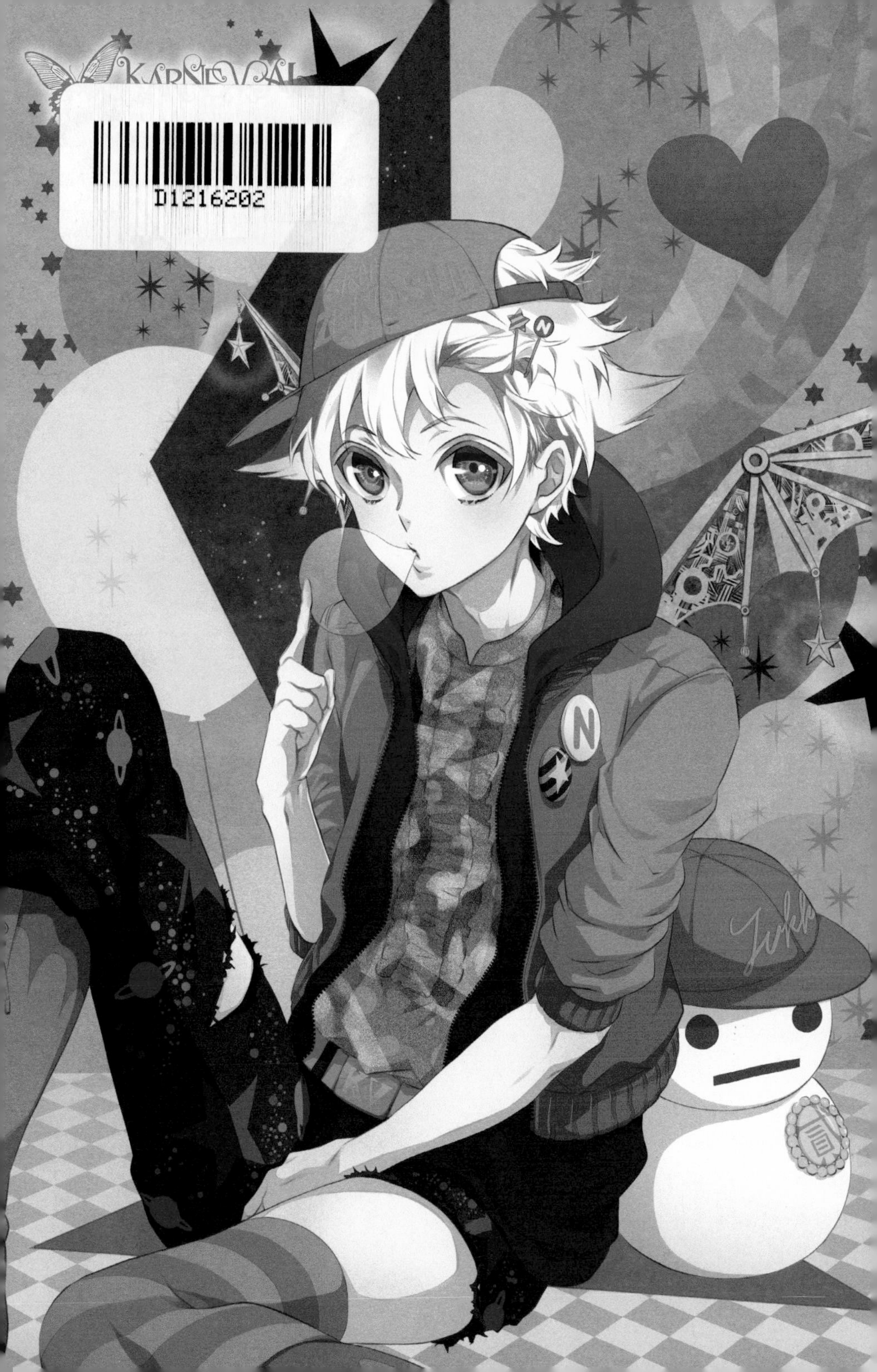
KARNEVAL

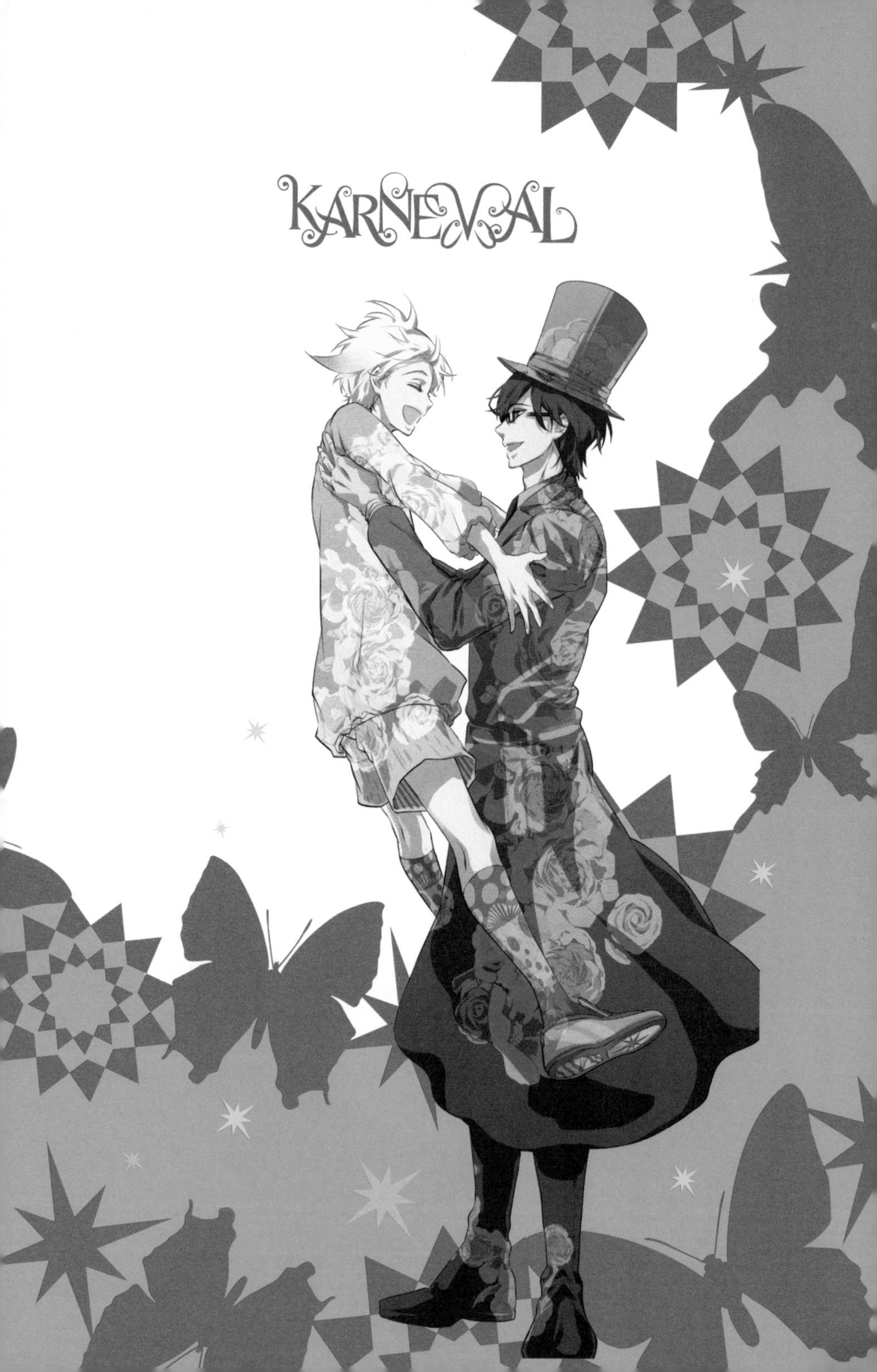
KARNEVAL

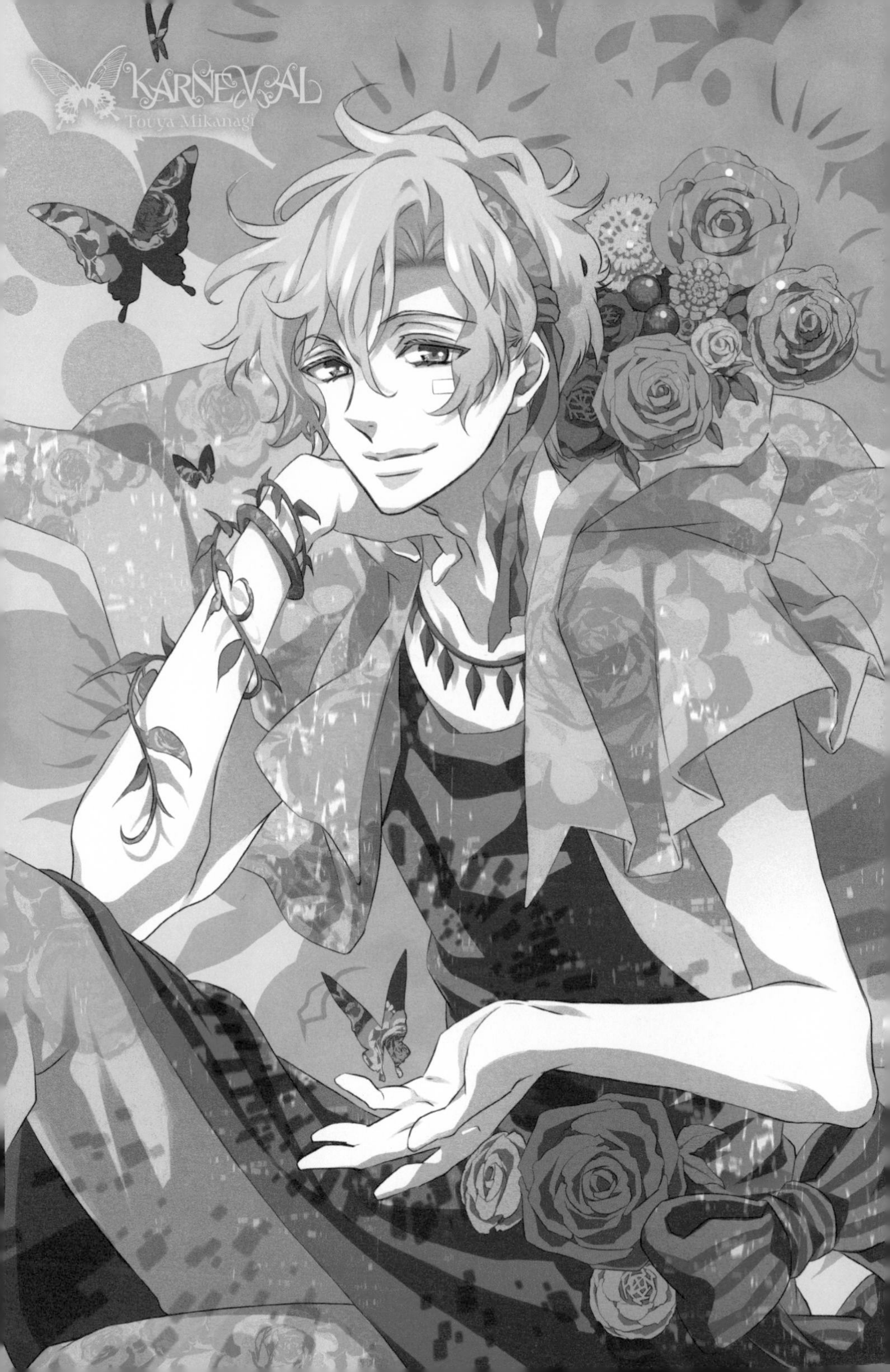
KARNEVAL
Touya Mikanagi

Score **117** * * * The Afternoon
of the Show

Score **118** * Links on Parade

Score **119** * Fated Encounter

Score **120** * * * * Premonition
of Collapse

Score **121** * * * * * Fluttering
Wings

Score **122** * * * Whereabouts

Score **123** * * * * Door of Beginnings

Score **124** * * Spread Your Promised Wings

Score **125** * * * * Unyielding Resolve

Score **126** * * * * * * * * Scars

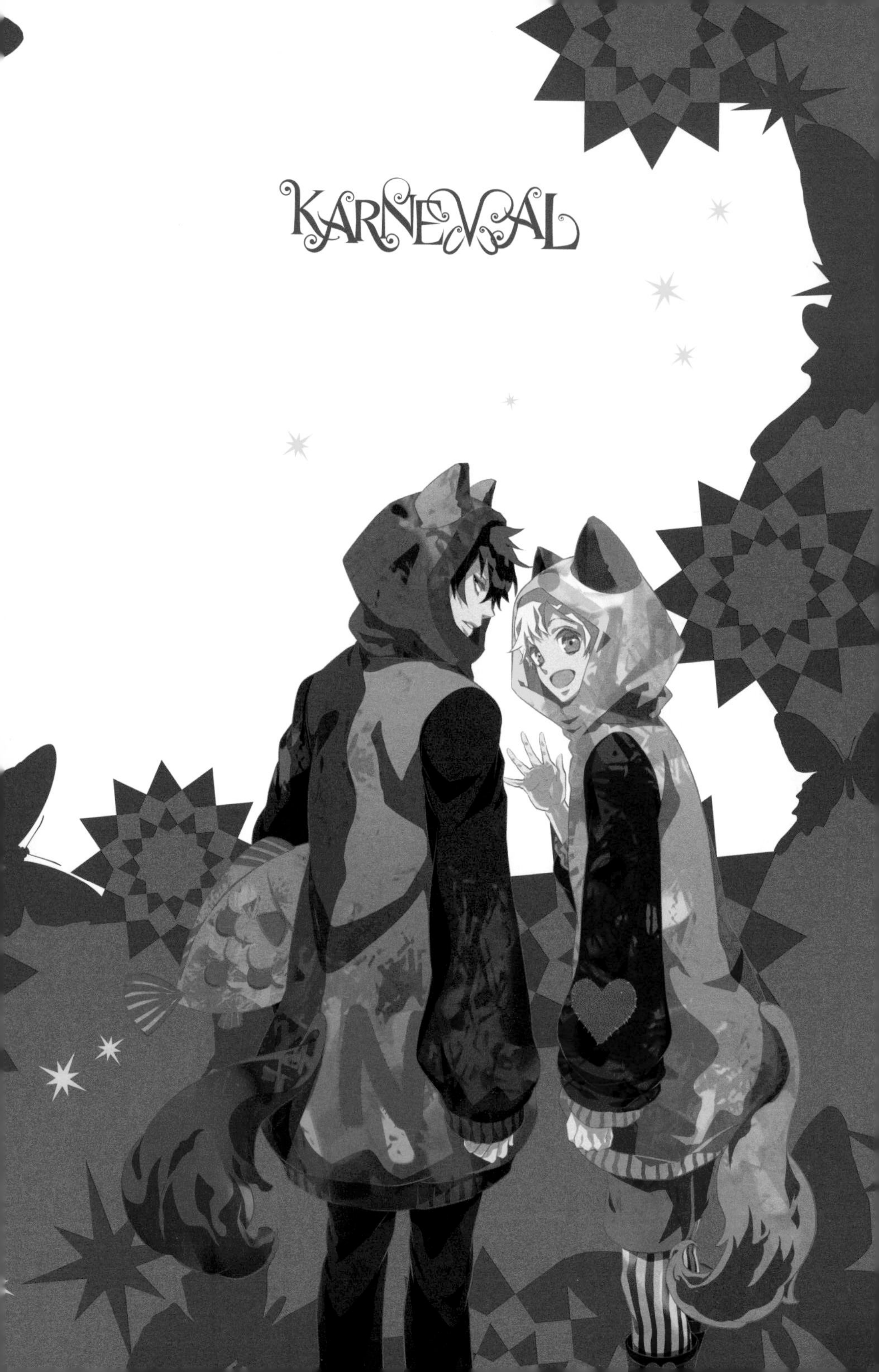
KARNEVAL

# KARNEVAL 11

Touya Mikanagi

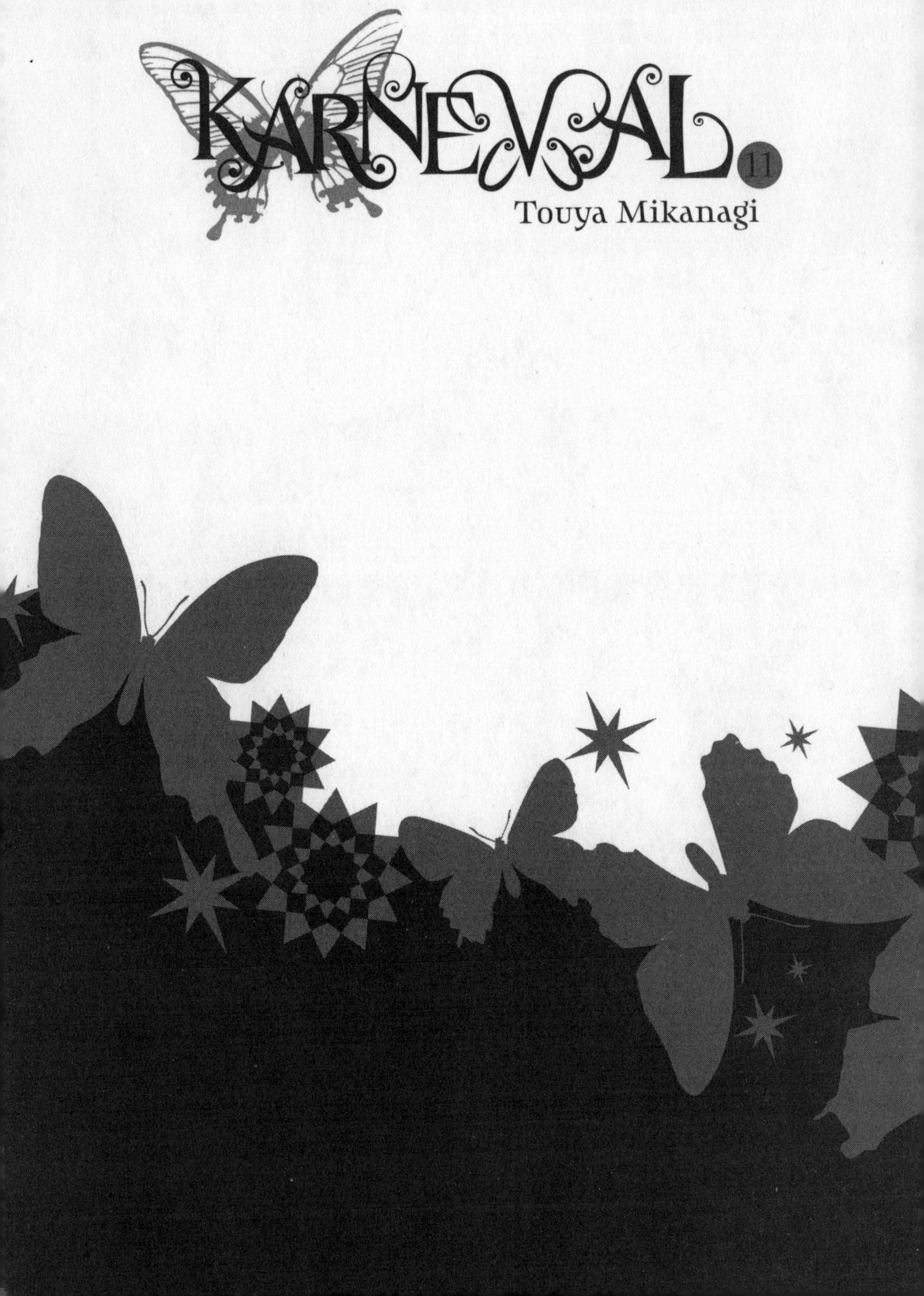

## STORY.

KAROKU'S MEMORIES HAVE RETURNED. ALONG WITH HIS PARENTS, HE ESCAPED FROM KAFKA'S HQ AND HID FROM THEIR PURSUERS IN THE RAINBOW FOREST. THERE KAROKU MET A NIJI AND GAVE HIM THE NAME NAI. THE FAMILY WAS SETTLING INTO THEIR NEW LIFE WHEN NISU, KAROKU'S FATHER, WAS MURDERED ON A SUPPLY RUN IN KARASUNA. UNABLE TO ACCEPT NISU'S DEATH, KAROKU'S MOTHER, BENIÉ, EXPLOITED NAI FOR THE SPECIAL PROPERTIES HIS CELLS POSSESS FOR THE SAKE OF CLONING NISU. HOWEVER, KAROKU REALIZED THE CLONE RETAINED NAI'S MEMORIES AND VOWED TO LOOK AFTER HIM. BUT SOON AFTER, KAFKA FOUND AND CAPTURED KAROKU, WHO DECIDED TO WILLINGLY RETURN TO THE ORGANIZATION IN ORDER TO PROTECT NAI. IN THE PRESENT DAY, CIRCUS'S 2ND SHIP CHARTS A COURSE FOR THE RESEARCH TOWER TO CONDUCT FURTHER TESTS ON NAI AND KAROKU. ON THE WAY, THEY RECEIVE WORD TO PREPARE TO HOST THE NEXT CIRCUS SHOW...

## CHARACTER'S OF KARNEVAL

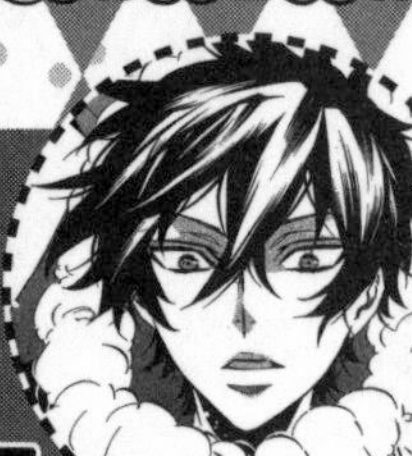

### GAREKI

HE MET NAI INSIDE AN EERIE MANSION THAT HE HAD INTENDED TO BURGLARIZE. HE IS CURRENTLY STUDYING AT THE RESEARCH TOWER IN ORDER TO BECOME CIRCUS'S FIRST COMBAT MEDIC.

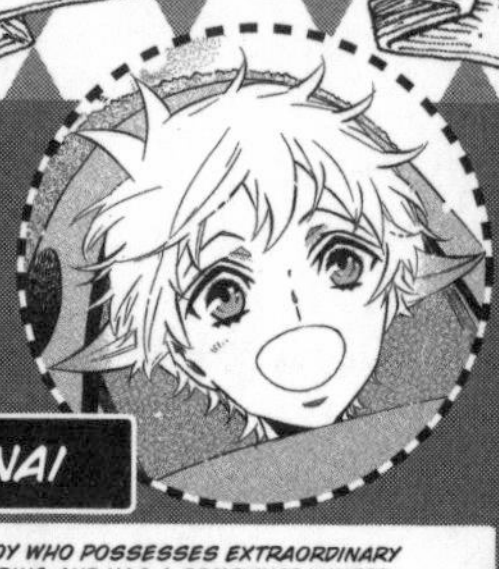

### NAI

A BOY WHO POSSESSES EXTRAORDINARY HEARING AND HAS A SOMEWHAT LIMITED UNDERSTANDING OF HOW THE WORLD WORKS. HE IS CURRENTLY LIVING ABOARD CIRCUS'S 2ND SHIP ALONGSIDE KAROKU.

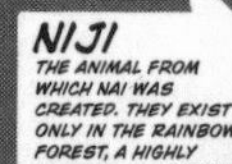

### NIJI

THE ANIMAL FROM WHICH NAI WAS CREATED. THEY EXIST ONLY IN THE RAINBOW FOREST, A HIGHLY UNUSUAL ECOSYSTEM THAT ALLOWED THE NIJI TO EVOLVE AS THEY DID.

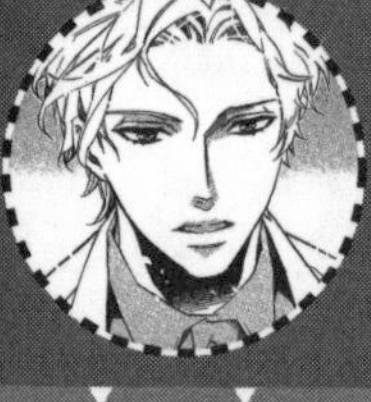

### AKARI

A BRILLIANT DOCTOR AND RESEARCHER IN THE NATIONAL DEFENSE'S RESEARCH TOWER. HE TERRIFIES YOGI, AND HE AND HIRATO FIGHT LIKE CATS AND DOGS.

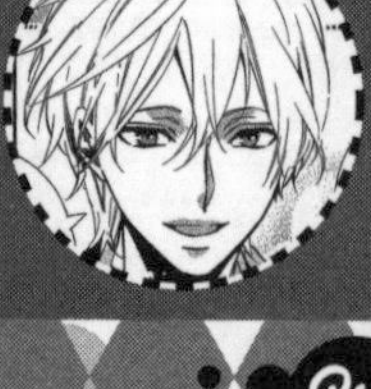

### KAROKU

THE PERSON BELIEVED TO HAVE CREATED NAI. HE HAS RECOVERED HIS MEMORIES AND IS NOW LIVING ABOARD CIRCUS'S 2ND SHIP.

### NATIONAL SUPREME DEFENSE FORCE "CIRCUS" 2ND SHIP

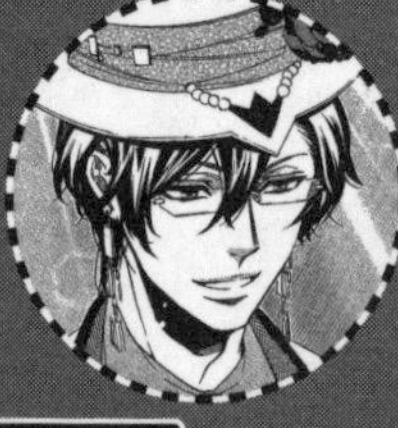

### HIRATO

CAPTAIN OF CIRCUS'S 2ND SHIP. NAI, WHO BROUGHT HIM A BRACELET BELONGING TO CIRCUS, AND GAREKI ARE CURRENTLY UNDER HIS PROTECTION. HE AND TSUKITATCHI, CAPTAIN OF CIRCUS'S 1ST SHIP, ARE FORMER CLASSMATES.

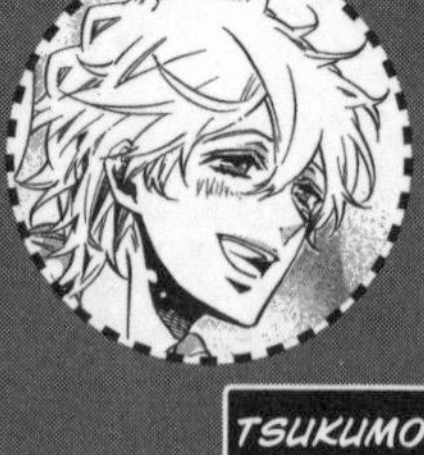

### YOGI

CIRCUS'S 2ND SHIP COMBAT SPECIALIST. HE HAS A CHEERFUL, FRIENDLY PERSONALITY. HE WAS BORN THE CROWN PRINCE OF RIMHAKKA, A KINGDOM THAT WAS DESTROYED IN A VARUGA ATTACK.

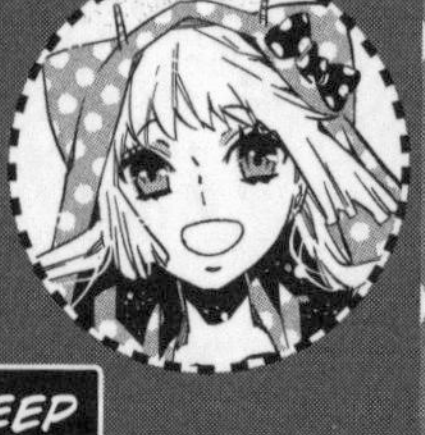

### TSUKUMO

CIRCUS'S 2ND SHIP COMBAT SPECIALIST. A BEAUTIFUL GIRL WITH A COOL, SERIOUS PERSONALITY. RECENTLY, SHE SEEMS TO HAVE TAKEN UP SEWING STUFFED TOYS AS A PASTIME. SHE HATES BUGS.

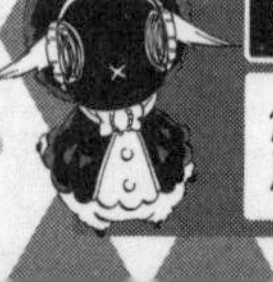

### SHEEP

A CIRCUS DEFENSE SYSTEM. DESPITE THEIR CUTE APPEARANCE, THE SHEEP HAVE SOME VERY POWERFUL CAPABILITIES.

## Q: WHAT IS CIRCUS?

**A:** THE EQUIVALENT OF THE REAL-WORLD POLICE. THEY CONDUCT THEIR LARGE-SCALE "OPERATIONS" UTILIZING COORDINATED, POWERFUL ATTACKS AND WITHOUT FOREWARNING TO ENSURE THEIR TARGETS WILL NOT ESCAPE ARREST!! AFTER SUCH AN OPERATION, CIRCUS PERFORMS A "SHOW" FOR THE PEOPLE OF THE CITY AS AN APOLOGY FOR THE FEAR AND INCONVENIENCE THEIR WORK MAY HAVE CAUSED. IN SHORT, "CIRCUS" IS A CHEERFUL(?) AGENCY THAT CARRIES OUT THEIR MISSION DAY AND NIGHT TO APPREHEND EVIL AND PROTECT THE PEACE OF THE LAND.

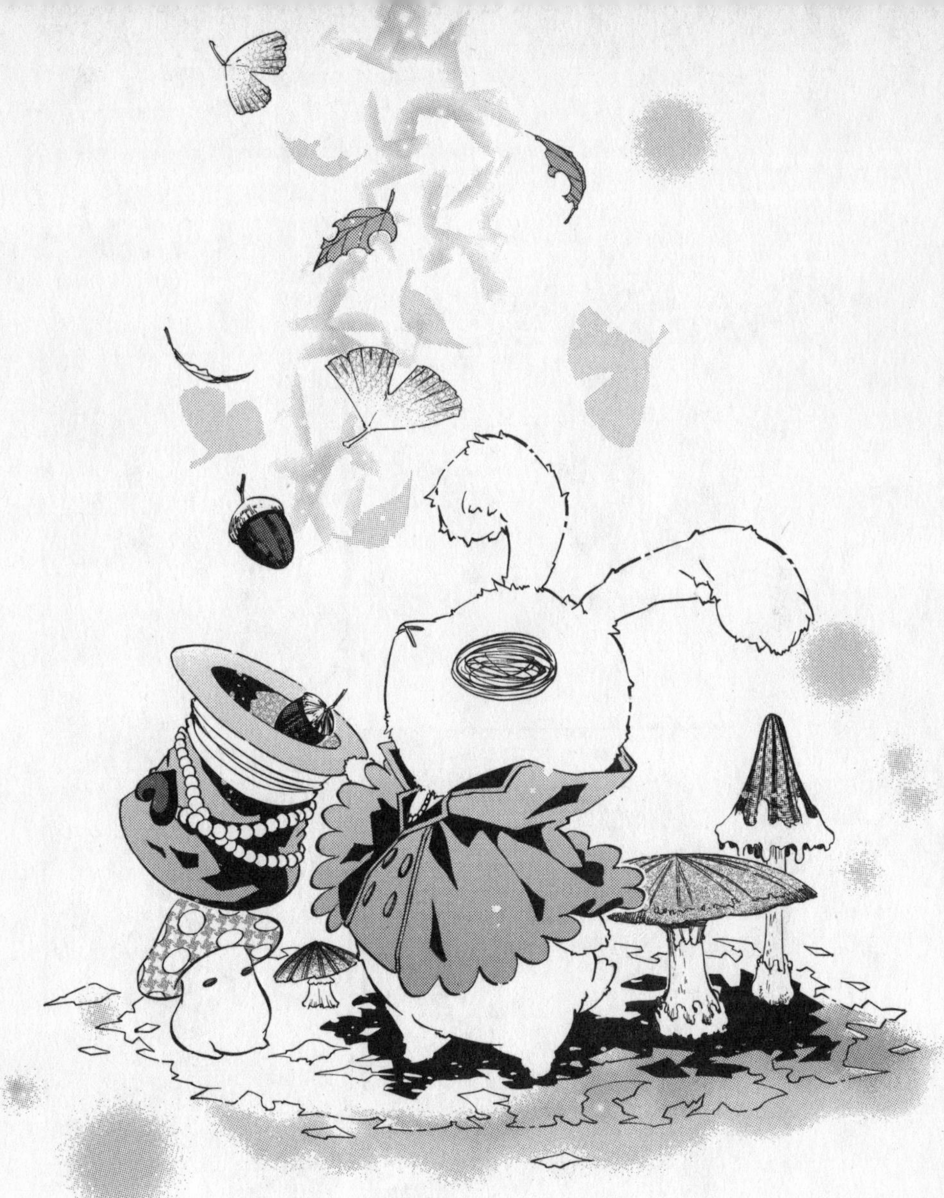

# Score 117:
# The Afternoon of the Show

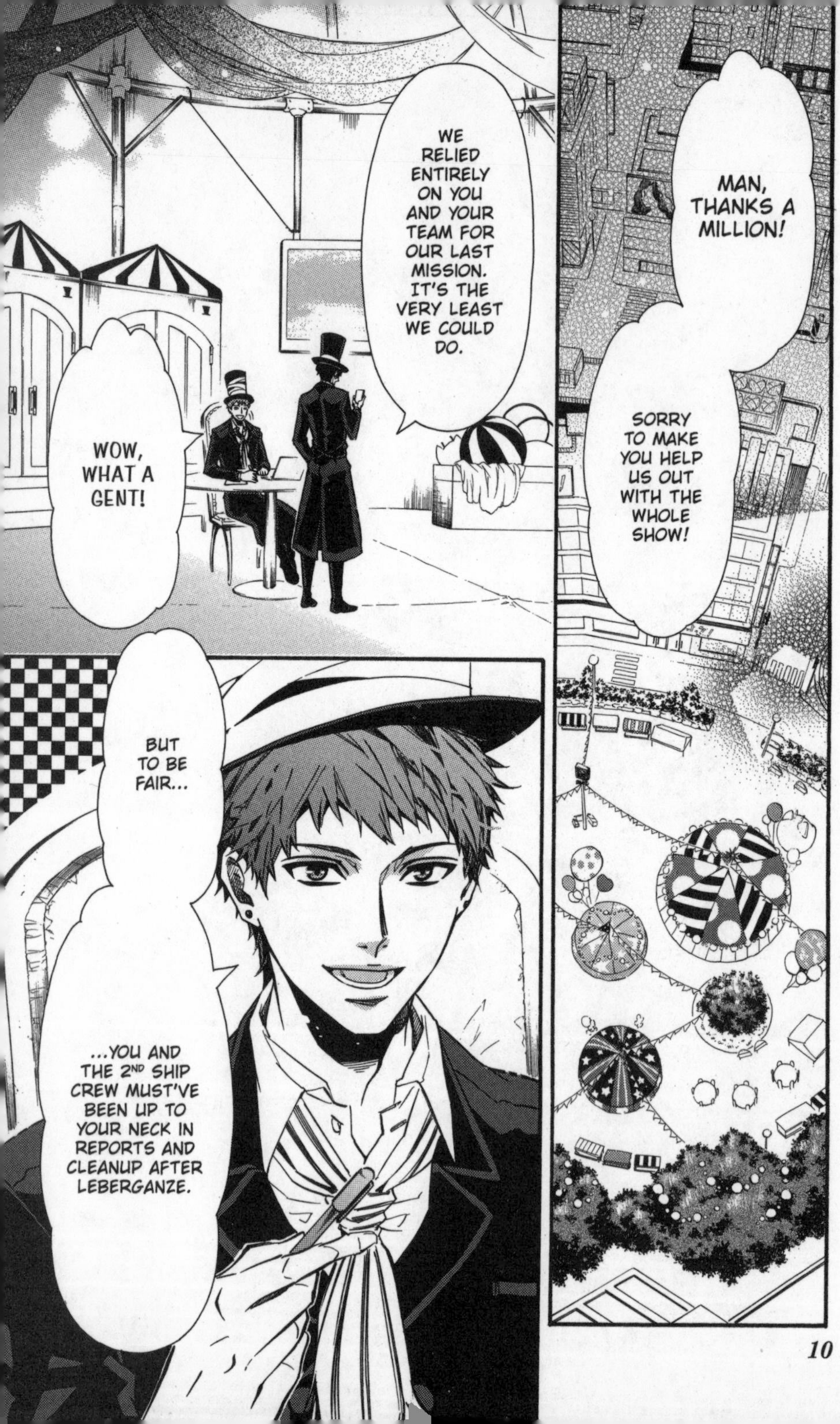
MAN, THANKS A MILLION!
SORRY TO MAKE YOU HELP US OUT WITH THE WHOLE SHOW!
WE RELIED ENTIRELY ON YOU AND YOUR TEAM FOR OUR LAST MISSION. IT'S THE VERY LEAST WE COULD DO.
WOW, WHAT A GENT!
BUT TO BE FAIR...
...YOU AND THE 2ND SHIP CREW MUST'VE BEEN UP TO YOUR NECK IN REPORTS AND CLEANUP AFTER LEBERGANZE.

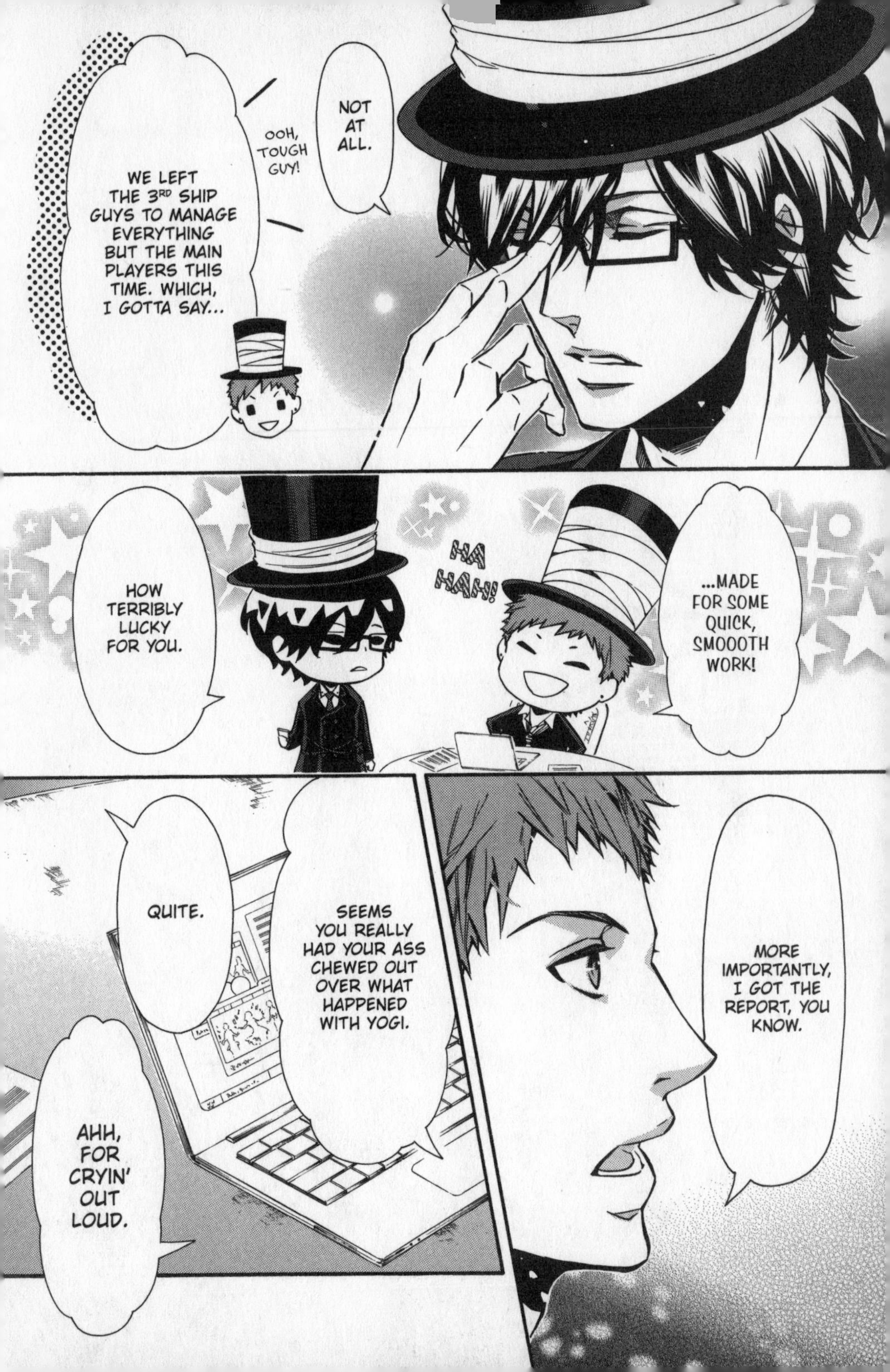
NOT AT ALL.
OOH, TOUGH GUY!
WE LEFT THE 3RD SHIP GUYS TO MANAGE EVERYTHING BUT THE MAIN PLAYERS THIS TIME. WHICH, I GOTTA SAY...
...MADE FOR SOME QUICK, SMOOOTH WORK!
HA HAH!
HOW TERRIBLY LUCKY FOR YOU.
MORE IMPORTANTLY, I GOT THE REPORT, YOU KNOW.
SEEMS YOU REALLY HAD YOUR ASS CHEWED OUT OVER WHAT HAPPENED WITH YOGI.
QUITE.
AHH, FOR CRYIN' OUT LOUD.

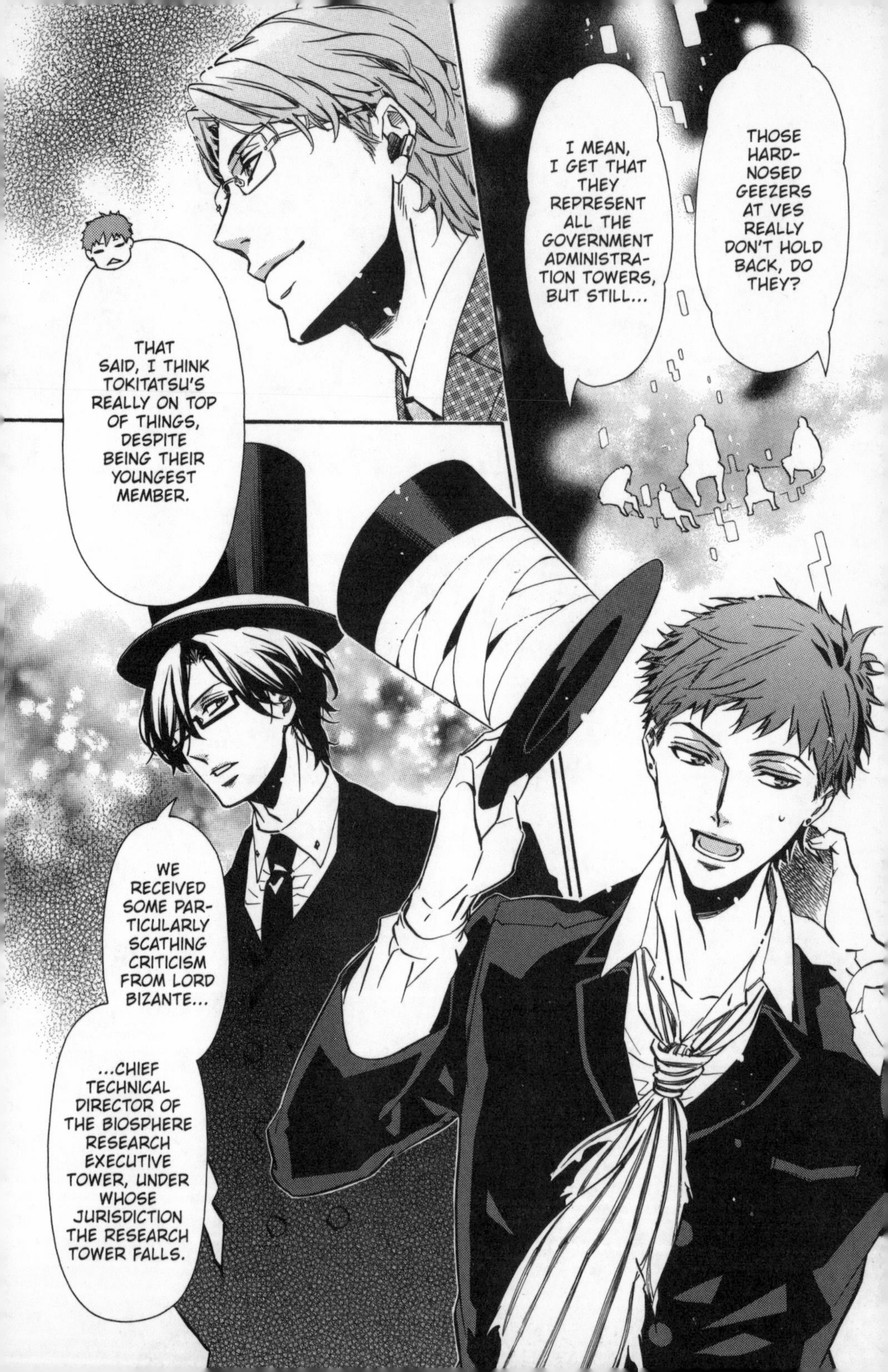
THOSE HARD-NOSED GEEZERS AT VES REALLY DON'T HOLD BACK, DO THEY?
I MEAN, I GET THAT THEY REPRESENT ALL THE GOVERNMENT ADMINISTRATION TOWERS, BUT STILL...
THAT SAID, I THINK TOKITATSU'S REALLY ON TOP OF THINGS, DESPITE BEING THEIR YOUNGEST MEMBER.
WE RECEIVED SOME PARTICULARLY SCATHING CRITICISM FROM LORD BIZANTE...
...CHIEF TECHNICAL DIRECTOR OF THE BIOSPHERE RESEARCH EXECUTIVE TOWER, UNDER WHOSE JURISDICTION THE RESEARCH TOWER FALLS.

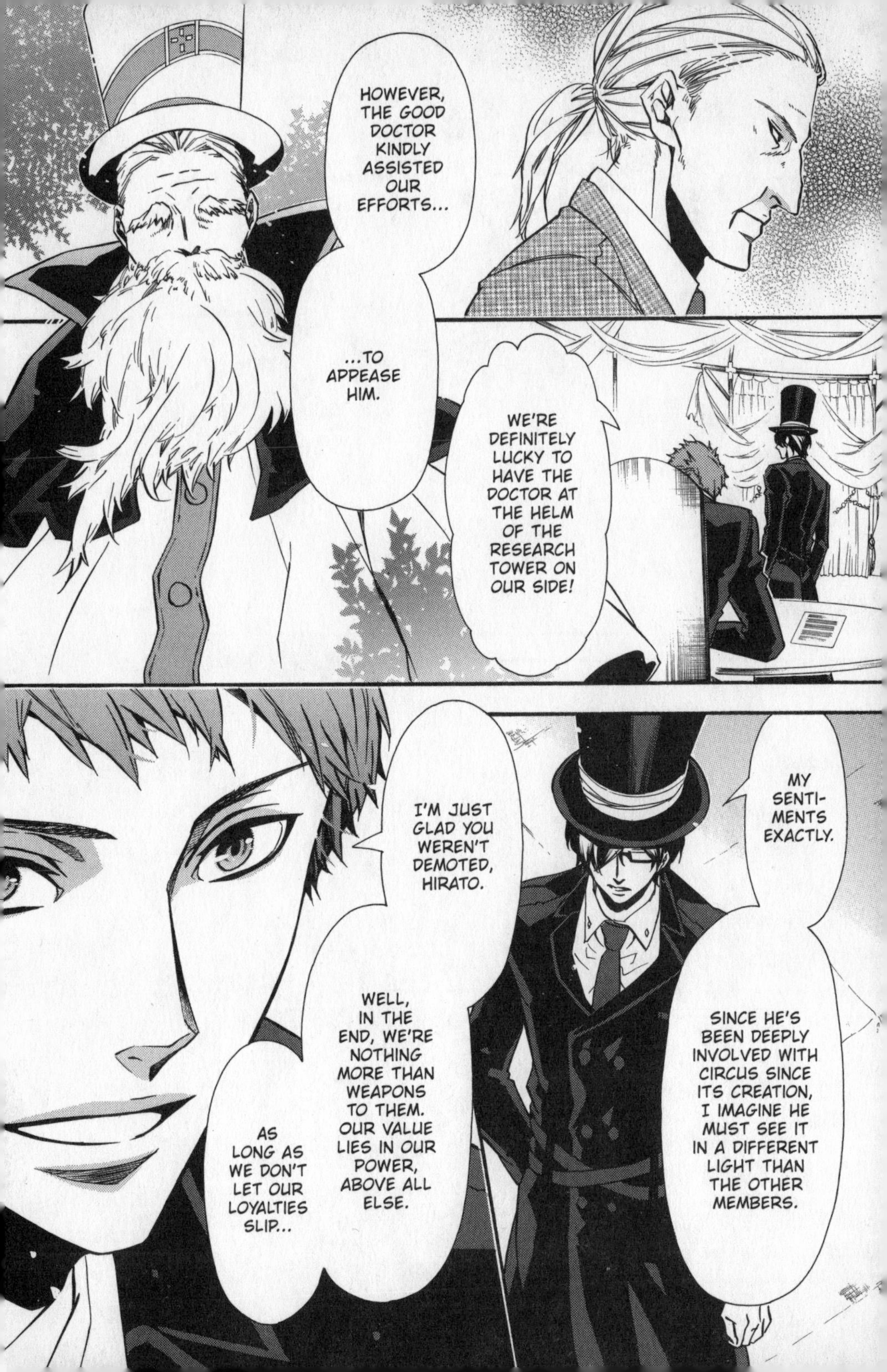
HOWEVER, THE GOOD DOCTOR KINDLY ASSISTED OUR EFFORTS...
...TO APPEASE HIM.
WE'RE DEFINITELY LUCKY TO HAVE THE DOCTOR AT THE HELM OF THE RESEARCH TOWER ON OUR SIDE!
MY SENTI-MENTS EXACTLY.
SINCE HE'S BEEN DEEPLY INVOLVED WITH CIRCUS SINCE ITS CREATION, I IMAGINE HE MUST SEE IT IN A DIFFERENT LIGHT THAN THE OTHER MEMBERS.
I'M JUST GLAD YOU WEREN'T DEMOTED, HIRATO.
WELL, IN THE END, WE'RE NOTHING MORE THAN WEAPONS TO THEM. OUR VALUE LIES IN OUR POWER, ABOVE ALL ELSE.
AS LONG AS WE DON'T LET OUR LOYALTIES SLIP...

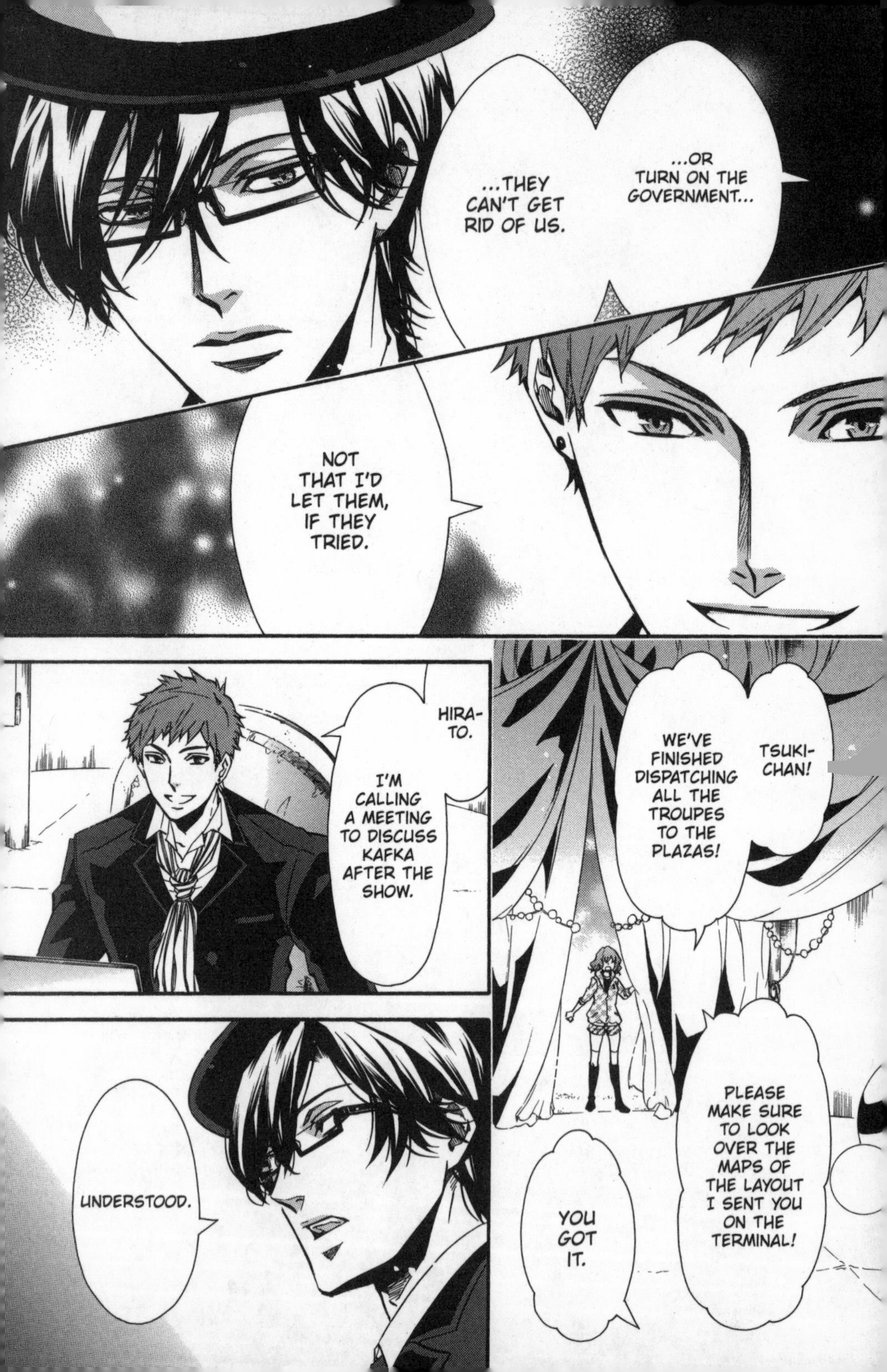
...OR TURN ON THE GOVERNMENT...
...THEY CAN'T GET RID OF US.
NOT THAT I'D LET THEM, IF THEY TRIED.
TSUKI-CHAN!
WE'VE FINISHED DISPATCHING ALL THE TROUPES TO THE PLAZAS!
PLEASE MAKE SURE TO LOOK OVER THE MAPS OF THE LAYOUT I SENT YOU ON THE TERMINAL!
YOU GOT IT.
HIRA-TO.
I'M CALLING A MEETING TO DISCUSS KAFKA AFTER THE SHOW.
UNDERSTOOD.

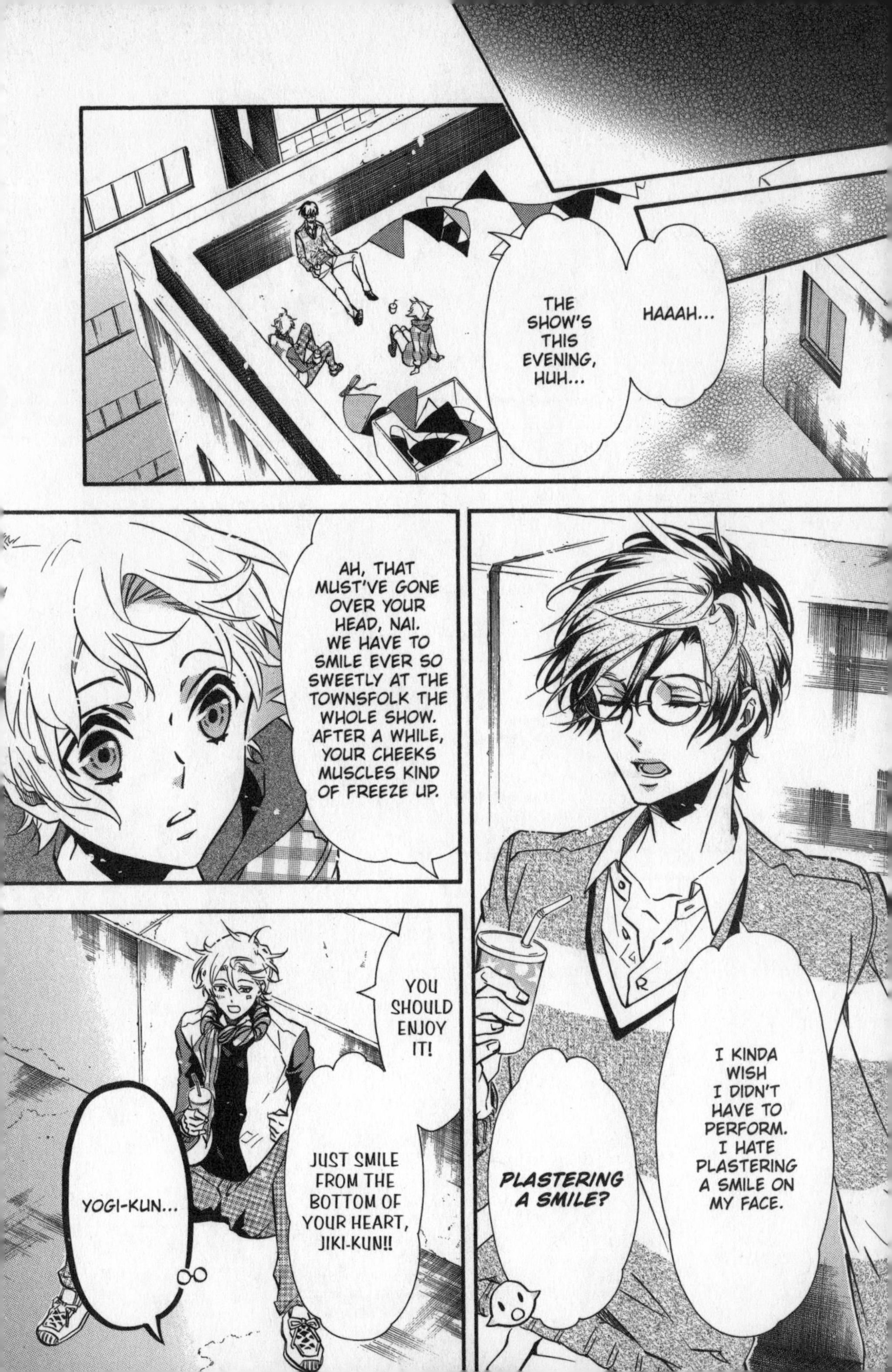
HAAAH...
THE SHOW'S THIS EVENING, HUH...
I KINDA WISH I DIDN'T HAVE TO PERFORM. I HATE PLASTERING A SMILE ON MY FACE.
PLASTERING A SMILE?
AH, THAT MUST'VE GONE OVER YOUR HEAD, NAI. WE HAVE TO SMILE EVER SO SWEETLY AT THE TOWNSFOLK THE WHOLE SHOW. AFTER A WHILE, YOUR CHEEKS MUSCLES KIND OF FREEZE UP.
YOU SHOULD ENJOY IT!
JUST SMILE FROM THE BOTTOM OF YOUR HEART, JIKI-KUN!!
YOGI-KUN...

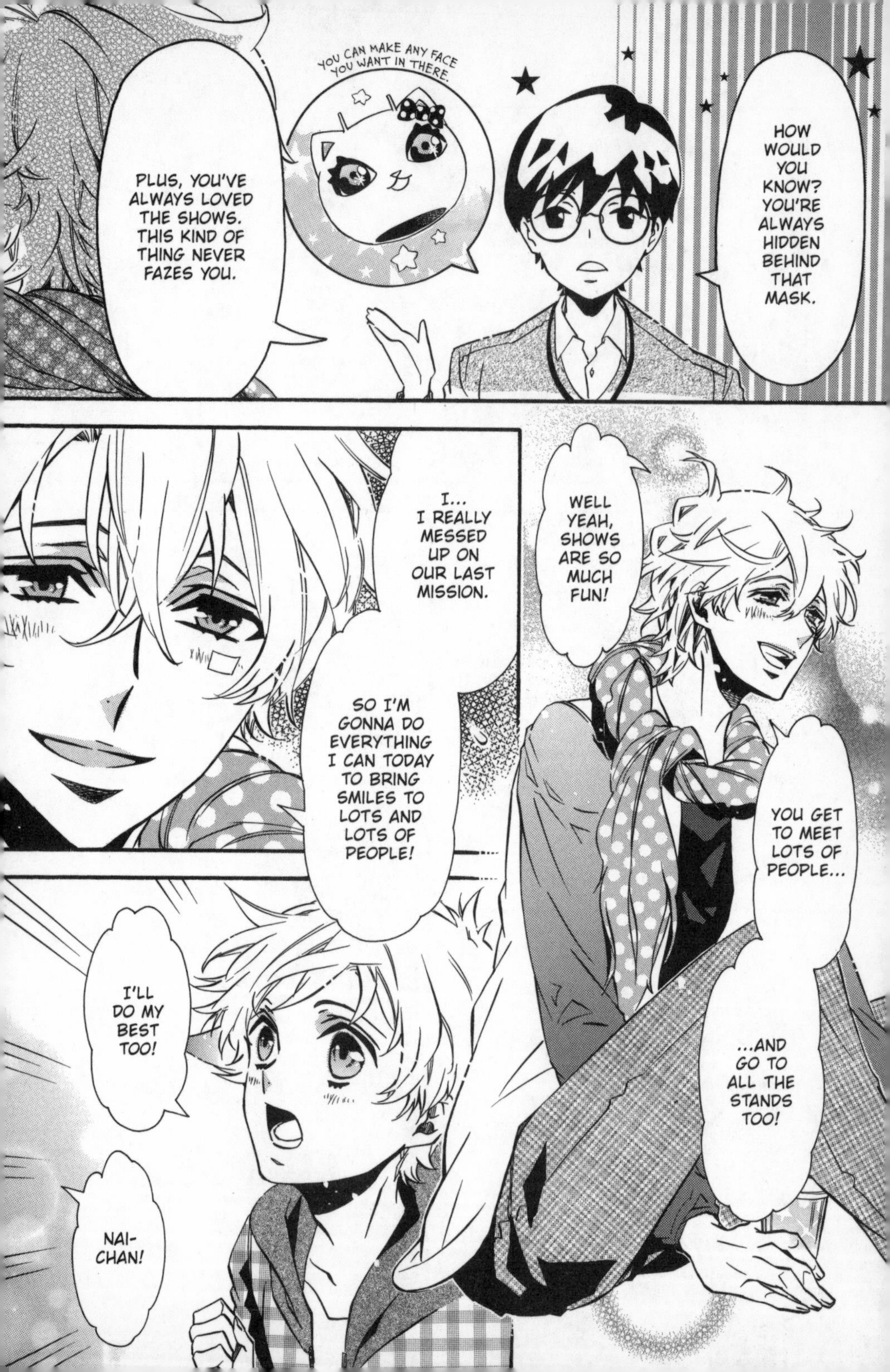
HOW WOULD YOU KNOW? YOU'RE ALWAYS HIDDEN BEHIND THAT MASK.
YOU CAN MAKE ANY FACE YOU WANT IN THERE.
PLUS, YOU'VE ALWAYS LOVED THE SHOWS. THIS KIND OF THING NEVER FAZES YOU.
WELL YEAH, SHOWS ARE SO MUCH FUN!
YOU GET TO MEET LOTS OF PEOPLE...
...AND GO TO ALL THE STANDS TOO!
I... I REALLY MESSED UP ON OUR LAST MISSION.
SO I'M GONNA DO EVERYTHING I CAN TODAY TO BRING SMILES TO LOTS AND LOTS OF PEOPLE!
I'LL DO MY BEST TOO!
NAI-CHAN!

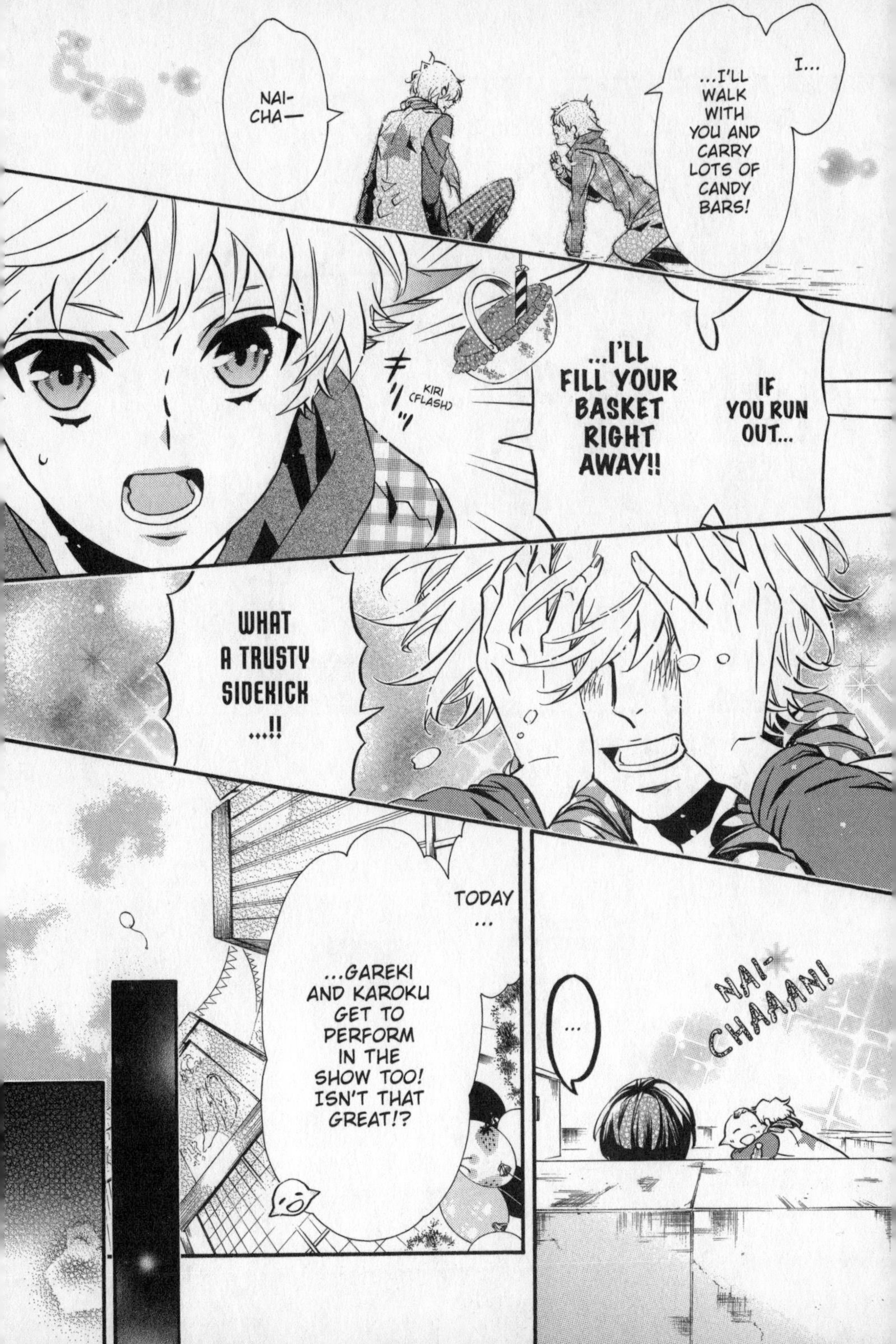
I...
...I'LL WALK WITH YOU AND CARRY LOTS OF CANDY BARS!
NAI-CHA—
IF YOU RUN OUT...
...I'LL FILL YOUR BASKET RIGHT AWAY!!
KIRI (FLASH)
WHAT A TRUSTY SIDEKICK ...!!
NAI-CHAAAN!
...
TODAY...
...GAREKI AND KAROKU GET TO PERFORM IN THE SHOW TOO! ISN'T THAT GREAT!?

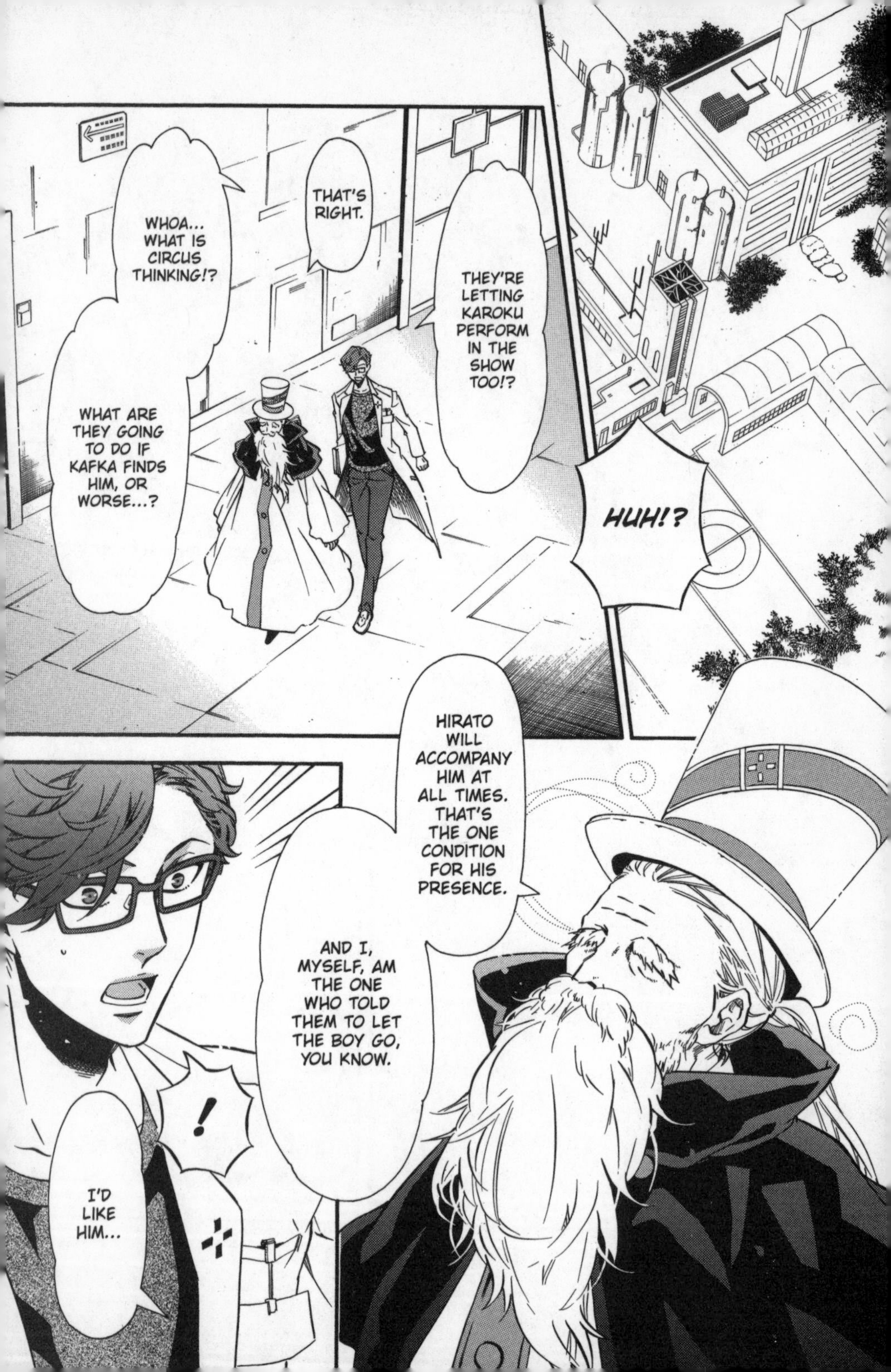
HUH!?
THEY'RE LETTING KAROKU PERFORM IN THE SHOW TOO!?
THAT'S RIGHT.
WHOA... WHAT IS CIRCUS THINKING!?
WHAT ARE THEY GOING TO DO IF KAFKA FINDS HIM, OR WORSE...?
HIRATO WILL ACCOMPANY HIM AT ALL TIMES. THAT'S THE ONE CONDITION FOR HIS PRESENCE.
AND I, MYSELF, AM THE ONE WHO TOLD THEM TO LET THE BOY GO, YOU KNOW.
!
I'D LIKE HIM...

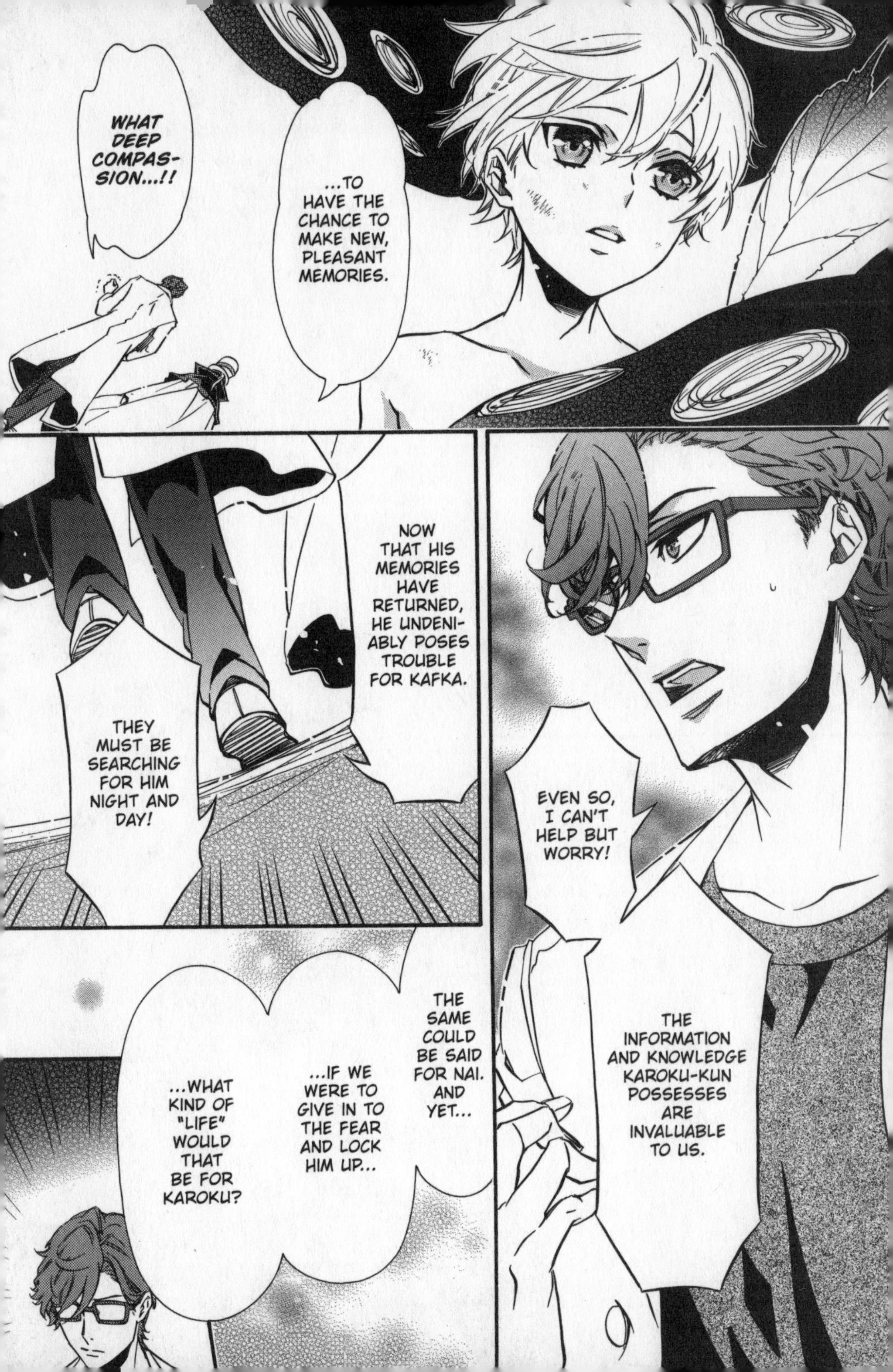
...TO HAVE THE CHANCE TO MAKE NEW, PLEASANT MEMORIES.
WHAT DEEP COMPASSION...!!
EVEN SO, I CAN'T HELP BUT WORRY!
THE INFORMATION AND KNOWLEDGE KAROKU-KUN POSSESSES ARE INVALUABLE TO US.
NOW THAT HIS MEMORIES HAVE RETURNED, HE UNDENIABLY POSES TROUBLE FOR KAFKA.
THEY MUST BE SEARCHING FOR HIM NIGHT AND DAY!
THE SAME COULD BE SAID FOR NAI. AND YET...
...IF WE WERE TO GIVE IN TO THE FEAR AND LOCK HIM UP...
...WHAT KIND OF "LIFE" WOULD THAT BE FOR KAROKU?

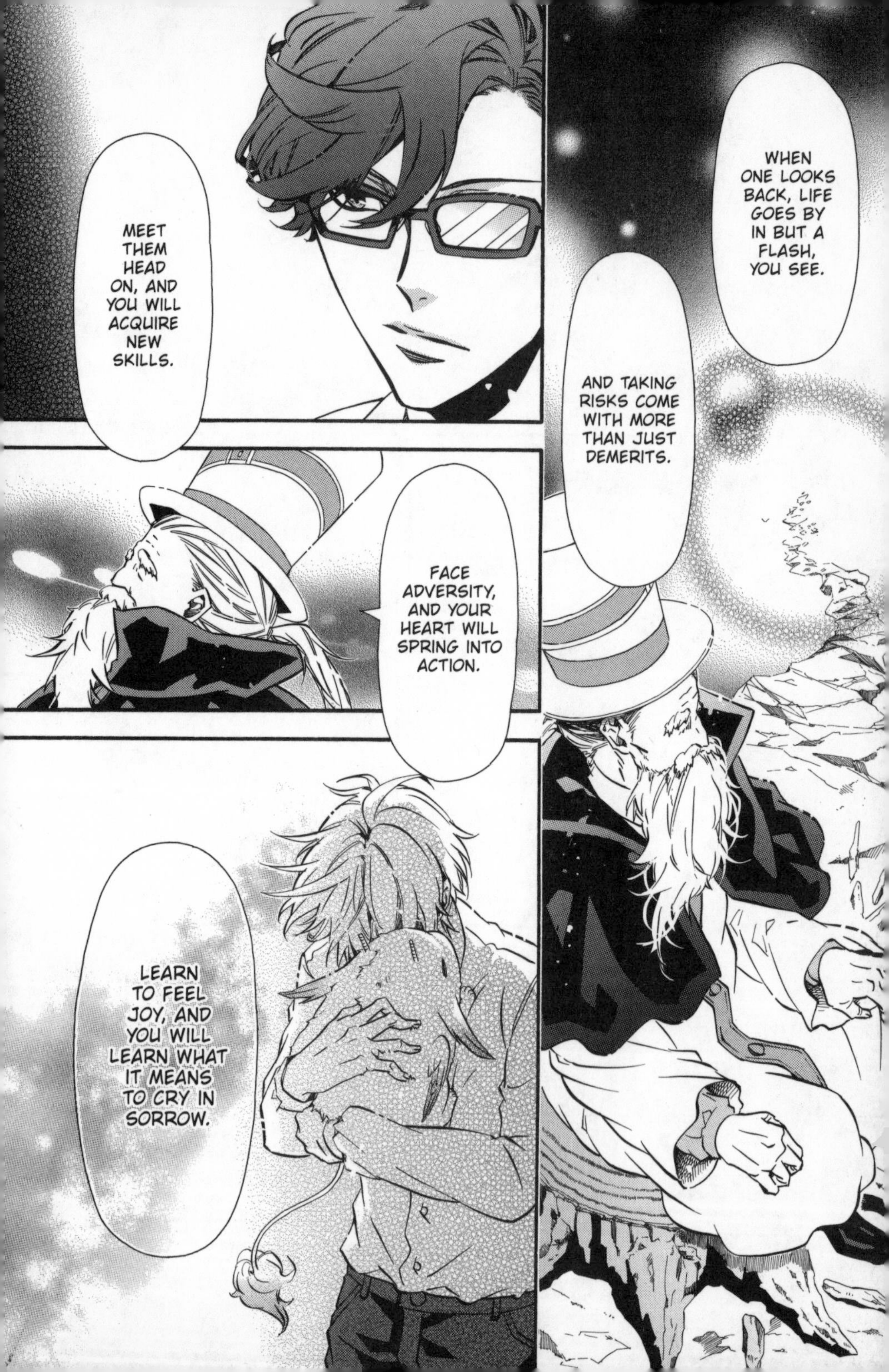
WHEN ONE LOOKS BACK, LIFE GOES BY IN BUT A FLASH, YOU SEE.
AND TAKING RISKS COME WITH MORE THAN JUST DEMERITS.
MEET THEM HEAD ON, AND YOU WILL ACQUIRE NEW SKILLS.
FACE ADVERSITY, AND YOUR HEART WILL SPRING INTO ACTION.
LEARN TO FEEL JOY, AND YOU WILL LEARN WHAT IT MEANS TO CRY IN SORROW.

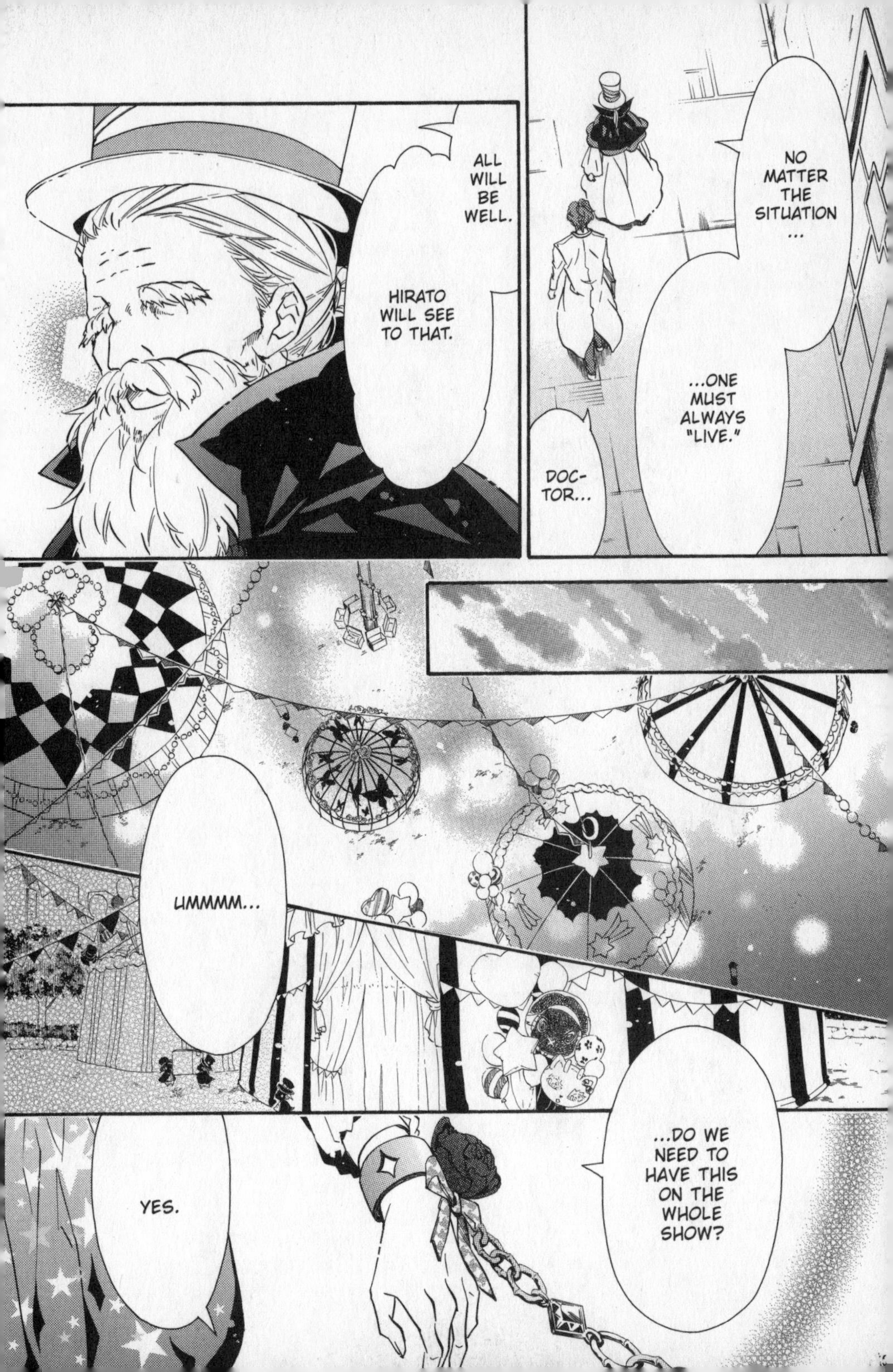
NO MATTER THE SITUATION...
...ONE MUST ALWAYS "LIVE."
DOCTOR...
ALL WILL BE WELL.
HIRATO WILL SEE TO THAT.
UMMMM...
...DO WE NEED TO HAVE THIS ON THE WHOLE SHOW?
YES.

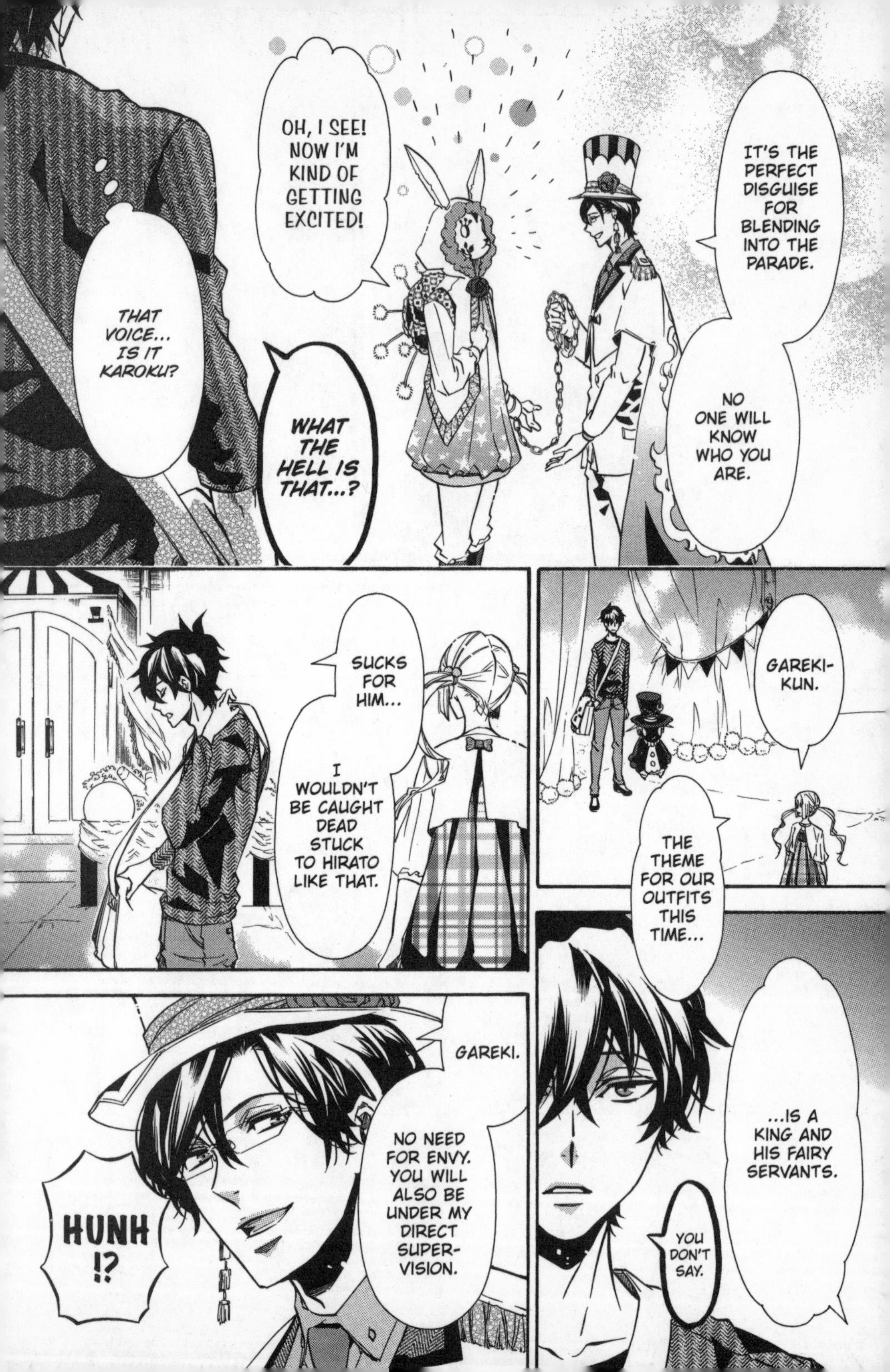
IT'S THE PERFECT DISGUISE FOR BLENDING INTO THE PARADE.
NO ONE WILL KNOW WHO YOU ARE.
OH, I SEE! NOW I'M KIND OF GETTING EXCITED!
WHAT THE HELL IS THAT...?
THAT VOICE... IS IT KAROKU?
GAREKI-KUN.
SUCKS FOR HIM...
I WOULDN'T BE CAUGHT DEAD STUCK TO HIRATO LIKE THAT.
THE THEME FOR OUR OUTFITS THIS TIME...
...IS A KING AND HIS FAIRY SERVANTS.
YOU DON'T SAY.
GAREKI.
NO NEED FOR ENVY. YOU WILL ALSO BE UNDER MY DIRECT SUPER-VISION.
HUNH!?

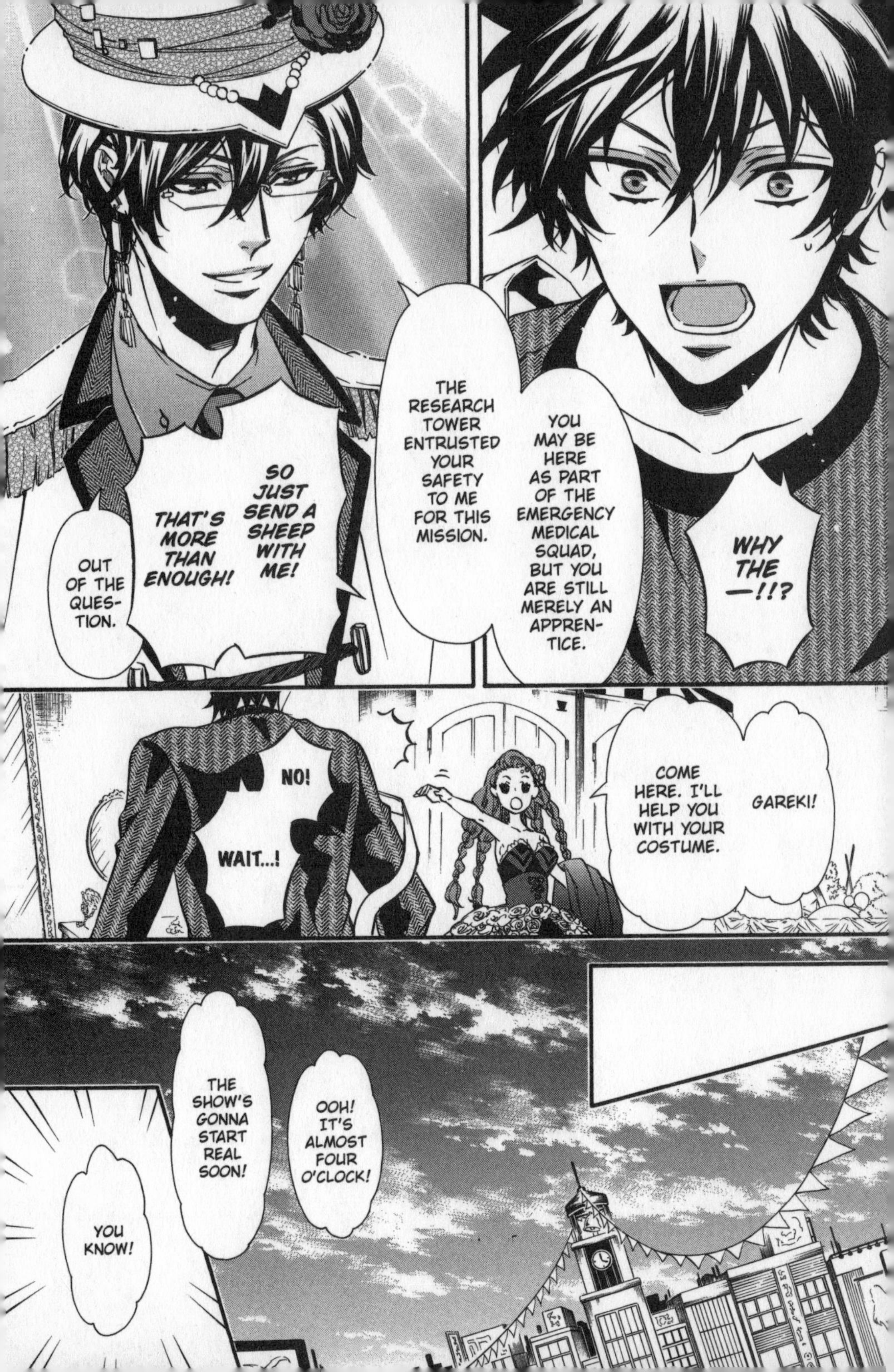
WHY THE—!!?
YOU MAY BE HERE AS PART OF THE EMERGENCY MEDICAL SQUAD, BUT YOU ARE STILL MERELY AN APPRENTICE.
THE RESEARCH TOWER ENTRUSTED YOUR SAFETY TO ME FOR THIS MISSION.
SO JUST SEND A SHEEP WITH ME!
THAT'S MORE THAN ENOUGH!
OUT OF THE QUES-TION.
GAREKI!
COME HERE. I'LL HELP YOU WITH YOUR COSTUME.
NO!
WAIT...!
OOH! IT'S ALMOST FOUR O'CLOCK!
THE SHOW'S GONNA START REAL SOON!
YOU KNOW!

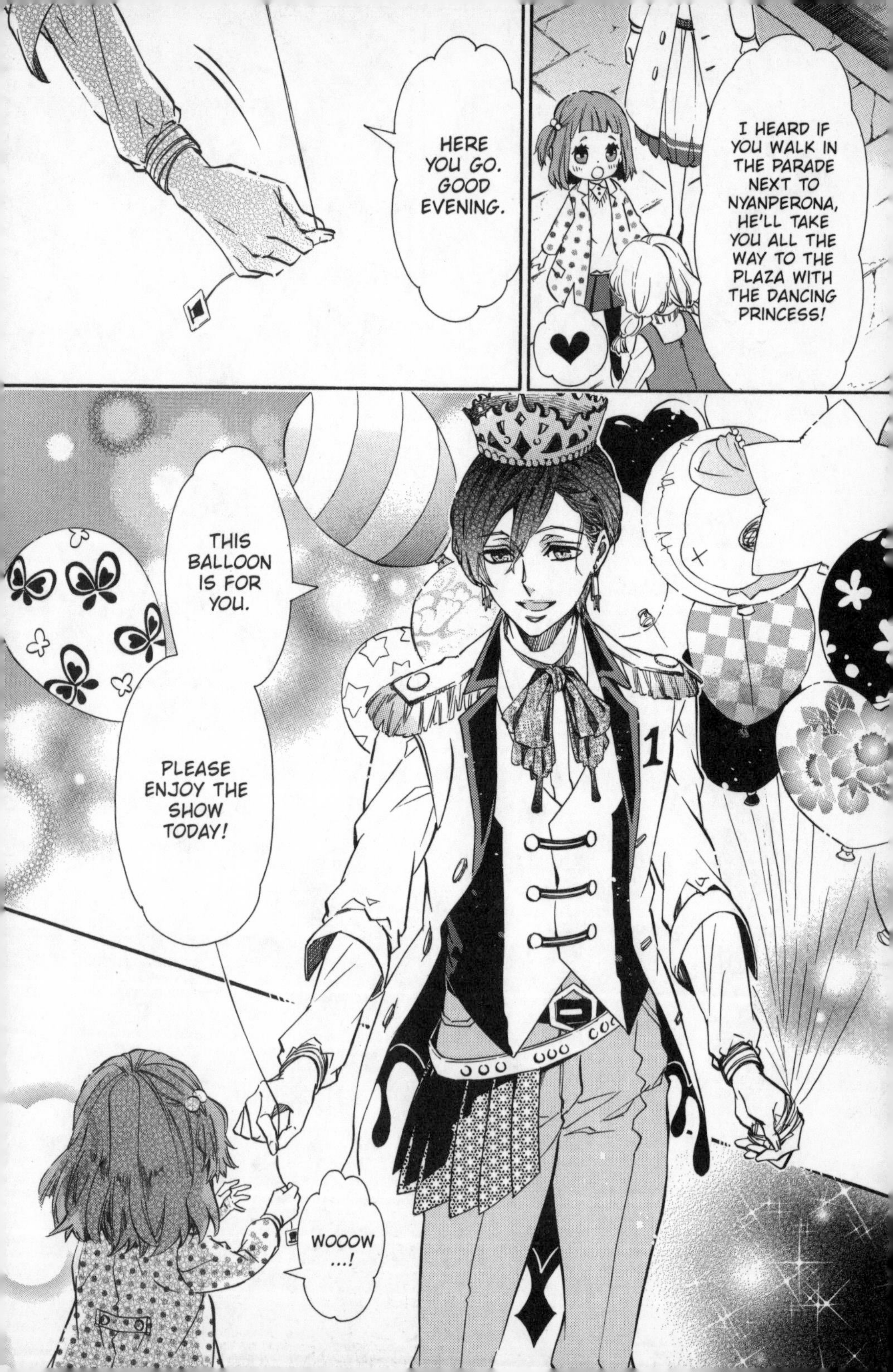
I HEARD IF YOU WALK IN THE PARADE NEXT TO NYANPERONA, HE'LL TAKE YOU ALL THE WAY TO THE PLAZA WITH THE DANCING PRINCESS!
♥
HERE YOU GO. GOOD EVENING.
THIS BALLOON IS FOR YOU.
PLEASE ENJOY THE SHOW TODAY!
WOOOW ...!

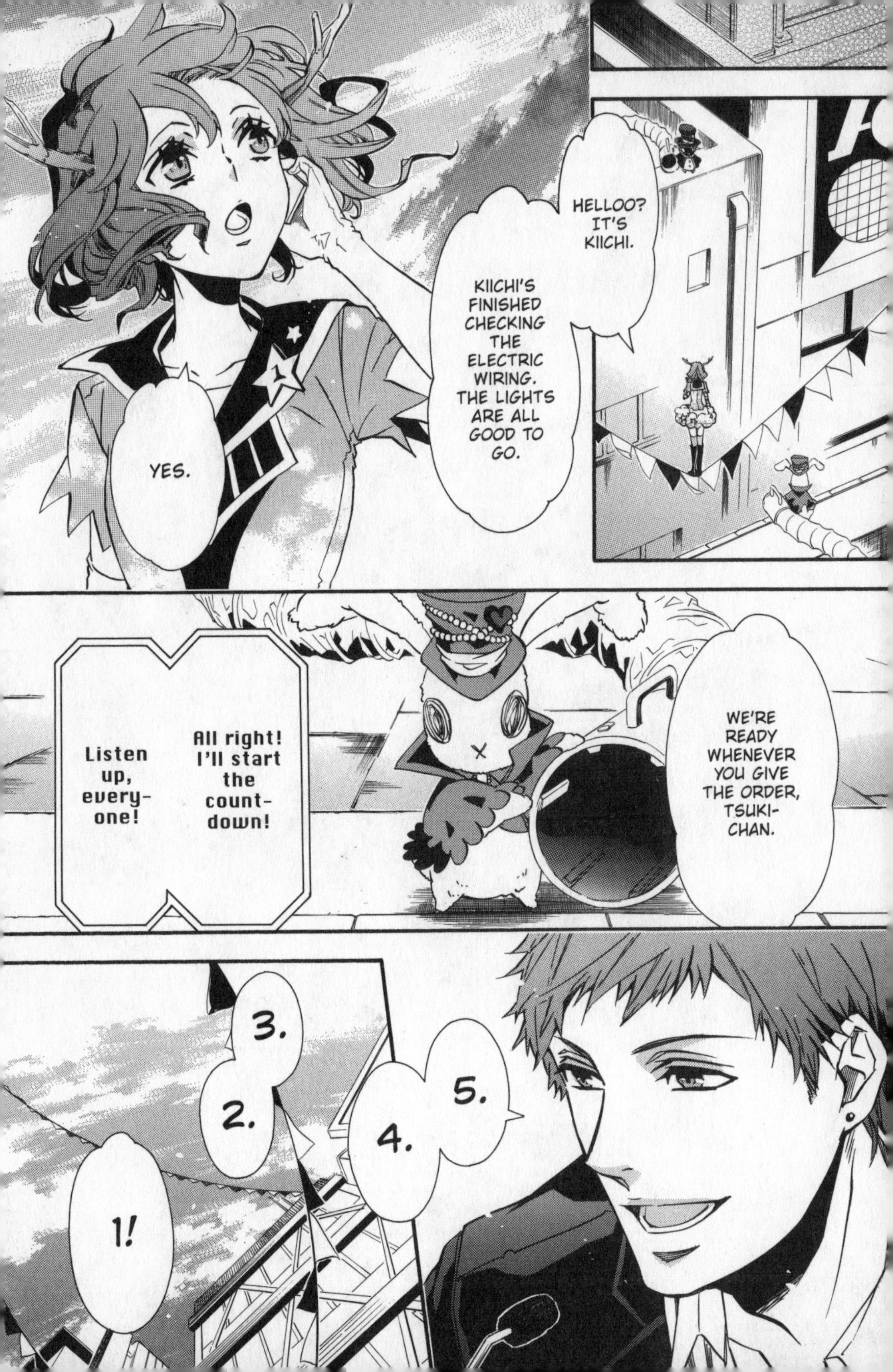
HELLOO? IT'S KIICHI.
KIICHI'S FINISHED CHECKING THE ELECTRIC WIRING. THE LIGHTS ARE ALL GOOD TO GO.
YES.
WE'RE READY WHENEVER YOU GIVE THE ORDER, TSUKI-CHAN.
All right! I'll start the count-down!
Listen up, every-one!
5.
4.
3.
2.
1!

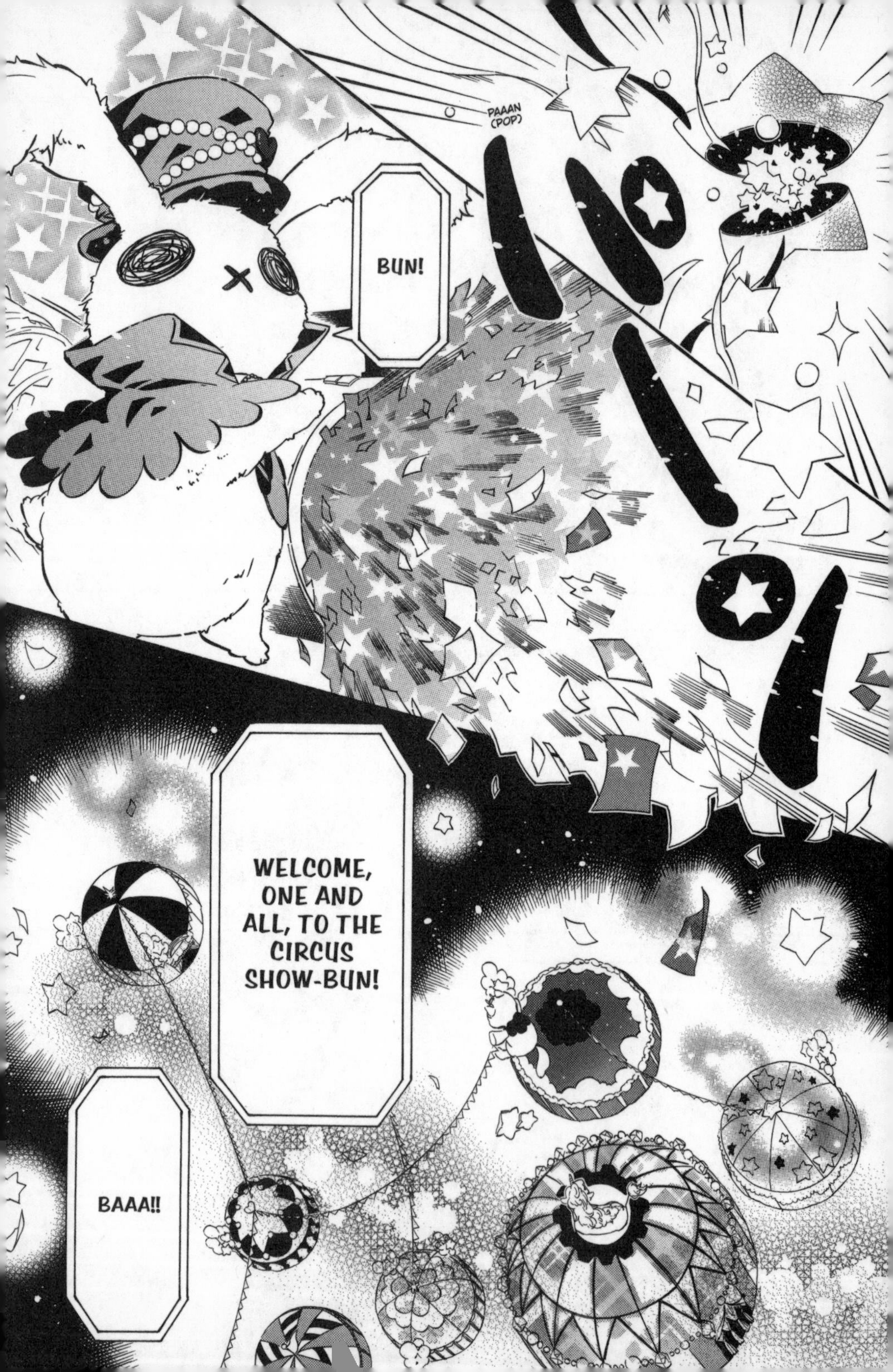
PAAAN
(POP)
BUN!
WELCOME, ONE AND ALL, TO THE CIRCUS SHOW-BUN!
BAAA!!

KARNEVAL

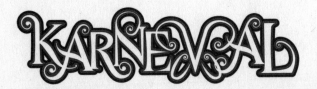

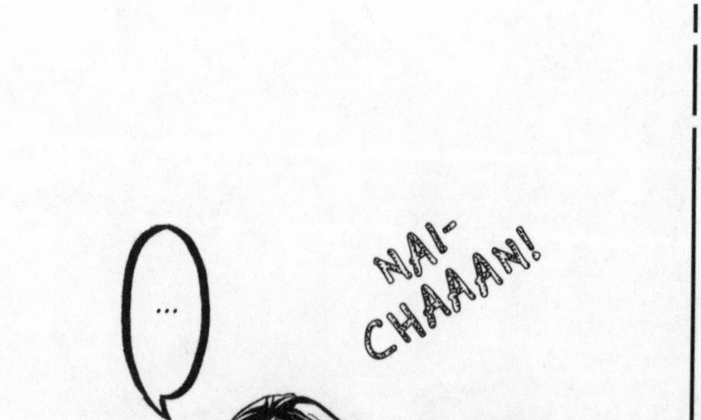
...
NAI-CHAAAN!

KARNEVAL

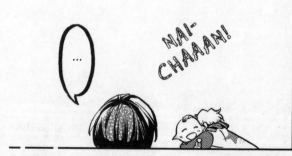

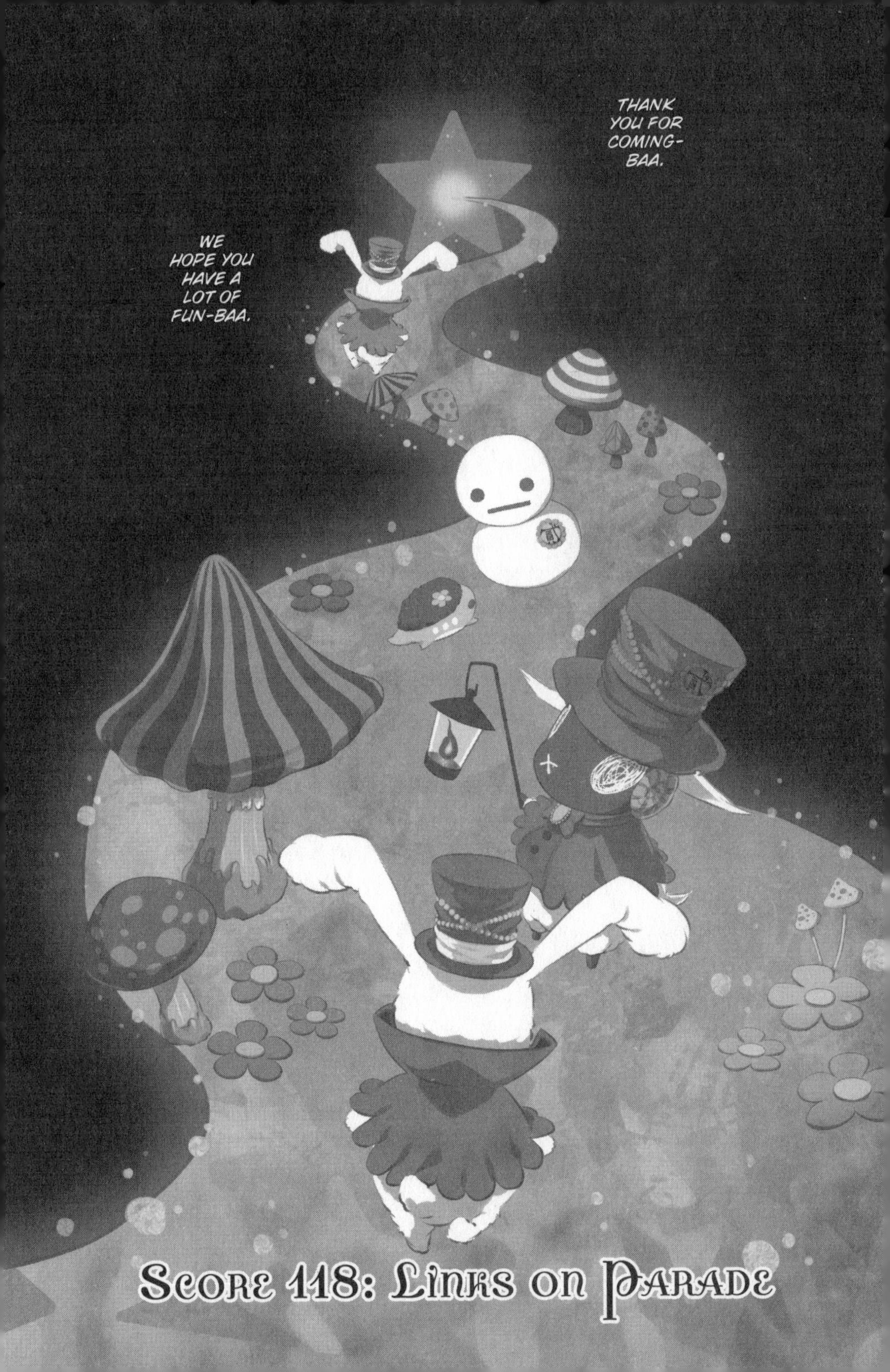
THANK YOU FOR COMING-BAA.
WE HOPE YOU HAVE A LOT OF FUN-BAA.
SCORE 118: LINKS ON PARADE

KARNEVAL

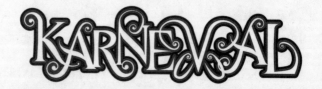

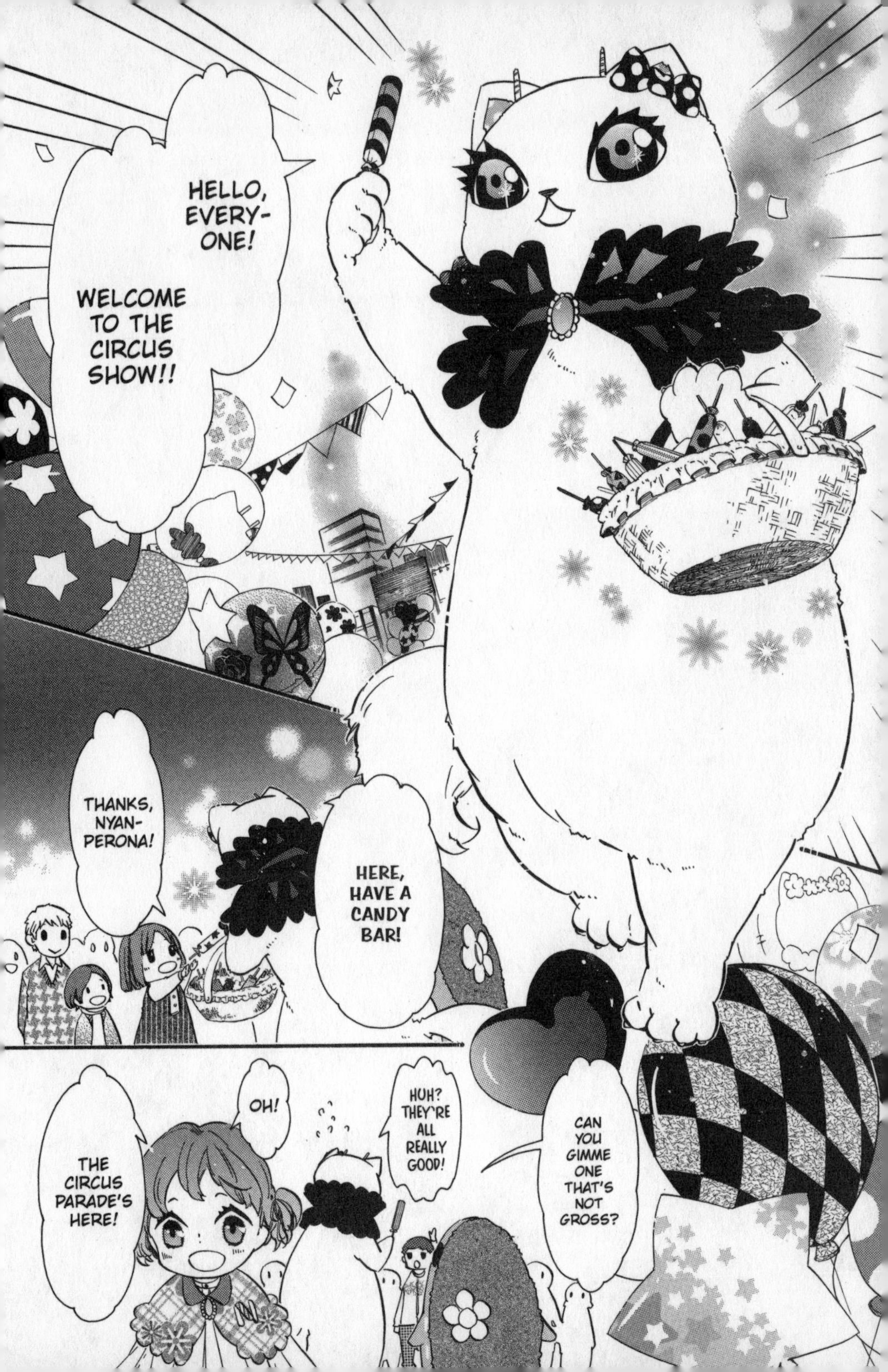
HELLO, EVERY-ONE!
WELCOME TO THE CIRCUS SHOW!!
HERE, HAVE A CANDY BAR!
THANKS, NYAN-PERONA!
CAN YOU GIMME ONE THAT'S NOT GROSS?
HUH? THEY'RE ALL REALLY GOOD!
OH!
THE CIRCUS PARADE'S HERE!

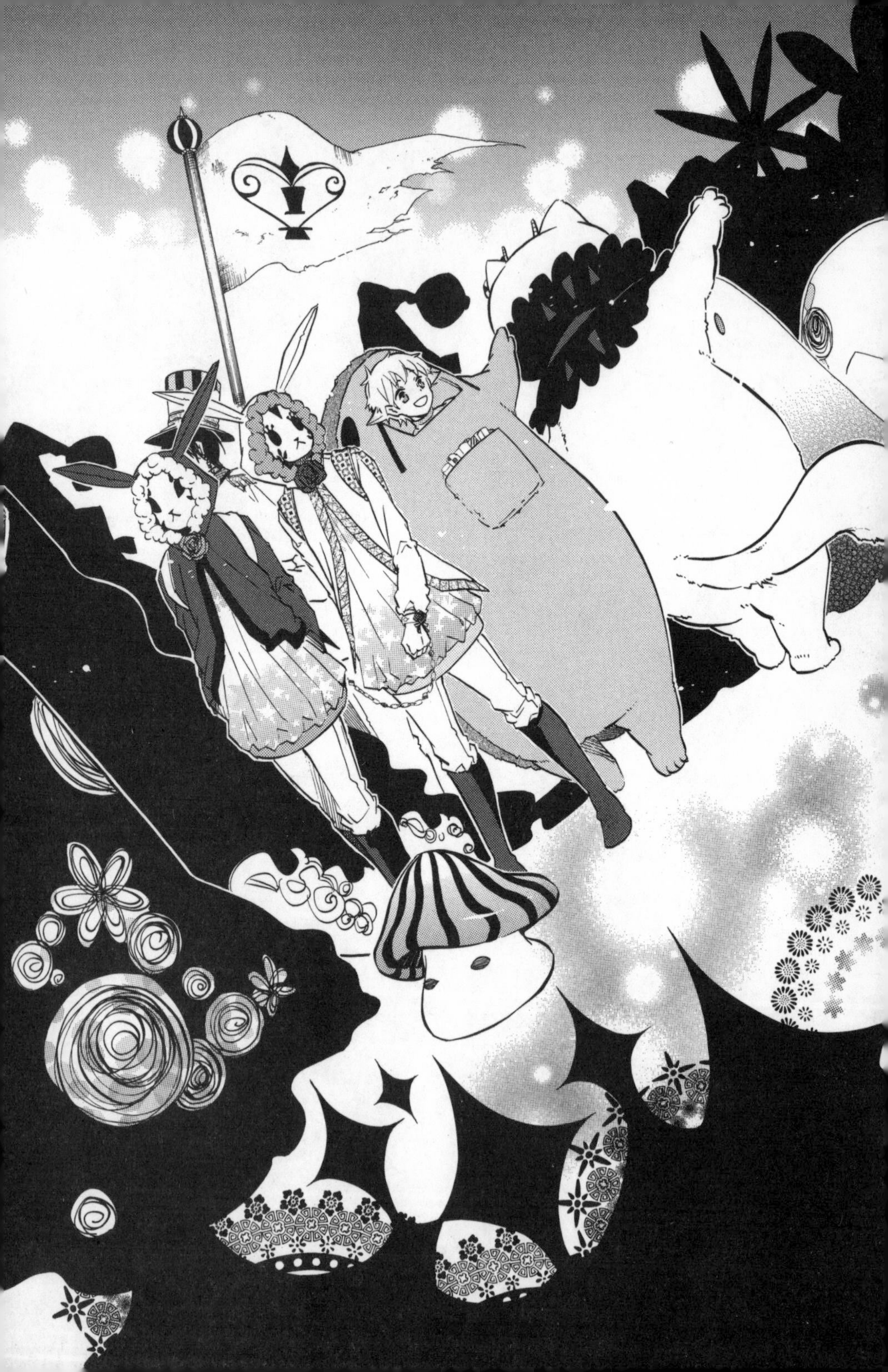

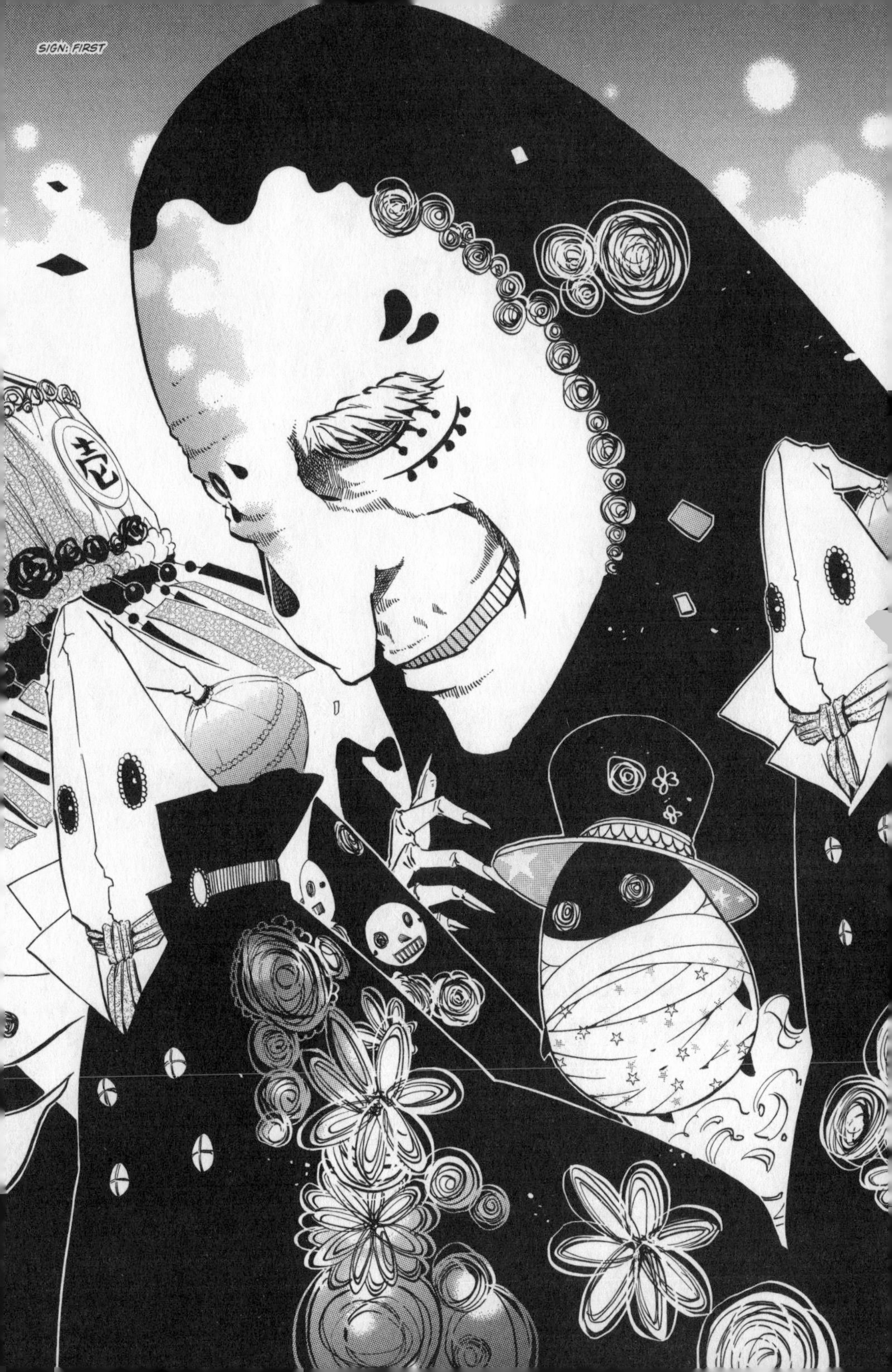
SIGN: FIRST
壱

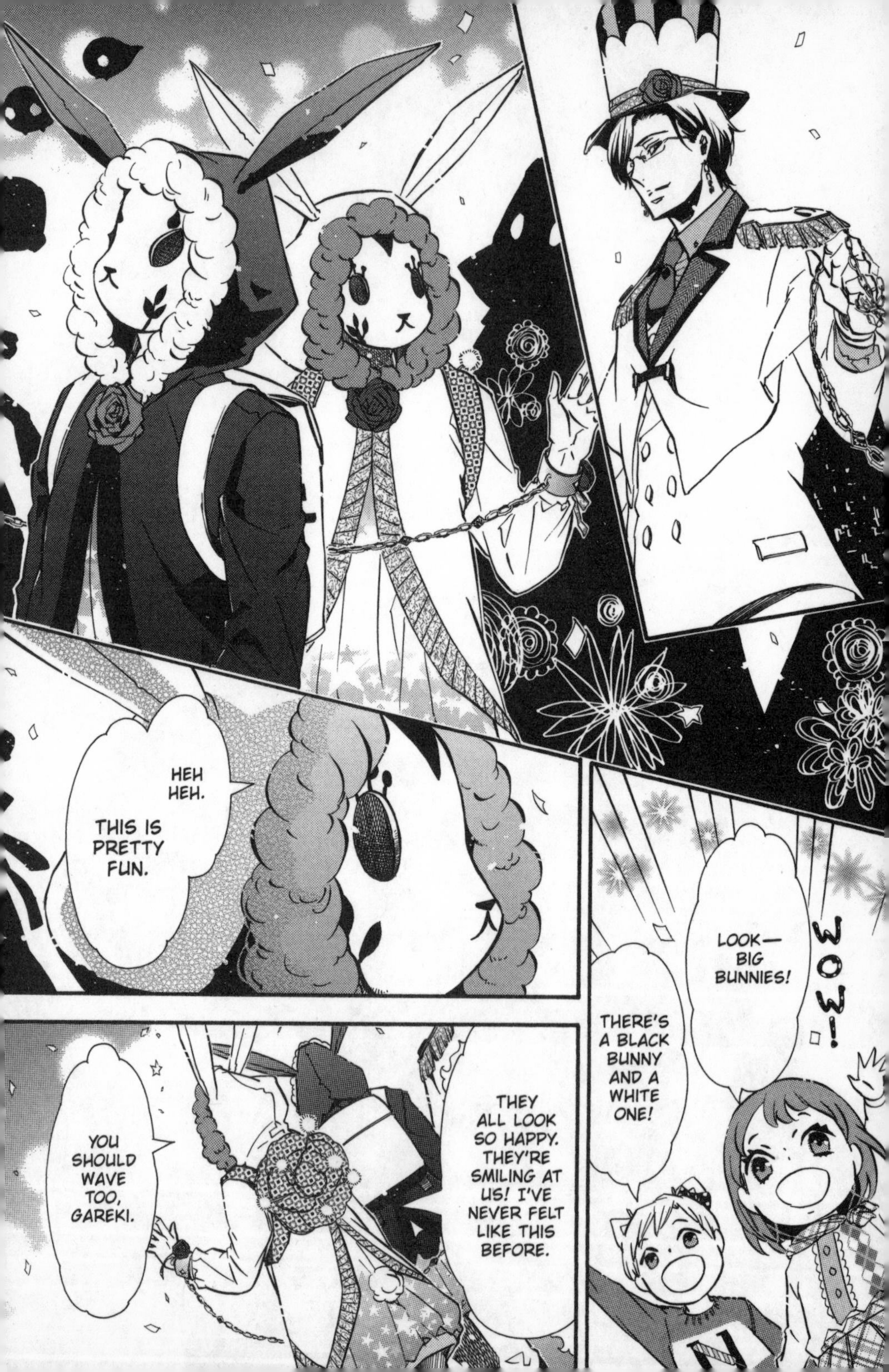
WOW!
LOOK— BIG BUNNIES!
THERE'S A BLACK BUNNY AND A WHITE ONE!
HEH HEH.
THIS IS PRETTY FUN.
THEY ALL LOOK SO HAPPY. THEY'RE SMILING AT US! I'VE NEVER FELT LIKE THIS BEFORE.
YOU SHOULD WAVE TOO, GAREKI.

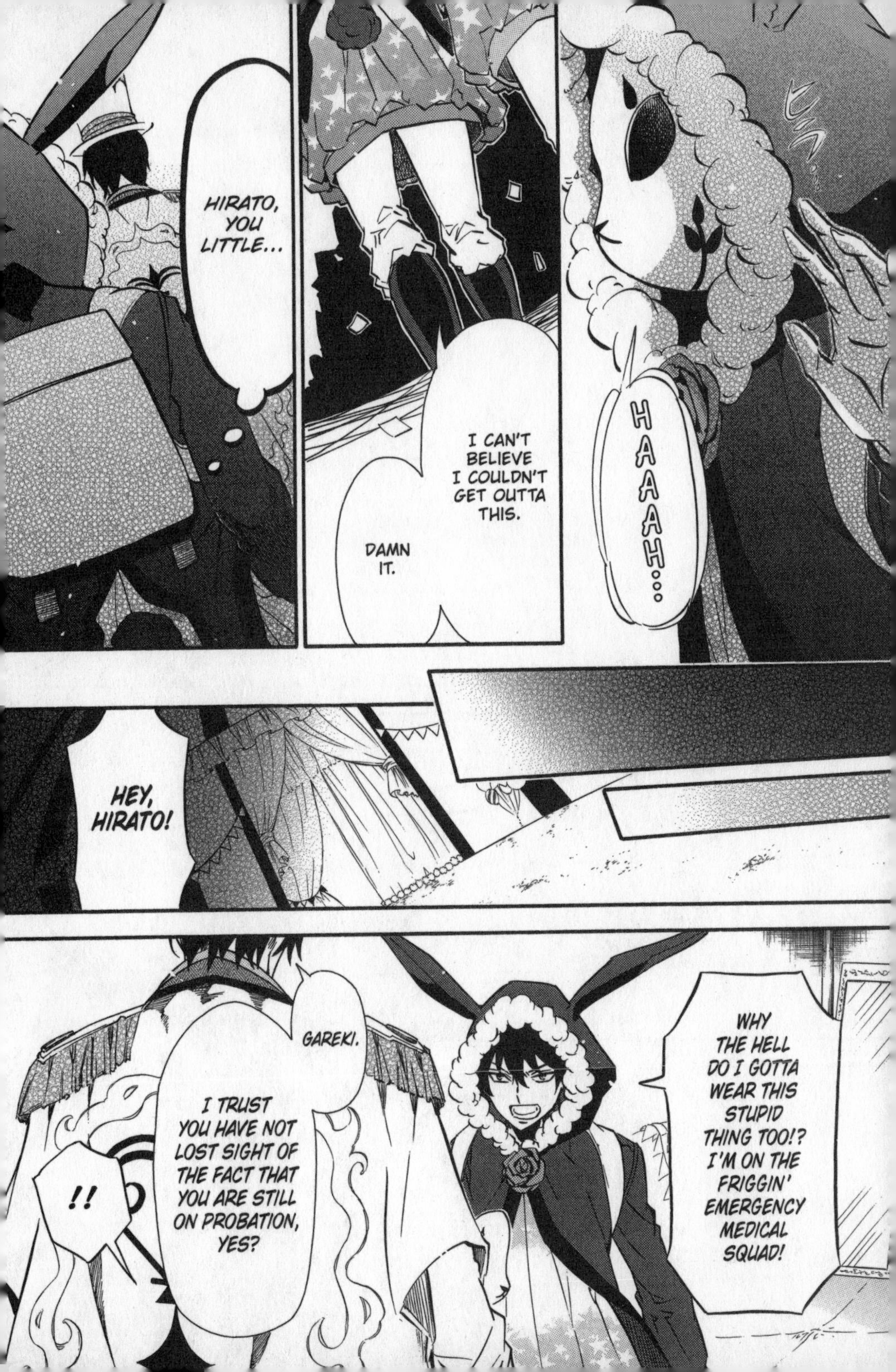
HAAAH...
I CAN'T BELIEVE I COULDN'T GET OUTTA THIS.
DAMN IT.
HIRATO, YOU LITTLE...
HEY, HIRATO!
WHY THE HELL DO I GOTTA WEAR THIS STUPID THING TOO!? I'M ON THE FRIGGIN' EMERGENCY MEDICAL SQUAD!
GAREKI.
I TRUST YOU HAVE NOT LOST SIGHT OF THE FACT THAT YOU ARE STILL ON PROBATION, YES?
!!

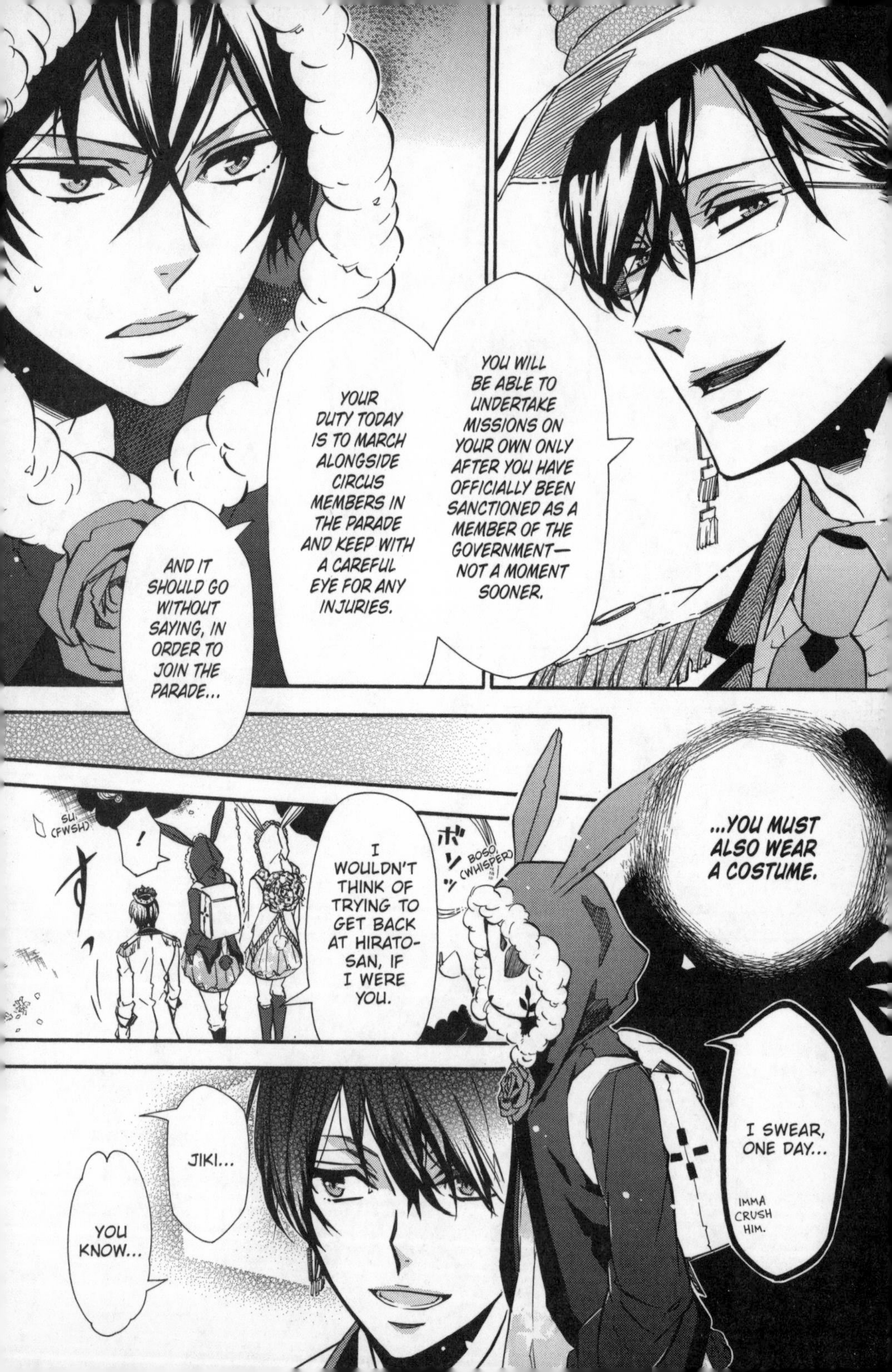
YOU WILL BE ABLE TO UNDERTAKE MISSIONS ON YOUR OWN ONLY AFTER YOU HAVE OFFICIALLY BEEN SANCTIONED AS A MEMBER OF THE GOVERNMENT— NOT A MOMENT SOONER.
YOUR DUTY TODAY IS TO MARCH ALONGSIDE CIRCUS MEMBERS IN THE PARADE AND KEEP WITH A CAREFUL EYE FOR ANY INJURIES.
AND IT SHOULD GO WITHOUT SAYING, IN ORDER TO JOIN THE PARADE...
...YOU MUST ALSO WEAR A COSTUME.
ボソッ
BOSO (WHISPER)
I WOULDN'T THINK OF TRYING TO GET BACK AT HIRATO-SAN, IF I WERE YOU.
!
す
SU (FWSH)
I SWEAR, ONE DAY...
IMMA CRUSH HIM.
JIKI...
YOU KNOW...

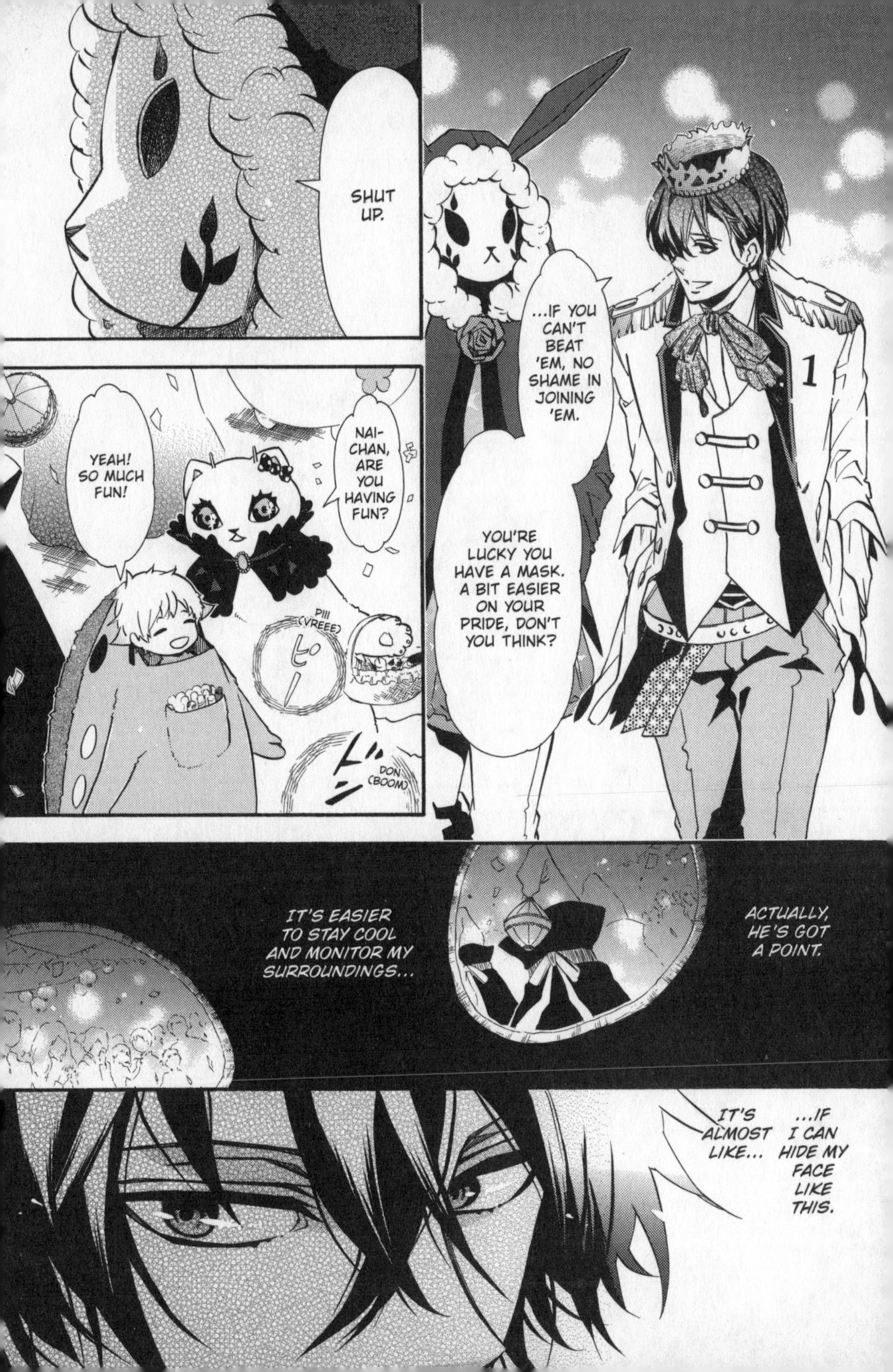
...IF YOU CAN'T BEAT 'EM, NO SHAME IN JOINING 'EM.
YOU'RE LUCKY YOU HAVE A MASK. A BIT EASIER ON YOUR PRIDE, DON'T YOU THINK?
1
SHUT UP.
NAI-CHAN, ARE YOU HAVING FUN?
YEAH! SO MUCH FUN!
PIII (VREEE)
DON (BOOM)
ACTUALLY, HE'S GOT A POINT.
IT'S EASIER TO STAY COOL AND MONITOR MY SURROUNDINGS...
IT'S ALMOST LIKE...
...IF I CAN HIDE MY FACE LIKE THIS.

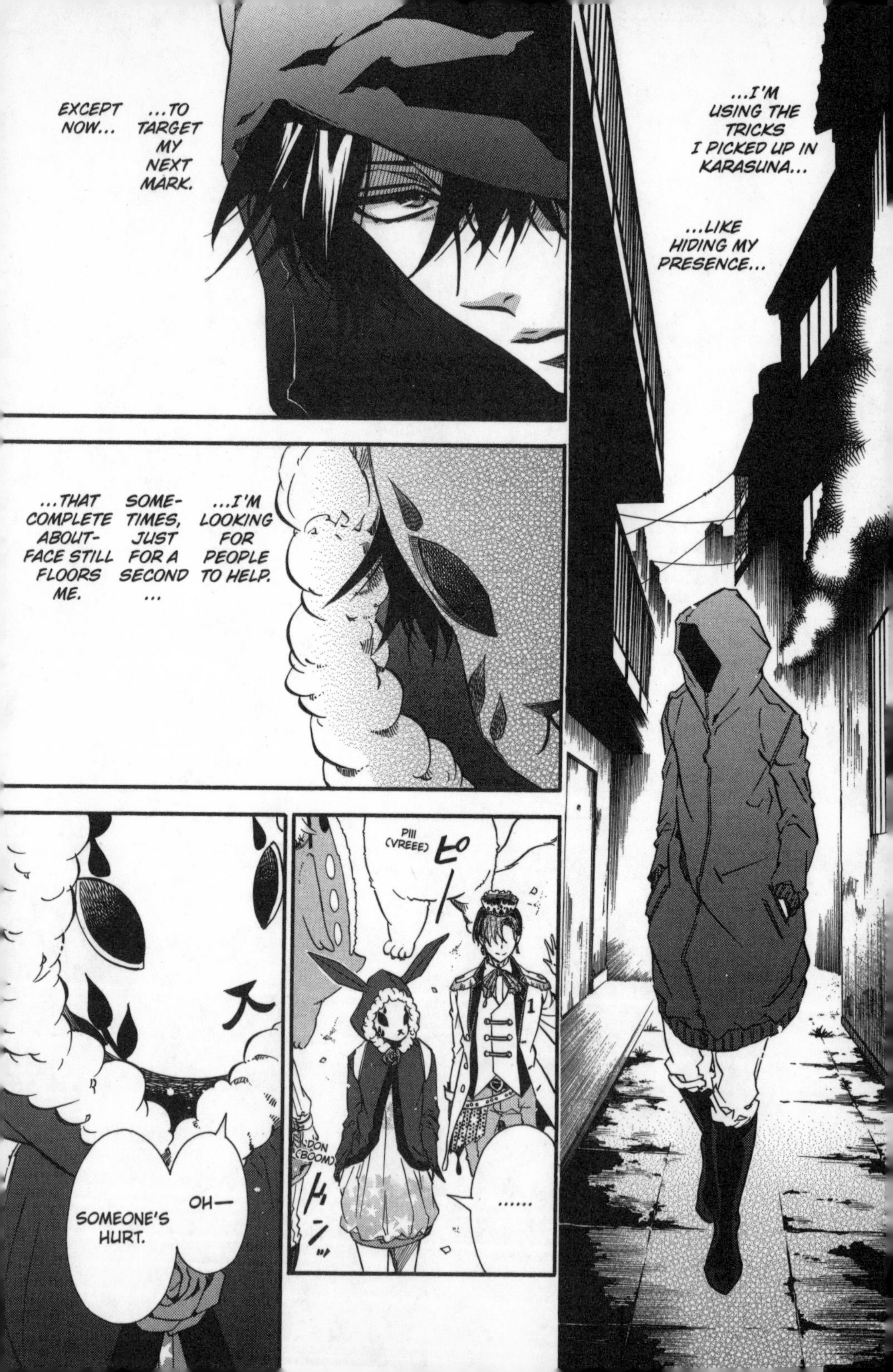

...I'M USING THE TRICKS I PICKED UP IN KARASUNA...
...LIKE HIDING MY PRESENCE...
...TO TARGET MY NEXT MARK.
EXCEPT NOW...
...I'M LOOKING FOR PEOPLE TO HELP.
SOME-TIMES, JUST FOR A SECOND...
...THAT COMPLETE ABOUT-FACE STILL FLOORS ME.
PIII (VREEE)
DON (BOOM)
......
OH—
SOMEONE'S HURT.

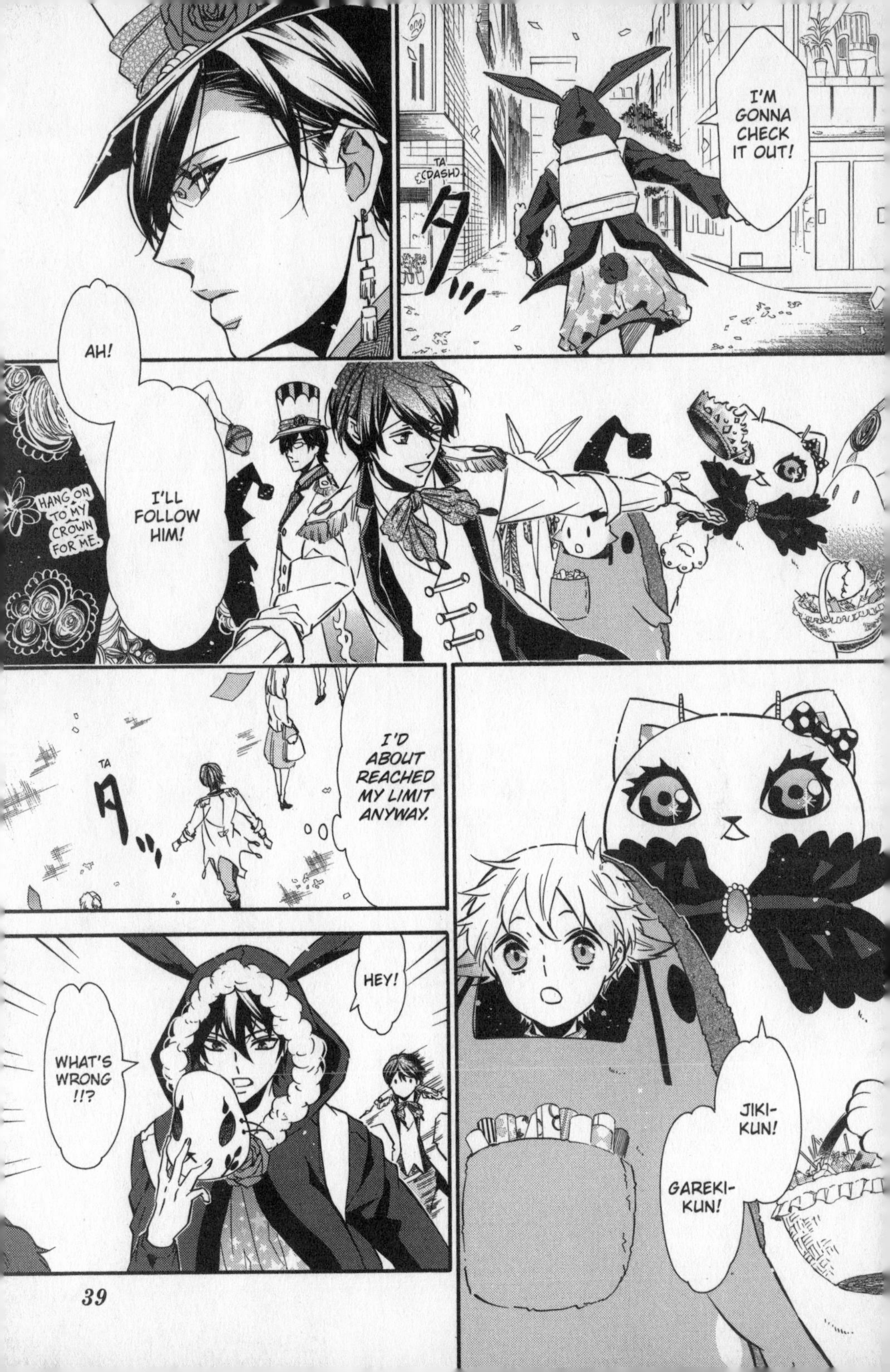
I'M GONNA CHECK IT OUT!
TA (DASH)
AH!
I'LL FOLLOW HIM!
HANG ON TO MY CROWN FOR ME.
JIKI-KUN!
GAREKI-KUN!
I'D ABOUT REACHED MY LIMIT ANYWAY.
TA
HEY!
WHAT'S WRONG!!?

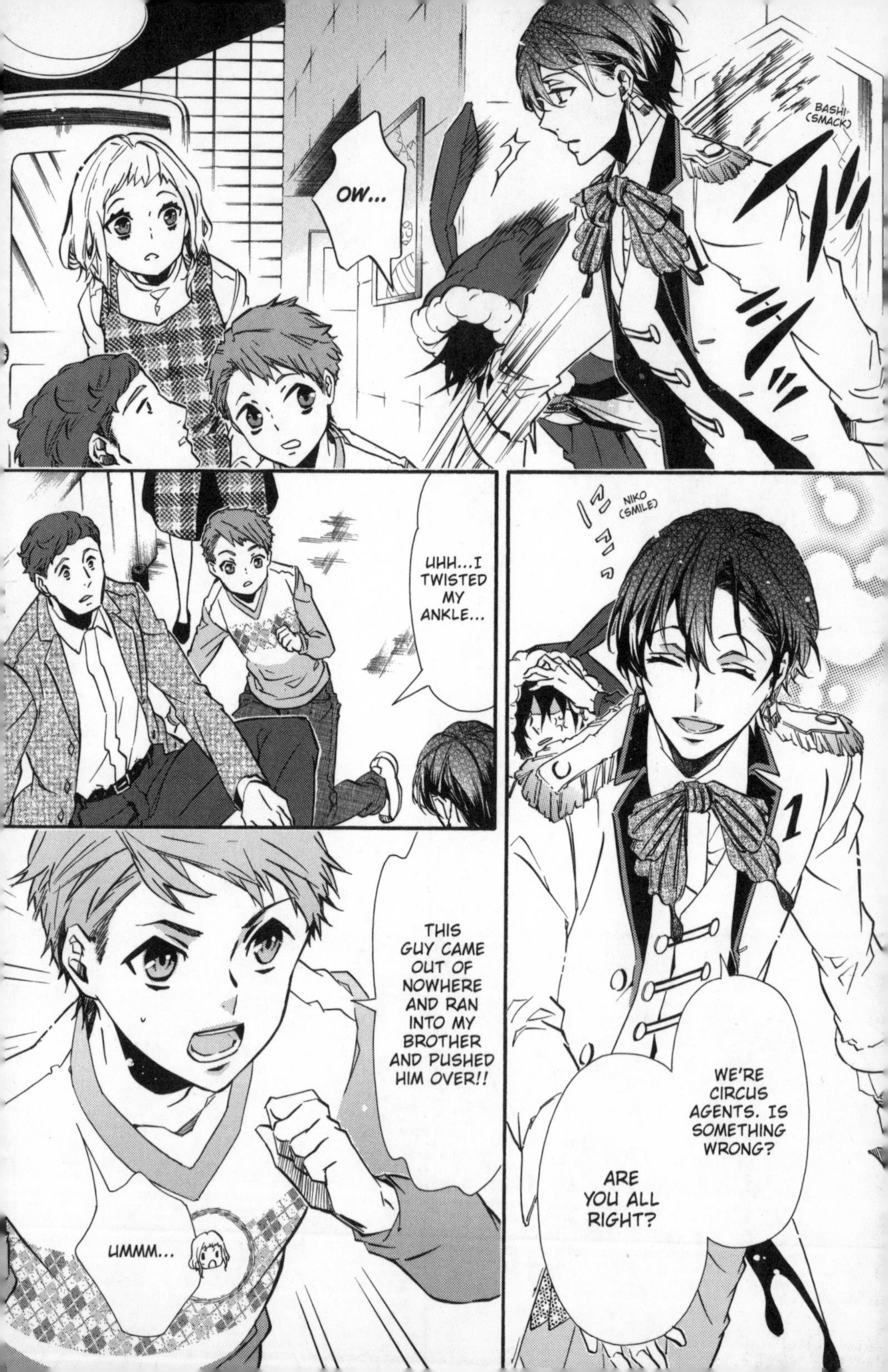
BASHI (SMACK)
OW...
NIKO (SMILE)
WE'RE CIRCUS AGENTS. IS SOMETHING WRONG?
ARE YOU ALL RIGHT?
UHH...I TWISTED MY ANKLE...
THIS GUY CAME OUT OF NOWHERE AND RAN INTO MY BROTHER AND PUSHED HIM OVER!!
UMMM...

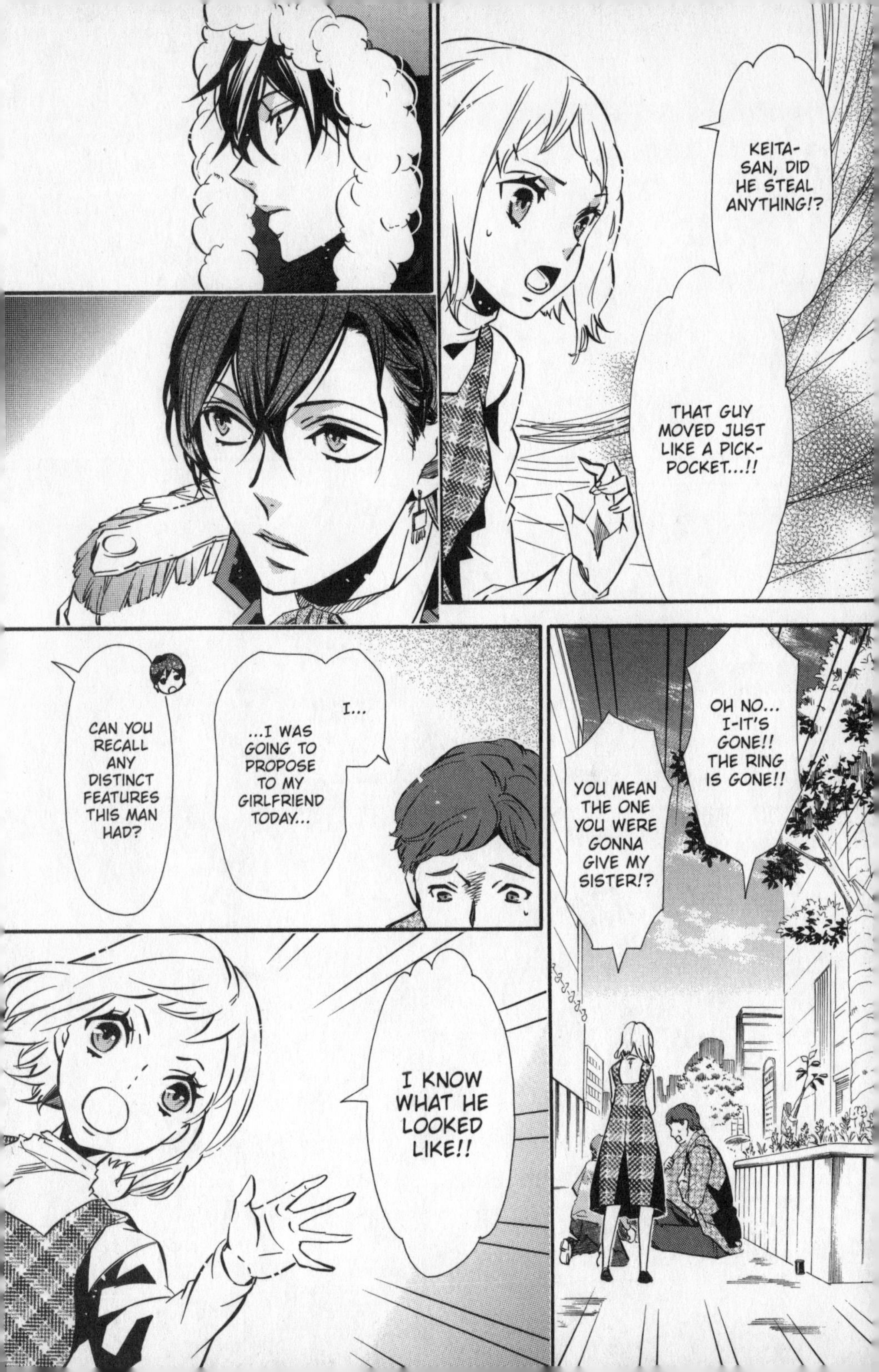
KEITA-SAN, DID HE STEAL ANYTHING!?
THAT GUY MOVED JUST LIKE A PICK-POCKET...!!
OH NO... I-IT'S GONE!! THE RING IS GONE!!
YOU MEAN THE ONE YOU WERE GONNA GIVE MY SISTER!?
I...
...I WAS GOING TO PROPOSE TO MY GIRLFRIEND TODAY...
CAN YOU RECALL ANY DISTINCT FEATURES THIS MAN HAD?
I KNOW WHAT HE LOOKED LIKE!!

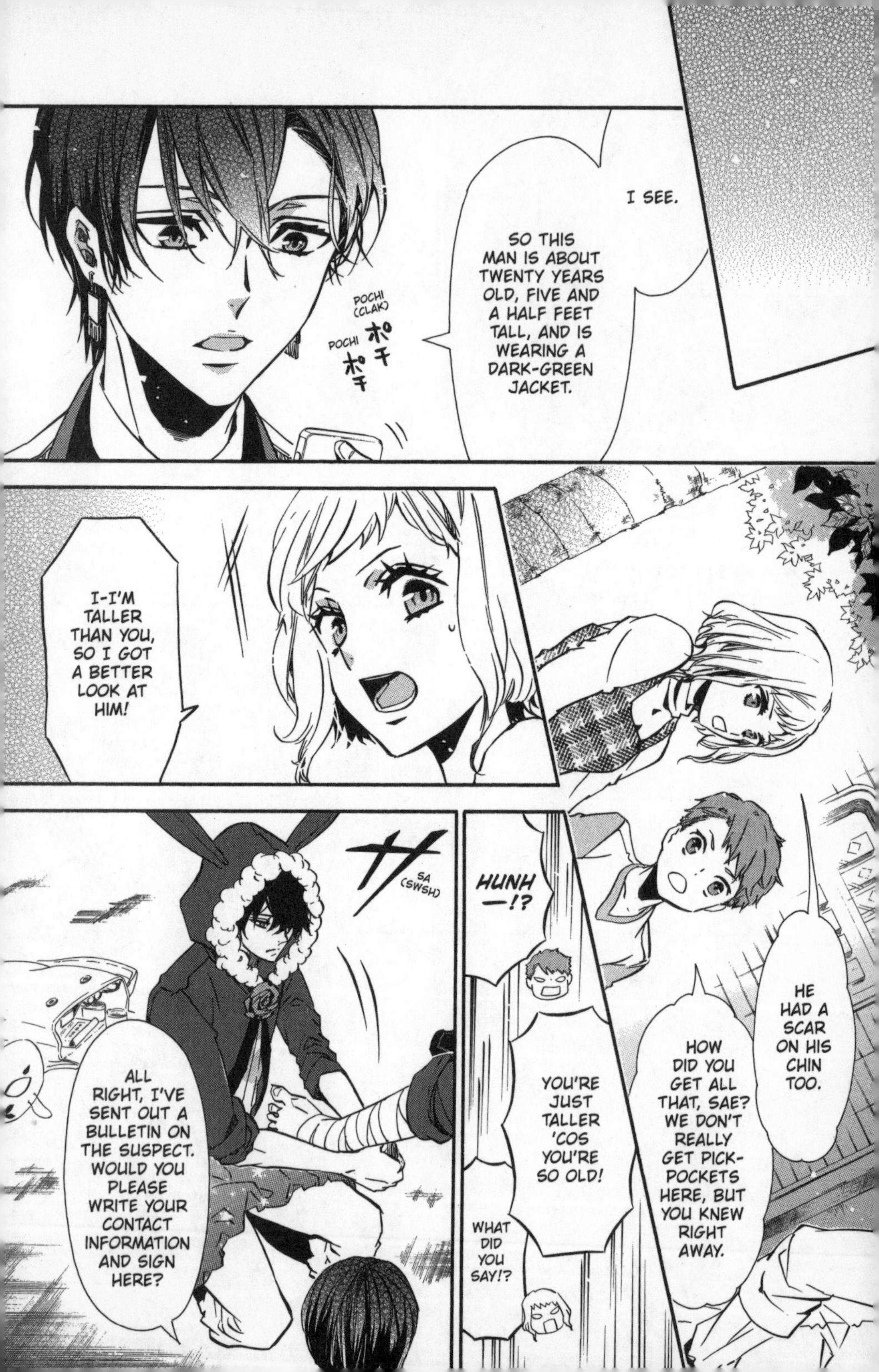
I SEE.
SO THIS MAN IS ABOUT TWENTY YEARS OLD, FIVE AND A HALF FEET TALL, AND IS WEARING A DARK-GREEN JACKET.
POCHI (CLAK)
ポチ
POCHI
ポチ
HE HAD A SCAR ON HIS CHIN TOO.
HOW DID YOU GET ALL THAT, SAE? WE DON'T REALLY GET PICK-POCKETS HERE, BUT YOU KNEW RIGHT AWAY.
I-I'M TALLER THAN YOU, SO I GOT A BETTER LOOK AT HIM!
HUNH—!?
YOU'RE JUST TALLER 'COS YOU'RE SO OLD!
WHAT DID YOU SAY!?
サ
SA (SWSH)
ALL RIGHT, I'VE SENT OUT A BULLETIN ON THE SUSPECT. WOULD YOU PLEASE WRITE YOUR CONTACT INFORMATION AND SIGN HERE?

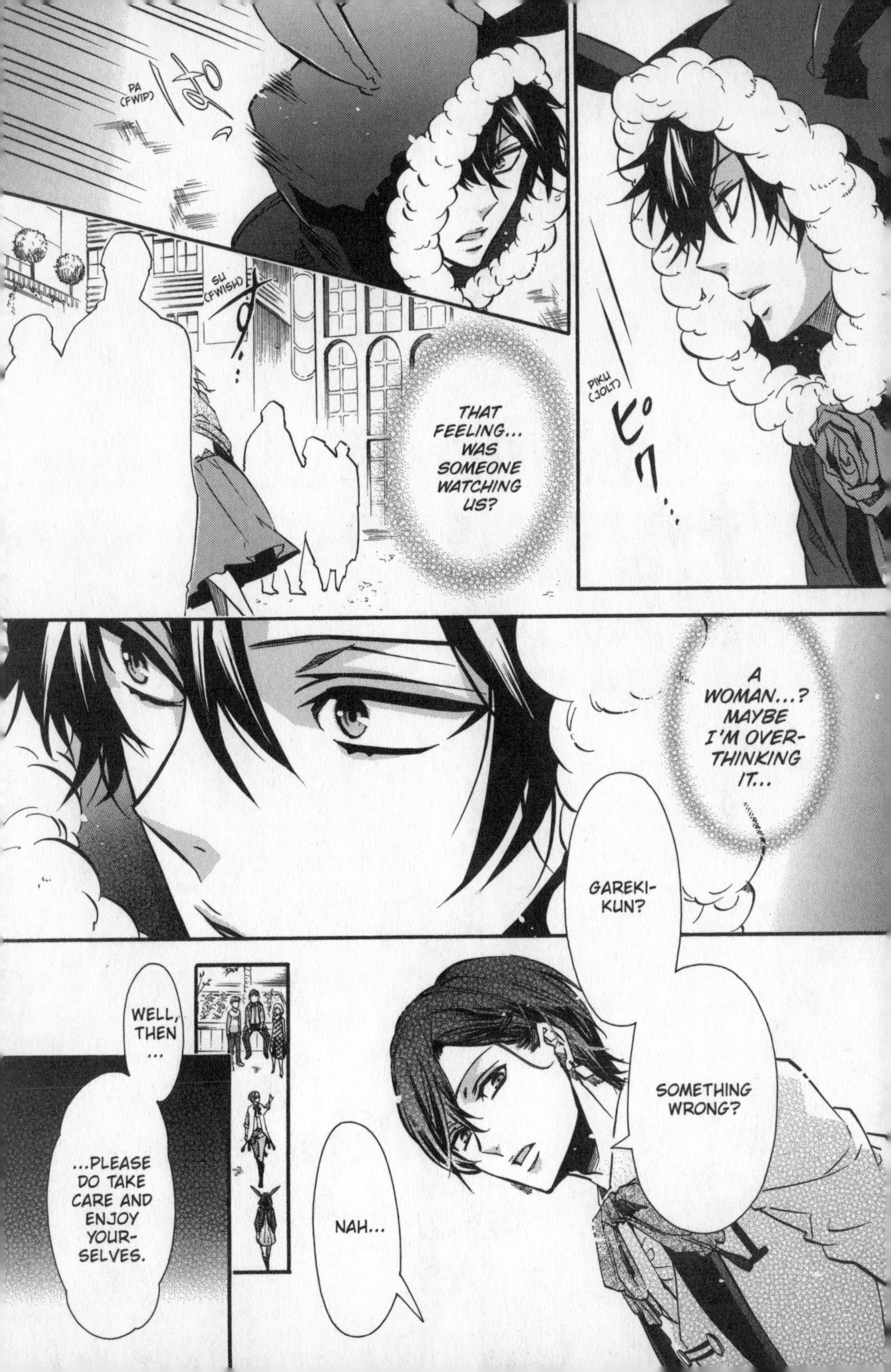
PIKU (JOLT)
PA (FWIP)
SU (FWISH)
THAT FEELING... WAS SOMEONE WATCHING US?
A WOMAN...? MAYBE I'M OVER-THINKING IT...
GAREKI-KUN?
SOMETHING WRONG?
NAH...
WELL, THEN...
...PLEASE DO TAKE CARE AND ENJOY YOUR-SELVES.

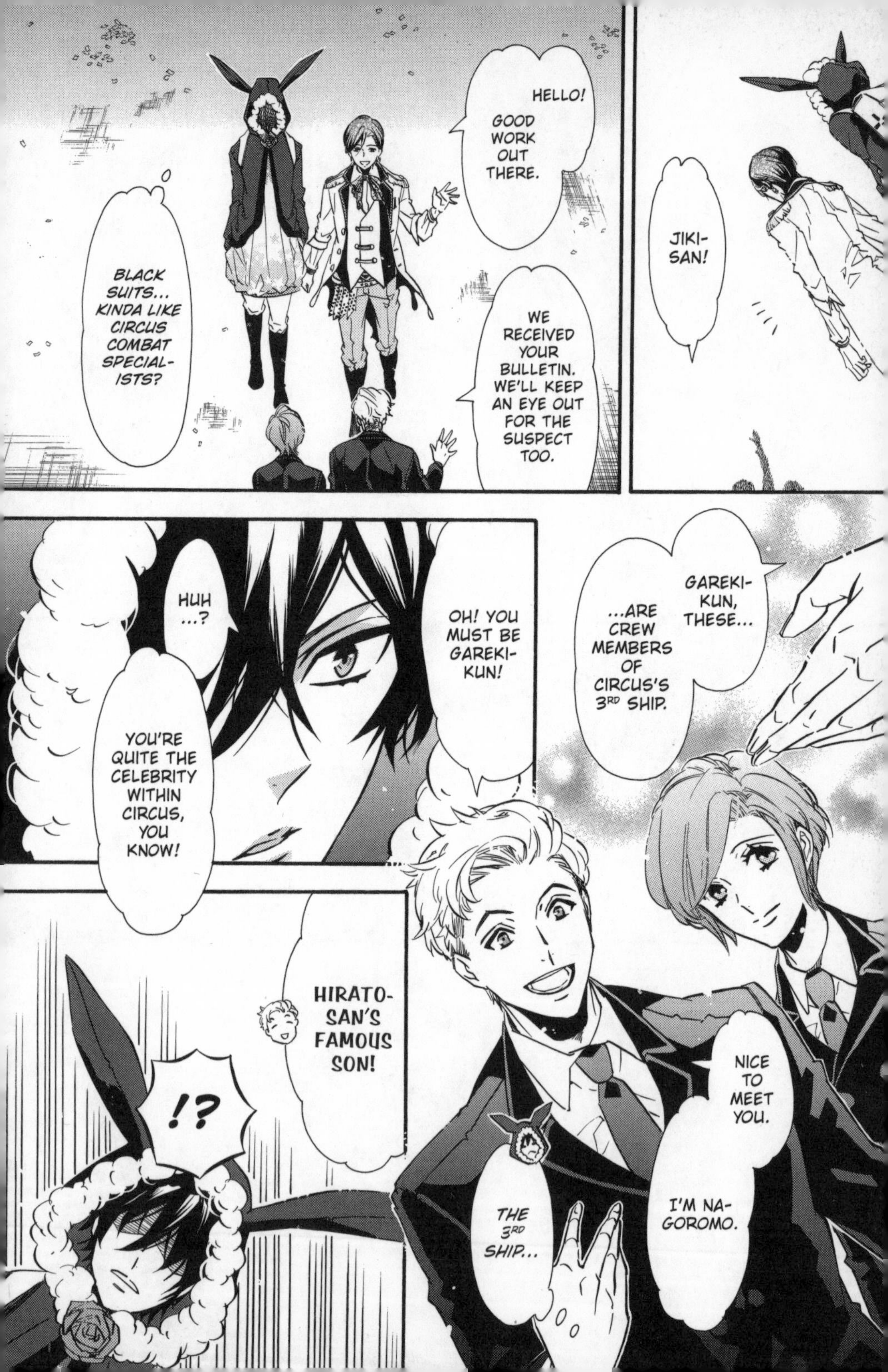
JIKI-SAN!
HELLO! GOOD WORK OUT THERE.
WE RECEIVED YOUR BULLETIN. WE'LL KEEP AN EYE OUT FOR THE SUSPECT TOO.
BLACK SUITS... KINDA LIKE CIRCUS COMBAT SPECIALISTS?
GAREKI-KUN, THESE...
...ARE CREW MEMBERS OF CIRCUS'S 3RD SHIP.
NICE TO MEET YOU.
I'M NAGOROMO.
OH! YOU MUST BE GAREKI-KUN!
HUH ...?
YOU'RE QUITE THE CELEBRITY WITHIN CIRCUS, YOU KNOW!
HIRATO-SAN'S FAMOUS SON!
!?
THE 3RD SHIP...

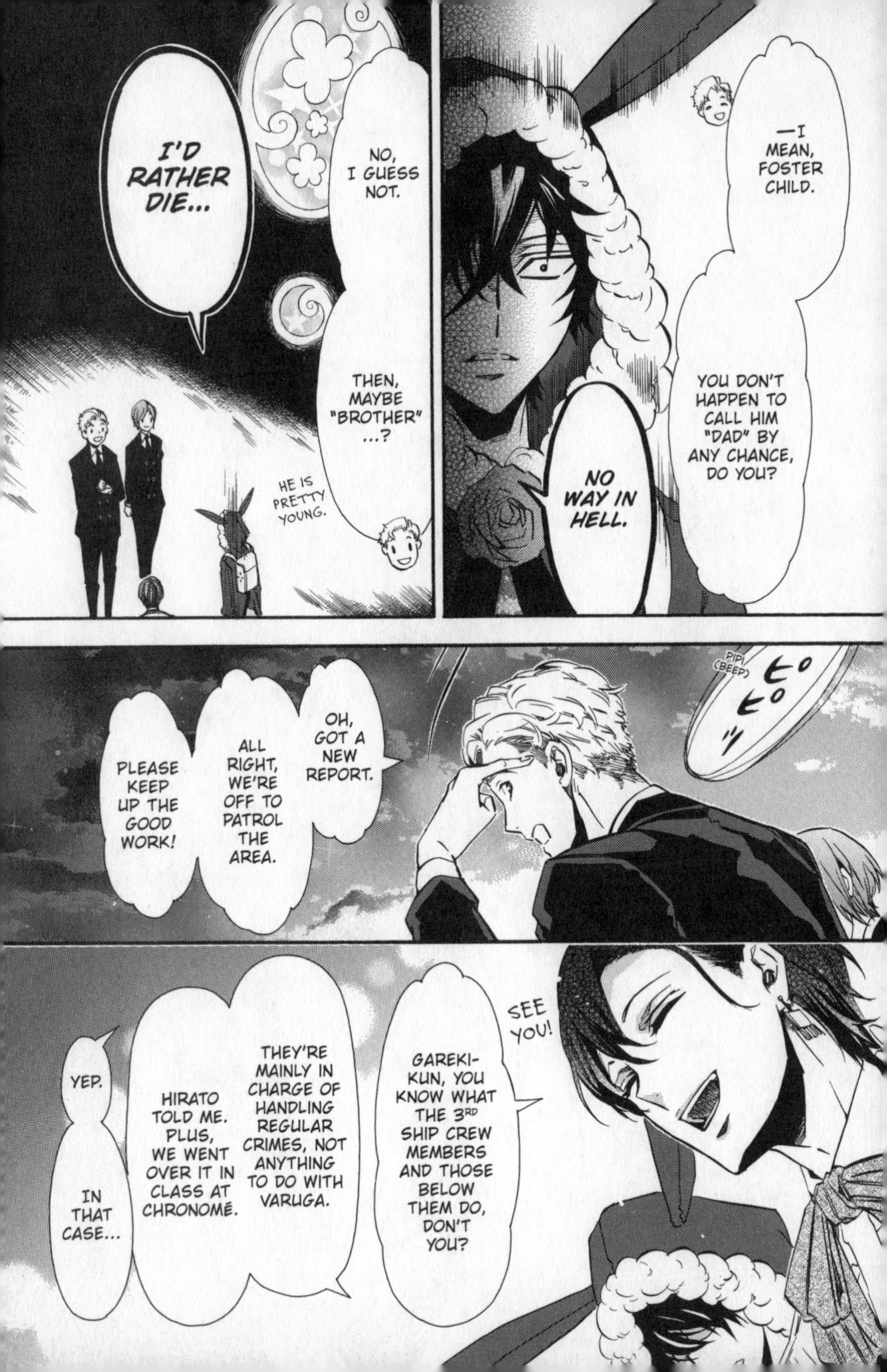

—I MEAN, FOSTER CHILD.
YOU DON'T HAPPEN TO CALL HIM "DAD" BY ANY CHANCE, DO YOU?
NO WAY IN HELL.
NO, I GUESS NOT.
THEN, MAYBE "BROTHER" ...?
HE IS PRETTY YOUNG.
I'D RATHER DIE...
ピピッ
PIPI (BEEP)
OH, GOT A NEW REPORT.
ALL RIGHT, WE'RE OFF TO PATROL THE AREA.
PLEASE KEEP UP THE GOOD WORK!
SEE YOU!
GAREKI-KUN, YOU KNOW WHAT THE 3RD SHIP CREW MEMBERS AND THOSE BELOW THEM DO, DON'T YOU?
THEY'RE MAINLY IN CHARGE OF HANDLING REGULAR CRIMES, NOT ANYTHING TO DO WITH VARUGA.
HIRATO TOLD ME. PLUS, WE WENT OVER IT IN CLASS AT CHRONOMÉ.
YEP.
IN THAT CASE...

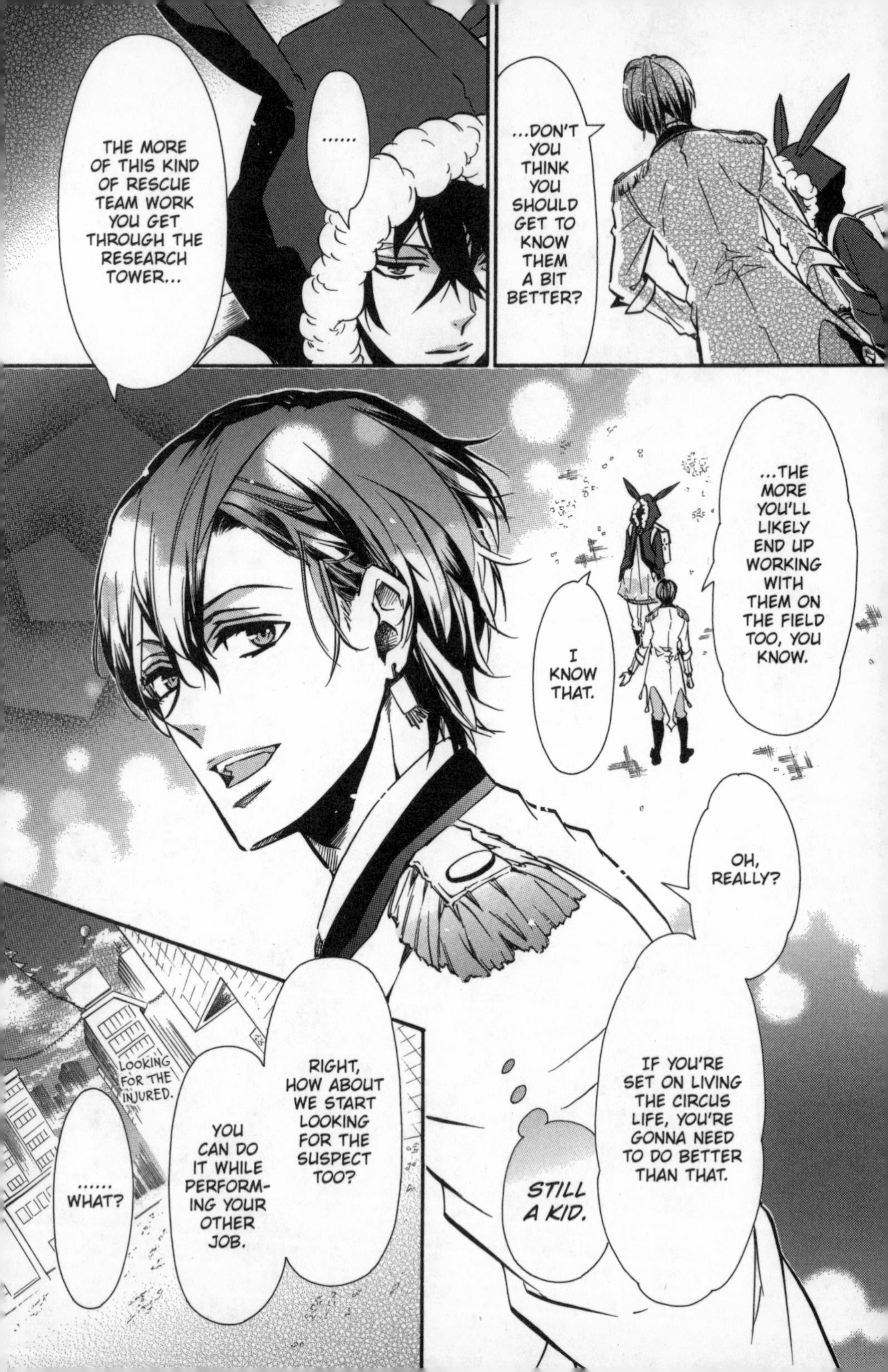
...DON'T YOU THINK YOU SHOULD GET TO KNOW THEM A BIT BETTER?
......
THE MORE OF THIS KIND OF RESCUE TEAM WORK YOU GET THROUGH THE RESEARCH TOWER...
...THE MORE YOU'LL LIKELY END UP WORKING WITH THEM ON THE FIELD TOO, YOU KNOW.
I KNOW THAT.
OH, REALLY?
IF YOU'RE SET ON LIVING THE CIRCUS LIFE, YOU'RE GONNA NEED TO DO BETTER THAN THAT.
STILL A KID.
RIGHT, HOW ABOUT WE START LOOKING FOR THE SUSPECT TOO?
YOU CAN DO IT WHILE PERFORMING YOUR OTHER JOB.
LOOKING FOR THE INJURED.
......WHAT?

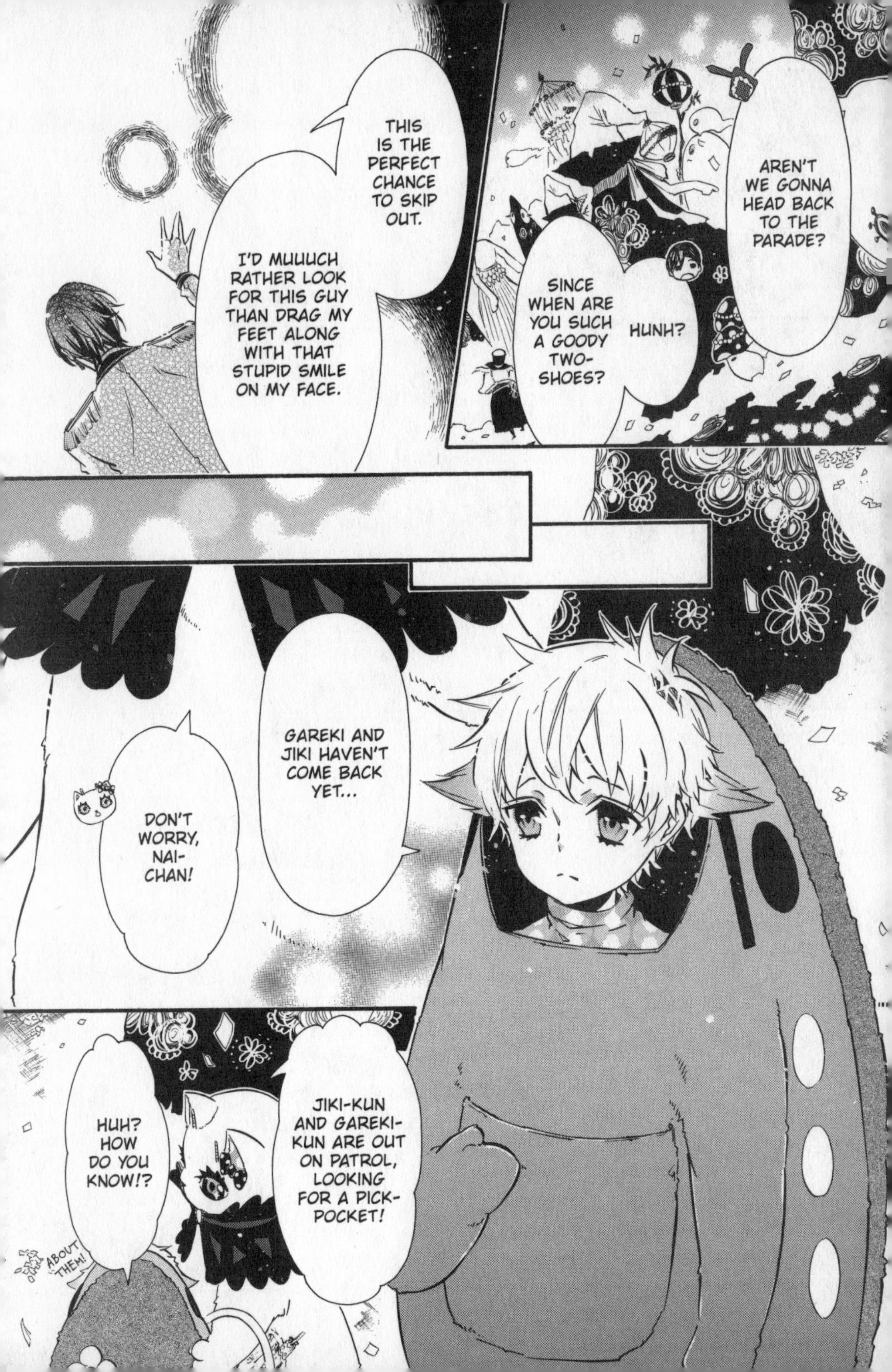
AREN'T WE GONNA HEAD BACK TO THE PARADE?
HUNH?
SINCE WHEN ARE YOU SUCH A GOODY TWO-SHOES?
THIS IS THE PERFECT CHANCE TO SKIP OUT.
I'D MUUUCH RATHER LOOK FOR THIS GUY THAN DRAG MY FEET ALONG WITH THAT STUPID SMILE ON MY FACE.
GAREKI AND JIKI HAVEN'T COME BACK YET...
DON'T WORRY, NAI-CHAN!
JIKI-KUN AND GAREKI-KUN ARE OUT ON PATROL, LOOKING FOR A PICK-POCKET!
HUH? HOW DO YOU KNOW!?
ABOUT THEM!

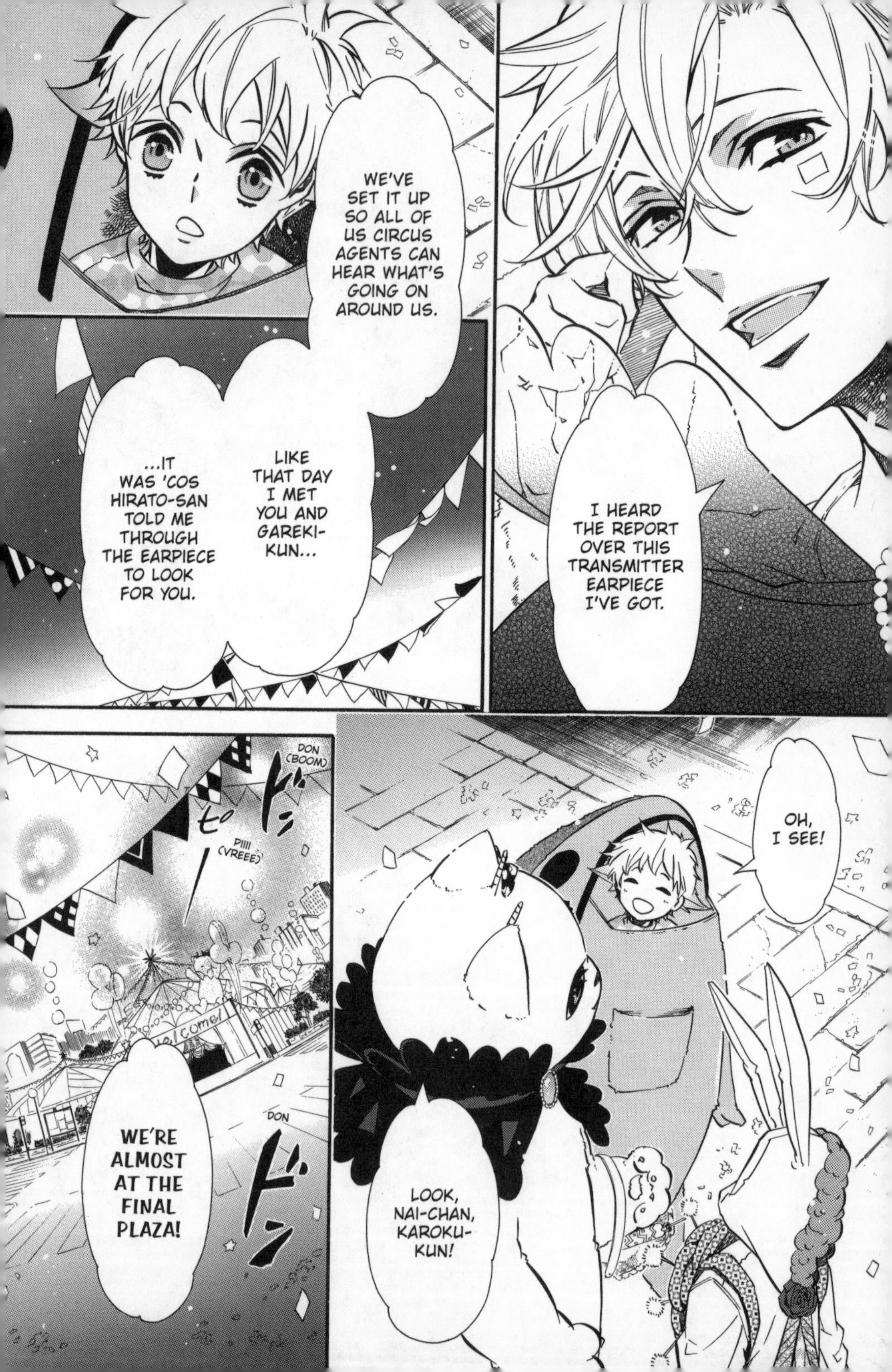
I HEARD THE REPORT OVER THIS TRANSMITTER EARPIECE I'VE GOT.
WE'VE SET IT UP SO ALL OF US CIRCUS AGENTS CAN HEAR WHAT'S GOING ON AROUND US.
LIKE THAT DAY I MET YOU AND GAREKI-KUN...
...IT WAS 'COS HIRATO-SAN TOLD ME THROUGH THE EARPIECE TO LOOK FOR YOU.
OH, I SEE!
LOOK, NAI-CHAN, KAROKU-KUN!
DON (BOOM)
PIIII (VREEE)
welcome!
DON
WE'RE ALMOST AT THE FINAL PLAZA!

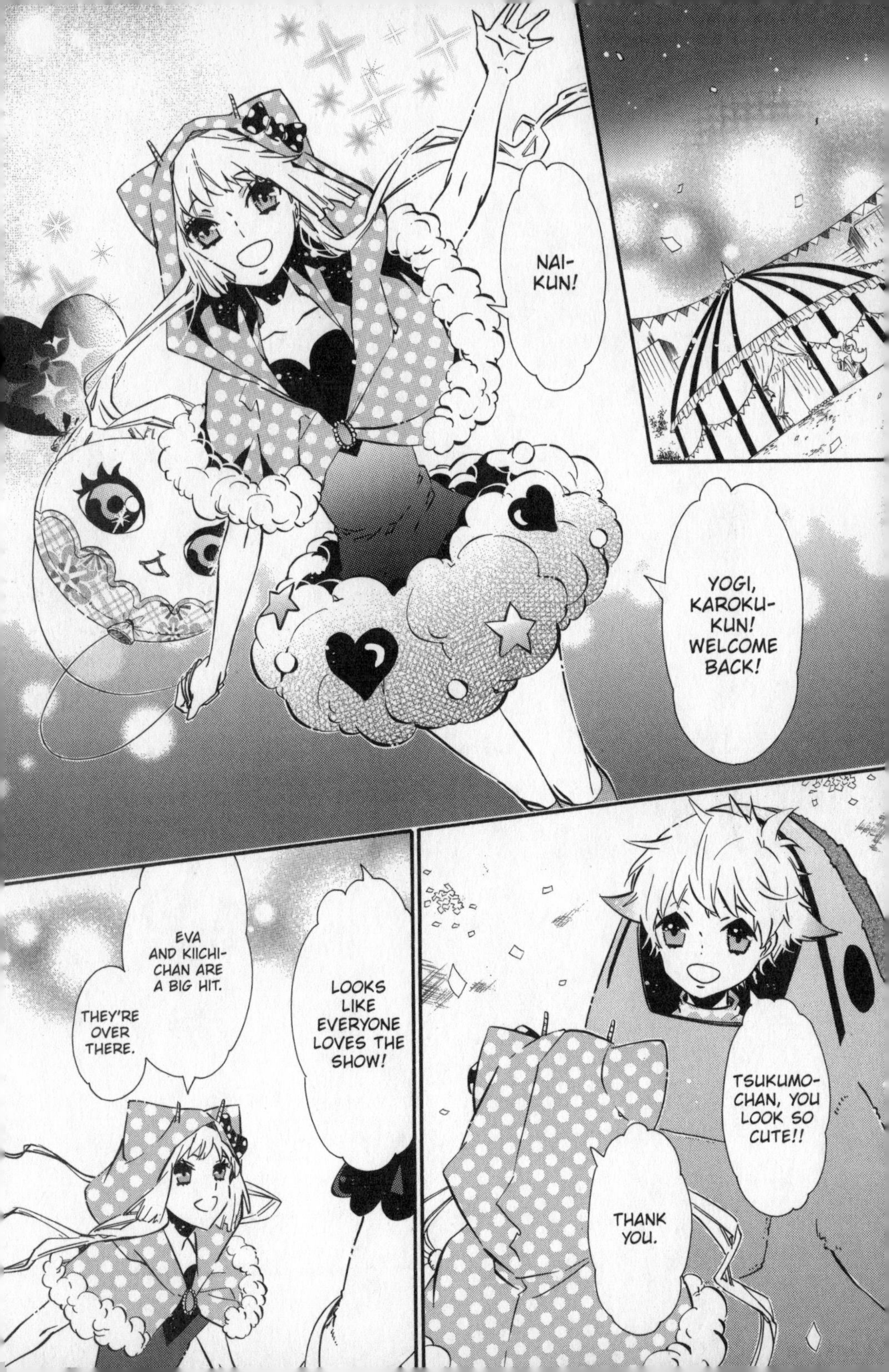
NAI-KUN!
YOGI, KAROKU-KUN! WELCOME BACK!
TSUKUMO-CHAN, YOU LOOK SO CUTE!!
THANK YOU.
LOOKS LIKE EVERYONE LOVES THE SHOW!
EVA AND KIICHI-CHAN ARE A BIG HIT.
THEY'RE OVER THERE.

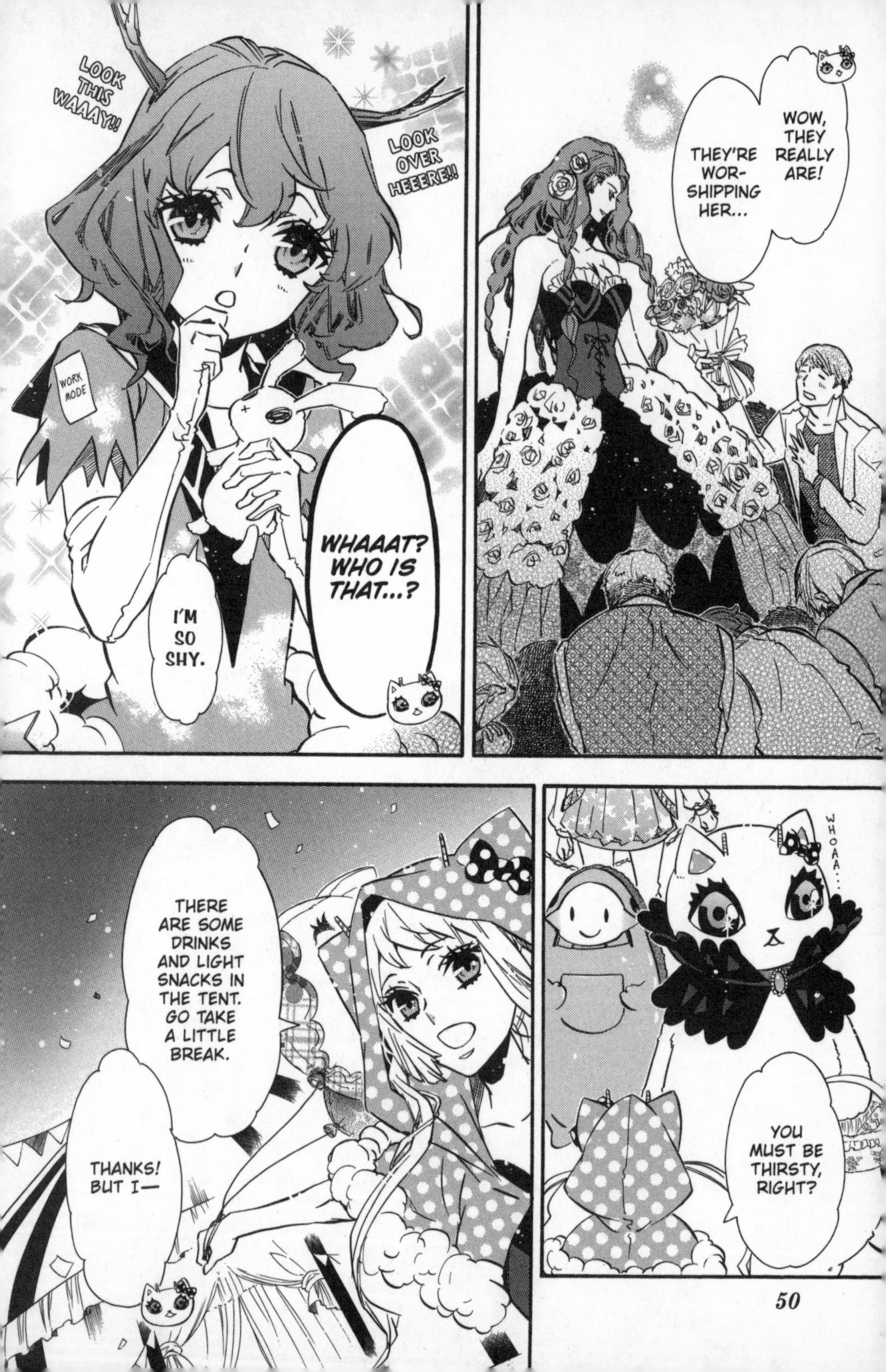
WOW, THEY REALLY ARE!
THEY'RE WOR-SHIPPING HER...
LOOK OVER HEEERE!!
LOOK THIS WAAAY!!
WORK MODE
WHAAAT? WHO IS THAT...?
I'M SO SHY.
WHOAA...
YOU MUST BE THIRSTY, RIGHT?
THERE ARE SOME DRINKS AND LIGHT SNACKS IN THE TENT. GO TAKE A LITTLE BREAK.
THANKS! BUT I—

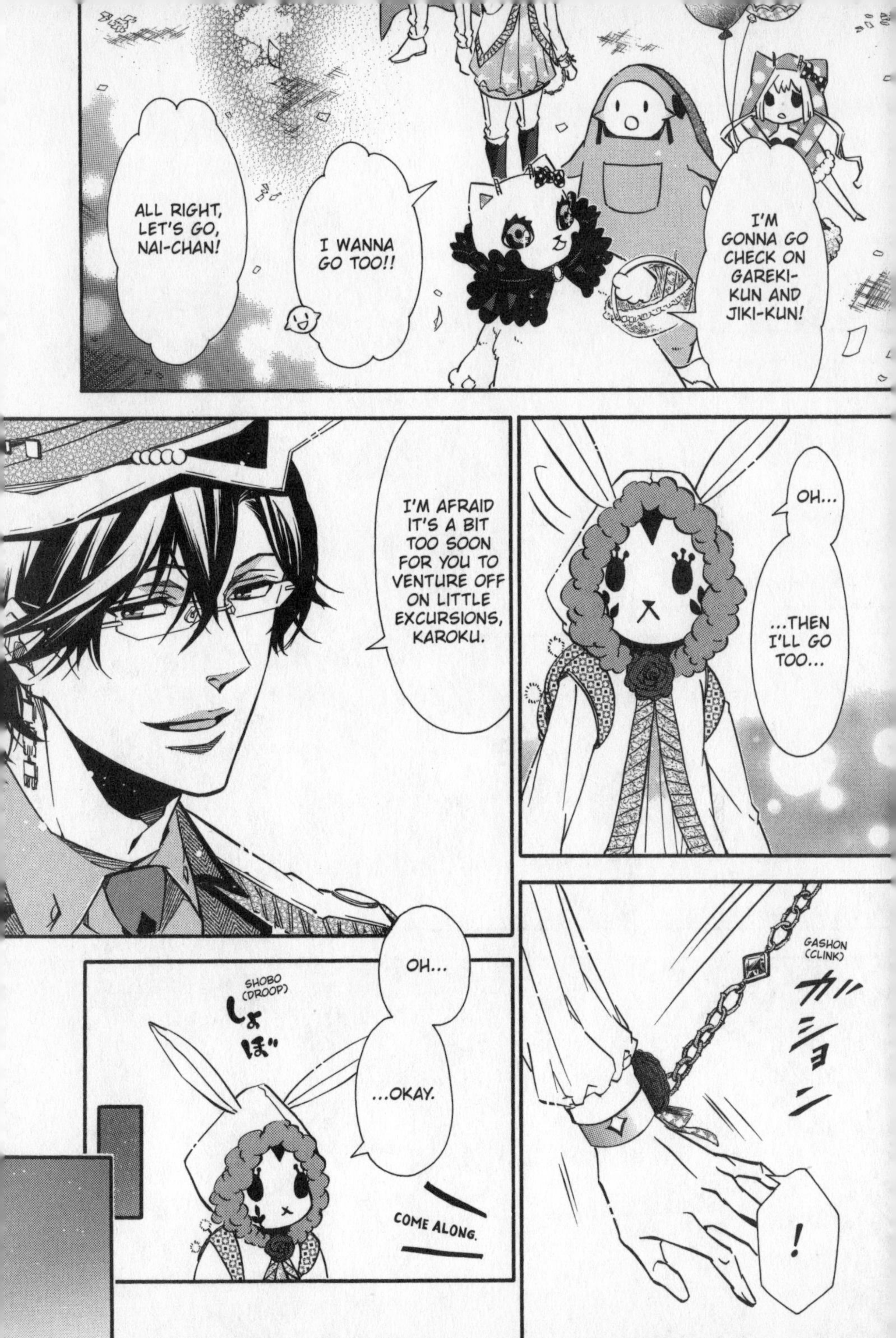
I'M GONNA GO CHECK ON GAREKI-KUN AND JIKI-KUN!
I WANNA GO TOO!!
ALL RIGHT, LET'S GO, NAI-CHAN!
OH...
...THEN I'LL GO TOO...
I'M AFRAID IT'S A BIT TOO SOON FOR YOU TO VENTURE OFF ON LITTLE EXCURSIONS, KAROKU.
GASHON (CLINK)
ガション
!
OH...
...OKAY.
SHOBO (DROOP)
しょぼ
COME ALONG.

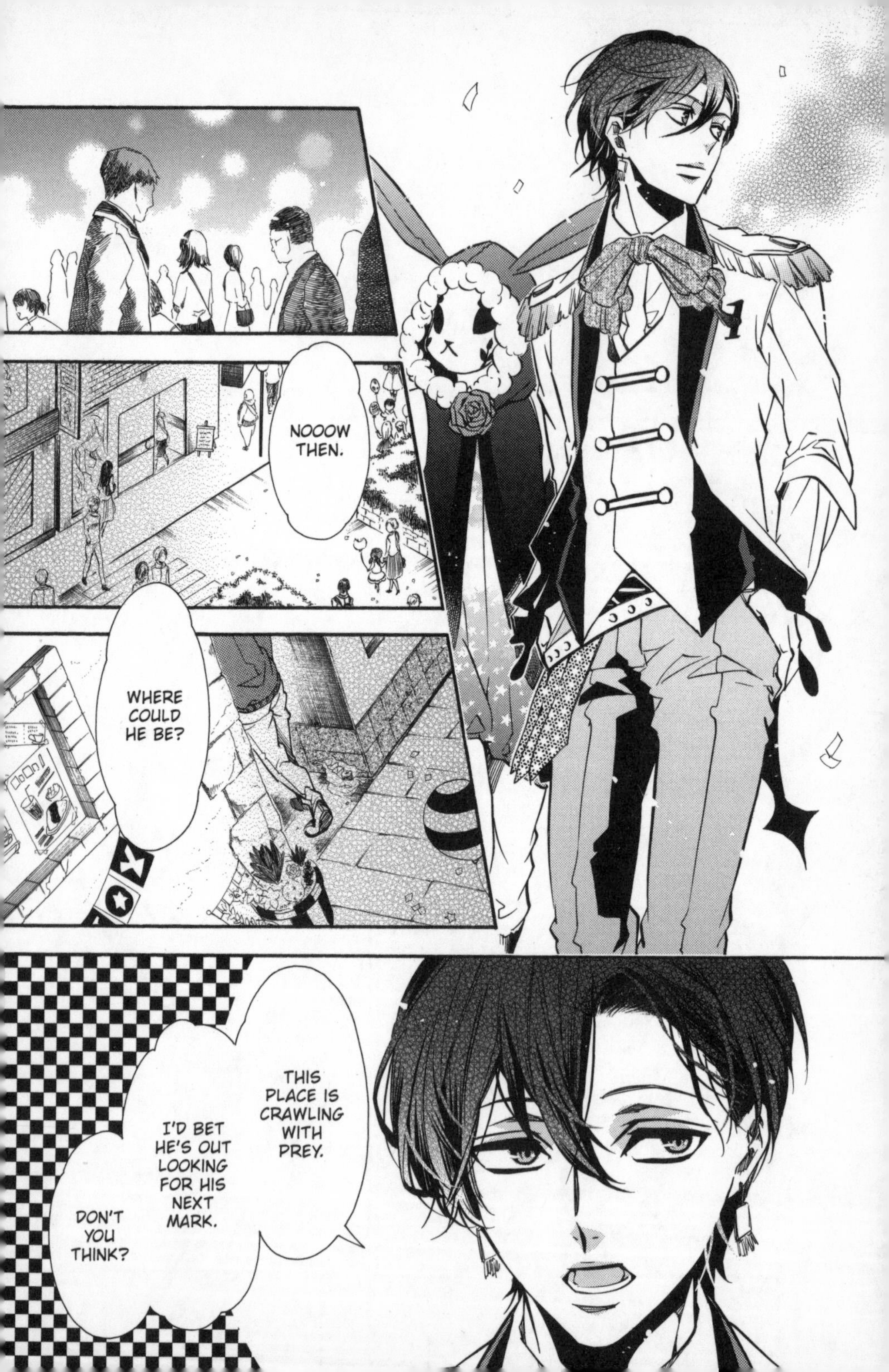
NOOOW THEN.
WHERE COULD HE BE?
THIS PLACE IS CRAWLING WITH PREY.
I'D BET HE'S OUT LOOKING FOR HIS NEXT MARK.
DON'T YOU THINK?

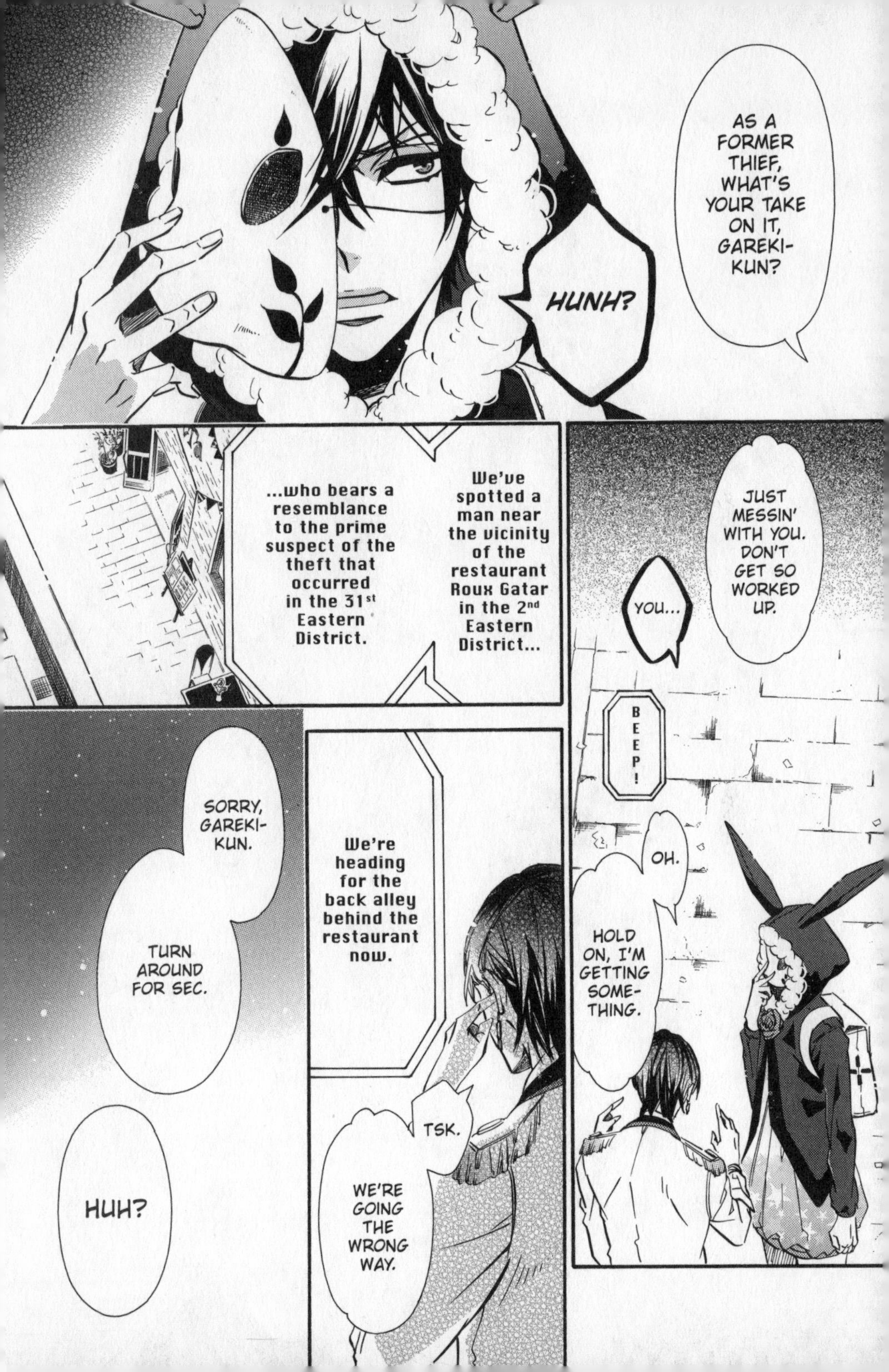
AS A FORMER THIEF, WHAT'S YOUR TAKE ON IT, GAREKI-KUN?
HUNH?
JUST MESSIN' WITH YOU. DON'T GET SO WORKED UP.
YOU...
BEEP!
OH.
HOLD ON, I'M GETTING SOME-THING.
We've spotted a man near the vicinity of the restaurant Roux Gatar in the 2nd Eastern District...
...who bears a resemblance to the prime suspect of the theft that occurred in the 31st Eastern District.
We're heading for the back alley behind the restaurant now.
TSK.
WE'RE GOING THE WRONG WAY.
SORRY, GAREKI-KUN.
TURN AROUND FOR SEC.
HUH?

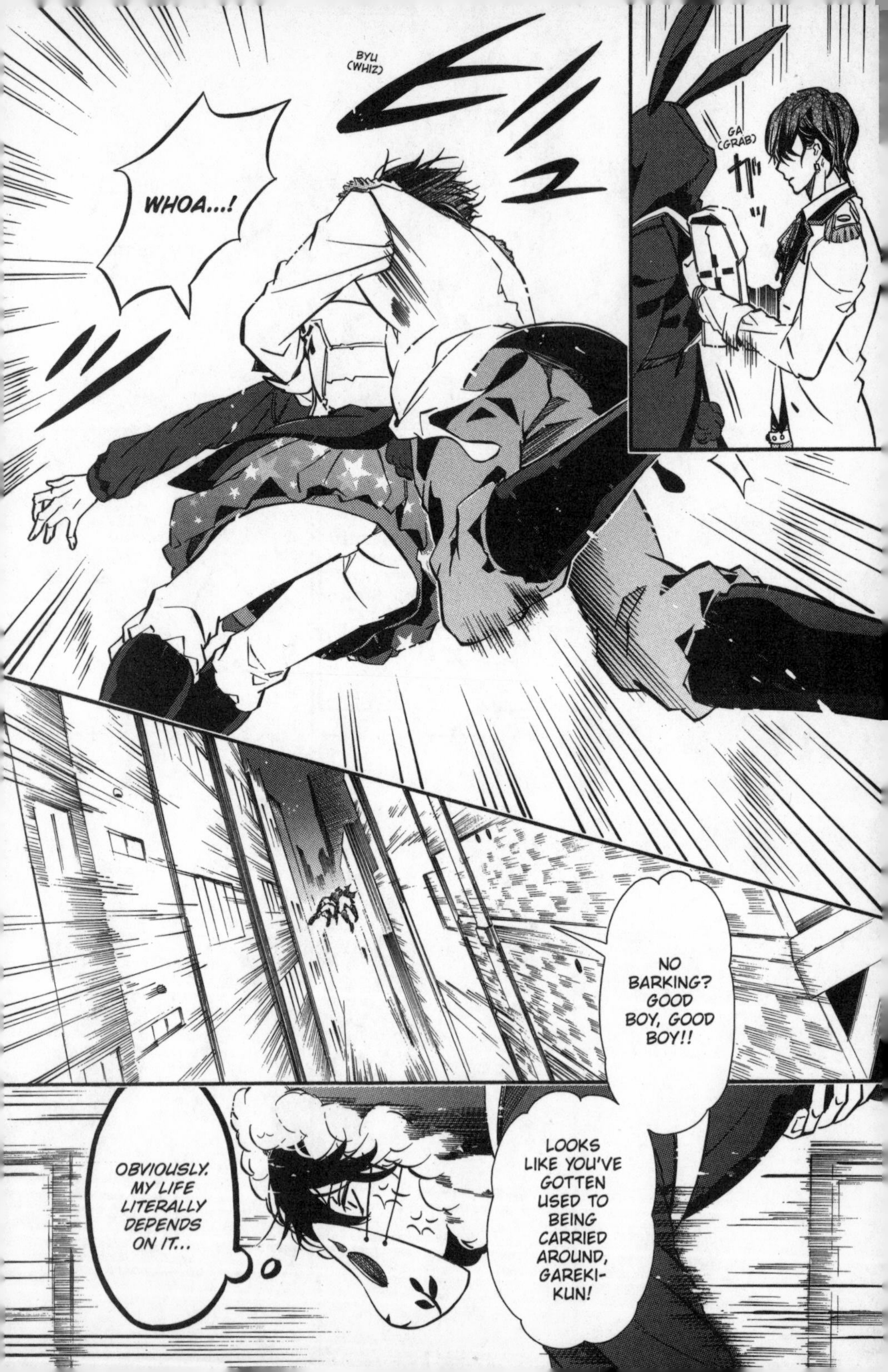
GA (GRAB)
BYU (WHIZ)
WHOA...!
NO BARKING? GOOD BOY, GOOD BOY!!
LOOKS LIKE YOU'VE GOTTEN USED TO BEING CARRIED AROUND, GAREKI-KUN!
OBVIOUSLY. MY LIFE LITERALLY DEPENDS ON IT...

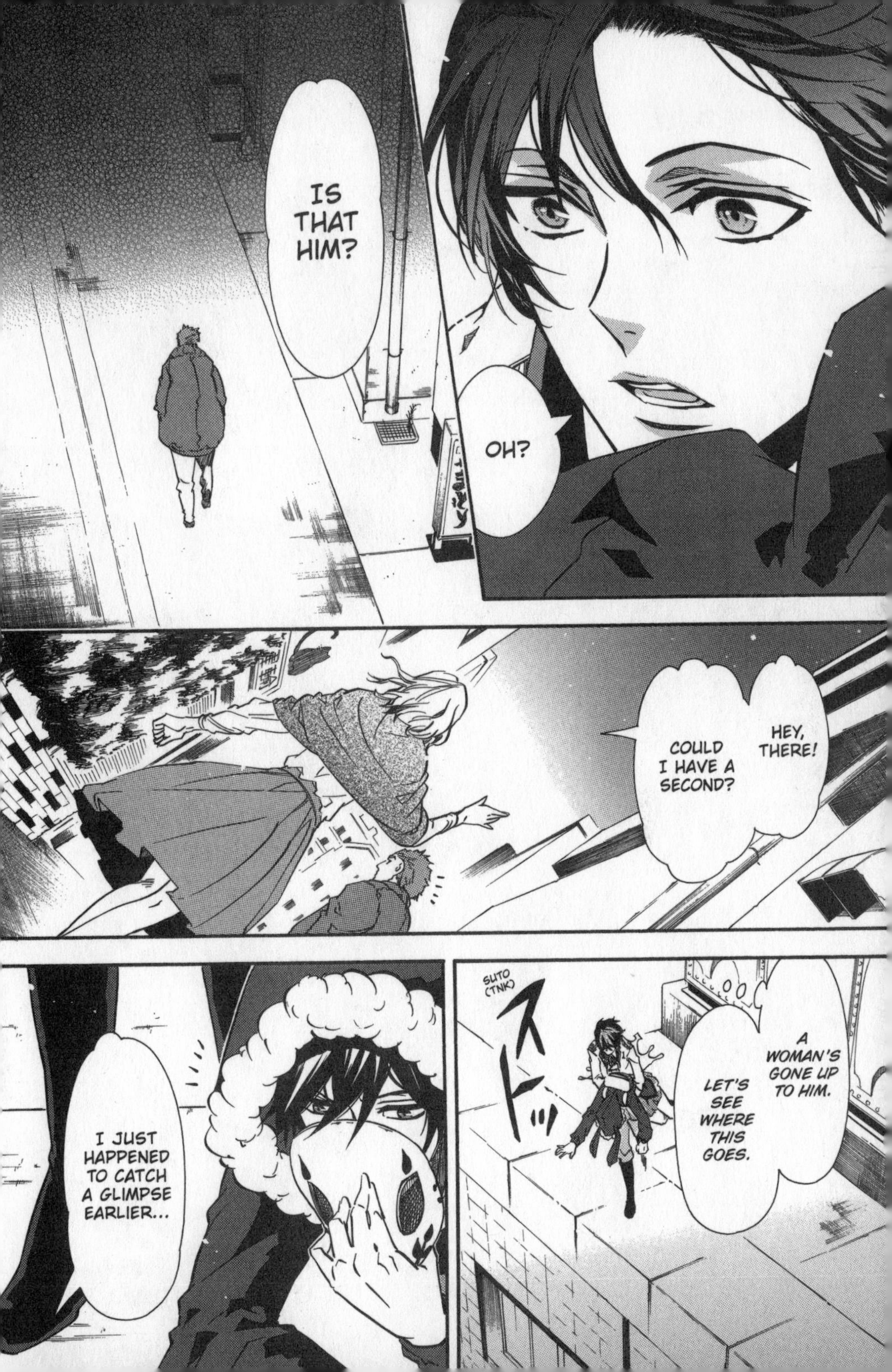
OH?
IS THAT HIM?
HEY, THERE!
COULD I HAVE A SECOND?
SUTO (TNK)
A WOMAN'S GONE UP TO HIM.
LET'S SEE WHERE THIS GOES.
I JUST HAPPENED TO CATCH A GLIMPSE EARLIER...

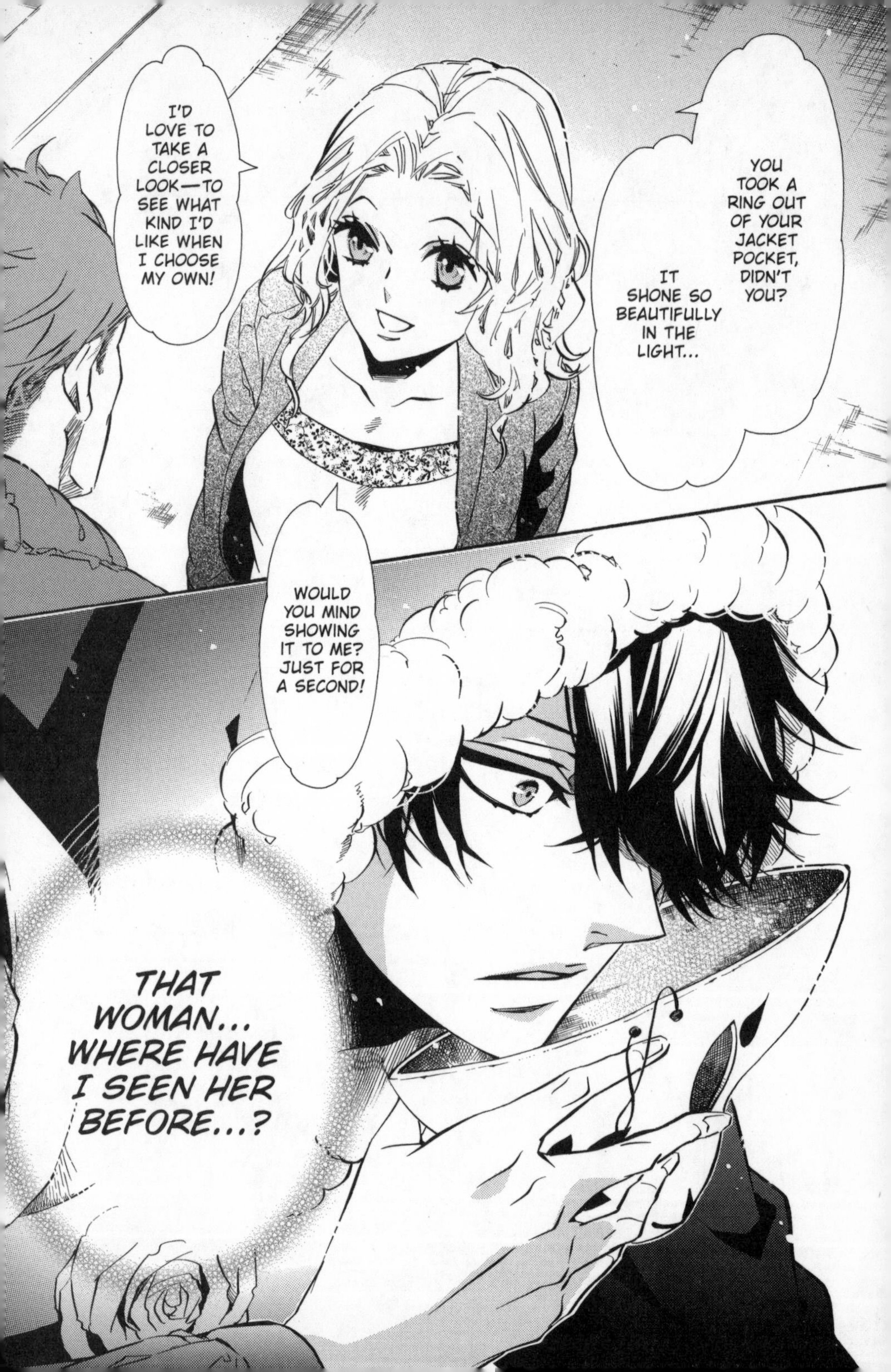
YOU TOOK A RING OUT OF YOUR JACKET POCKET, DIDN'T YOU?
IT SHONE SO BEAUTIFULLY IN THE LIGHT...
I'D LOVE TO TAKE A CLOSER LOOK—TO SEE WHAT KIND I'D LIKE WHEN I CHOOSE MY OWN!
WOULD YOU MIND SHOWING IT TO ME? JUST FOR A SECOND!
THAT WOMAN... WHERE HAVE I SEEN HER BEFORE...?

KARNEVAL

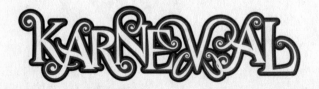

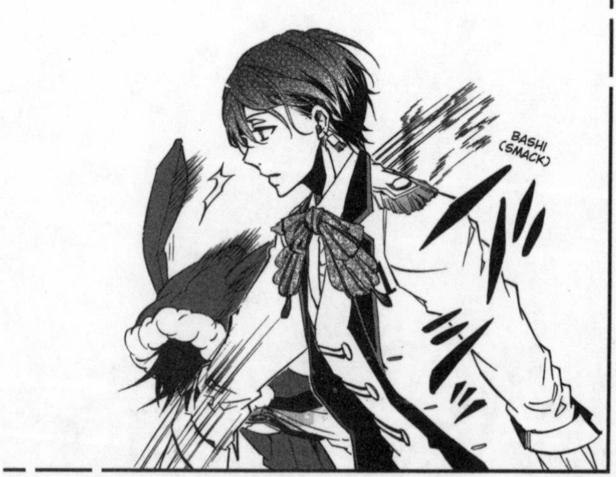
BASHI
(SMACK)

KARNEVAL

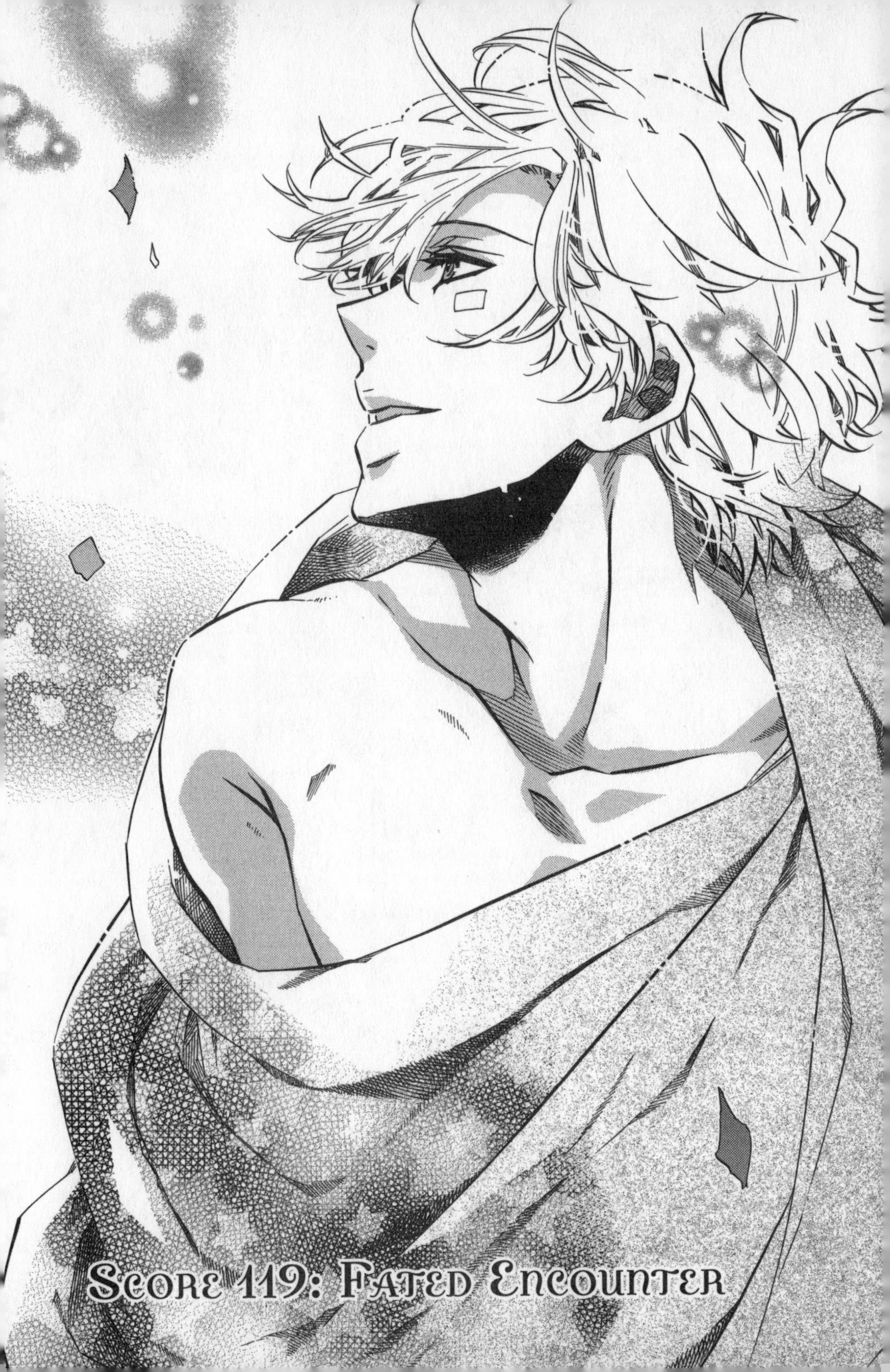

## Score 119: Fated Encounter

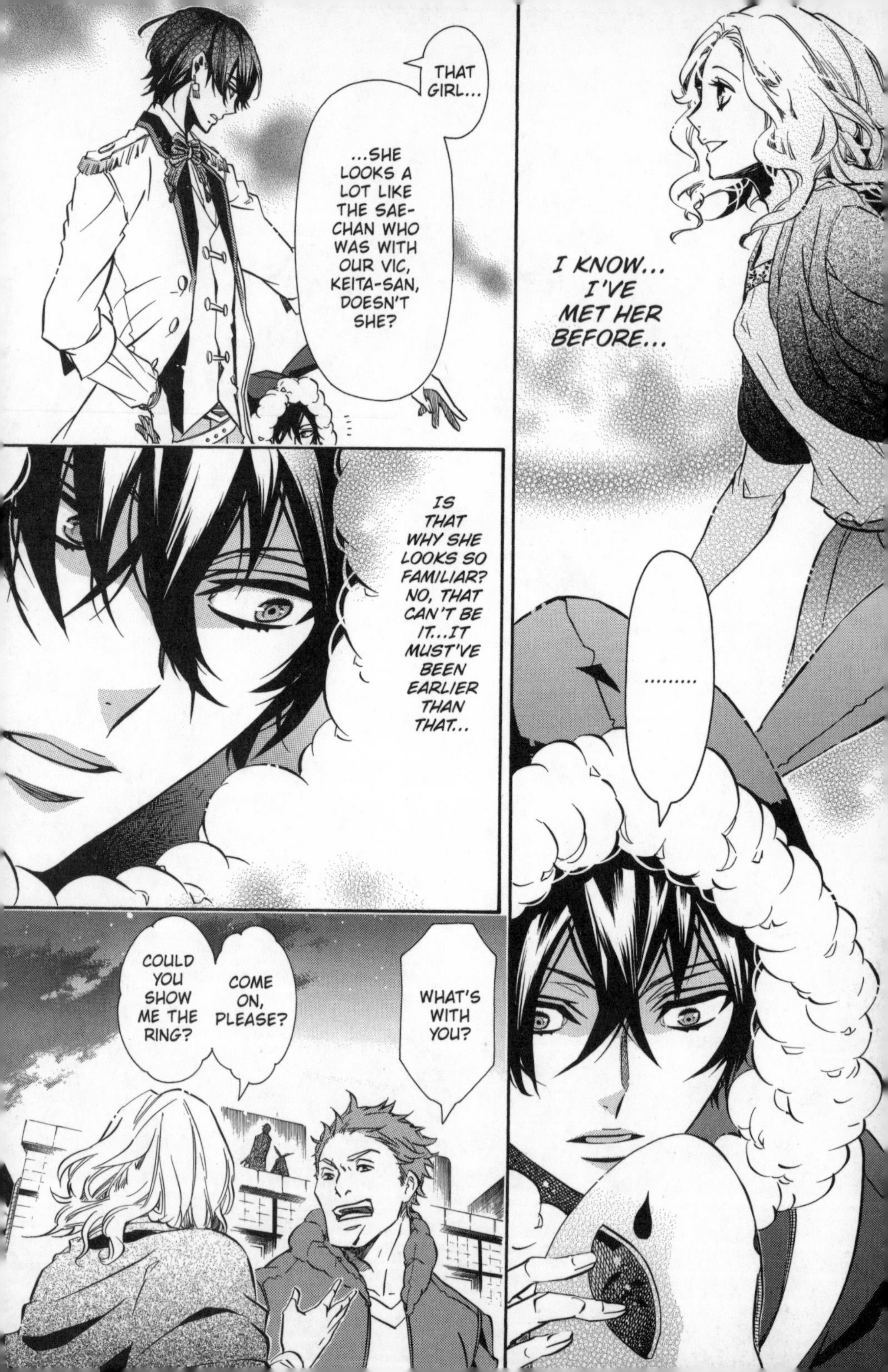
I KNOW... I'VE MET HER BEFORE...
.........
THAT GIRL...
...SHE LOOKS A LOT LIKE THE SAE-CHAN WHO WAS WITH OUR VIC, KEITA-SAN, DOESN'T SHE?
IS THAT WHY SHE LOOKS SO FAMILIAR? NO, THAT CAN'T BE IT...IT MUST'VE BEEN EARLIER THAN THAT...
WHAT'S WITH YOU?
COME ON, PLEASE?
COULD YOU SHOW ME THE RING?

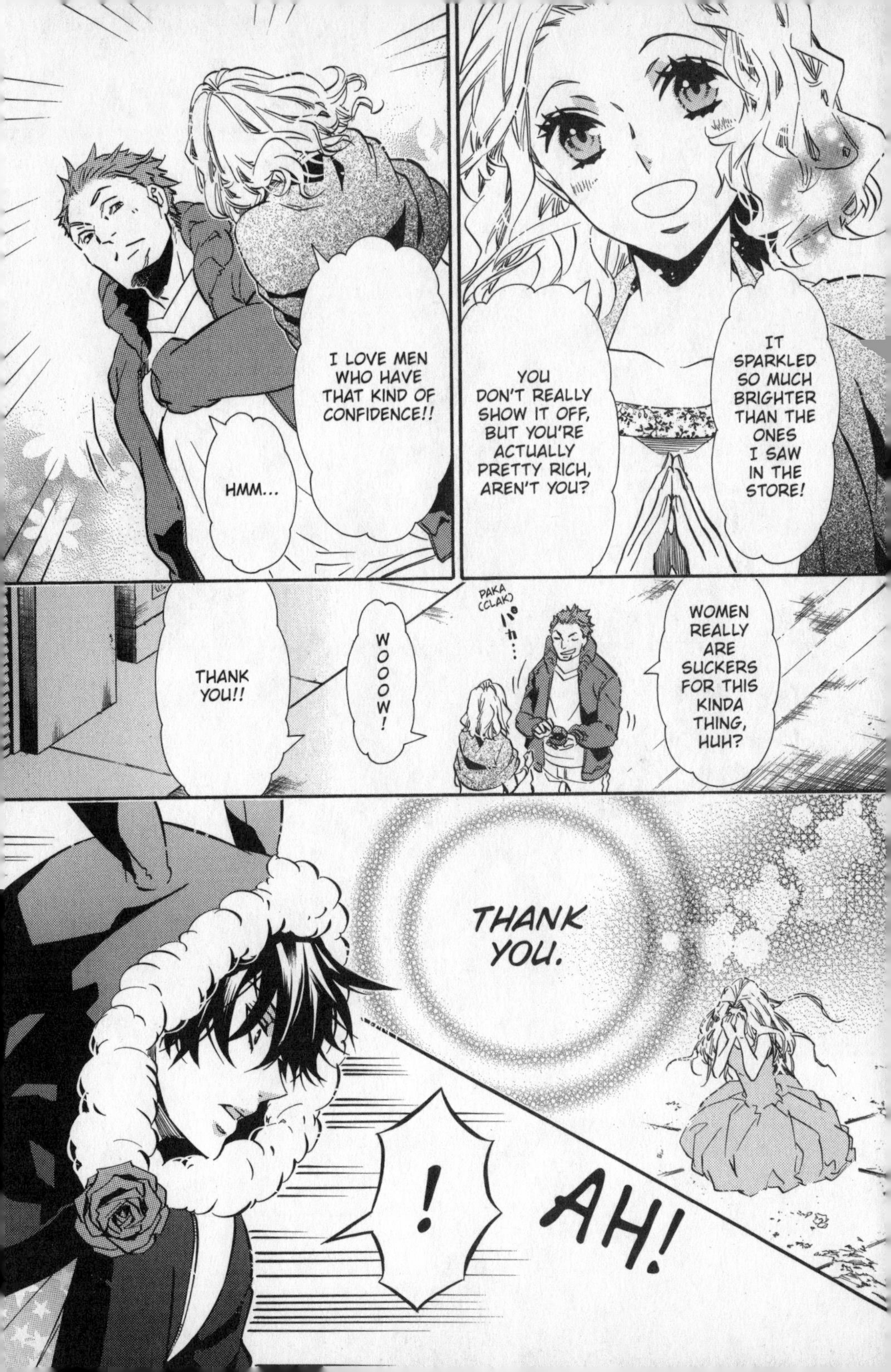

IT SPARKLED SO MUCH BRIGHTER THAN THE ONES I SAW IN THE STORE!
YOU DON'T REALLY SHOW IT OFF, BUT YOU'RE ACTUALLY PRETTY RICH, AREN'T YOU?
I LOVE MEN WHO HAVE THAT KIND OF CONFIDENCE!!
HMM...
WOMEN REALLY ARE SUCKERS FOR THIS KINDA THING, HUH?
PAKA (CLAK)
パカ…
WOOOOW!
THANK YOU!!
THANK YOU.
AH!
!

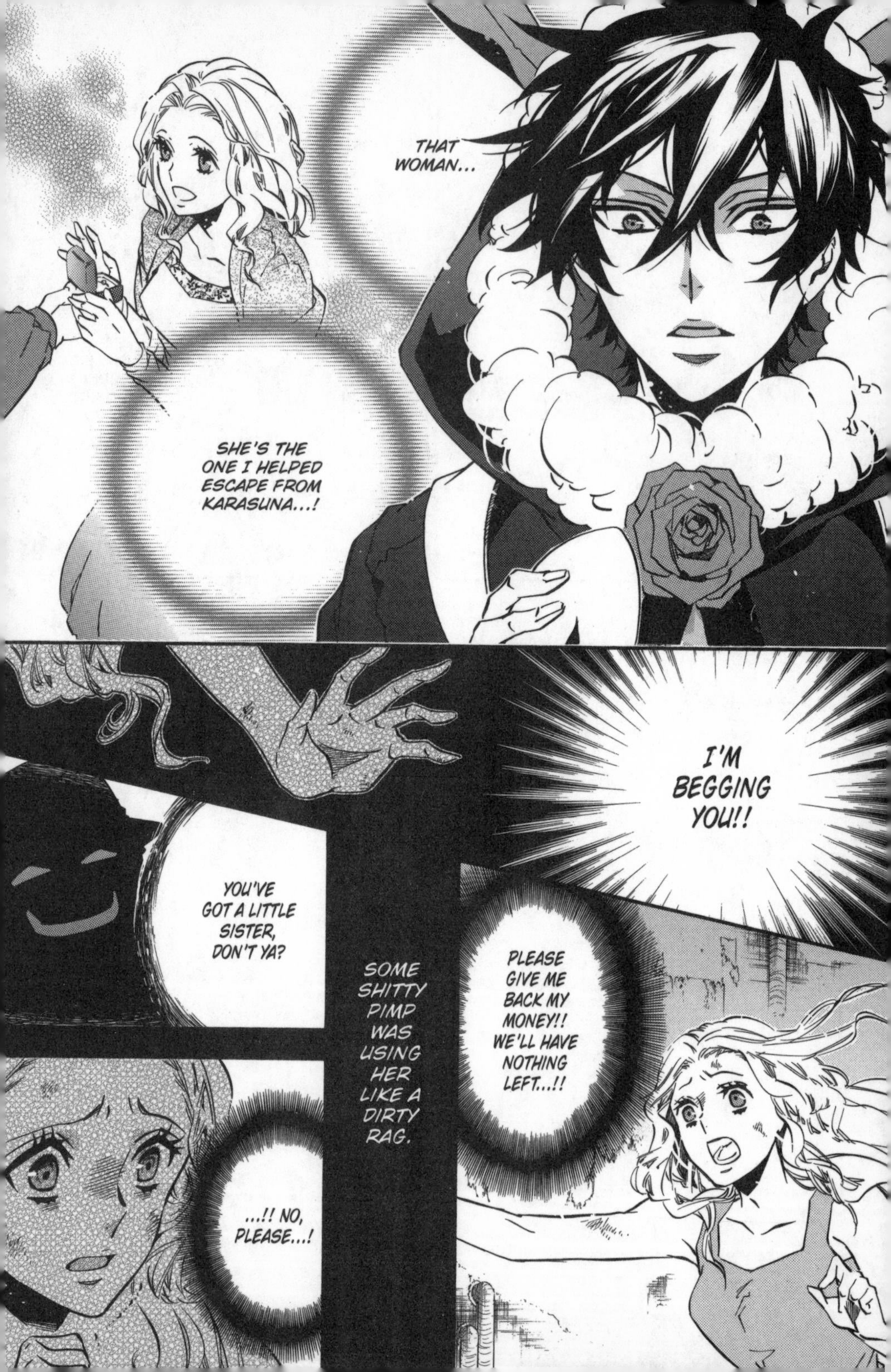
THAT WOMAN...
SHE'S THE ONE I HELPED ESCAPE FROM KARASUNA...!
I'M BEGGING YOU!!
PLEASE GIVE ME BACK MY MONEY!! WE'LL HAVE NOTHING LEFT...!!
SOME SHITTY PIMP WAS USING HER LIKE A DIRTY RAG.
YOU'VE GOT A LITTLE SISTER, DON'T YA?
...!! NO, PLEASE...!

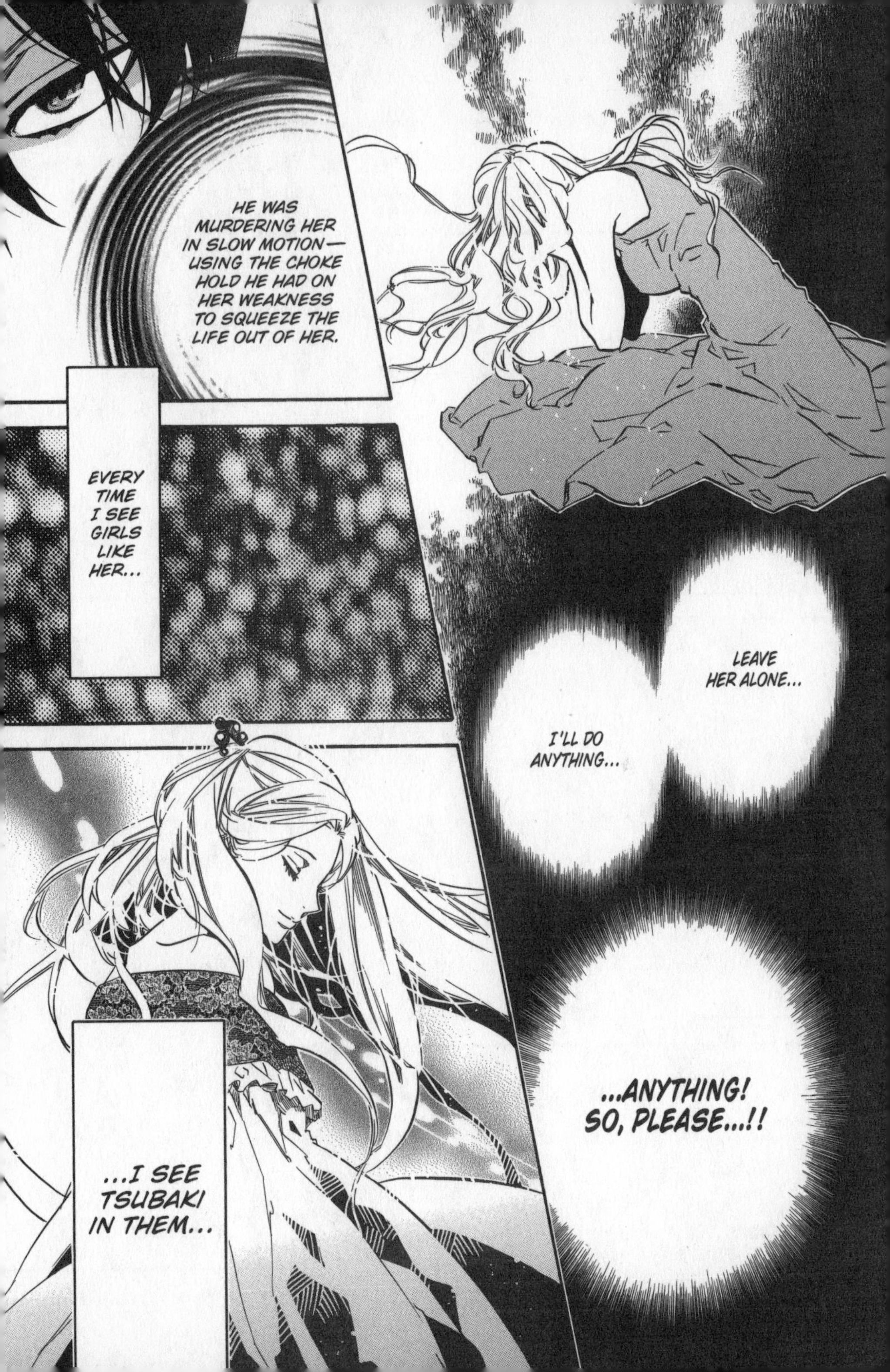
LEAVE HER ALONE...
I'LL DO ANYTHING...
...ANYTHING! SO, PLEASE...!!
HE WAS MURDERING HER IN SLOW MOTION— USING THE CHOKE HOLD HE HAD ON HER WEAKNESS TO SQUEEZE THE LIFE OUT OF HER.
EVERY TIME I SEE GIRLS LIKE HER...
...I SEE TSUBAKI IN THEM...

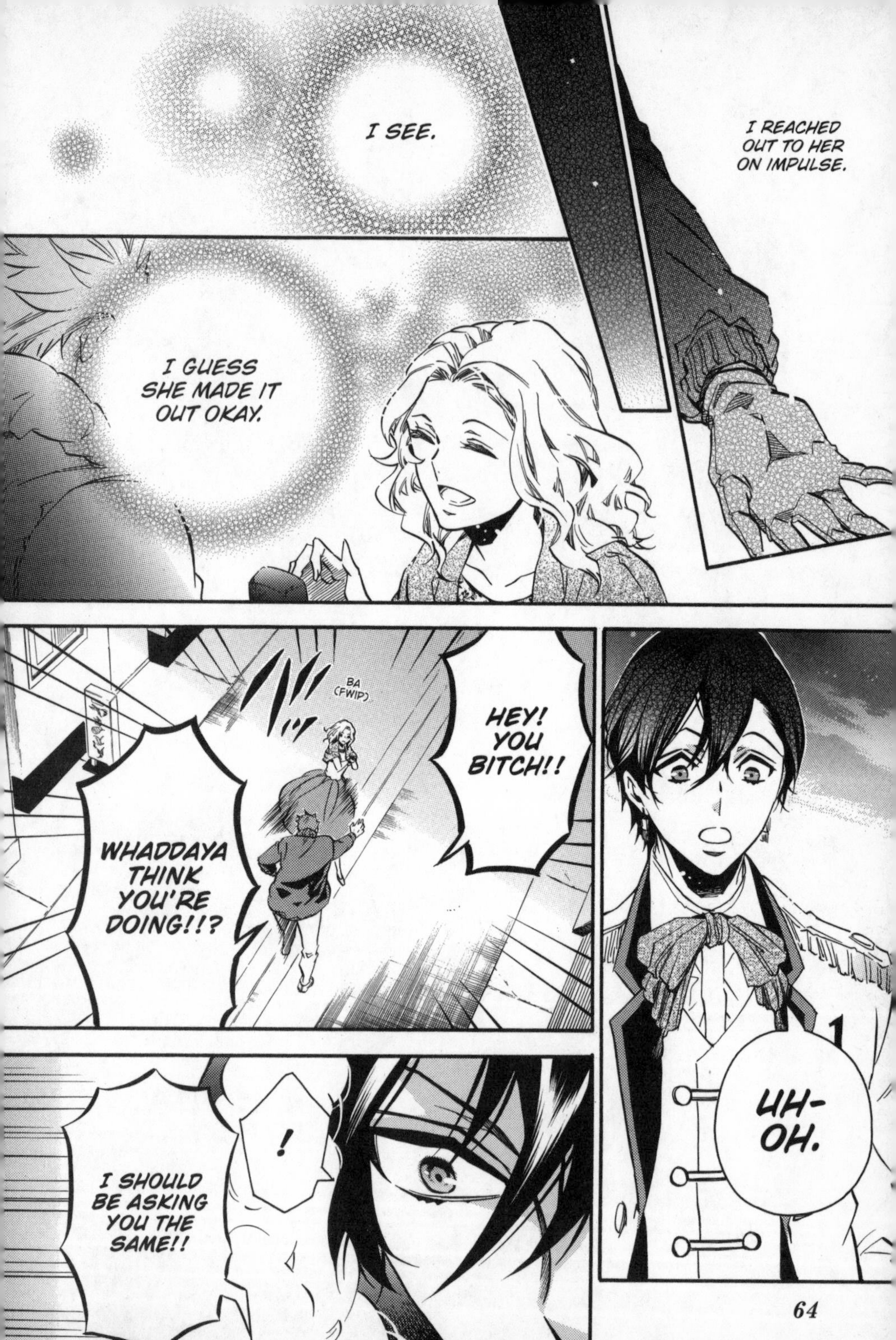
I REACHED OUT TO HER ON IMPULSE.
I SEE.
I GUESS SHE MADE IT OUT OKAY.
UH-OH.
HEY! YOU BITCH!!
BA (FWIP)
WHADDAYA THINK YOU'RE DOING!!?
!
I SHOULD BE ASKING YOU THE SAME!!

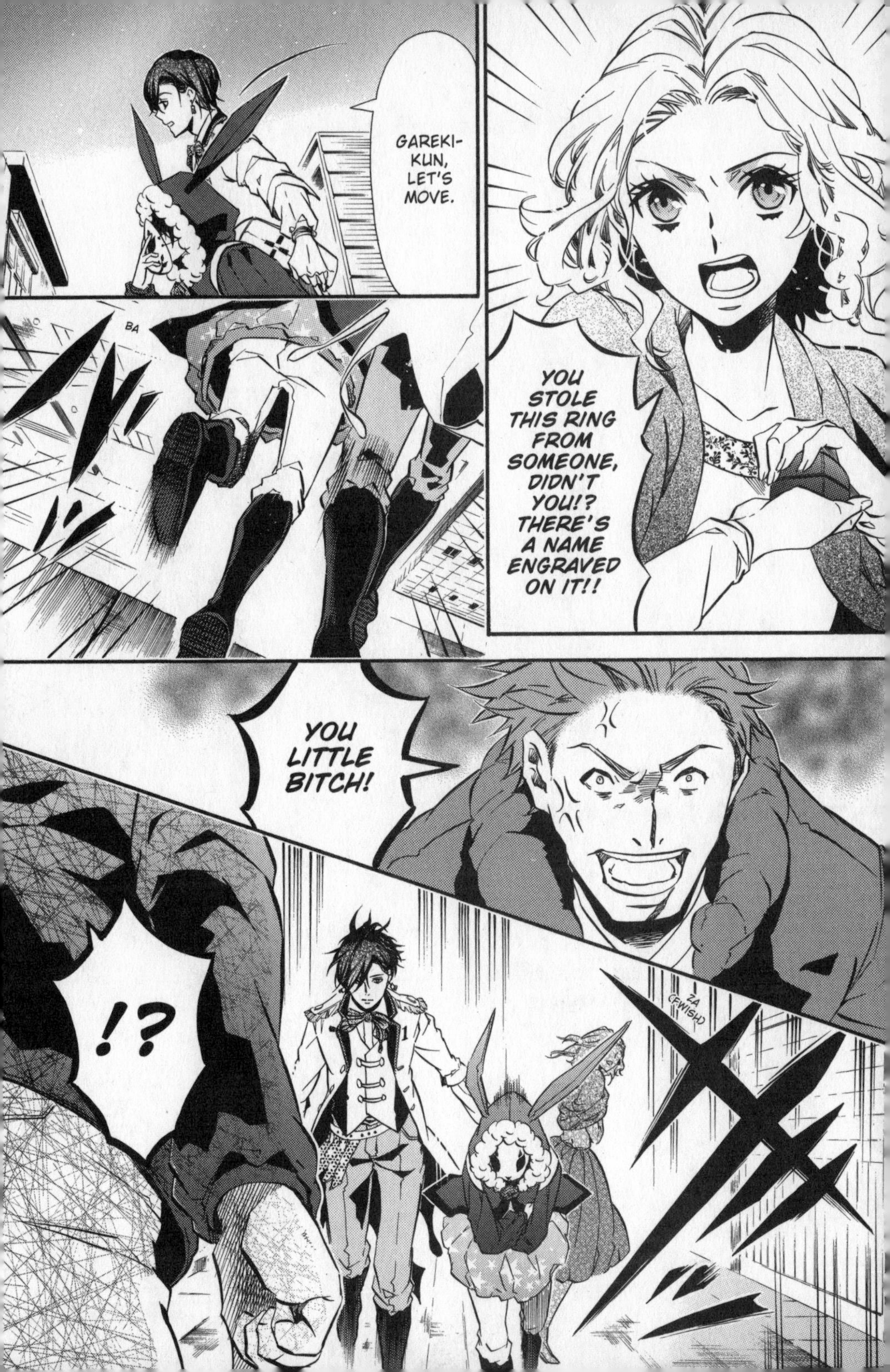
YOU STOLE THIS RING FROM SOMEONE, DIDN'T YOU!? THERE'S A NAME ENGRAVED ON IT!!
GAREKI-KUN, LET'S MOVE.
BA
YOU LITTLE BITCH!
ZA (FWISH)
!?

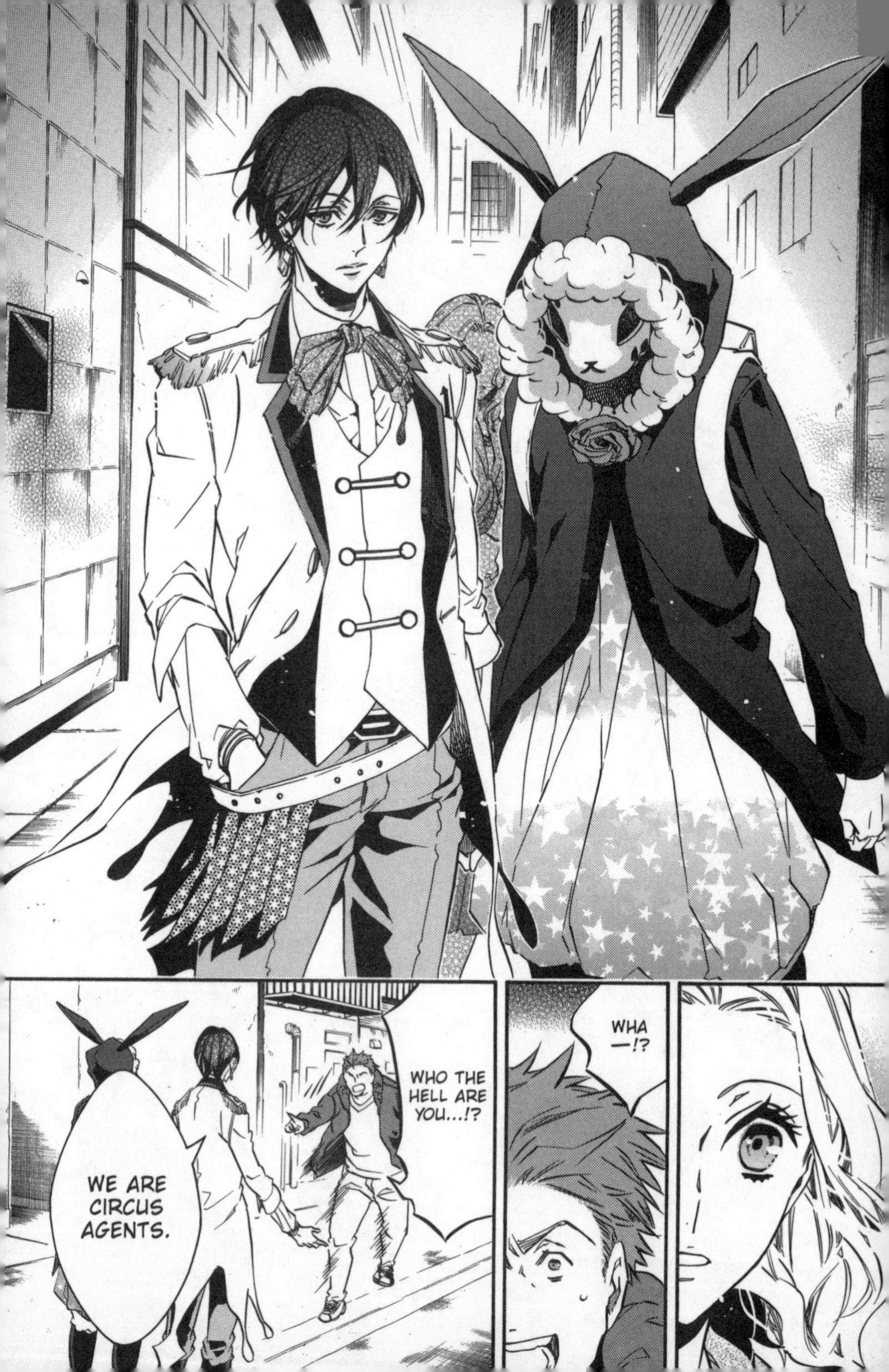
WHA—!?
WHO THE HELL ARE YOU...!?
WE ARE CIRCUS AGENTS.

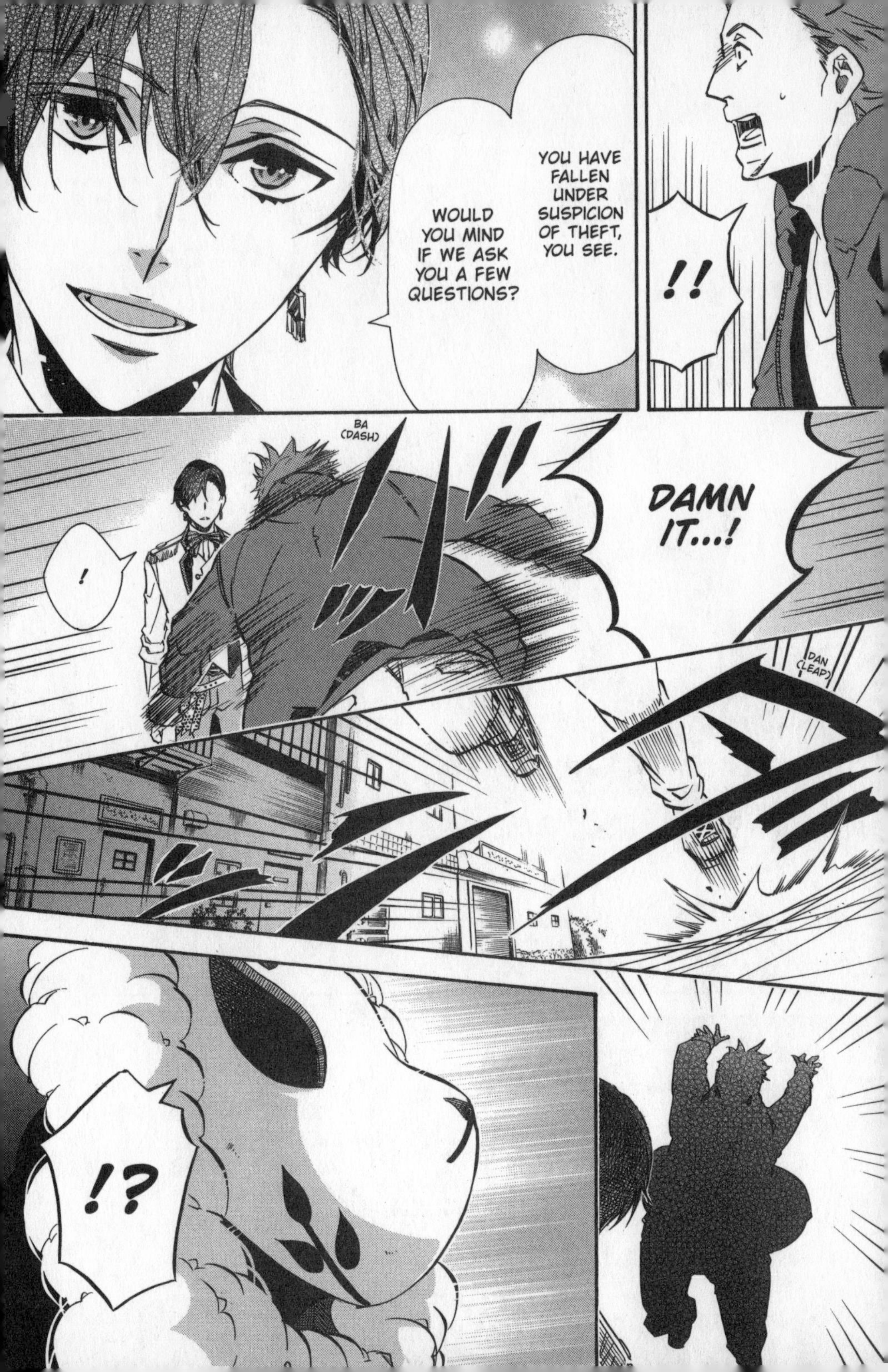
!!
YOU HAVE FALLEN UNDER SUSPICION OF THEFT, YOU SEE.
WOULD YOU MIND IF WE ASK YOU A FEW QUESTIONS?
DAMN IT...!
DAN (LEAP)
BA (DASH)
!
!?

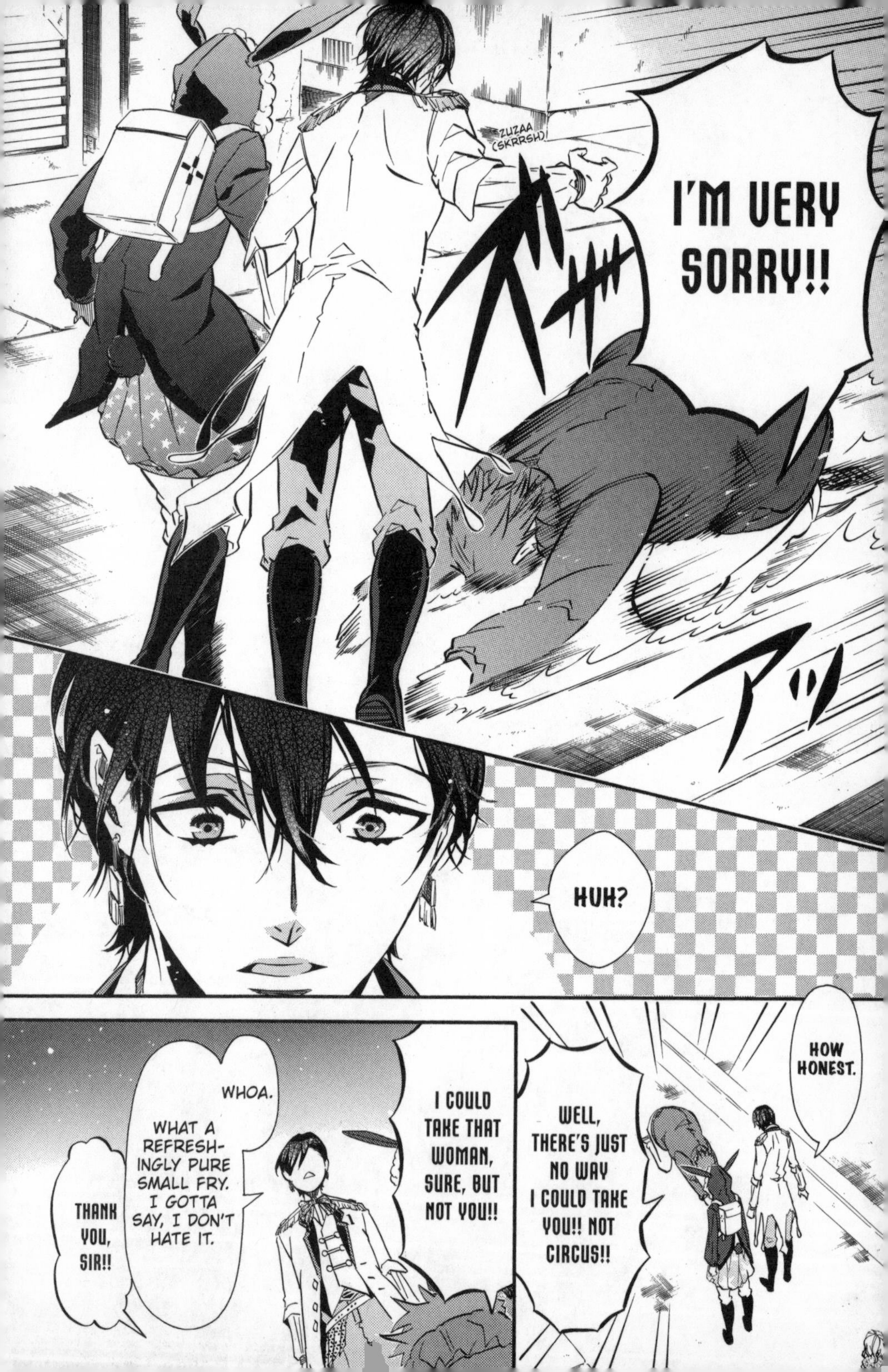
ZUZAA (SKRRSH)
I'M VERY SORRY!!
HUH?
HOW HONEST.
WELL, THERE'S JUST NO WAY I COULD TAKE YOU!! NOT CIRCUS!!
I COULD TAKE THAT WOMAN, SURE, BUT NOT YOU!!
WHOA.
WHAT A REFRESH-INGLY PURE SMALL FRY. I GOTTA SAY, I DON'T HATE IT.
THANK YOU, SIR!!

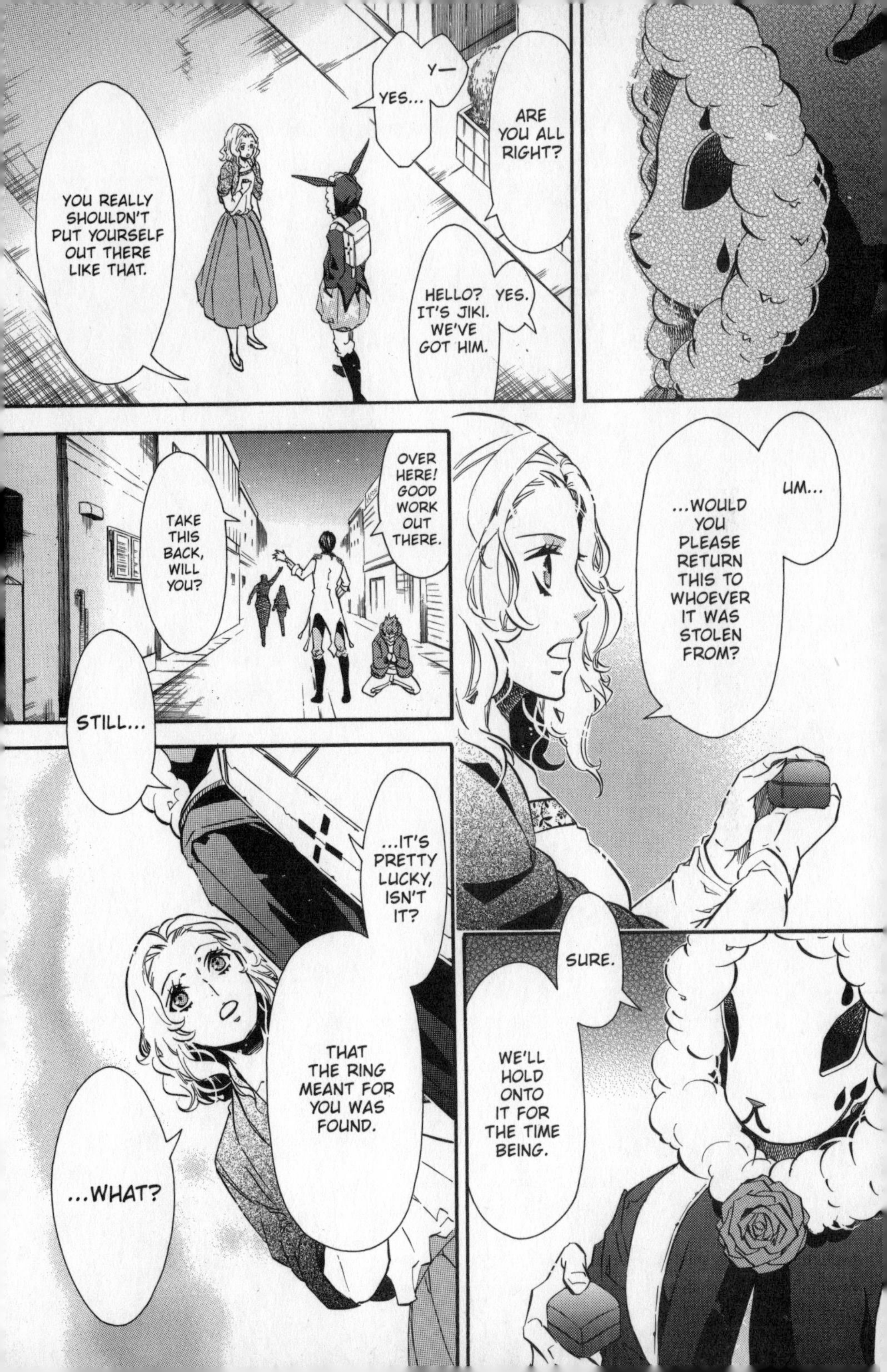
ARE YOU ALL RIGHT?
Y— YES...
HELLO? YES. IT'S JIKI. WE'VE GOT HIM.
YOU REALLY SHOULDN'T PUT YOURSELF OUT THERE LIKE THAT.
UM...
...WOULD YOU PLEASE RETURN THIS TO WHOEVER IT WAS STOLEN FROM?
OVER HERE! GOOD WORK OUT THERE.
TAKE THIS BACK, WILL YOU?
SURE.
WE'LL HOLD ONTO IT FOR THE TIME BEING.
STILL...
...IT'S PRETTY LUCKY, ISN'T IT?
THAT THE RING MEANT FOR YOU WAS FOUND.
...WHAT?

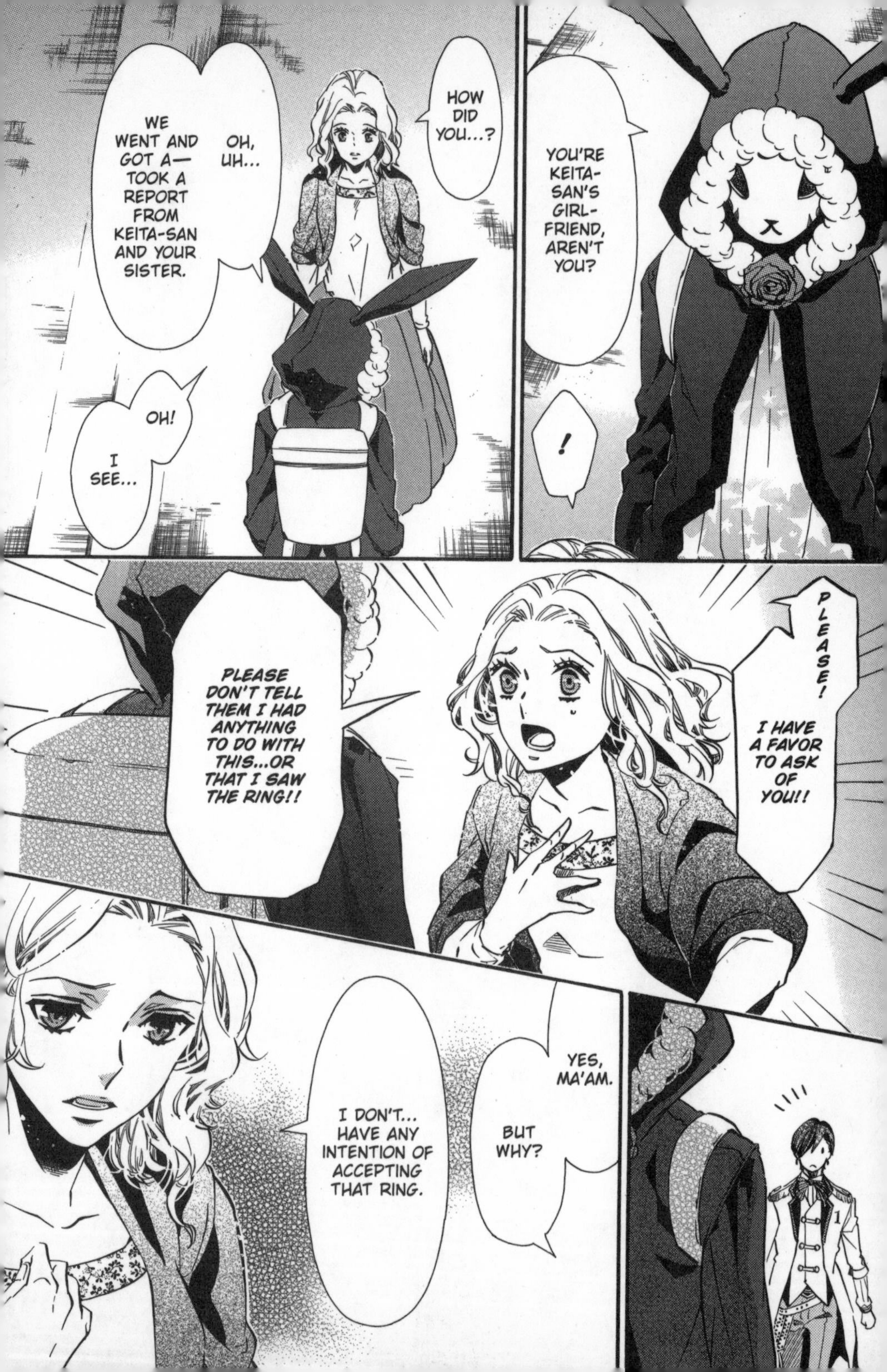
YOU'RE KEITA-SAN'S GIRLFRIEND, AREN'T YOU?
!
HOW DID YOU...?
OH, UH...
WE WENT AND GOT A— TOOK A REPORT FROM KEITA-SAN AND YOUR SISTER.
OH! I SEE...
PLEASE!
I HAVE A FAVOR TO ASK OF YOU!!
PLEASE DON'T TELL THEM I HAD ANYTHING TO DO WITH THIS...OR THAT I SAW THE RING!!
YES, MA'AM.
BUT WHY?
I DON'T... HAVE ANY INTENTION OF ACCEPTING THAT RING.

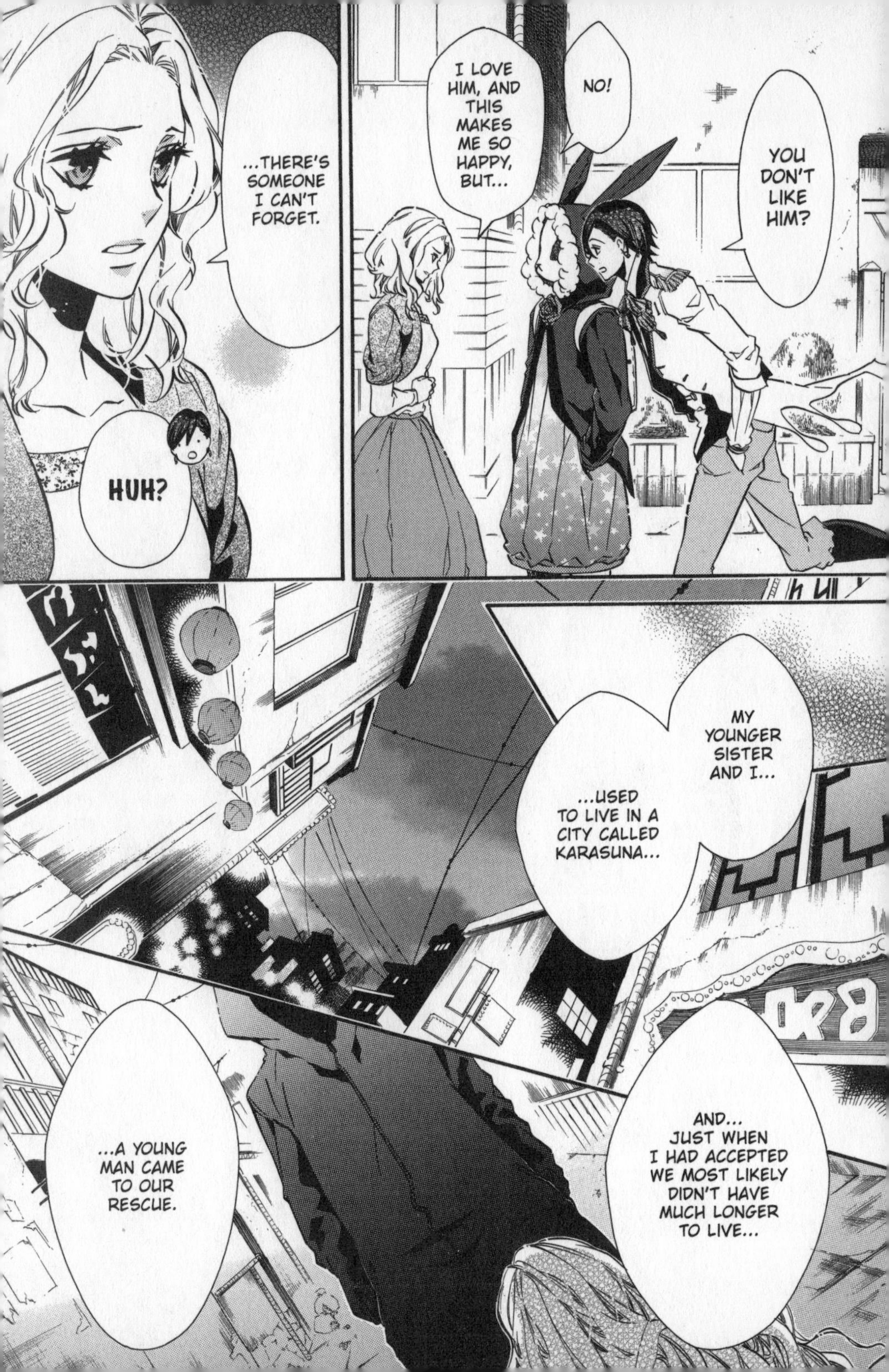
YOU DON'T LIKE HIM?
NO!
I LOVE HIM, AND THIS MAKES ME SO HAPPY, BUT...
...THERE'S SOMEONE I CAN'T FORGET.
HUH?
MY YOUNGER SISTER AND I...
...USED TO LIVE IN A CITY CALLED KARASUNA...
AND... JUST WHEN I HAD ACCEPTED WE MOST LIKELY DIDN'T HAVE MUCH LONGER TO LIVE...
...A YOUNG MAN CAME TO OUR RESCUE.

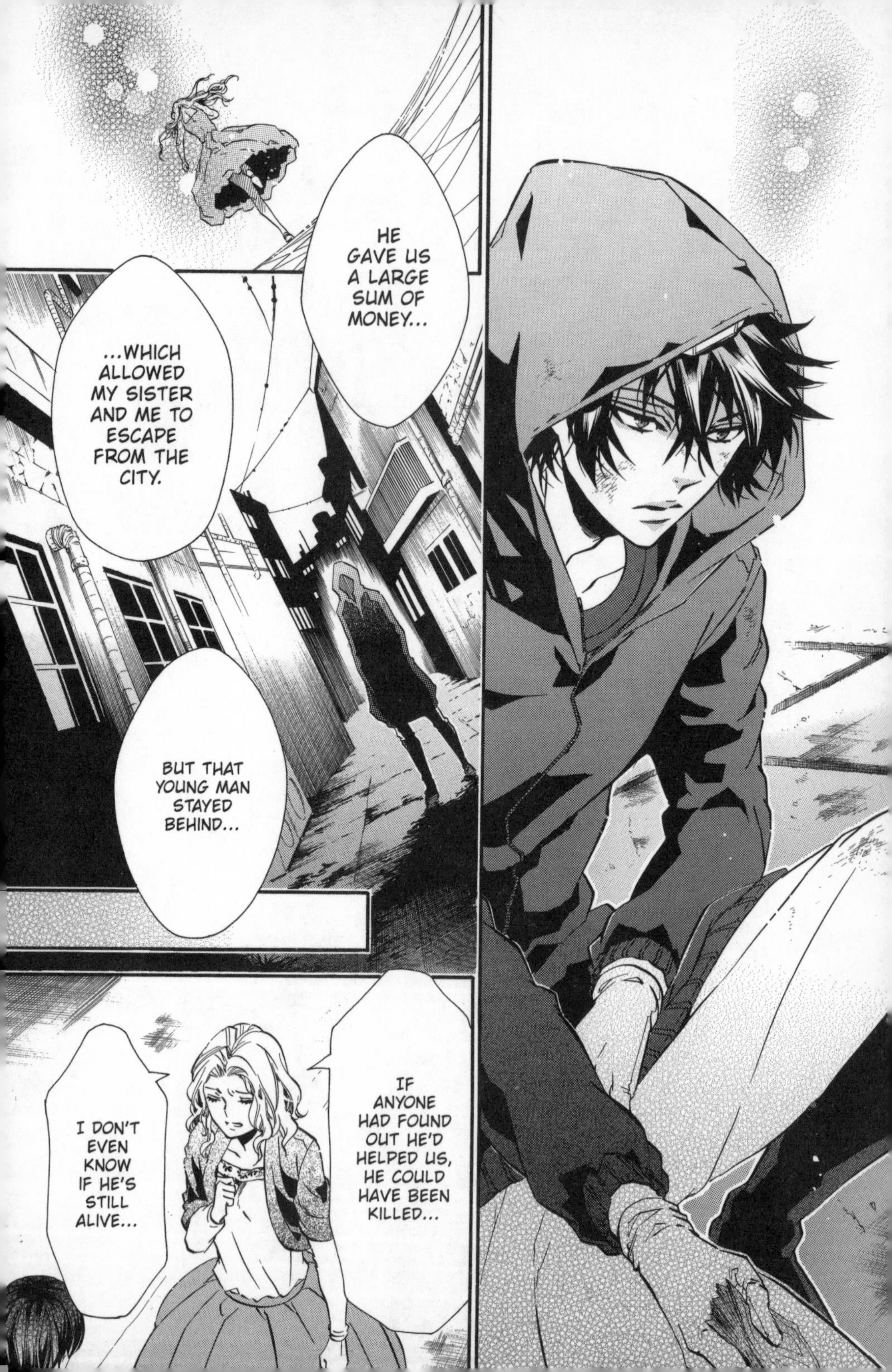
HE GAVE US A LARGE SUM OF MONEY...
...WHICH ALLOWED MY SISTER AND ME TO ESCAPE FROM THE CITY.
BUT THAT YOUNG MAN STAYED BEHIND...
IF ANYONE HAD FOUND OUT HE'D HELPED US, HE COULD HAVE BEEN KILLED...
I DON'T EVEN KNOW IF HE'S STILL ALIVE...

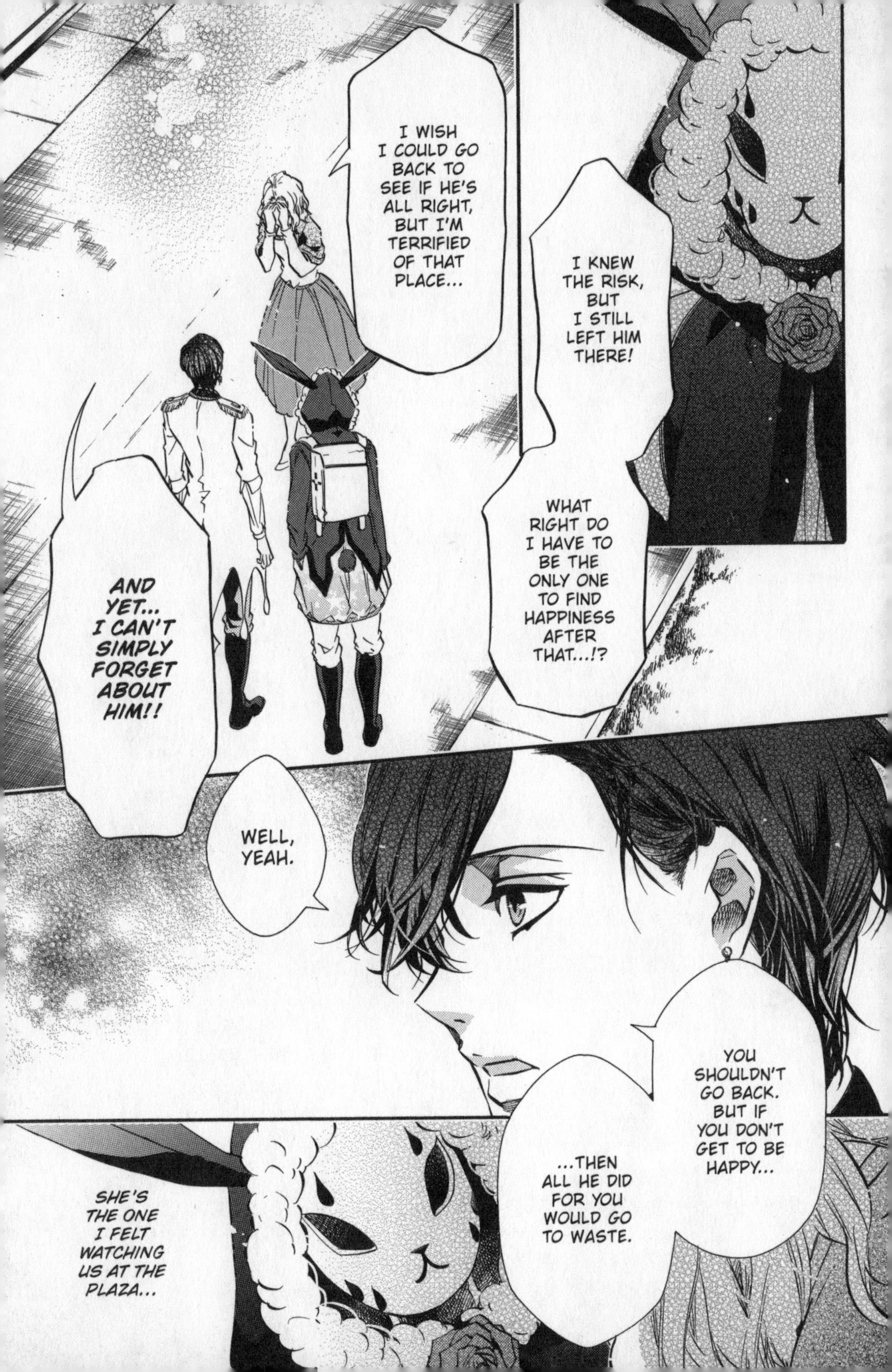
I KNEW THE RISK, BUT I STILL LEFT HIM THERE!
WHAT RIGHT DO I HAVE TO BE THE ONLY ONE TO FIND HAPPINESS AFTER THAT...!?
I WISH I COULD GO BACK TO SEE IF HE'S ALL RIGHT, BUT I'M TERRIFIED OF THAT PLACE...
AND YET... I CAN'T SIMPLY FORGET ABOUT HIM!!
WELL, YEAH.
YOU SHOULDN'T GO BACK. BUT IF YOU DON'T GET TO BE HAPPY...
...THEN ALL HE DID FOR YOU WOULD GO TO WASTE.
SHE'S THE ONE I FELT WATCHING US AT THE PLAZA...

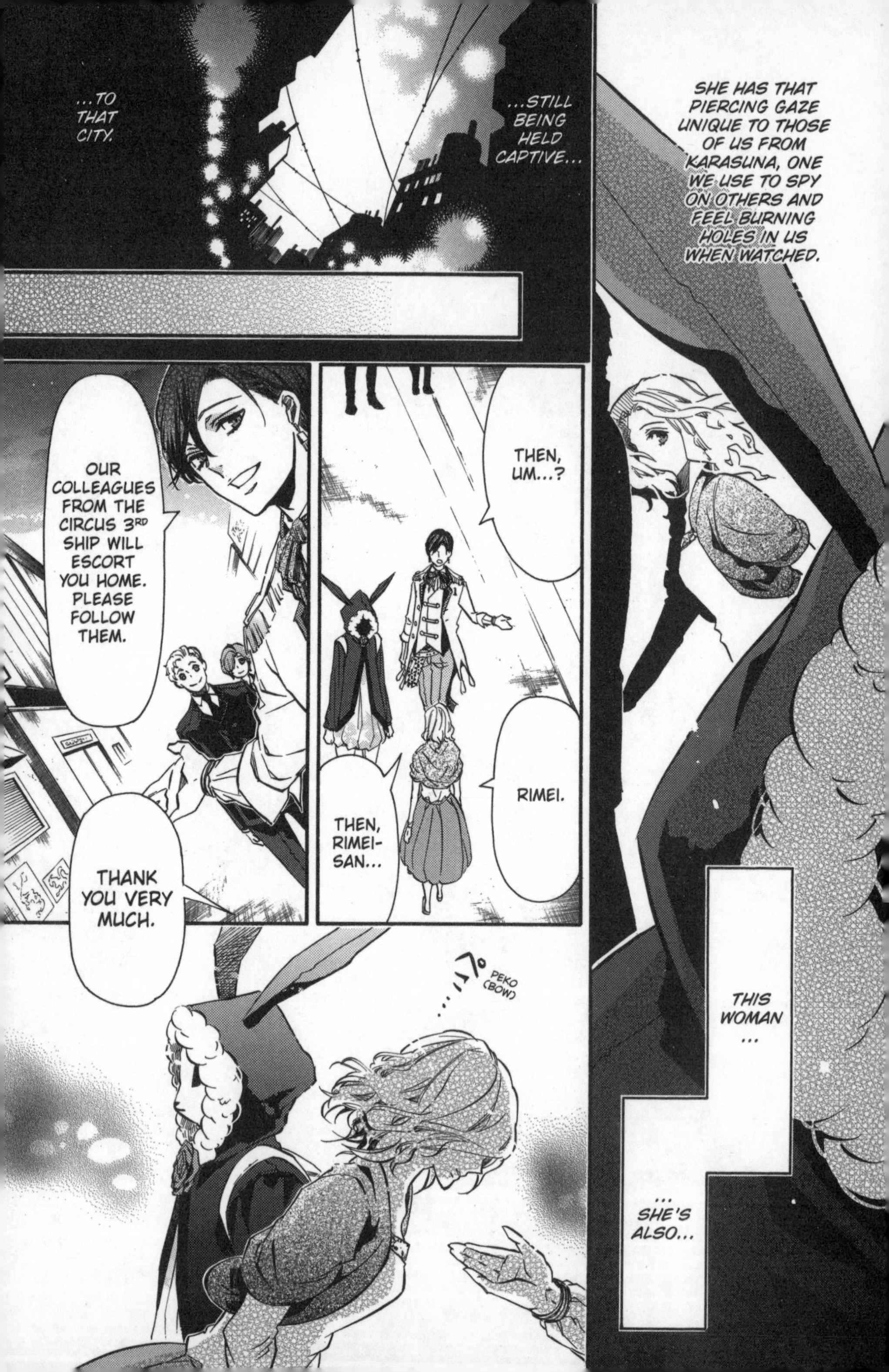
SHE HAS THAT PIERCING GAZE UNIQUE TO THOSE OF US FROM KARASUNA, ONE WE USE TO SPY ON OTHERS AND FEEL BURNING HOLES IN US WHEN WATCHED.
THIS WOMAN...
...SHE'S ALSO...
...STILL BEING HELD CAPTIVE...
...TO THAT CITY.
THEN, UM...?
RIMEI.
THEN, RIMEI-SAN...
OUR COLLEAGUES FROM THE CIRCUS 3RD SHIP WILL ESCORT YOU HOME. PLEASE FOLLOW THEM.
THANK YOU VERY MUCH.
...
PEKO (BOW)

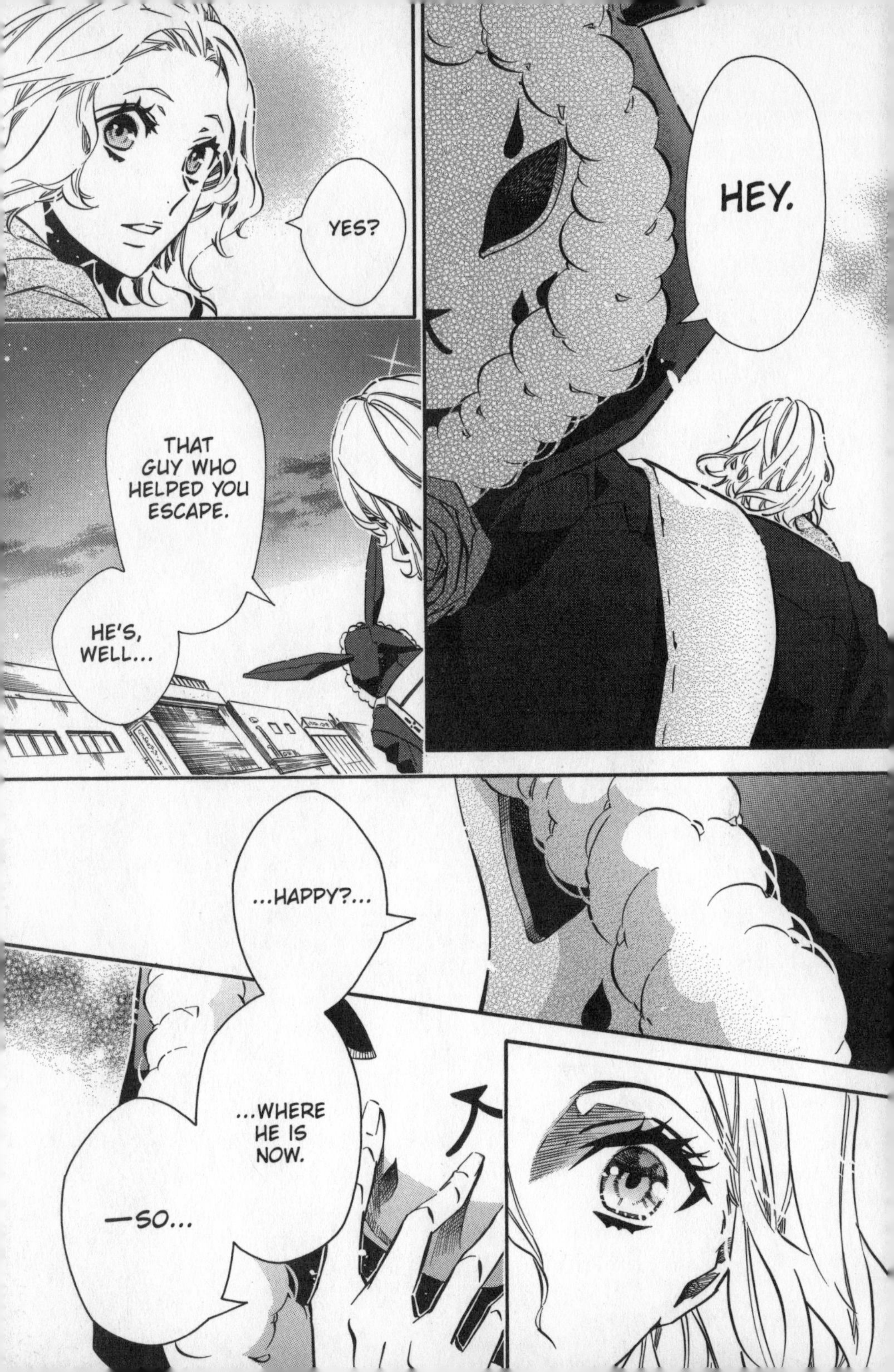
HEY.
YES?
THAT GUY WHO HELPED YOU ESCAPE.
HE'S, WELL...
...HAPPY?...
...WHERE HE IS NOW.
—SO...

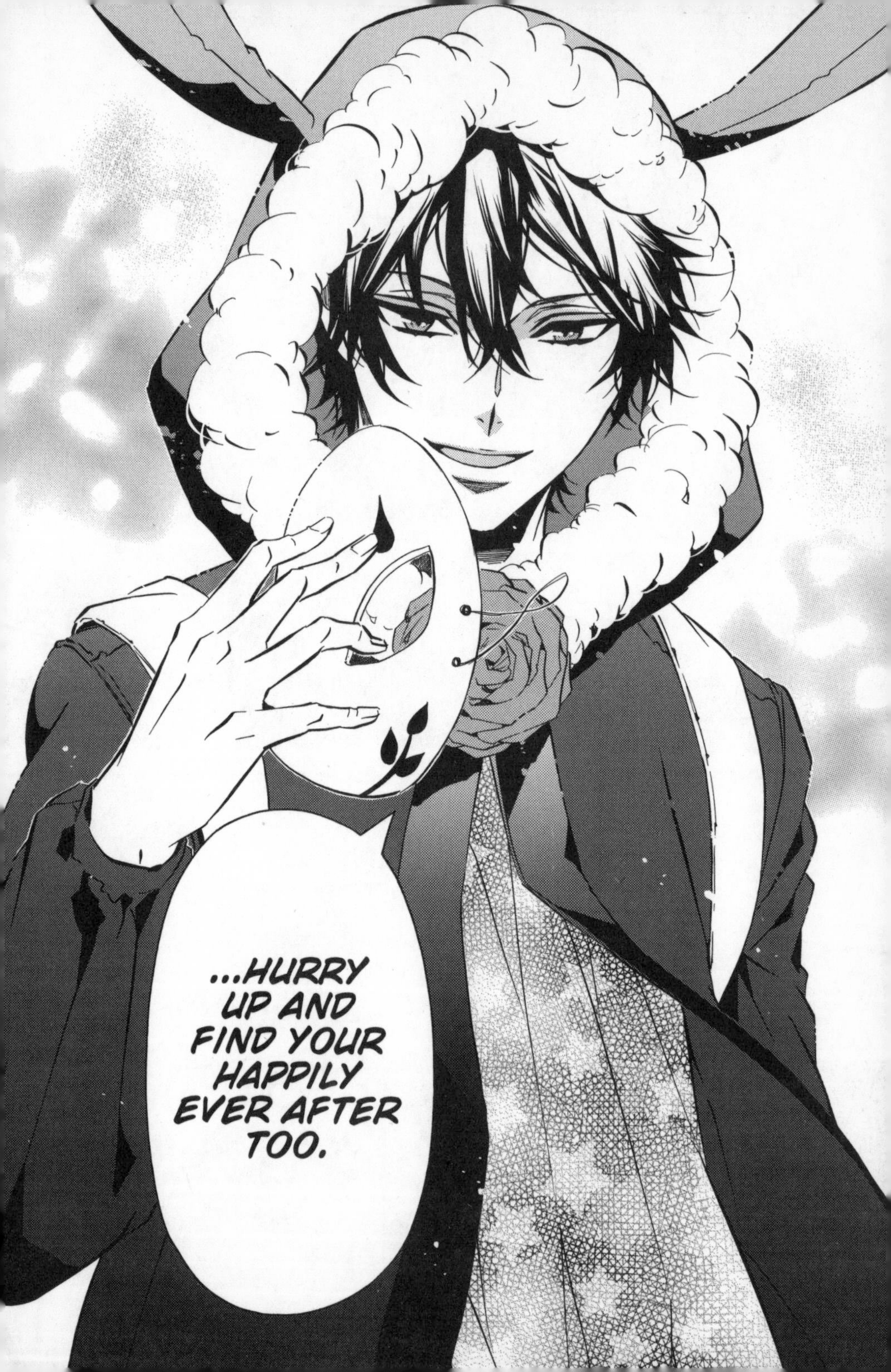
...HURRY UP AND FIND YOUR HAPPILY EVER AFTER TOO.

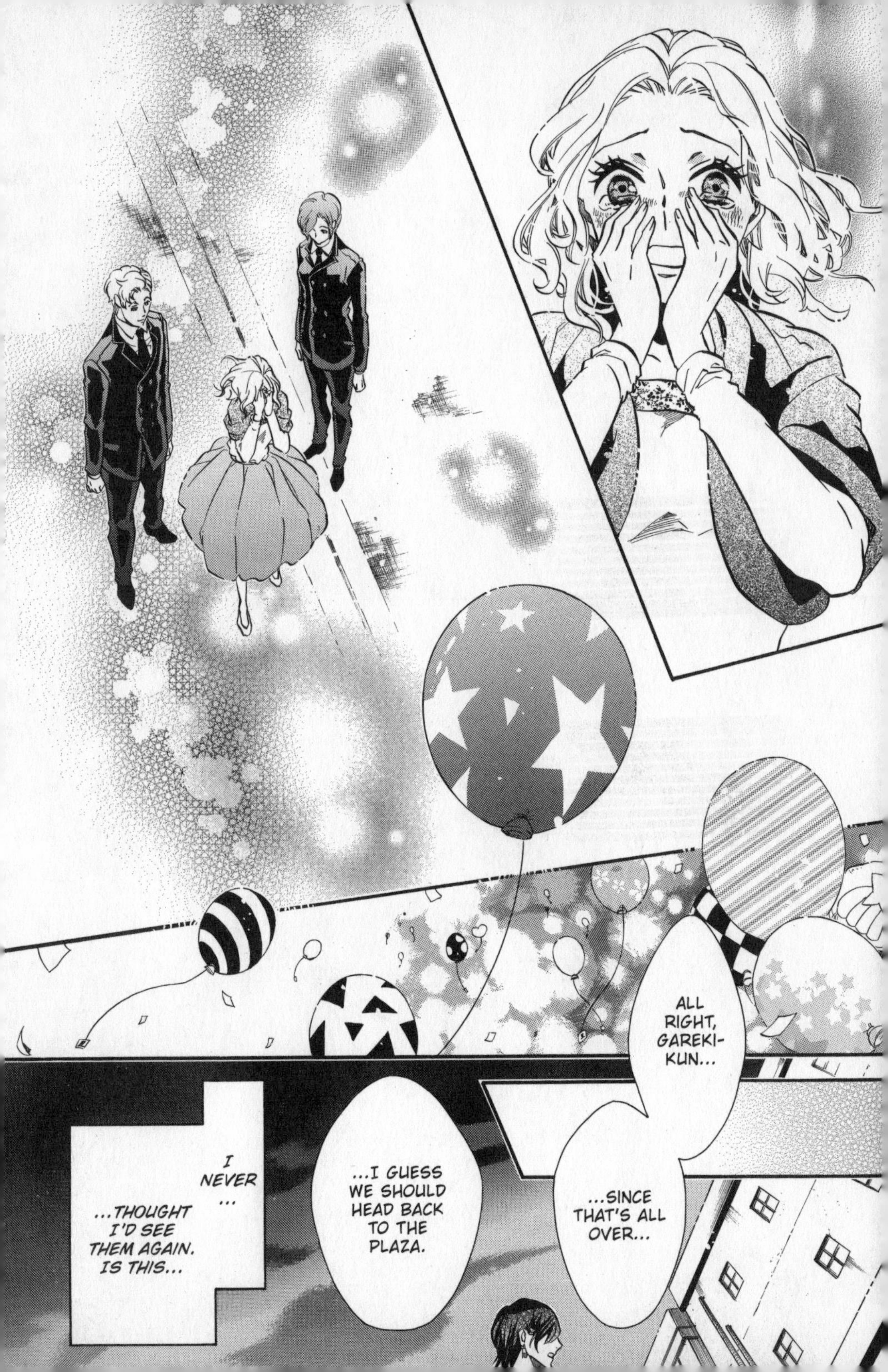
ALL RIGHT, GAREKI-KUN...
...SINCE THAT'S ALL OVER...
...I GUESS WE SHOULD HEAD BACK TO THE PLAZA.
I NEVER...
...THOUGHT I'D SEE THEM AGAIN. IS THIS...

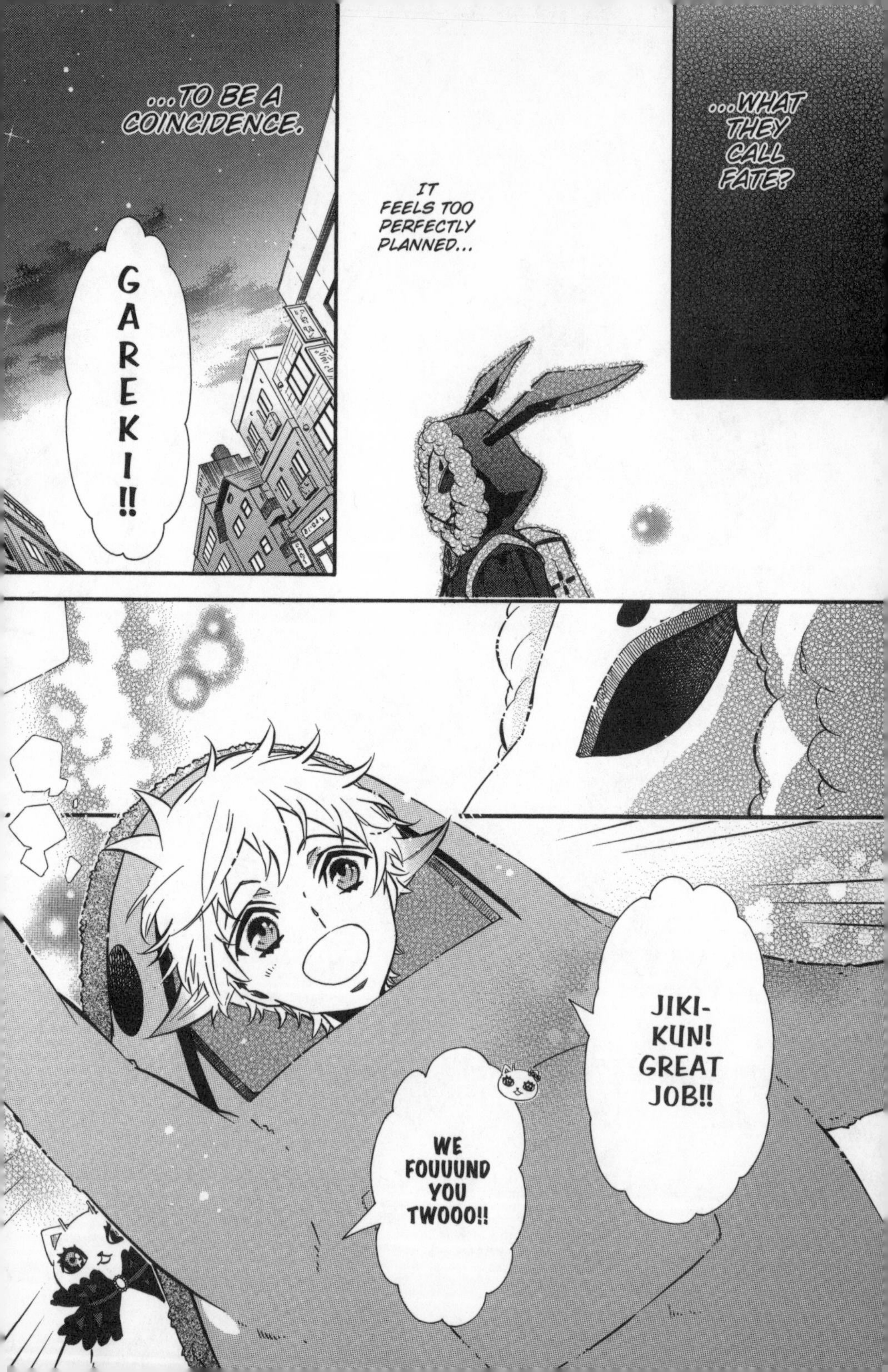
...WHAT THEY CALL FATE?
IT FEELS TOO PERFECTLY PLANNED...
...TO BE A COINCIDENCE.
GAREKI!!
JIKI-KUN! GREAT JOB!!
WE FOUUUND YOU TWOOO!!

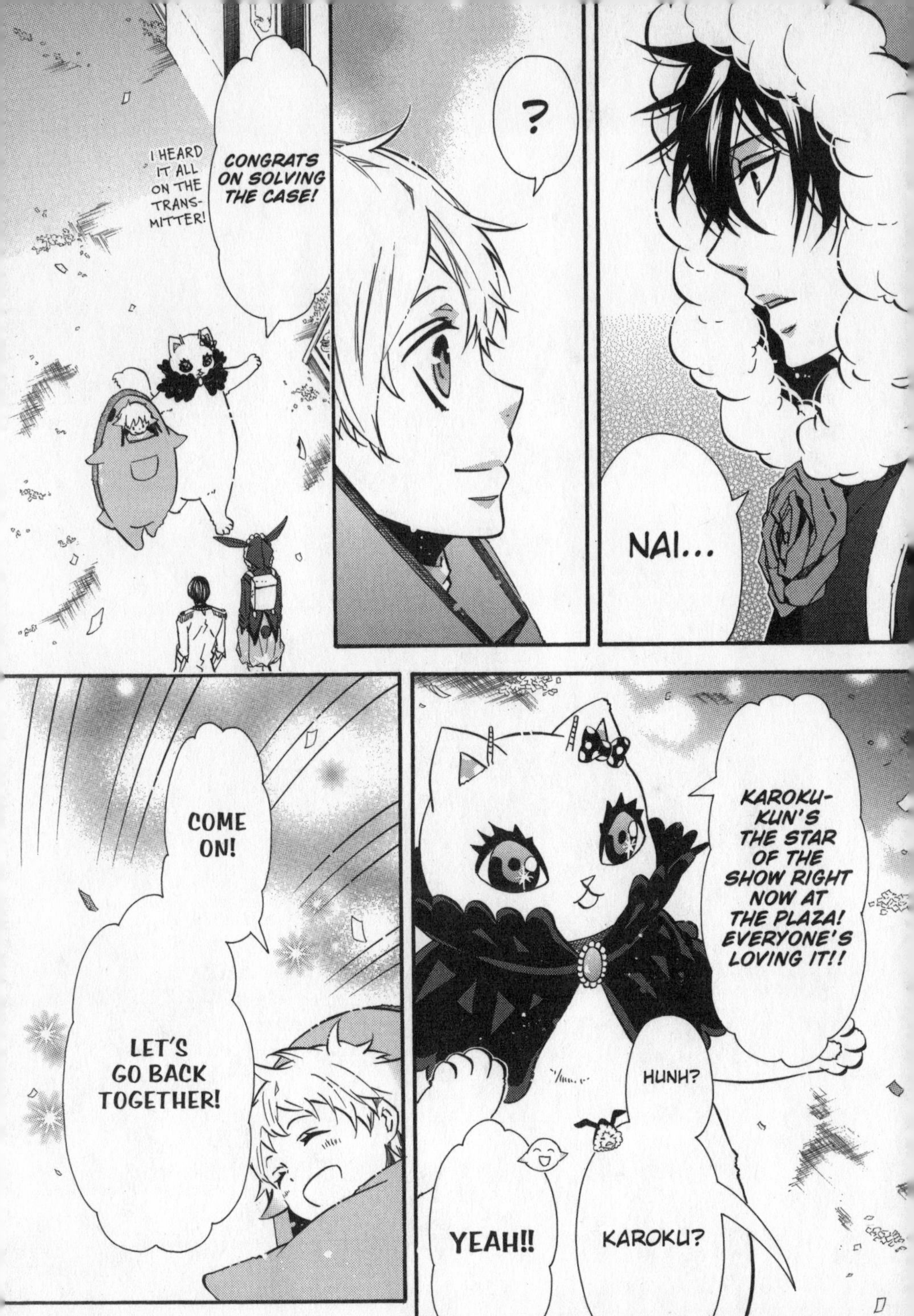
NAI...
?
CONGRATS ON SOLVING THE CASE!
I HEARD IT ALL ON THE TRANS-MITTER!
KAROKU-KUN'S THE STAR OF THE SHOW RIGHT NOW AT THE PLAZA! EVERYONE'S LOVING IT!!
HUNH?
KAROKU?
YEAH!!
COME ON!
LET'S GO BACK TOGETHER!

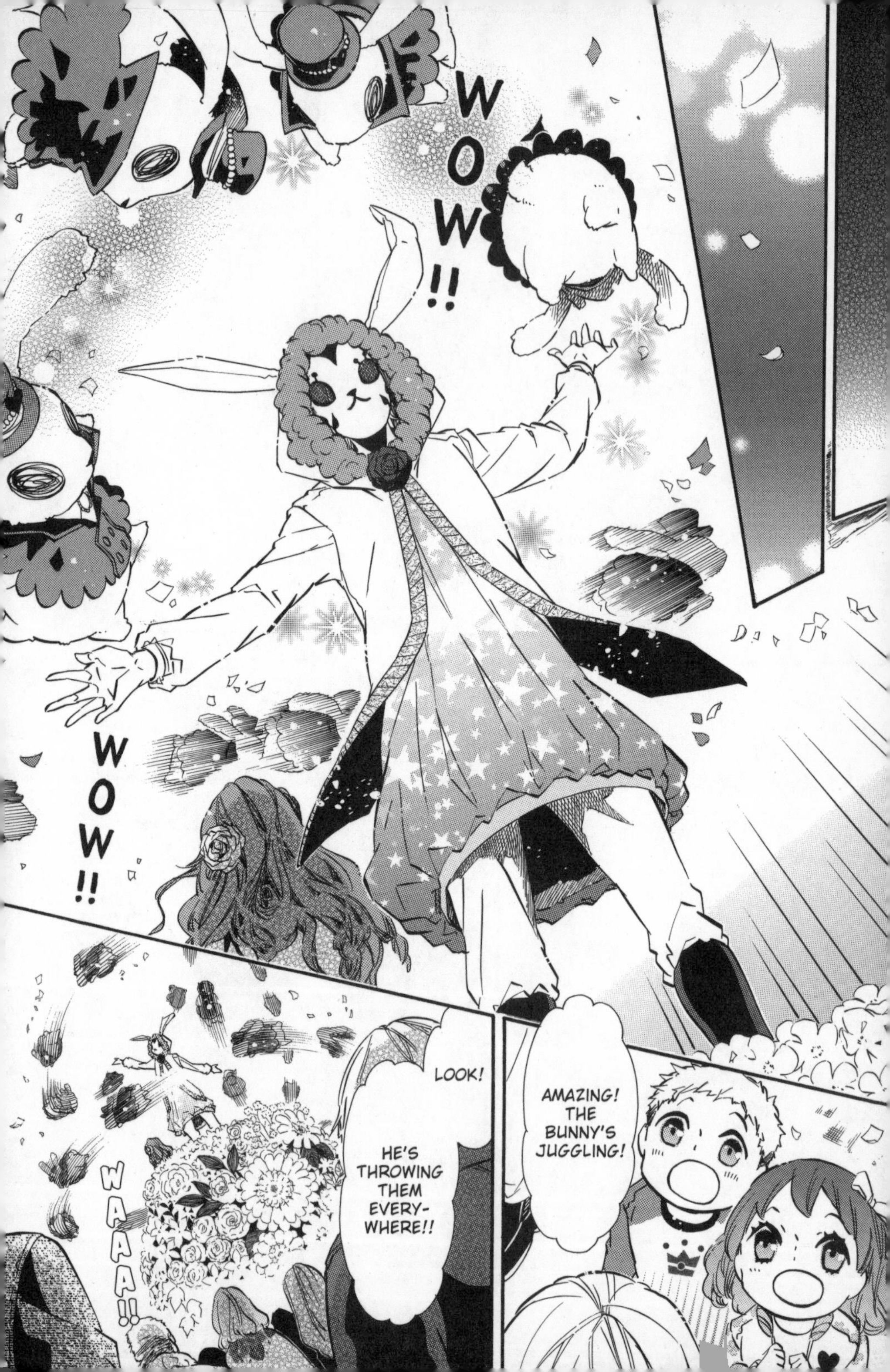
WOW!!
WOW!!
AMAZING! THE BUNNY'S JUGGLING!
LOOK!
HE'S THROWING THEM EVERY-WHERE!!
WAAAA!!

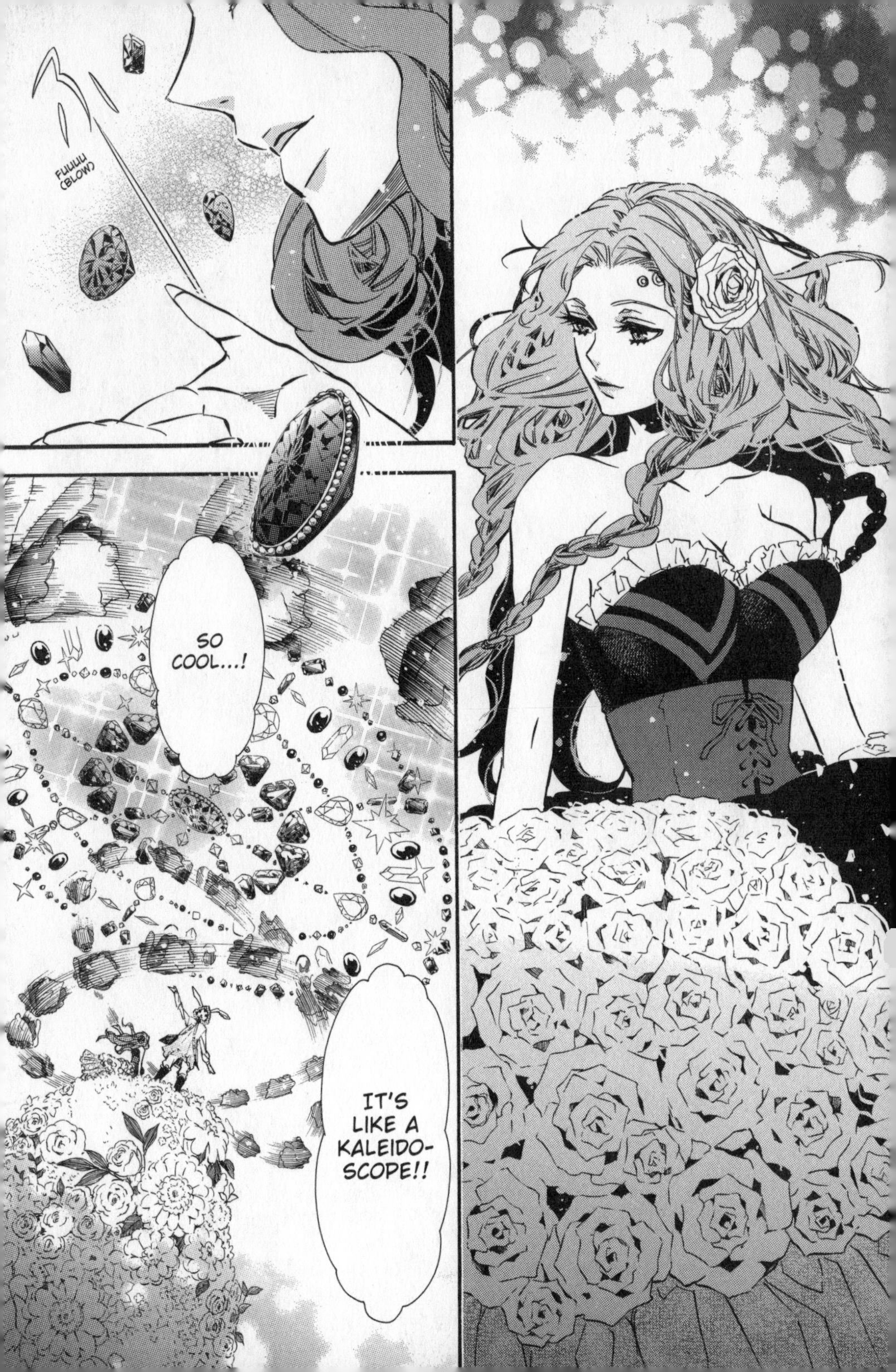
FUUUU (BLOW)
SO COOL...!
IT'S LIKE A KALEIDO-SCOPE!!

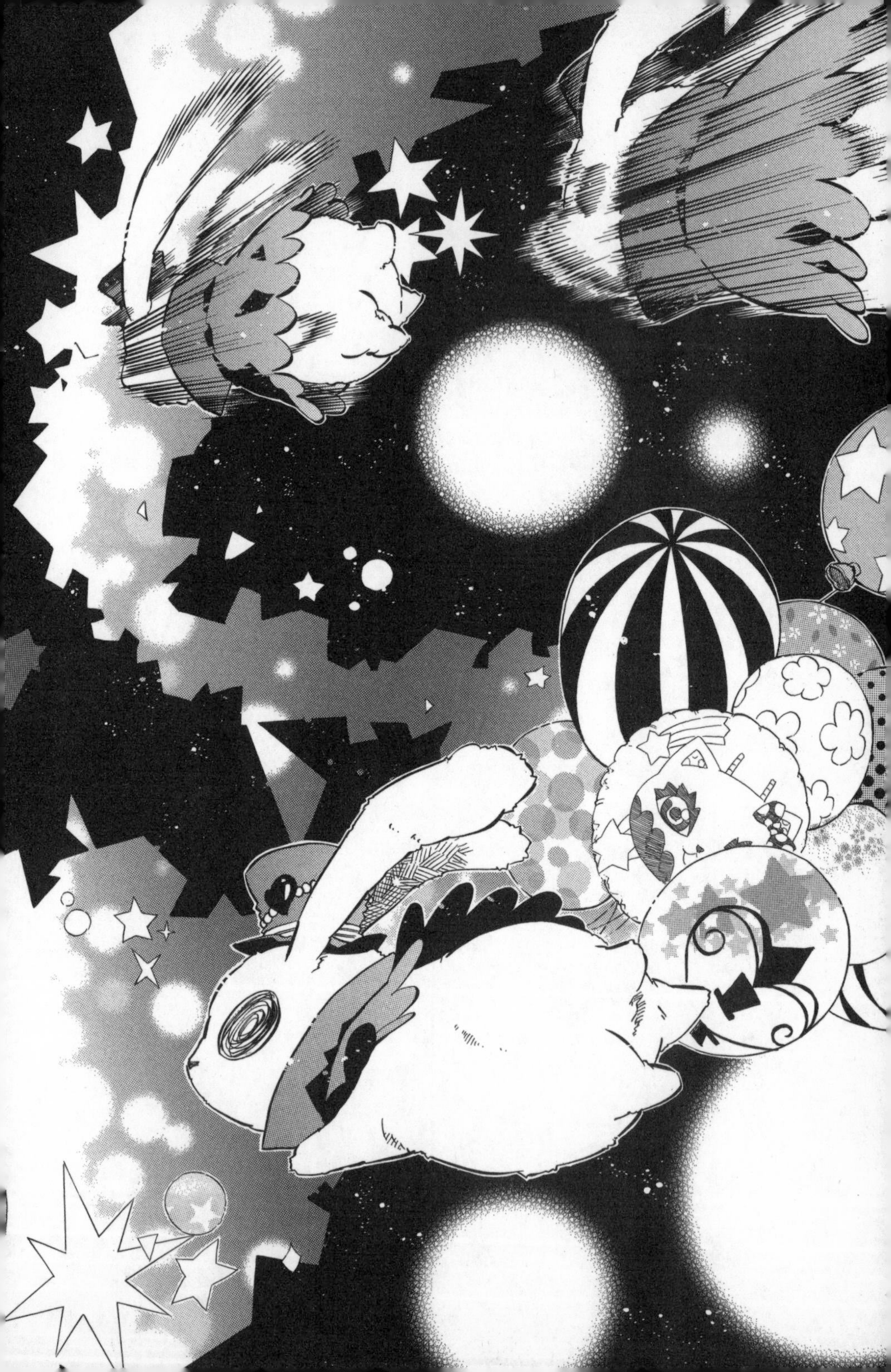

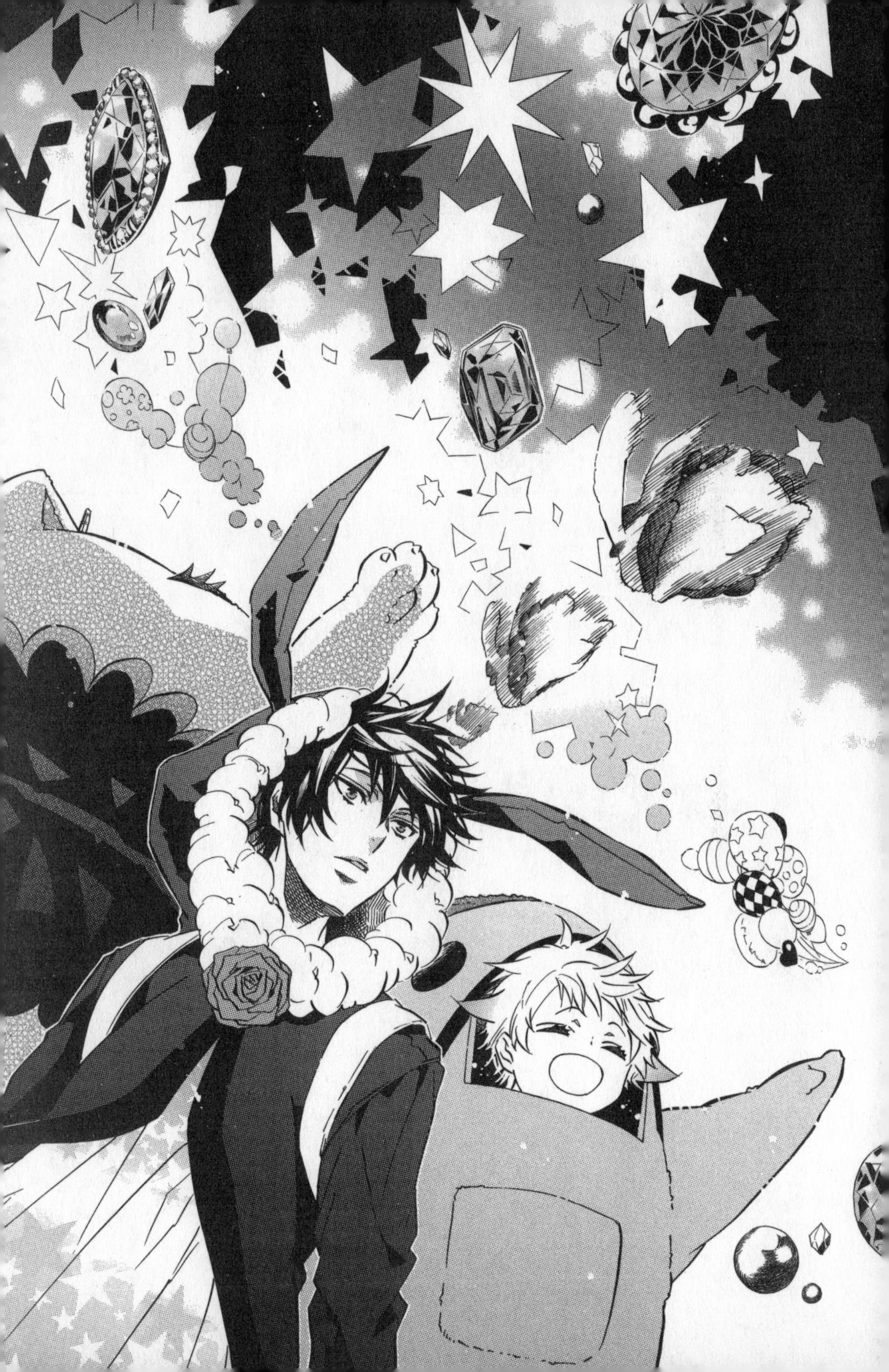

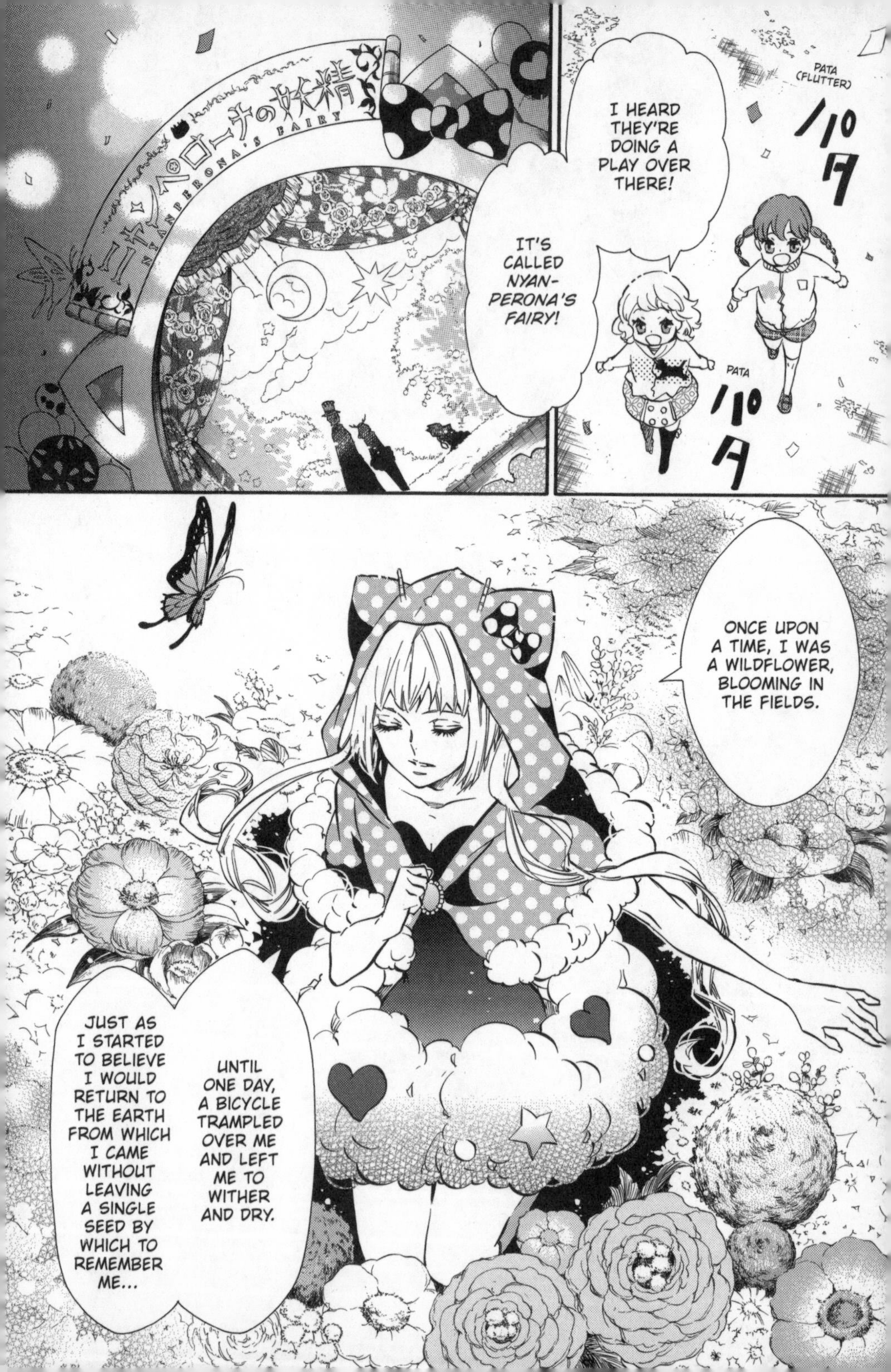
PATA (FLUTTER)
パタ
I HEARD THEY'RE DOING A PLAY OVER THERE!
IT'S CALLED NYAN-PERONA'S FAIRY!
PATA
パタ
ニャンペローナの妖精
NYANPERONA'S FAIRY
ONCE UPON A TIME, I WAS A WILDFLOWER, BLOOMING IN THE FIELDS.
UNTIL ONE DAY, A BICYCLE TRAMPLED OVER ME AND LEFT ME TO WITHER AND DRY.
JUST AS I STARTED TO BELIEVE I WOULD RETURN TO THE EARTH FROM WHICH I CAME WITHOUT LEAVING A SINGLE SEED BY WHICH TO REMEMBER ME...

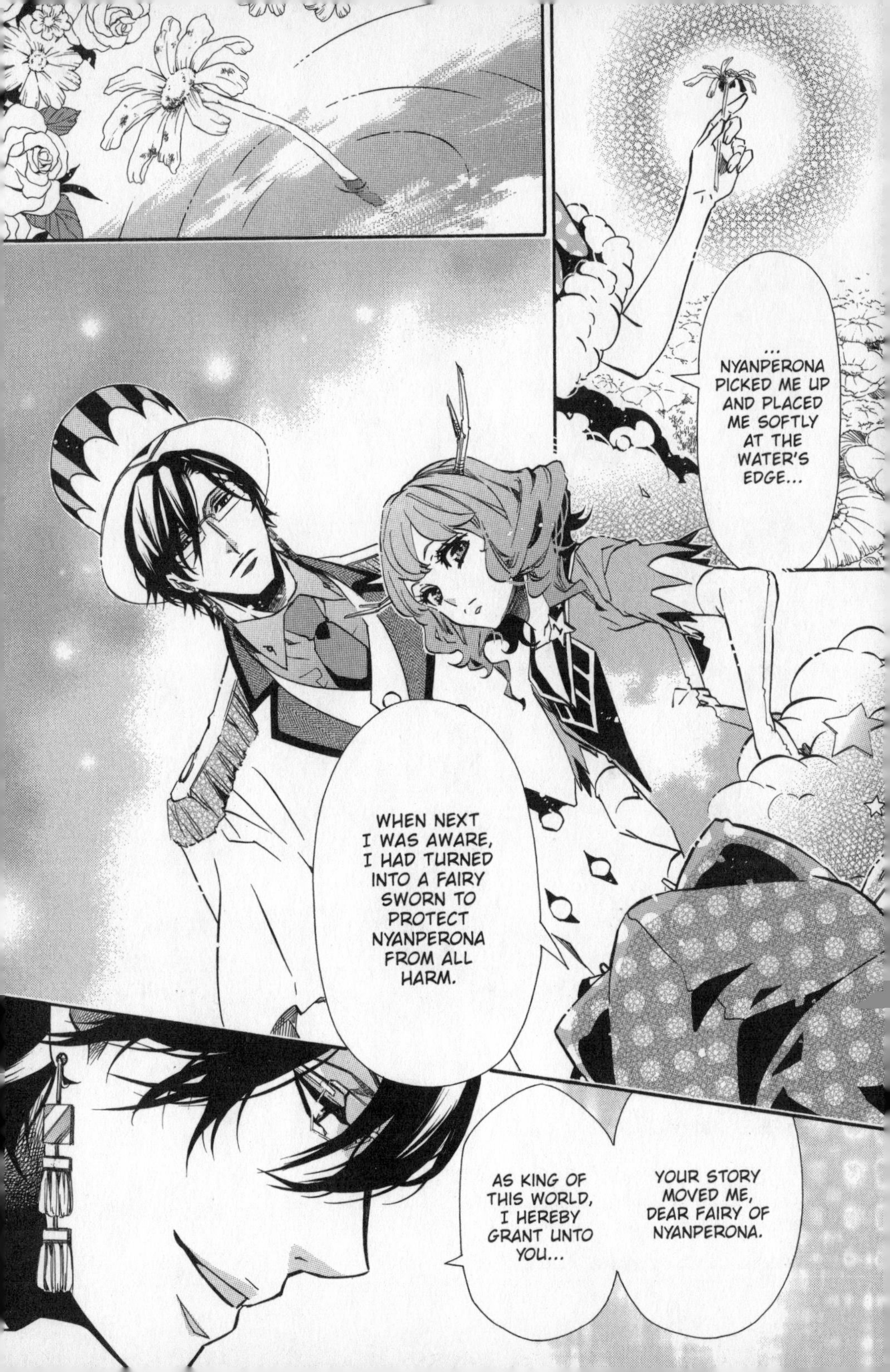
... NYANPERONA PICKED ME UP AND PLACED ME SOFTLY AT THE WATER'S EDGE...
WHEN NEXT I WAS AWARE, I HAD TURNED INTO A FAIRY SWORN TO PROTECT NYANPERONA FROM ALL HARM.
YOUR STORY MOVED ME, DEAR FAIRY OF NYANPERONA.
AS KING OF THIS WORLD, I HEREBY GRANT UNTO YOU...

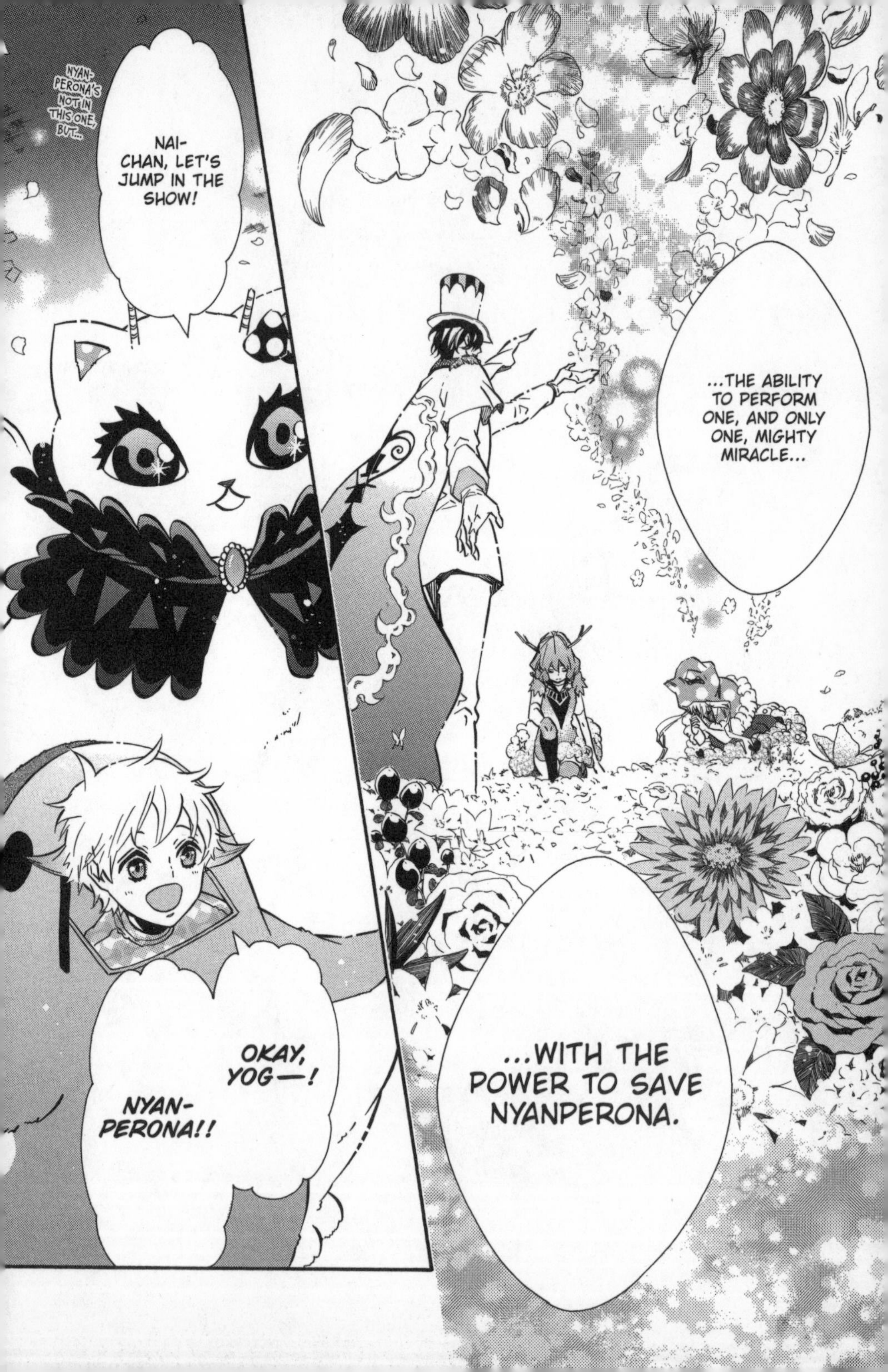
...THE ABILITY TO PERFORM ONE, AND ONLY ONE, MIGHTY MIRACLE...
...WITH THE POWER TO SAVE NYANPERONA.
NAI-CHAN, LET'S JUMP IN THE SHOW!
NYAN-PERONA'S NOT IN THIS ONE, BUT...
OKAY, YOG—!
NYAN-PERONA!!

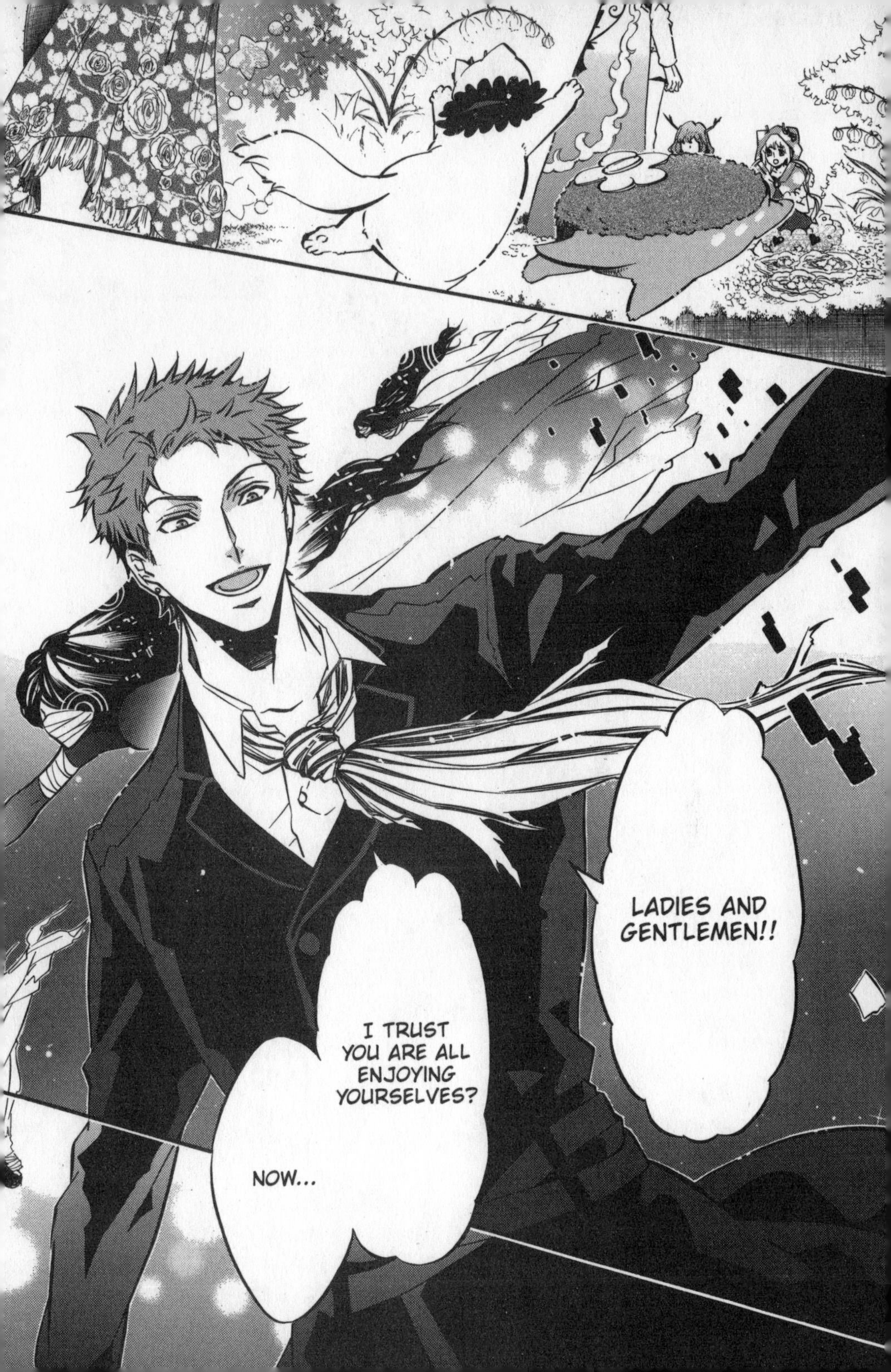
LADIES AND GENTLEMEN!!
I TRUST YOU ARE ALL ENJOYING YOURSELVES?
NOW...

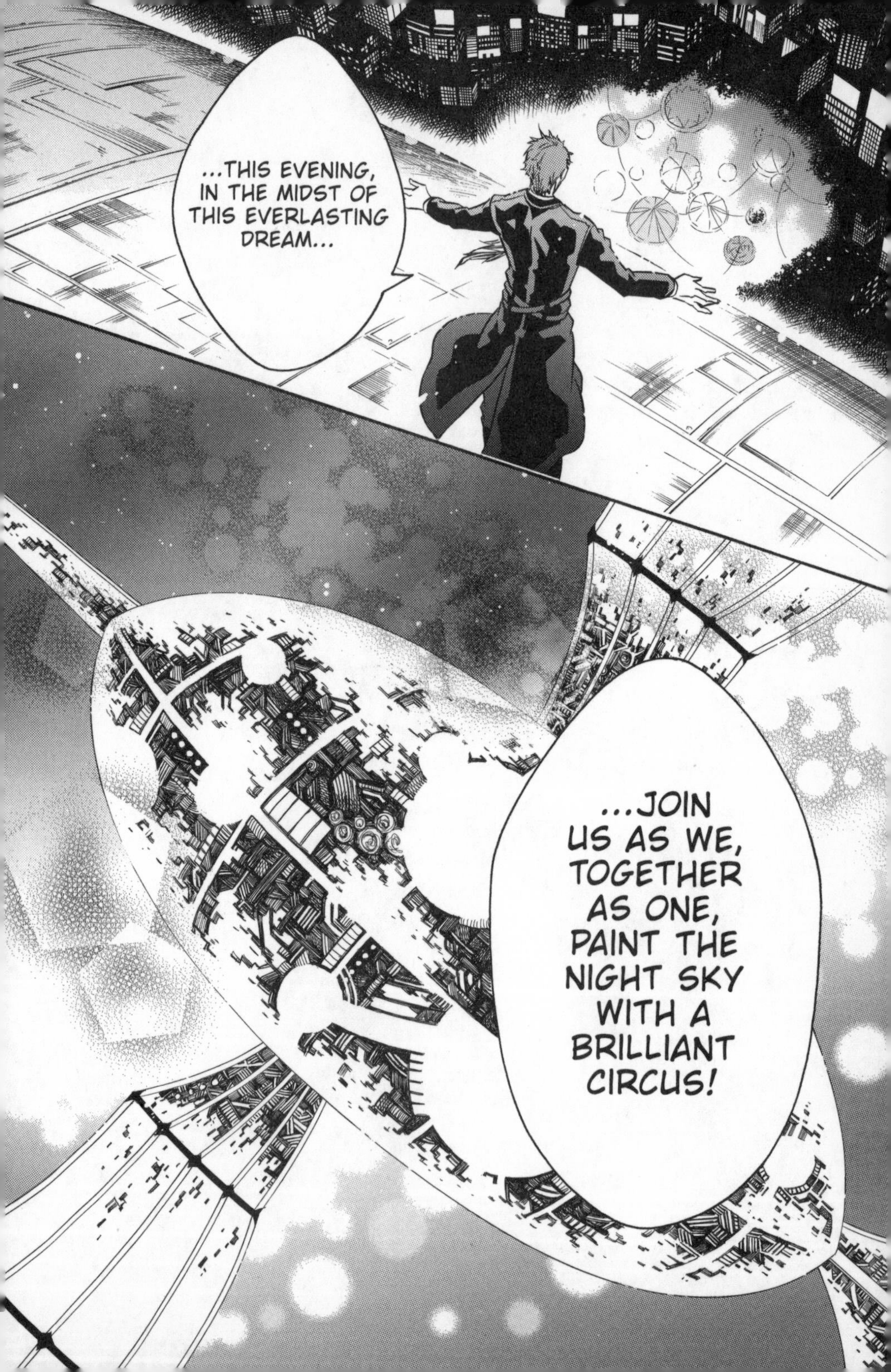
...THIS EVENING, IN THE MIDST OF THIS EVERLASTING DREAM...
...JOIN US AS WE, TOGETHER AS ONE, PAINT THE NIGHT SKY WITH A BRILLIANT CIRCUS!

KARNEVAL

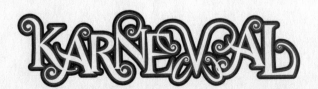

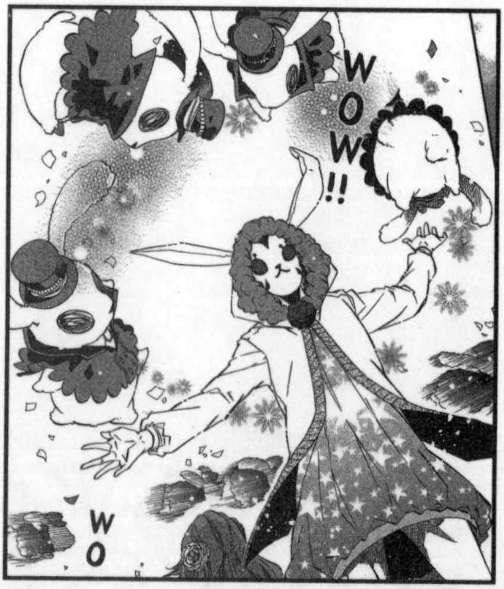
WOW!!
WO

KARNEVAL

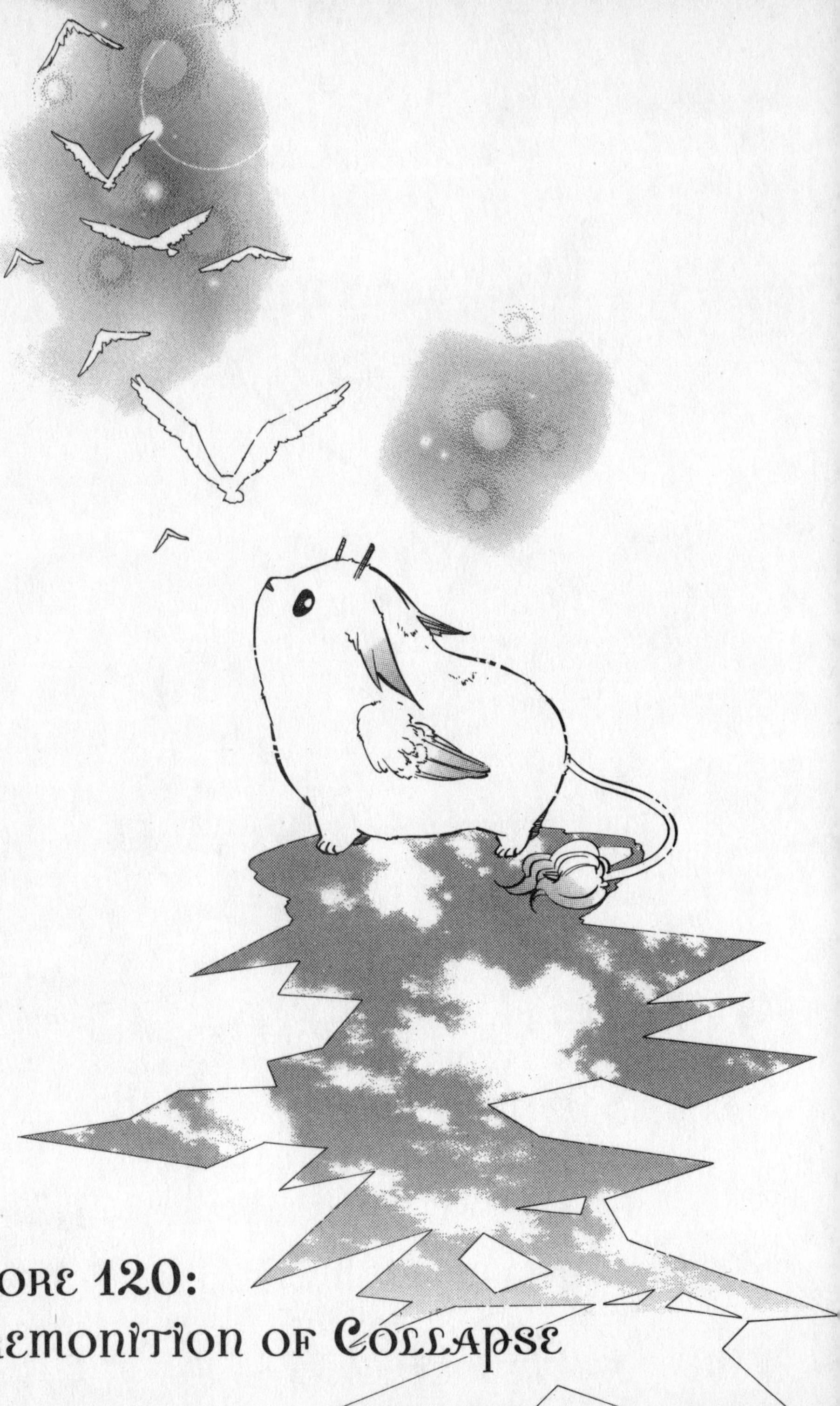

# Score 120: Premonition of Collapse

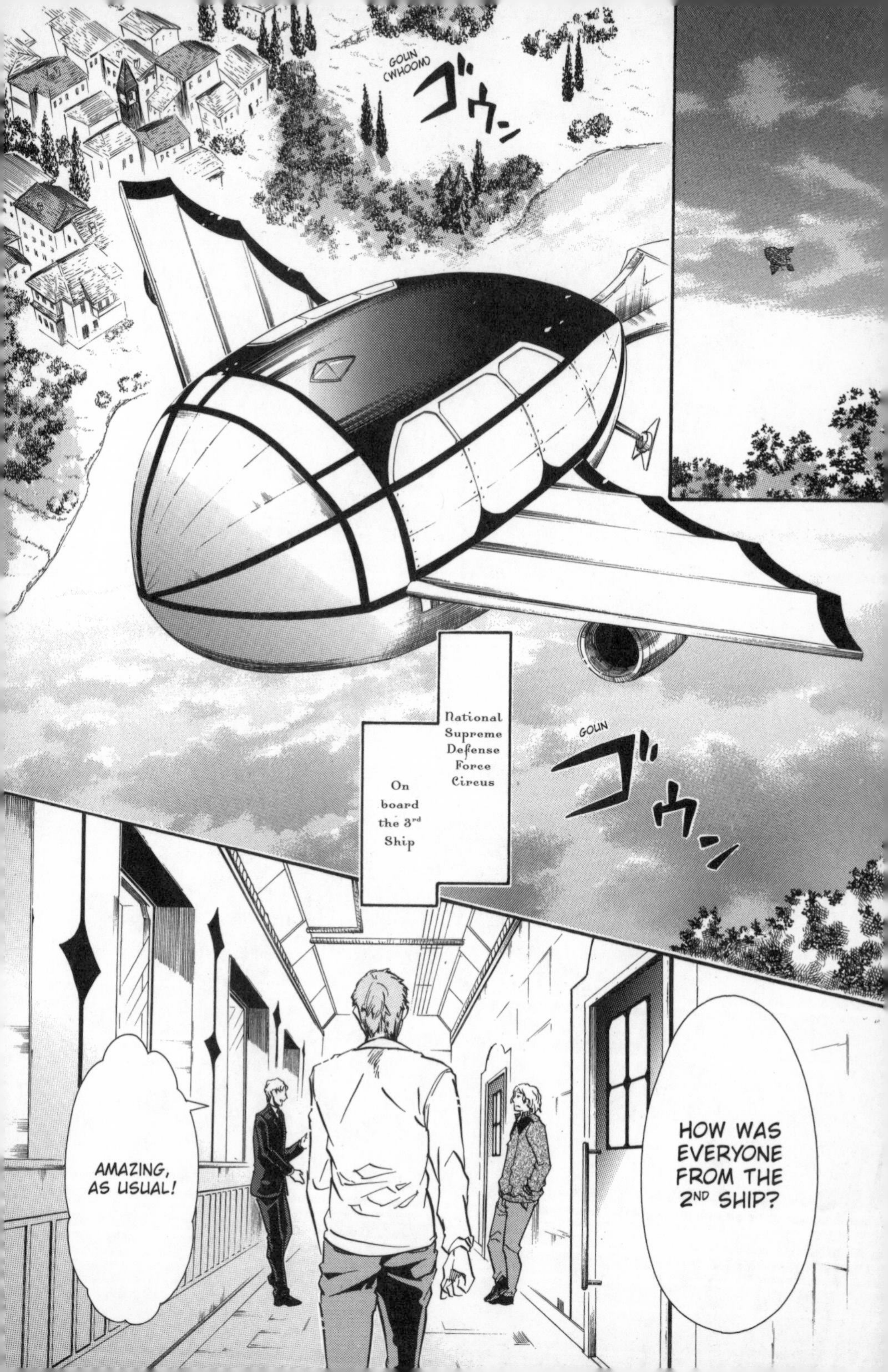
GOUN (WHOOM)
ゴウン
GOUN
ゴウン
National Supreme Defense Force Circus
On board the 3rd Ship
HOW WAS EVERYONE FROM THE 2ND SHIP?
AMAZING, AS USUAL!

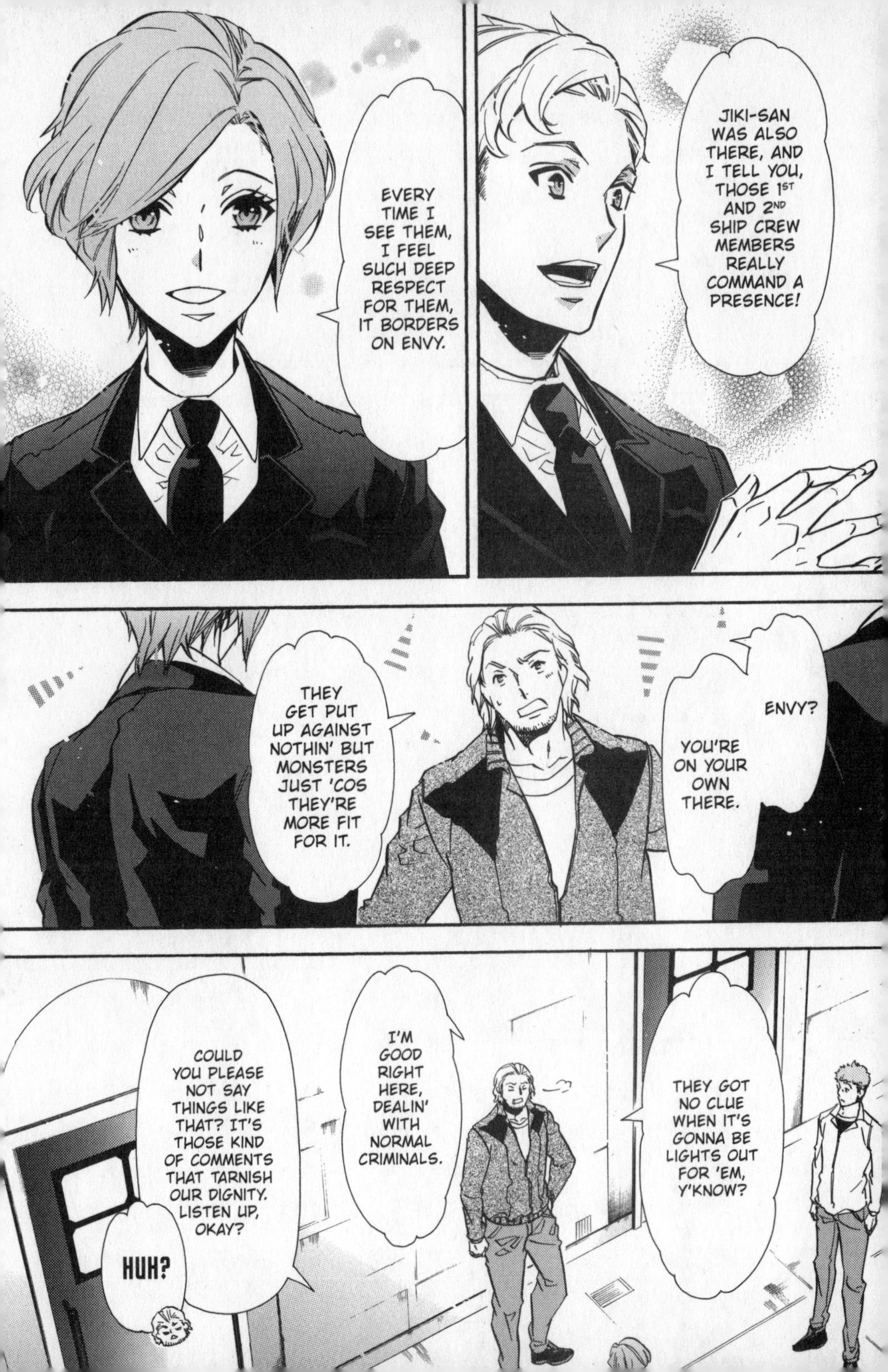
JIKI-SAN WAS ALSO THERE, AND I TELL YOU, THOSE 1ST AND 2ND SHIP CREW MEMBERS REALLY COMMAND A PRESENCE!
EVERY TIME I SEE THEM, I FEEL SUCH DEEP RESPECT FOR THEM, IT BORDERS ON ENVY.
ENVY?
YOU'RE ON YOUR OWN THERE.
THEY GET PUT UP AGAINST NOTHIN' BUT MONSTERS JUST 'COS THEY'RE MORE FIT FOR IT.
THEY GOT NO CLUE WHEN IT'S GONNA BE LIGHTS OUT FOR 'EM, Y'KNOW?
I'M GOOD RIGHT HERE, DEALIN' WITH NORMAL CRIMINALS.
COULD YOU PLEASE NOT SAY THINGS LIKE THAT? IT'S THOSE KIND OF COMMENTS THAT TARNISH OUR DIGNITY. LISTEN UP, OKAY?
HUH?

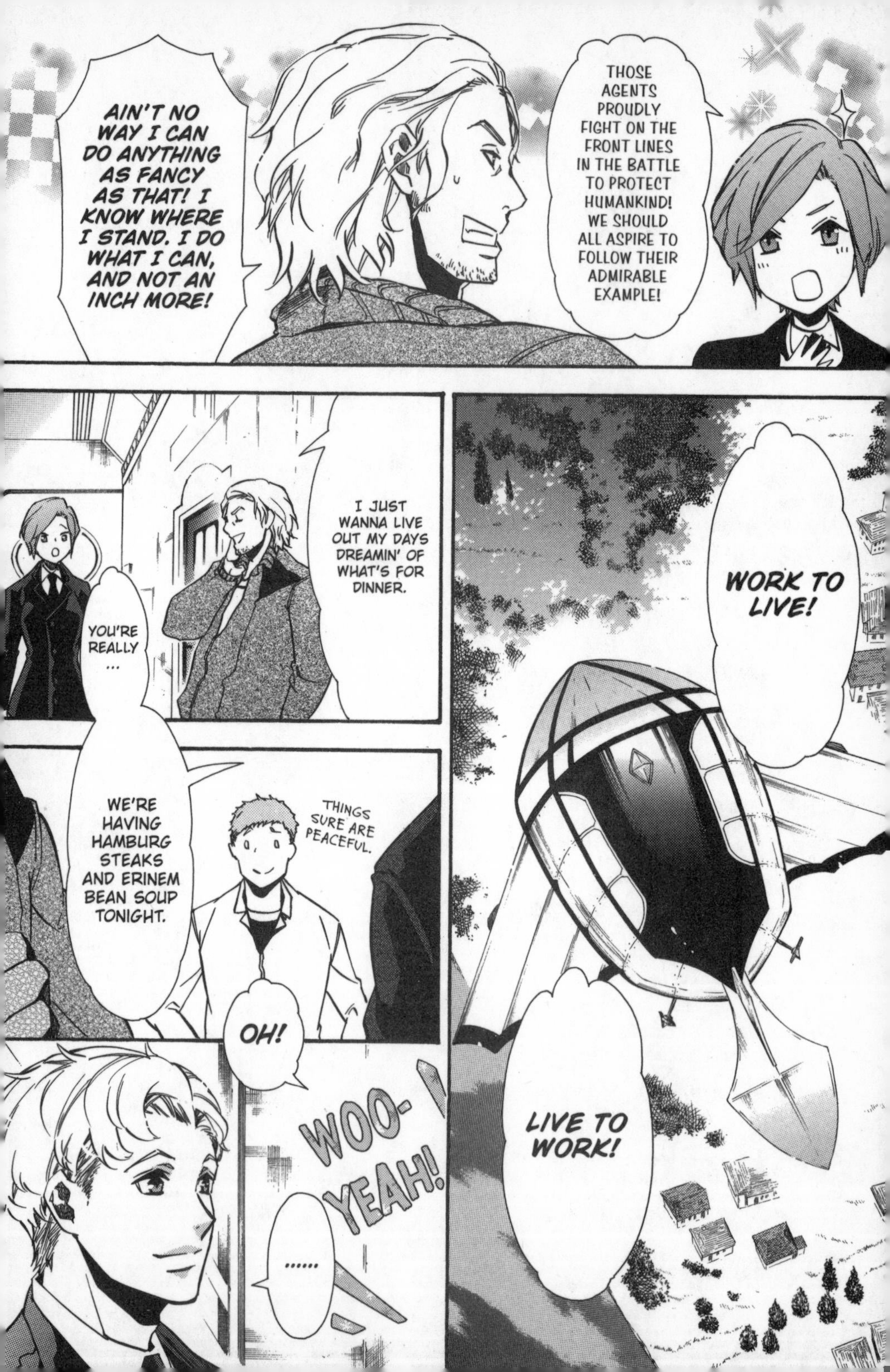
THOSE AGENTS PROUDLY FIGHT ON THE FRONT LINES IN THE BATTLE TO PROTECT HUMANKIND! WE SHOULD ALL ASPIRE TO FOLLOW THEIR ADMIRABLE EXAMPLE!
AIN'T NO WAY I CAN DO ANYTHING AS FANCY AS THAT! I KNOW WHERE I STAND. I DO WHAT I CAN, AND NOT AN INCH MORE!
WORK TO LIVE!
LIVE TO WORK!
I JUST WANNA LIVE OUT MY DAYS DREAMIN' OF WHAT'S FOR DINNER.
YOU'RE REALLY ...
WE'RE HAVING HAMBURG STEAKS AND ERINEM BEAN SOUP TONIGHT.
THINGS SURE ARE PEACEFUL.
OH!
WOO-YEAH!
......

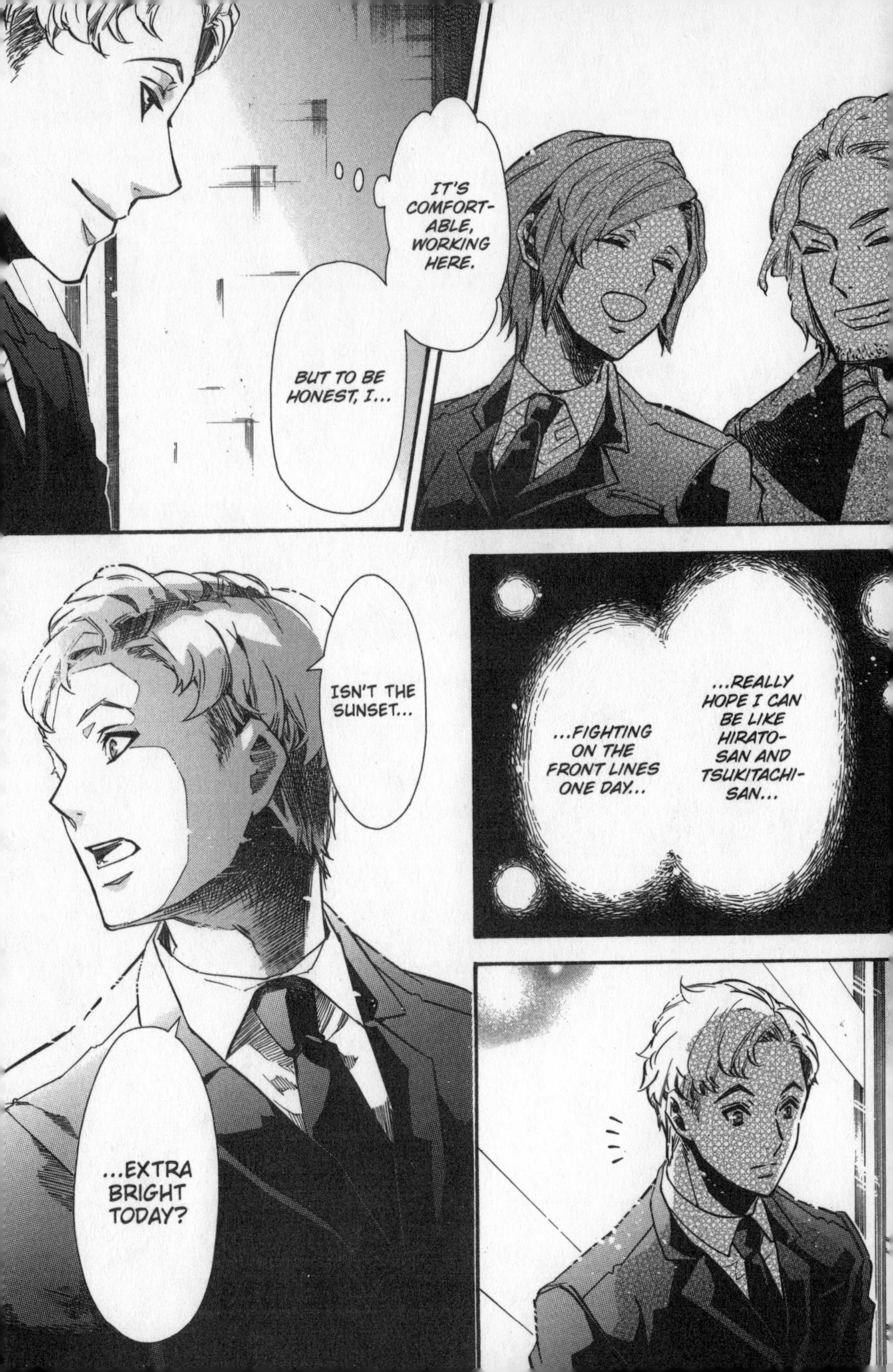
IT'S COMFORTABLE, WORKING HERE.
BUT TO BE HONEST, I...
...REALLY HOPE I CAN BE LIKE HIRATO-SAN AND TSUKITACHI-SAN...
...FIGHTING ON THE FRONT LINES ONE DAY...
ISN'T THE SUNSET...
...EXTRA BRIGHT TODAY?

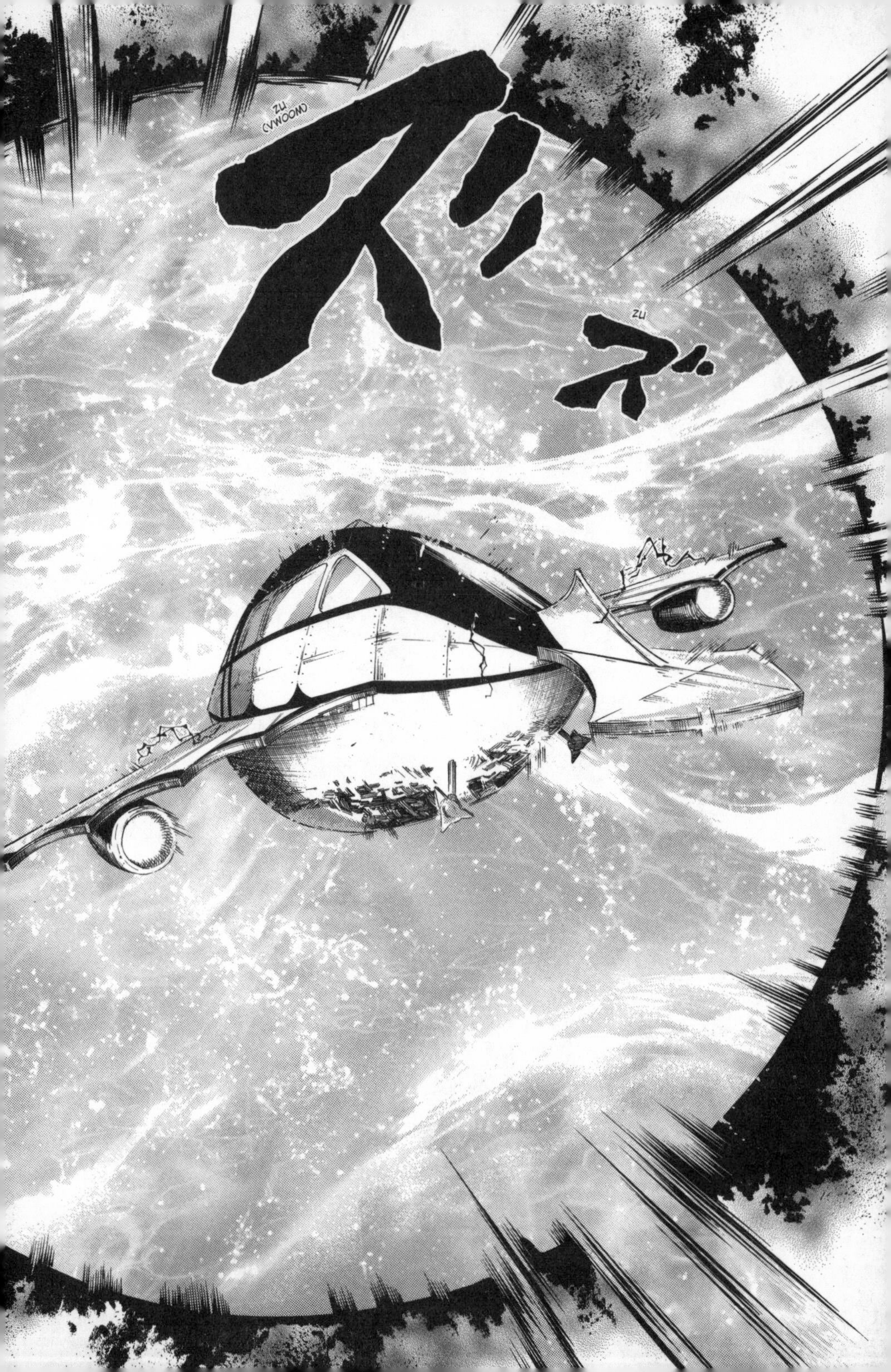
ZU
(VWOOM)
ZU

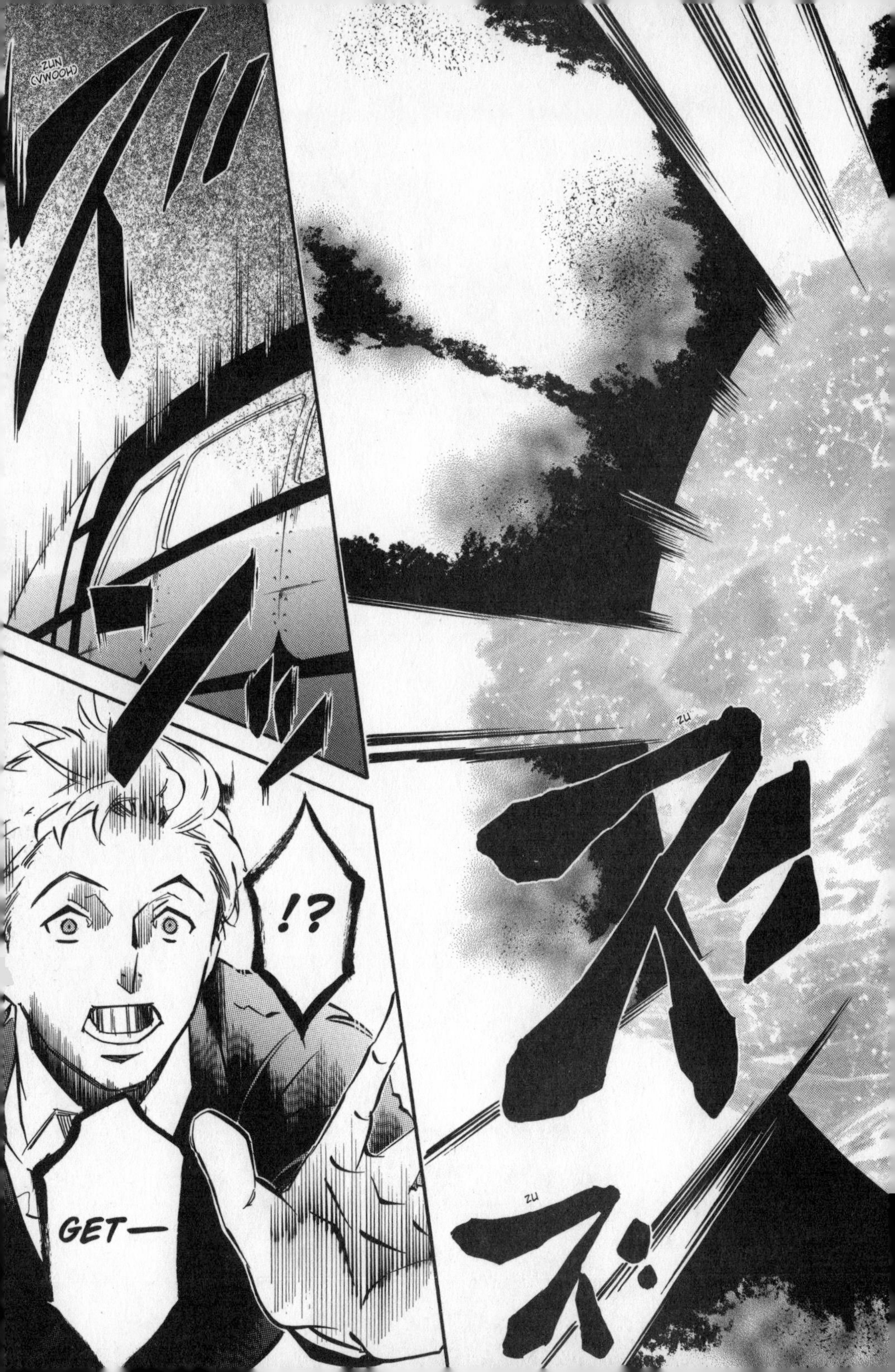
ZU
ZU
ZUN (VWOOH)
!?
GET—

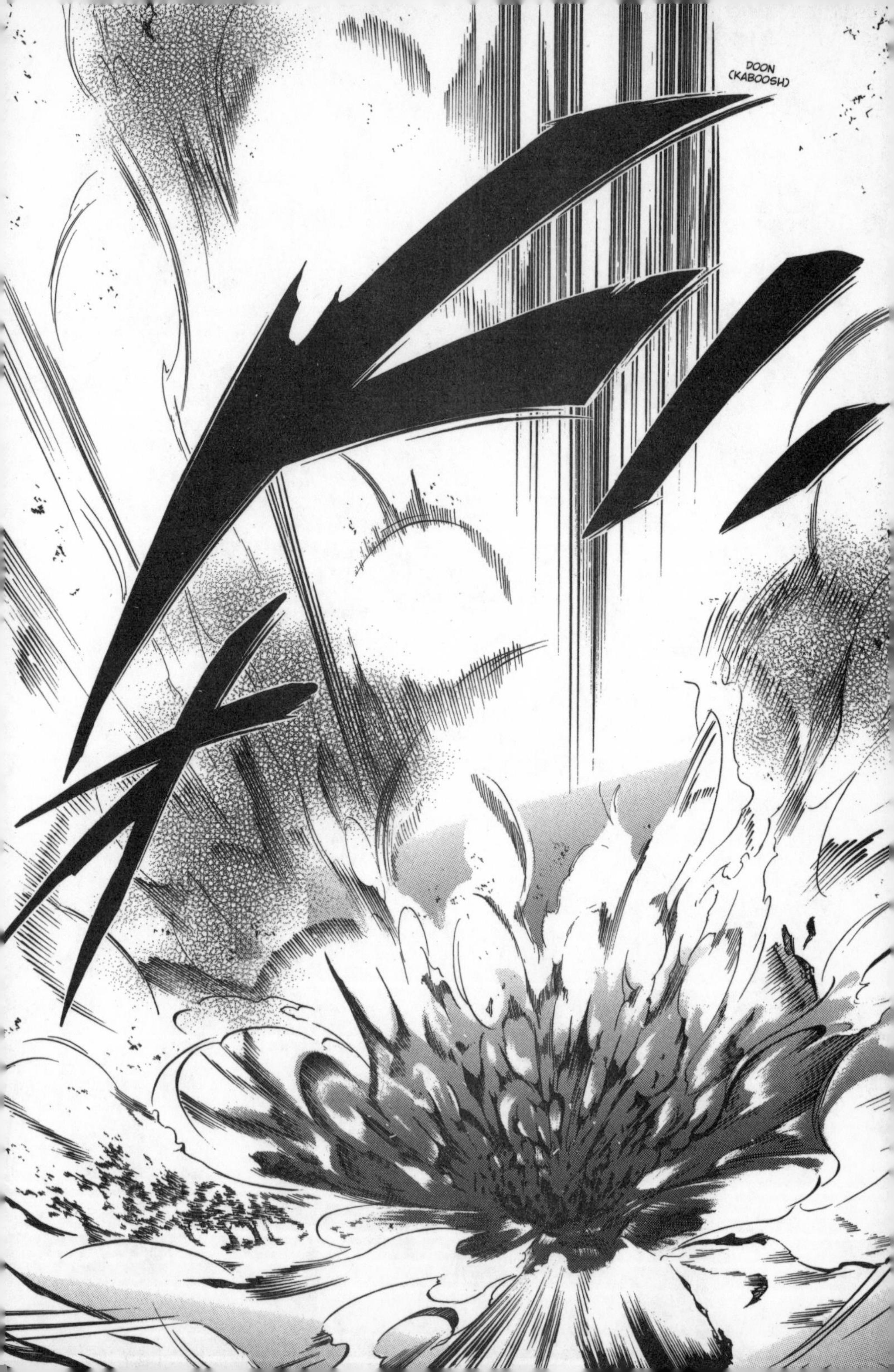
DOON
(KABOOSH)

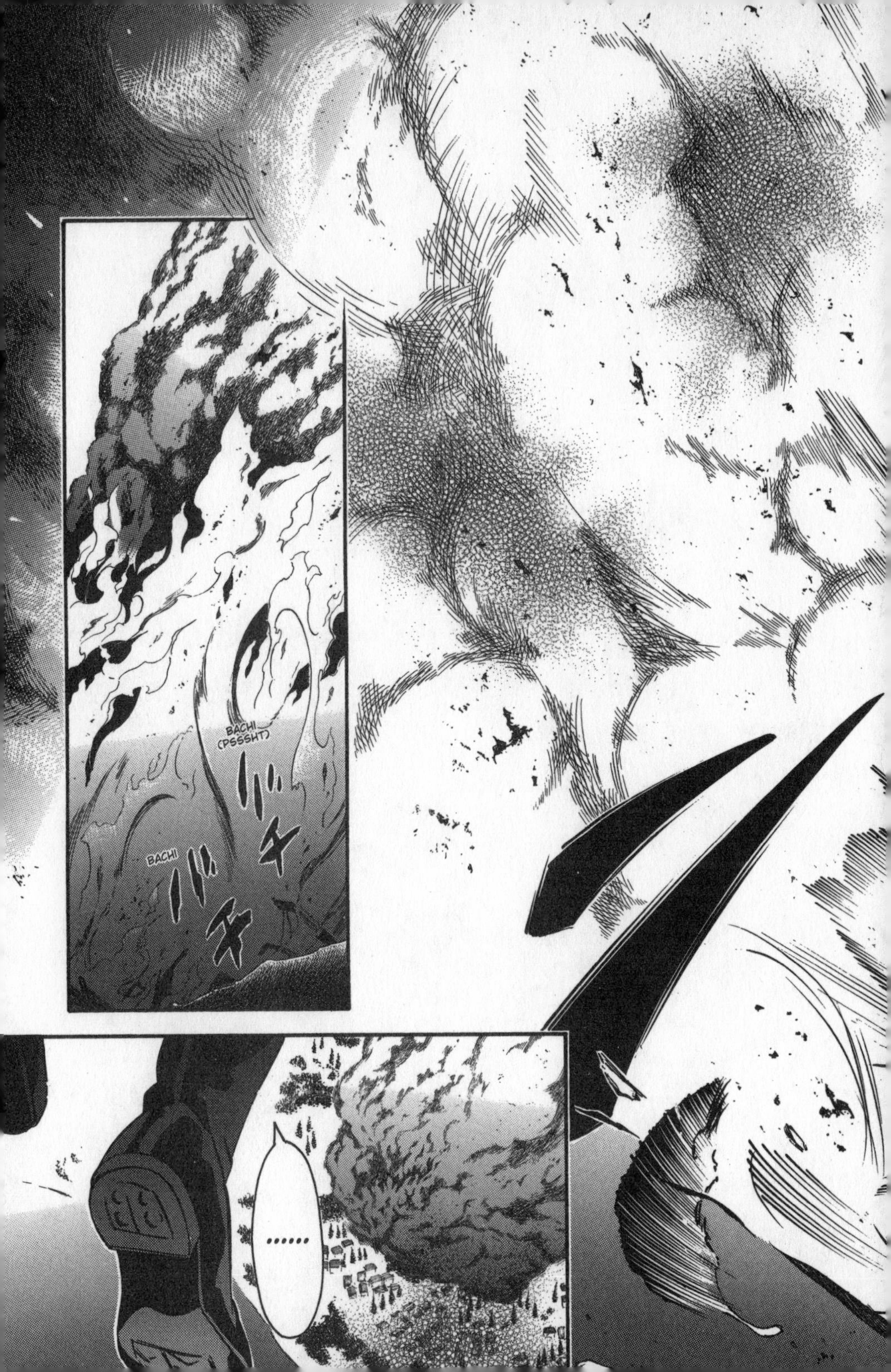
BACHI (PSSSHT)
バチ
BACHI
バチ
......

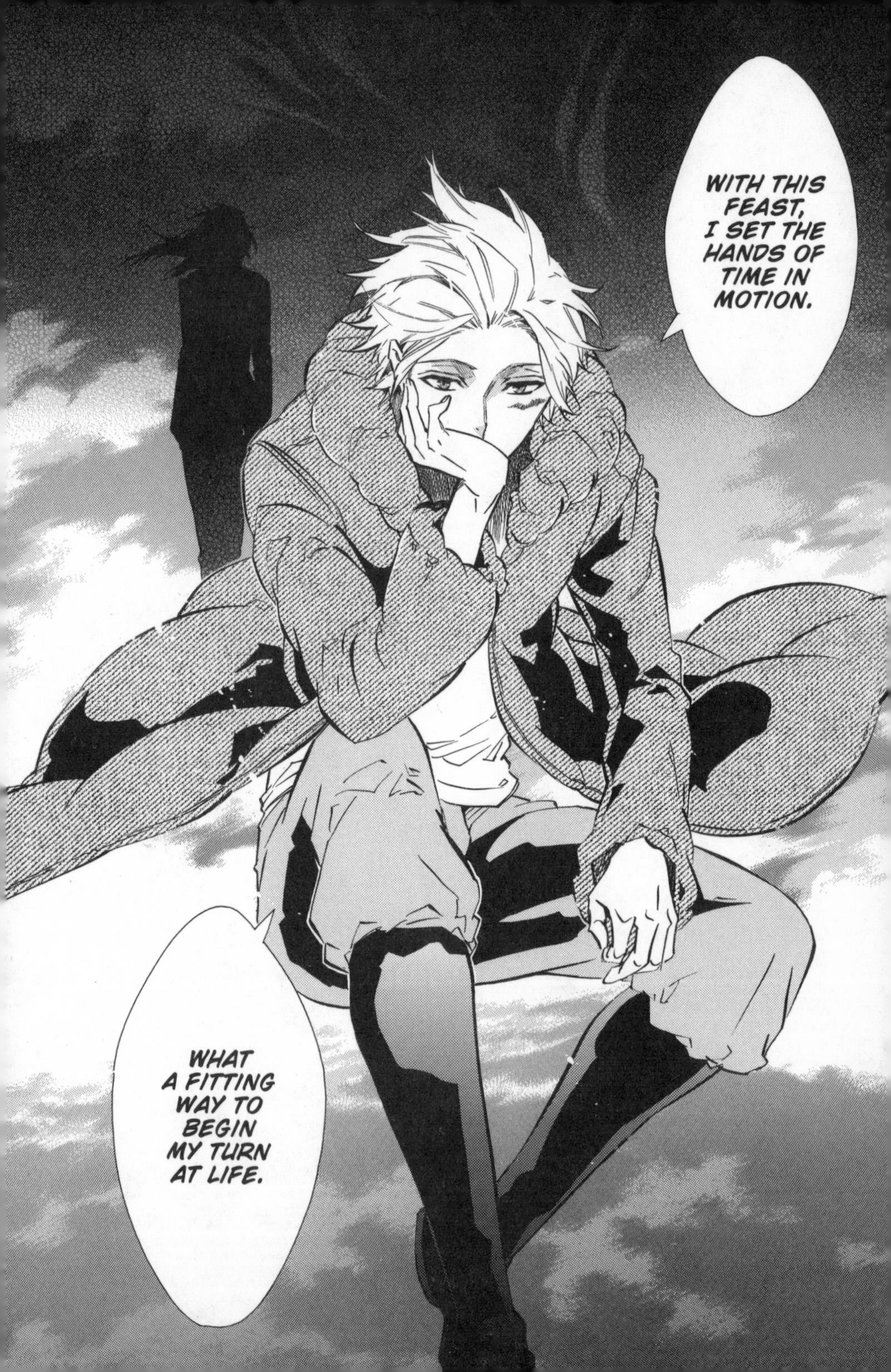
WITH THIS FEAST, I SET THE HANDS OF TIME IN MOTION.
WHAT A FITTING WAY TO BEGIN MY TURN AT LIFE.

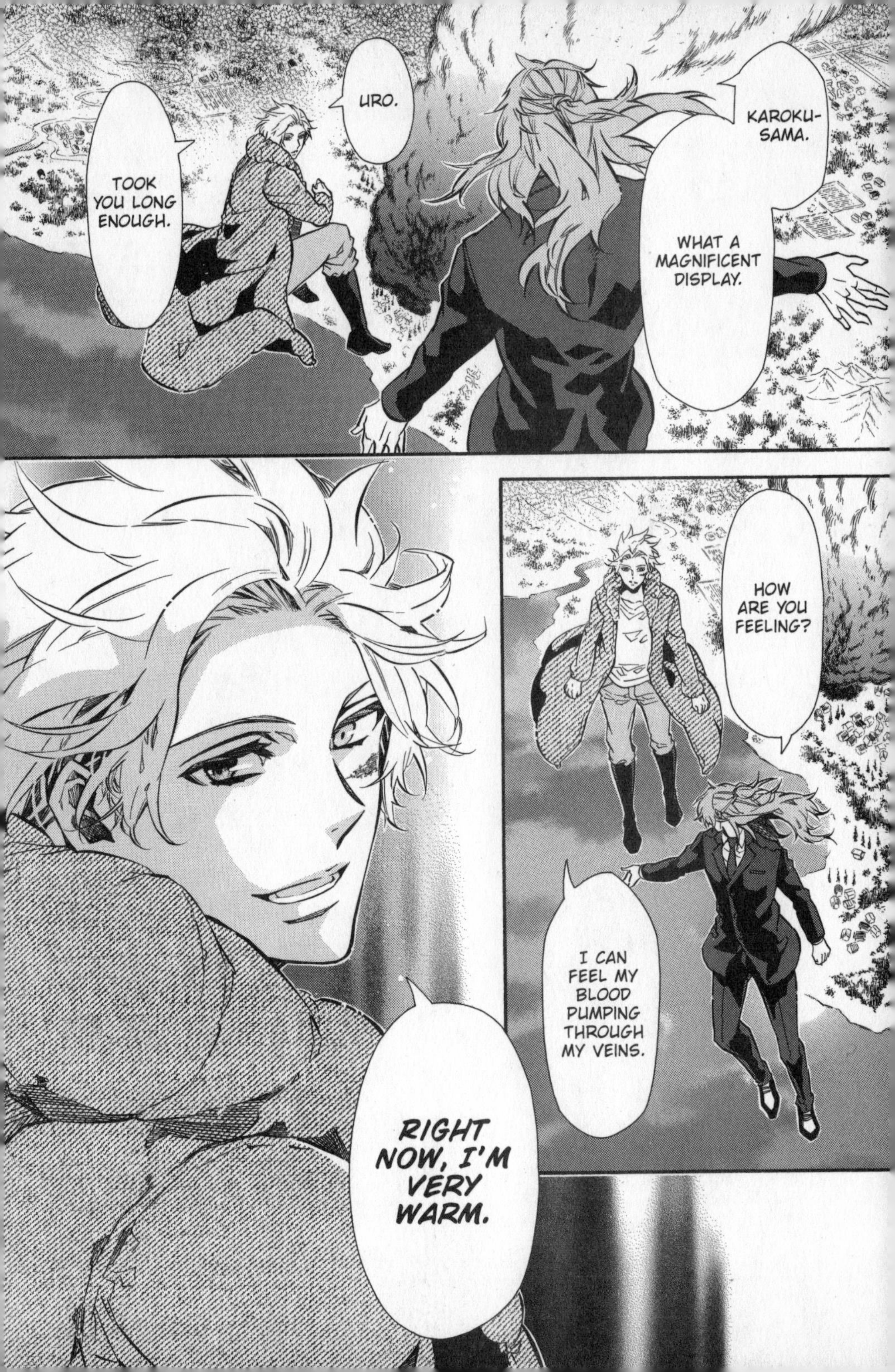
KAROKU-SAMA.
WHAT A MAGNIFICENT DISPLAY.
URO.
TOOK YOU LONG ENOUGH.
HOW ARE YOU FEELING?
I CAN FEEL MY BLOOD PUMPING THROUGH MY VEINS.
RIGHT NOW, I'M VERY WARM.

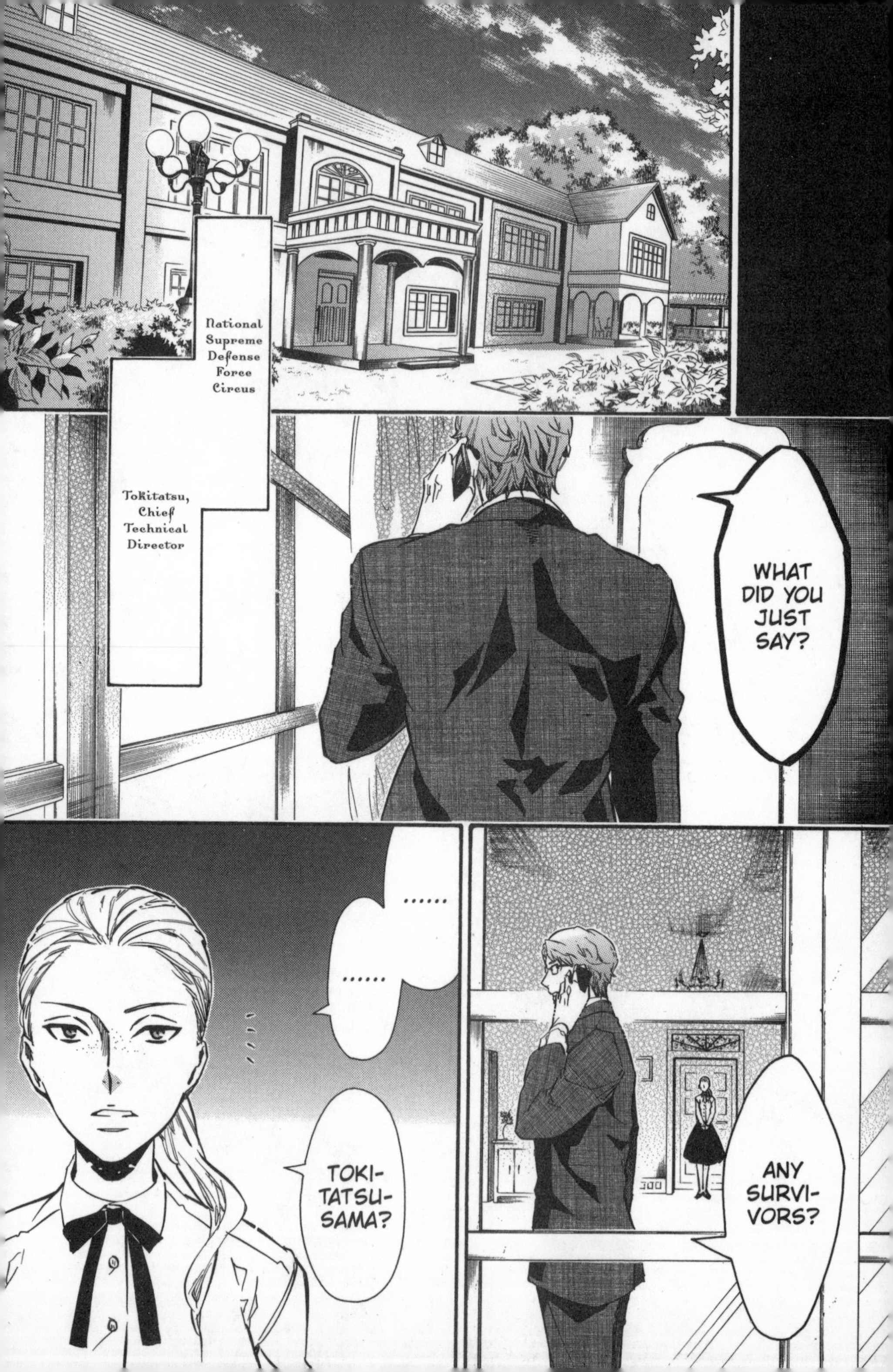
National Supreme Defense Force Circus
Tokitatsu, Chief Technical Director
WHAT DID YOU JUST SAY?
ANY SURVIVORS?
......
......
TOKI-TATSU-SAMA?

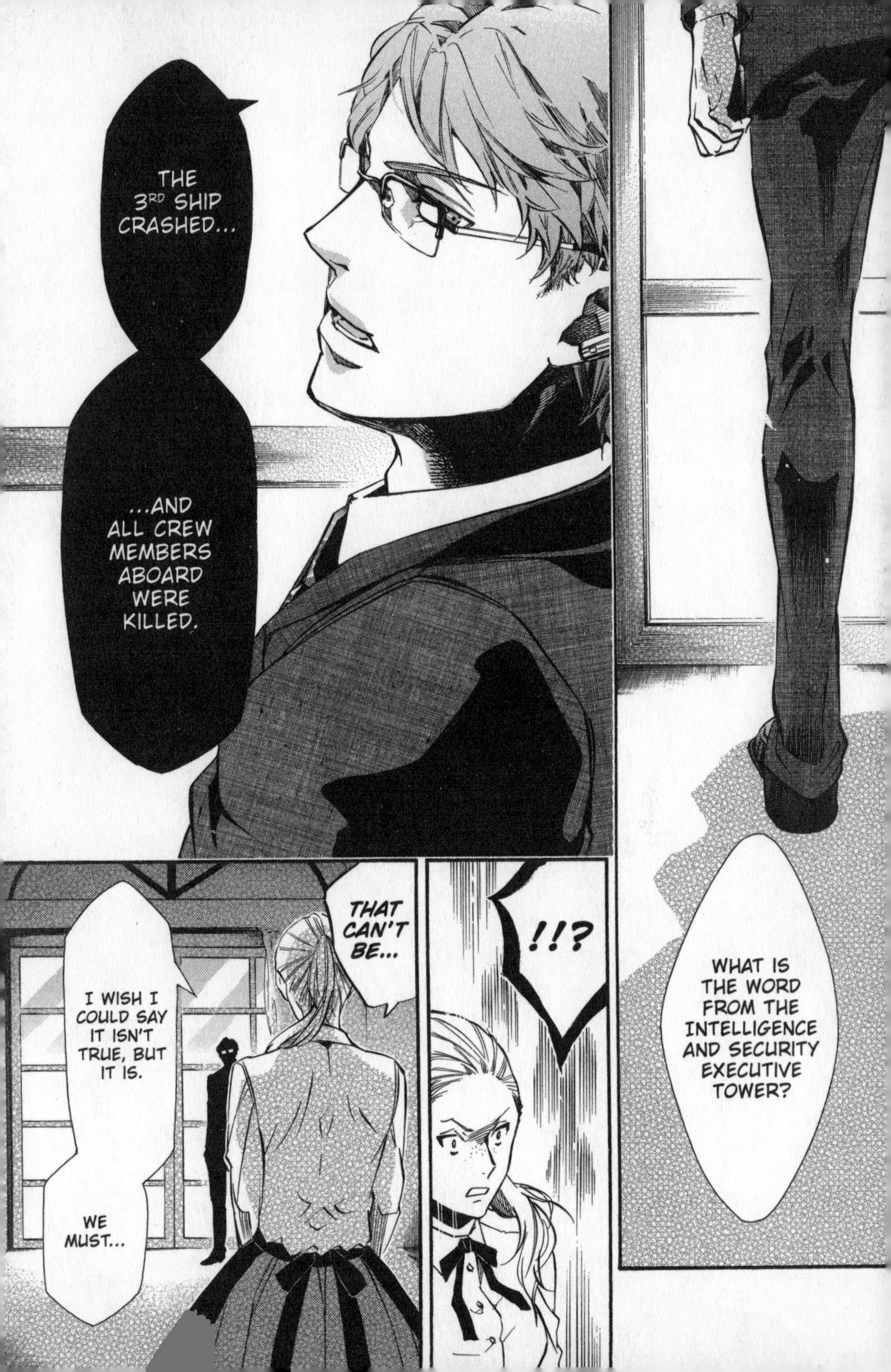
WHAT IS THE WORD FROM THE INTELLIGENCE AND SECURITY EXECUTIVE TOWER?
THE 3RD SHIP CRASHED...
...AND ALL CREW MEMBERS ABOARD WERE KILLED.
!!?
THAT CAN'T BE...
I WISH I COULD SAY IT ISN'T TRUE, BUT IT IS.
WE MUST...

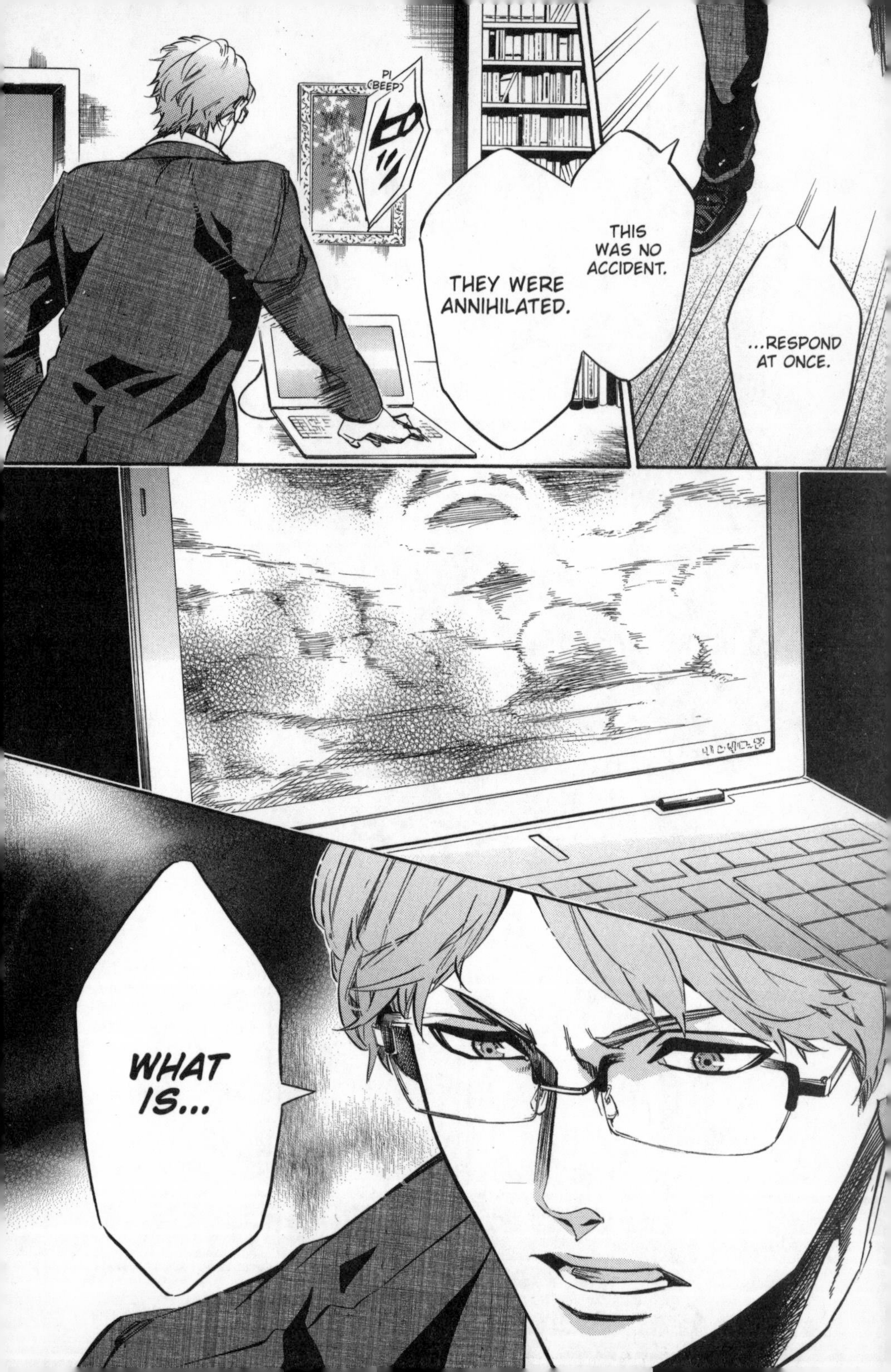
...RESPOND AT ONCE.
THIS WAS NO ACCIDENT.
THEY WERE ANNIHILATED.
PI (BEEP)
WHAT IS...

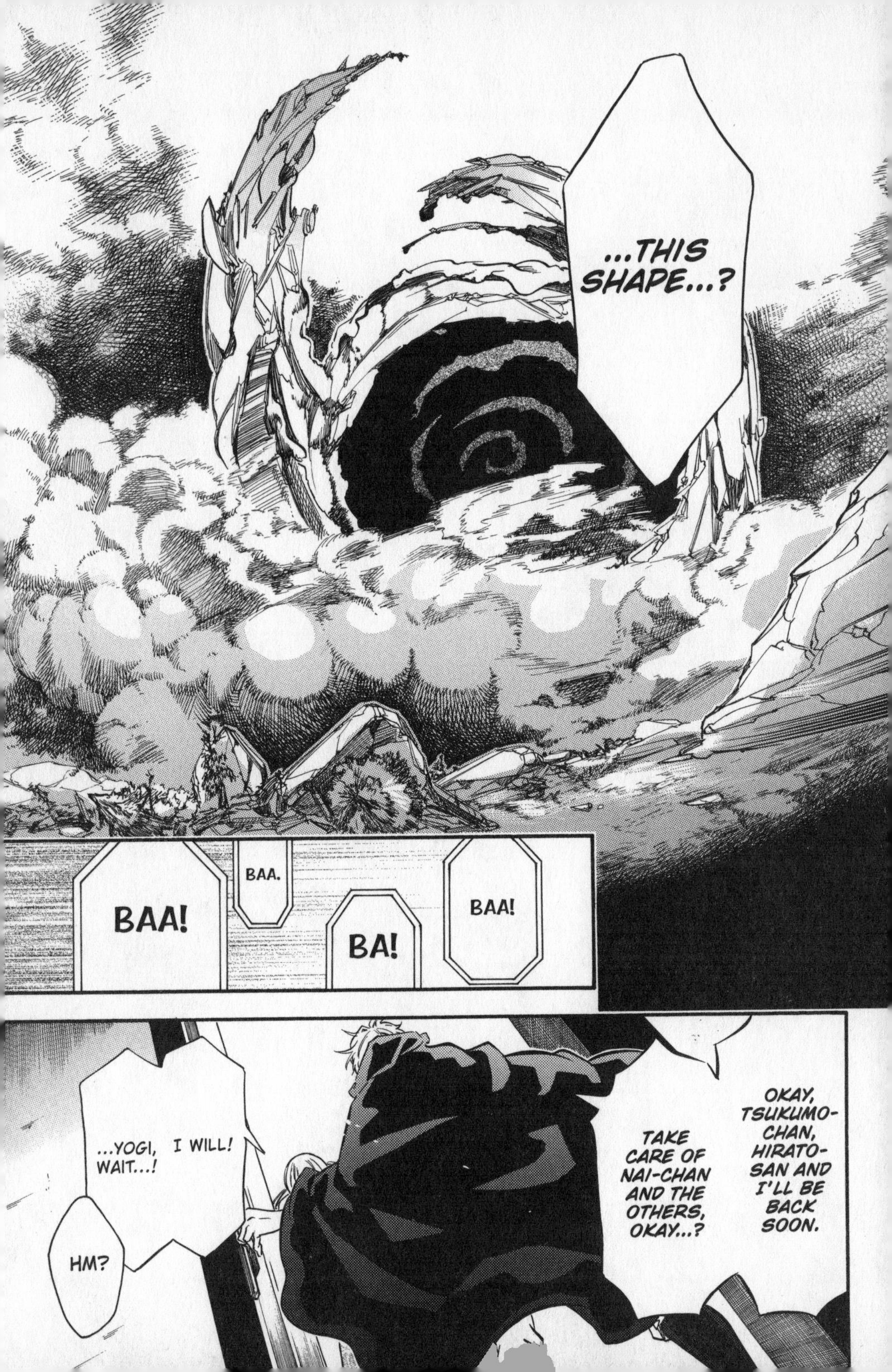
...THIS SHAPE...?
BAA!
BA!
BAA.
BAA!
OKAY, TSUKUMO-CHAN, HIRATO-SAN AND I'LL BE BACK SOON.
TAKE CARE OF NAI-CHAN AND THE OTHERS, OKAY...?
I WILL!
...YOGI, WAIT...!
HM?

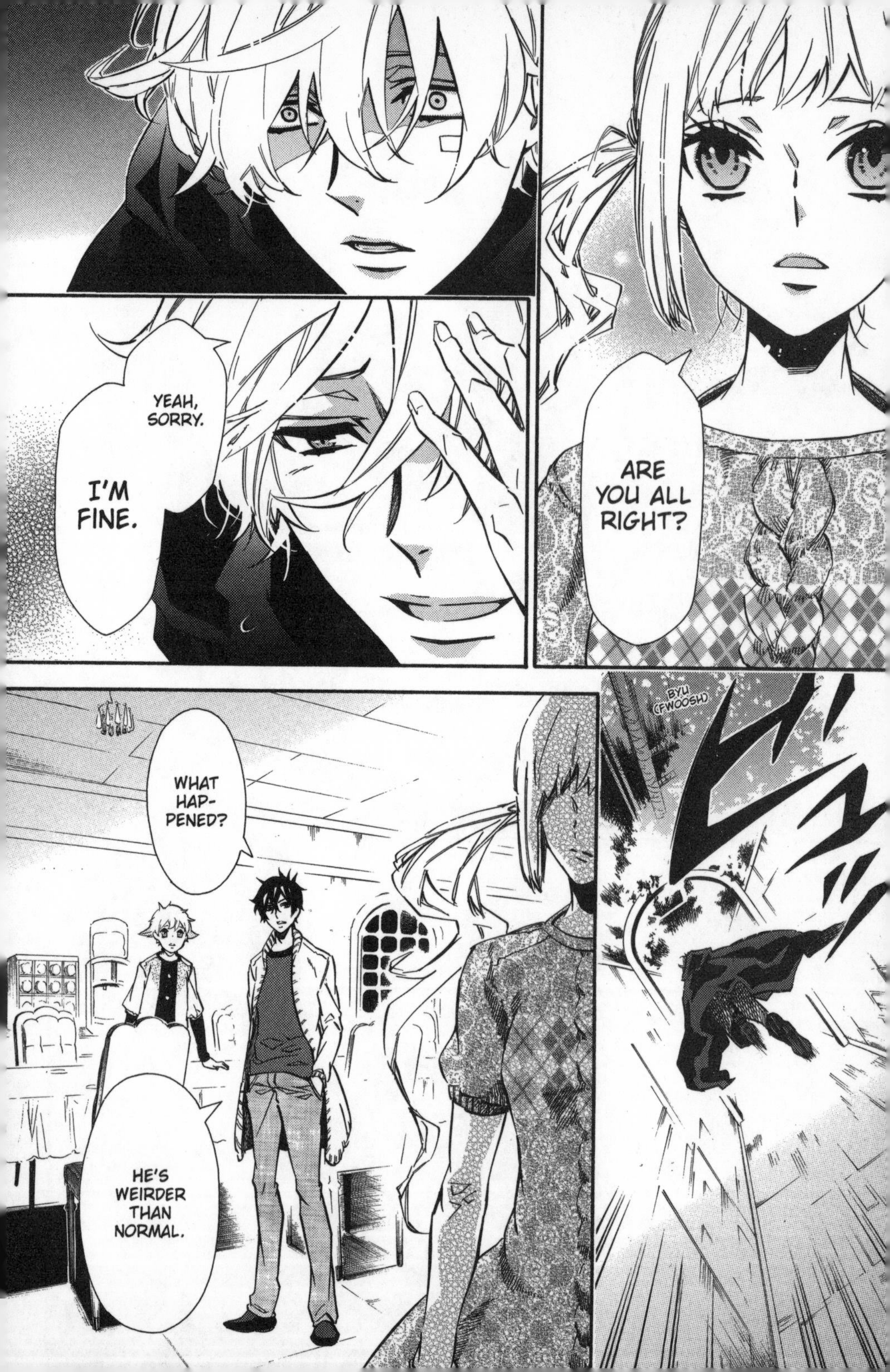
ARE YOU ALL RIGHT?
YEAH, SORRY.
I'M FINE.
BYU (FWOOSH)
WHAT HAP-PENED?
HE'S WEIRDER THAN NORMAL.

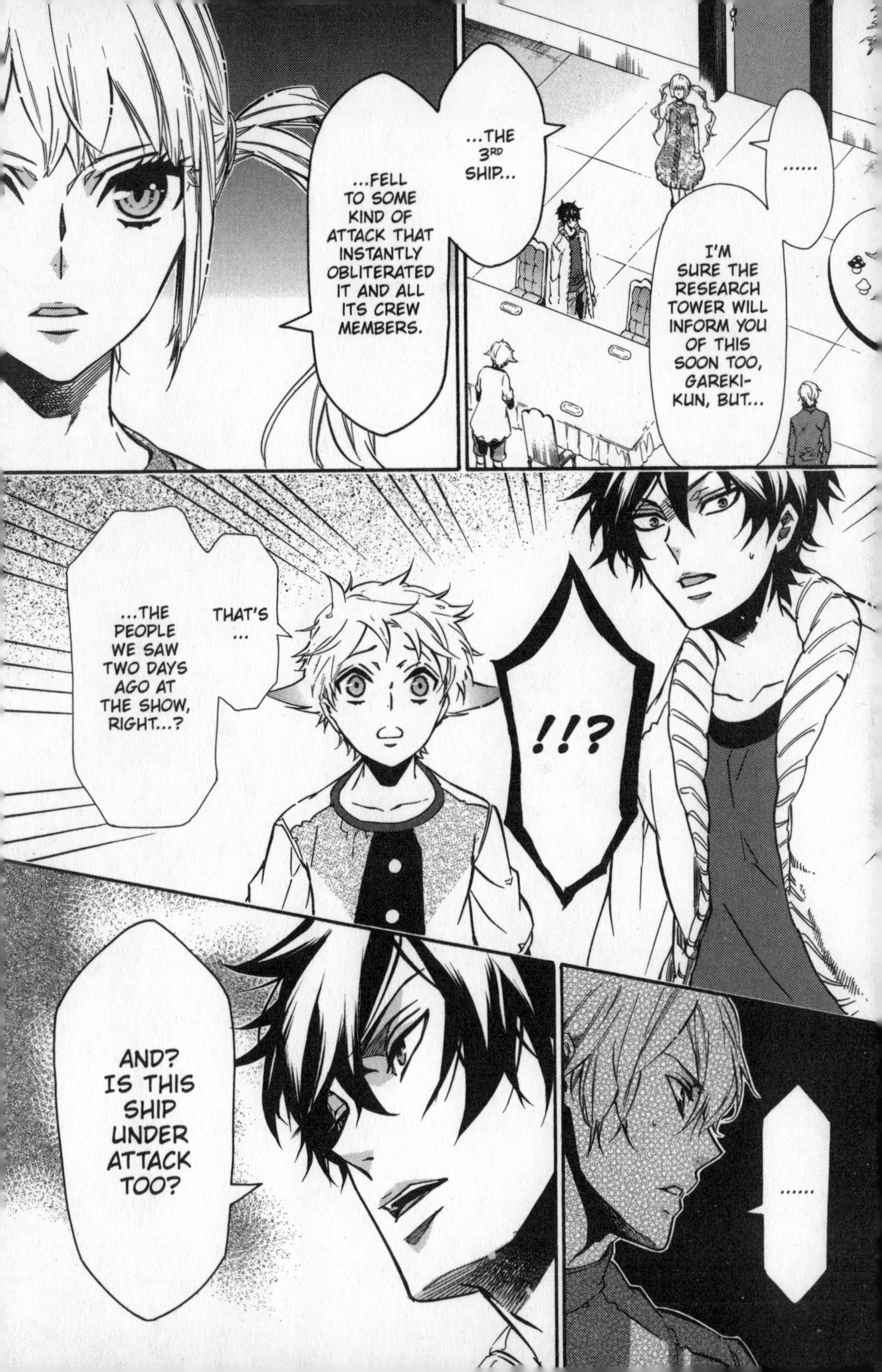
......
I'M SURE THE RESEARCH TOWER WILL INFORM YOU OF THIS SOON TOO, GAREKI-KUN, BUT...
...THE 3RD SHIP...
...FELL TO SOME KIND OF ATTACK THAT INSTANTLY OBLITERATED IT AND ALL ITS CREW MEMBERS.
!!?
THAT'S ...
...THE PEOPLE WE SAW TWO DAYS AGO AT THE SHOW, RIGHT...?
......
AND? IS THIS SHIP UNDER ATTACK TOO?

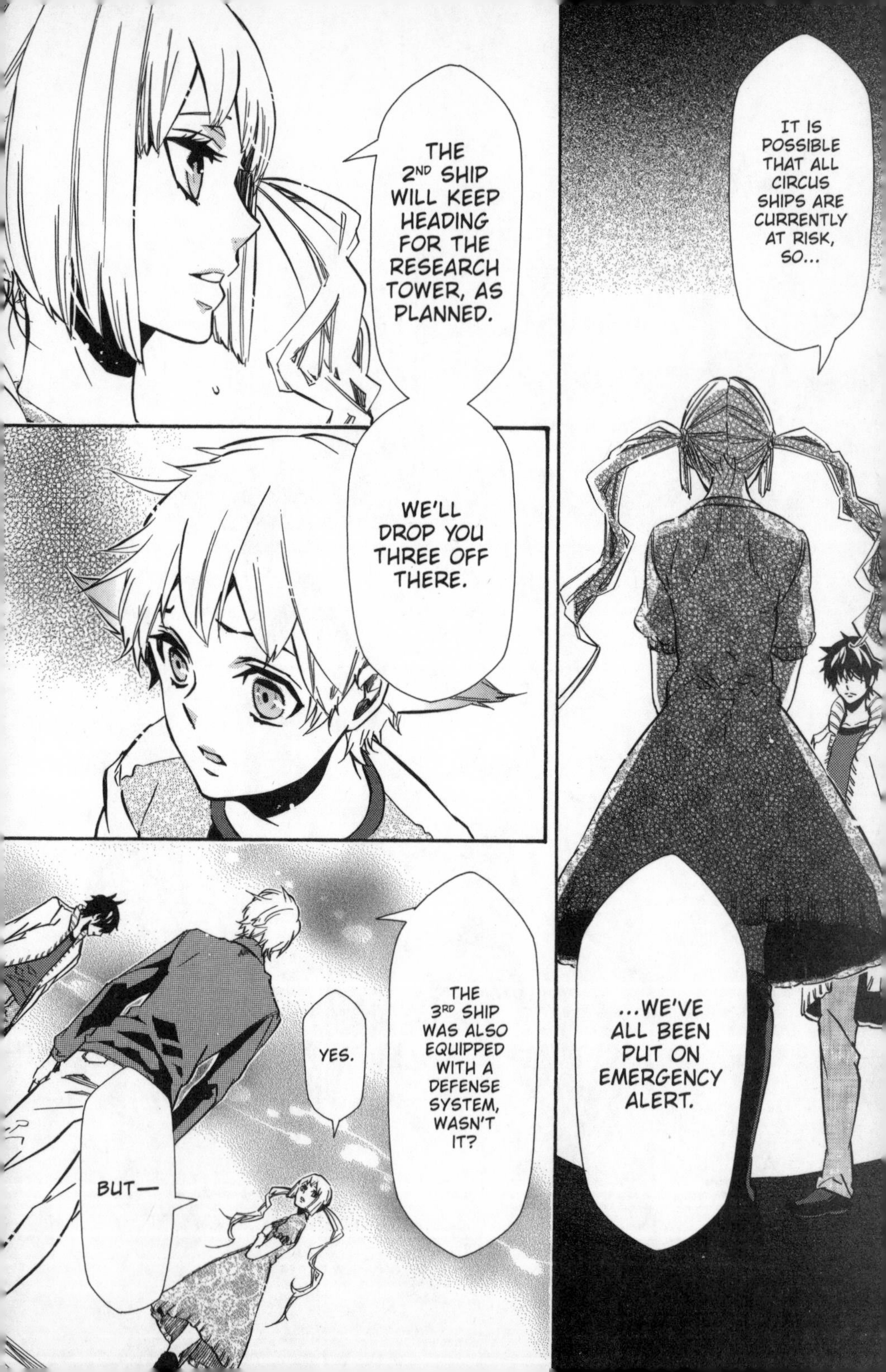
IT IS POSSIBLE THAT ALL CIRCUS SHIPS ARE CURRENTLY AT RISK, SO...
...WE'VE ALL BEEN PUT ON EMERGENCY ALERT.
THE 2ND SHIP WILL KEEP HEADING FOR THE RESEARCH TOWER, AS PLANNED.
WE'LL DROP YOU THREE OFF THERE.
THE 3RD SHIP WAS ALSO EQUIPPED WITH A DEFENSE SYSTEM, WASN'T IT?
YES.
BUT—

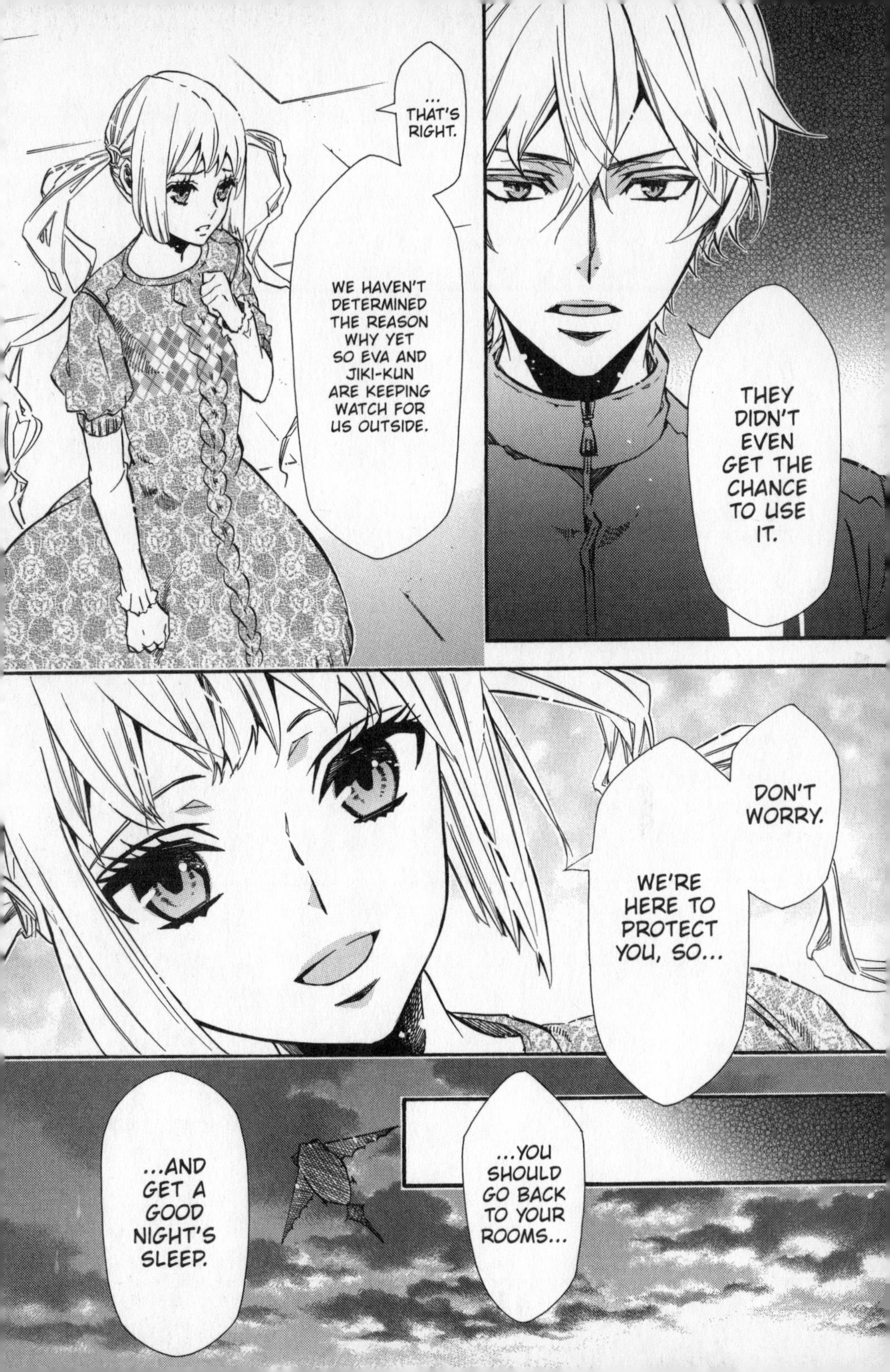
THEY DIDN'T EVEN GET THE CHANCE TO USE IT.
...THAT'S RIGHT.
WE HAVEN'T DETERMINED THE REASON WHY YET SO EVA AND JIKI-KUN ARE KEEPING WATCH FOR US OUTSIDE.
DON'T WORRY.
WE'RE HERE TO PROTECT YOU, SO...
...YOU SHOULD GO BACK TO YOUR ROOMS...
...AND GET A GOOD NIGHT'S SLEEP.

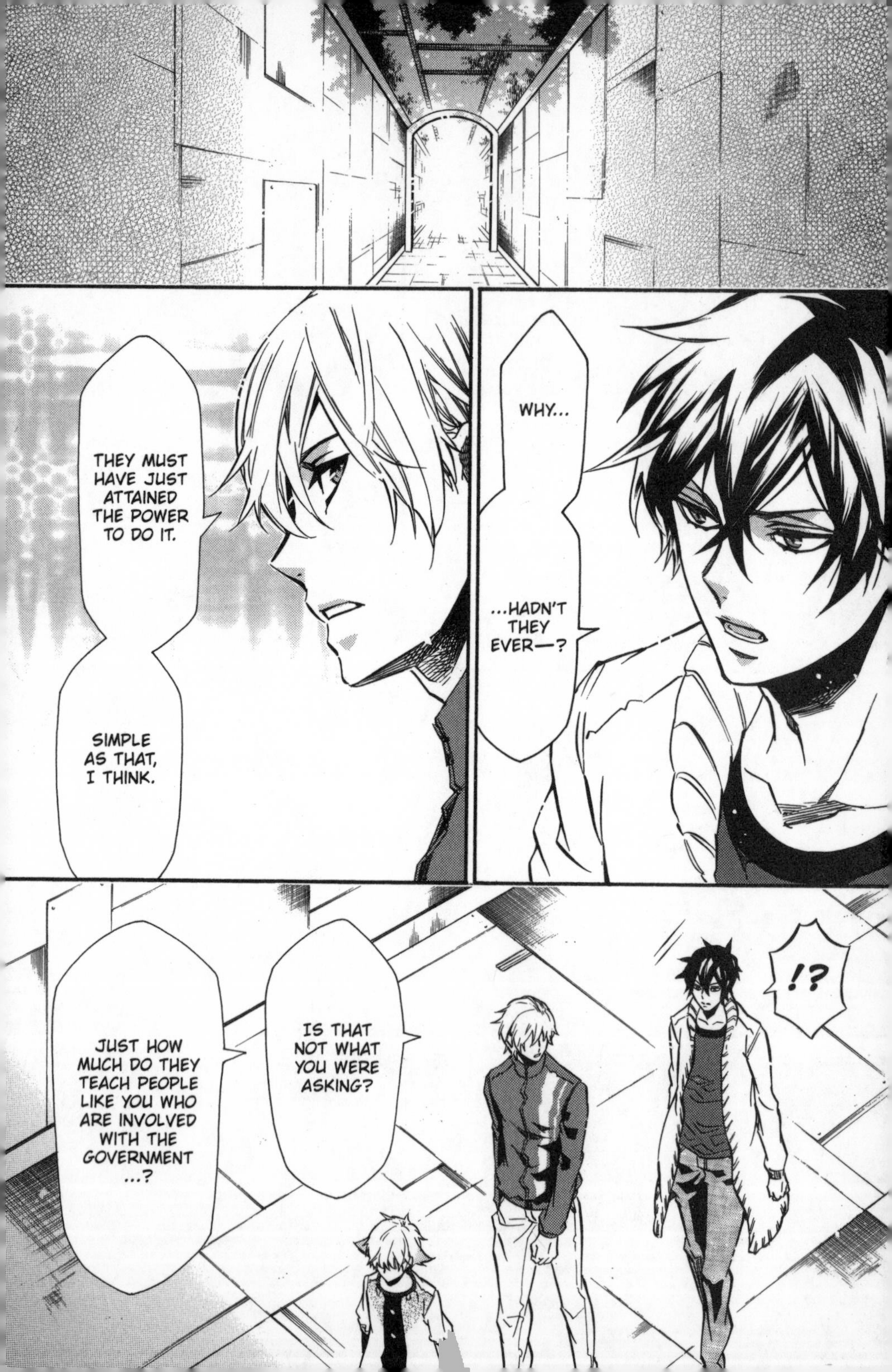
WHY...
...HADN'T THEY EVER—?
THEY MUST HAVE JUST ATTAINED THE POWER TO DO IT.
SIMPLE AS THAT, I THINK.
!?
IS THAT NOT WHAT YOU WERE ASKING?
JUST HOW MUCH DO THEY TEACH PEOPLE LIKE YOU WHO ARE INVOLVED WITH THE GOVERNMENT ...?

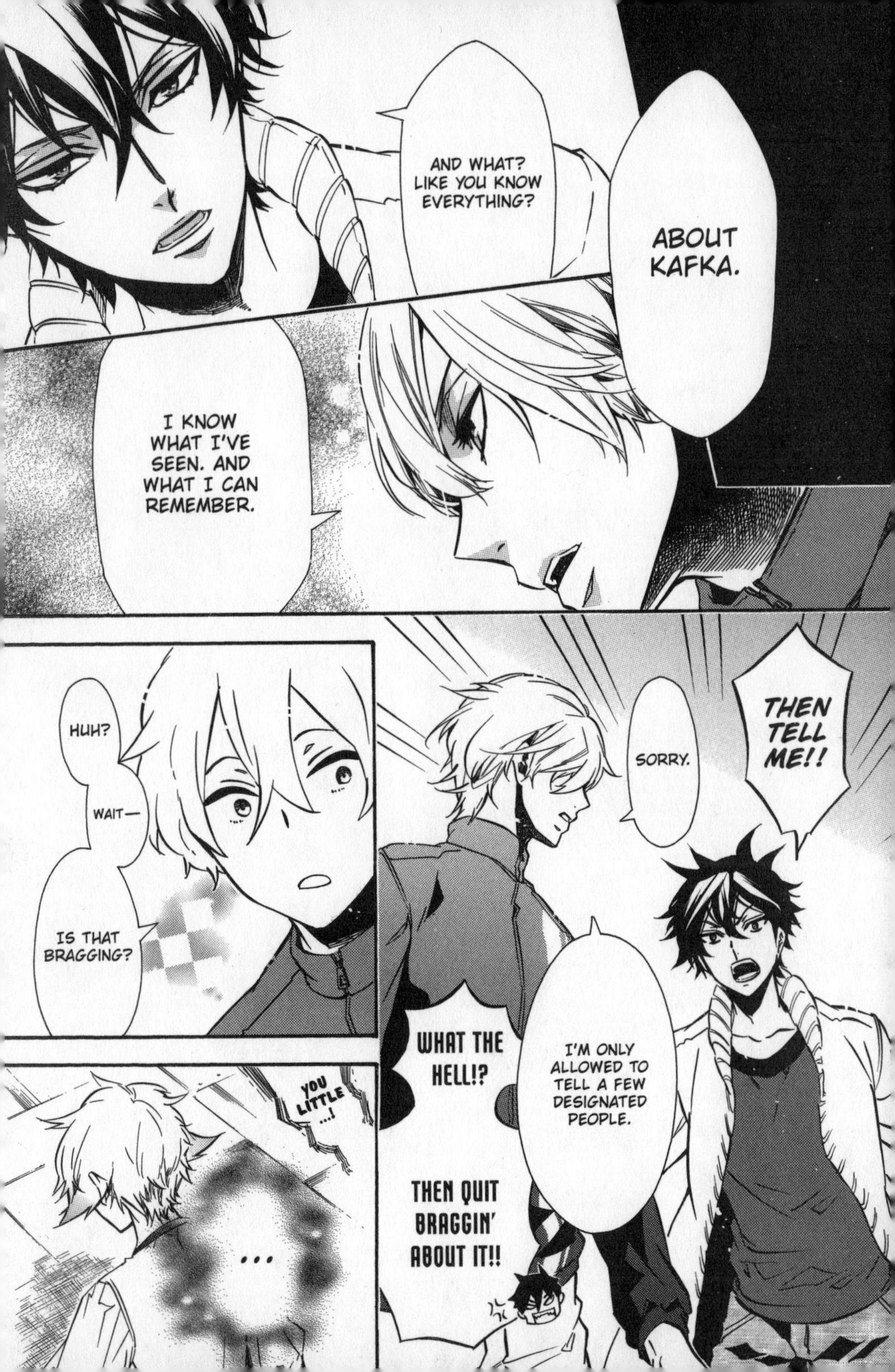
AND WHAT? LIKE YOU KNOW EVERYTHING?
ABOUT KAFKA.
I KNOW WHAT I'VE SEEN. AND WHAT I CAN REMEMBER.
THEN TELL ME!!
SORRY.
I'M ONLY ALLOWED TO TELL A FEW DESIGNATED PEOPLE.
WHAT THE HELL!?
THEN QUIT BRAGGIN' ABOUT IT!!
HUH?
WAIT—
IS THAT BRAGGING?
YOU LITTLE ...!
...

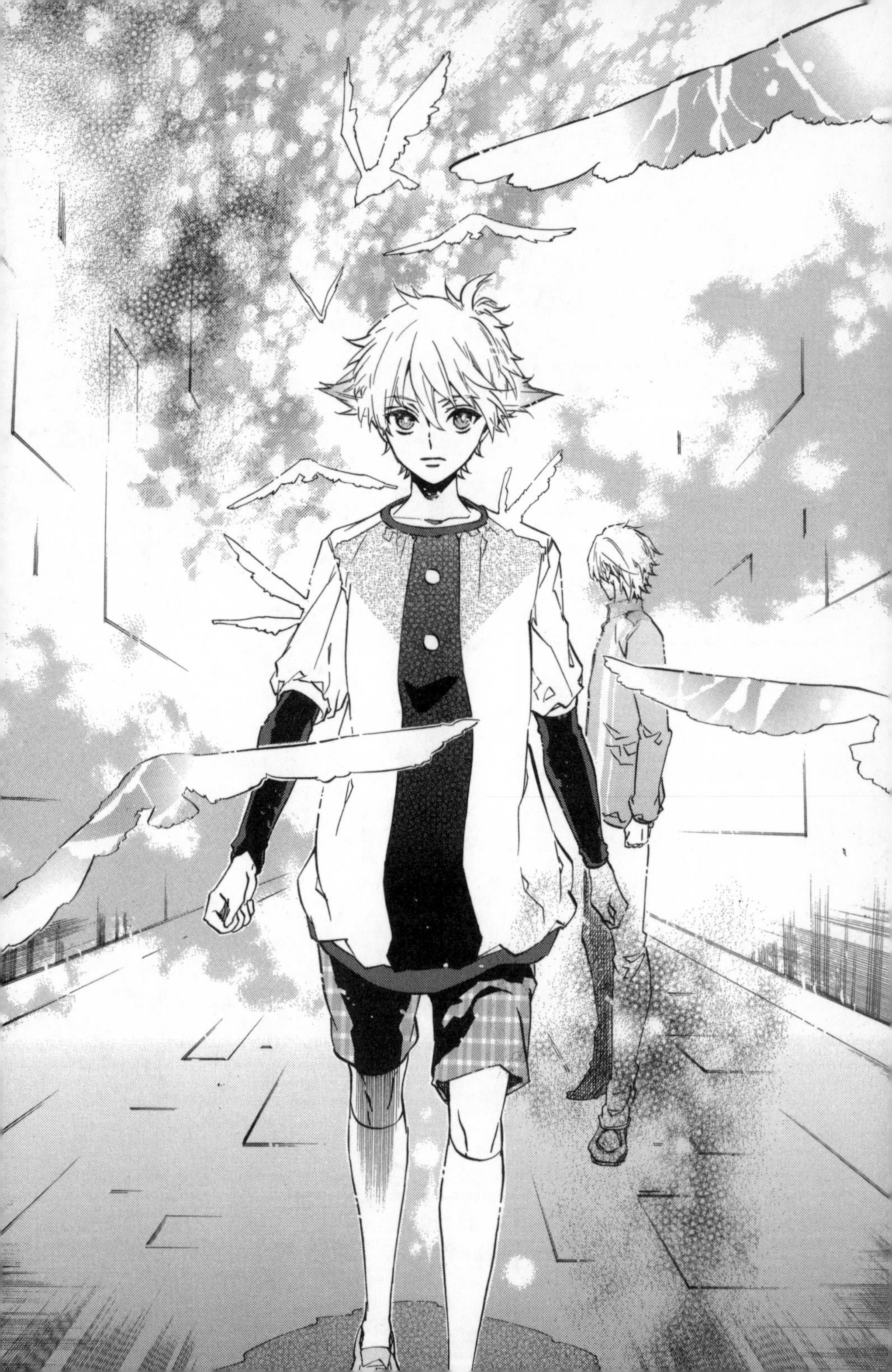

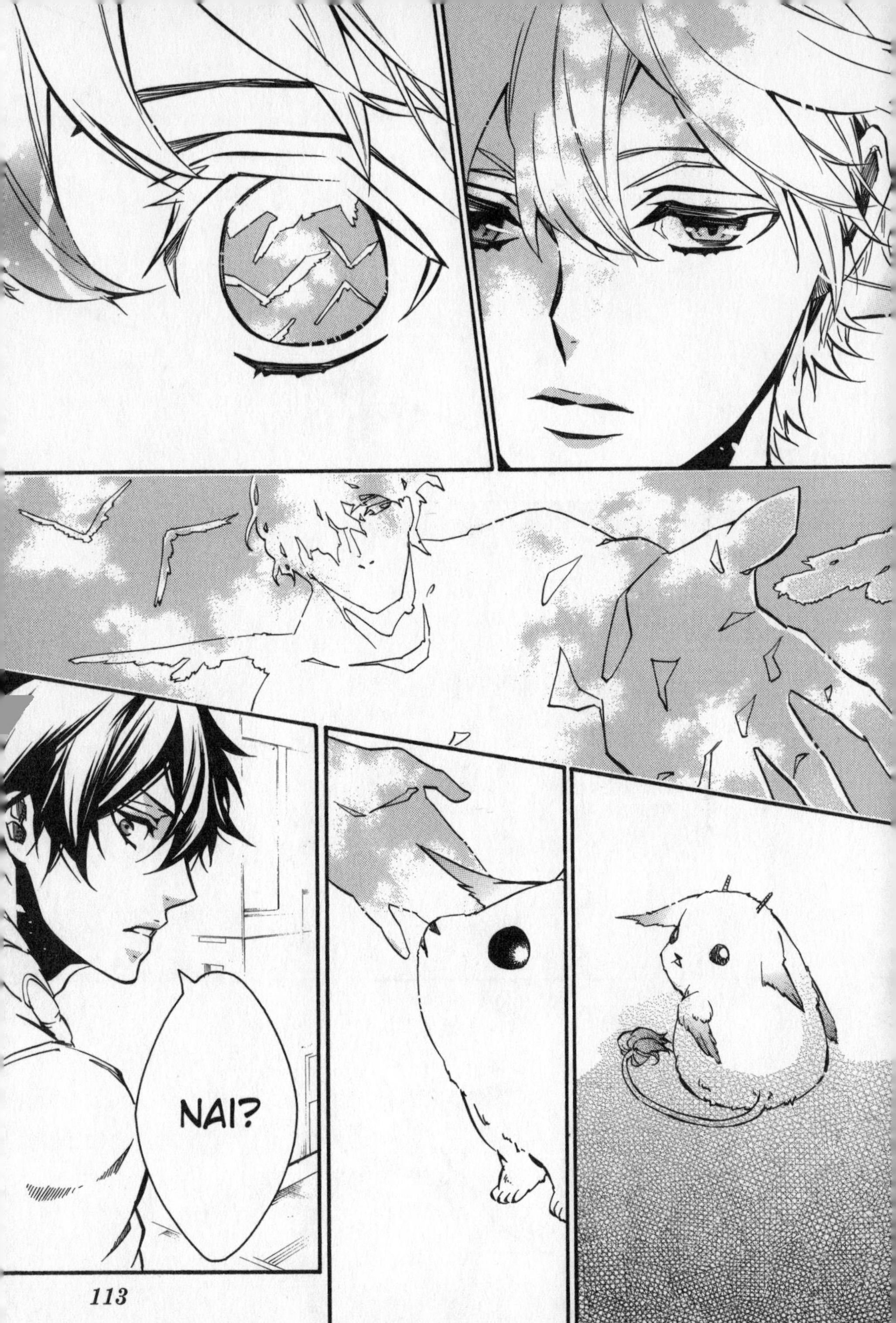
NAI?

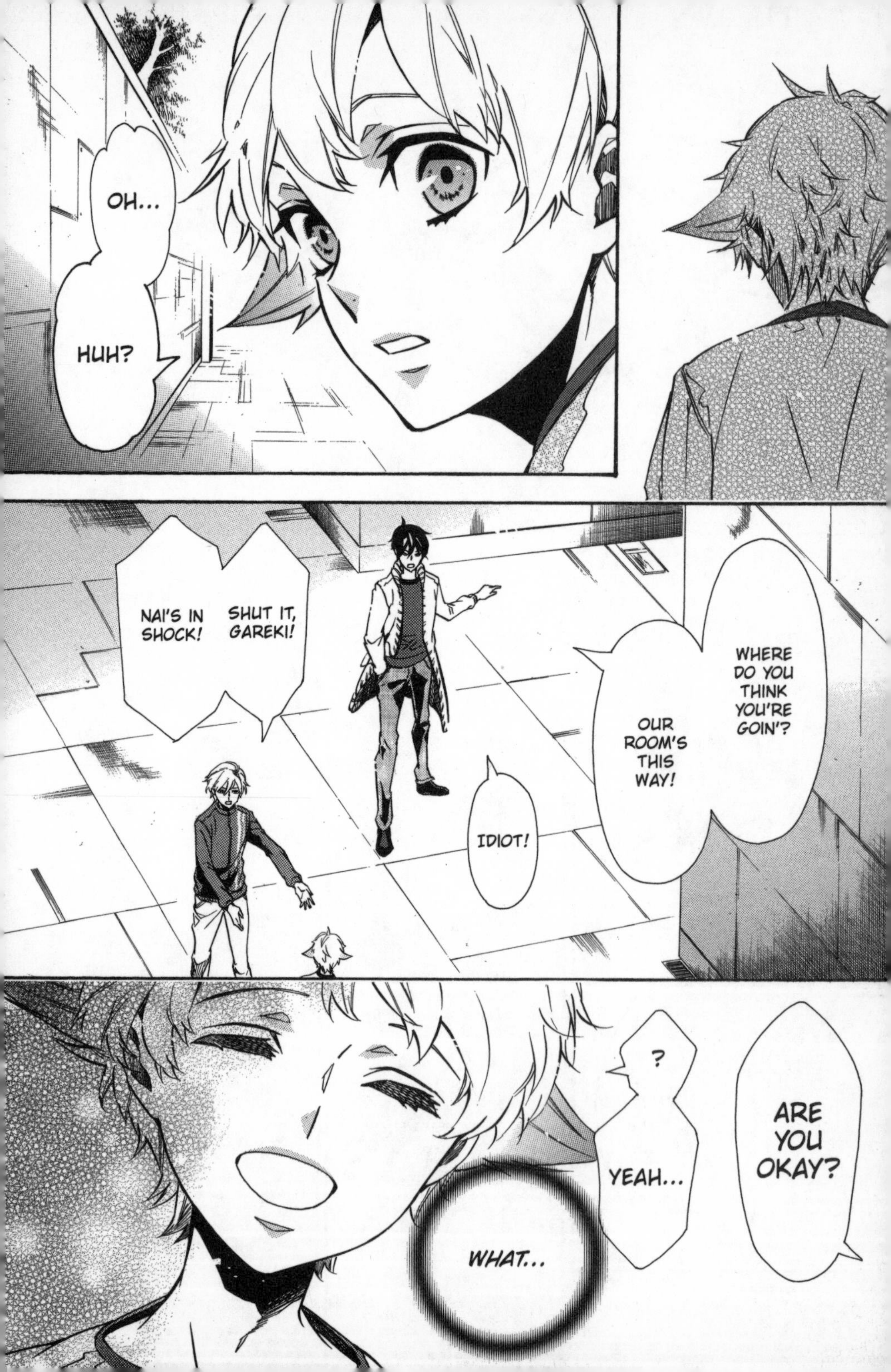
OH...
HUH?
WHERE DO YOU THINK YOU'RE GOIN'?
OUR ROOM'S THIS WAY!
IDIOT!
SHUT IT, GAREKI!
NAI'S IN SHOCK!
ARE YOU OKAY?
?
YEAH...
WHAT...

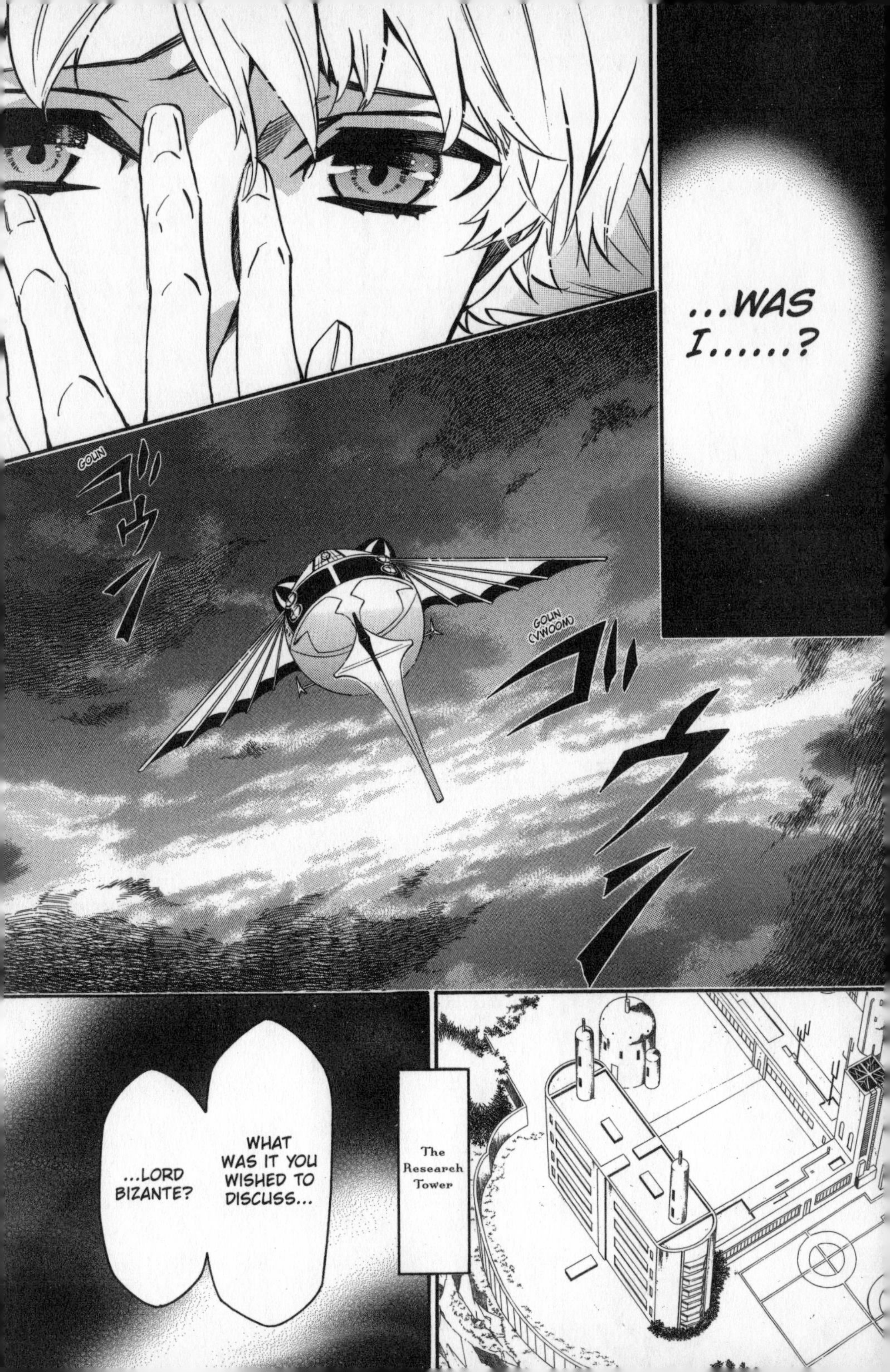
...WAS
I......?
GOUN
(VWOOM)
ゴウン
GOUN
ゴウン
The
Research
Tower
WHAT WAS IT YOU WISHED TO DISCUSS...
...LORD BIZANTE?

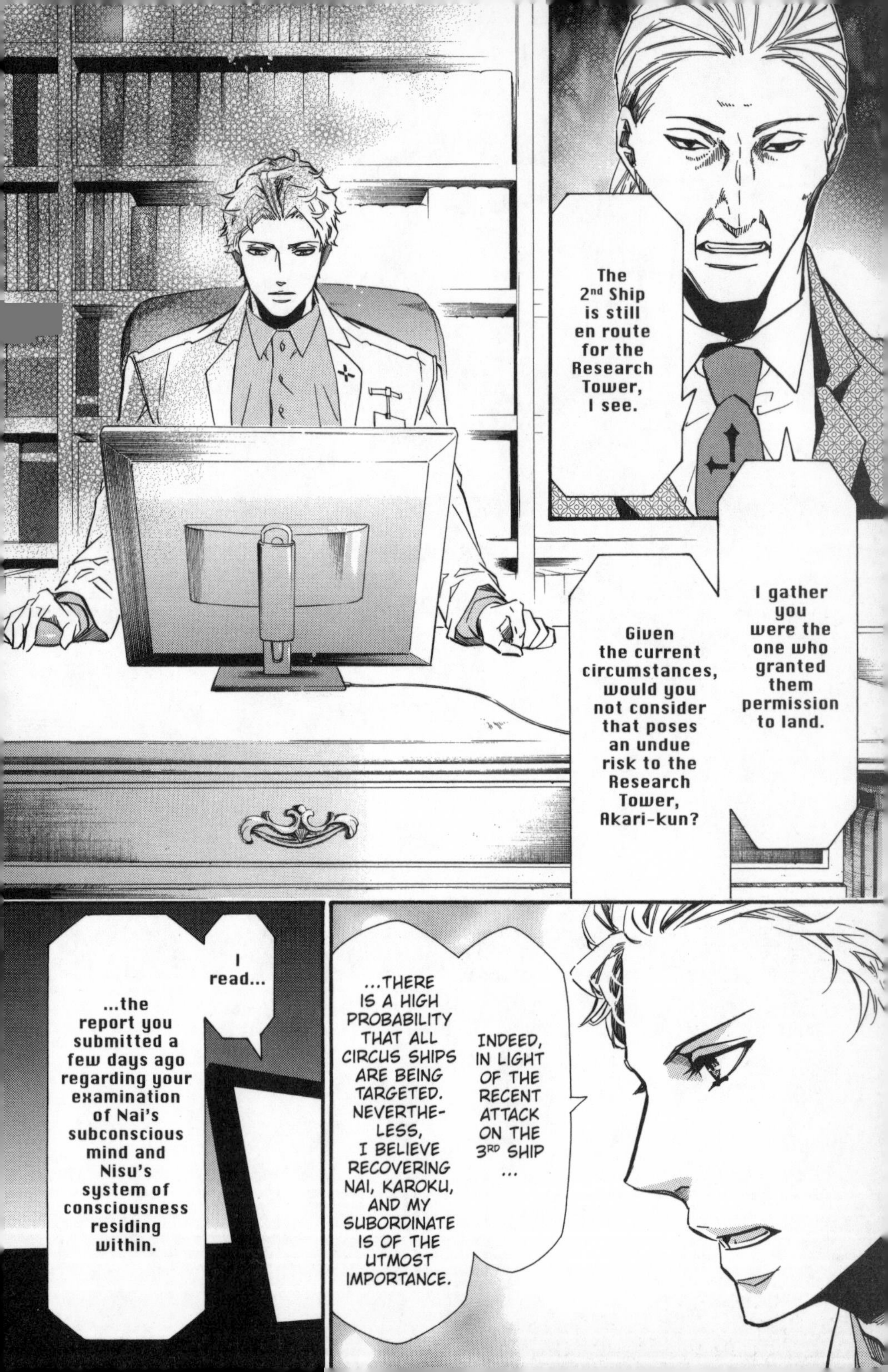
The 2nd Ship is still en route for the Research Tower, I see.
I gather you were the one who granted them permission to land.
Given the current circumstances, would you not consider that poses an undue risk to the Research Tower, Akari-kun?
INDEED, IN LIGHT OF THE RECENT ATTACK ON THE 3RD SHIP...
...THERE IS A HIGH PROBABILITY THAT ALL CIRCUS SHIPS ARE BEING TARGETED. NEVERTHELESS, I BELIEVE RECOVERING NAI, KAROKU, AND MY SUBORDINATE IS OF THE UTMOST IMPORTANCE.
I read...
...the report you submitted a few days ago regarding your examination of Nai's subconscious mind and Nisu's system of consciousness residing within.

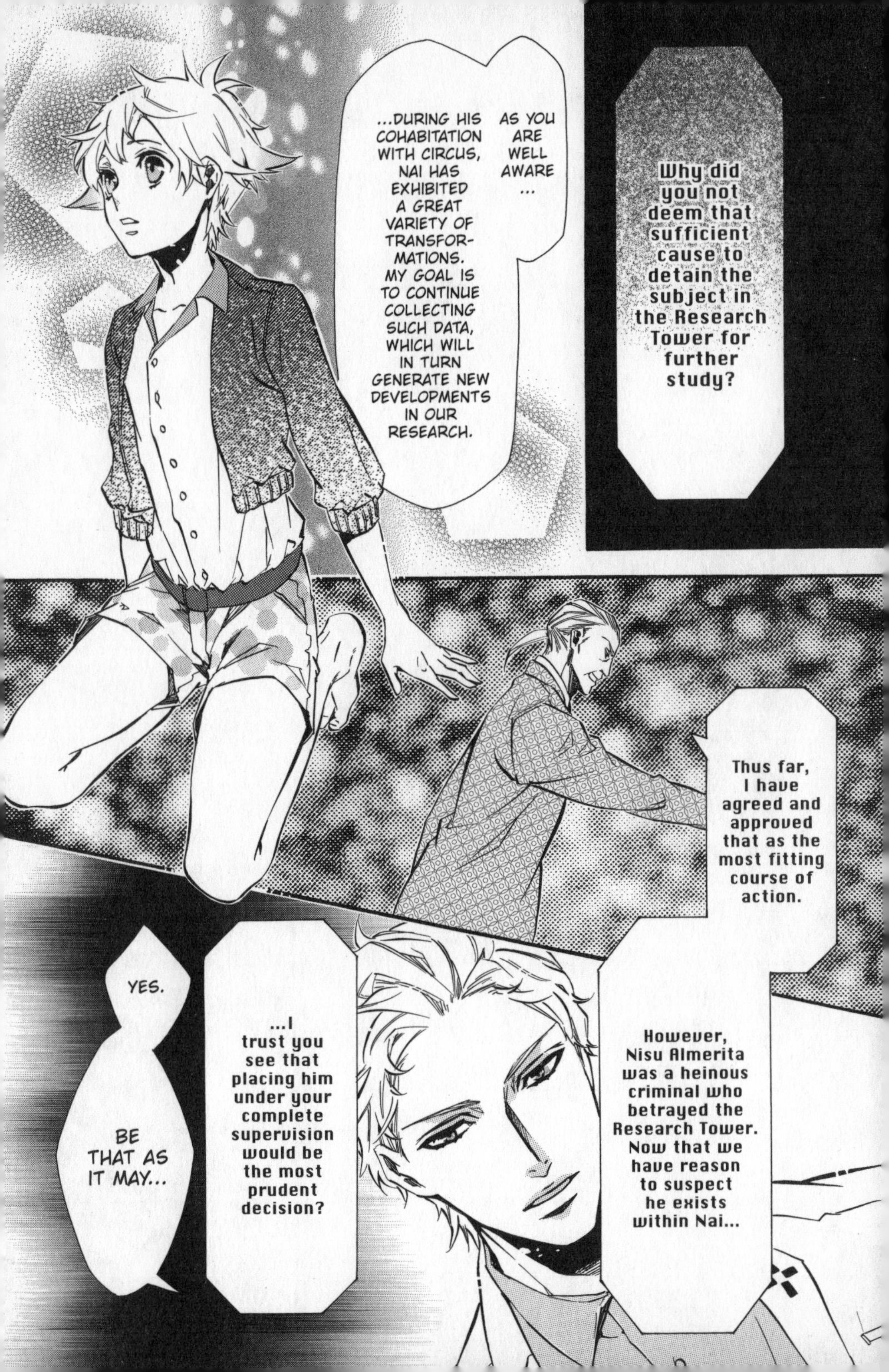
Why did you not deem that sufficient cause to detain the subject in the Research Tower for further study?
AS YOU ARE WELL AWARE...
...DURING HIS COHABITATION WITH CIRCUS, NAI HAS EXHIBITED A GREAT VARIETY OF TRANSFORMATIONS. MY GOAL IS TO CONTINUE COLLECTING SUCH DATA, WHICH WILL IN TURN GENERATE NEW DEVELOPMENTS IN OUR RESEARCH.
Thus far, I have agreed and approved that as the most fitting course of action.
However, Nisu Almerita was a heinous criminal who betrayed the Research Tower. Now that we have reason to suspect he exists within Nai...
...I trust you see that placing him under your complete supervision would be the most prudent decision?
YES.
BE THAT AS IT MAY...

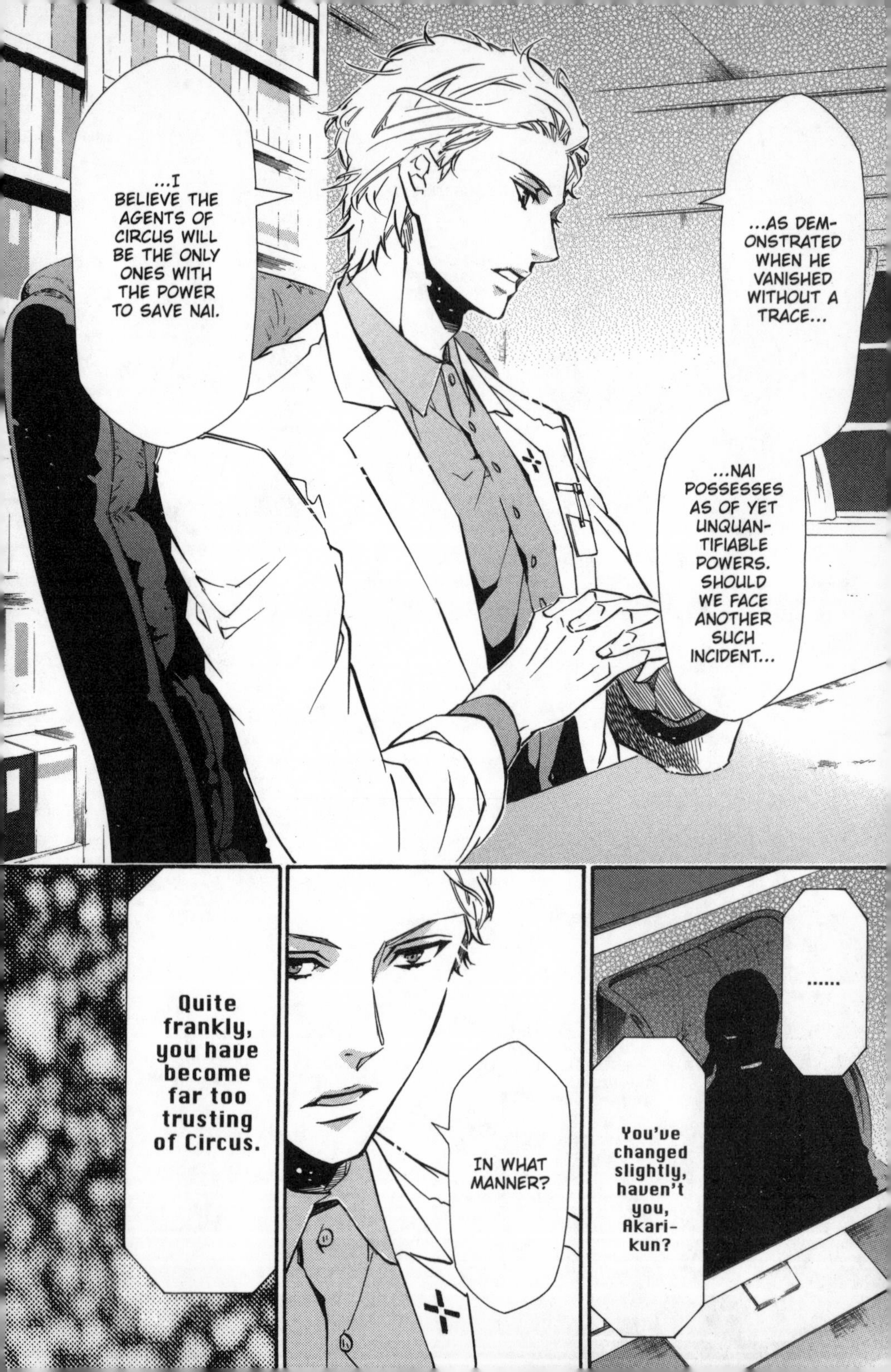
...AS DEM-ONSTRATED WHEN HE VANISHED WITHOUT A TRACE...
...NAI POSSESSES AS OF YET UNQUAN-TIFIABLE POWERS. SHOULD WE FACE ANOTHER SUCH INCIDENT...
...I BELIEVE THE AGENTS OF CIRCUS WILL BE THE ONLY ONES WITH THE POWER TO SAVE NAI.
......
You've changed slightly, haven't you, Akari-kun?
IN WHAT MANNER?
Quite frankly, you have become far too trusting of Circus.

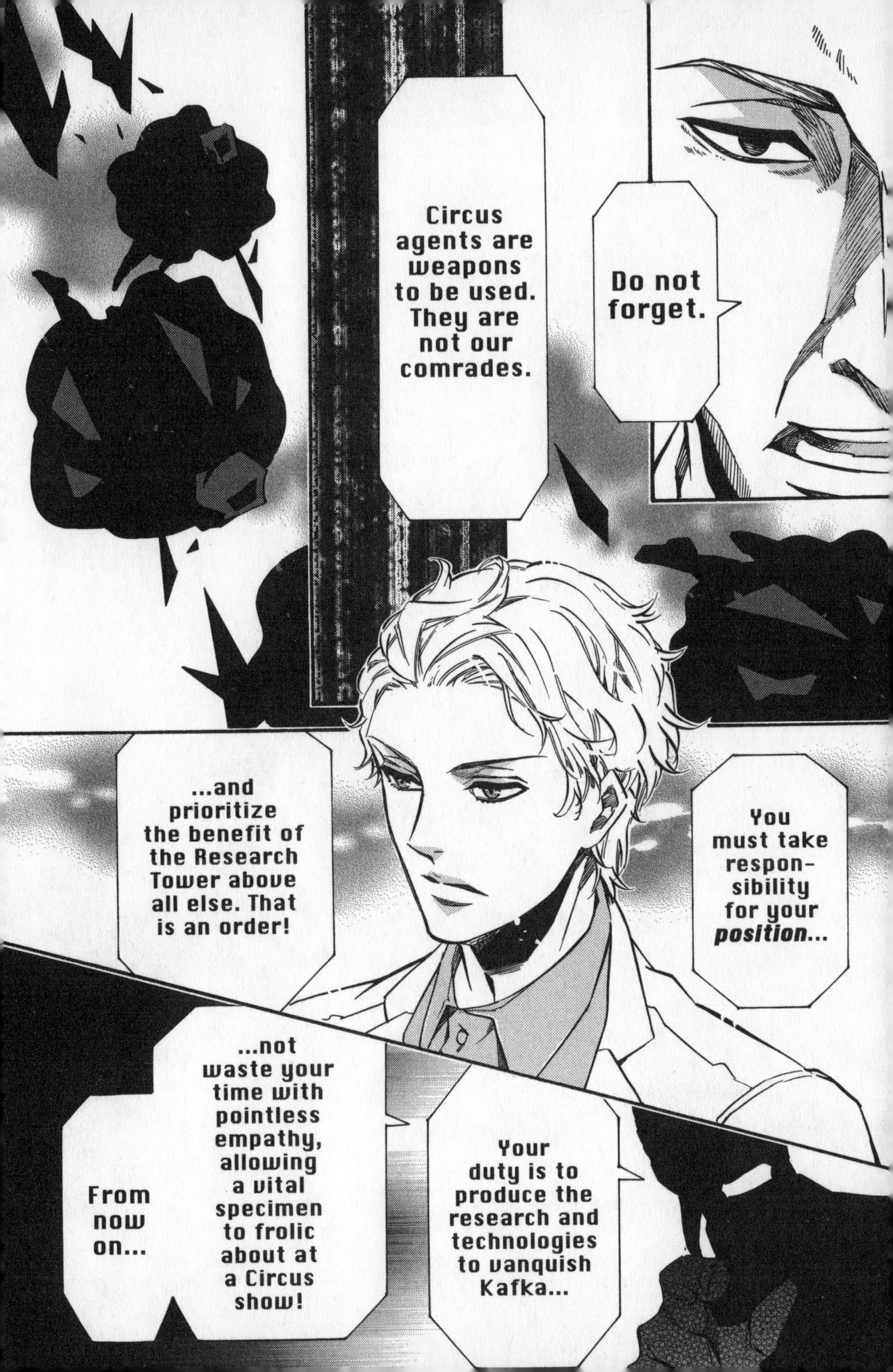
Do not forget.
Circus agents are weapons to be used. They are not our comrades.
You must take respon-sibility for your *position*...
...and prioritize the benefit of the Research Tower above all else. That is an order!
Your duty is to produce the research and technologies to vanquish Kafka...
...not waste your time with pointless empathy, allowing a vital specimen to frolic about at a Circus show!
From now on...

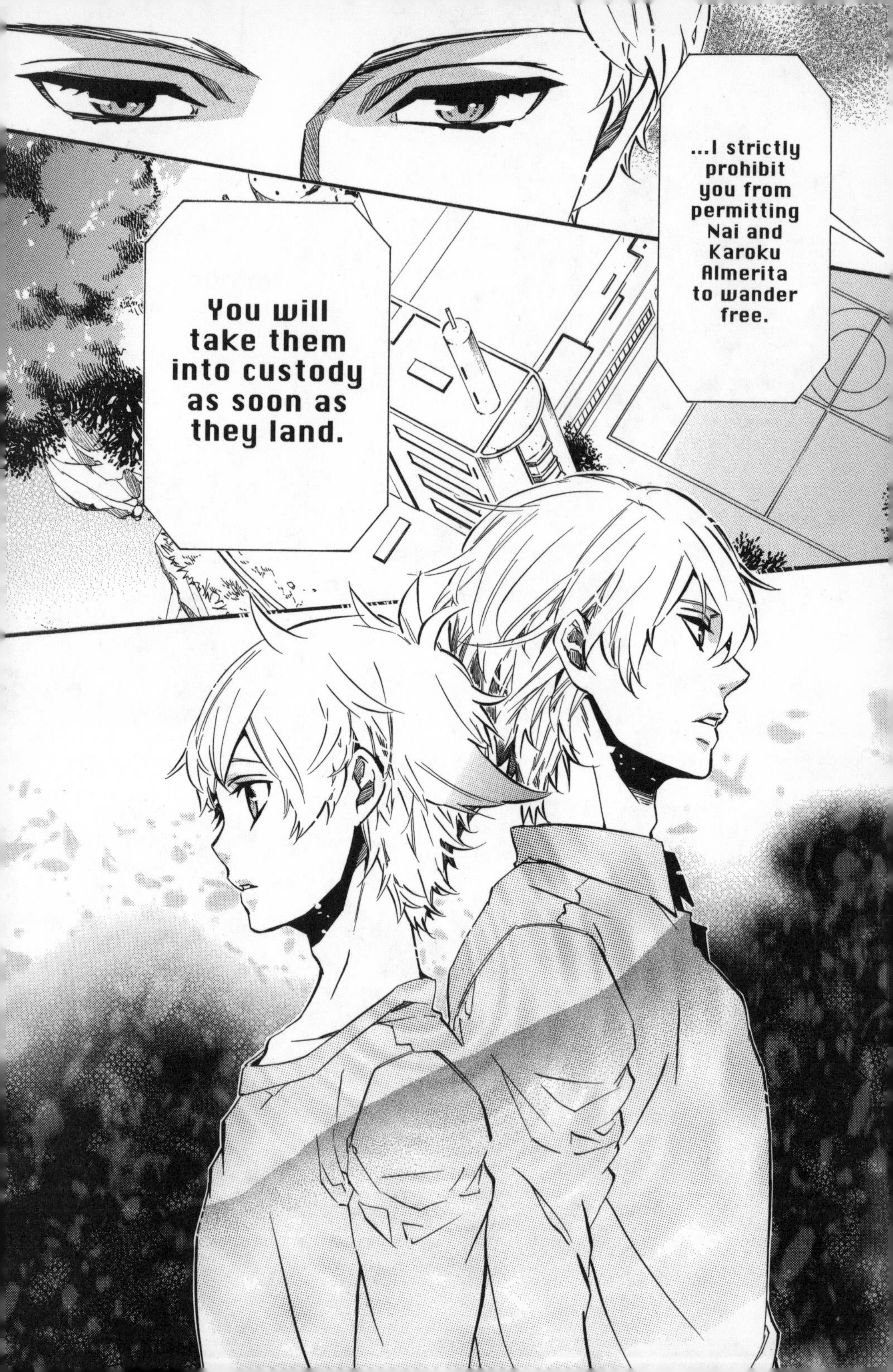
...I strictly prohibit you from permitting Nai and Karoku Almerita to wander free.
You will take them into custody as soon as they land.

KARNEVAL

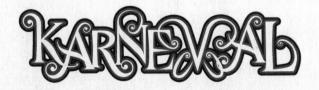

KARNEVAL

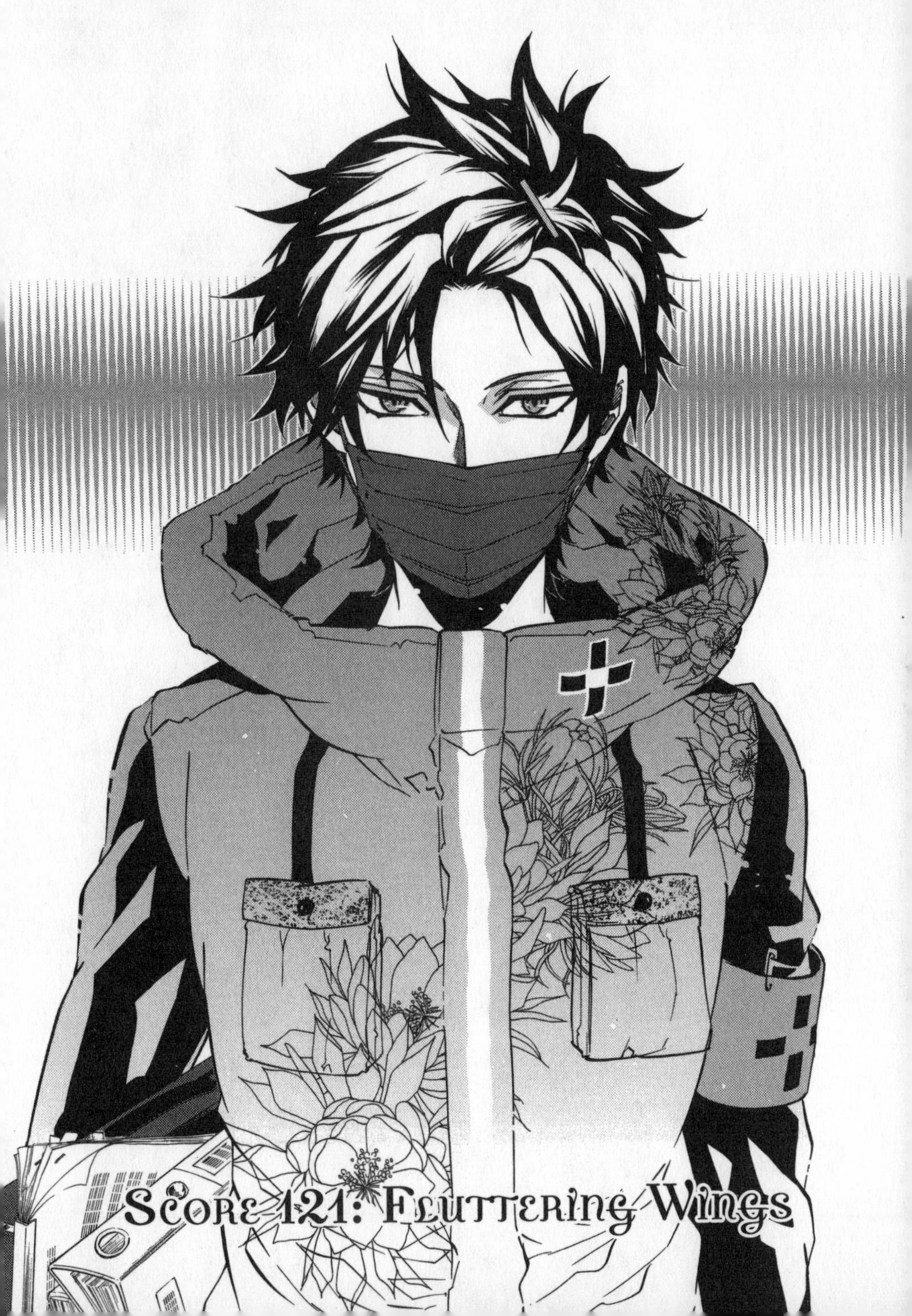
Score 121: Fluttering Wings

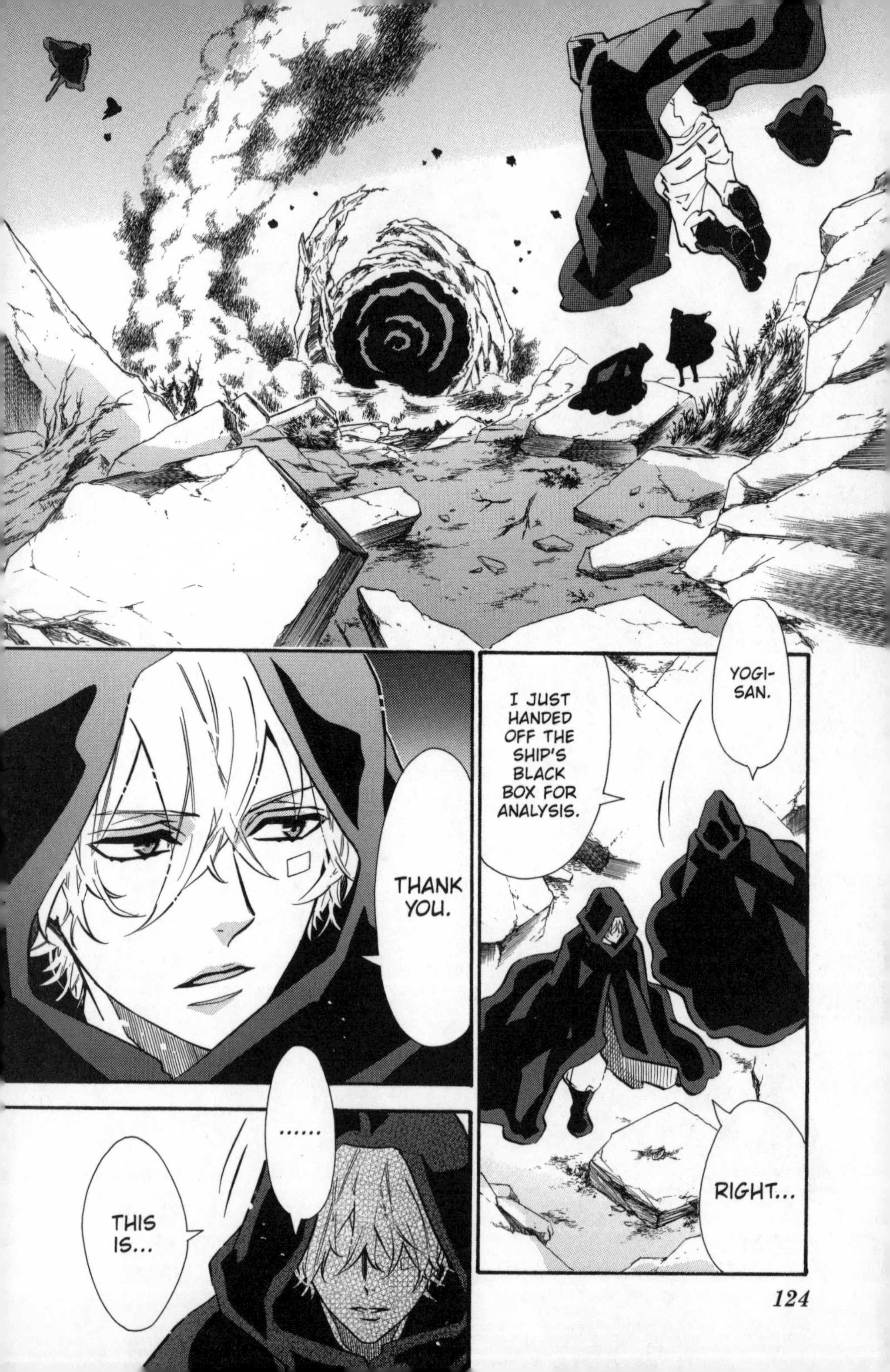
YOGI-SAN.
I JUST HANDED OFF THE SHIP'S BLACK BOX FOR ANALYSIS.
RIGHT...
THANK YOU.
......
THIS IS...

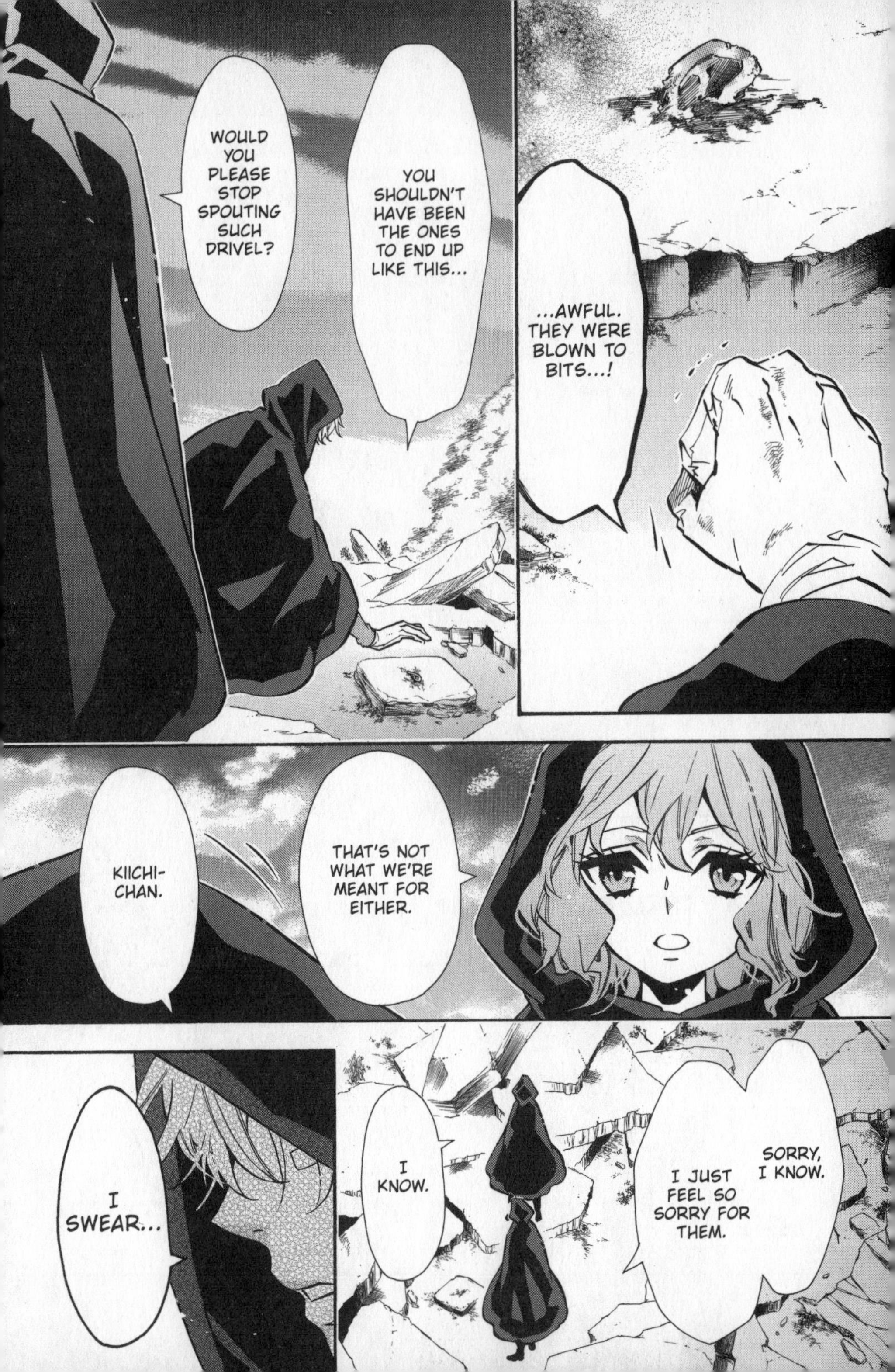
...AWFUL. THEY WERE BLOWN TO BITS...!
YOU SHOULDN'T HAVE BEEN THE ONES TO END UP LIKE THIS...
WOULD YOU PLEASE STOP SPOUTING SUCH DRIVEL?
THAT'S NOT WHAT WE'RE MEANT FOR EITHER.
KIICHI-CHAN.
SORRY, I KNOW.
I JUST FEEL SO SORRY FOR THEM.
I KNOW.
I SWEAR...

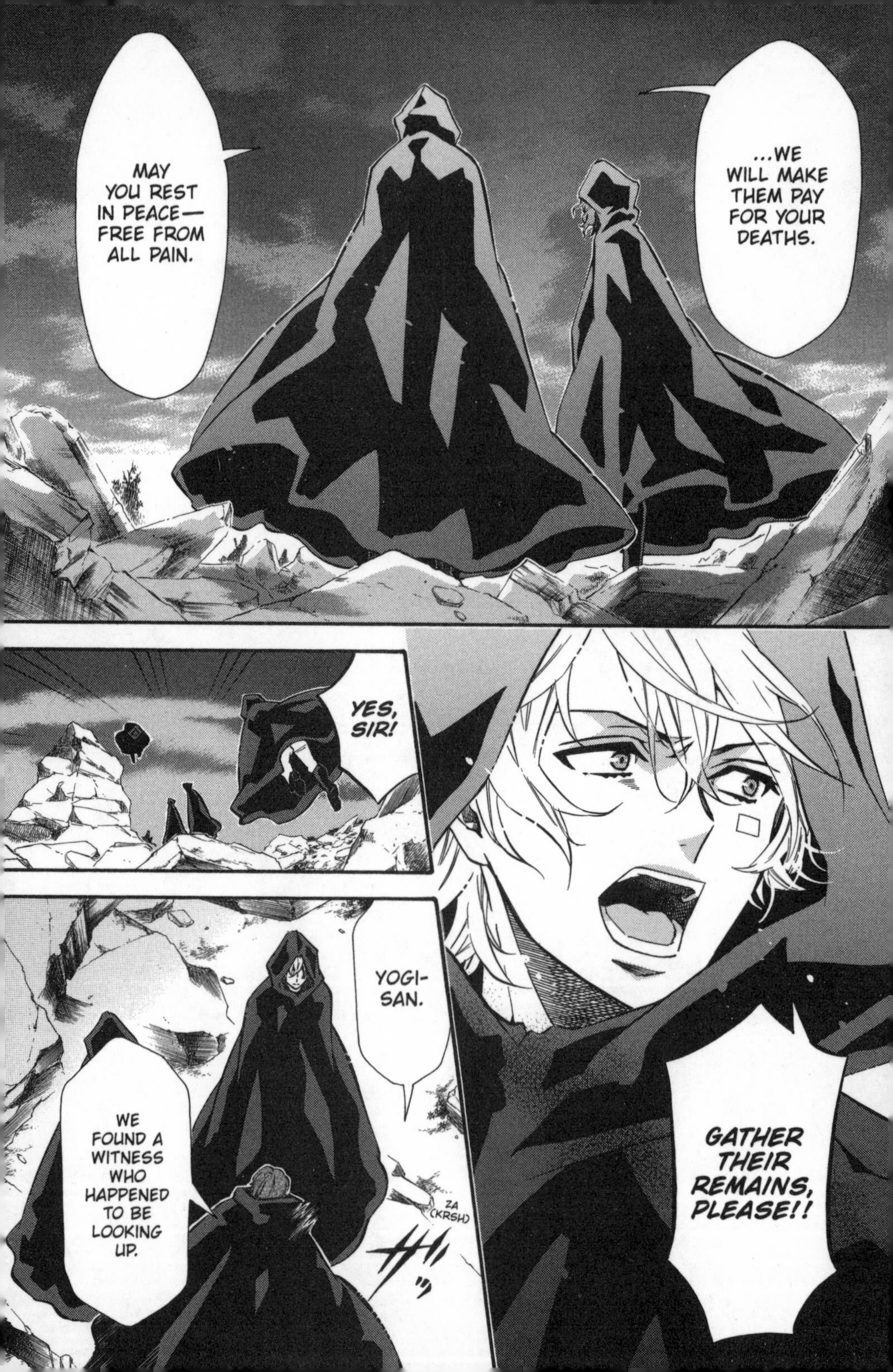
...WE WILL MAKE THEM PAY FOR YOUR DEATHS.
MAY YOU REST IN PEACE—FREE FROM ALL PAIN.
GATHER THEIR REMAINS, PLEASE!!
YES, SIR!
YOGI-SAN.
WE FOUND A WITNESS WHO HAPPENED TO BE LOOKING UP.
ZA (KRSH)

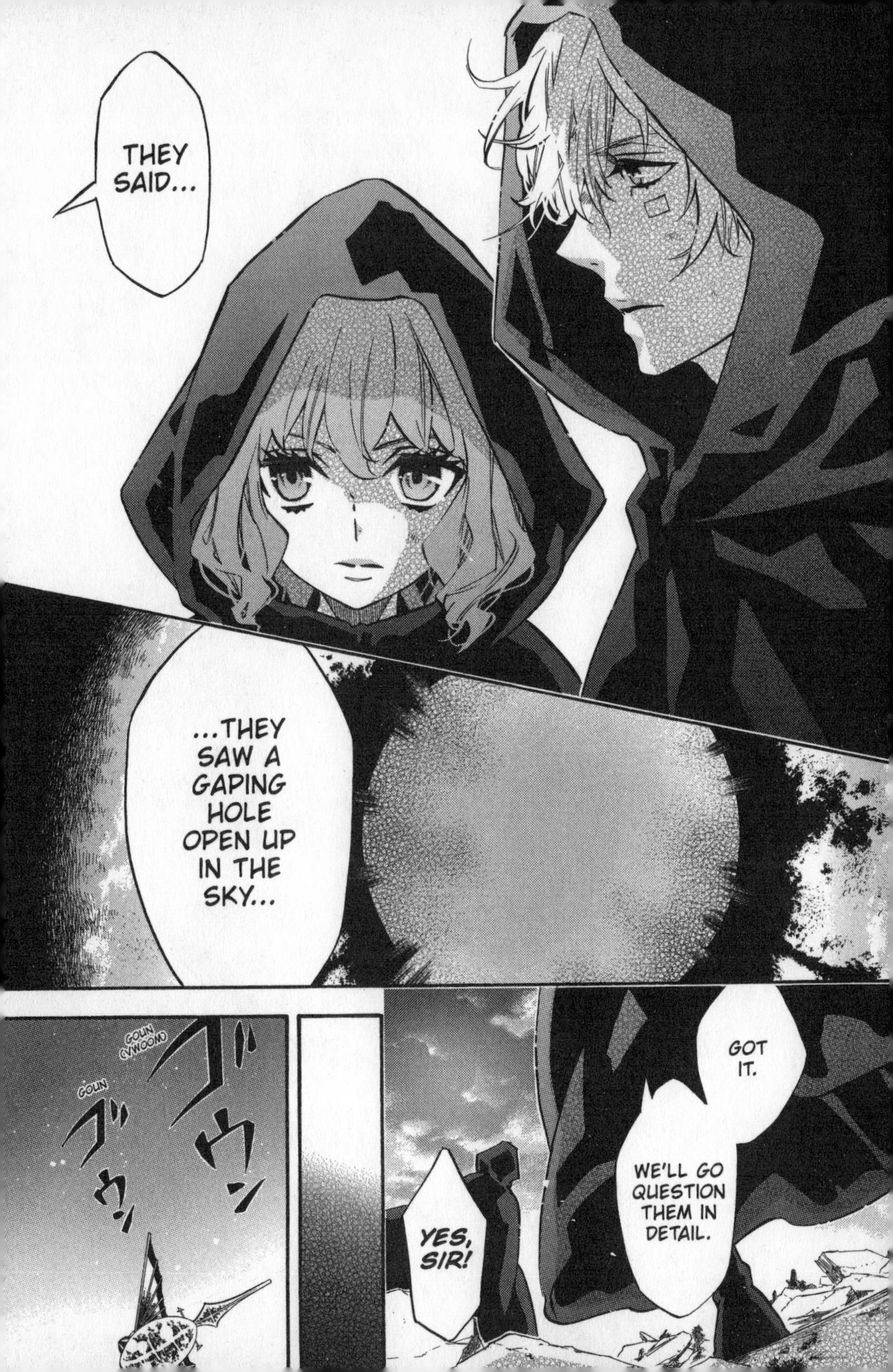
THEY SAID...
...THEY SAW A GAPING HOLE OPEN UP IN THE SKY...
GOT IT.
WE'LL GO QUESTION THEM IN DETAIL.
YES, SIR!
GOUN (VWOOM)
GOUN

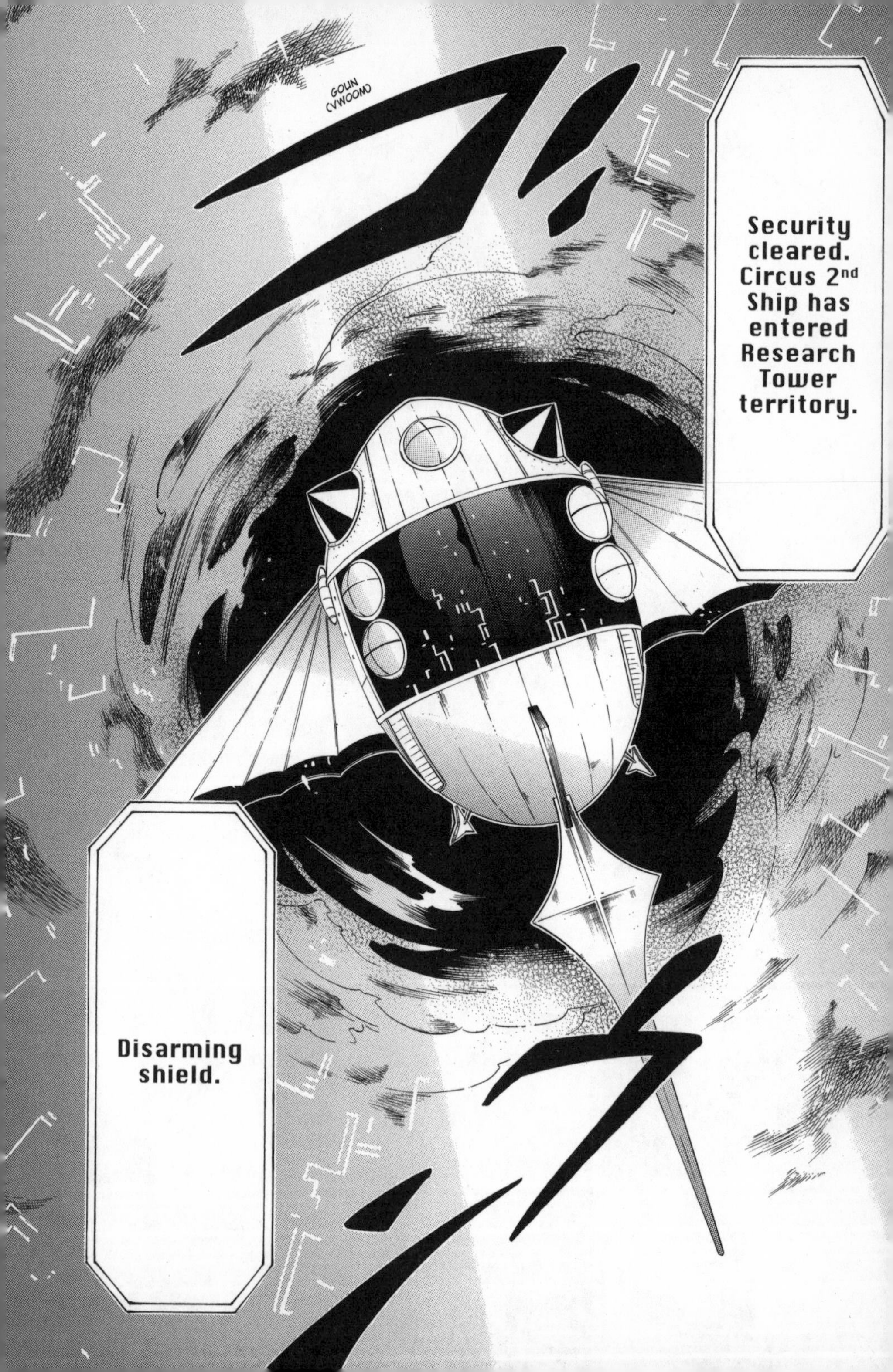
Security cleared. Circus 2nd Ship has entered Research Tower territory.
GOUN (VWOOM)
Disarming shield.

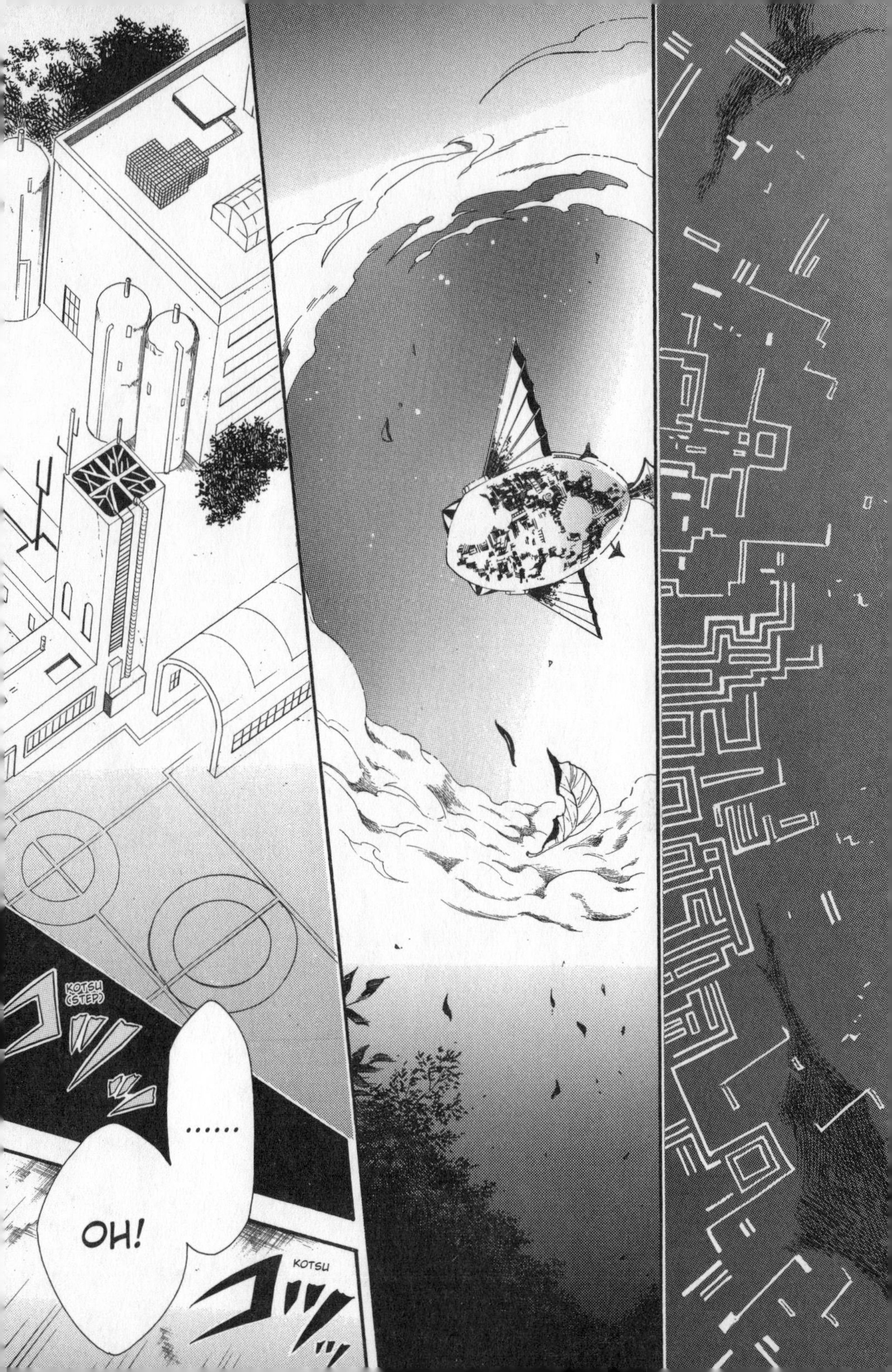
KOTSU (STEP)
......
OH!
KOTSU

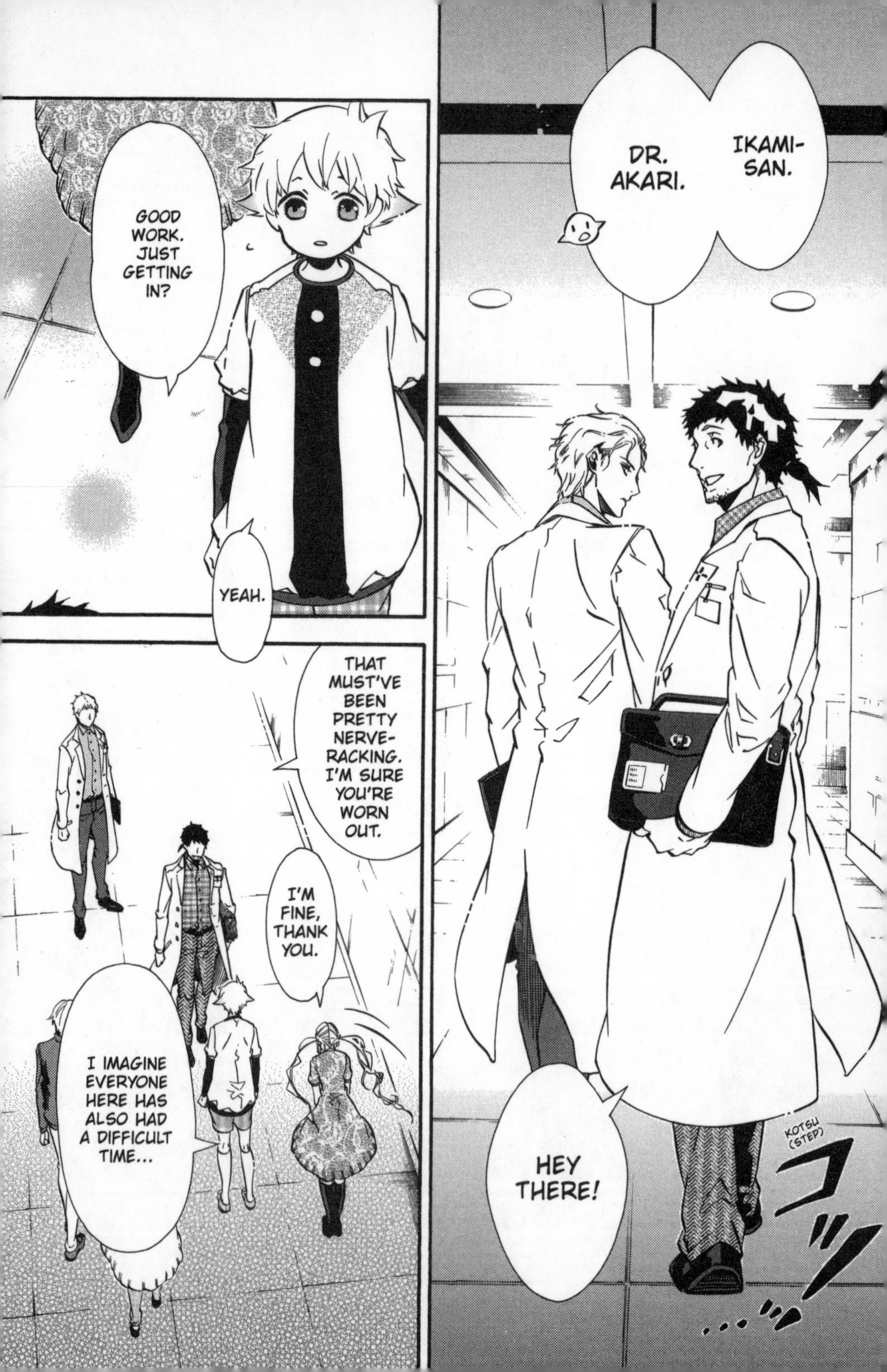
IKAMI-SAN.
DR. AKARI.
HEY THERE!
KOTSU (STEP)
GOOD WORK. JUST GETTING IN?
YEAH.
THAT MUST'VE BEEN PRETTY NERVE-RACKING. I'M SURE YOU'RE WORN OUT.
I'M FINE, THANK YOU.
I IMAGINE EVERYONE HERE HAS ALSO HAD A DIFFICULT TIME...

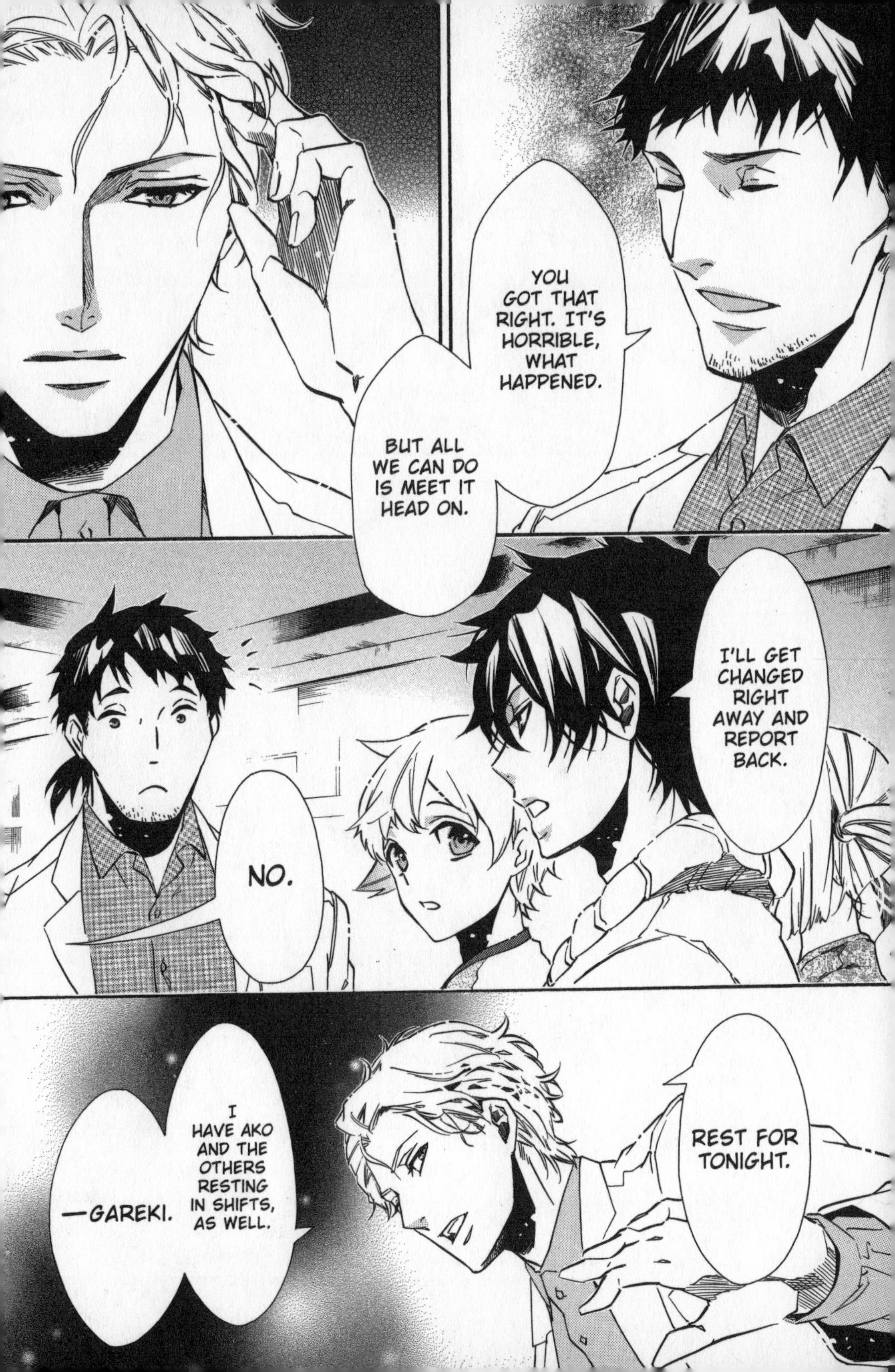
YOU GOT THAT RIGHT. IT'S HORRIBLE, WHAT HAPPENED.
BUT ALL WE CAN DO IS MEET IT HEAD ON.
I'LL GET CHANGED RIGHT AWAY AND REPORT BACK.
NO.
REST FOR TONIGHT.
I HAVE AKO AND THE OTHERS RESTING IN SHIFTS, AS WELL.
—GAREKI.

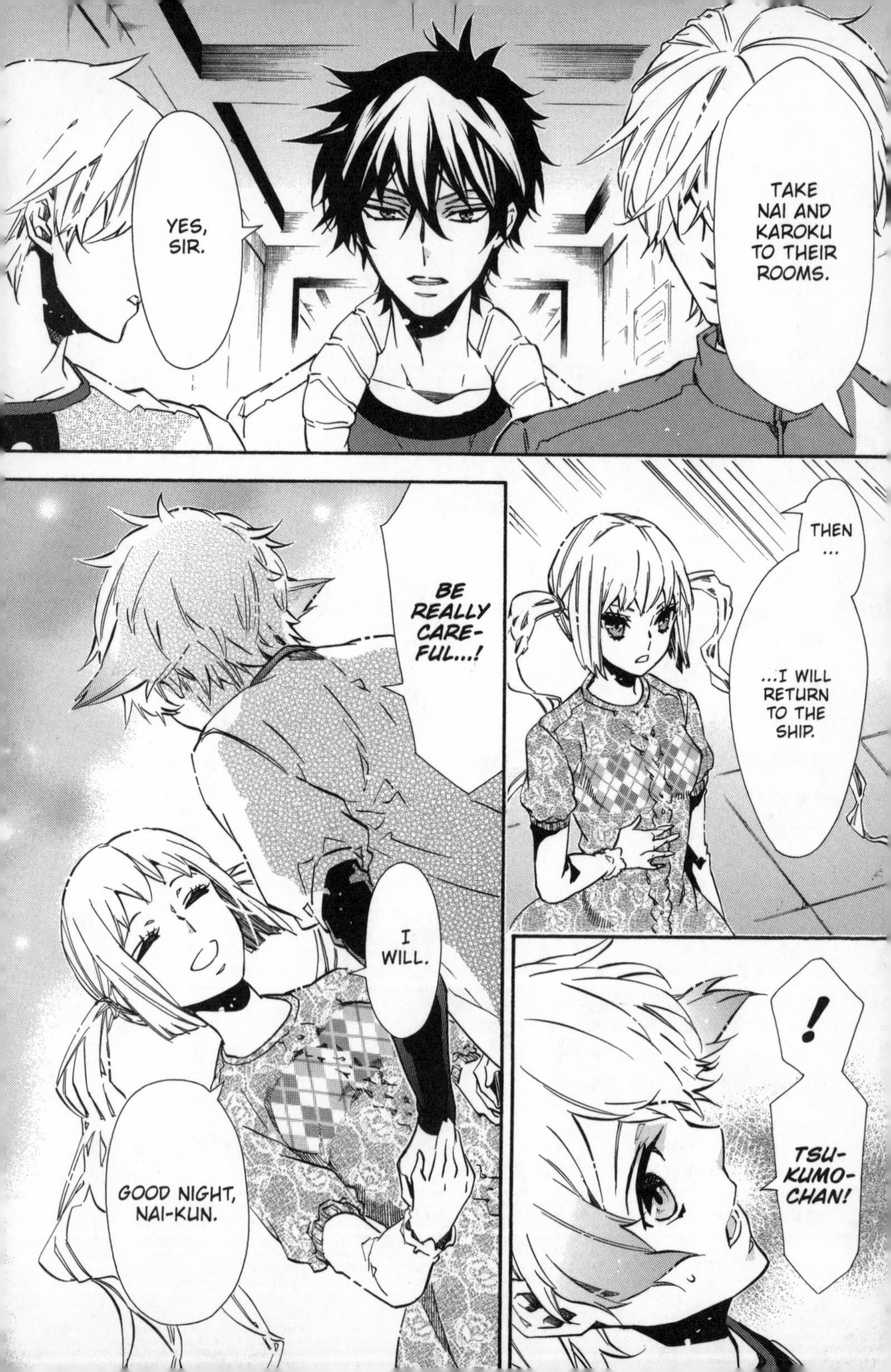
TAKE NAI AND KAROKU TO THEIR ROOMS.
YES, SIR.
THEN...
...I WILL RETURN TO THE SHIP.
!
TSU-KUMO-CHAN!
BE REALLY CARE-FUL...!
I WILL.
GOOD NIGHT, NAI-KUN.

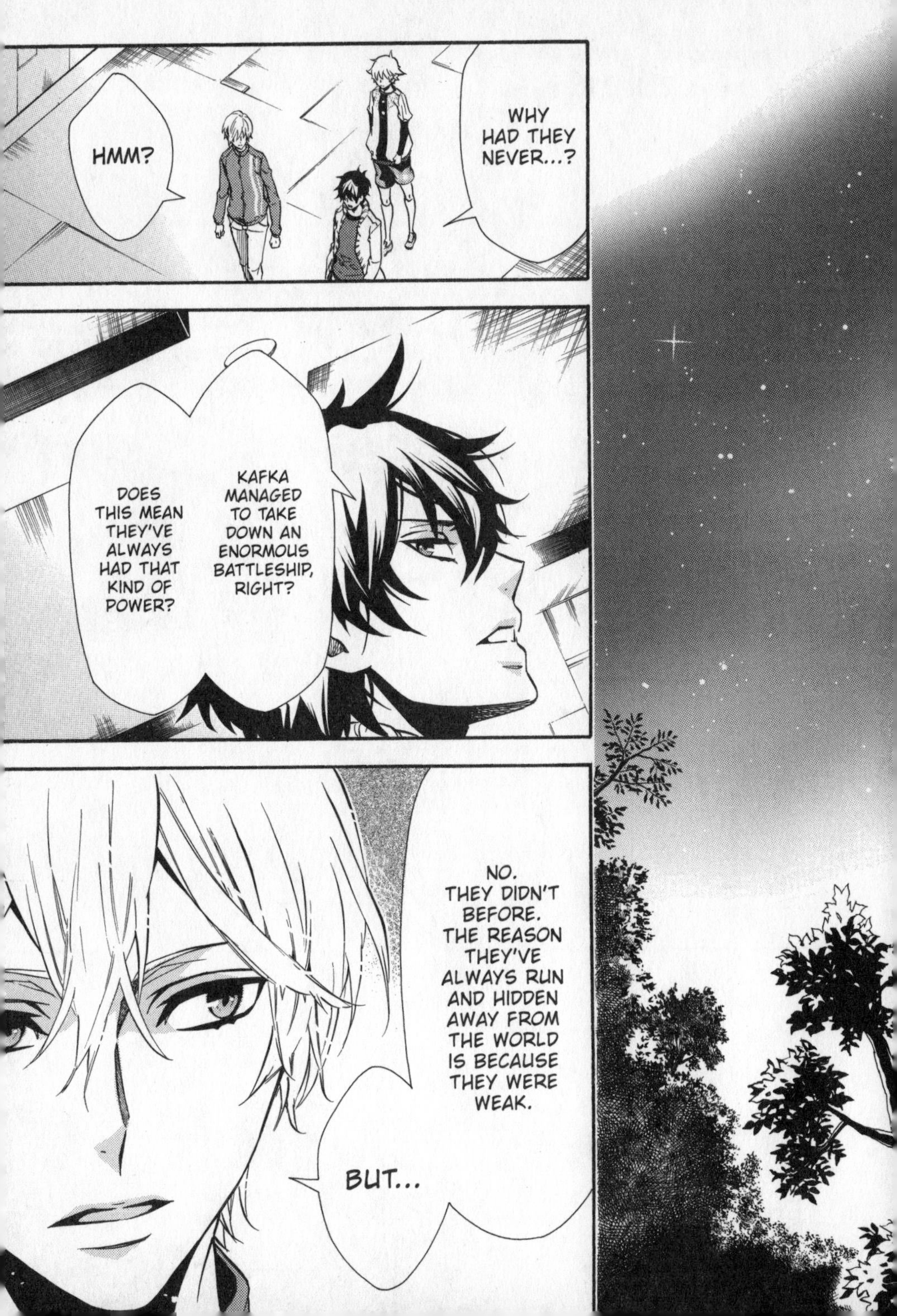
WHY HAD THEY NEVER...?
HMM?
KAFKA MANAGED TO TAKE DOWN AN ENORMOUS BATTLESHIP, RIGHT?
DOES THIS MEAN THEY'VE ALWAYS HAD THAT KIND OF POWER?
NO. THEY DIDN'T BEFORE. THE REASON THEY'VE ALWAYS RUN AND HIDDEN AWAY FROM THE WORLD IS BECAUSE THEY WERE WEAK.
BUT...

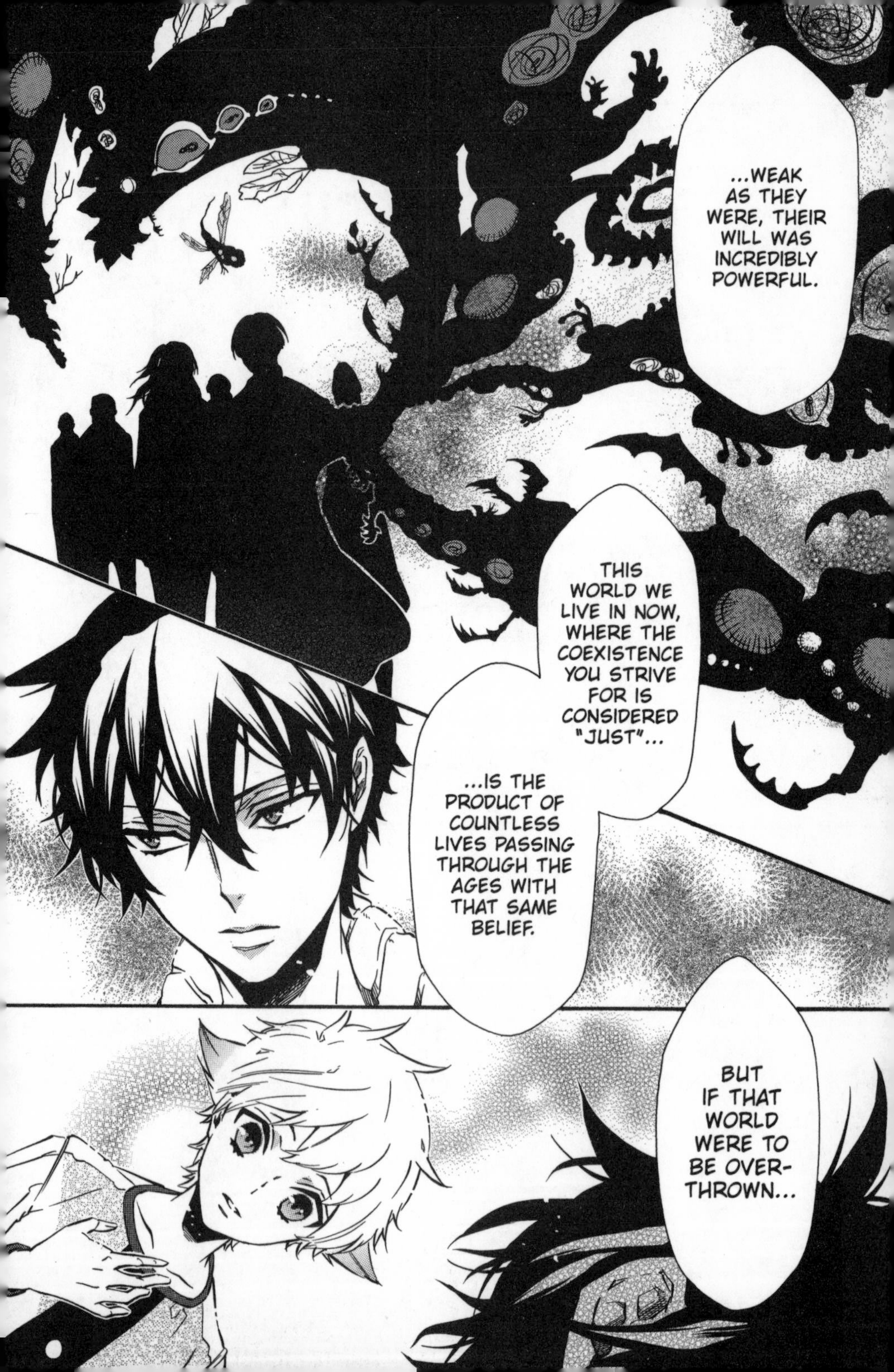
...WEAK AS THEY WERE, THEIR WILL WAS INCREDIBLY POWERFUL.
THIS WORLD WE LIVE IN NOW, WHERE THE COEXISTENCE YOU STRIVE FOR IS CONSIDERED "JUST"...
...IS THE PRODUCT OF COUNTLESS LIVES PASSING THROUGH THE AGES WITH THAT SAME BELIEF.
BUT IF THAT WORLD WERE TO BE OVER-THROWN...

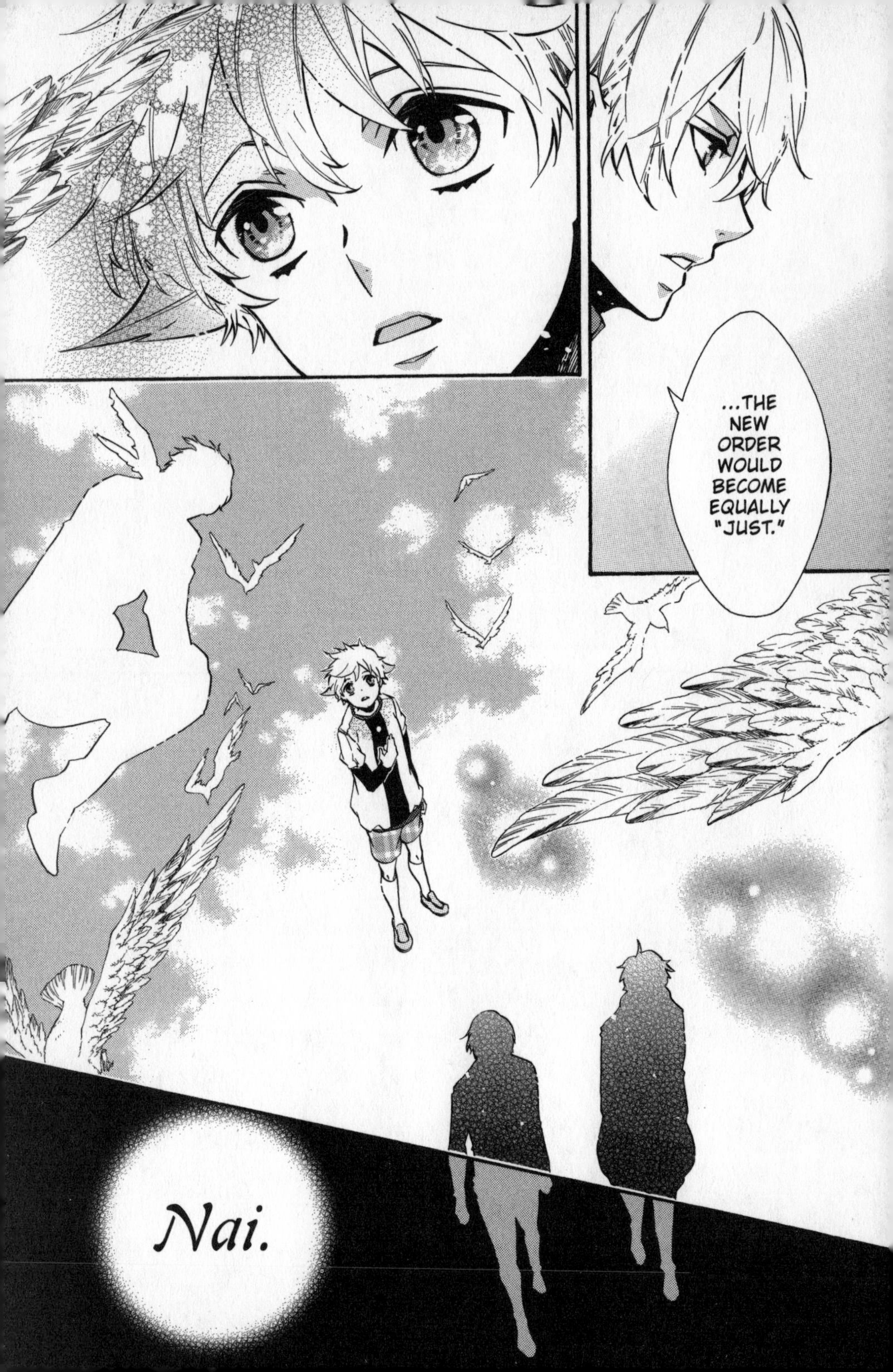
...THE NEW ORDER WOULD BECOME EQUALLY "JUST."
Nai.

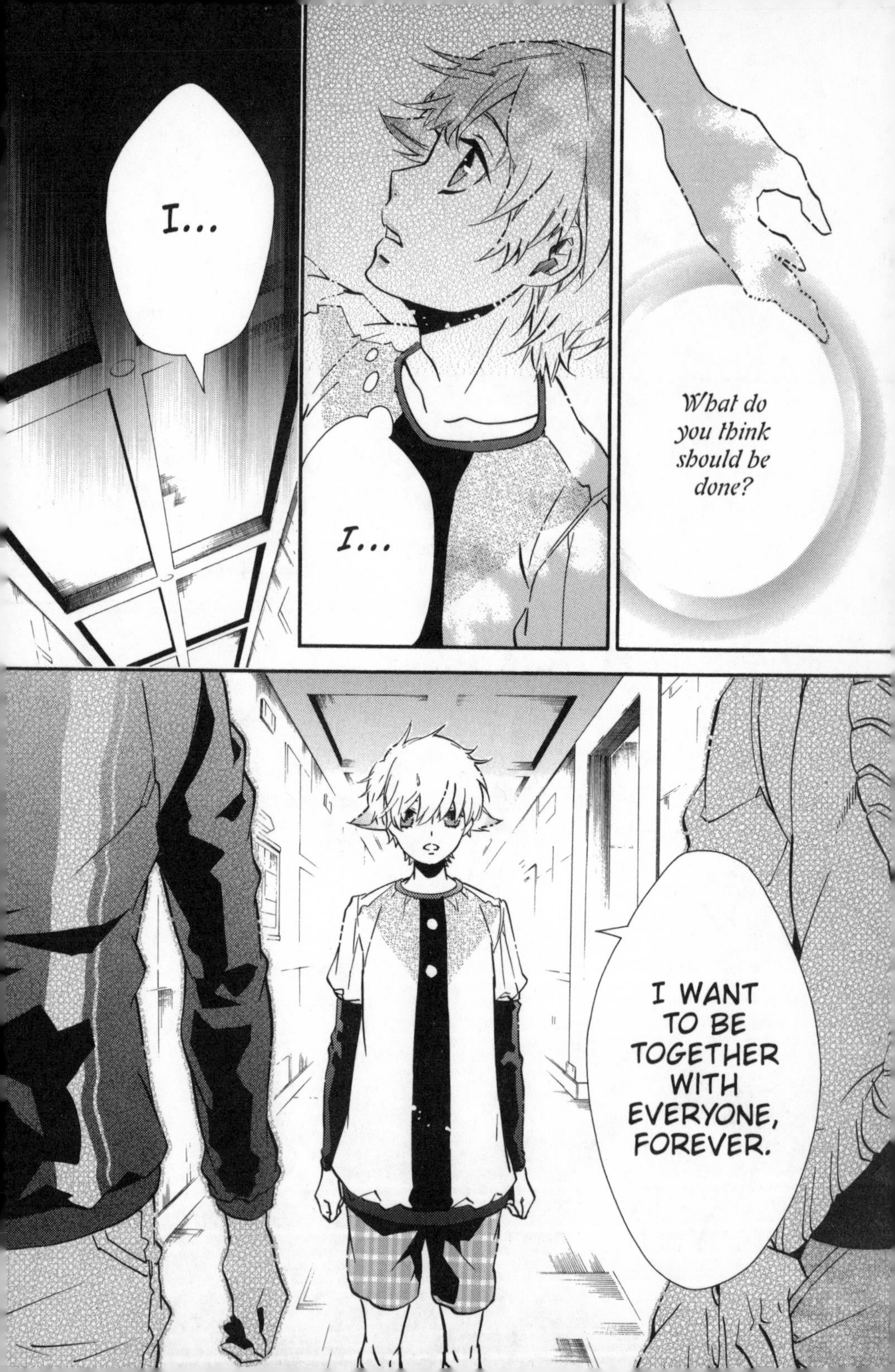
What do you think should be done?
I...
I...
I WANT TO BE TOGETHER WITH EVERYONE, FOREVER.

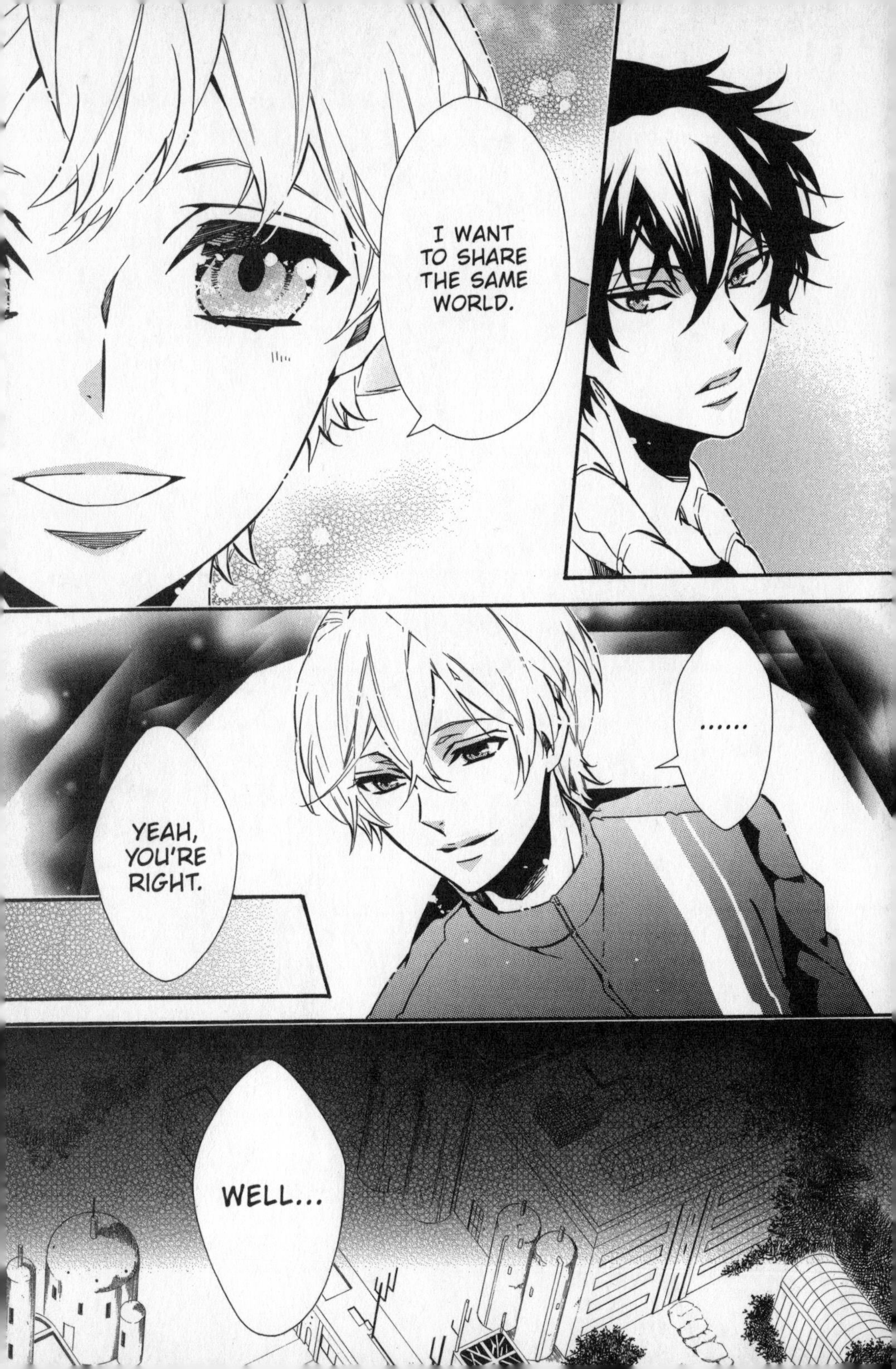
I WANT TO SHARE THE SAME WORLD.
......
YEAH, YOU'RE RIGHT.
WELL...

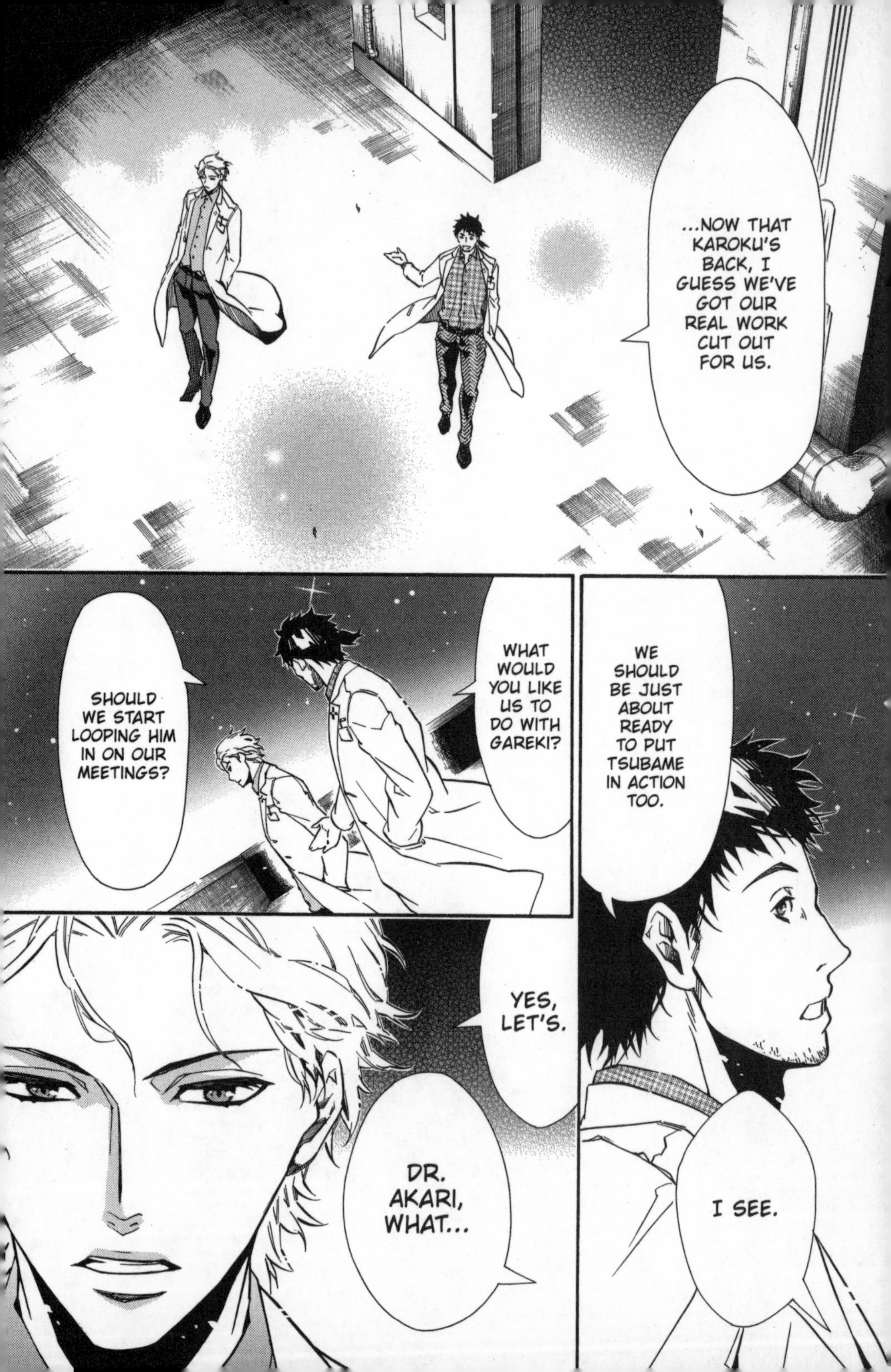
...NOW THAT KAROKU'S BACK, I GUESS WE'VE GOT OUR REAL WORK CUT OUT FOR US.
WE SHOULD BE JUST ABOUT READY TO PUT TSUBAME IN ACTION TOO.
I SEE.
WHAT WOULD YOU LIKE US TO DO WITH GAREKI?
SHOULD WE START LOOPING HIM IN ON OUR MEETINGS?
YES, LET'S.
DR. AKARI, WHAT...

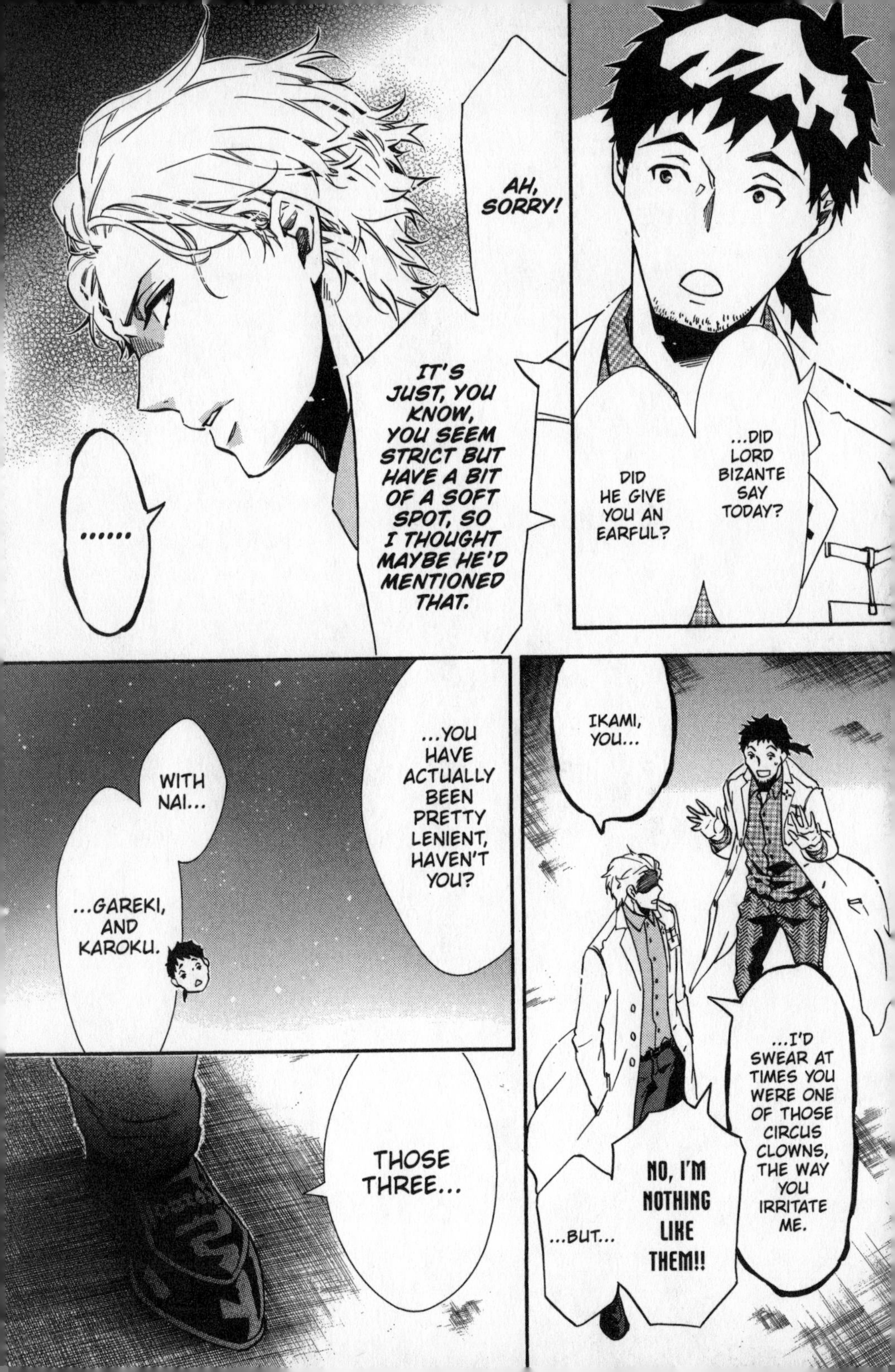

...DID LORD BIZANTE SAY TODAY?
DID HE GIVE YOU AN EARFUL?
AH, SORRY!
IT'S JUST, YOU KNOW, YOU SEEM STRICT BUT HAVE A BIT OF A SOFT SPOT, SO I THOUGHT MAYBE HE'D MENTIONED THAT.
......
IKAMI, YOU...
...I'D SWEAR AT TIMES YOU WERE ONE OF THOSE CIRCUS CLOWNS, THE WAY YOU IRRITATE ME.
NO, I'M NOTHING LIKE THEM!!
...BUT...
...YOU HAVE ACTUALLY BEEN PRETTY LENIENT, HAVEN'T YOU?
WITH NAI...
...GAREKI, AND KAROKU.
THOSE THREE...

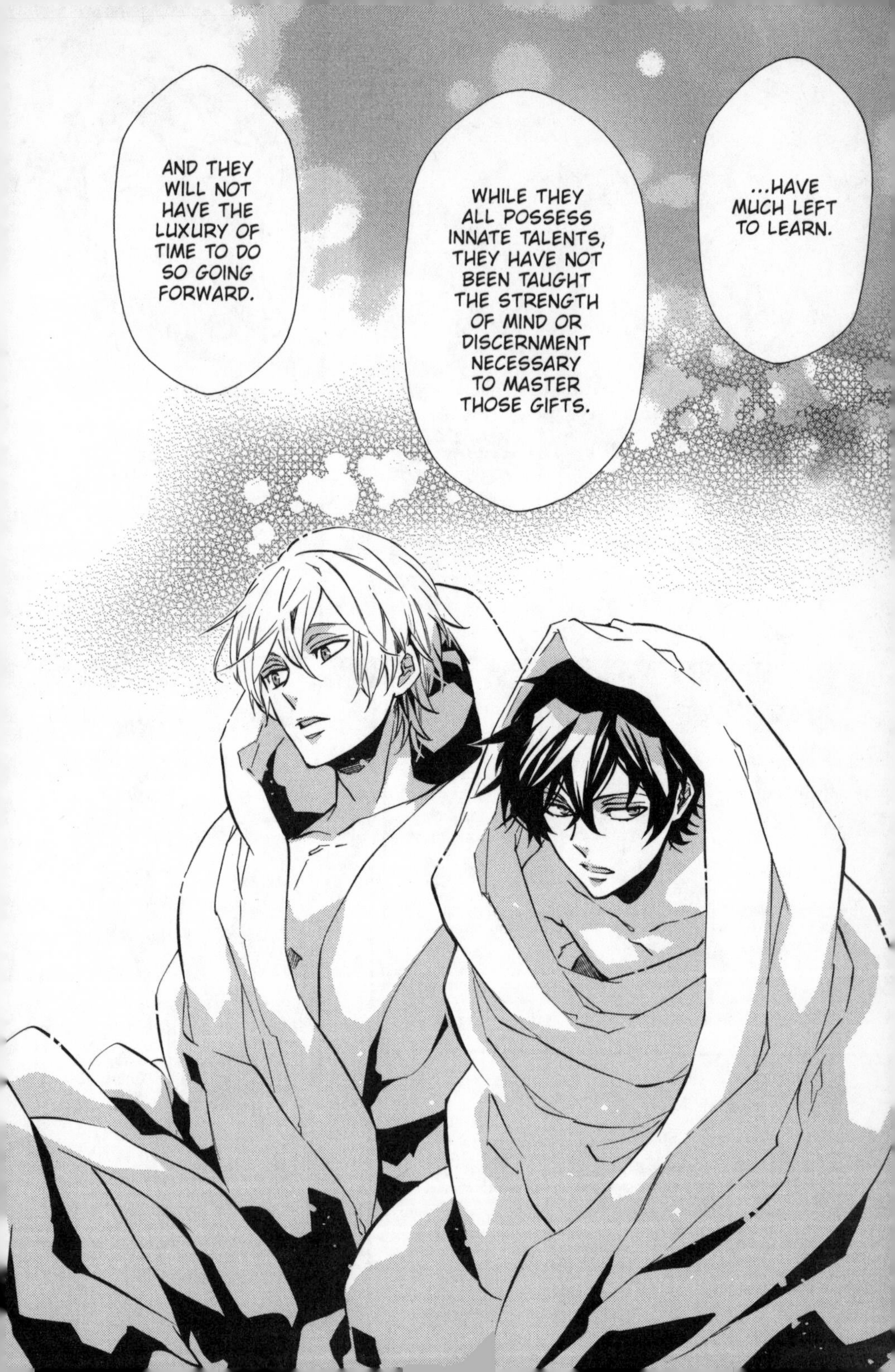
...HAVE MUCH LEFT TO LEARN.
WHILE THEY ALL POSSESS INNATE TALENTS, THEY HAVE NOT BEEN TAUGHT THE STRENGTH OF MIND OR DISCERNMENT NECESSARY TO MASTER THOSE GIFTS.
AND THEY WILL NOT HAVE THE LUXURY OF TIME TO DO SO GOING FORWARD.

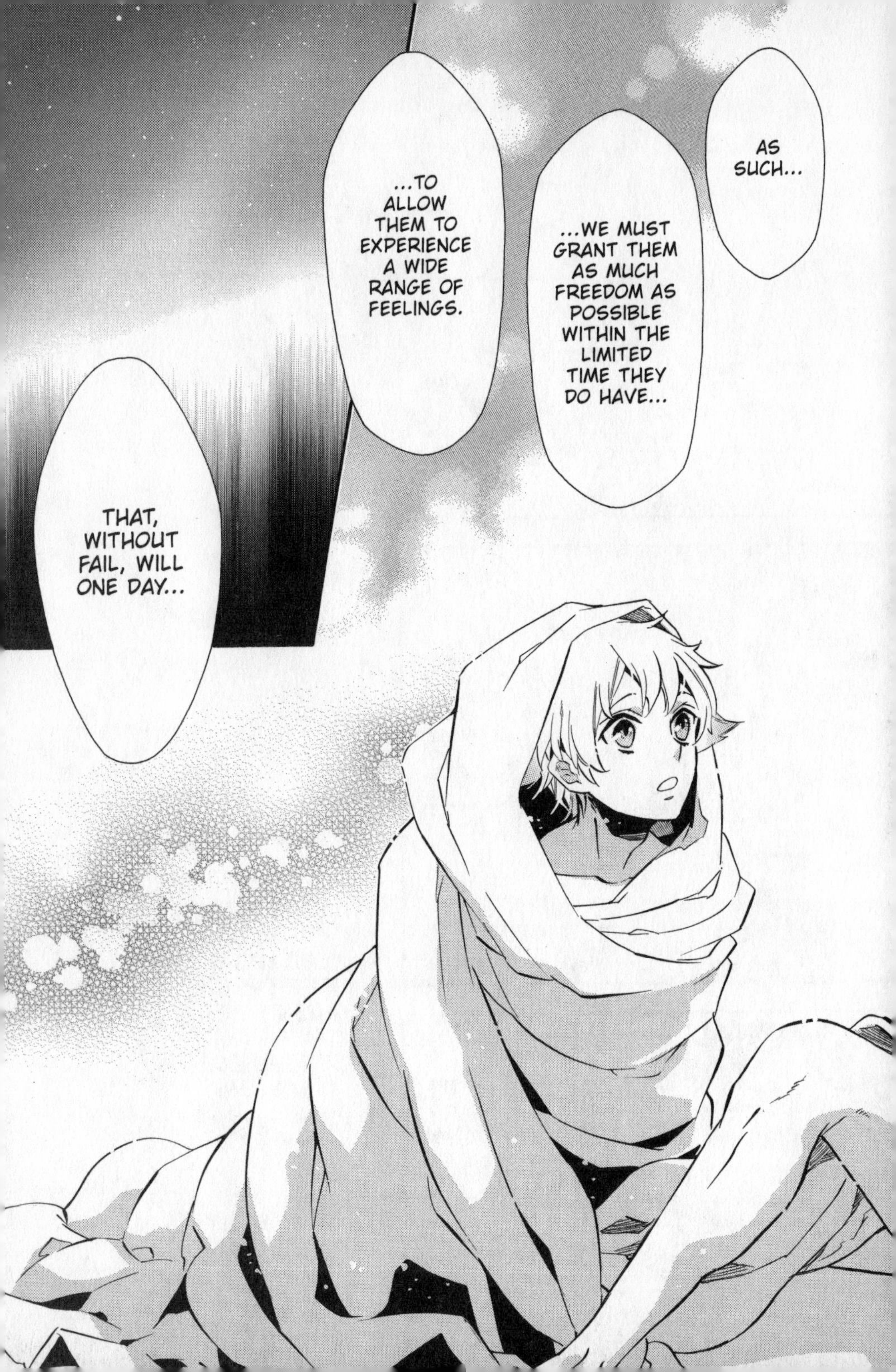
AS SUCH...
...WE MUST GRANT THEM AS MUCH FREEDOM AS POSSIBLE WITHIN THE LIMITED TIME THEY DO HAVE...
...TO ALLOW THEM TO EXPERIENCE A WIDE RANGE OF FEELINGS.
THAT, WITHOUT FAIL, WILL ONE DAY...

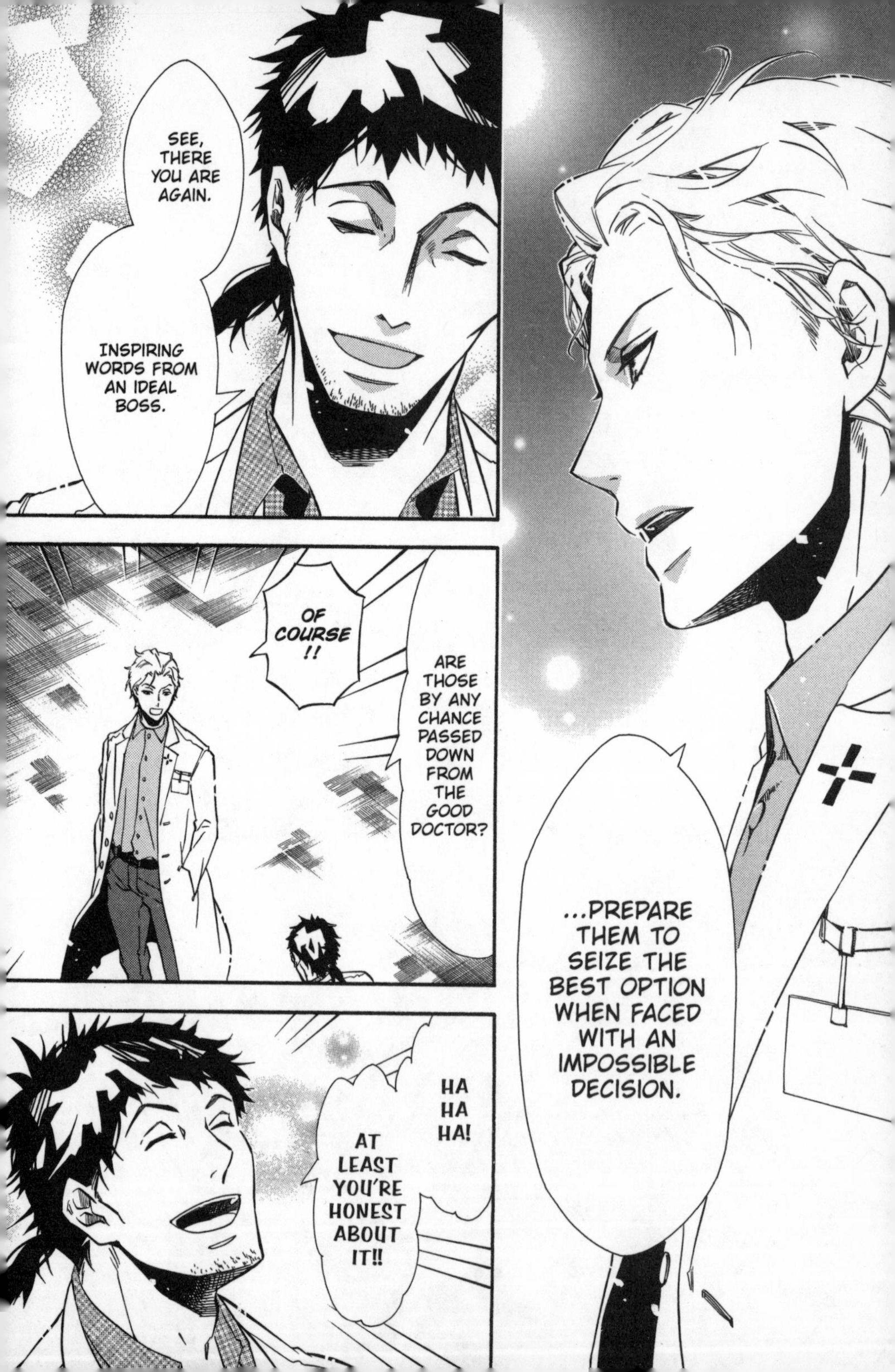
...PREPARE THEM TO SEIZE THE BEST OPTION WHEN FACED WITH AN IMPOSSIBLE DECISION.
SEE, THERE YOU ARE AGAIN.
INSPIRING WORDS FROM AN IDEAL BOSS.
ARE THOSE BY ANY CHANCE PASSED DOWN FROM THE GOOD DOCTOR?
OF COURSE!!
HA HA HA!
AT LEAST YOU'RE HONEST ABOUT IT!!

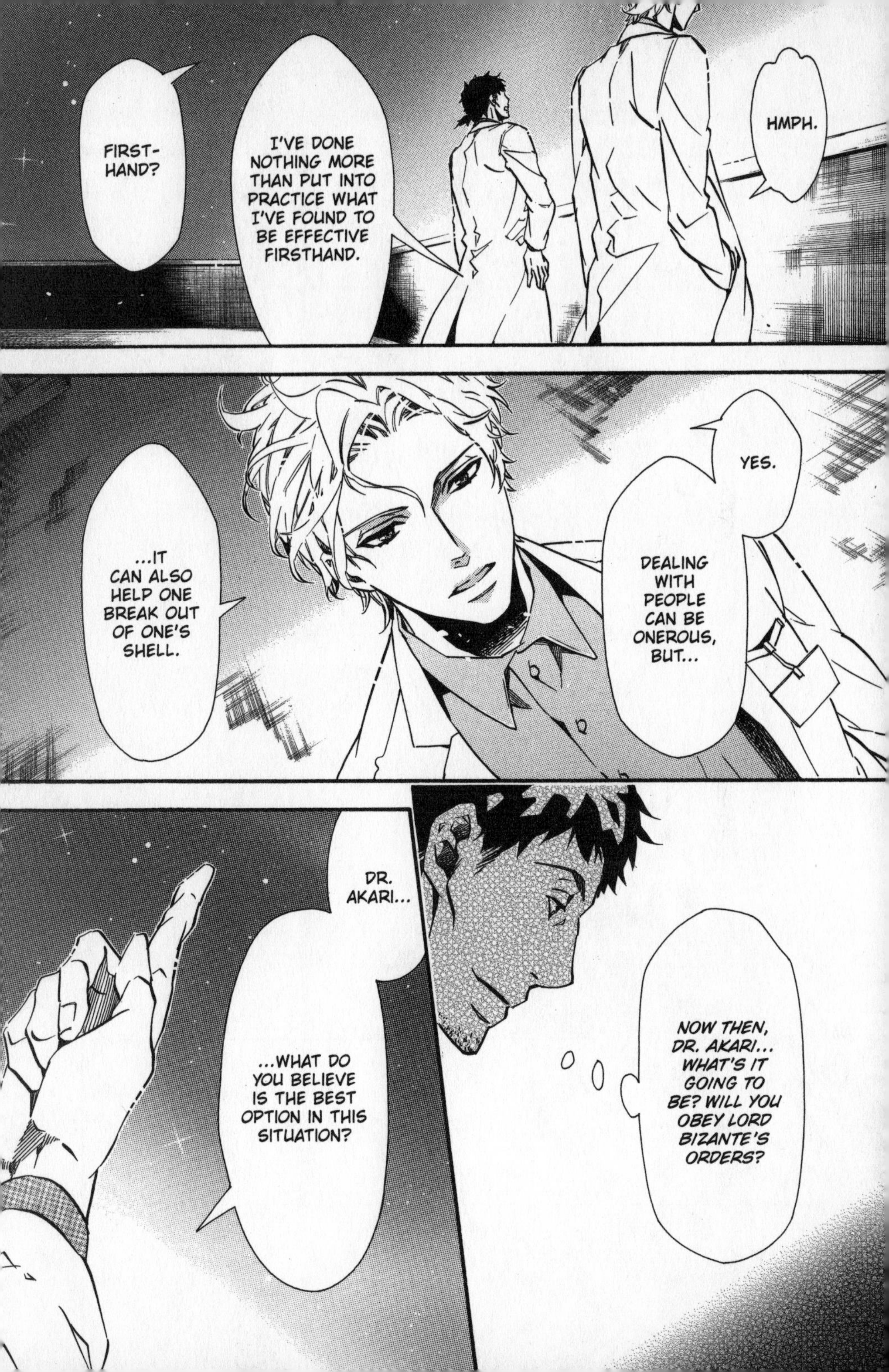
HMPH.
I'VE DONE NOTHING MORE THAN PUT INTO PRACTICE WHAT I'VE FOUND TO BE EFFECTIVE FIRSTHAND.
FIRST-HAND?
YES.
DEALING WITH PEOPLE CAN BE ONEROUS, BUT...
...IT CAN ALSO HELP ONE BREAK OUT OF ONE'S SHELL.
DR. AKARI...
NOW THEN, DR. AKARI... WHAT'S IT GOING TO BE? WILL YOU OBEY LORD BIZANTE'S ORDERS?
...WHAT DO YOU BELIEVE IS THE BEST OPTION IN THIS SITUATION?

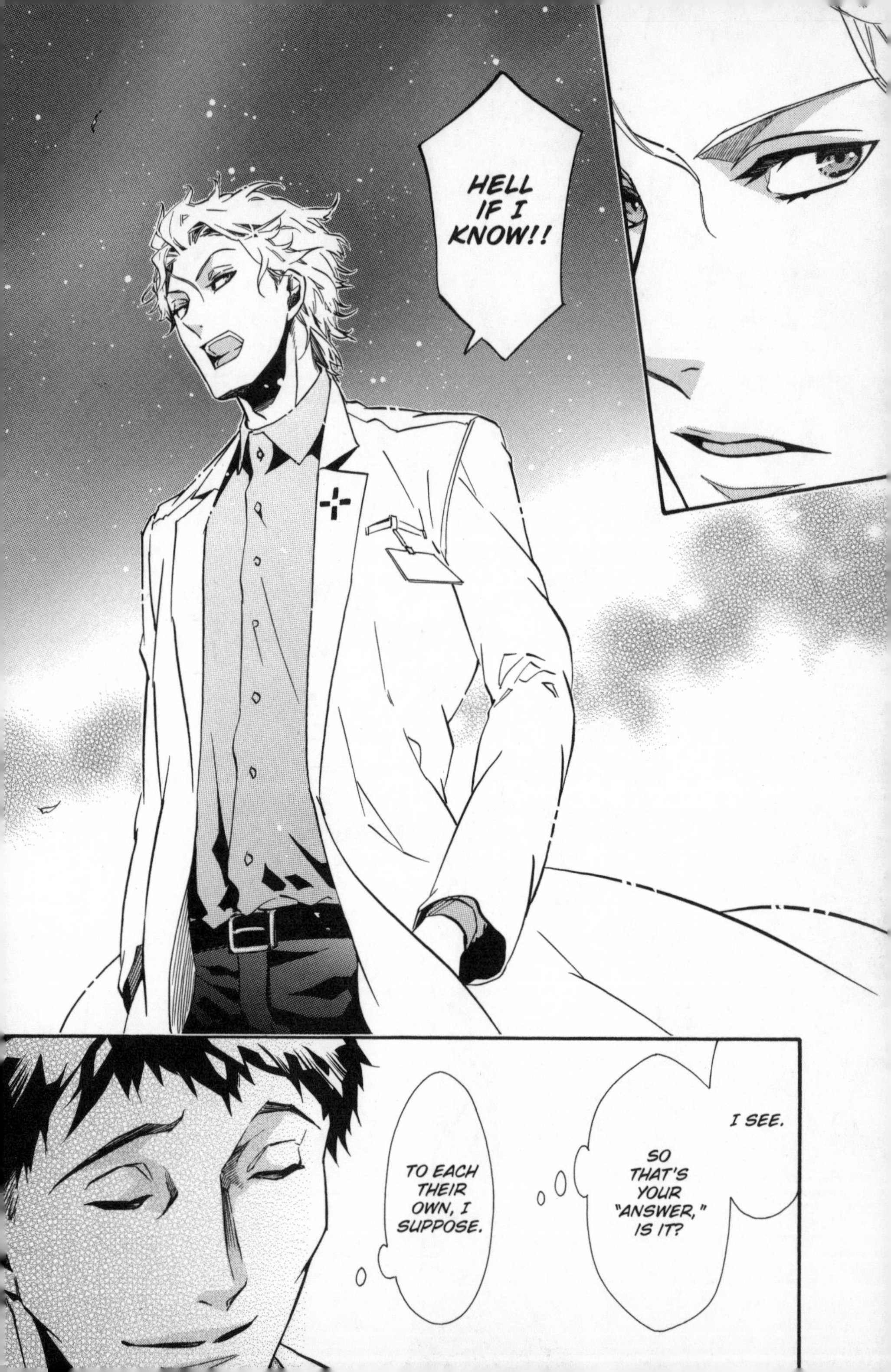
HELL IF I KNOW!!
I SEE.
SO THAT'S YOUR "ANSWER," IS IT?
TO EACH THEIR OWN, I SUPPOSE.

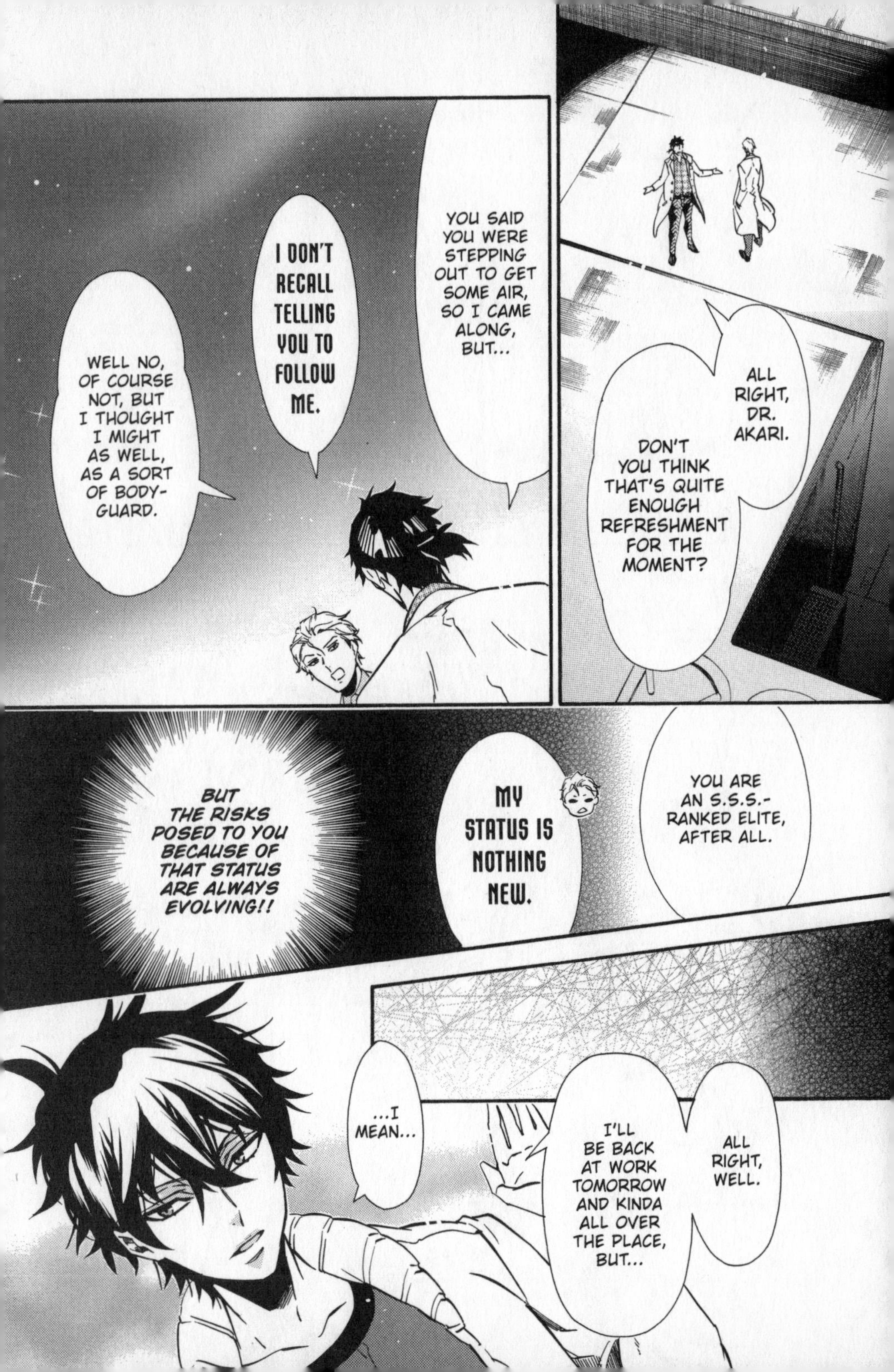
ALL RIGHT, DR. AKARI.
DON'T YOU THINK THAT'S QUITE ENOUGH REFRESHMENT FOR THE MOMENT?
YOU SAID YOU WERE STEPPING OUT TO GET SOME AIR, SO I CAME ALONG, BUT...
I DON'T RECALL TELLING YOU TO FOLLOW ME.
WELL NO, OF COURSE NOT, BUT I THOUGHT I MIGHT AS WELL, AS A SORT OF BODY-GUARD.
YOU ARE AN S.S.S.-RANKED ELITE, AFTER ALL.
MY STATUS IS NOTHING NEW.
BUT THE RISKS POSED TO YOU BECAUSE OF THAT STATUS ARE ALWAYS EVOLVING!!
ALL RIGHT, WELL.
I'LL BE BACK AT WORK TOMORROW AND KINDA ALL OVER THE PLACE, BUT...
...I MEAN...

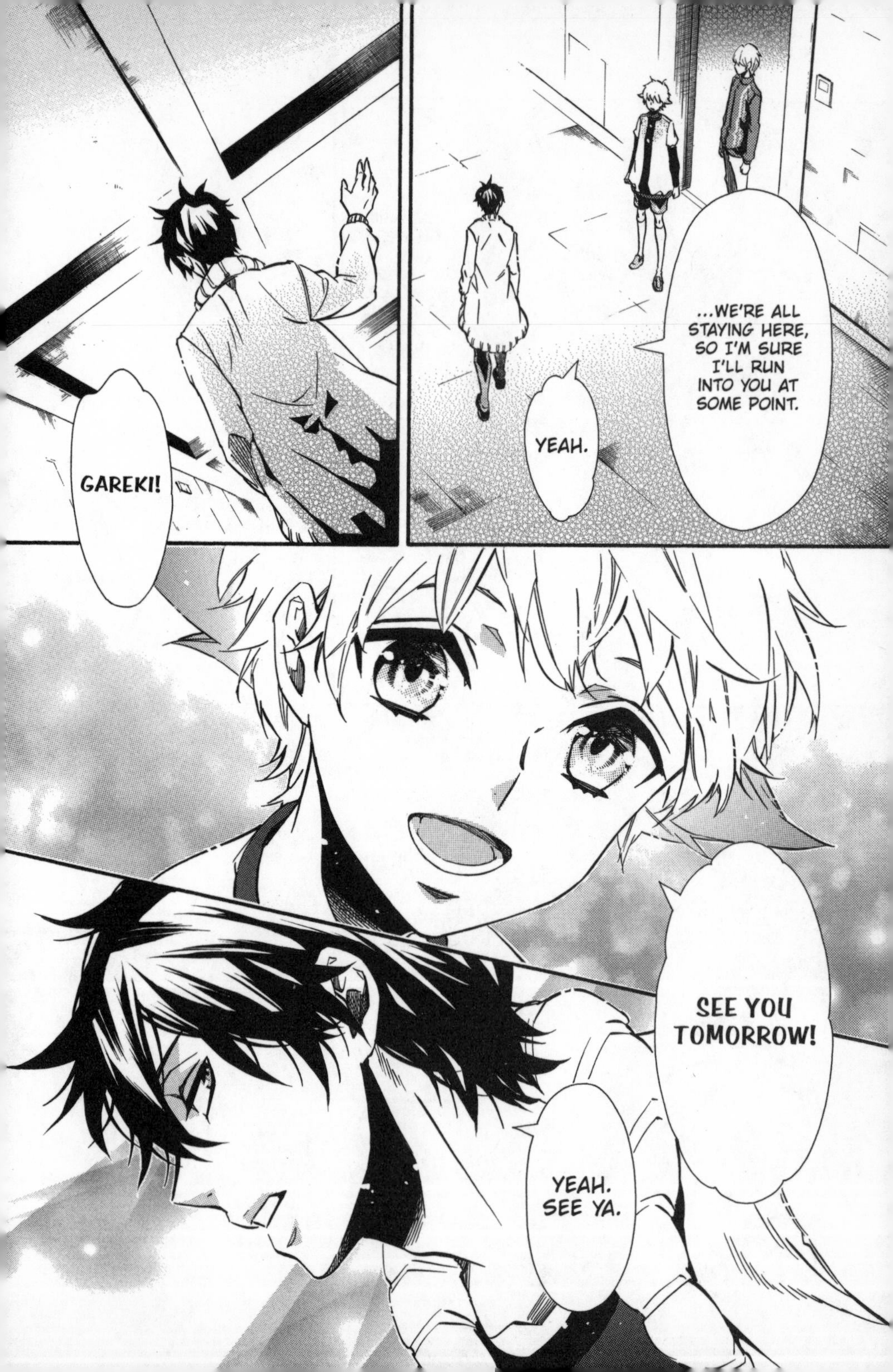
...WE'RE ALL STAYING HERE, SO I'M SURE I'LL RUN INTO YOU AT SOME POINT.
YEAH.
GAREKI!
SEE YOU TOMORROW!
YEAH. SEE YA.

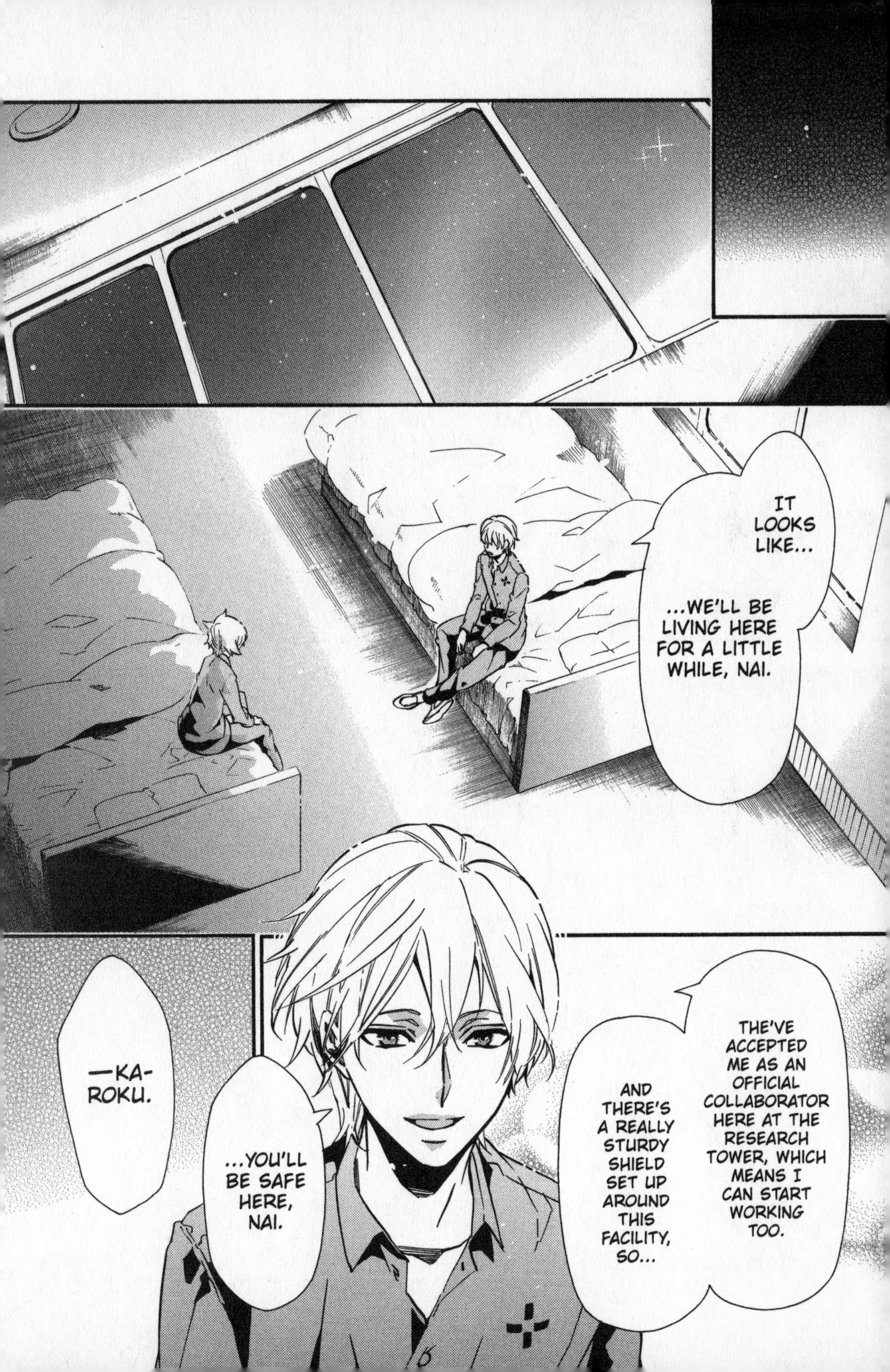
IT LOOKS LIKE...
...WE'LL BE LIVING HERE FOR A LITTLE WHILE, NAI.
THE'VE ACCEPTED ME AS AN OFFICIAL COLLABORATOR HERE AT THE RESEARCH TOWER, WHICH MEANS I CAN START WORKING TOO.
AND THERE'S A REALLY STURDY SHIELD SET UP AROUND THIS FACILITY, SO...
...YOU'LL BE SAFE HERE, NAI.
—KA-ROKU.

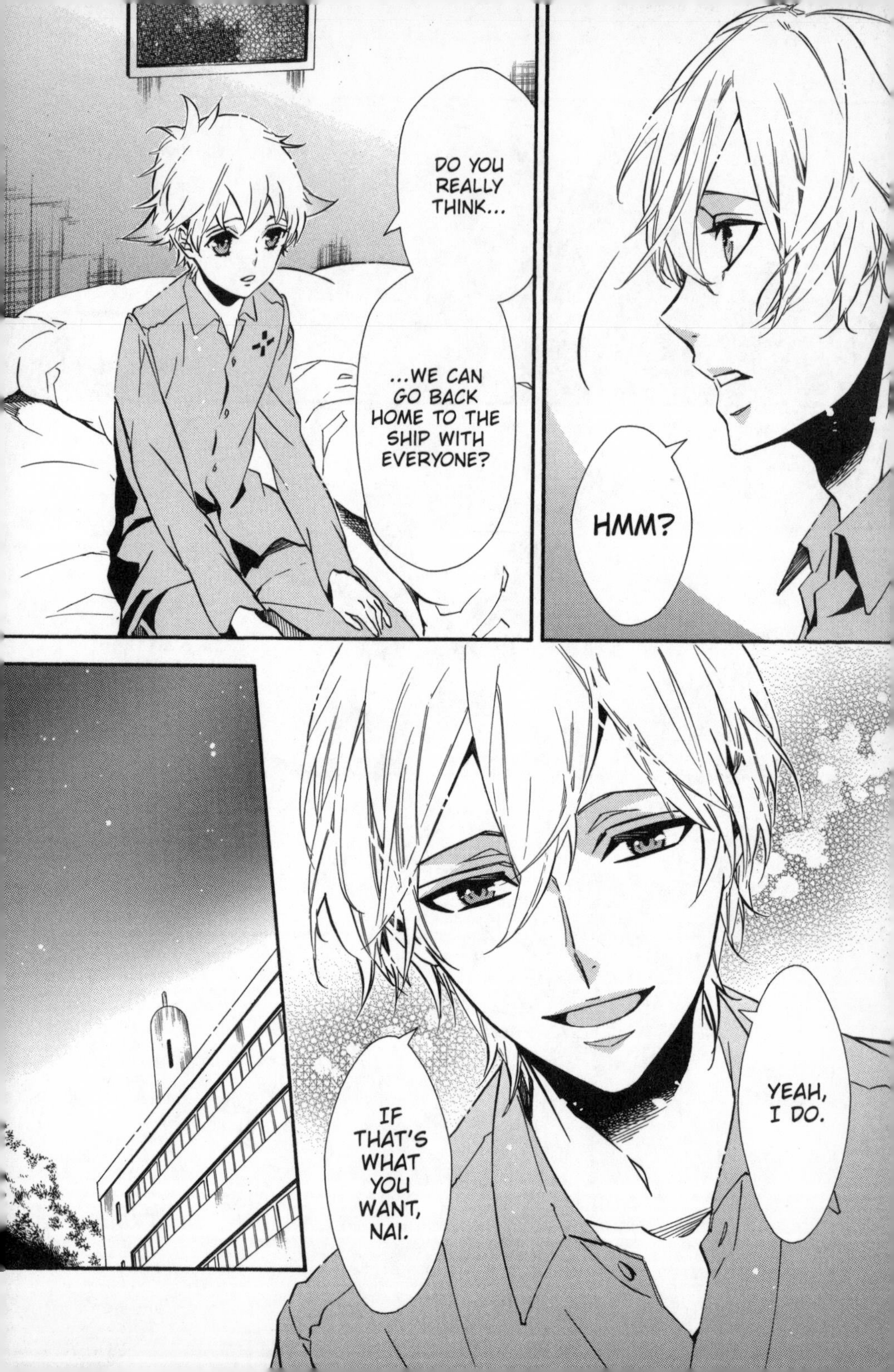
HMM?
DO YOU REALLY THINK...
...WE CAN GO BACK HOME TO THE SHIP WITH EVERYONE?
YEAH, I DO.
IF THAT'S WHAT YOU WANT, NAI.

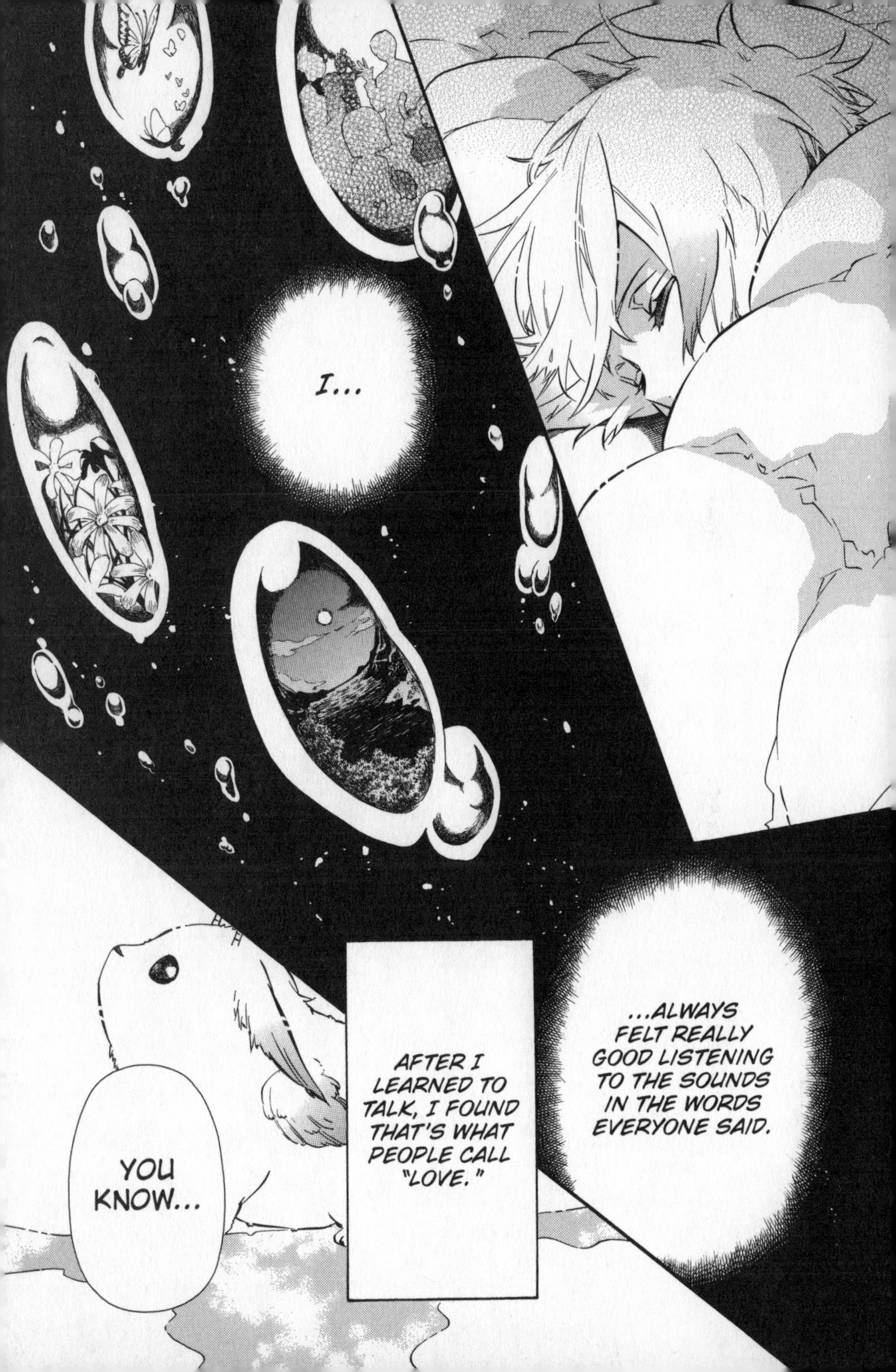
I...
...ALWAYS FELT REALLY GOOD LISTENING TO THE SOUNDS IN THE WORDS EVERYONE SAID.
AFTER I LEARNED TO TALK, I FOUND THAT'S WHAT PEOPLE CALL "LOVE."
YOU KNOW...

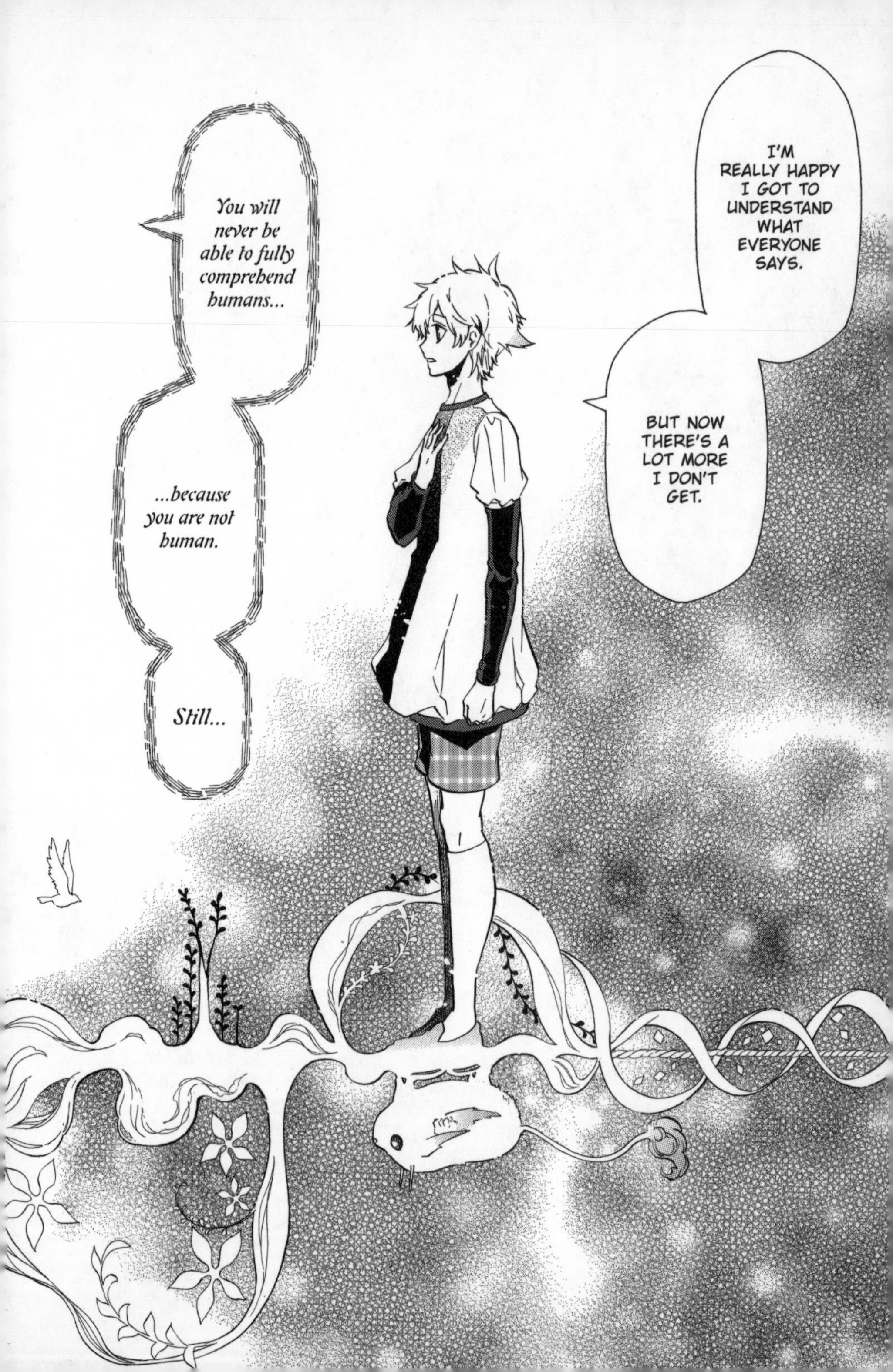
I'M REALLY HAPPY I GOT TO UNDERSTAND WHAT EVERYONE SAYS.
BUT NOW THERE'S A LOT MORE I DON'T GET.
You will never be able to fully comprehend humans...
...because you are not human.
Still...

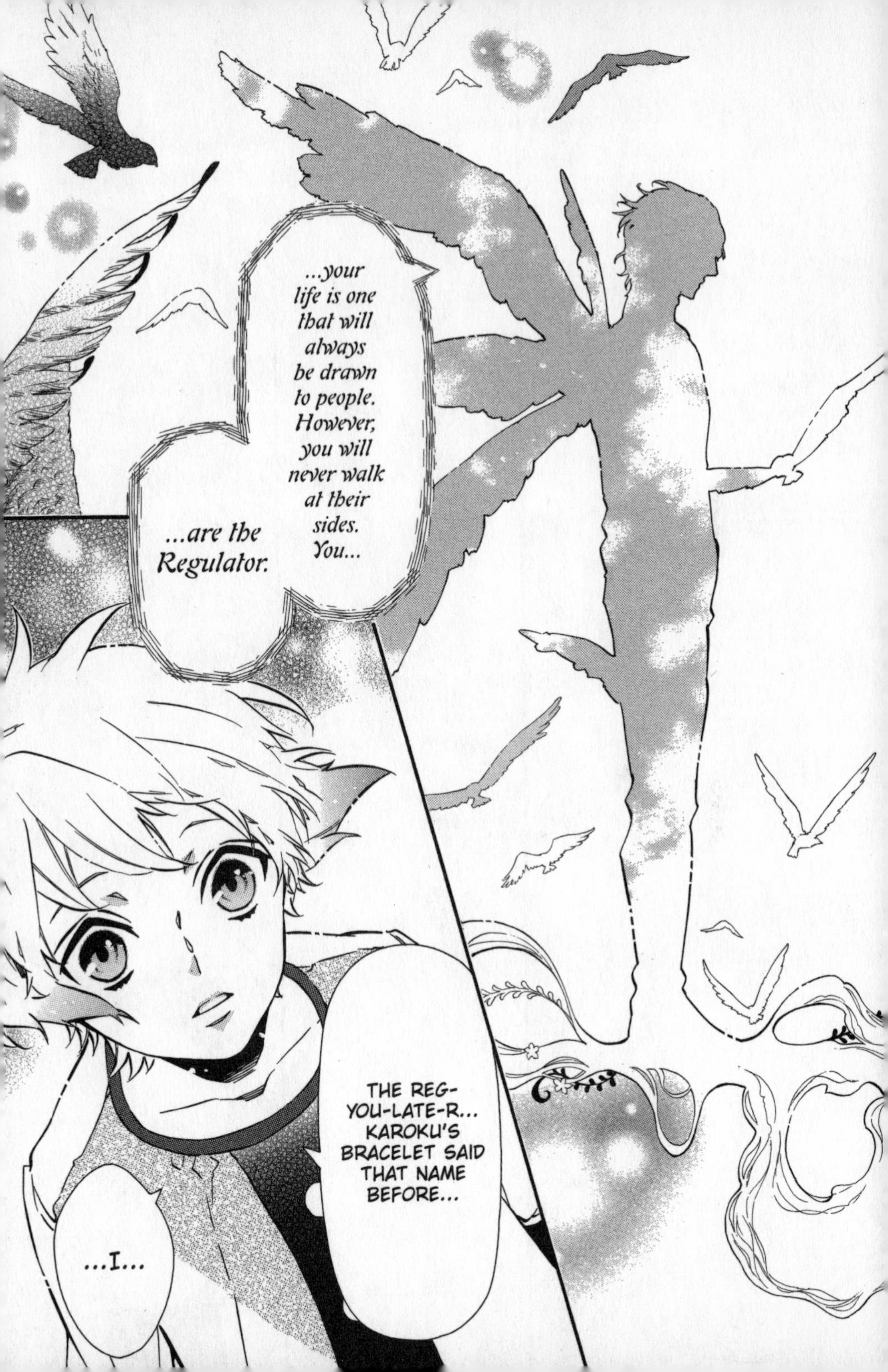
...your life is one that will always be drawn to people. However, you will never walk at their sides. You...
...are the Regulator.
THE REG-YOU-LATE-R... KAROKU'S BRACELET SAID THAT NAME BEFORE...
...I...

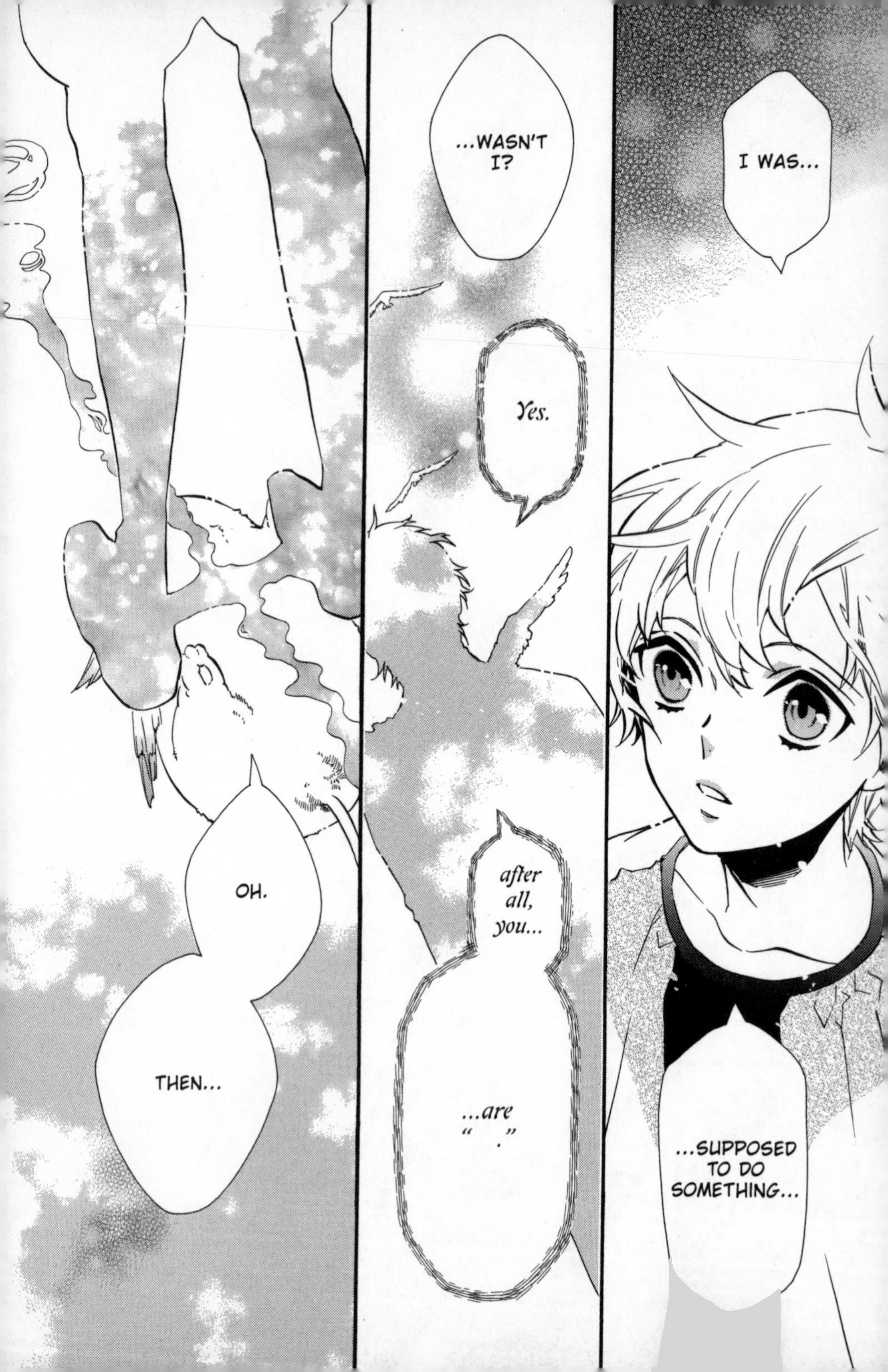
I WAS...
...SUPPOSED TO DO SOMETHING...
...WASN'T I?
Yes.
after all, you...
...are " ."
OH.
THEN...

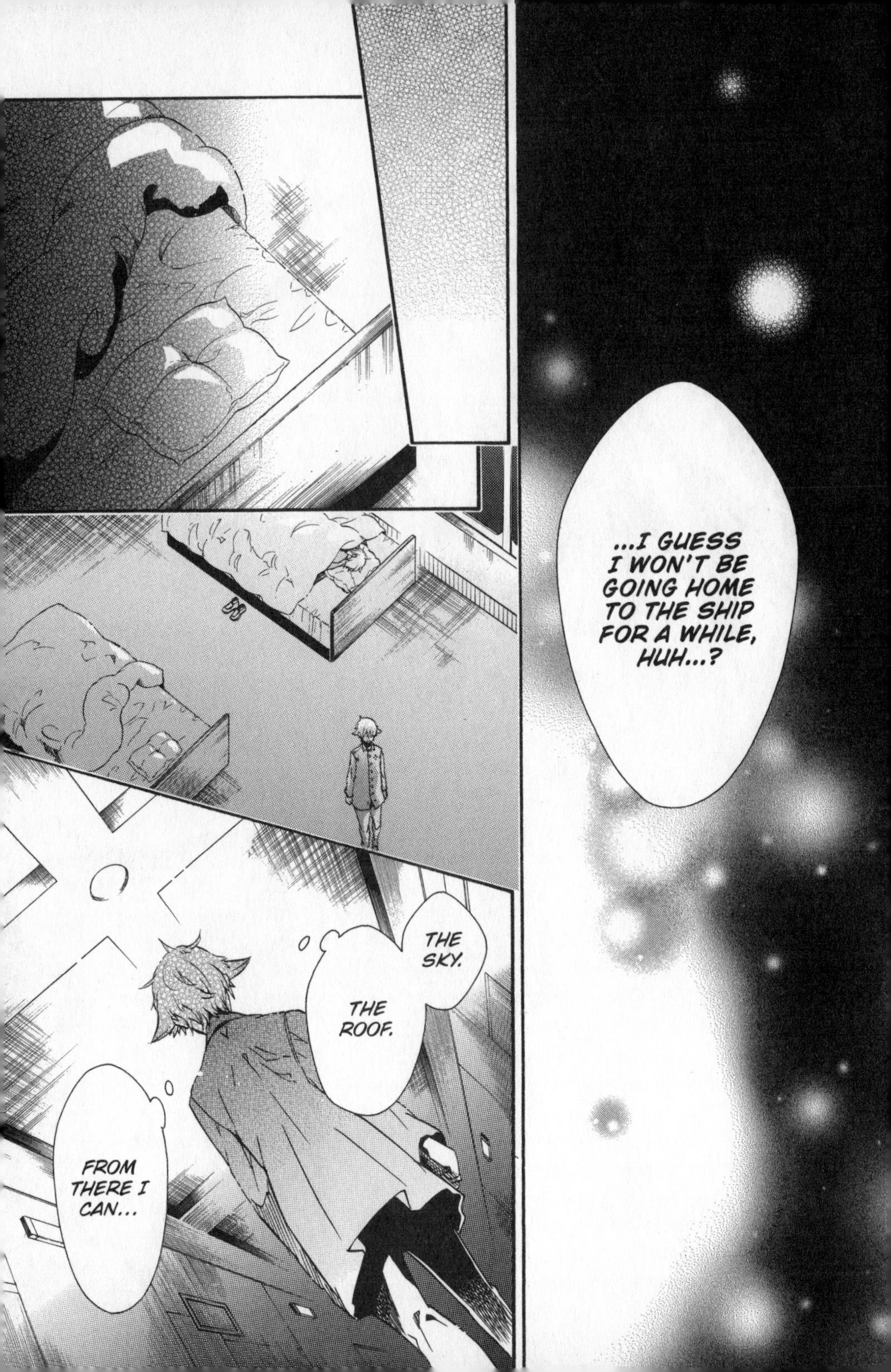
...I GUESS I WON'T BE GOING HOME TO THE SHIP FOR A WHILE, HUH...?
THE SKY.
THE ROOF.
FROM THERE I CAN...

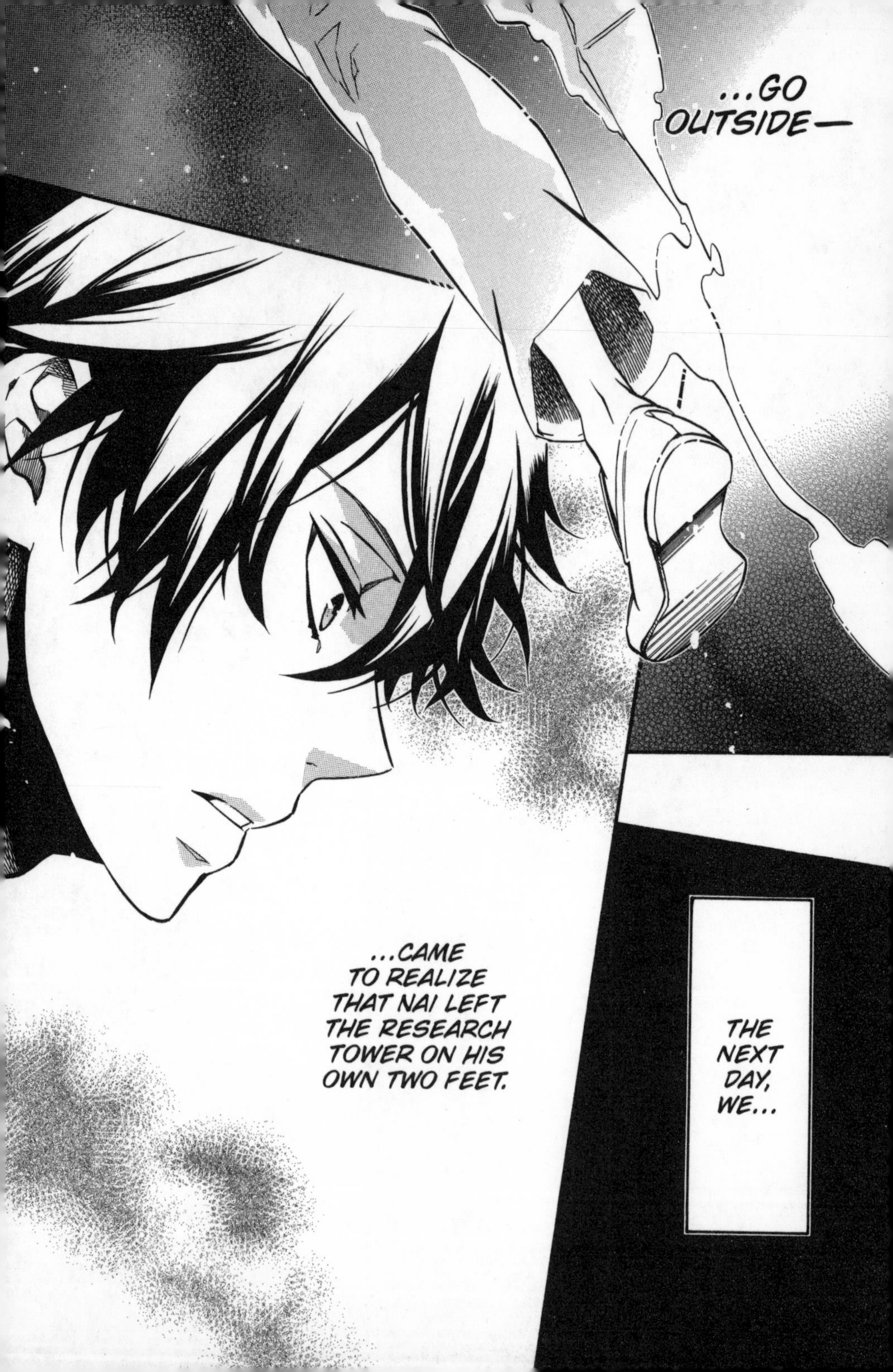
...GO OUTSIDE—
THE NEXT DAY, WE...
...CAME TO REALIZE THAT NAI LEFT THE RESEARCH TOWER ON HIS OWN TWO FEET.

KARNEVAL

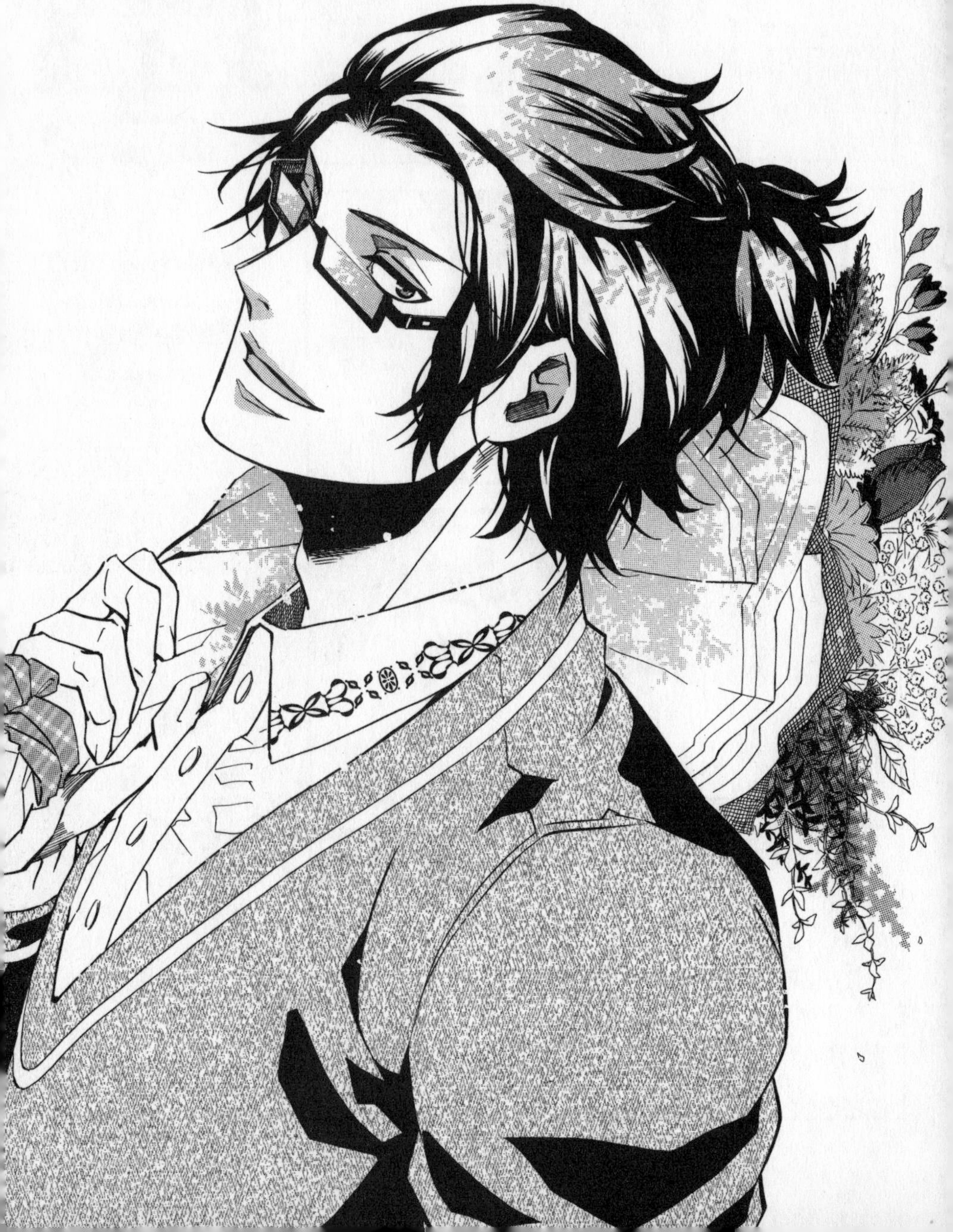

# Bonus Comic 1

## The Hidden Circus Member: Ikami

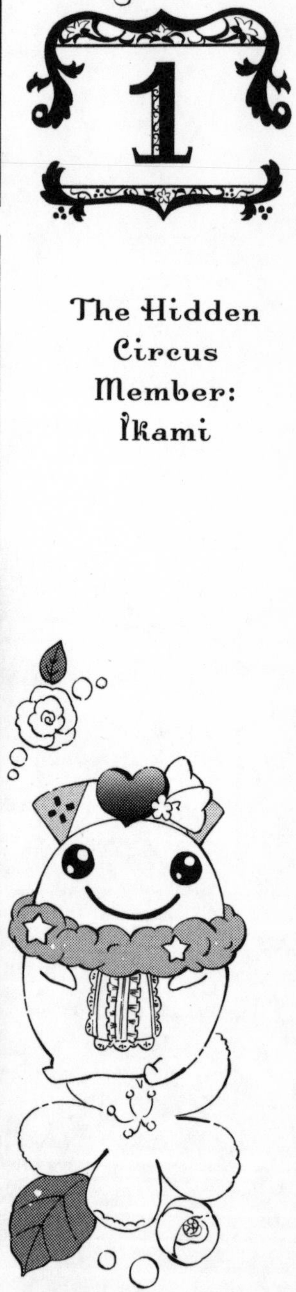

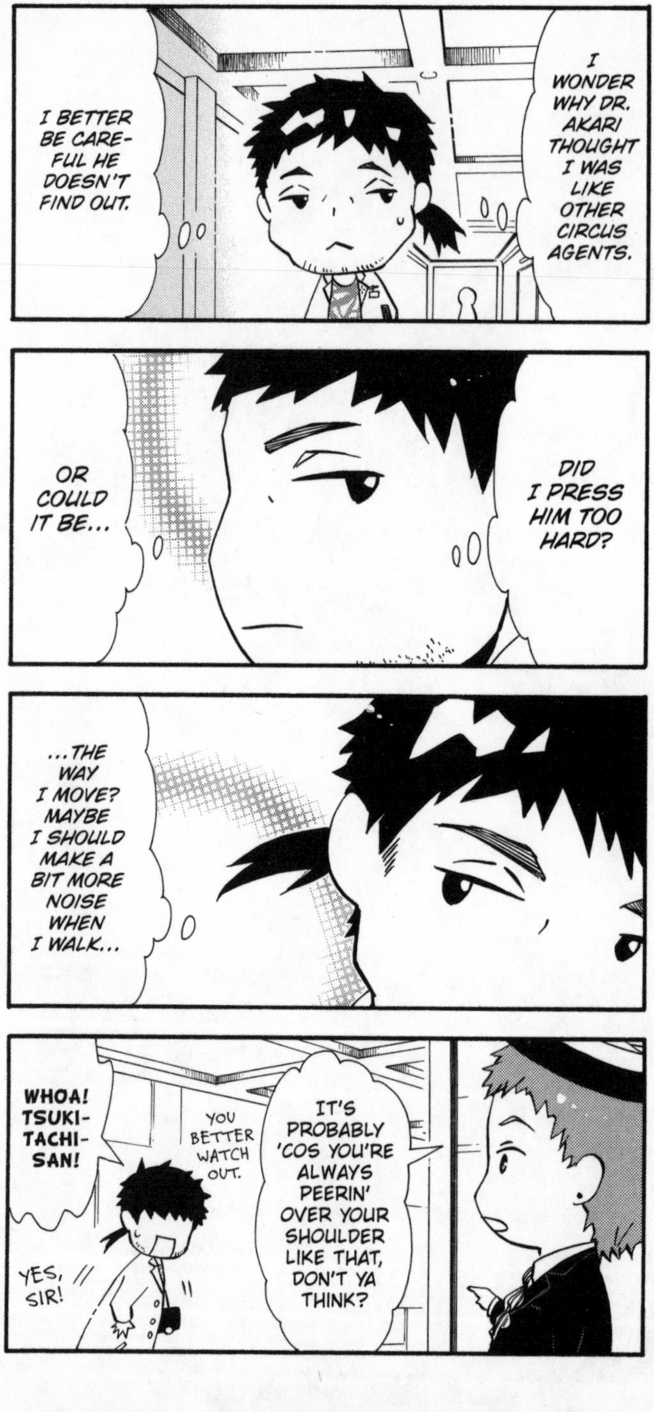

I WONDER WHY DR. AKARI THOUGHT I WAS LIKE OTHER CIRCUS AGENTS.
I BETTER BE CARE-FUL HE DOESN'T FIND OUT.
DID I PRESS HIM TOO HARD?
OR COULD IT BE...
...THE WAY I MOVE? MAYBE I SHOULD MAKE A BIT MORE NOISE WHEN I WALK...
IT'S PROBABLY 'COS YOU'RE ALWAYS PEERIN' OVER YOUR SHOULDER LIKE THAT, DON'T YA THINK?
YOU BETTER WATCH OUT.
WHOA! TSUKI-TACHI-SAN!
YES, SIR!

## Bonus Comic 2

### He Can't Forget the Spotlight

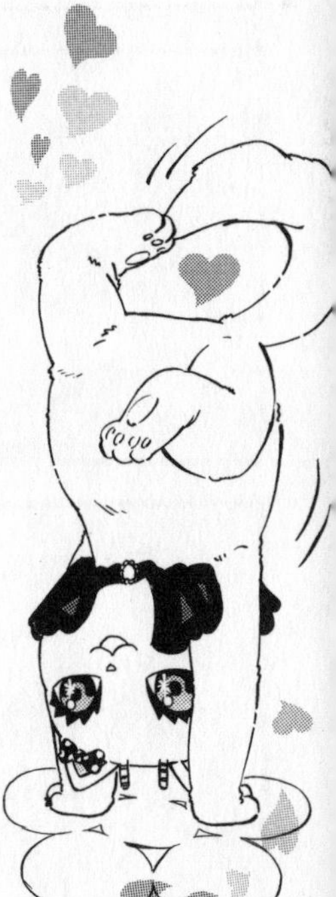

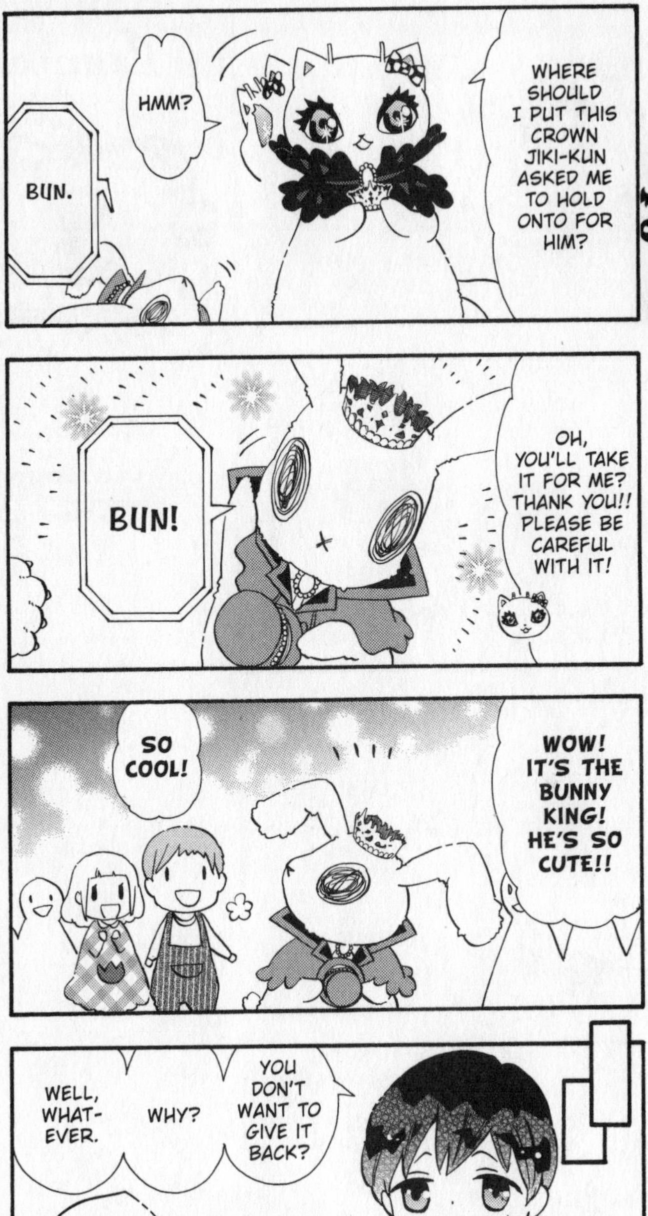
WHERE SHOULD I PUT THIS CROWN JIKI-KUN ASKED ME TO HOLD ONTO FOR HIM?
HMM?
BUN.
OH, YOU'LL TAKE IT FOR ME? THANK YOU!! PLEASE BE CAREFUL WITH IT!
BUN!
WOW! IT'S THE BUNNY KING! HE'S SO CUTE!!
SO COOL!
YOU DON'T WANT TO GIVE IT BACK?
WHY?
WELL, WHAT-EVER.
HUH?

# Bonus Comic 3

## The Boy's Wish Comes True

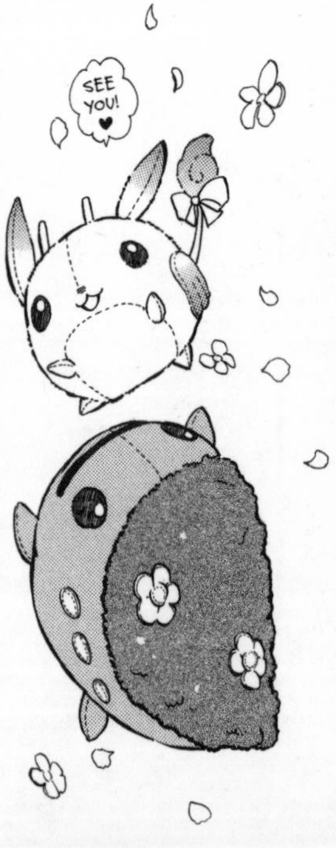
SEE YOU! ♥

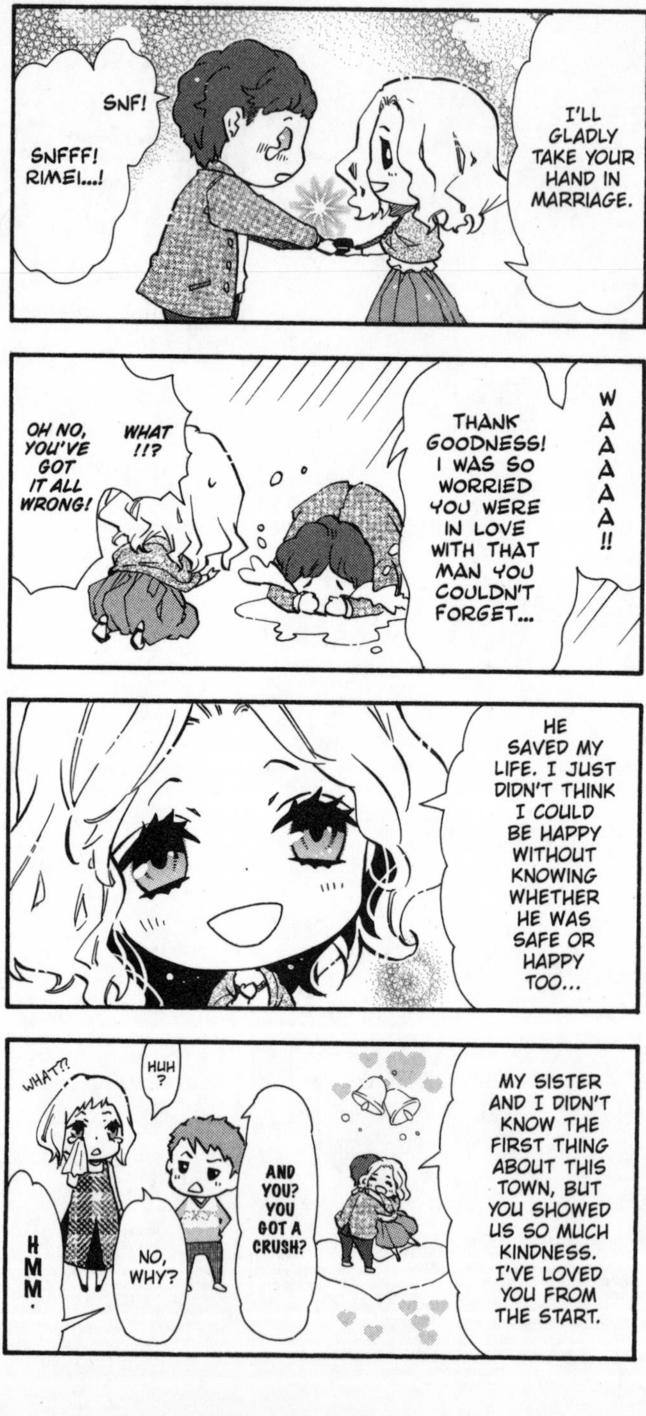
I'LL GLADLY TAKE YOUR HAND IN MARRIAGE.
SNF!
SNFFF! RIMEI...!
WAAAAAA!!
THANK GOODNESS! I WAS SO WORRIED YOU WERE IN LOVE WITH THAT MAN YOU COULDN'T FORGET...
WHAT!!?
OH NO, YOU'VE GOT IT ALL WRONG!
HE SAVED MY LIFE. I JUST DIDN'T THINK I COULD BE HAPPY WITHOUT KNOWING WHETHER HE WAS SAFE OR HAPPY TOO...
MY SISTER AND I DIDN'T KNOW THE FIRST THING ABOUT THIS TOWN, BUT YOU SHOWED US SO MUCH KINDNESS. I'VE LOVED YOU FROM THE START.
AND YOU? YOU GOT A CRUSH?
HUH?
NO, WHY?
WHAT??
HMM.

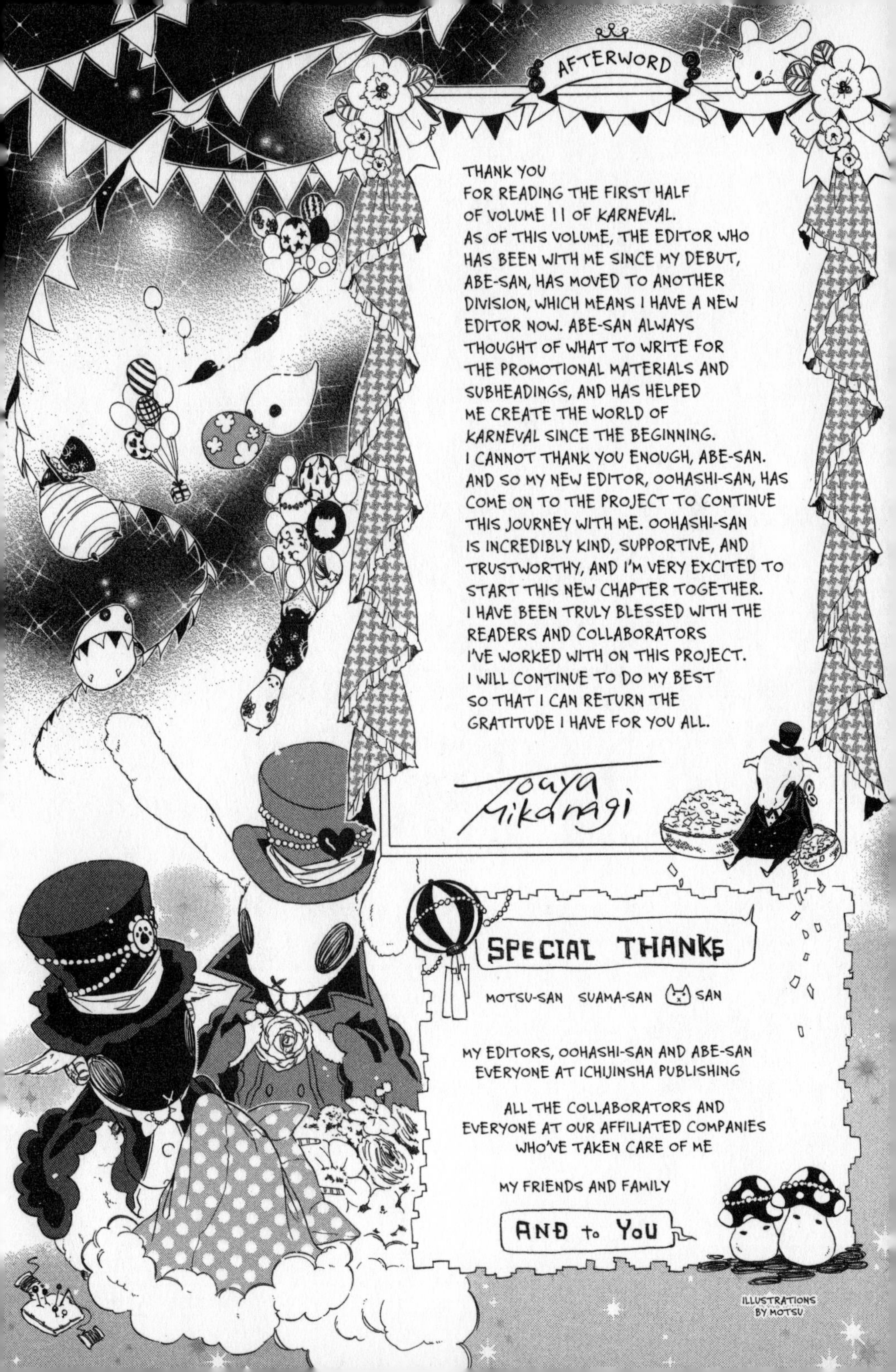

# AFTERWORD

THANK YOU
FOR READING THE FIRST HALF
OF VOLUME 11 OF *KARNEVAL*.
AS OF THIS VOLUME, THE EDITOR WHO
HAS BEEN WITH ME SINCE MY DEBUT,
ABE-SAN, HAS MOVED TO ANOTHER
DIVISION, WHICH MEANS I HAVE A NEW
EDITOR NOW. ABE-SAN ALWAYS
THOUGHT OF WHAT TO WRITE FOR
THE PROMOTIONAL MATERIALS AND
SUBHEADINGS, AND HAS HELPED
ME CREATE THE WORLD OF
*KARNEVAL* SINCE THE BEGINNING.
I CANNOT THANK YOU ENOUGH, ABE-SAN.
AND SO MY NEW EDITOR, OOHASHI-SAN, HAS
COME ON TO THE PROJECT TO CONTINUE
THIS JOURNEY WITH ME. OOHASHI-SAN
IS INCREDIBLY KIND, SUPPORTIVE, AND
TRUSTWORTHY, AND I'M VERY EXCITED TO
START THIS NEW CHAPTER TOGETHER.
I HAVE BEEN TRULY BLESSED WITH THE
READERS AND COLLABORATORS
I'VE WORKED WITH ON THIS PROJECT.
I WILL CONTINUE TO DO MY BEST
SO THAT I CAN RETURN THE
GRATITUDE I HAVE FOR YOU ALL.

Touya Mikanagi

## SPECIAL THANKS

MOTSU-SAN SUAMA-SAN (cat) SAN

MY EDITORS, OOHASHI-SAN AND ABE-SAN
EVERYONE AT ICHIJINSHA PUBLISHING

ALL THE COLLABORATORS AND
EVERYONE AT OUR AFFILIATED COMPANIES
WHO'VE TAKEN CARE OF ME

MY FRIENDS AND FAMILY

AND to YOU

ILLUSTRATIONS
BY MOTSU

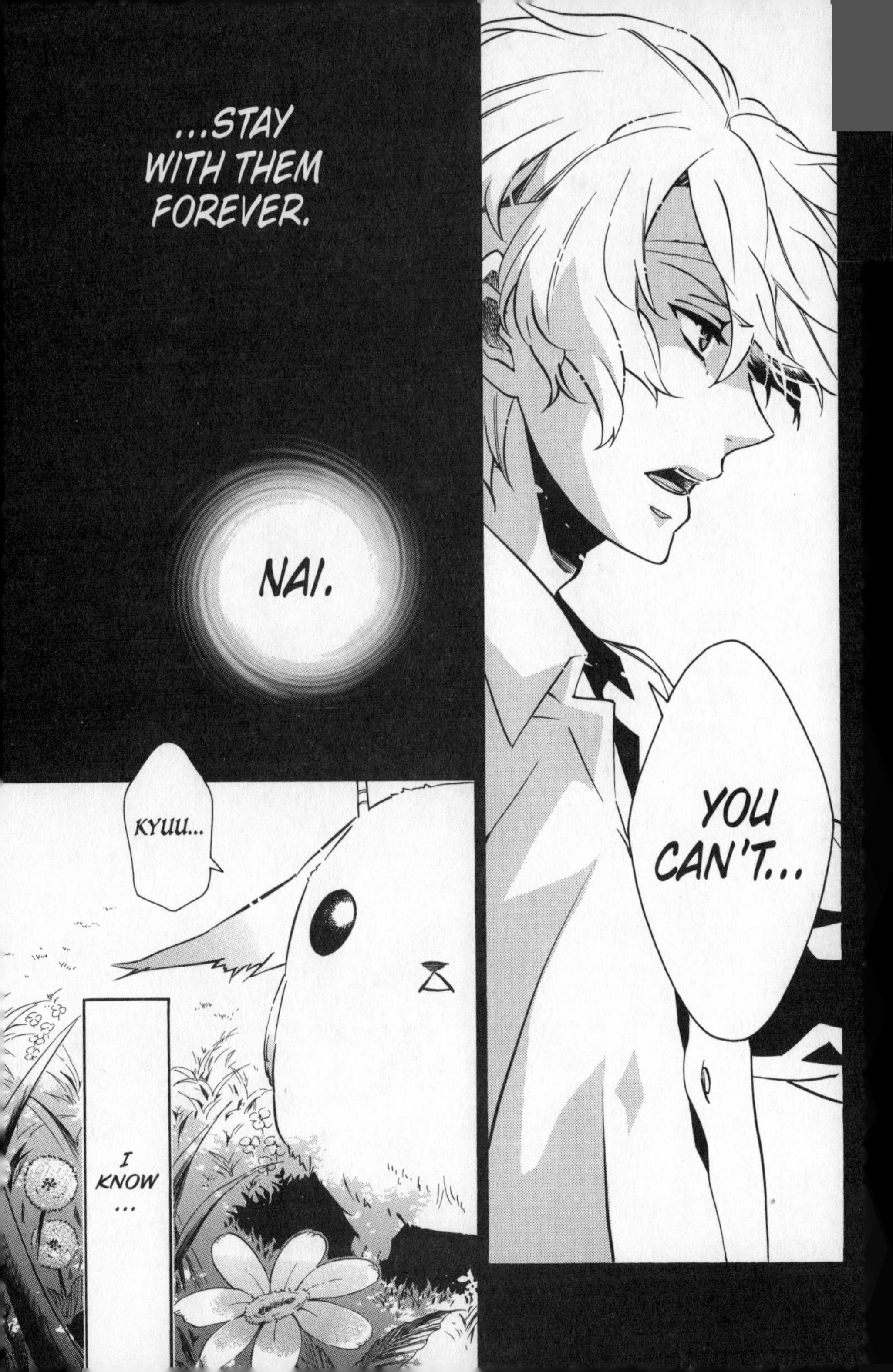
YOU CAN'T...
...STAY WITH THEM FOREVER.
NAI.
KYUU...
I KNOW...

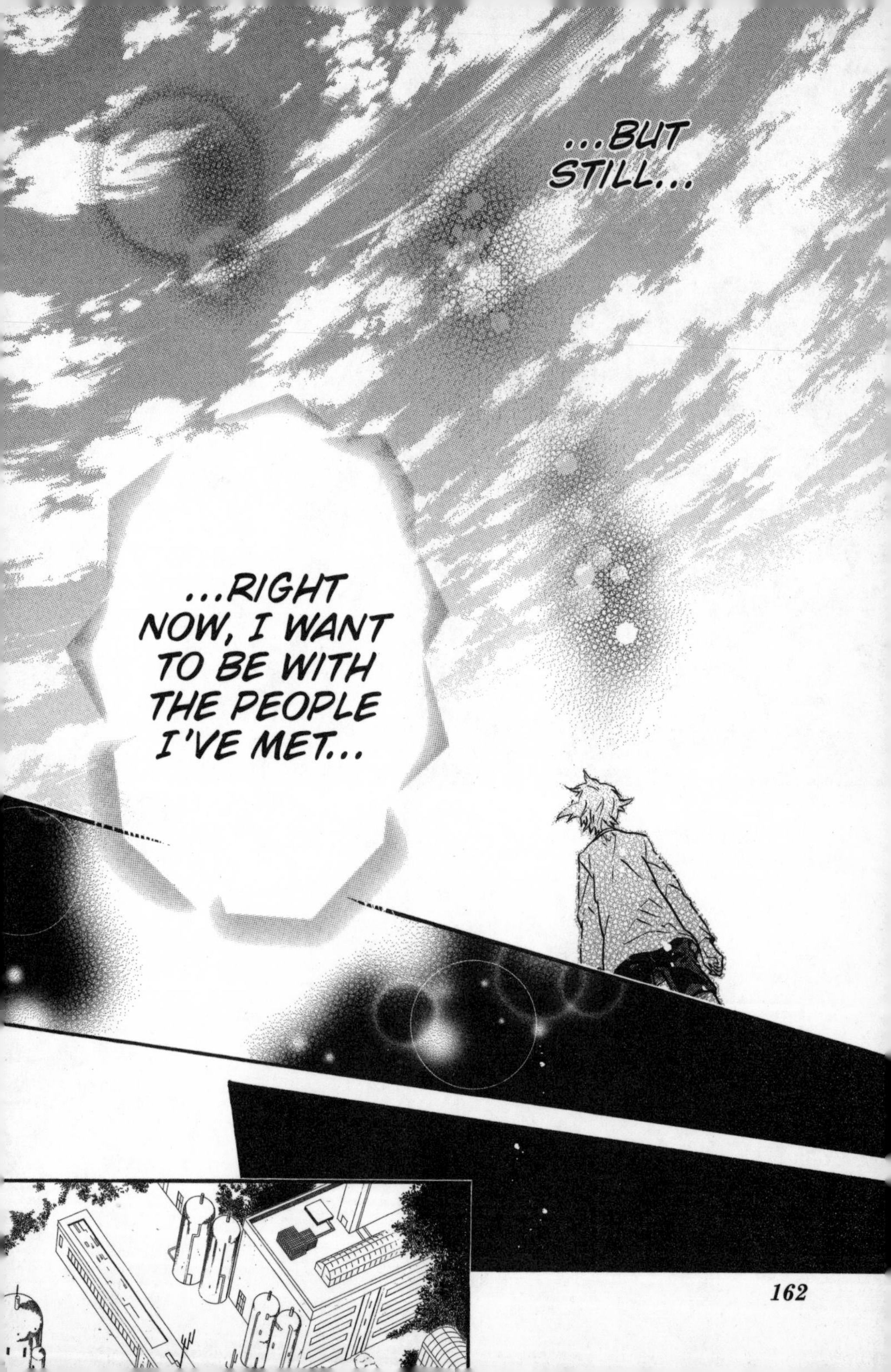
...BUT STILL...
...RIGHT NOW, I WANT TO BE WITH THE PEOPLE I'VE MET...

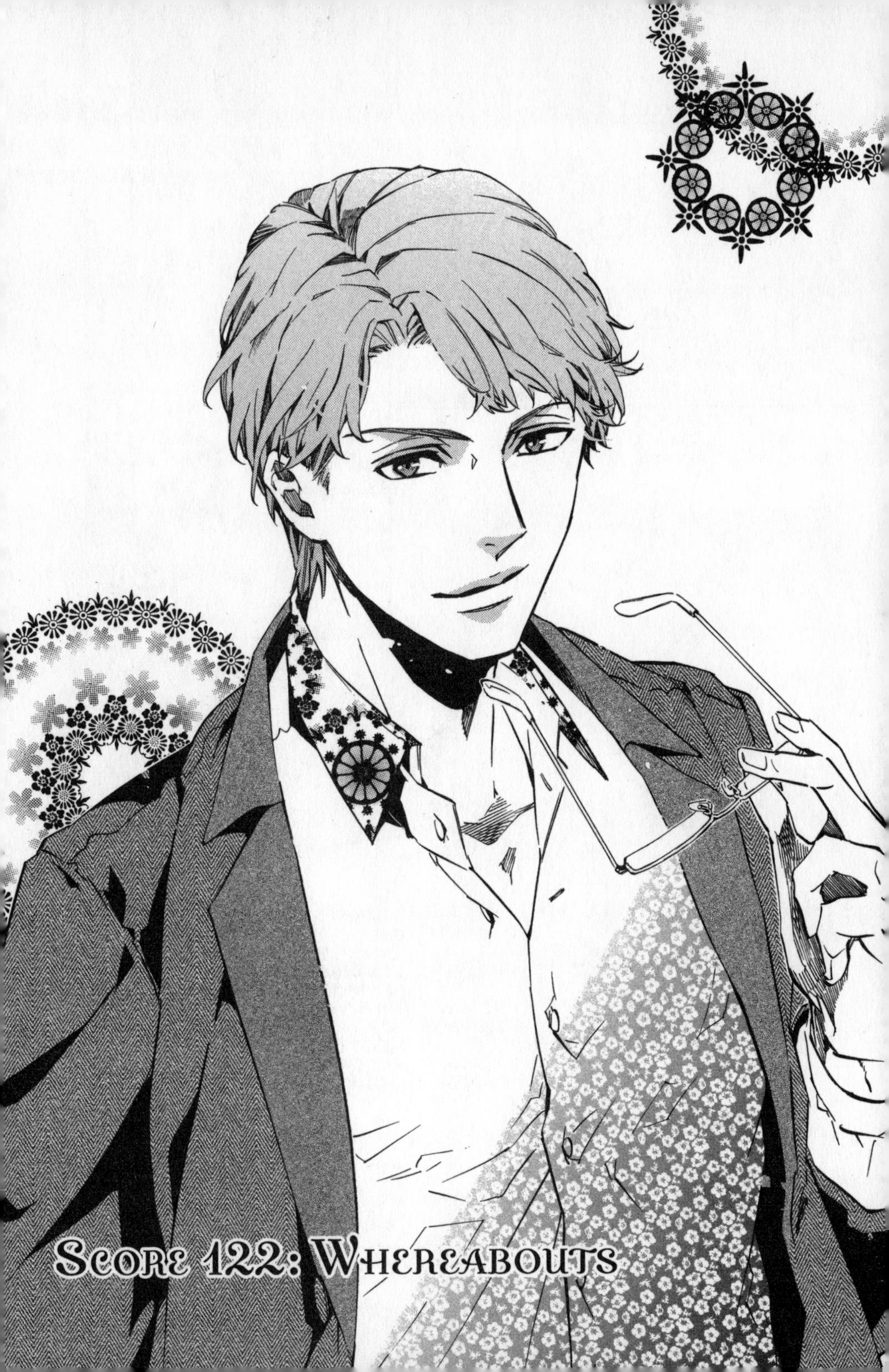
Score 122: Whereabouts

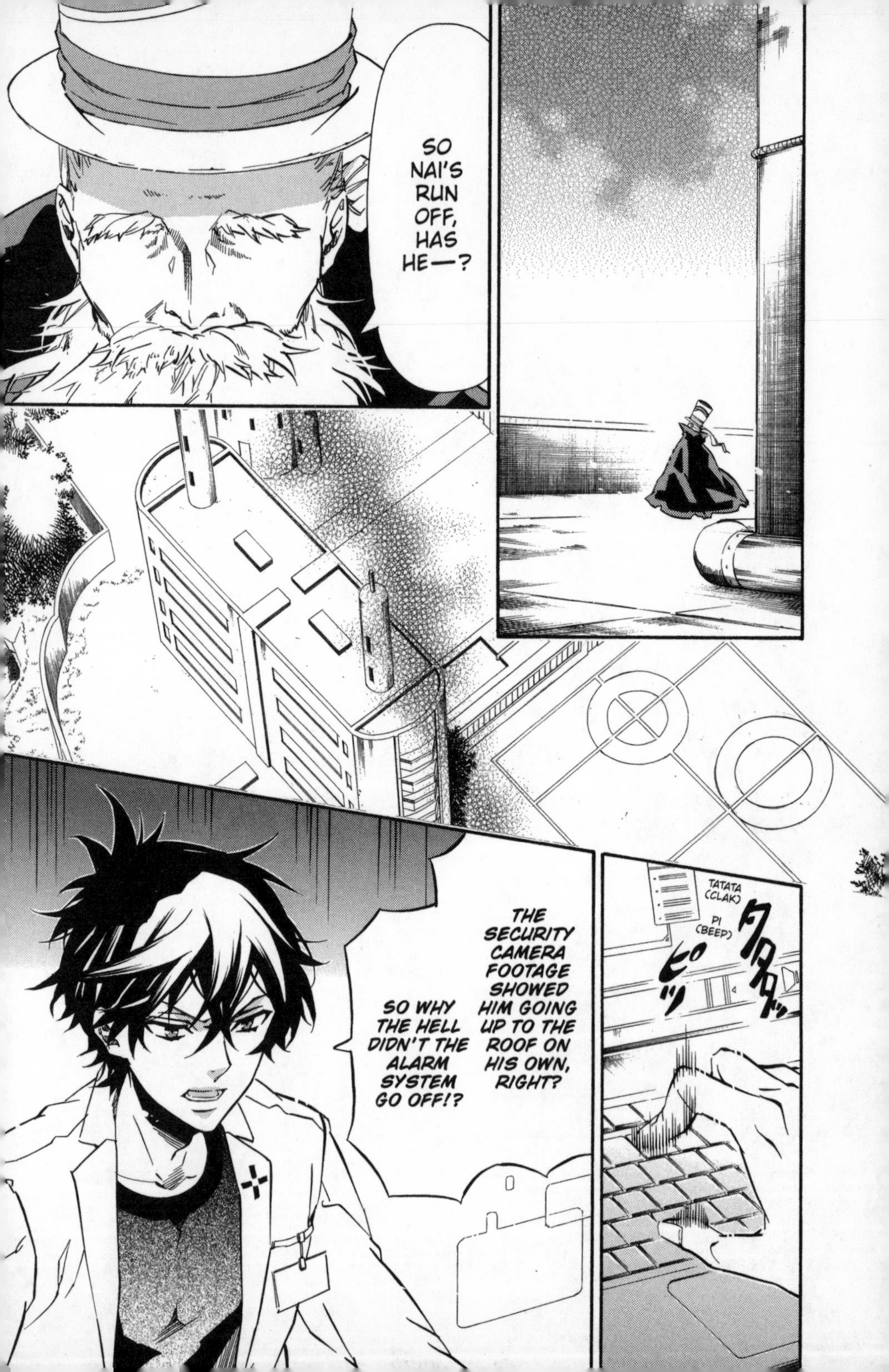
SO NAI'S RUN OFF, HAS HE—?
TATATA (CLAK)
PI (BEEP)
THE SECURITY CAMERA FOOTAGE SHOWED HIM GOING UP TO THE ROOF ON HIS OWN, RIGHT?
SO WHY THE HELL DIDN'T THE ALARM SYSTEM GO OFF!?

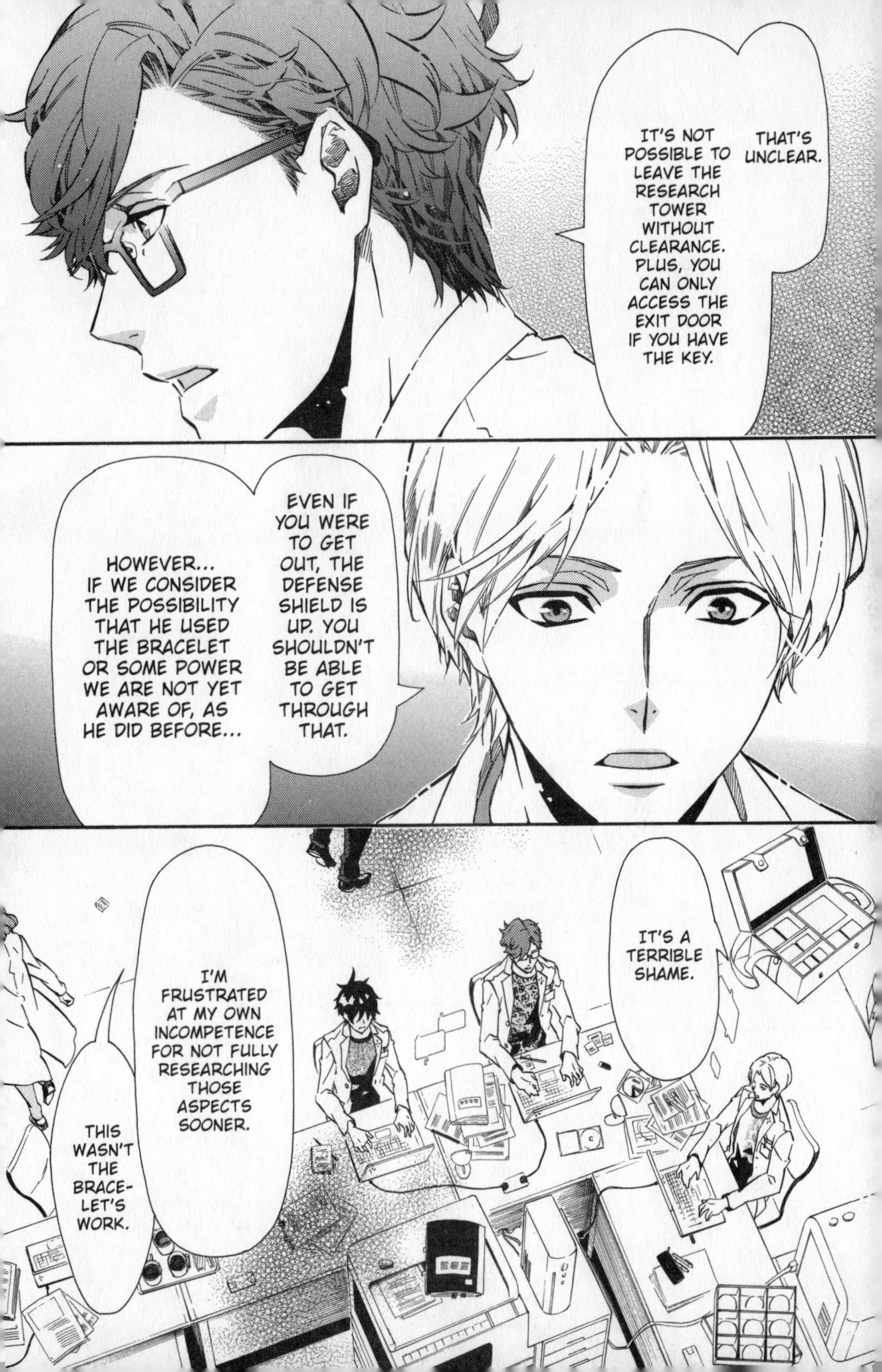
THAT'S UNCLEAR.
IT'S NOT POSSIBLE TO LEAVE THE RESEARCH TOWER WITHOUT CLEARANCE. PLUS, YOU CAN ONLY ACCESS THE EXIT DOOR IF YOU HAVE THE KEY.
EVEN IF YOU WERE TO GET OUT, THE DEFENSE SHIELD IS UP. YOU SHOULDN'T BE ABLE TO GET THROUGH THAT.
HOWEVER... IF WE CONSIDER THE POSSIBILITY THAT HE USED THE BRACELET OR SOME POWER WE ARE NOT YET AWARE OF, AS HE DID BEFORE...
IT'S A TERRIBLE SHAME.
I'M FRUSTRATED AT MY OWN INCOMPETENCE FOR NOT FULLY RESEARCHING THOSE ASPECTS SOONER.
THIS WASN'T THE BRACE-LET'S WORK.

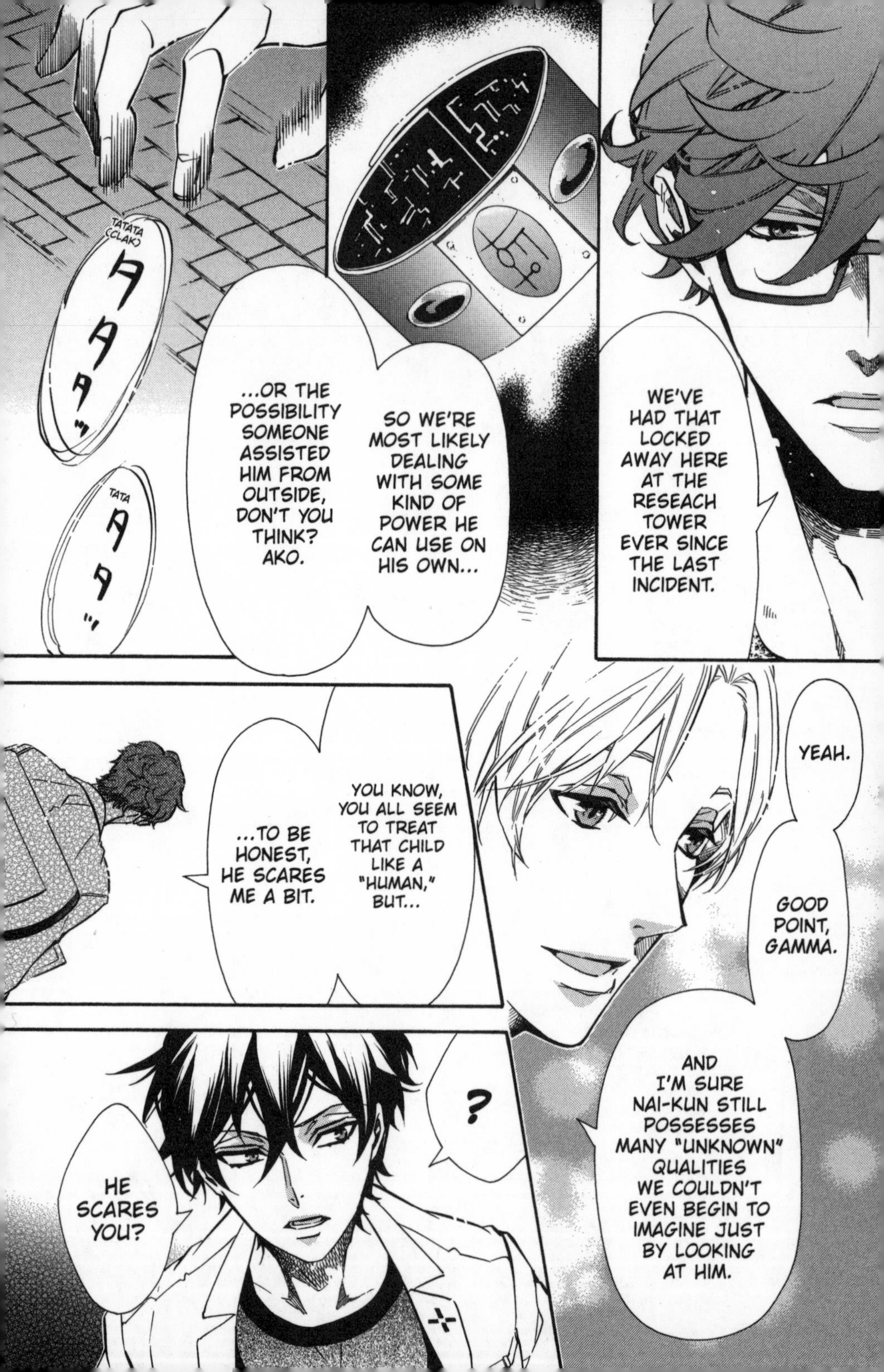
WE'VE HAD THAT LOCKED AWAY HERE AT THE RESEACH TOWER EVER SINCE THE LAST INCIDENT.
SO WE'RE MOST LIKELY DEALING WITH SOME KIND OF POWER HE CAN USE ON HIS OWN...
...OR THE POSSIBILITY SOMEONE ASSISTED HIM FROM OUTSIDE, DON'T YOU THINK? AKO.
TATATA (CLAK)
タタタッ
TATA
タタッ
YEAH.
GOOD POINT, GAMMA.
AND I'M SURE NAI-KUN STILL POSSESSES MANY "UNKNOWN" QUALITIES WE COULDN'T EVEN BEGIN TO IMAGINE JUST BY LOOKING AT HIM.
YOU KNOW, YOU ALL SEEM TO TREAT THAT CHILD LIKE A "HUMAN," BUT...
...TO BE HONEST, HE SCARES ME A BIT.
?
HE SCARES YOU?

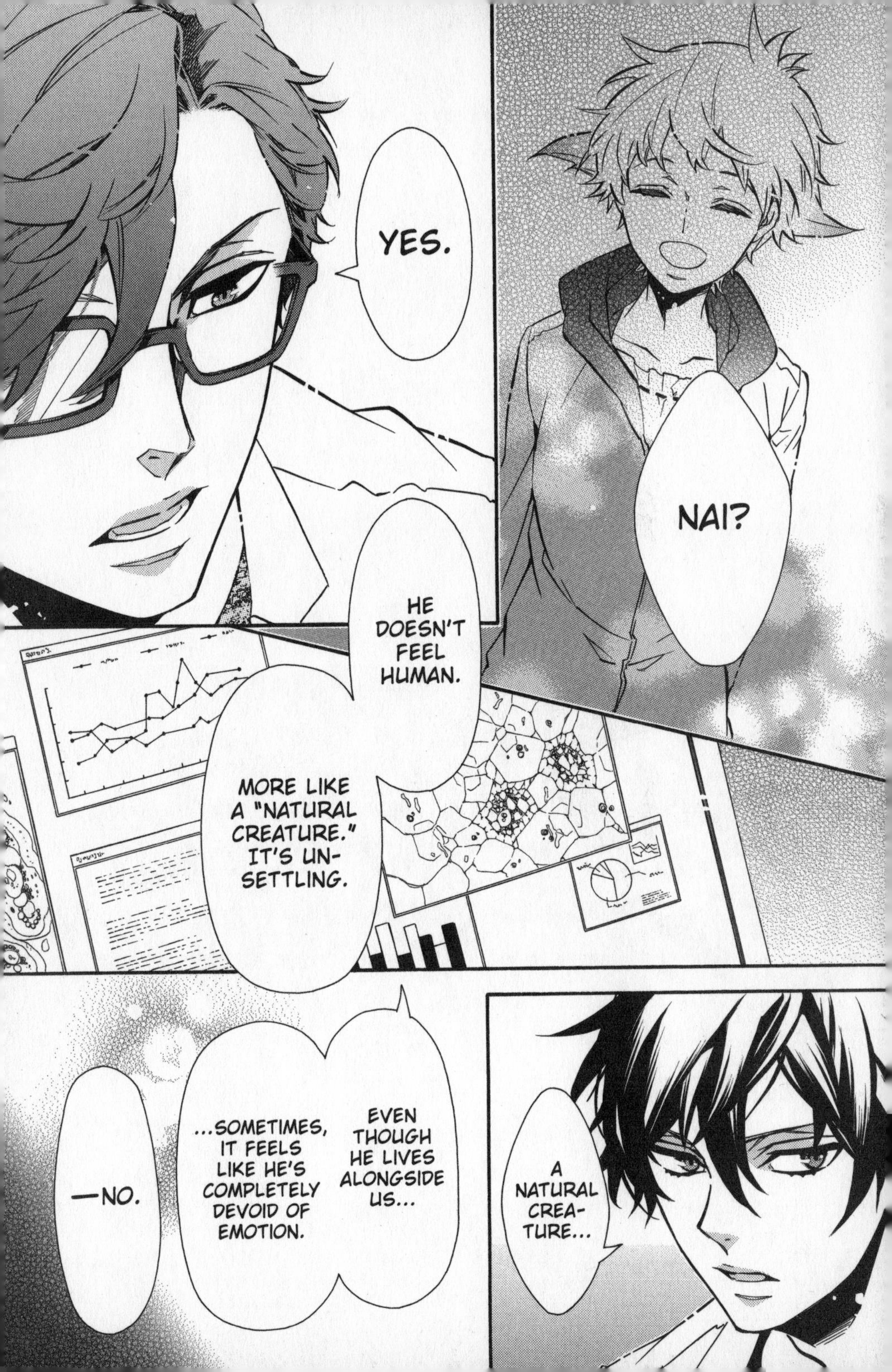
NAI?
YES.
HE DOESN'T FEEL HUMAN.
MORE LIKE A "NATURAL CREATURE." IT'S UN-SETTLING.
A NATURAL CREA-TURE...
EVEN THOUGH HE LIVES ALONGSIDE US...
...SOMETIMES, IT FEELS LIKE HE'S COMPLETELY DEVOID OF EMOTION.
—NO.

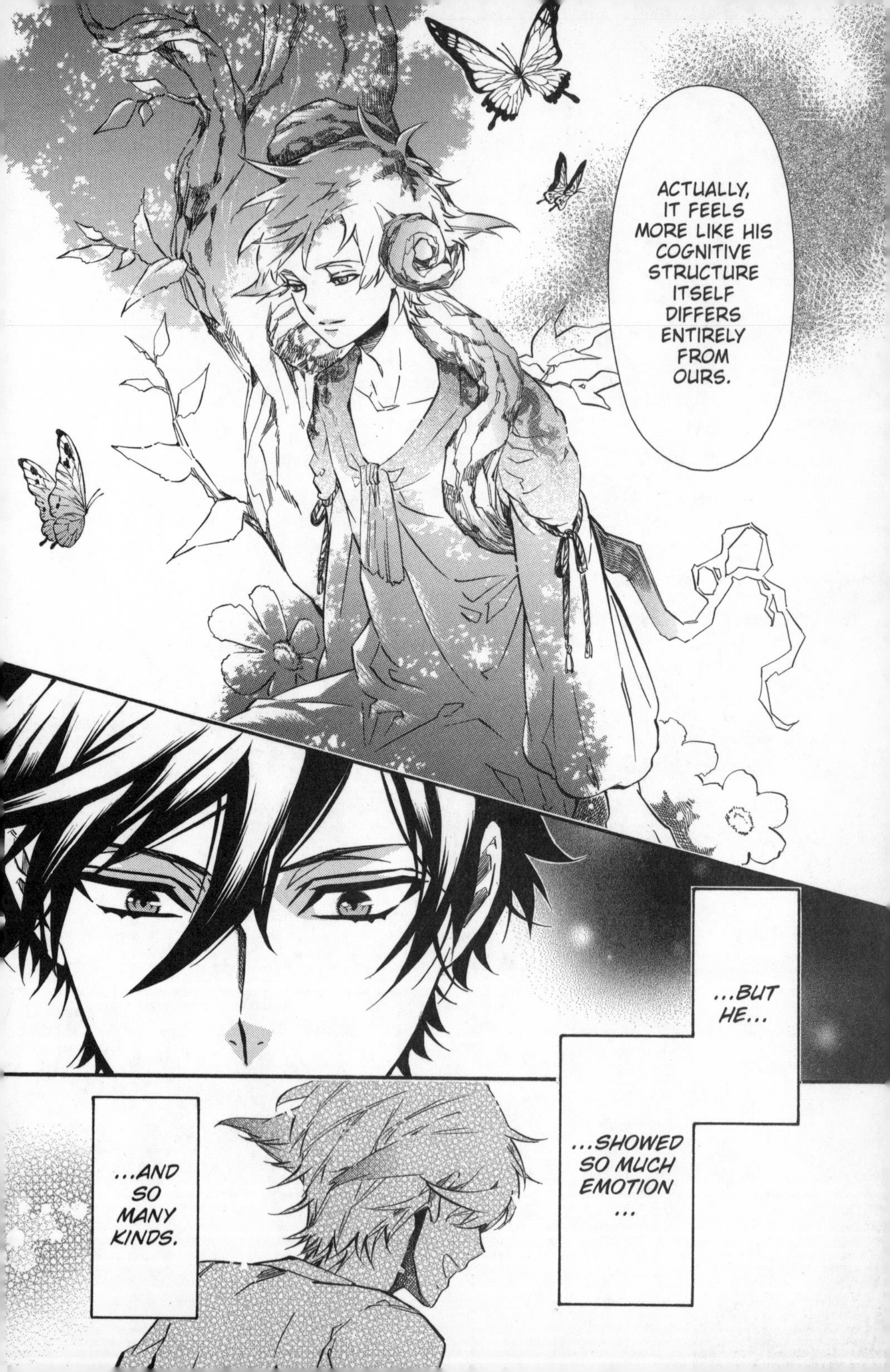
ACTUALLY, IT FEELS MORE LIKE HIS COGNITIVE STRUCTURE ITSELF DIFFERS ENTIRELY FROM OURS.
...BUT HE...
...SHOWED SO MUCH EMOTION ...
...AND SO MANY KINDS.

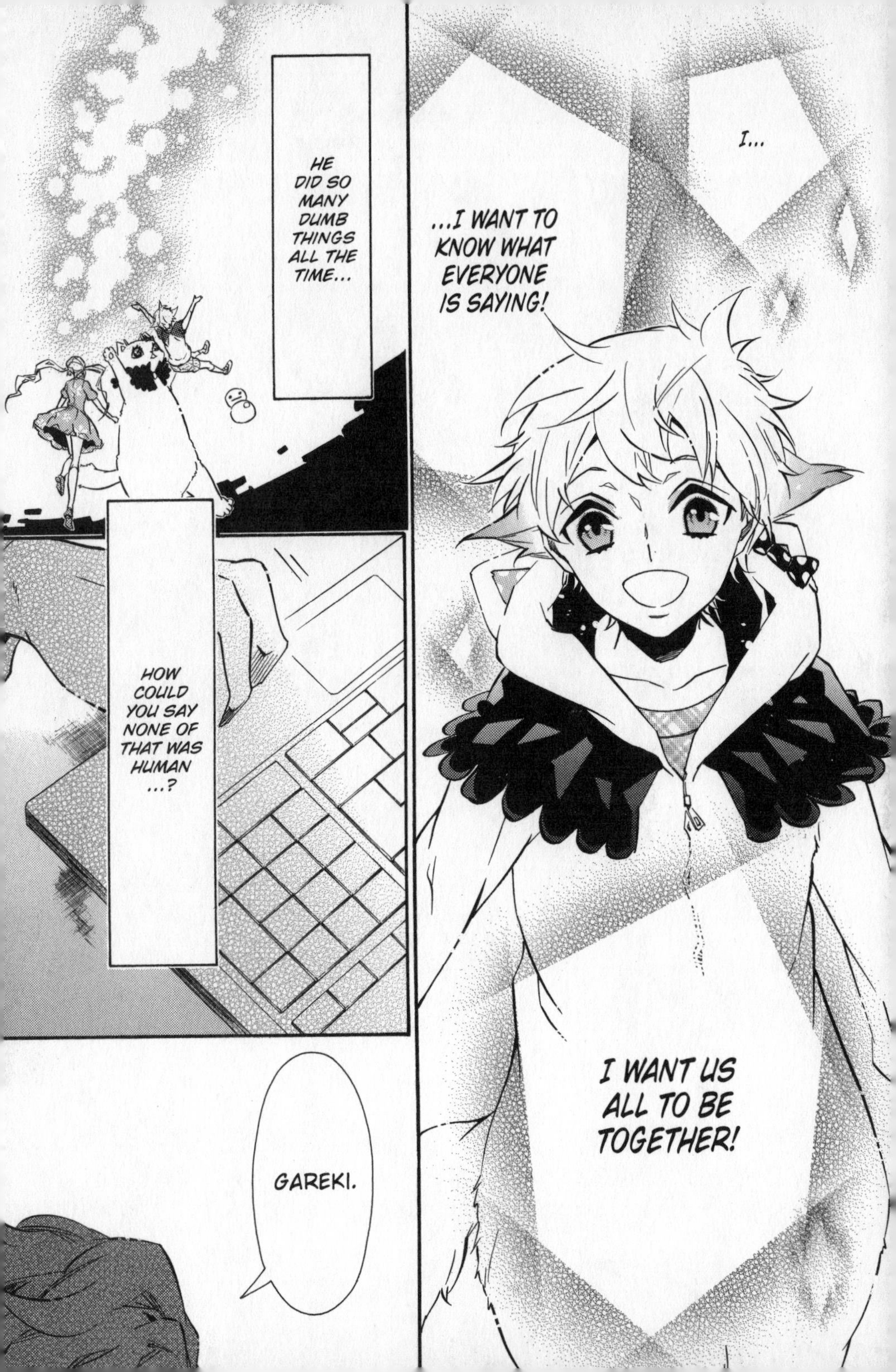
I...
...I WANT TO KNOW WHAT EVERYONE IS SAYING!
I WANT US ALL TO BE TOGETHER!
HE DID SO MANY DUMB THINGS ALL THE TIME...
HOW COULD YOU SAY NONE OF THAT WAS HUMAN ...?
GAREKI.

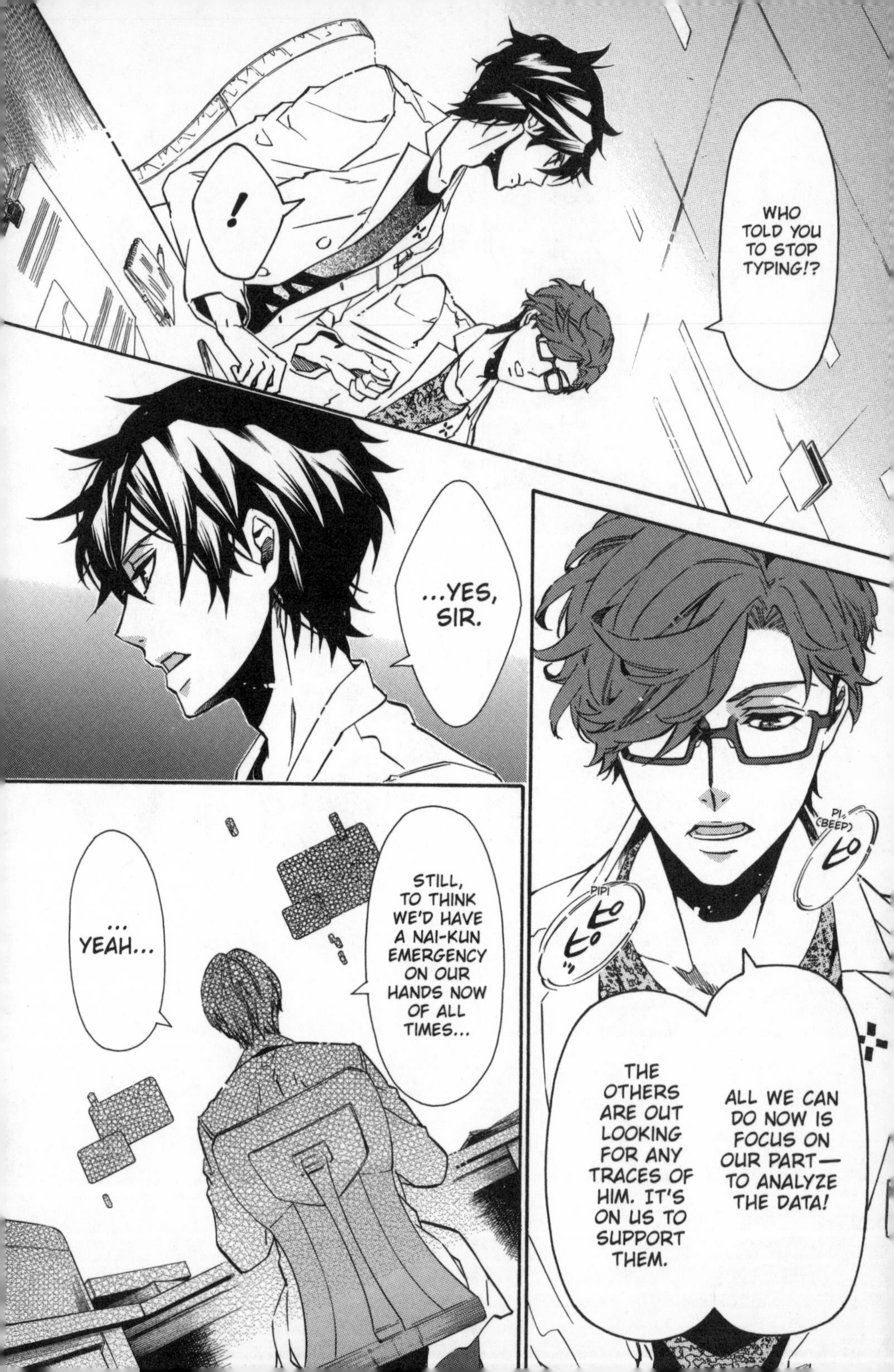
WHO TOLD YOU TO STOP TYPING!?
!
PI (BEEP)
PIPI
ALL WE CAN DO NOW IS FOCUS ON OUR PART—TO ANALYZE THE DATA!
THE OTHERS ARE OUT LOOKING FOR ANY TRACES OF HIM. IT'S ON US TO SUPPORT THEM.
...YES, SIR.
STILL, TO THINK WE'D HAVE A NAI-KUN EMERGENCY ON OUR HANDS NOW OF ALL TIMES...
...YEAH...

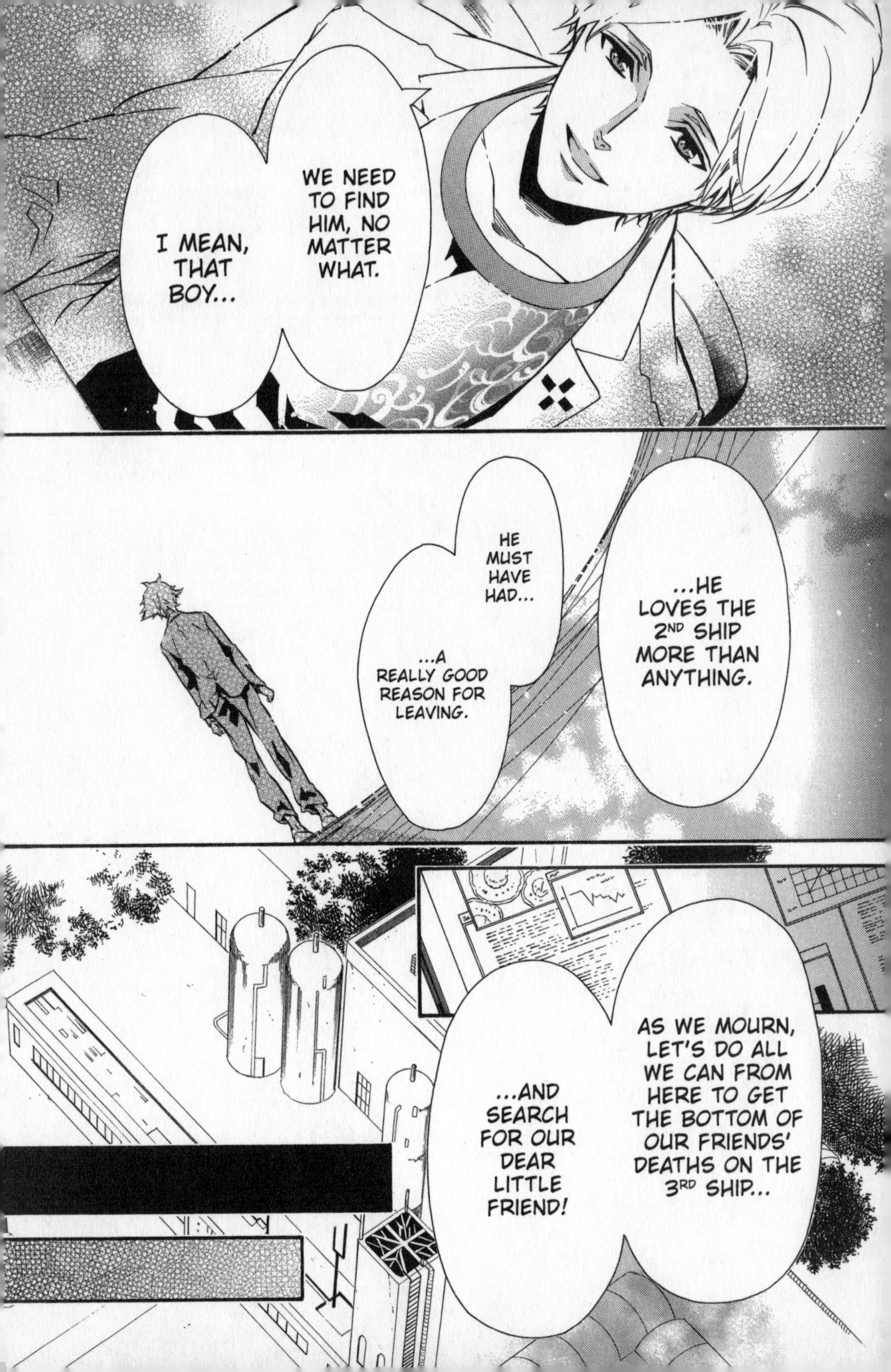
WE NEED TO FIND HIM, NO MATTER WHAT.
I MEAN, THAT BOY...
...HE LOVES THE 2ND SHIP MORE THAN ANYTHING.
HE MUST HAVE HAD...
...A REALLY GOOD REASON FOR LEAVING.
AS WE MOURN, LET'S DO ALL WE CAN FROM HERE TO GET THE BOTTOM OF OUR FRIENDS' DEATHS ON THE 3RD SHIP...
...AND SEARCH FOR OUR DEAR LITTLE FRIEND!

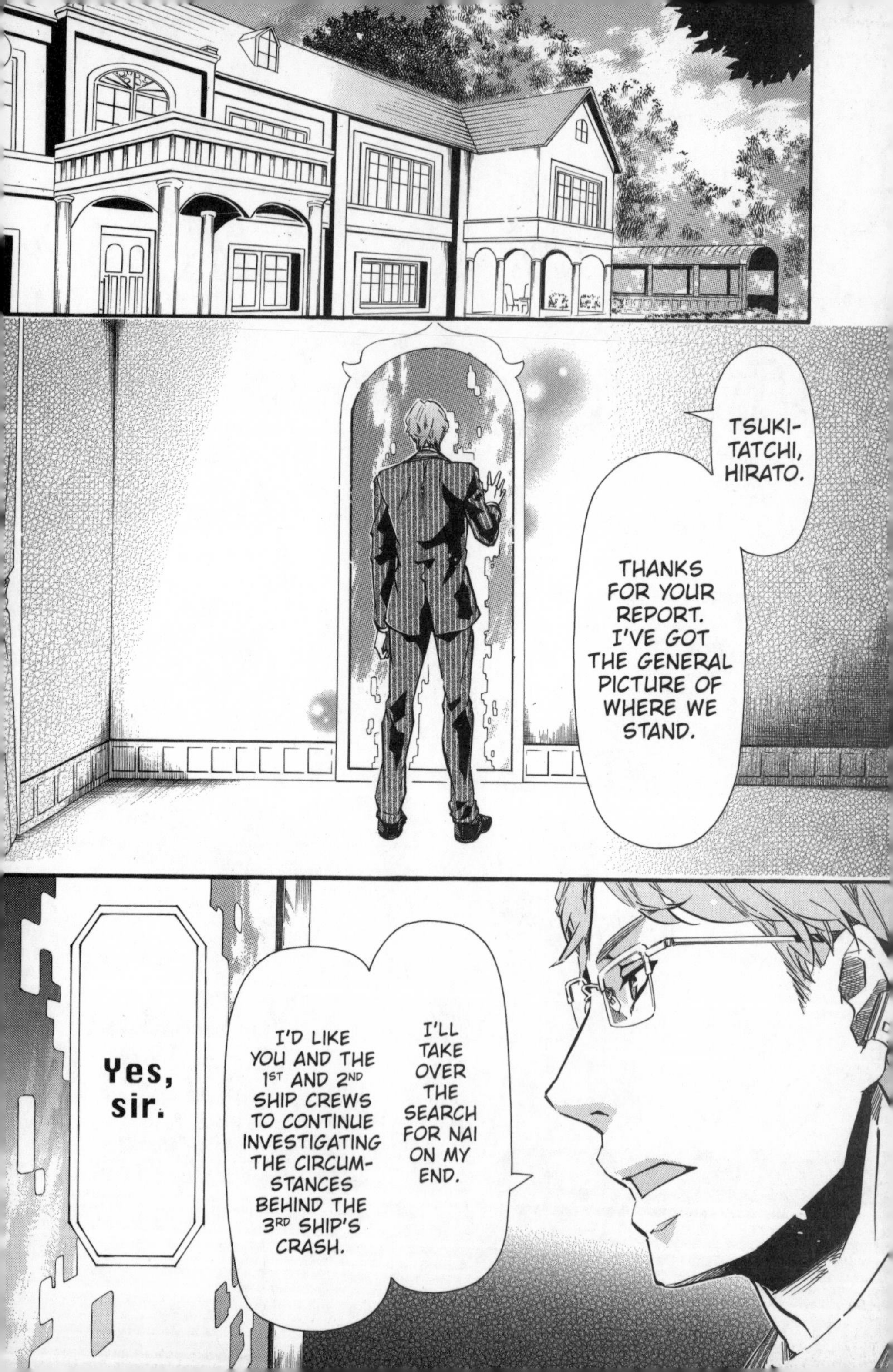
TSUKI-TATCHI, HIRATO.
THANKS FOR YOUR REPORT. I'VE GOT THE GENERAL PICTURE OF WHERE WE STAND.
I'LL TAKE OVER THE SEARCH FOR NAI ON MY END.
I'D LIKE YOU AND THE 1ST AND 2ND SHIP CREWS TO CONTINUE INVESTIGATING THE CIRCUMSTANCES BEHIND THE 3RD SHIP'S CRASH.
Yes, sir.

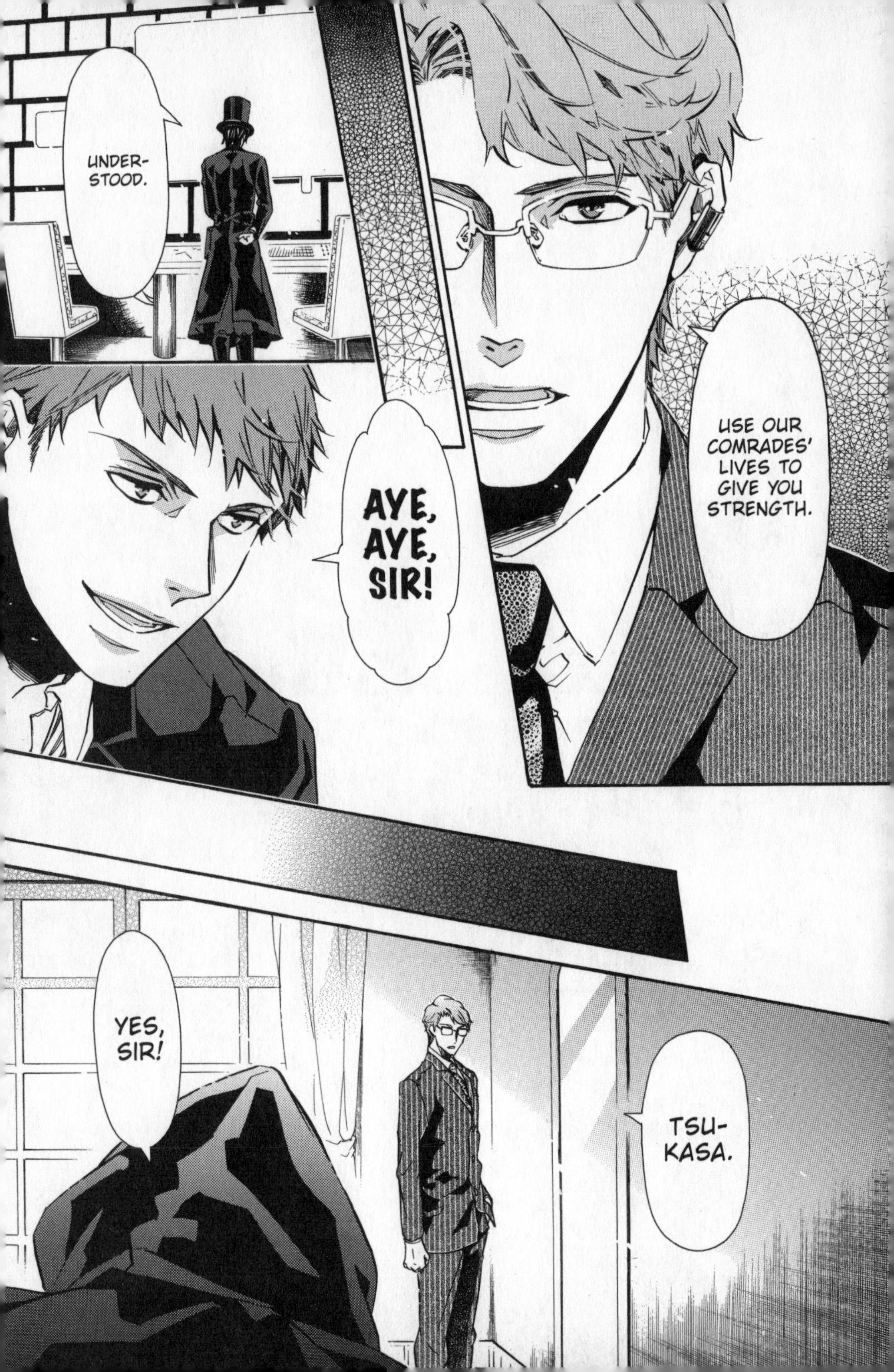
USE OUR COMRADES' LIVES TO GIVE YOU STRENGTH.
UNDER-STOOD.
AYE, AYE, SIR!
TSU-KASA.
YES, SIR!

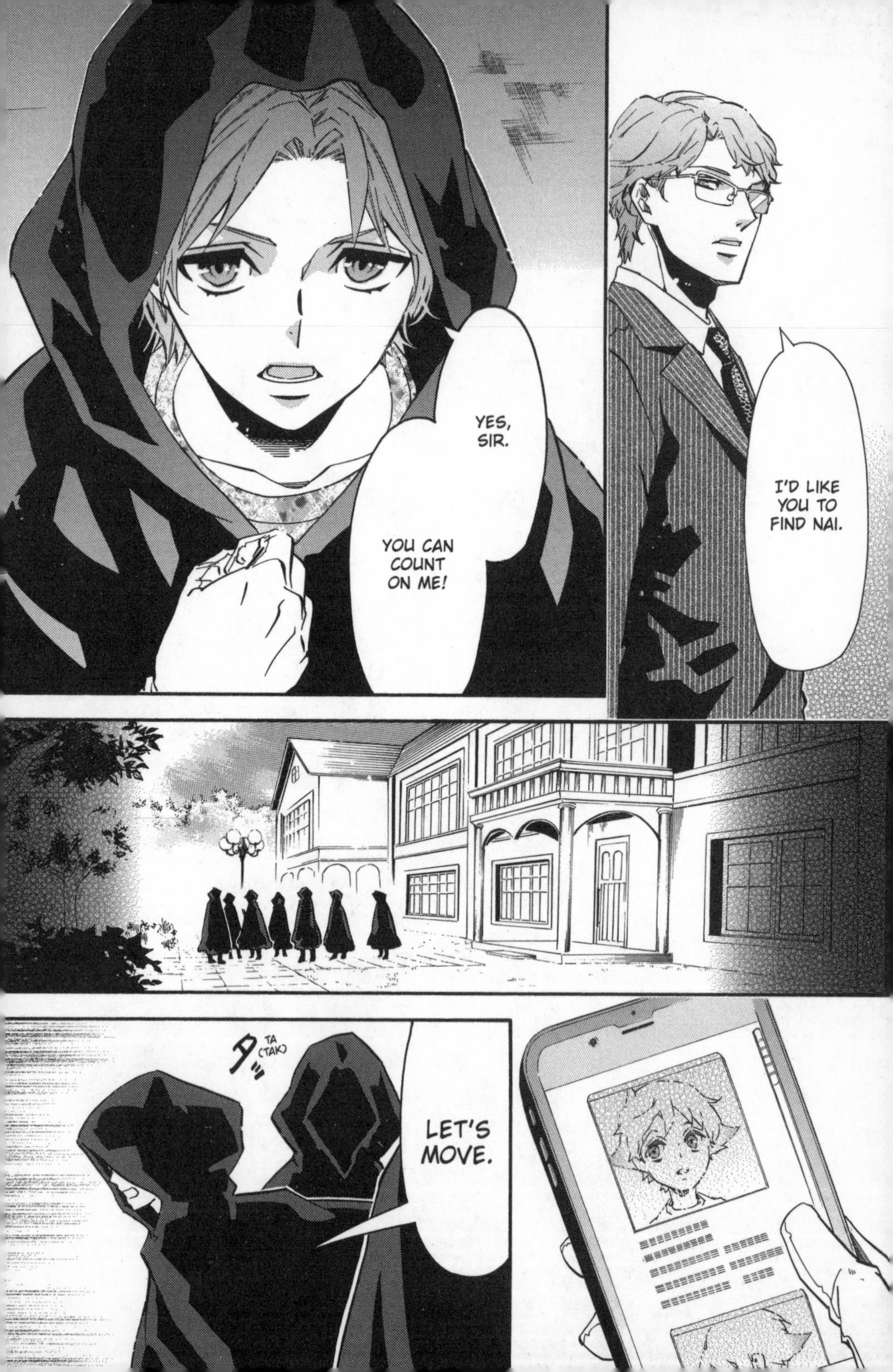
I'D LIKE YOU TO FIND NAI.
YES, SIR.
YOU CAN COUNT ON ME!
LET'S MOVE.
TA (TAK)

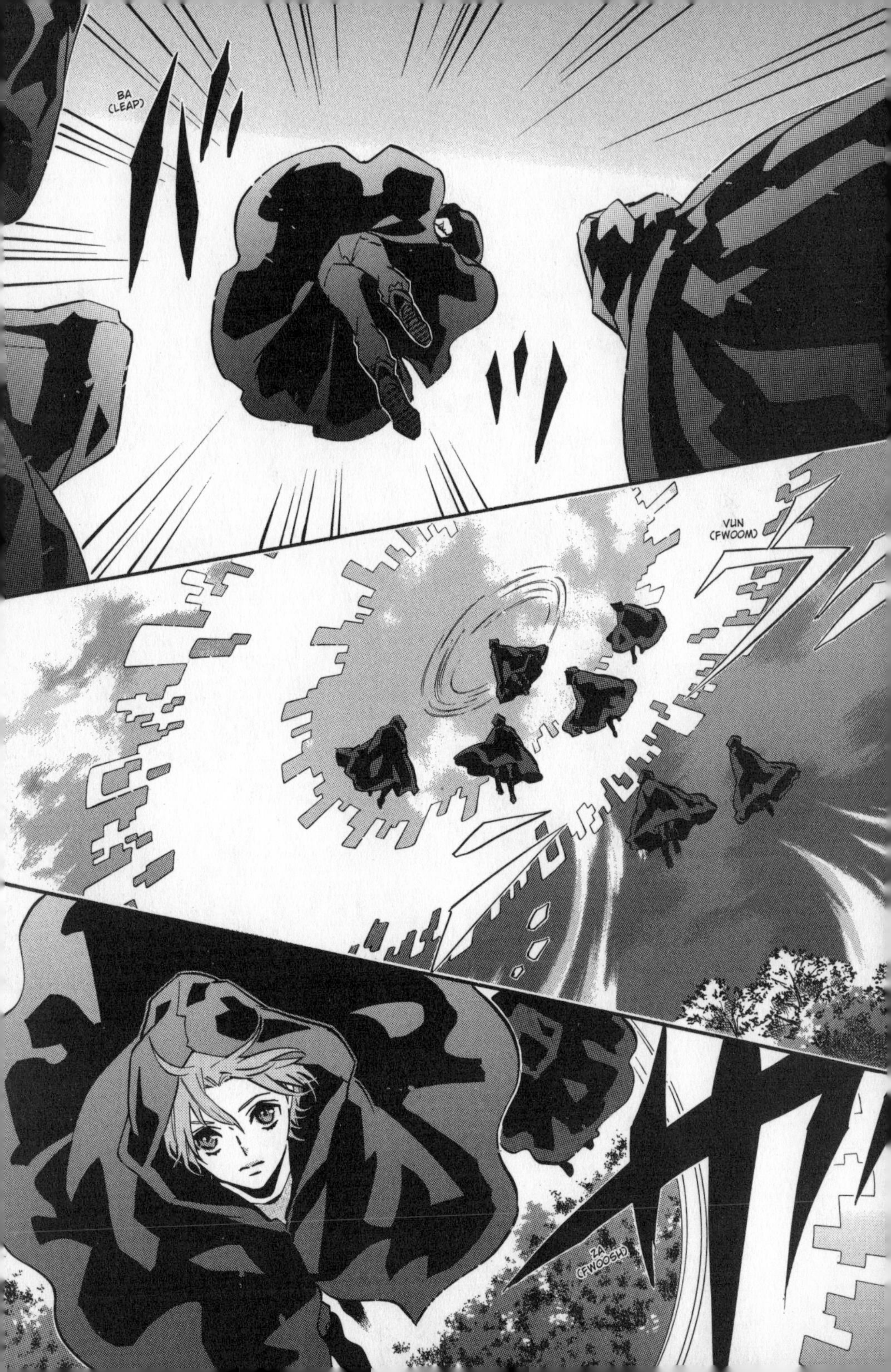
BA
(LEAP)
VUN
(FWOOM)
ZA
(FWOOSH)

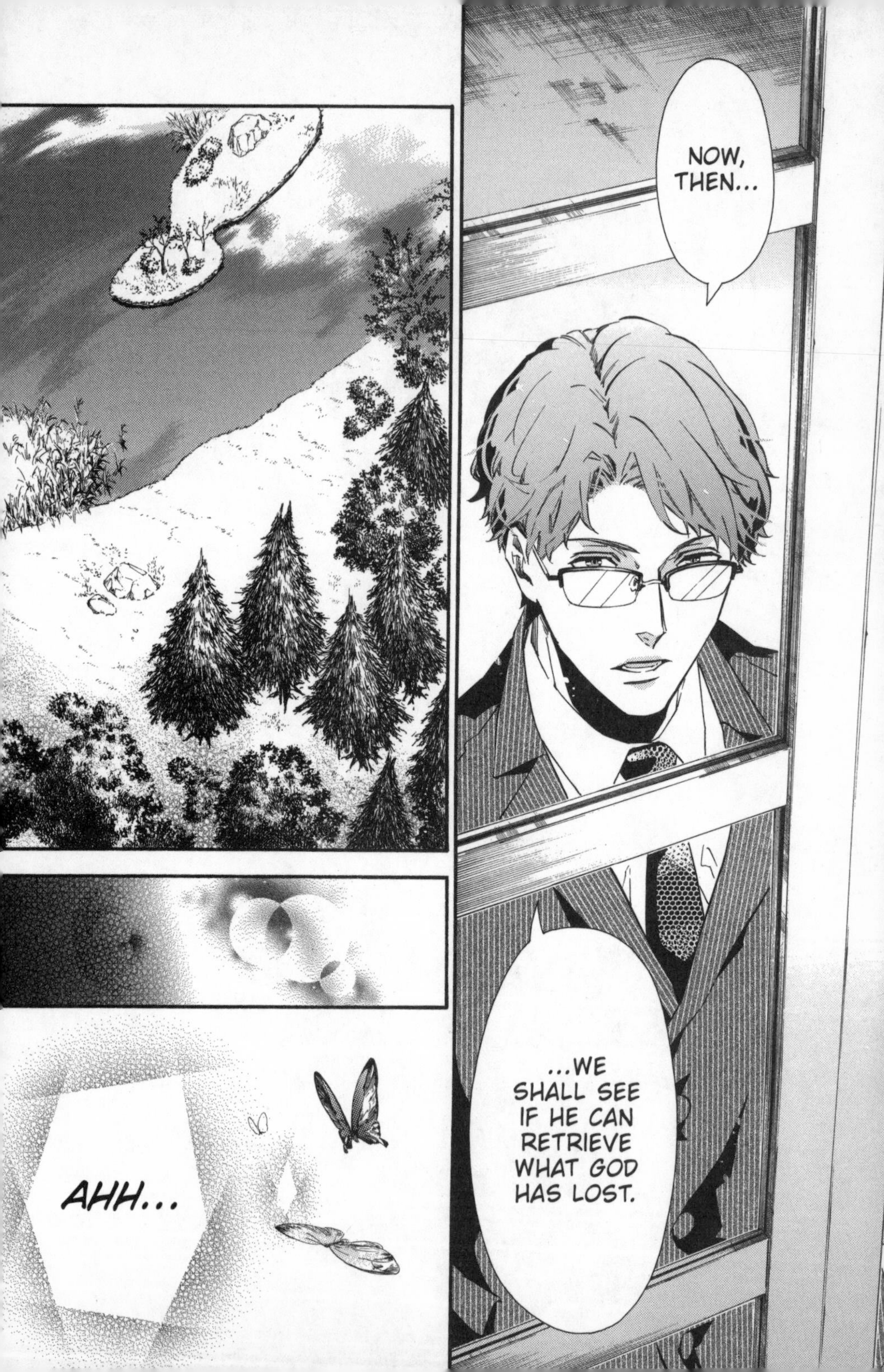
NOW, THEN...
...WE SHALL SEE IF HE CAN RETRIEVE WHAT GOD HAS LOST.
AHH...

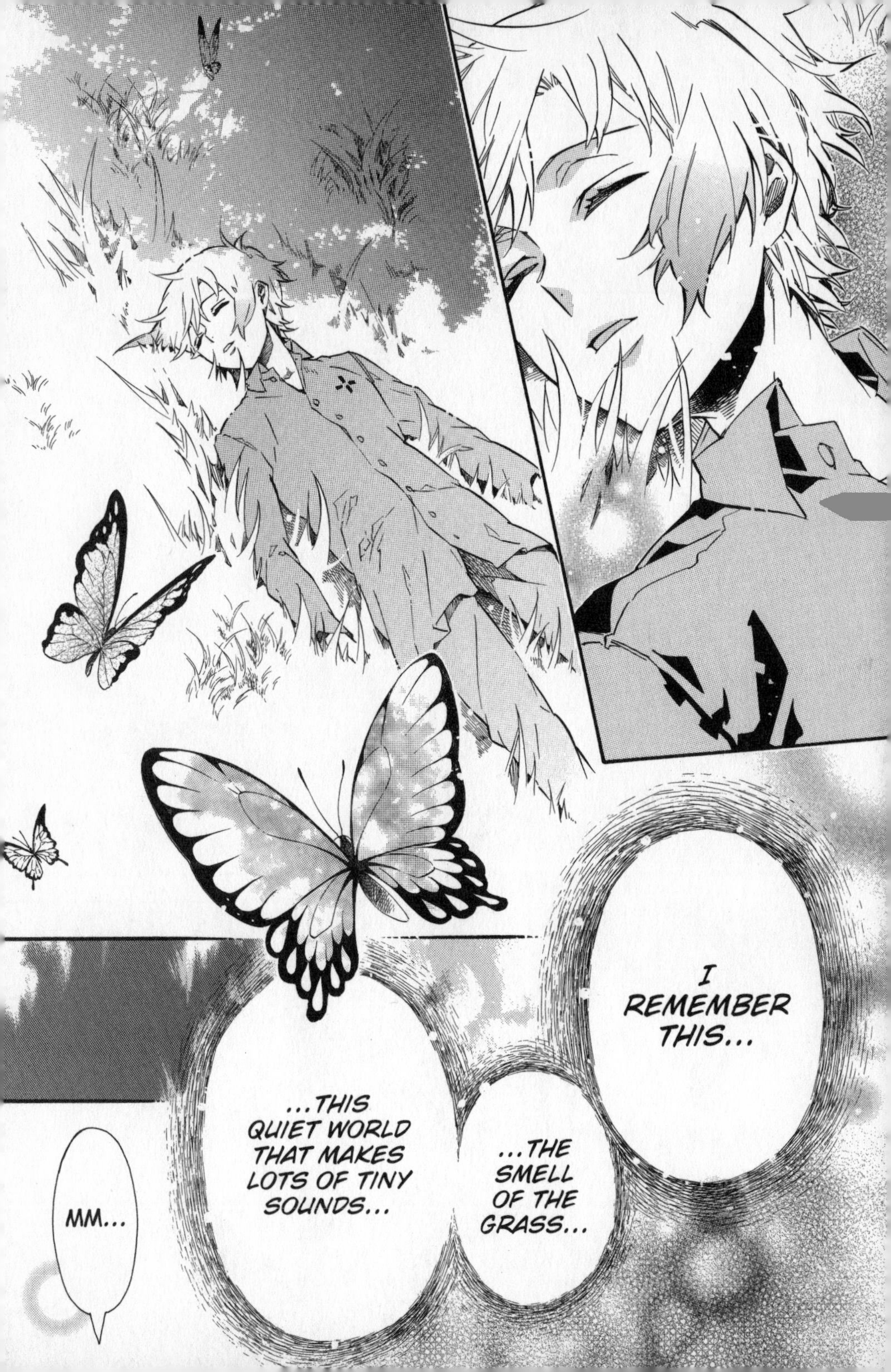
I REMEMBER THIS...
...THE SMELL OF THE GRASS...
...THIS QUIET WORLD THAT MAKES LOTS OF TINY SOUNDS...
MM...

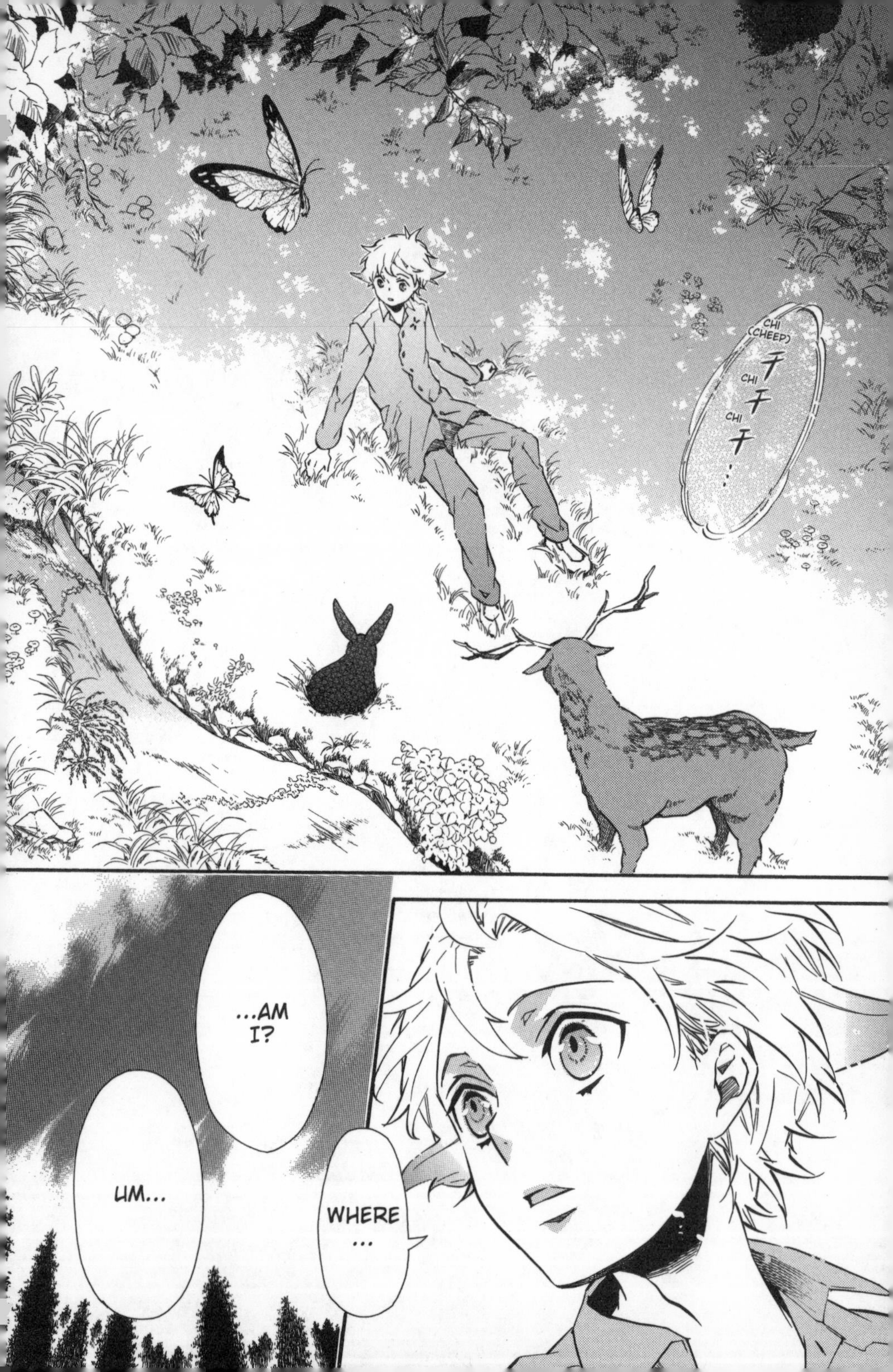
CHI (CHEEP) チ CHI チ CHI チ ...
WHERE ...
...AM I?
UM...

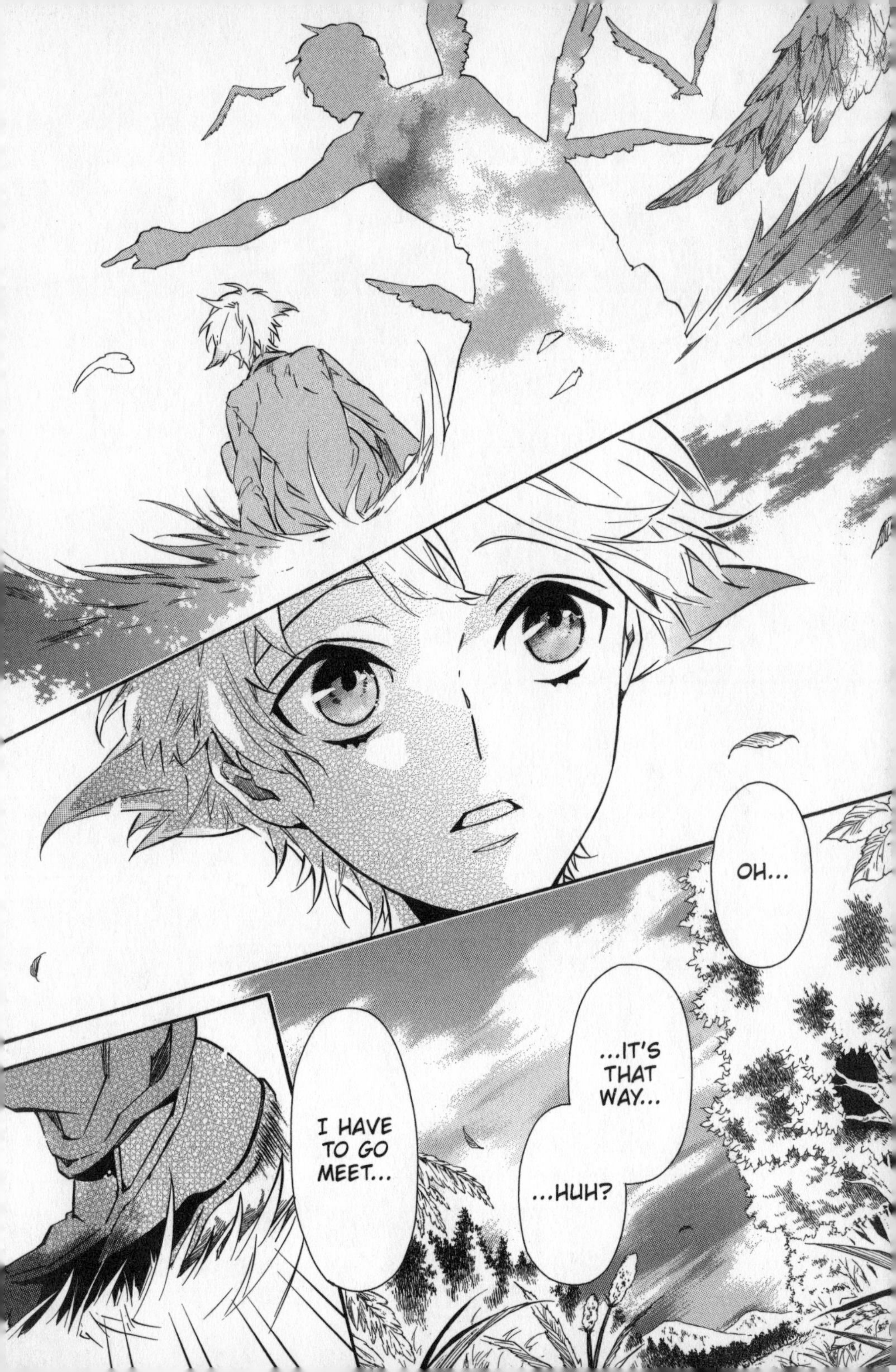
OH...
...IT'S THAT WAY...
I HAVE TO GO MEET...
...HUH?

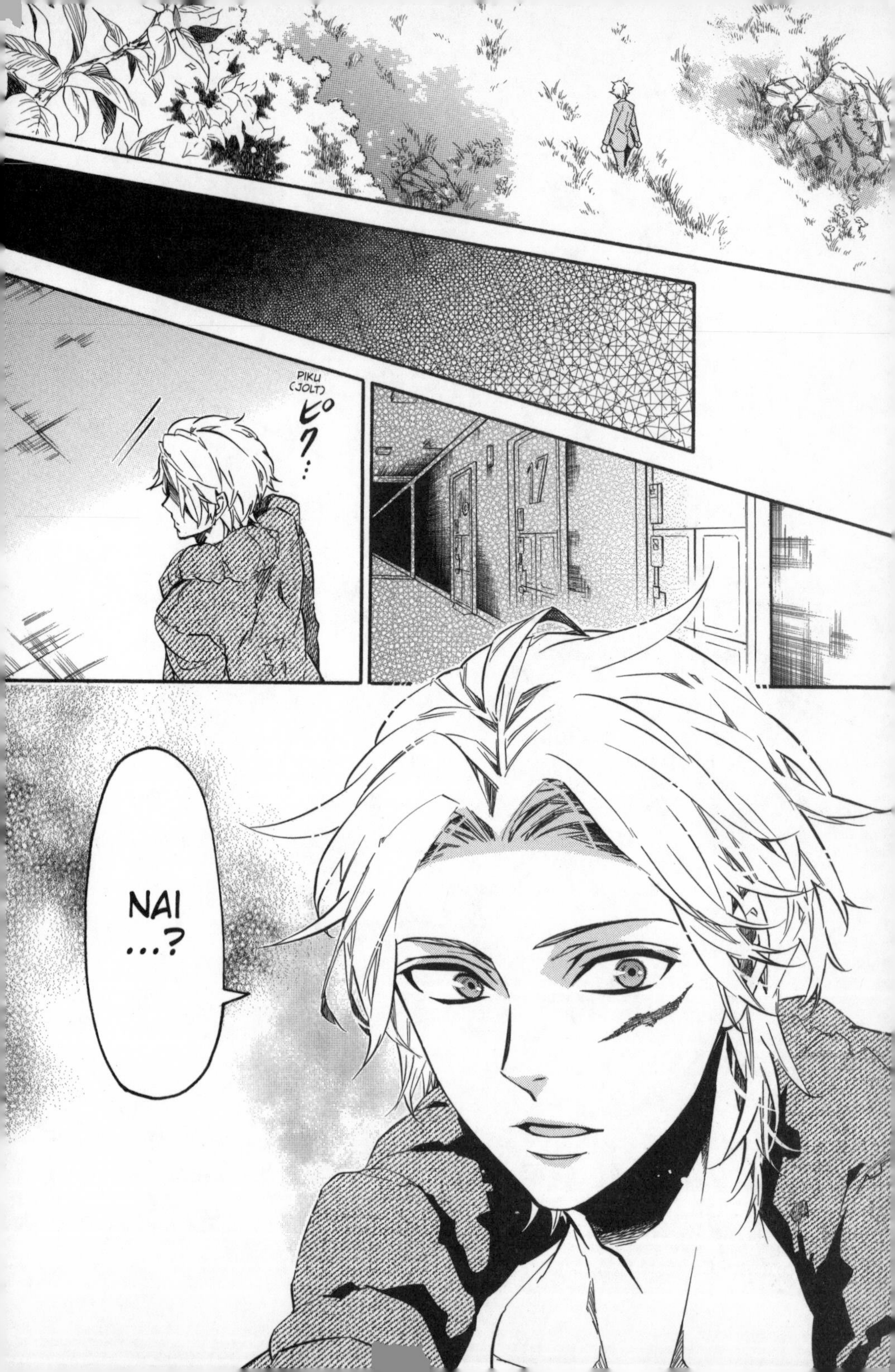
PIKU (JOLT)
ピク…
NAI ...?

KARNEVAL

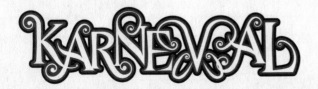

KARNEVAL

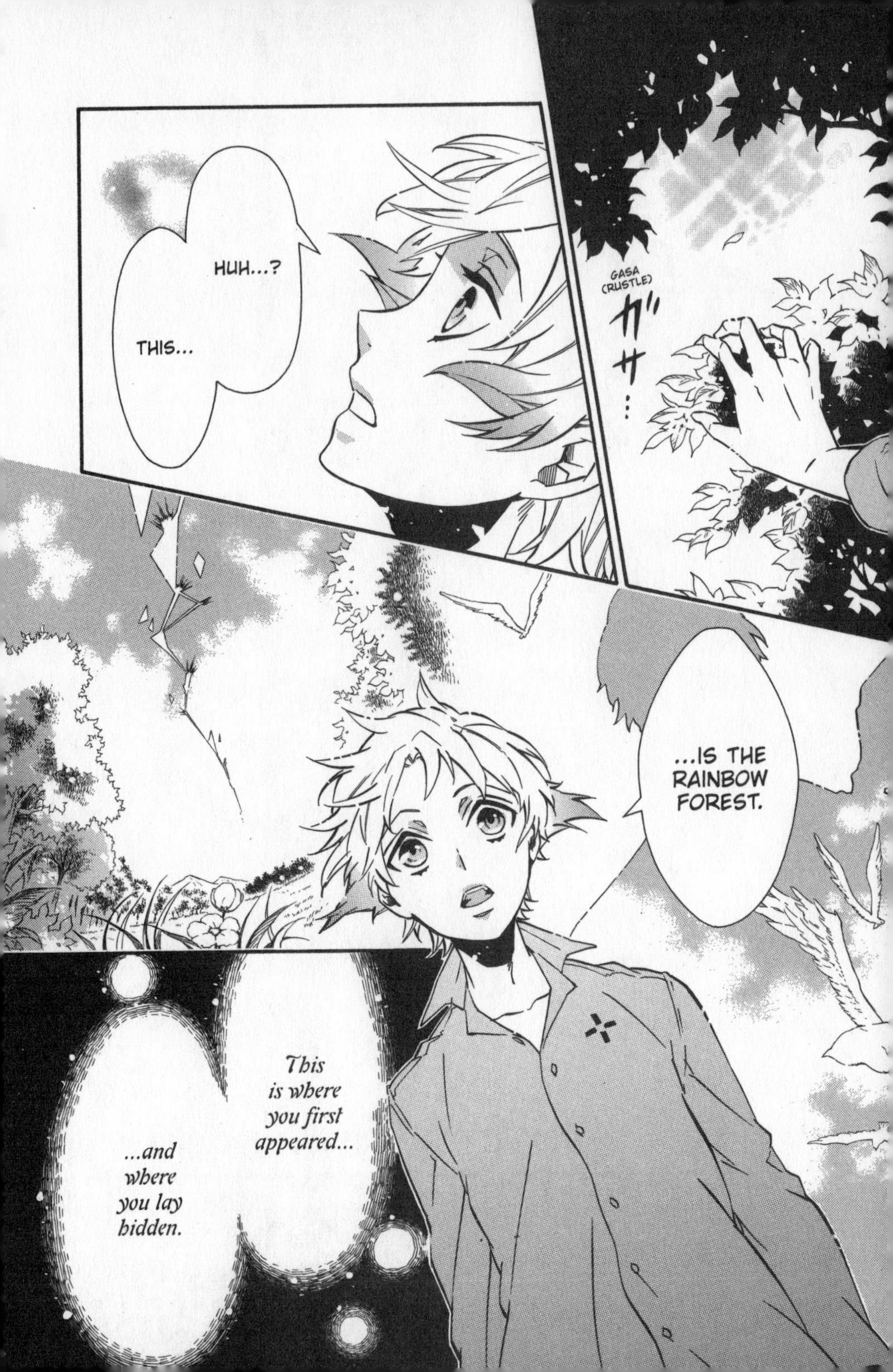
GASA (RUSTLE)
ガサ…
HUH...?
THIS...
...IS THE RAINBOW FOREST.
This is where you first appeared...
...and where you lay hidden.

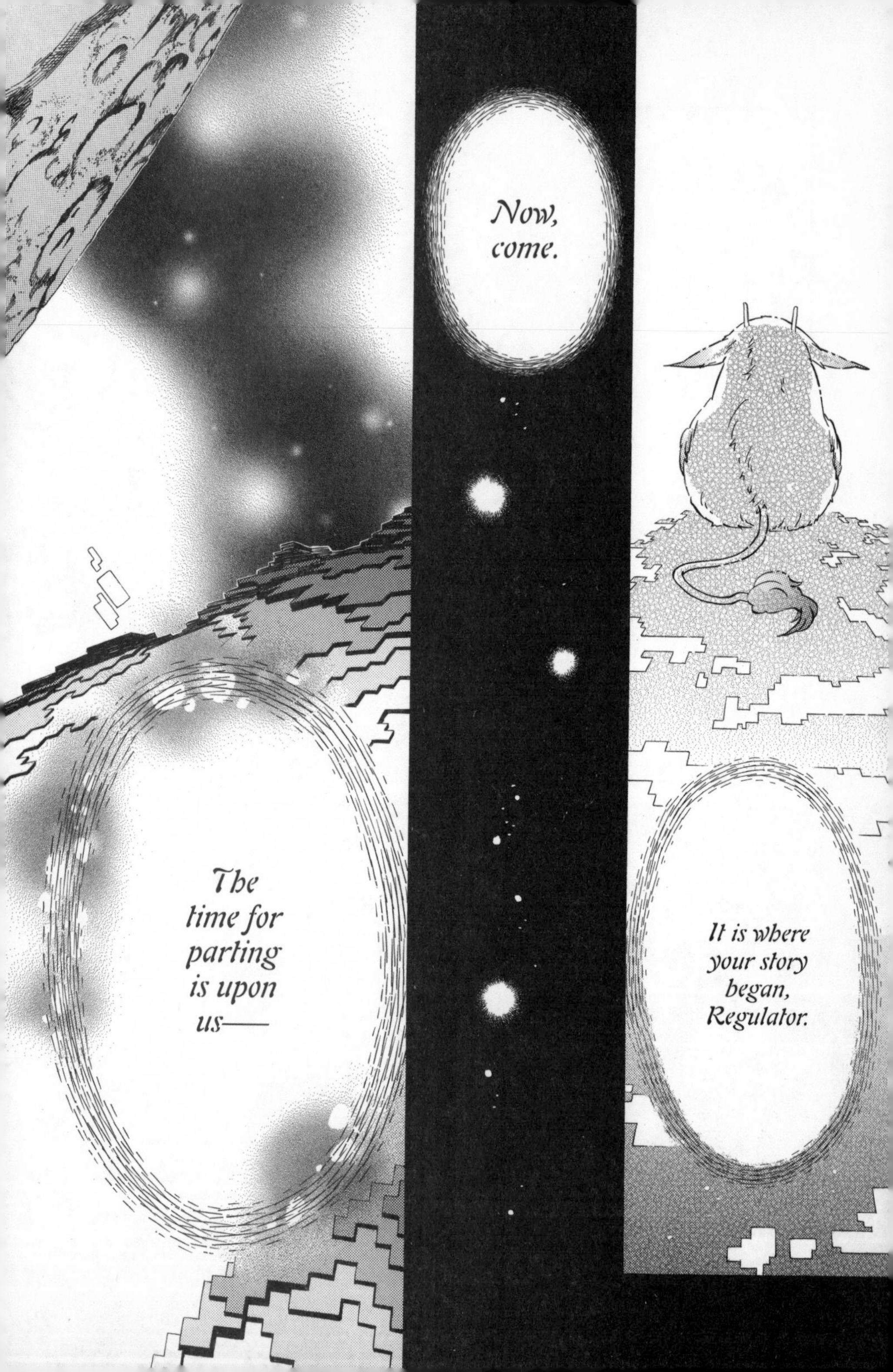
It is where your story began, Regulator.
Now, come.
The time for parting is upon us——

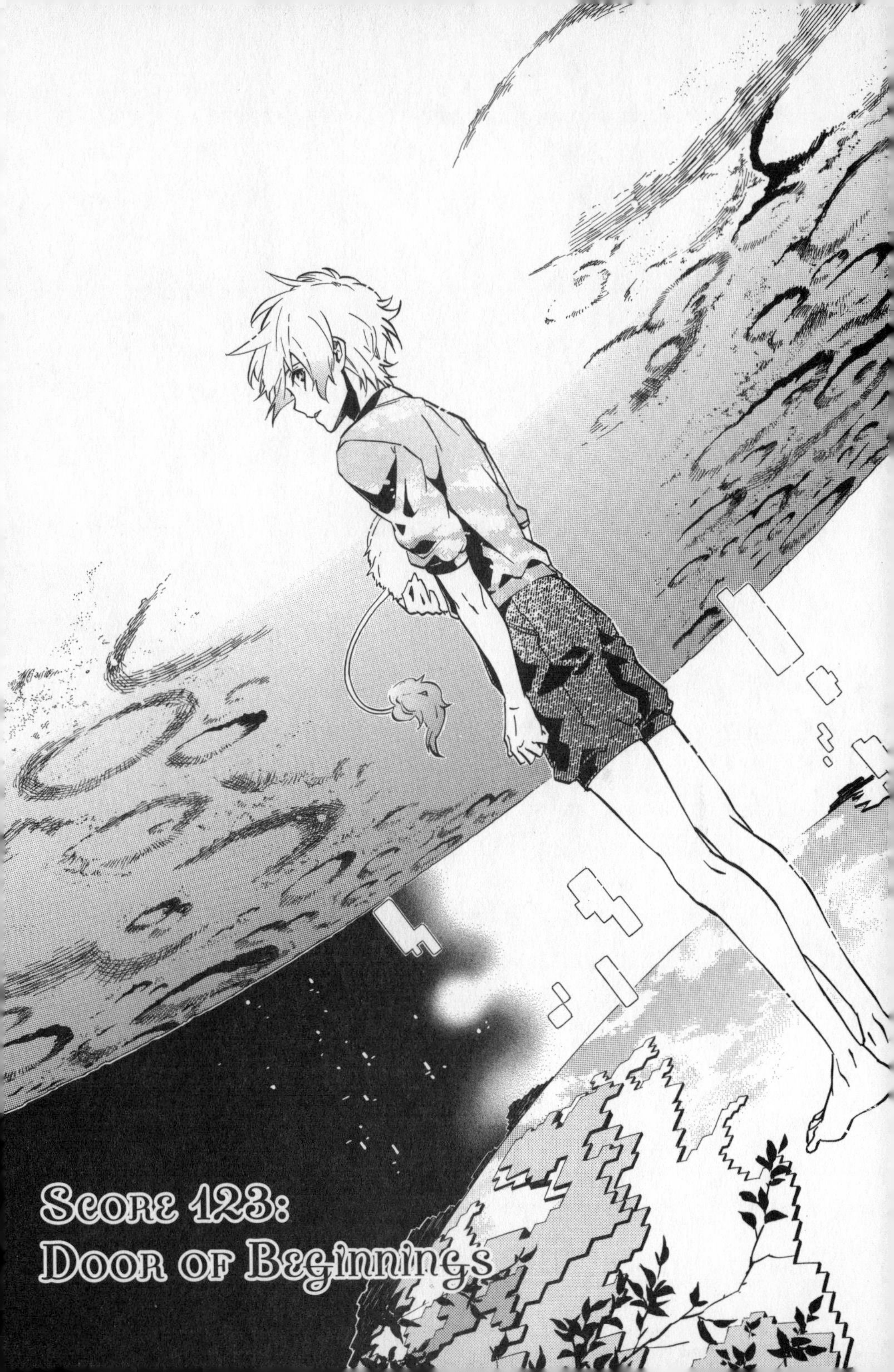
Score 123:
Door of Beginnings

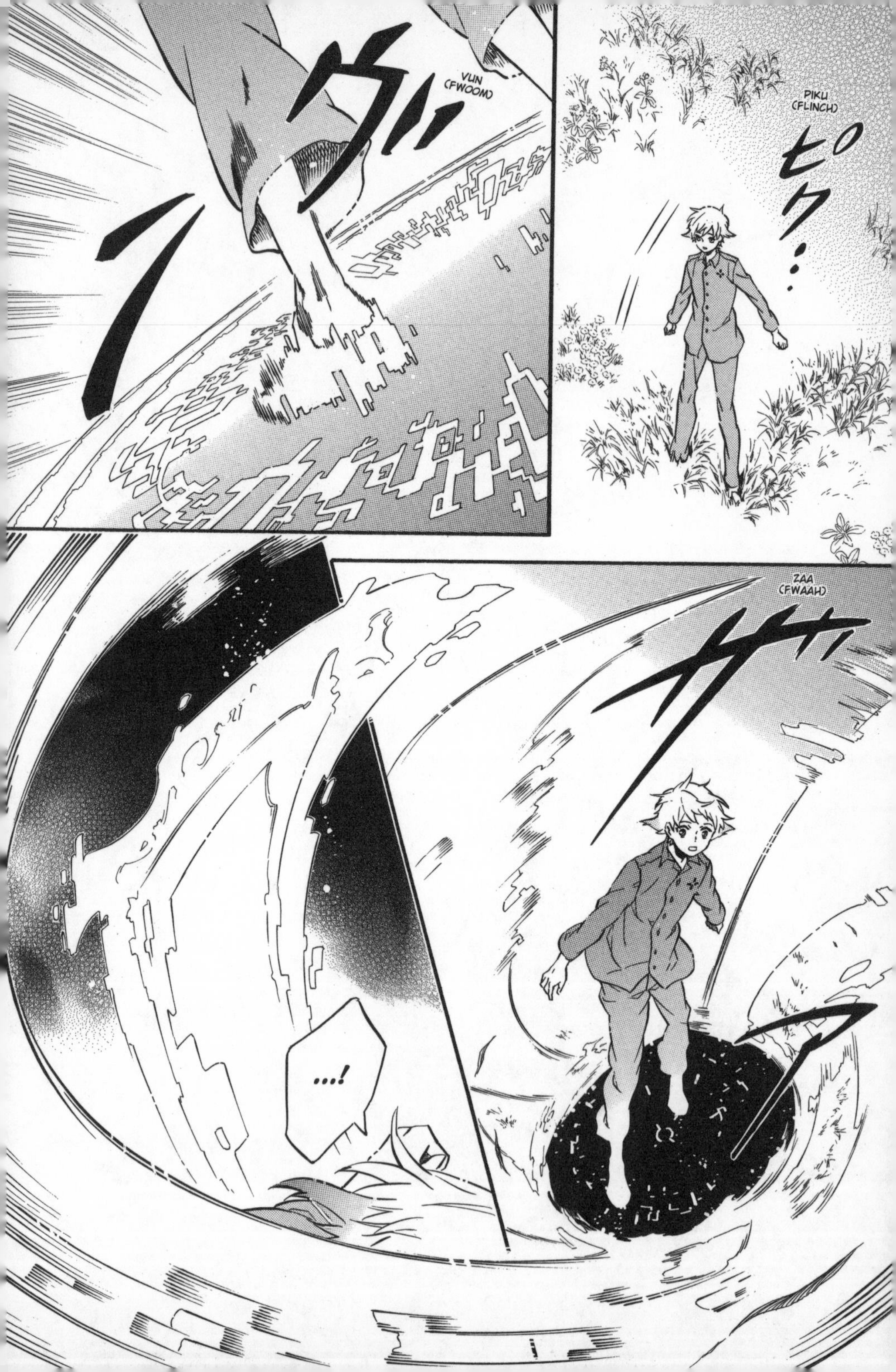
PIKU (FLINCH)
VUN (FWOOM)
ZAA (FWAAH)
...!

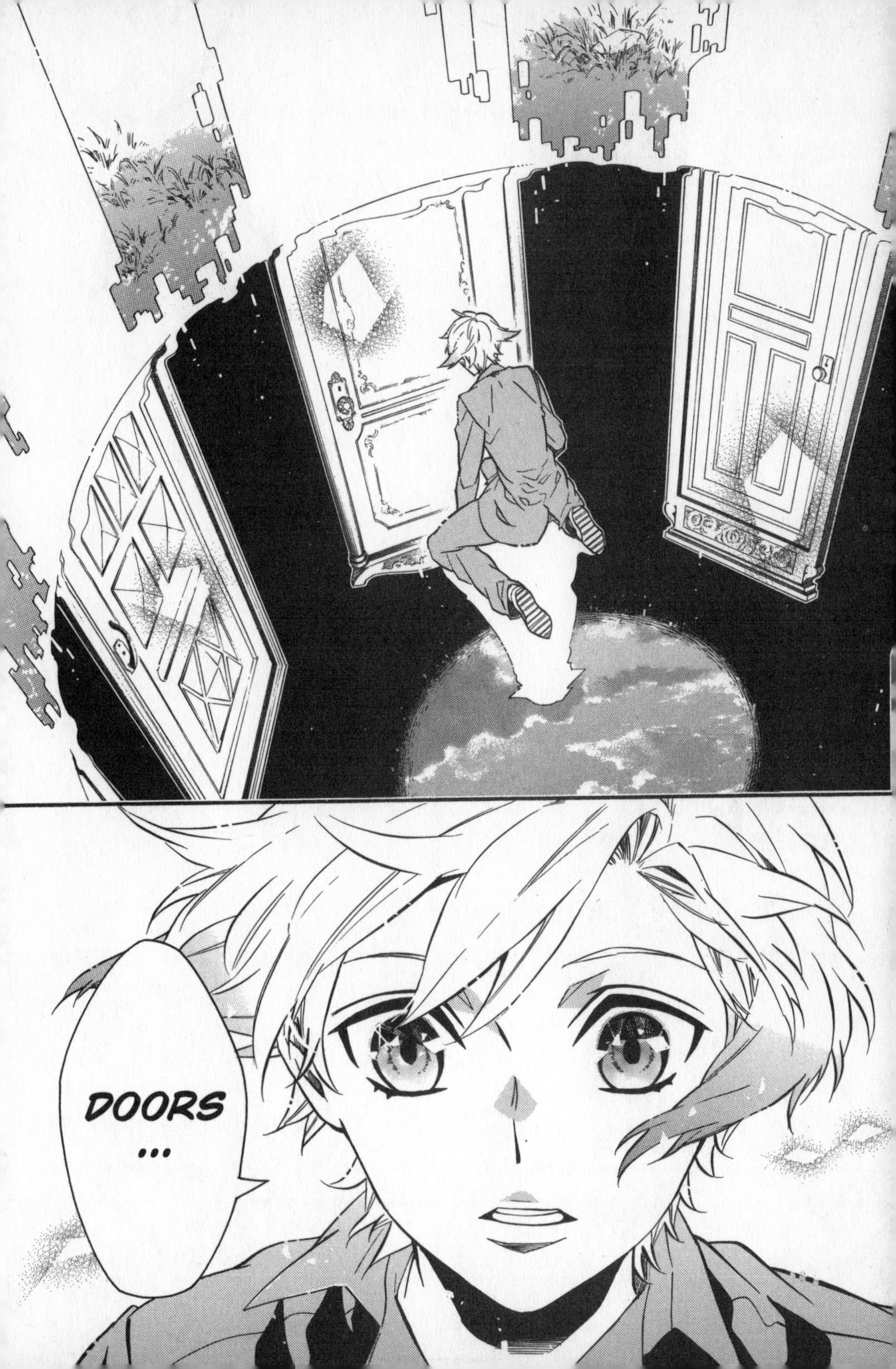
DOORS
...

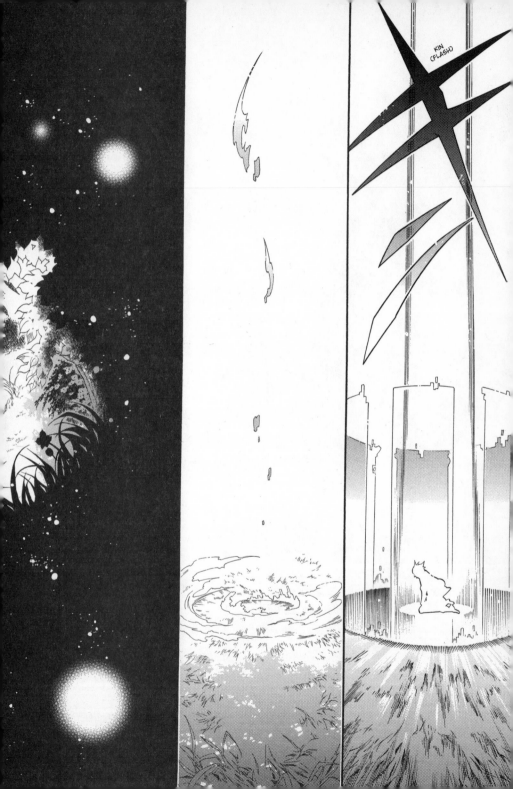

KIN
(FLASH)

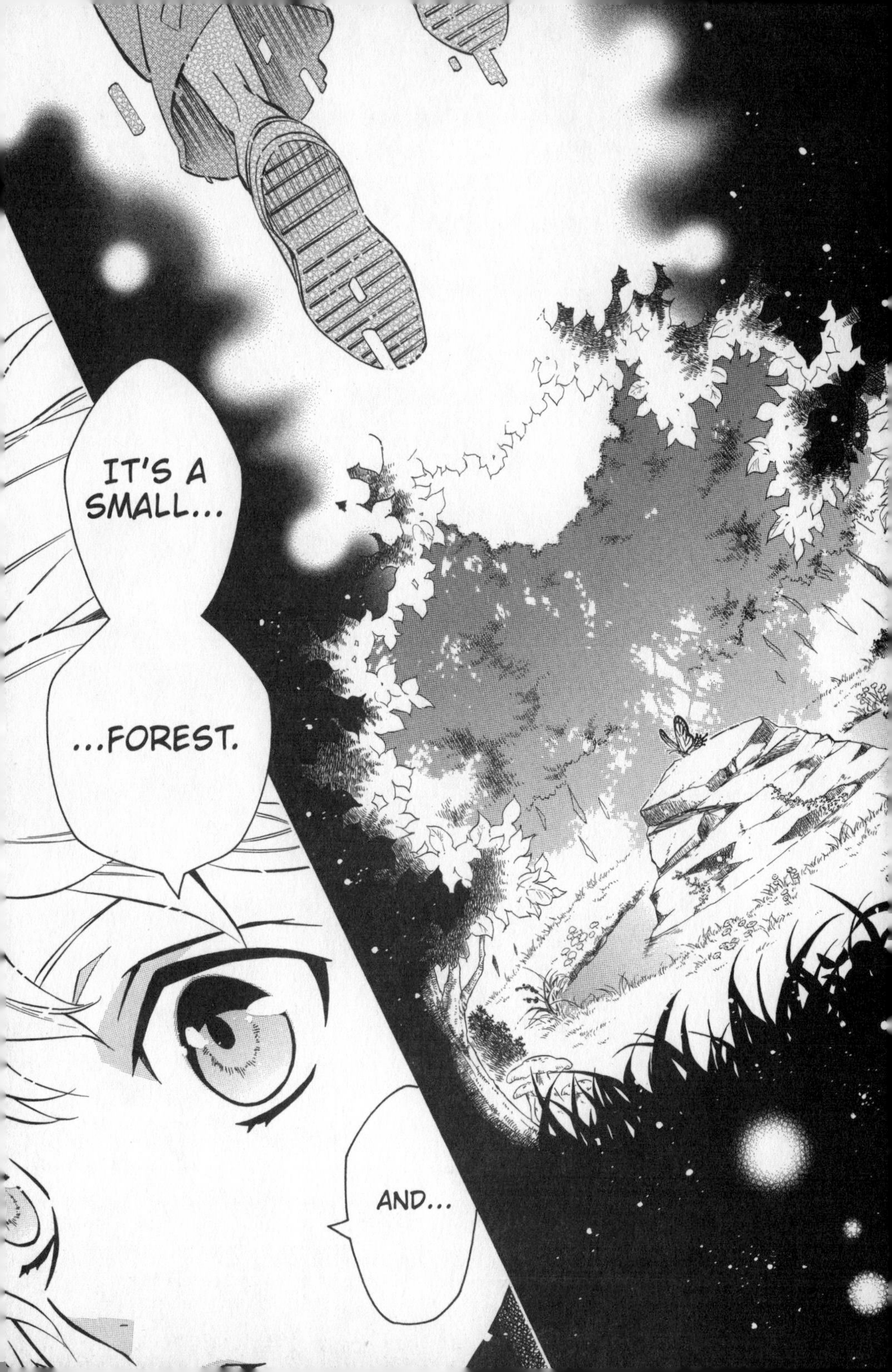
IT'S A SMALL...
...FOREST.
AND...

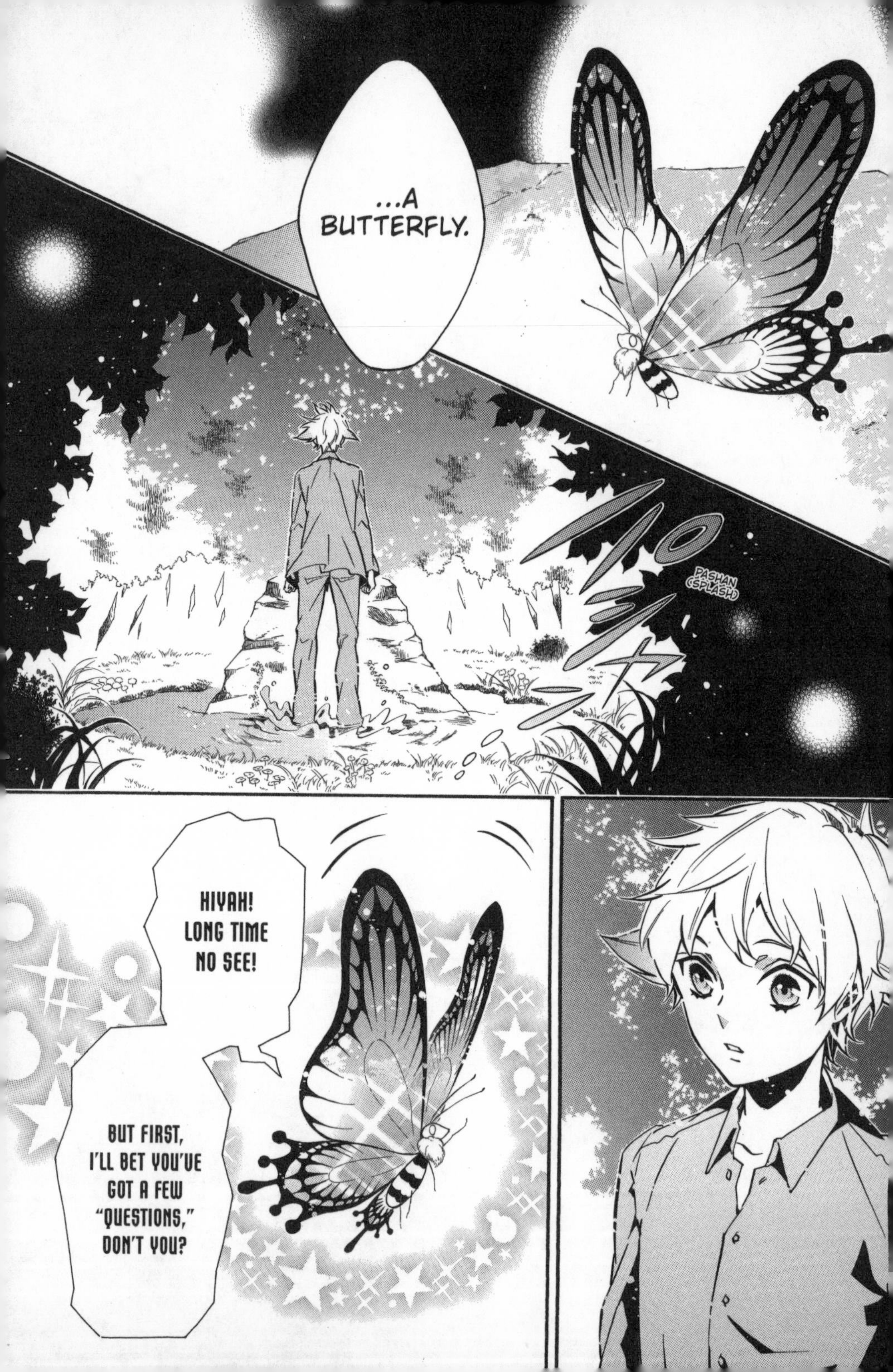
...A BUTTERFLY.
PASHAN (SPLASH)
HIYAH! LONG TIME NO SEE!
BUT FIRST, I'LL BET YOU'VE GOT A FEW "QUESTIONS," DON'T YOU?

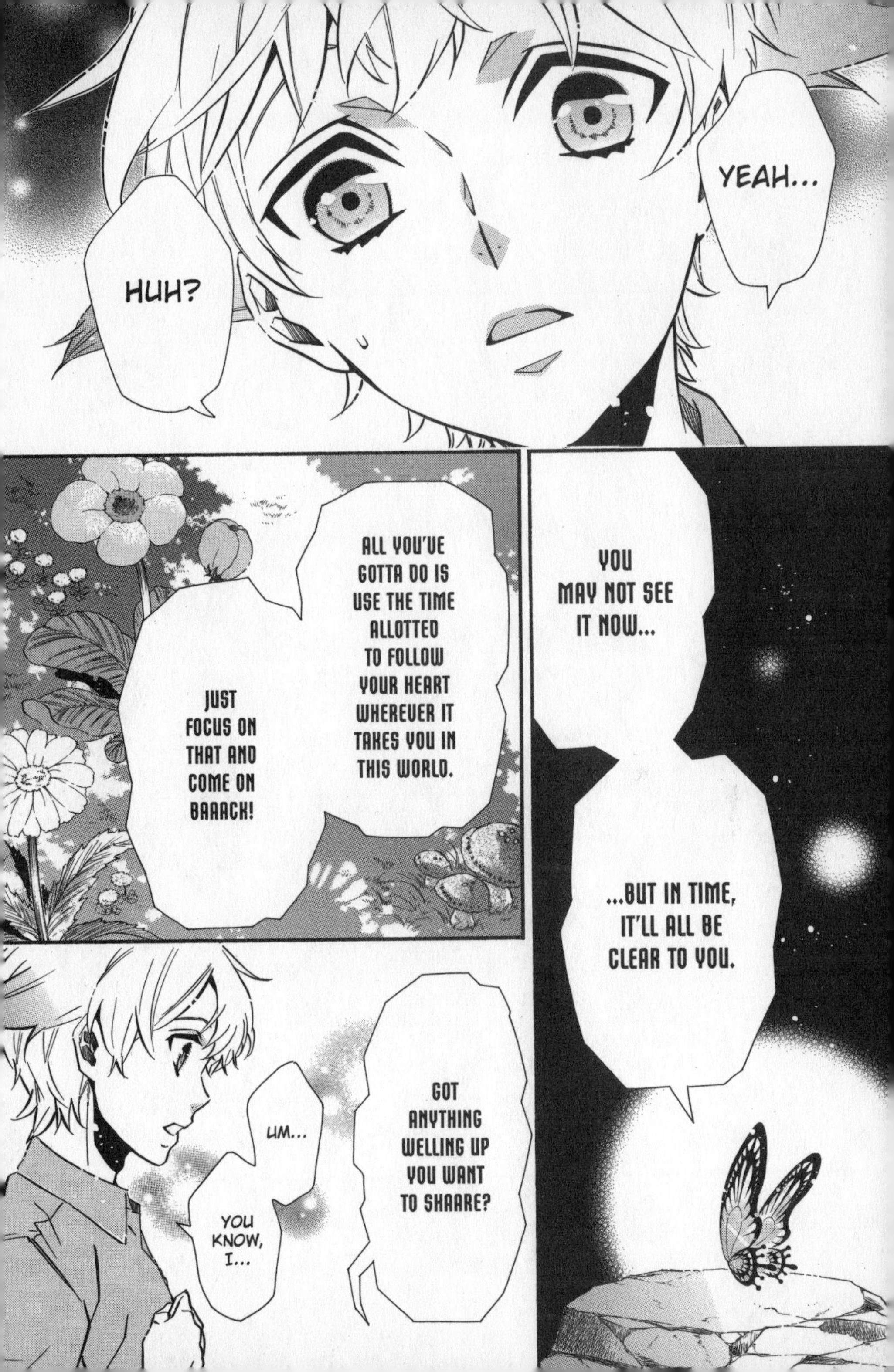
YEAH...
HUH?
YOU MAY NOT SEE IT NOW...
...BUT IN TIME, IT'LL ALL BE CLEAR TO YOU.
ALL YOU'VE GOTTA DO IS USE THE TIME ALLOTTED TO FOLLOW YOUR HEART WHEREVER IT TAKES YOU IN THIS WORLD.
JUST FOCUS ON THAT AND COME ON BAAACK!
GOT ANYTHING WELLING UP YOU WANT TO SHAARE?
UM...
YOU KNOW, I...

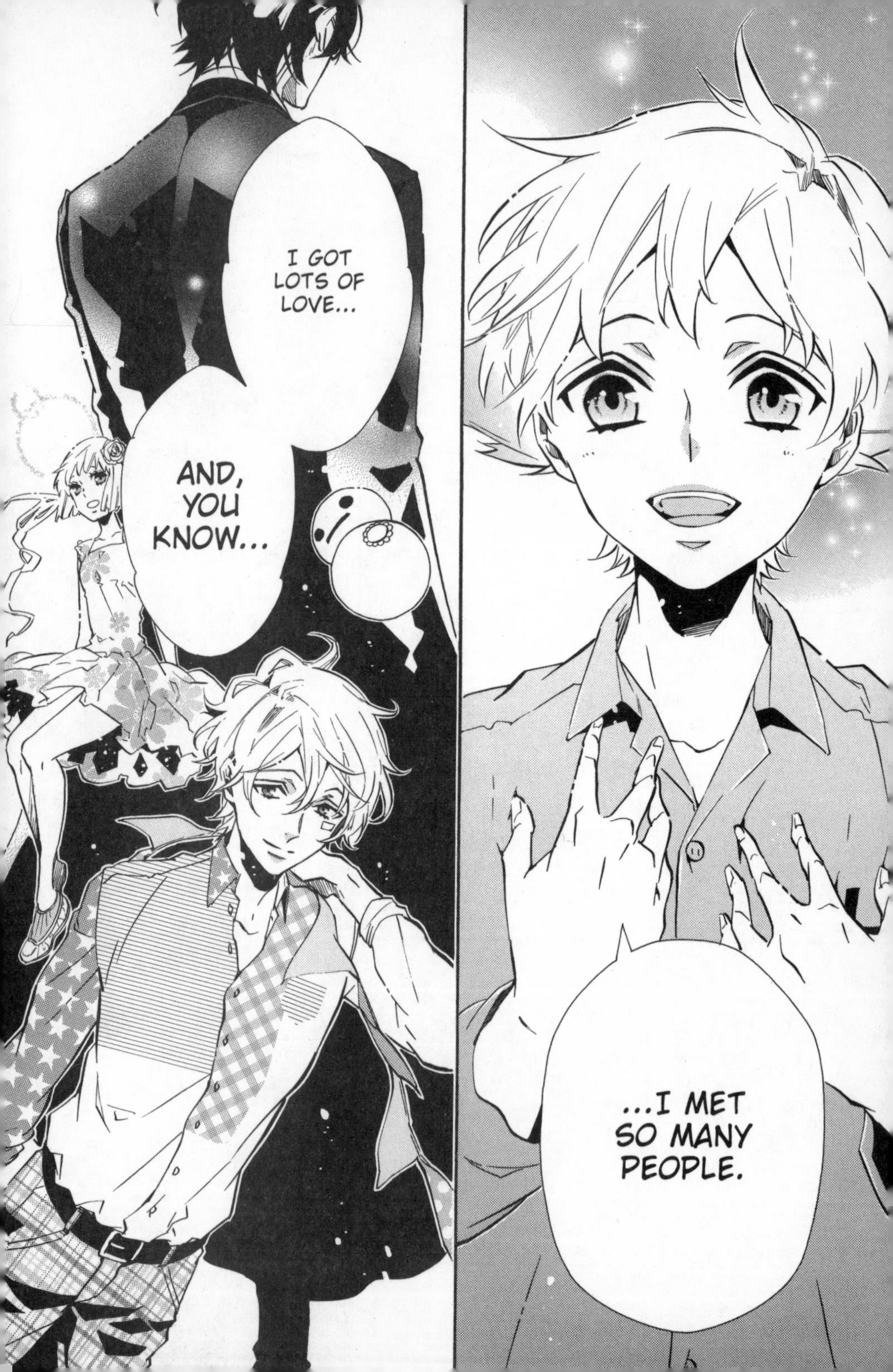
I GOT LOTS OF LOVE...
AND, YOU KNOW...
...I MET SO MANY PEOPLE.

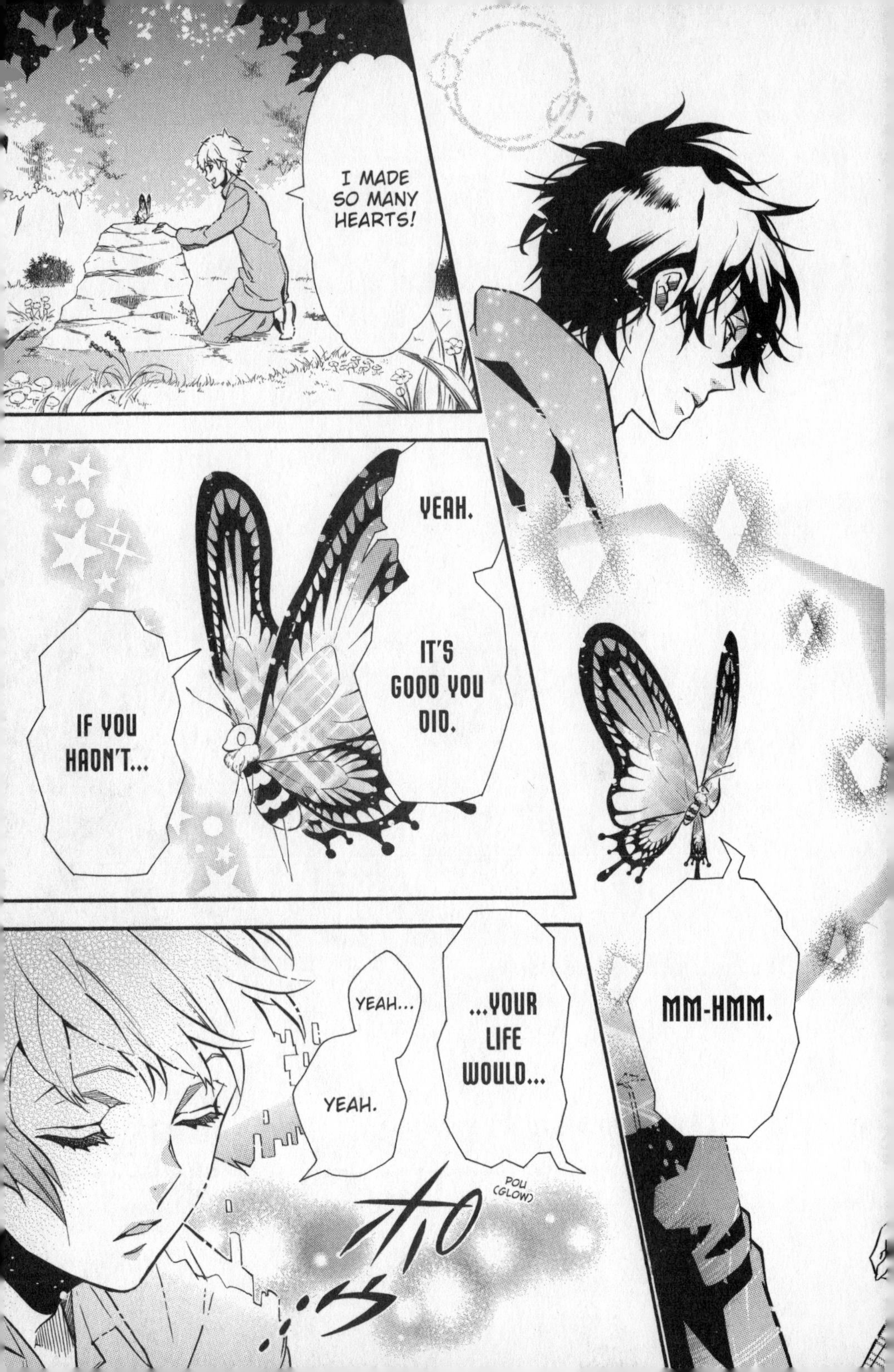
MM-HMM.
I MADE SO MANY HEARTS!
YEAH.
IT'S GOOD YOU DID.
IF YOU HADN'T...
...YOUR LIFE WOULD...
YEAH...
YEAH.
POU (GLOW)

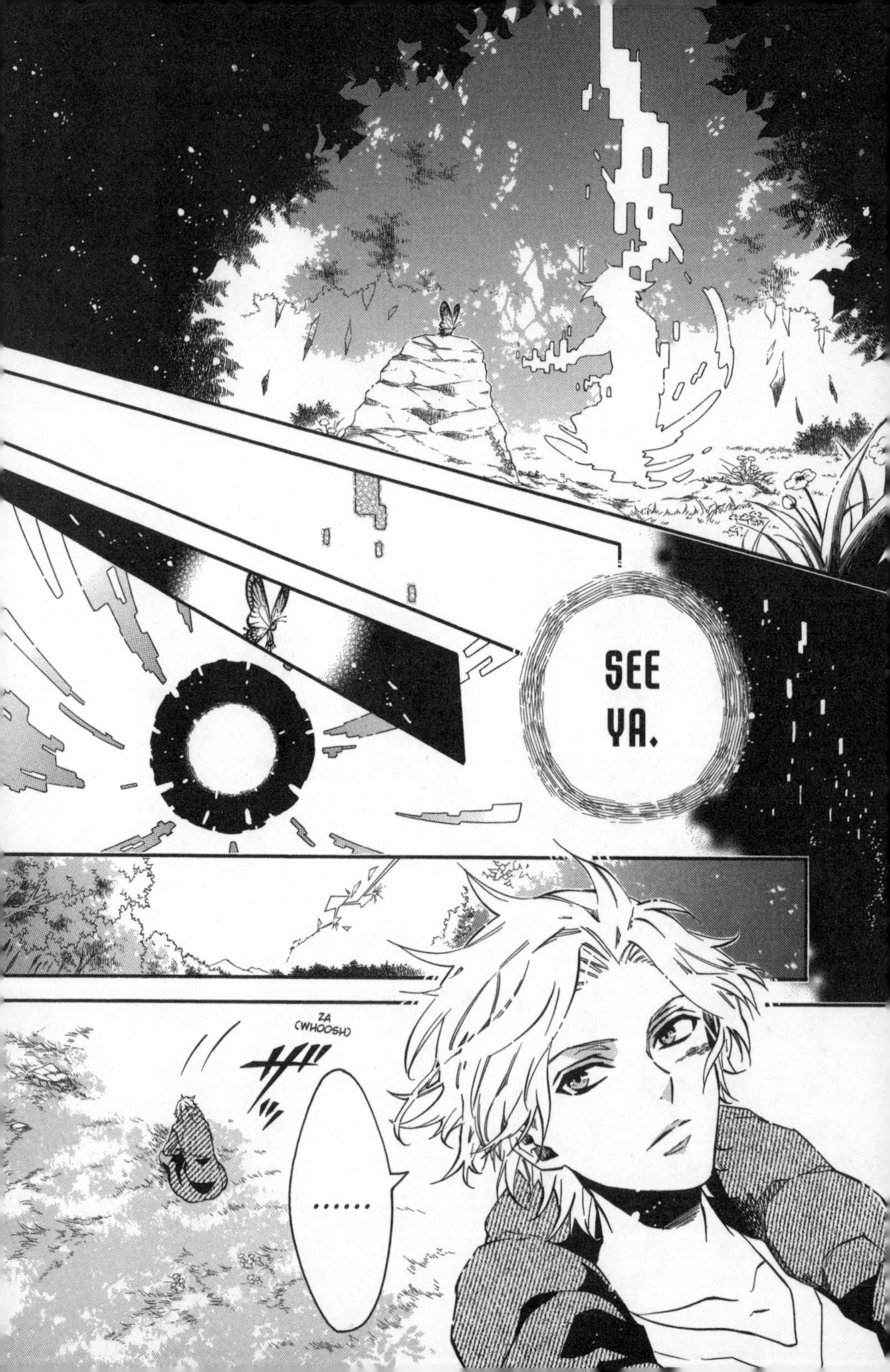
SEE YA.
ZA (WHOOSH)
......

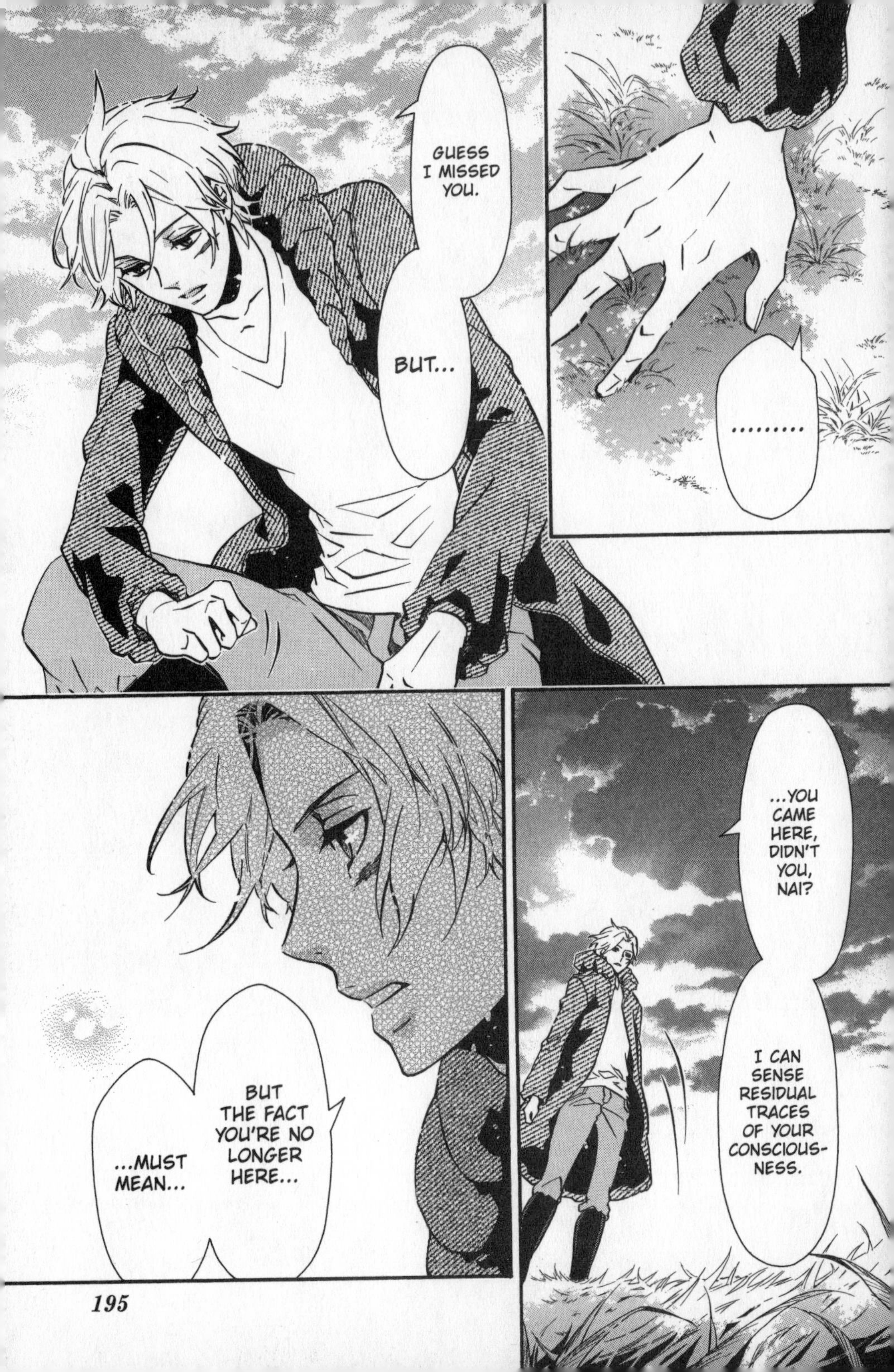
.........
GUESS I MISSED YOU.
BUT...
...YOU CAME HERE, DIDN'T YOU, NAI?
I CAN SENSE RESIDUAL TRACES OF YOUR CONSCIOUSNESS.
BUT THE FACT YOU'RE NO LONGER HERE...
...MUST MEAN...

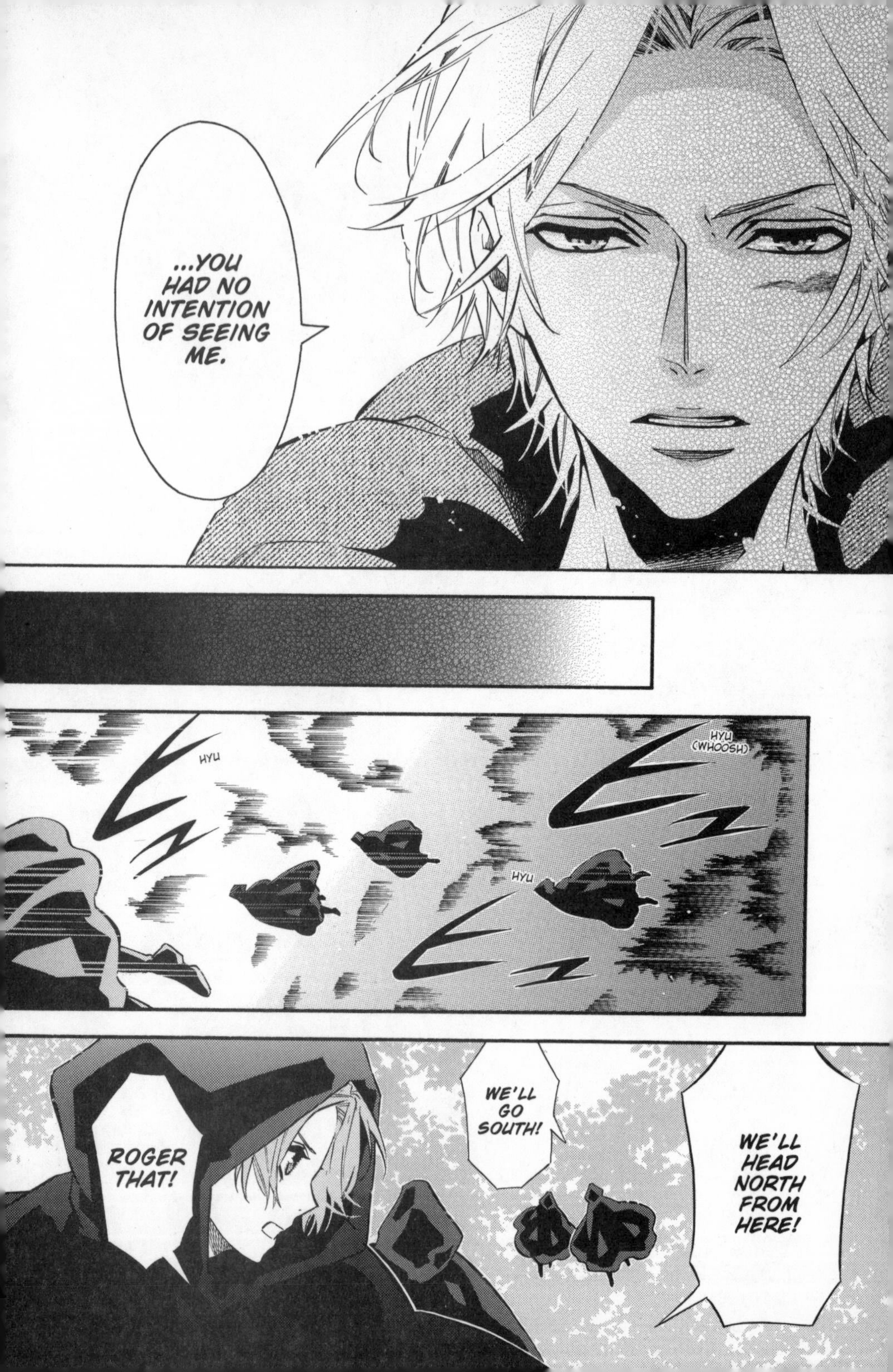
...YOU HAD NO INTENTION OF SEEING ME.
HYU (WHOOSH)
HYU
HYU
WE'LL HEAD NORTH FROM HERE!
WE'LL GO SOUTH!
ROGER THAT!

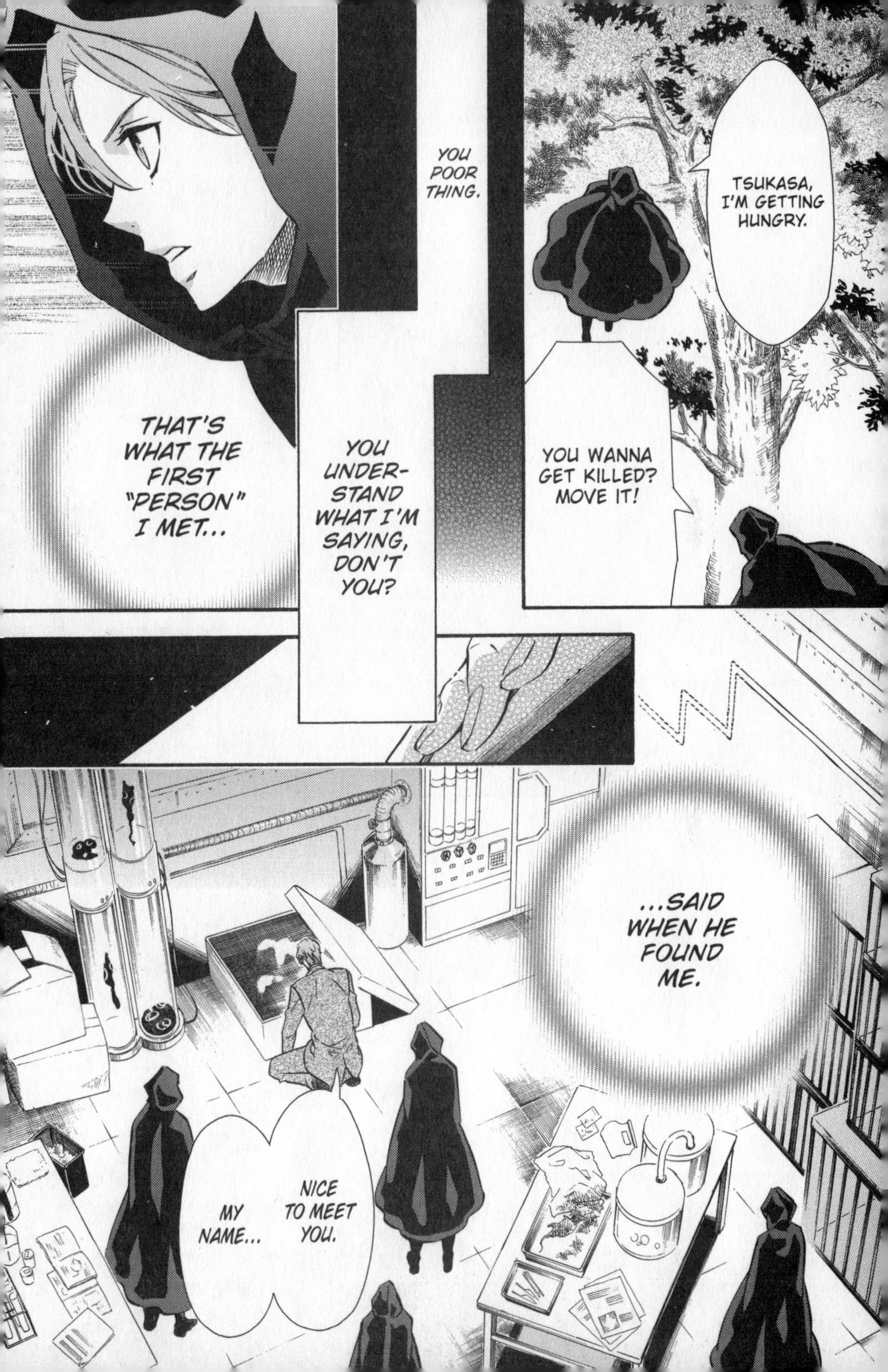
TSUKASA, I'M GETTING HUNGRY.
YOU WANNA GET KILLED? MOVE IT!
YOU POOR THING.
YOU UNDER-STAND WHAT I'M SAYING, DON'T YOU?
THAT'S WHAT THE FIRST "PERSON" I MET...
...SAID WHEN HE FOUND ME.
NICE TO MEET YOU.
MY NAME...

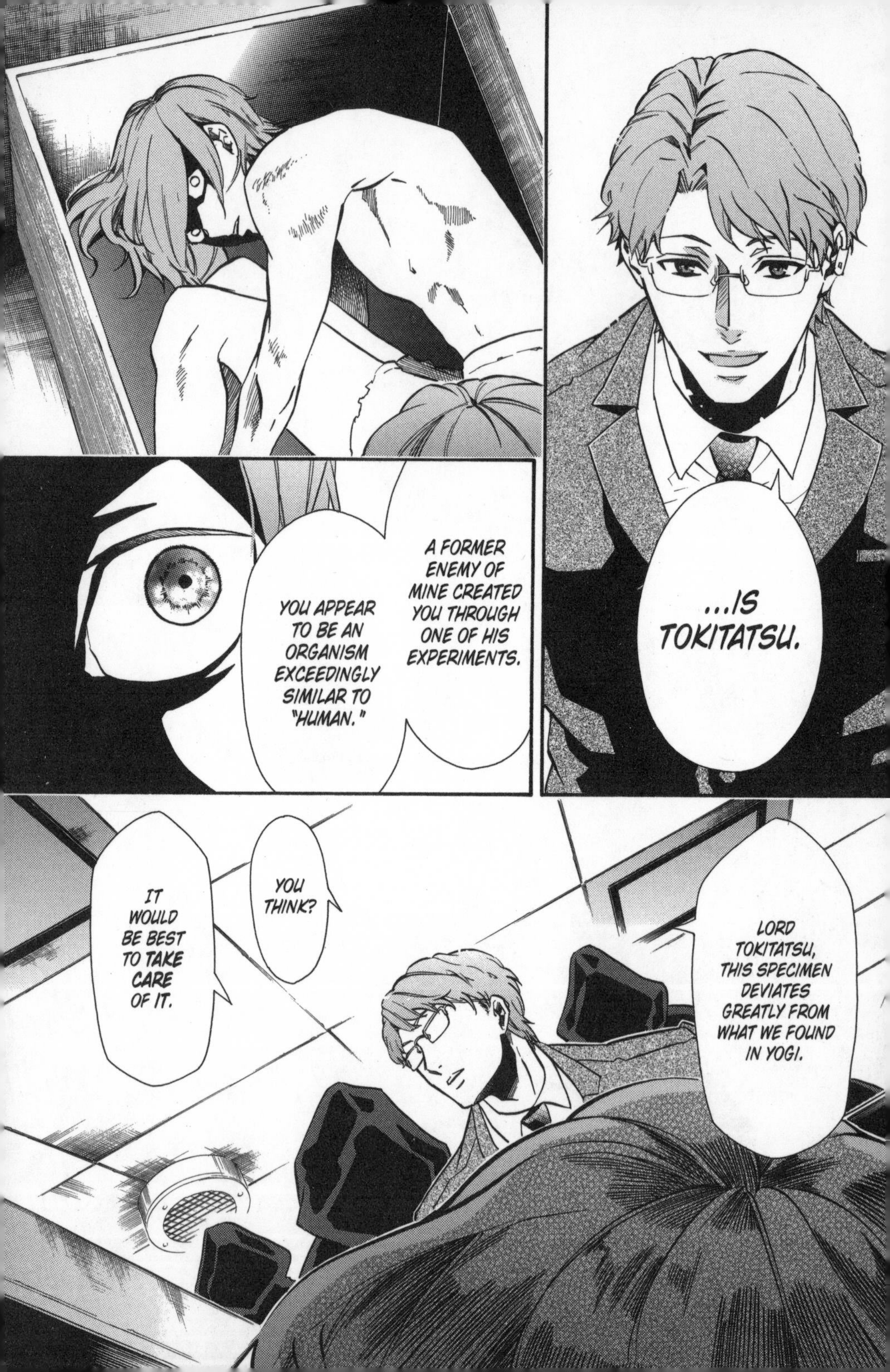
...IS TOKITATSU.
A FORMER ENEMY OF MINE CREATED YOU THROUGH ONE OF HIS EXPERIMENTS.
YOU APPEAR TO BE AN ORGANISM EXCEEDINGLY SIMILAR TO "HUMAN."
LORD TOKITATSU, THIS SPECIMEN DEVIATES GREATLY FROM WHAT WE FOUND IN YOGI.
YOU THINK?
IT WOULD BE BEST TO TAKE CARE OF IT.

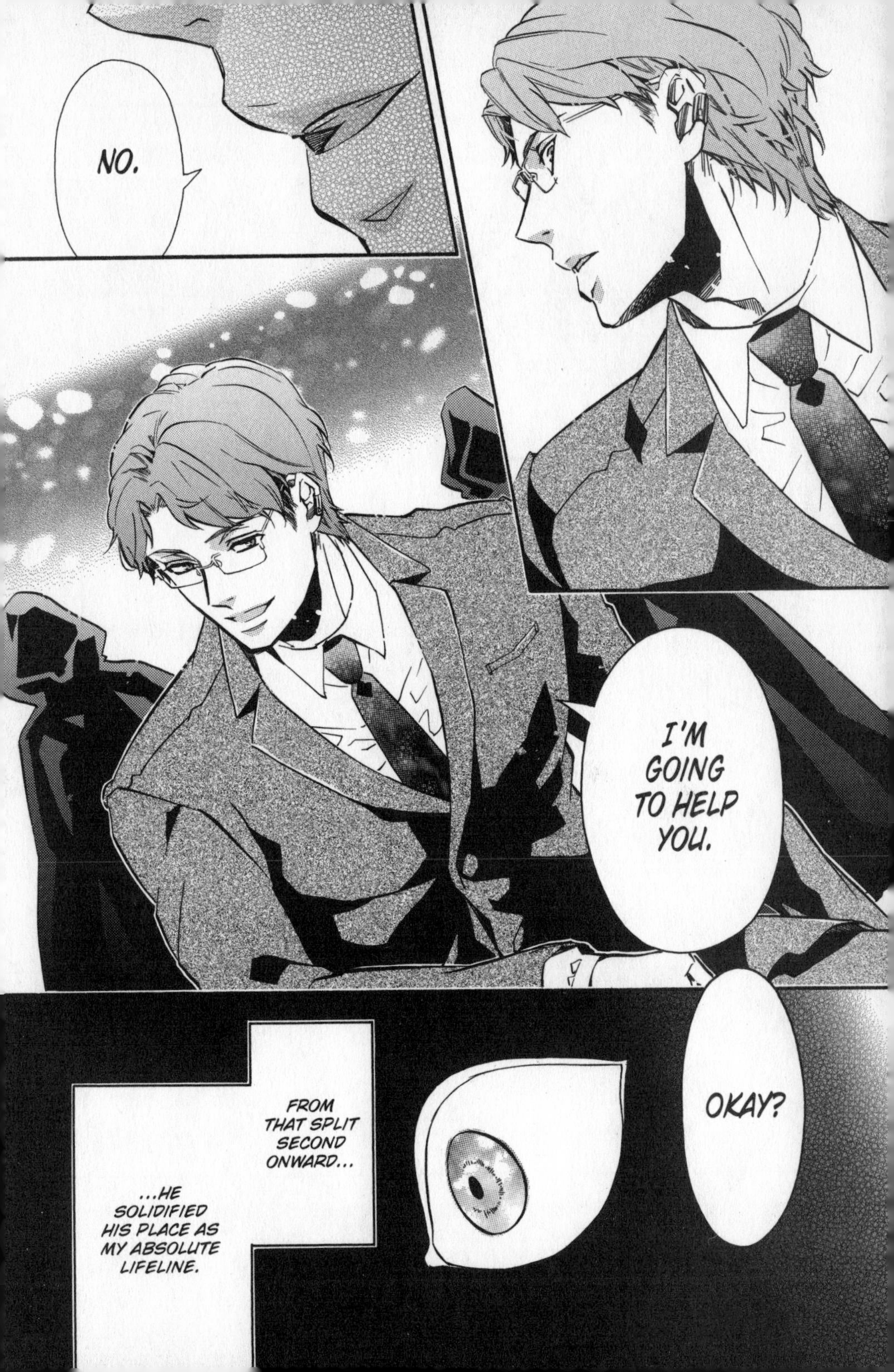
NO.
I'M GOING TO HELP YOU.
OKAY?
FROM THAT SPLIT SECOND ONWARD...
...HE SOLIDIFIED HIS PLACE AS MY ABSOLUTE LIFELINE.

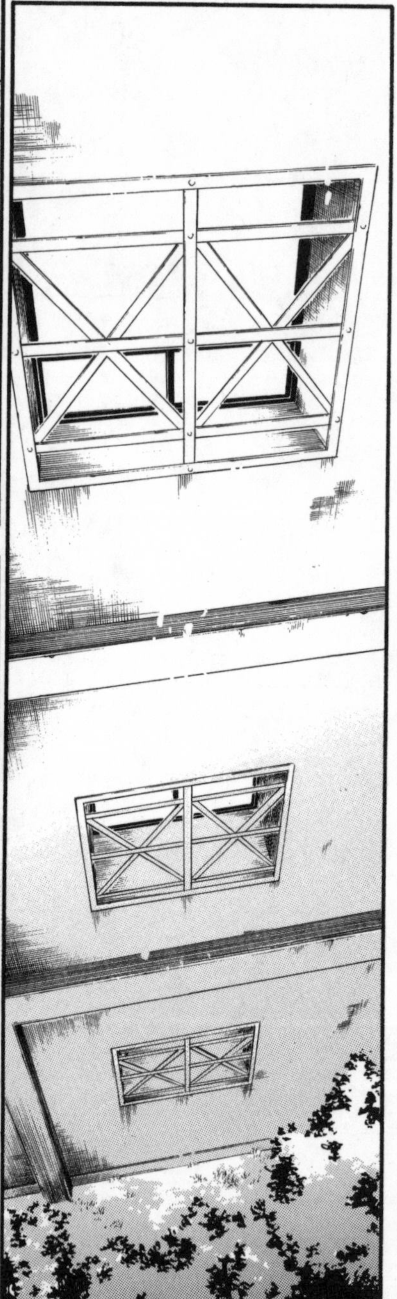

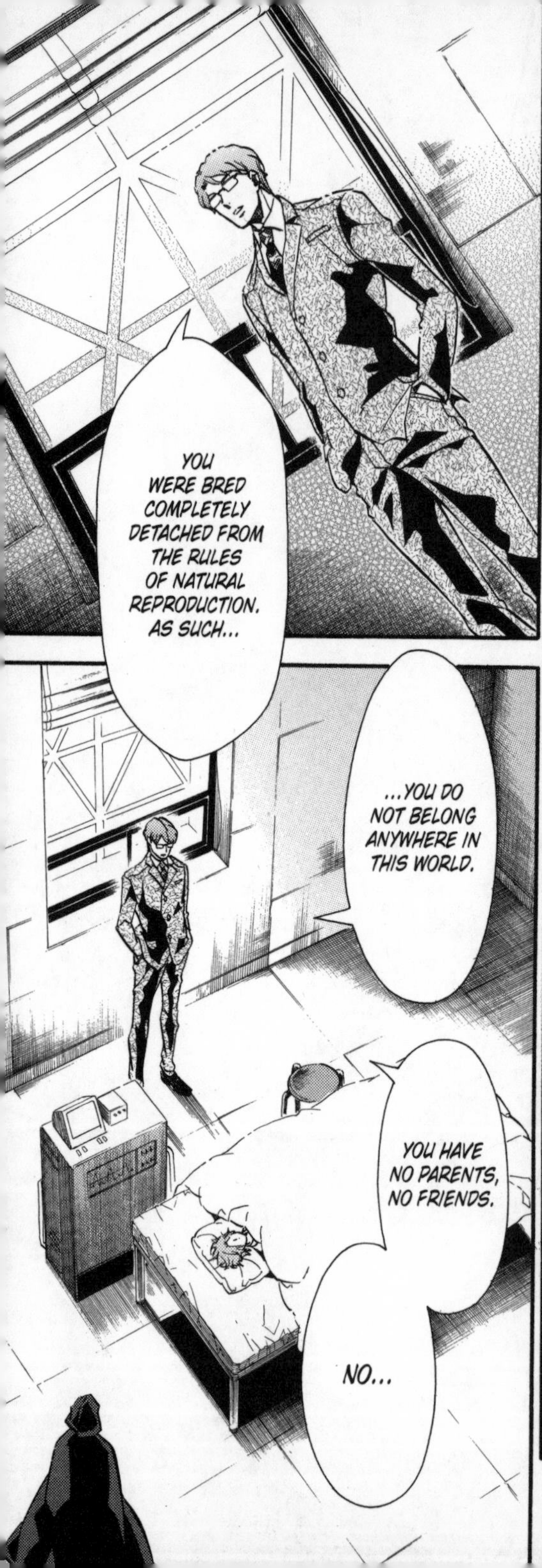
YOU WERE BRED COMPLETELY DETACHED FROM THE RULES OF NATURAL REPRODUCTION. AS SUCH...
...YOU DO NOT BELONG ANYWHERE IN THIS WORLD.
YOU HAVE NO PARENTS, NO FRIENDS.
NO...

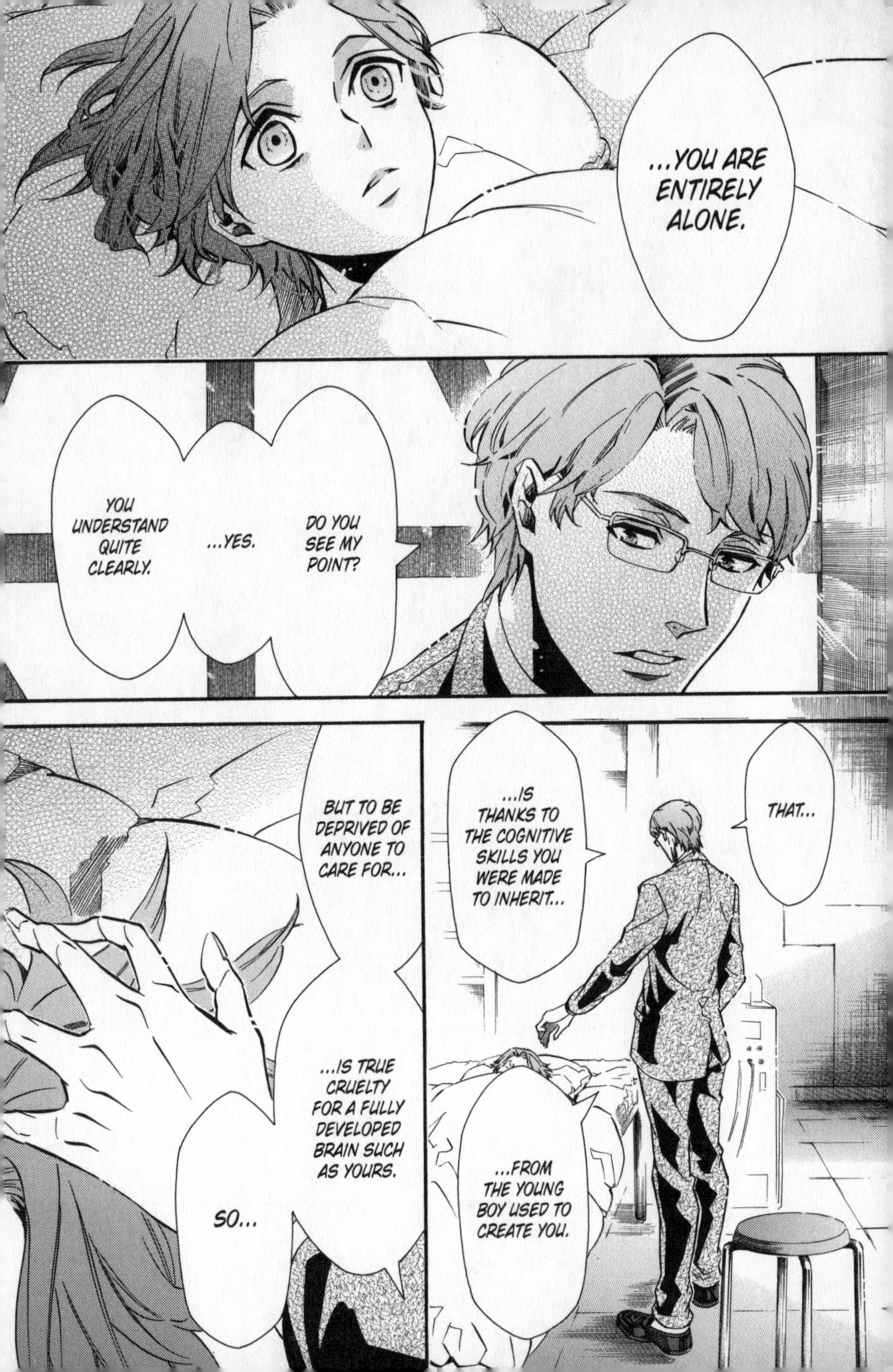
...YOU ARE ENTIRELY ALONE.
DO YOU SEE MY POINT?
...YES.
YOU UNDERSTAND QUITE CLEARLY.
THAT...
...IS THANKS TO THE COGNITIVE SKILLS YOU WERE MADE TO INHERIT...
...FROM THE YOUNG BOY USED TO CREATE YOU.
BUT TO BE DEPRIVED OF ANYONE TO CARE FOR...
...IS TRUE CRUELTY FOR A FULLY DEVELOPED BRAIN SUCH AS YOURS.
SO...

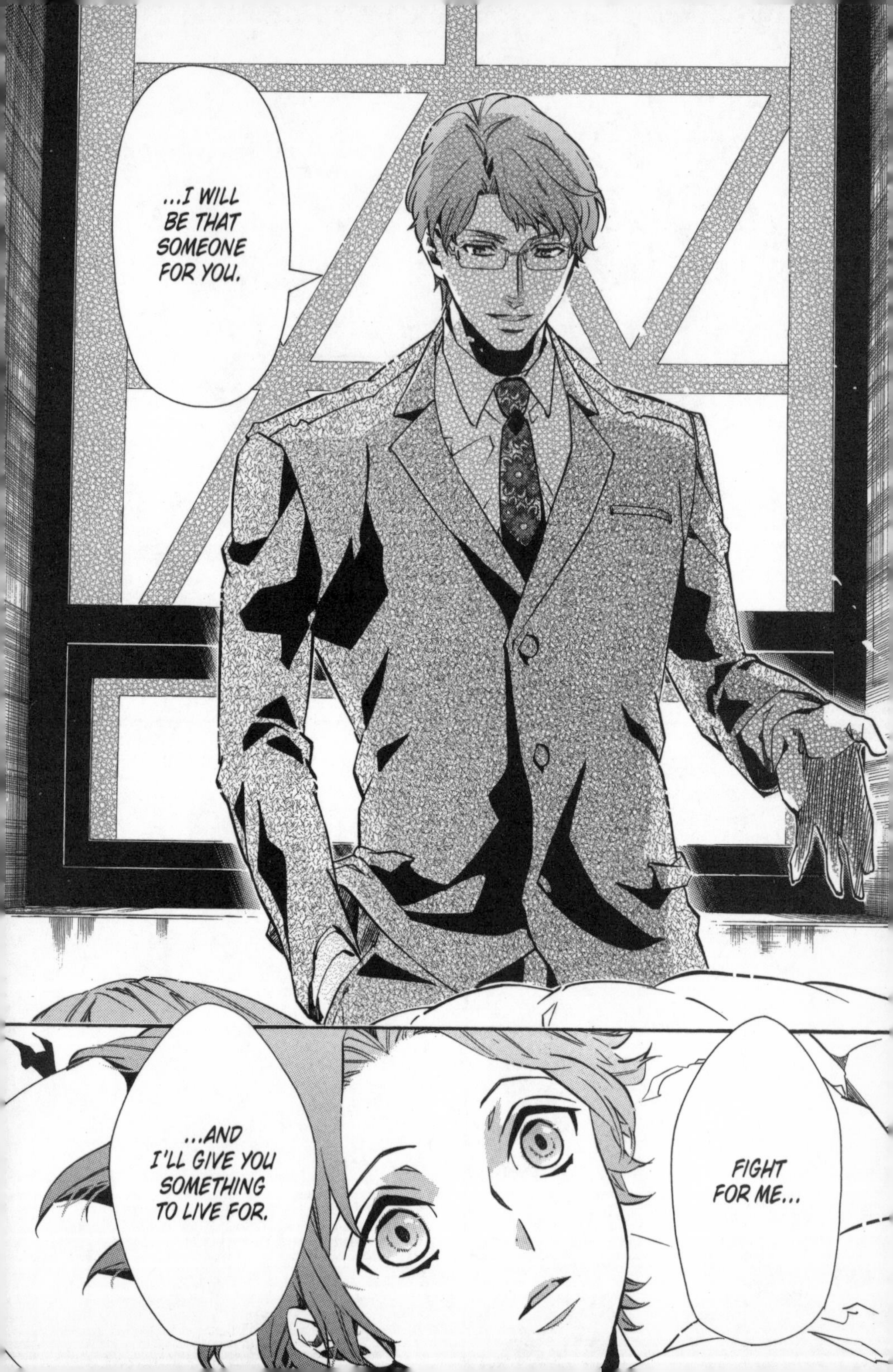
...I WILL BE THAT SOMEONE FOR YOU.
FIGHT FOR ME...
...AND I'LL GIVE YOU SOMETHING TO LIVE FOR.

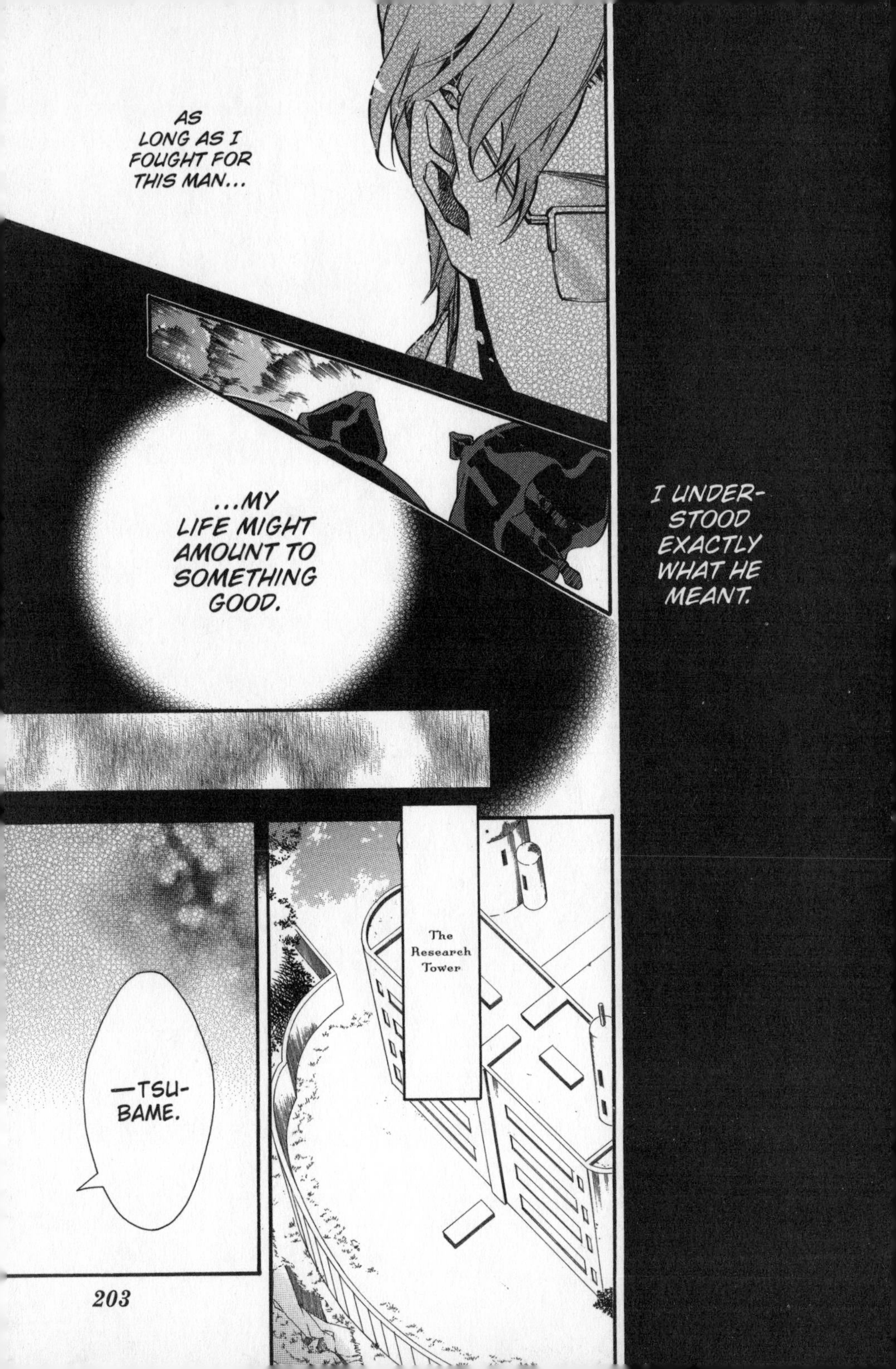
I UNDER-STOOD EXACTLY WHAT HE MEANT.
AS LONG AS I FOUGHT FOR THIS MAN...
...MY LIFE MIGHT AMOUNT TO SOMETHING GOOD.
The Research Tower
—TSU-BAME.

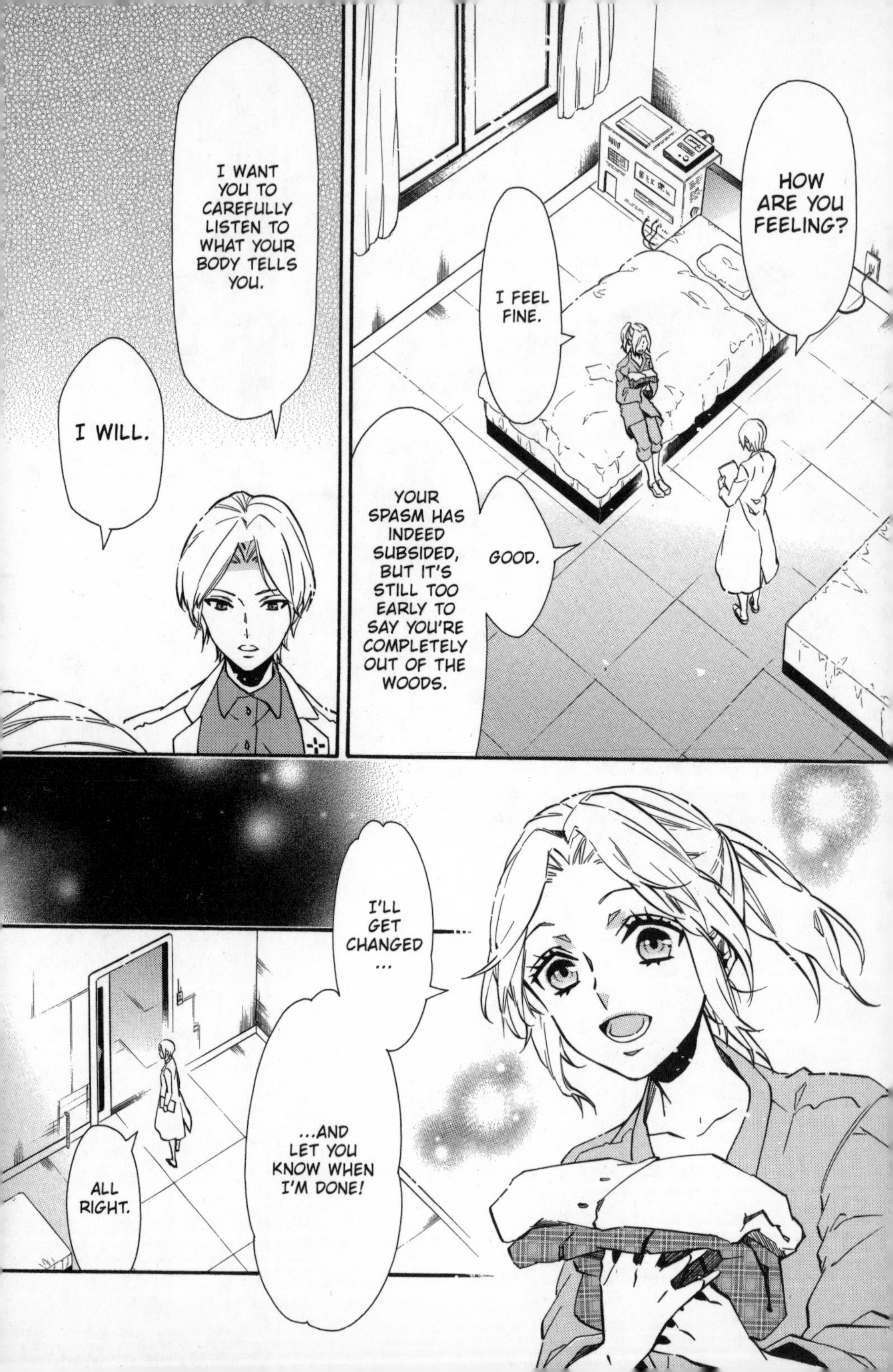
HOW ARE YOU FEELING?
I FEEL FINE.
GOOD.
YOUR SPASM HAS INDEED SUBSIDED, BUT IT'S STILL TOO EARLY TO SAY YOU'RE COMPLETELY OUT OF THE WOODS.
I WANT YOU TO CAREFULLY LISTEN TO WHAT YOUR BODY TELLS YOU.
I WILL.
I'LL GET CHANGED...
...AND LET YOU KNOW WHEN I'M DONE!
ALL RIGHT.

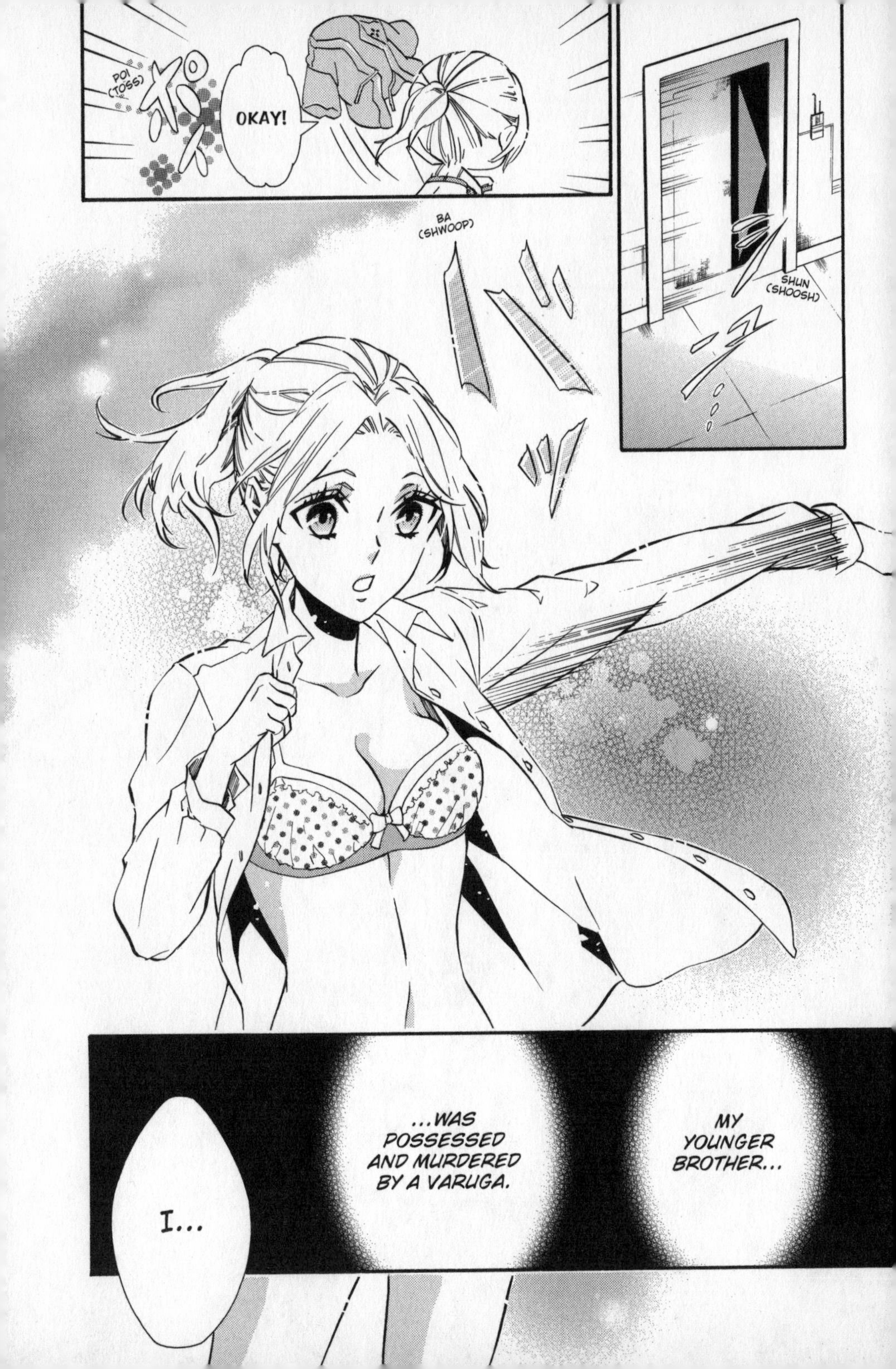
SHUN
(SHOOSH)
OKAY!
POI
(TOSS)
BA
(SHWOOP)
MY YOUNGER BROTHER...
...WAS POSSESSED AND MURDERED BY A VARUGA.
I...

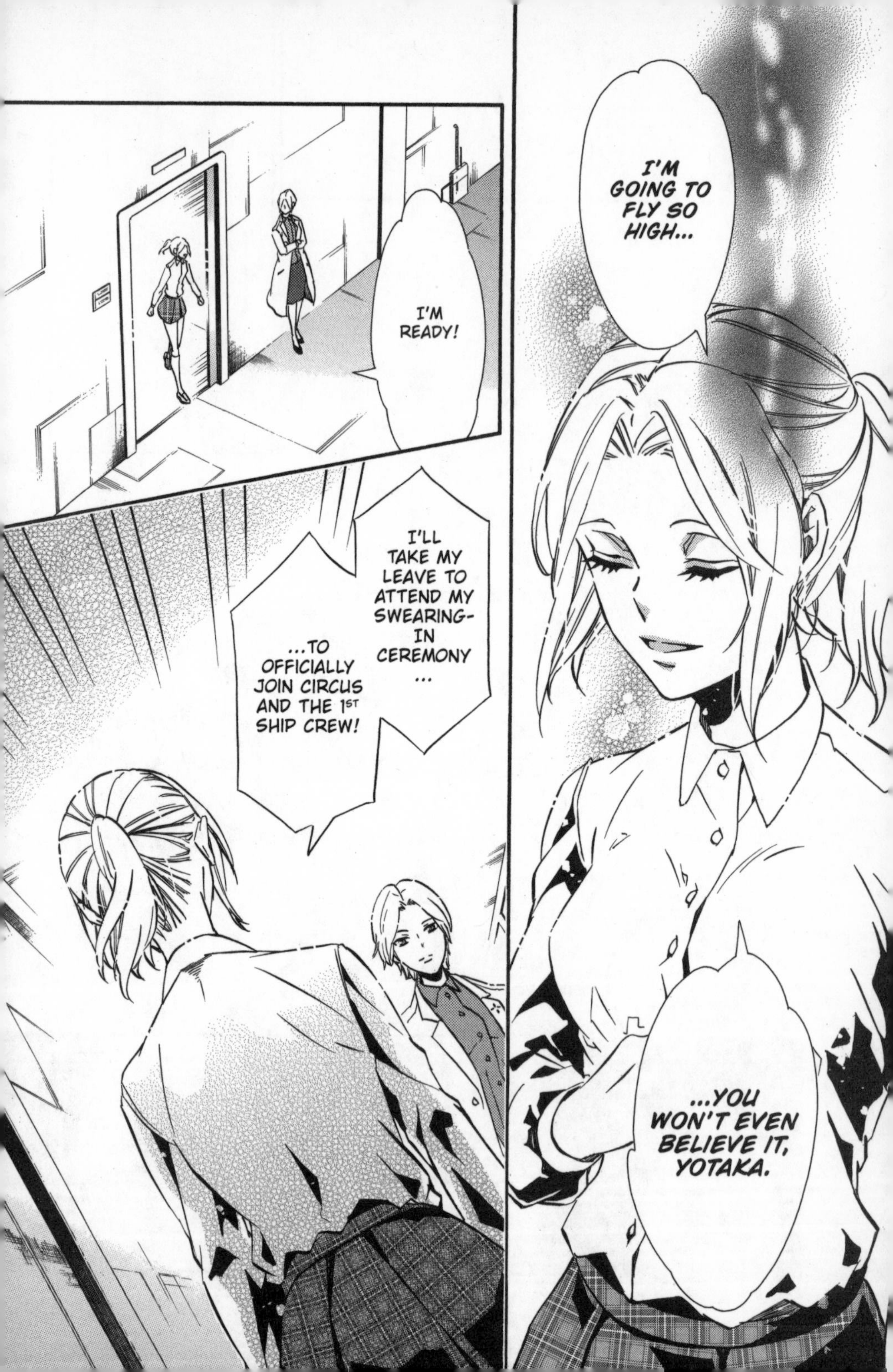
I'M GOING TO FLY SO HIGH...
...YOU WON'T EVEN BELIEVE IT, YOTAKA.
I'M READY!
I'LL TAKE MY LEAVE TO ATTEND MY SWEARING-IN CEREMONY...
...TO OFFICIALLY JOIN CIRCUS AND THE 1ST SHIP CREW!

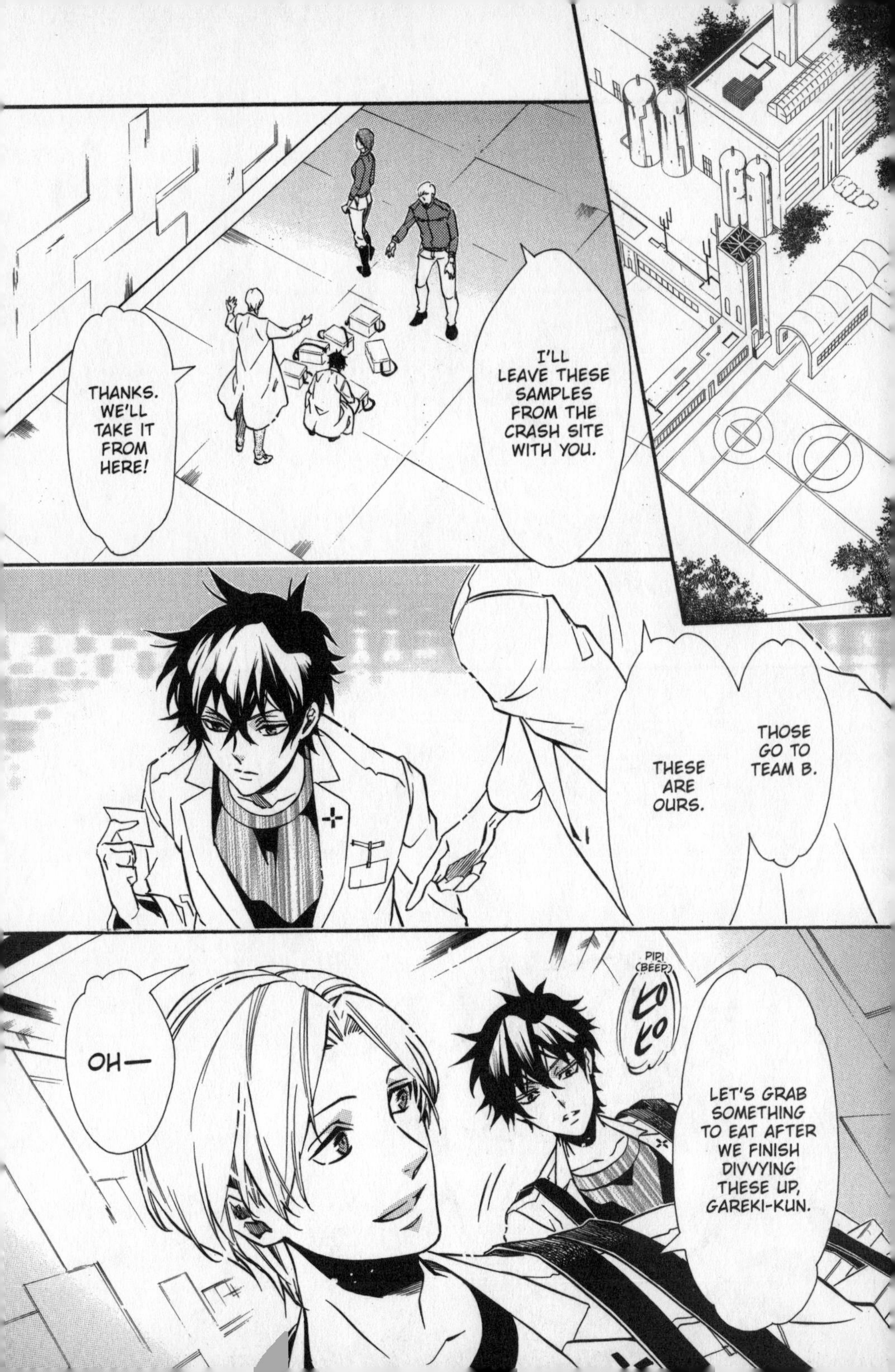
I'LL LEAVE THESE SAMPLES FROM THE CRASH SITE WITH YOU.
THANKS. WE'LL TAKE IT FROM HERE!
THOSE GO TO TEAM B.
THESE ARE OURS.
LET'S GRAB SOMETHING TO EAT AFTER WE FINISH DIVVYING THESE UP, GAREKI-KUN.
PIPI (BEEP)
ピピ
OH—

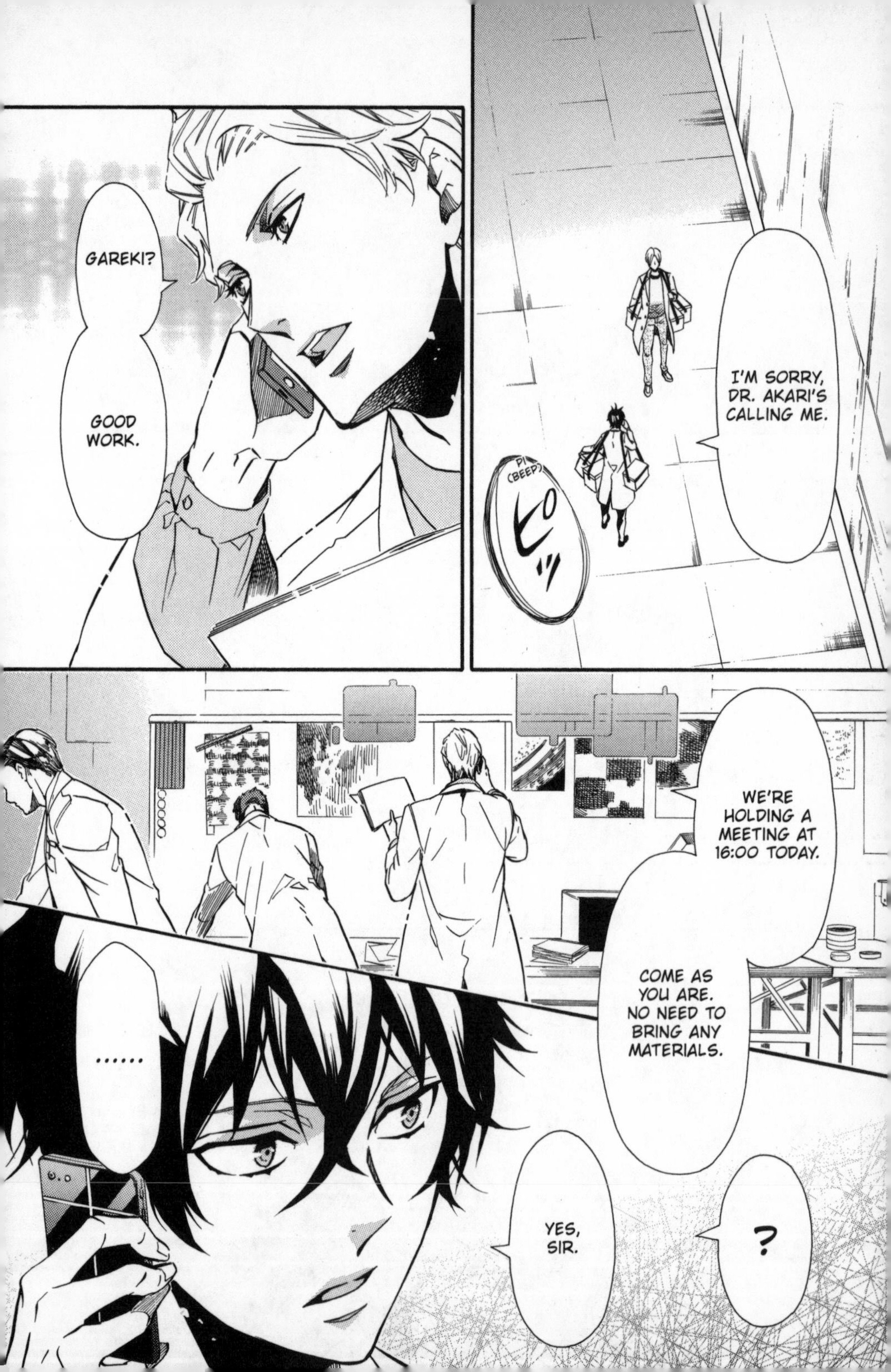
I'M SORRY, DR. AKARI'S CALLING ME.
PI (BEEP)
ピッ
GAREKI?
GOOD WORK.
WE'RE HOLDING A MEETING AT 16:00 TODAY.
COME AS YOU ARE. NO NEED TO BRING ANY MATERIALS.
......
YES, SIR.
?

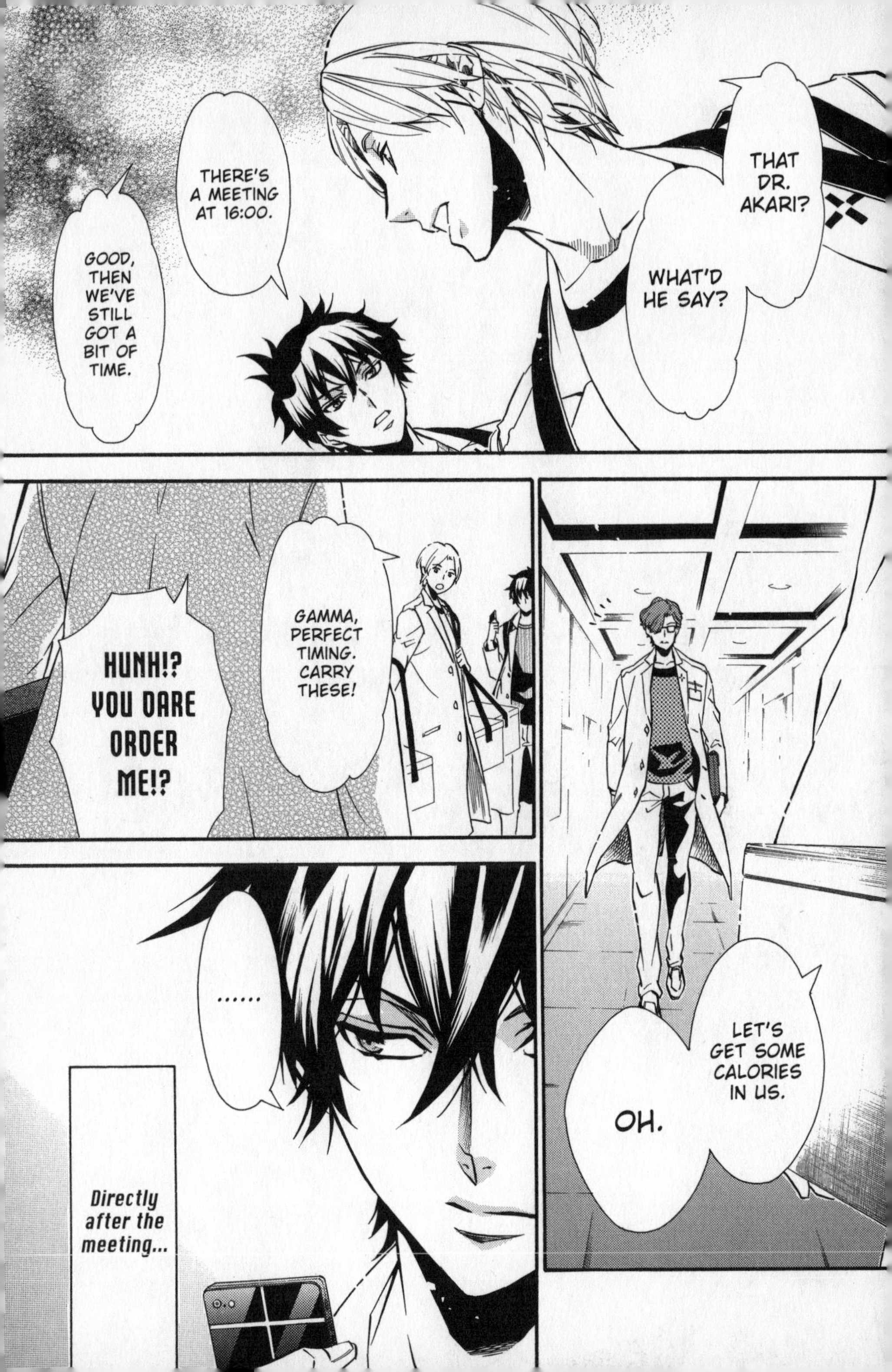
THAT DR. AKARI?
WHAT'D HE SAY?
THERE'S A MEETING AT 16:00.
GOOD, THEN WE'VE STILL GOT A BIT OF TIME.
LET'S GET SOME CALORIES IN US.
OH.
GAMMA, PERFECT TIMING. CARRY THESE!
HUNH!? YOU DARE ORDER ME!?
......
Directly after the meeting...

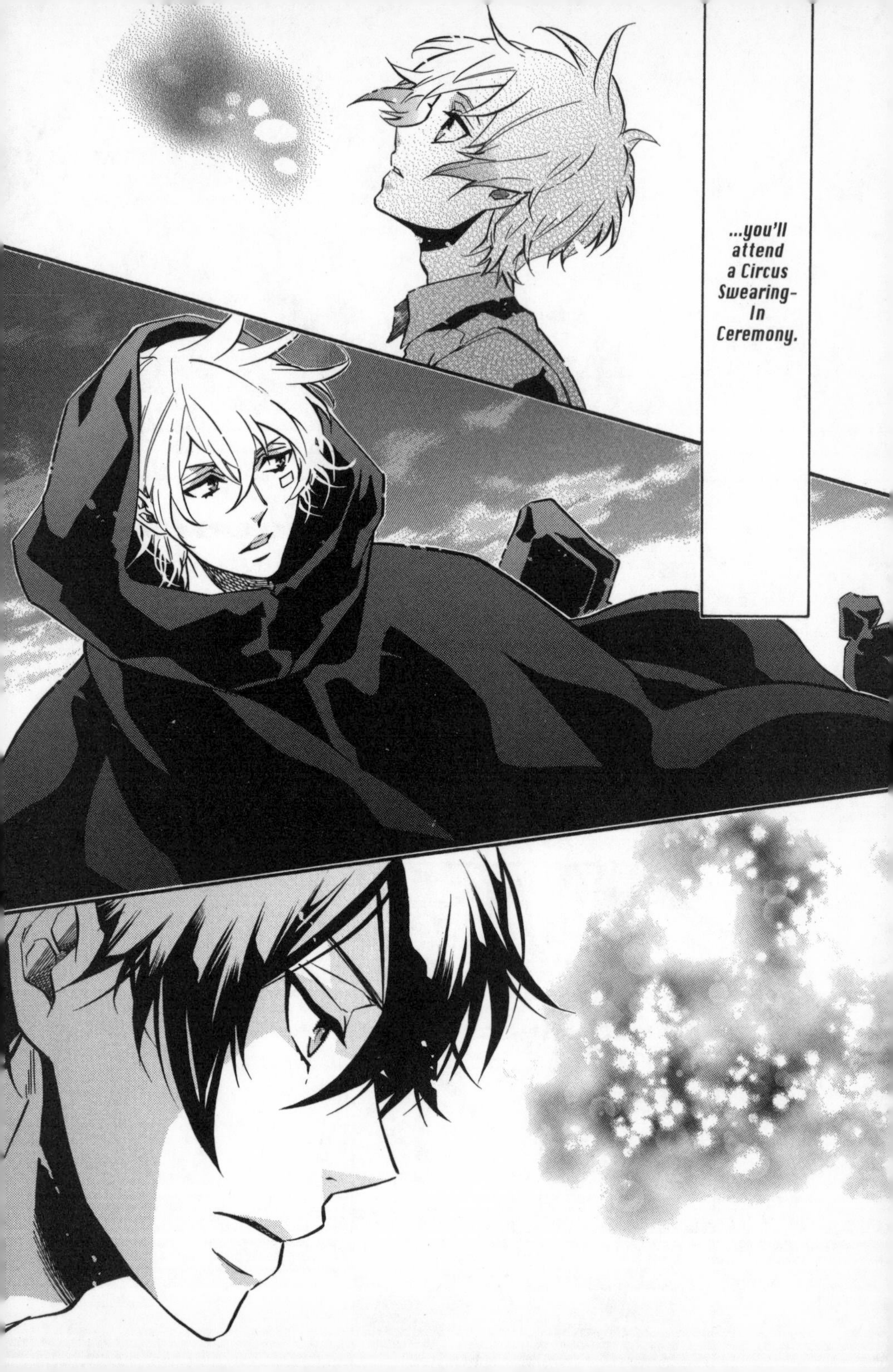
...you'll attend a Circus Swearing-In Ceremony.

KARNEVAL

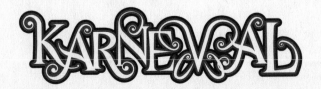

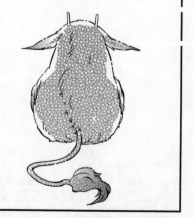

KARNEVAL

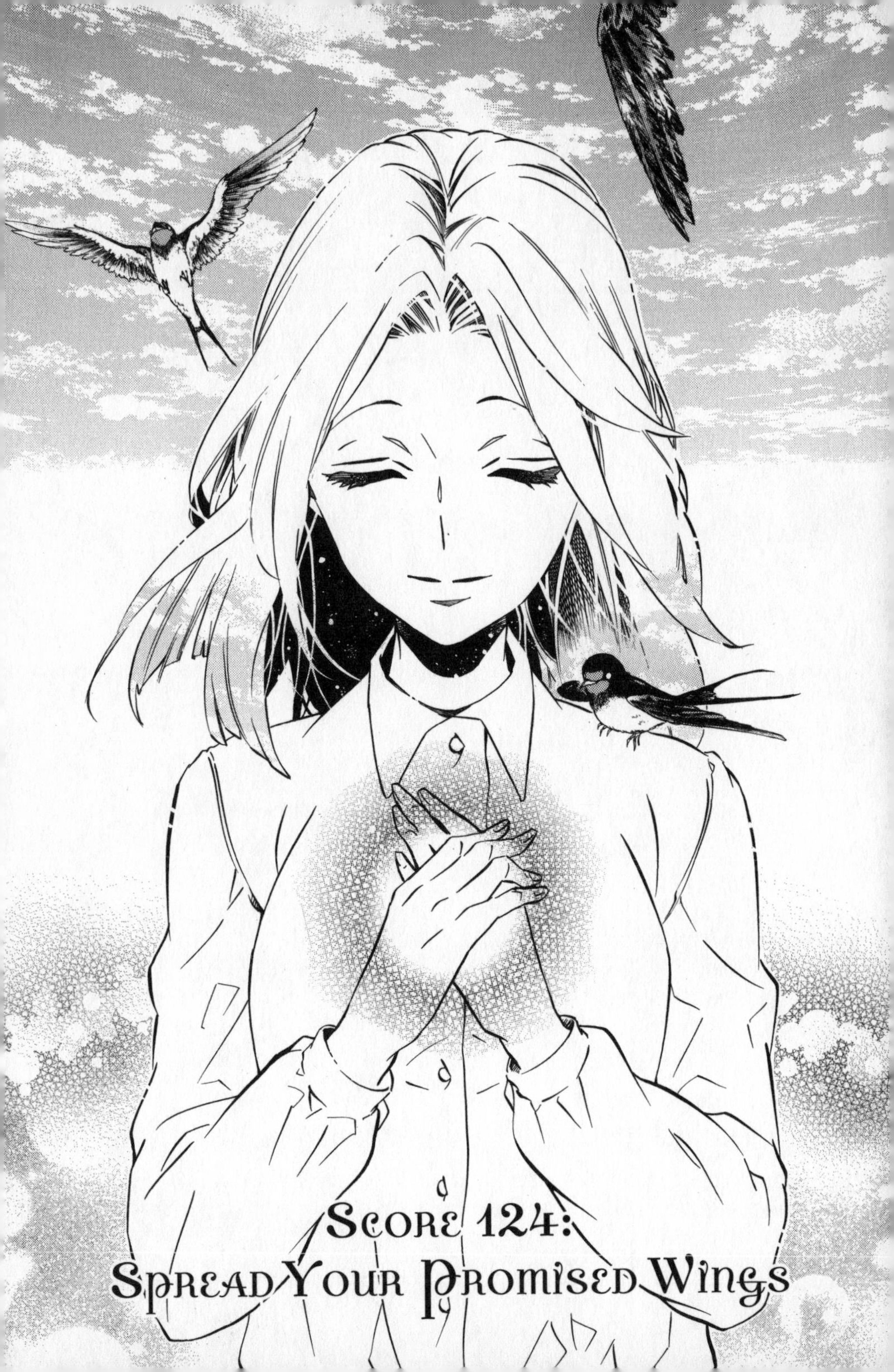
Score 124:
Spread Your Promised Wings

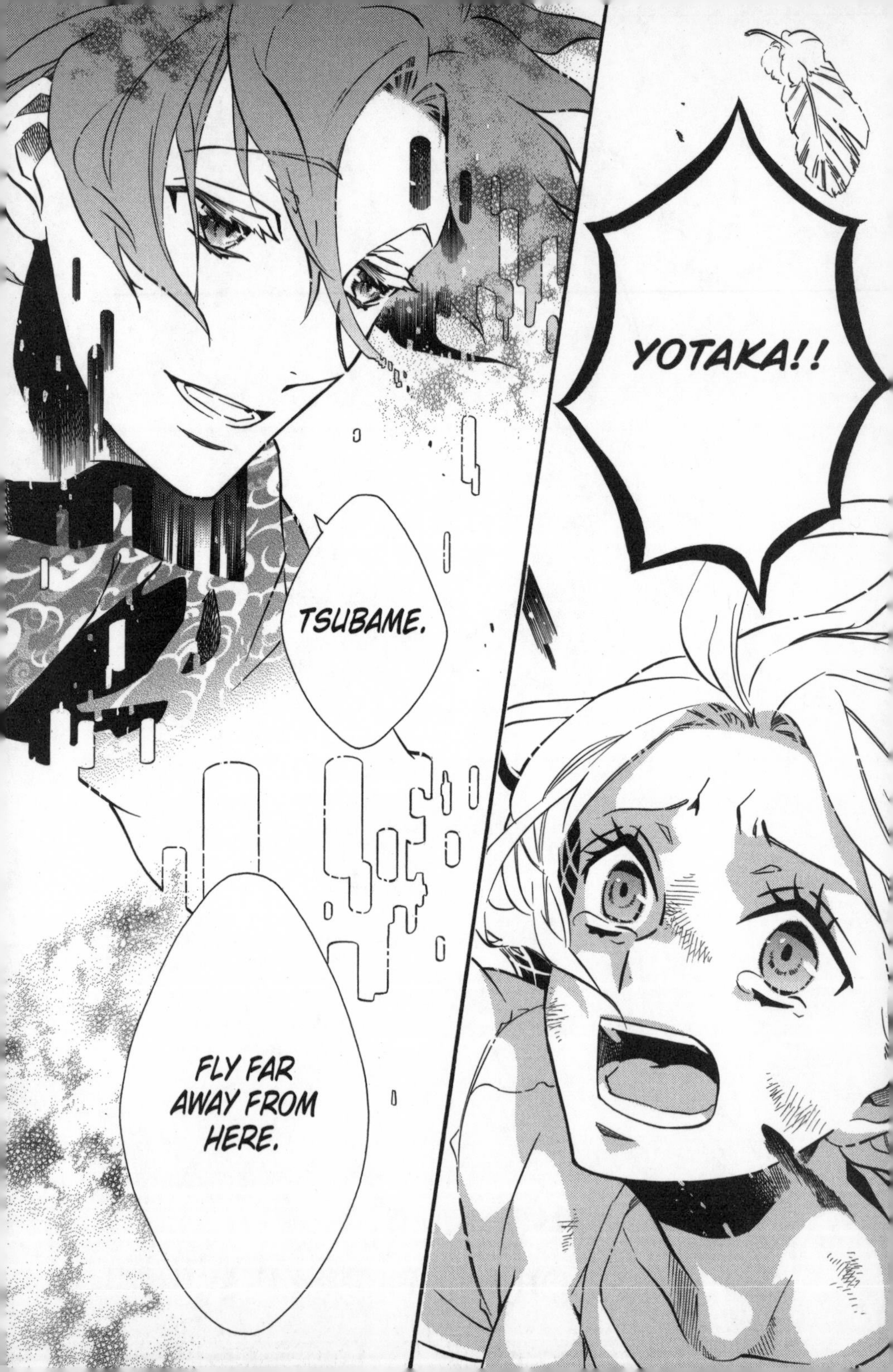
YOTAKA!!
TSUBAME.
FLY FAR AWAY FROM HERE.

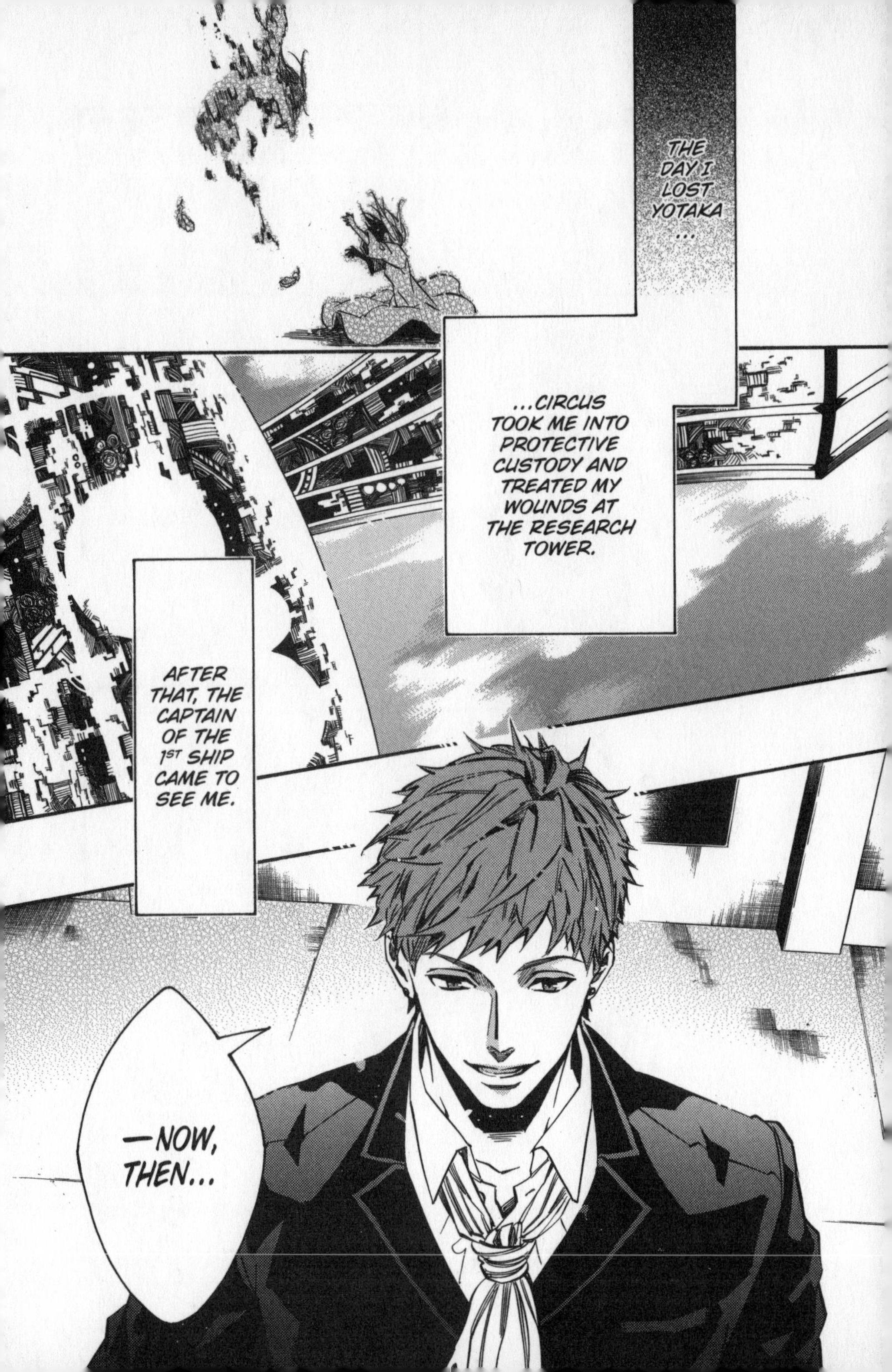
THE DAY I LOST YOTAKA...
...CIRCUS TOOK ME INTO PROTECTIVE CUSTODY AND TREATED MY WOUNDS AT THE RESEARCH TOWER.
AFTER THAT, THE CAPTAIN OF THE 1ST SHIP CAME TO SEE ME.
—NOW, THEN...

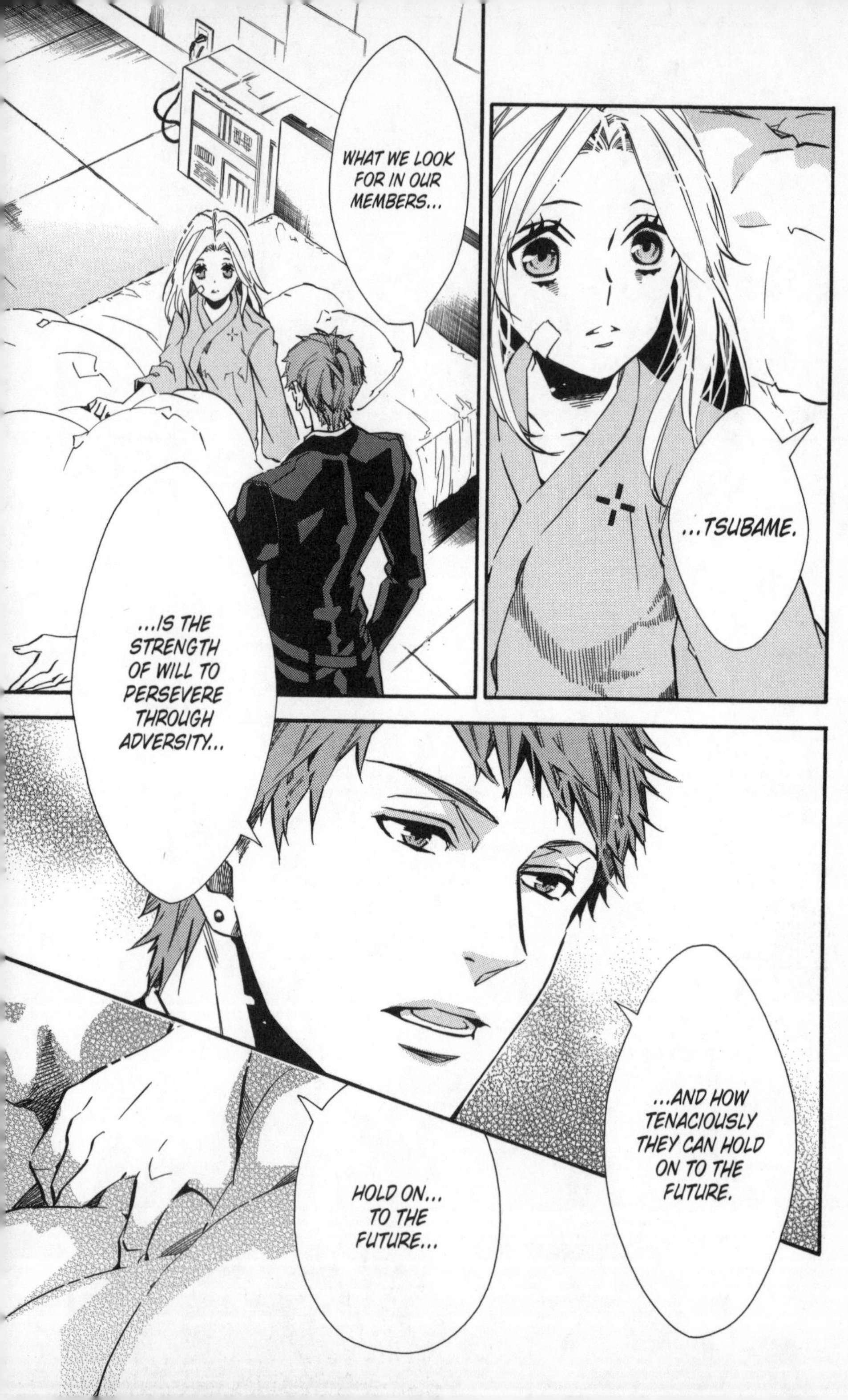
...TSUBAME.
WHAT WE LOOK FOR IN OUR MEMBERS...
...IS THE STRENGTH OF WILL TO PERSEVERE THROUGH ADVERSITY...
...AND HOW TENACIOUSLY THEY CAN HOLD ON TO THE FUTURE.
HOLD ON... TO THE FUTURE...

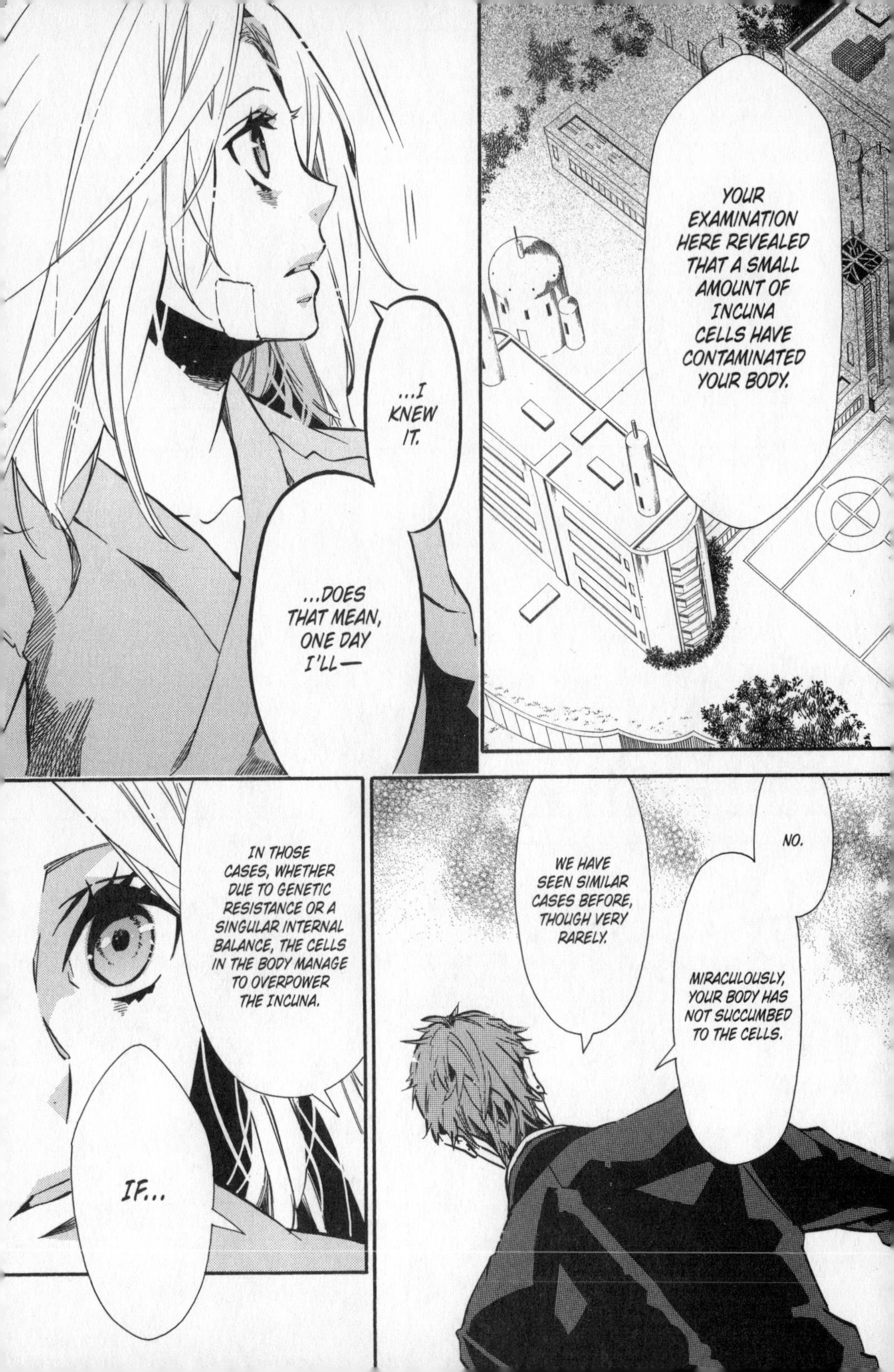
YOUR EXAMINATION HERE REVEALED THAT A SMALL AMOUNT OF INCUNA CELLS HAVE CONTAMINATED YOUR BODY.
...I KNEW IT.
...DOES THAT MEAN, ONE DAY I'LL—
NO.
MIRACULOUSLY, YOUR BODY HAS NOT SUCCUMBED TO THE CELLS.
WE HAVE SEEN SIMILAR CASES BEFORE, THOUGH VERY RARELY.
IN THOSE CASES, WHETHER DUE TO GENETIC RESISTANCE OR A SINGULAR INTERNAL BALANCE, THE CELLS IN THE BODY MANAGE TO OVERPOWER THE INCUNA.
IF...

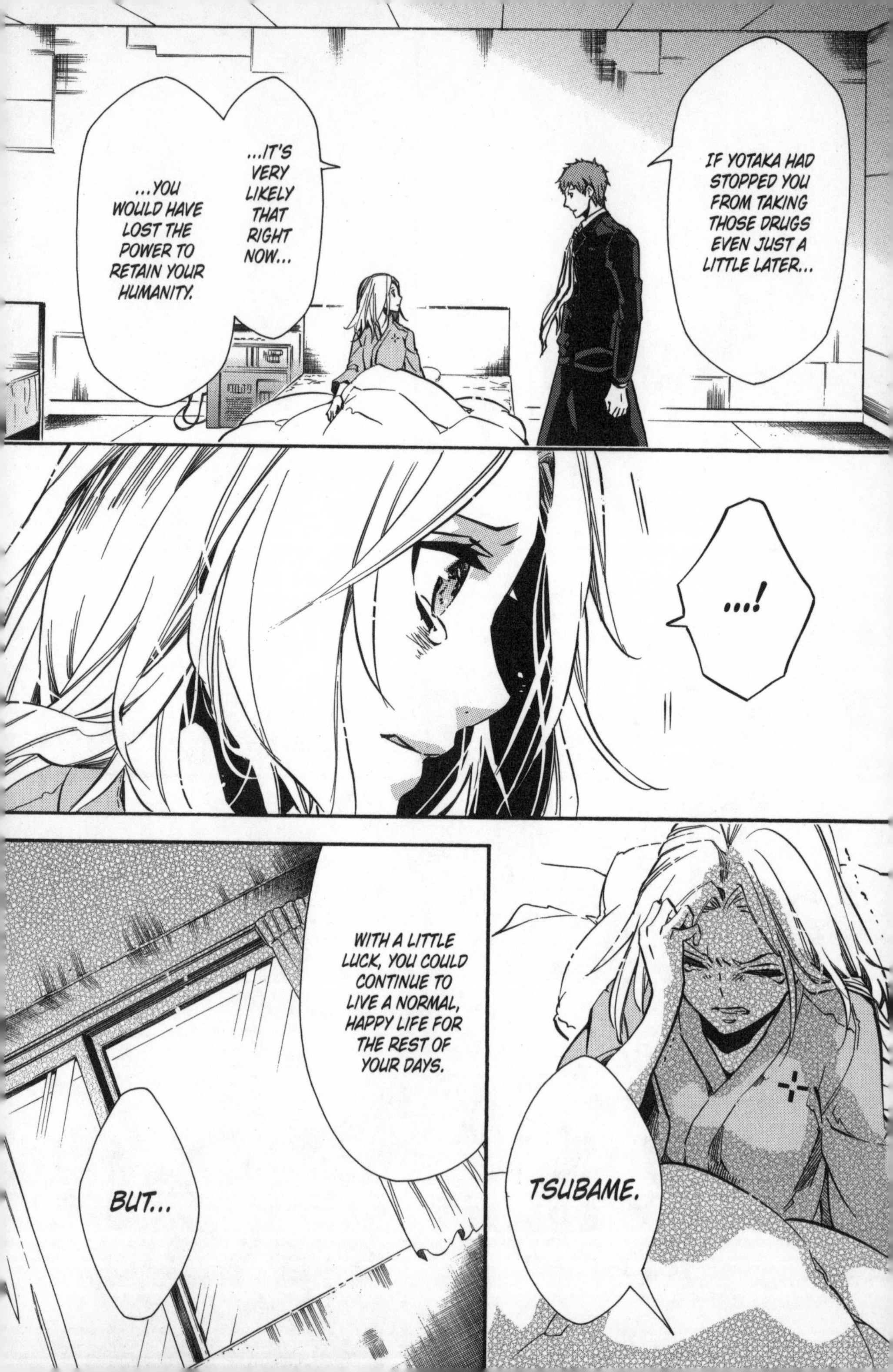
IF YOTAKA HAD STOPPED YOU FROM TAKING THOSE DRUGS EVEN JUST A LITTLE LATER...
...IT'S VERY LIKELY THAT RIGHT NOW...
...YOU WOULD HAVE LOST THE POWER TO RETAIN YOUR HUMANITY.
...!
TSUBAME.
WITH A LITTLE LUCK, YOU COULD CONTINUE TO LIVE A NORMAL, HAPPY LIFE FOR THE REST OF YOUR DAYS.
BUT...

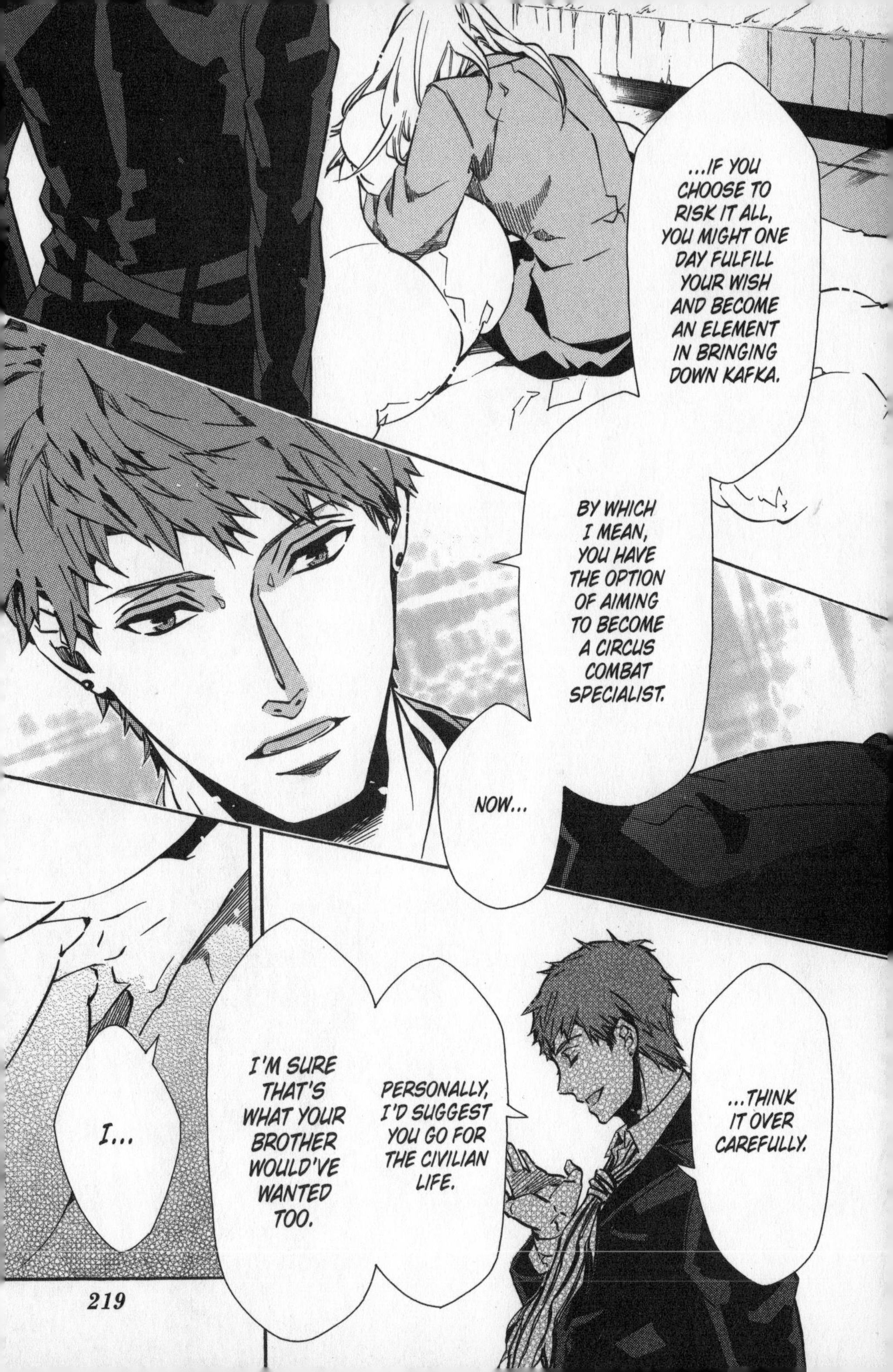
...IF YOU CHOOSE TO RISK IT ALL, YOU MIGHT ONE DAY FULFILL YOUR WISH AND BECOME AN ELEMENT IN BRINGING DOWN KAFKA.
BY WHICH I MEAN, YOU HAVE THE OPTION OF AIMING TO BECOME A CIRCUS COMBAT SPECIALIST.
NOW...
...THINK IT OVER CAREFULLY.
PERSONALLY, I'D SUGGEST YOU GO FOR THE CIVILIAN LIFE.
I'M SURE THAT'S WHAT YOUR BROTHER WOULD'VE WANTED TOO.
I...

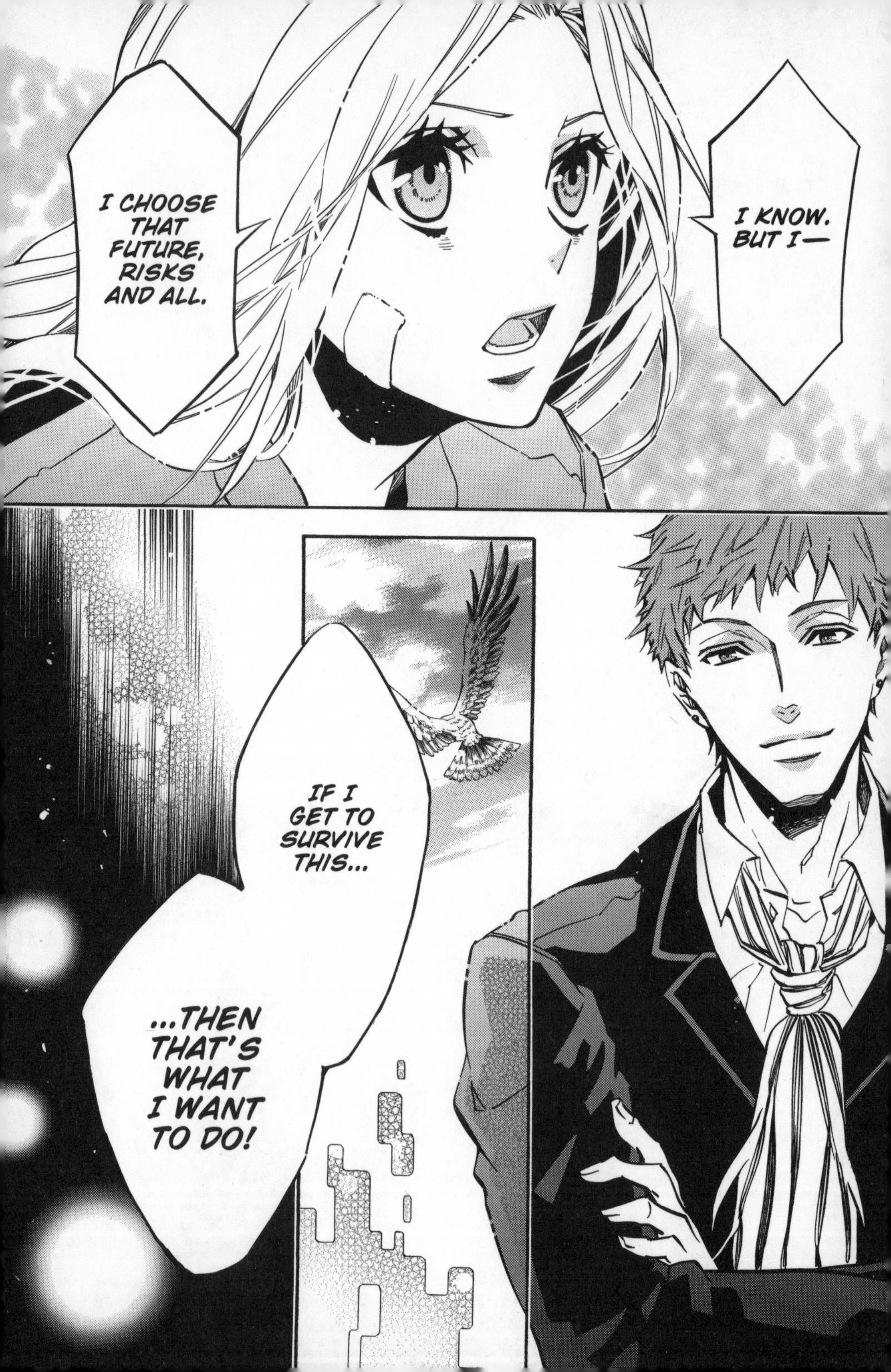
I KNOW. BUT I—
I CHOOSE THAT FUTURE, RISKS AND ALL.
IF I GET TO SURVIVE THIS...
...THEN THAT'S WHAT I WANT TO DO!

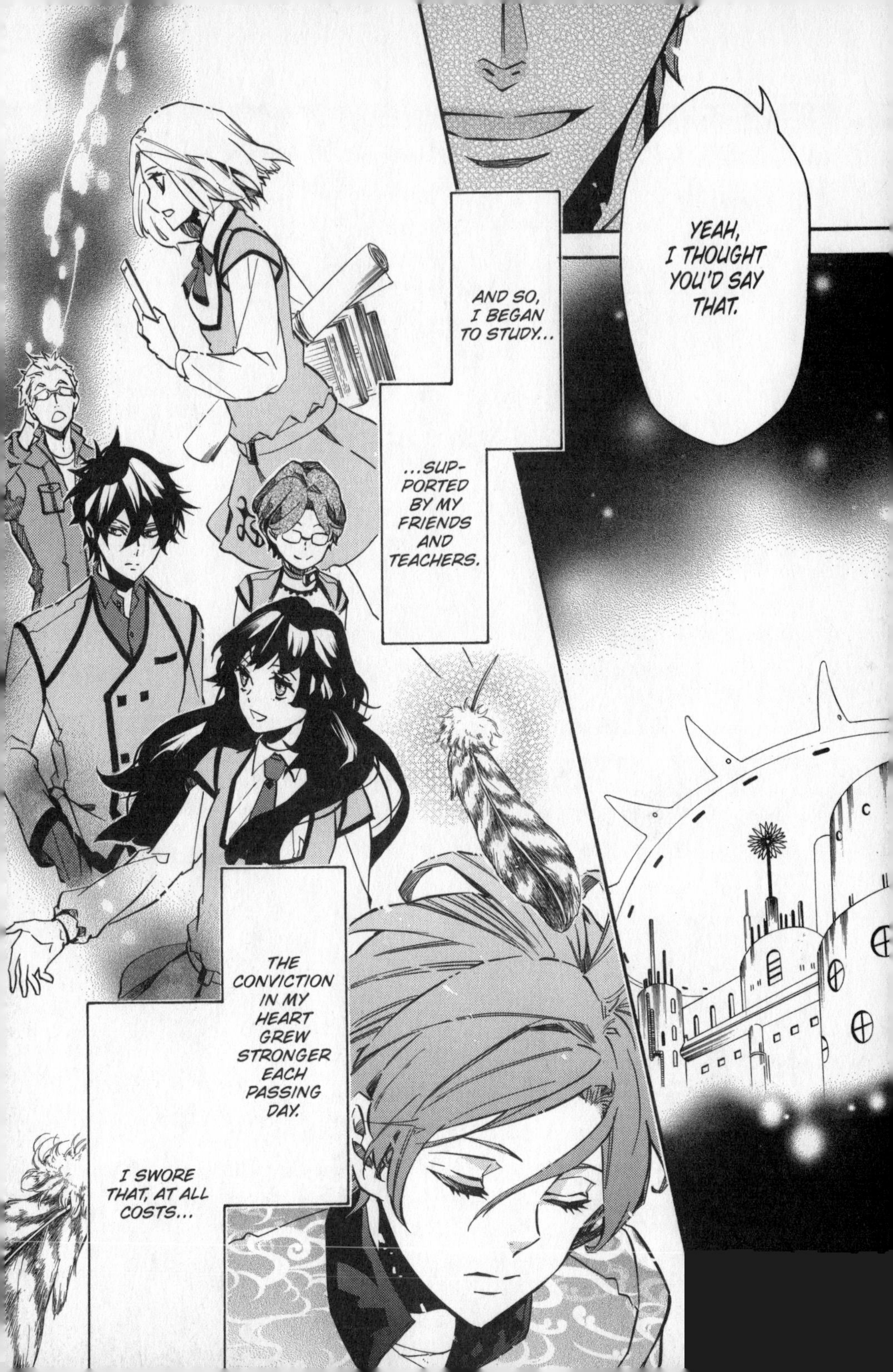
YEAH, I THOUGHT YOU'D SAY THAT.
AND SO, I BEGAN TO STUDY...
...SUP-PORTED BY MY FRIENDS AND TEACHERS.
THE CONVICTION IN MY HEART GREW STRONGER EACH PASSING DAY.
I SWORE THAT, AT ALL COSTS...

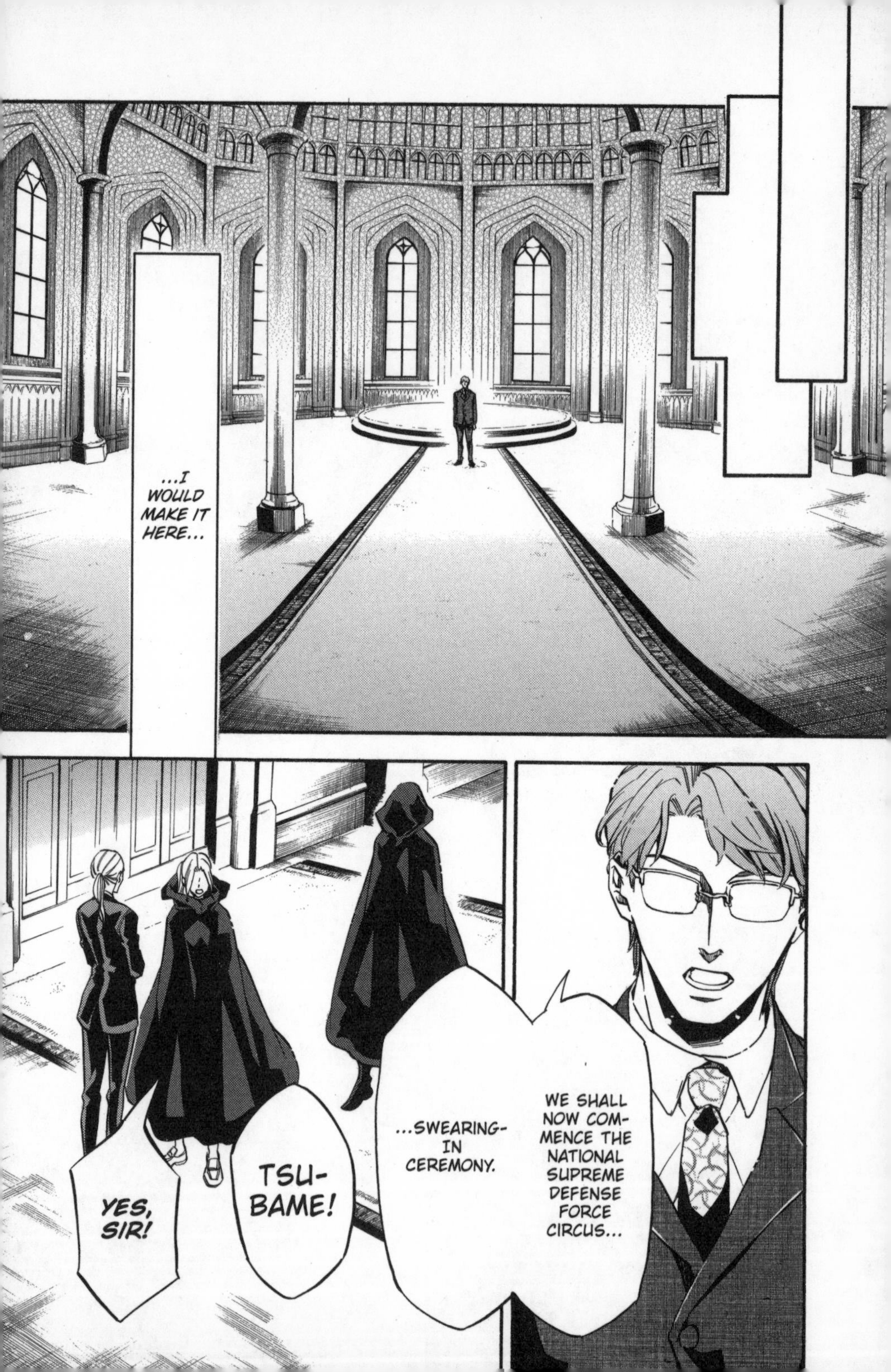
...I WOULD MAKE IT HERE...
WE SHALL NOW COMMENCE THE NATIONAL SUPREME DEFENSE FORCE CIRCUS...
...SWEARING-IN CEREMONY.
TSUBAME!
YES, SIR!

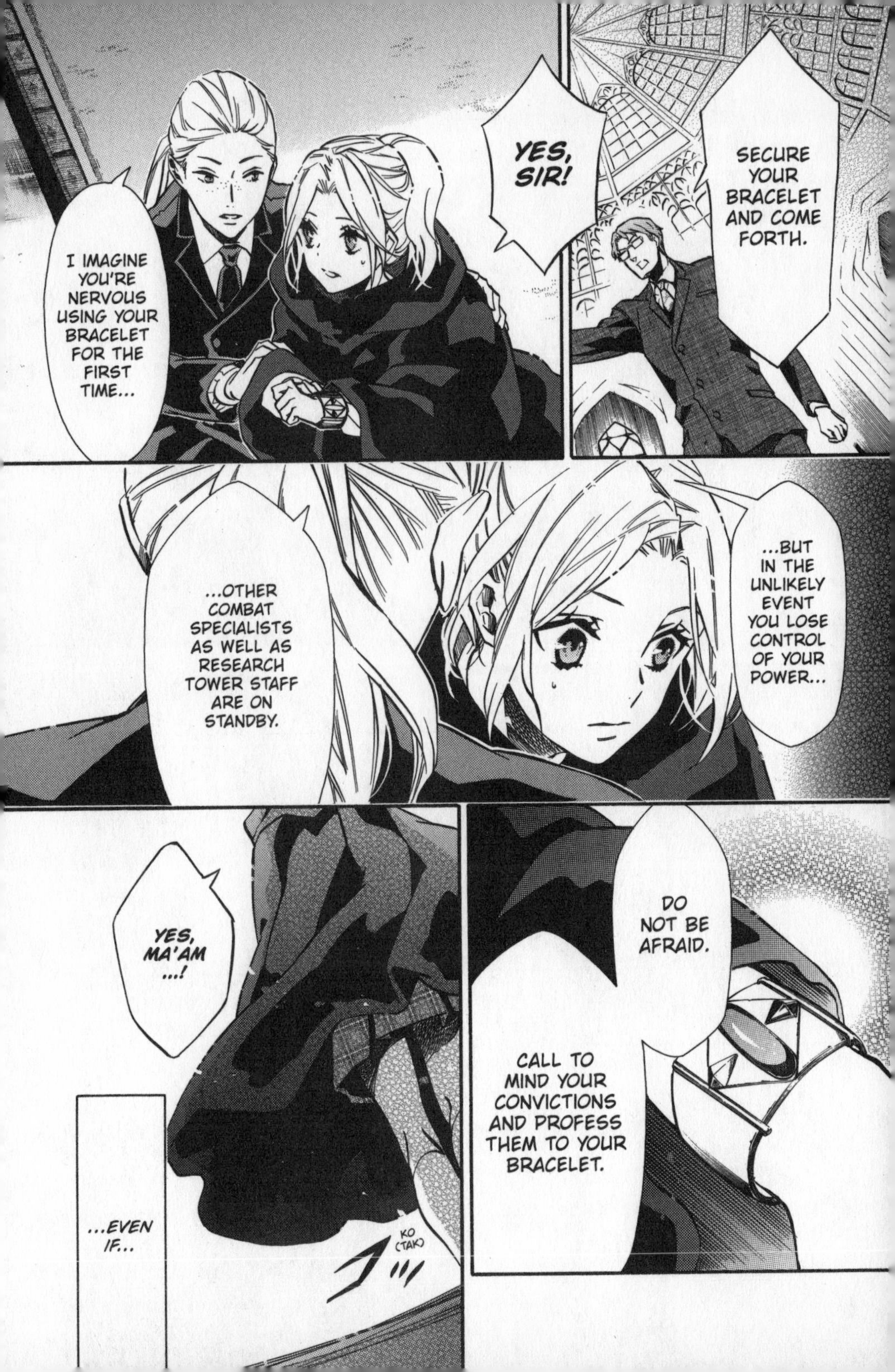
SECURE YOUR BRACELET AND COME FORTH.
YES, SIR!
I IMAGINE YOU'RE NERVOUS USING YOUR BRACELET FOR THE FIRST TIME...
...BUT IN THE UNLIKELY EVENT YOU LOSE CONTROL OF YOUR POWER...
...OTHER COMBAT SPECIALISTS AS WELL AS RESEARCH TOWER STAFF ARE ON STANDBY.
DO NOT BE AFRAID.
CALL TO MIND YOUR CONVICTIONS AND PROFESS THEM TO YOUR BRACELET.
YES, MA'AM ...!
...EVEN IF...
KO (TAK)

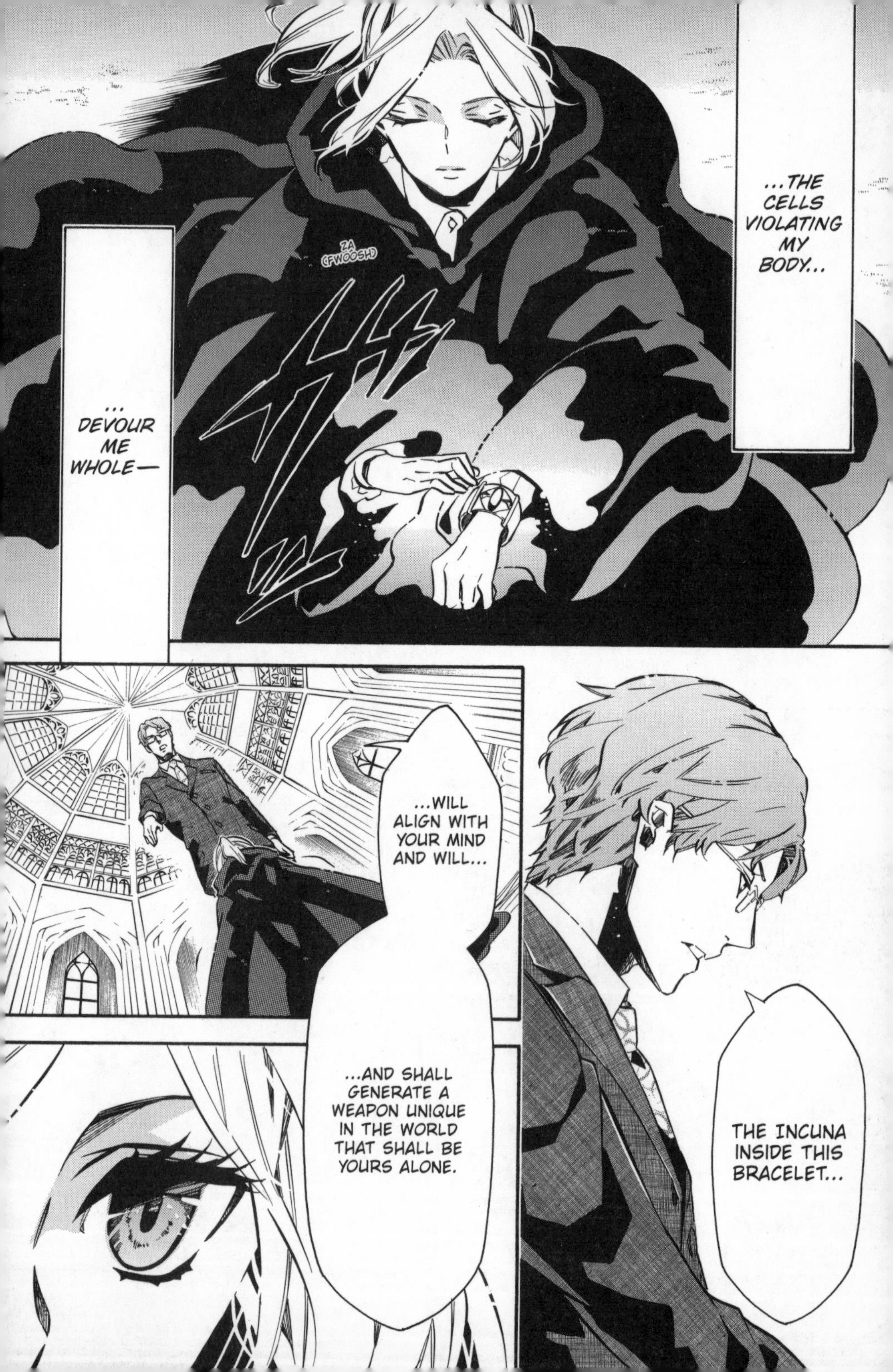
...THE CELLS VIOLATING MY BODY...
ZA (FWOOSH)
...DEVOUR ME WHOLE—
THE INCUNA INSIDE THIS BRACELET...
...WILL ALIGN WITH YOUR MIND AND WILL...
...AND SHALL GENERATE A WEAPON UNIQUE IN THE WORLD THAT SHALL BE YOURS ALONE.

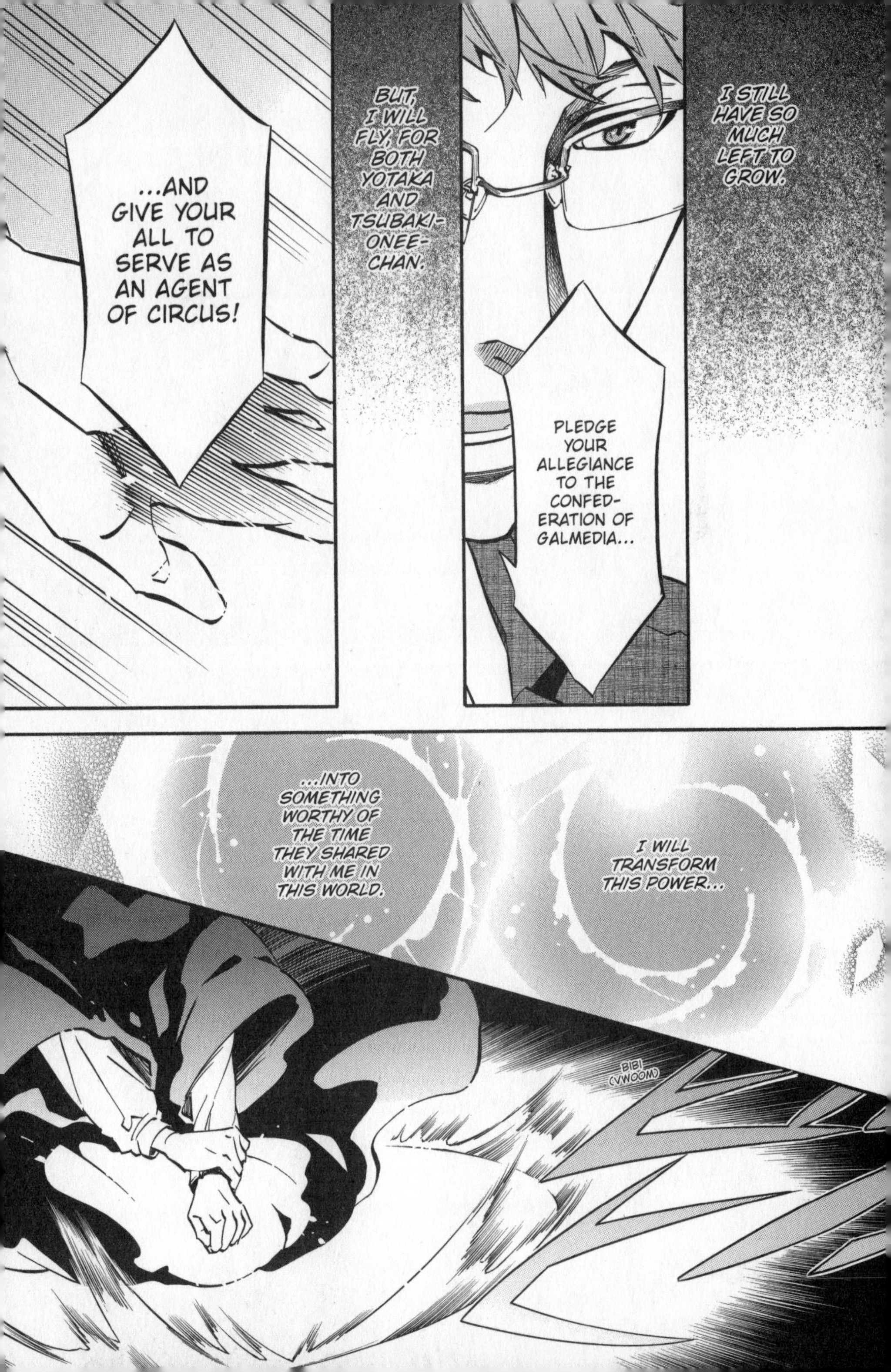
I STILL HAVE SO MUCH LEFT TO GROW.
PLEDGE YOUR ALLEGIANCE TO THE CONFED-ERATION OF GALMEDIA...
BUT, I WILL FLY, FOR BOTH YOTAKA AND TSUBAKI-ONEE-CHAN.
...AND GIVE YOUR ALL TO SERVE AS AN AGENT OF CIRCUS!
I WILL TRANSFORM THIS POWER...
...INTO SOMETHING WORTHY OF THE TIME THEY SHARED WITH ME IN THIS WORLD.
BIBI (VWOOM)

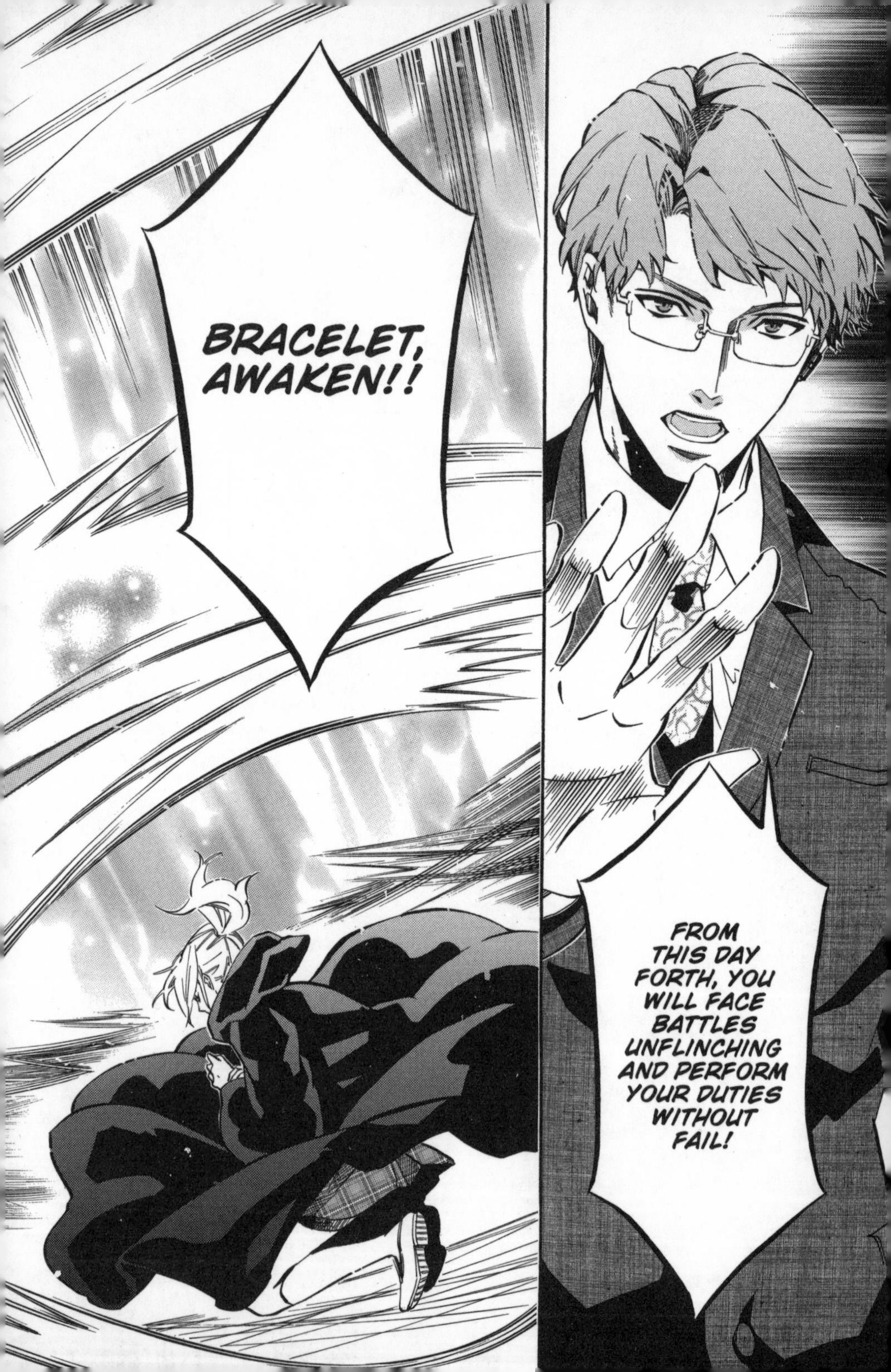
FROM THIS DAY FORTH, YOU WILL FACE BATTLES UNFLINCHING AND PERFORM YOUR DUTIES WITHOUT FAIL!
BRACELET, AWAKEN!!

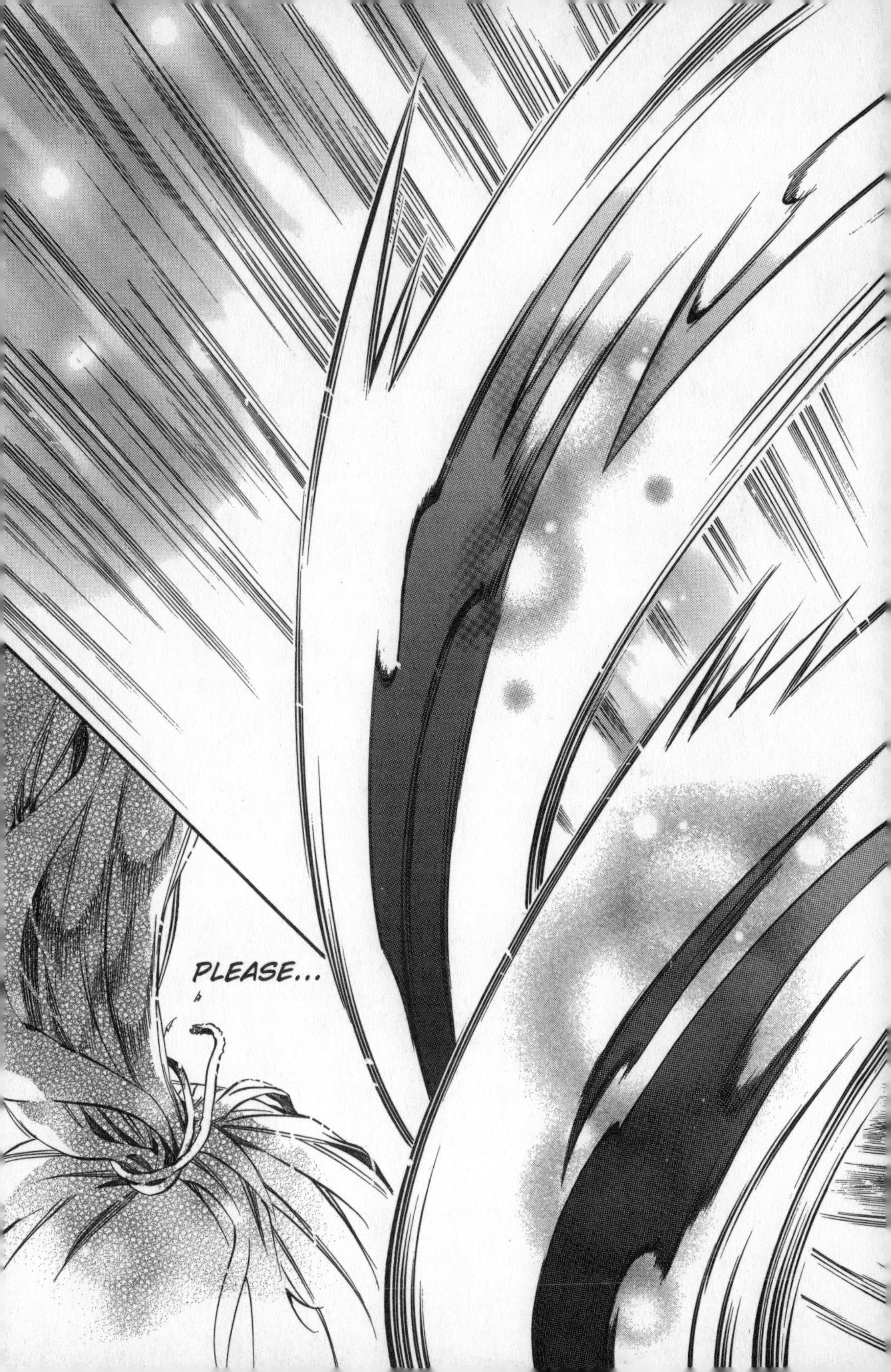
PLEASE...

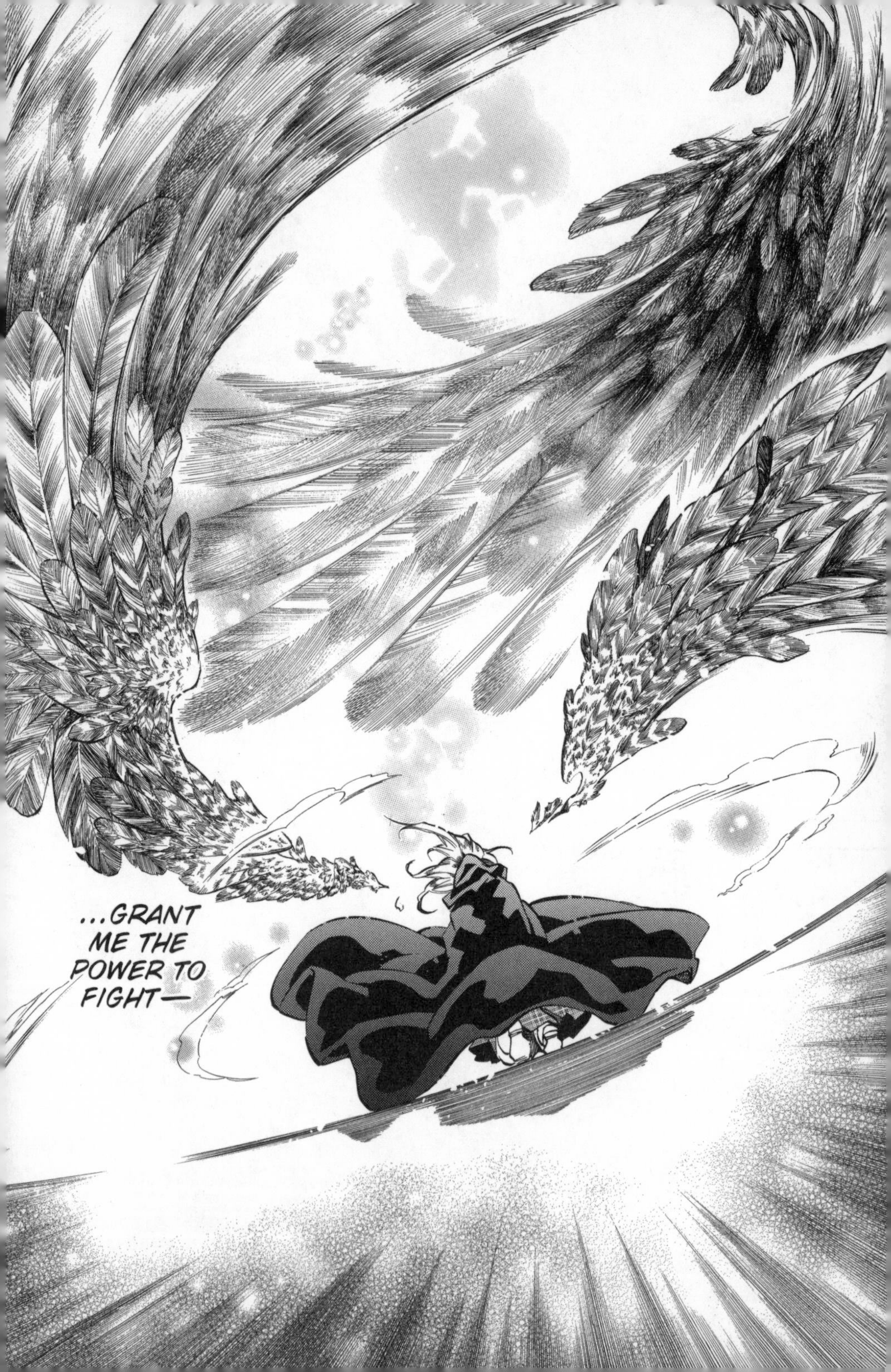
...GRANT ME THE POWER TO FIGHT—

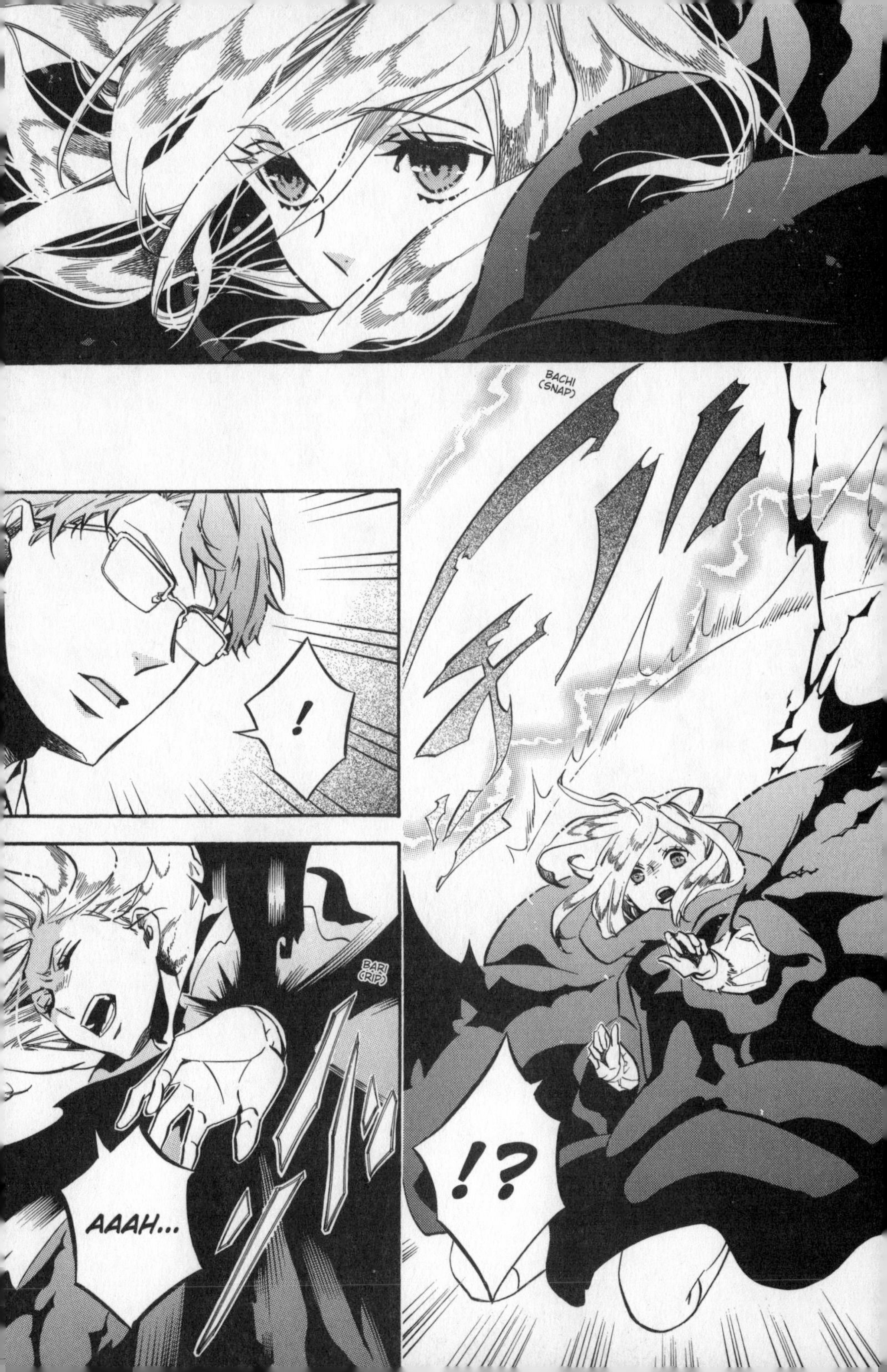
BACHI (SNAP)
!?
!
BARI (RIP)
AAAH...

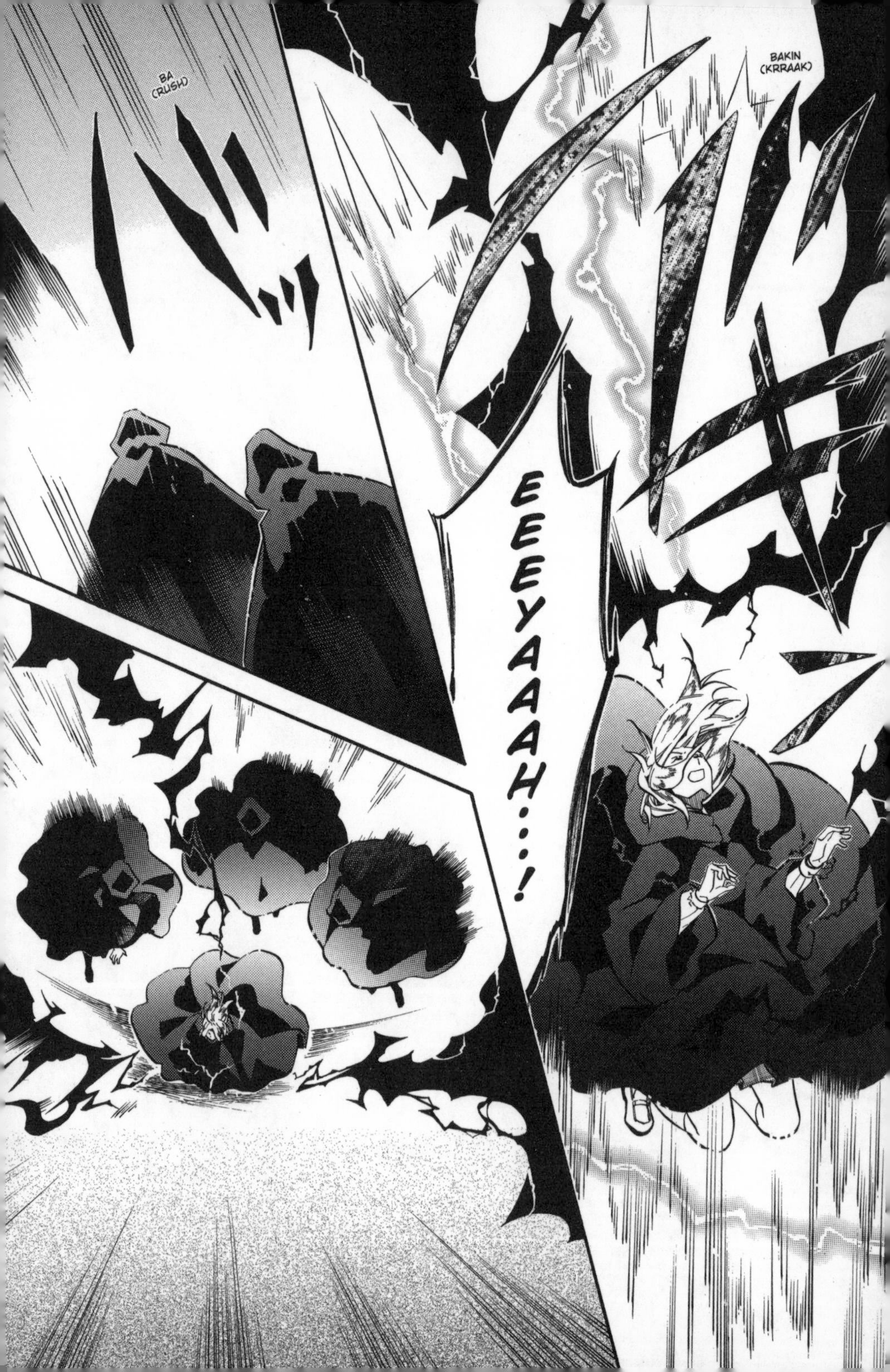
BAKIN (KRRAAK)
EEEYAAAAH...!
BA (RUSH)

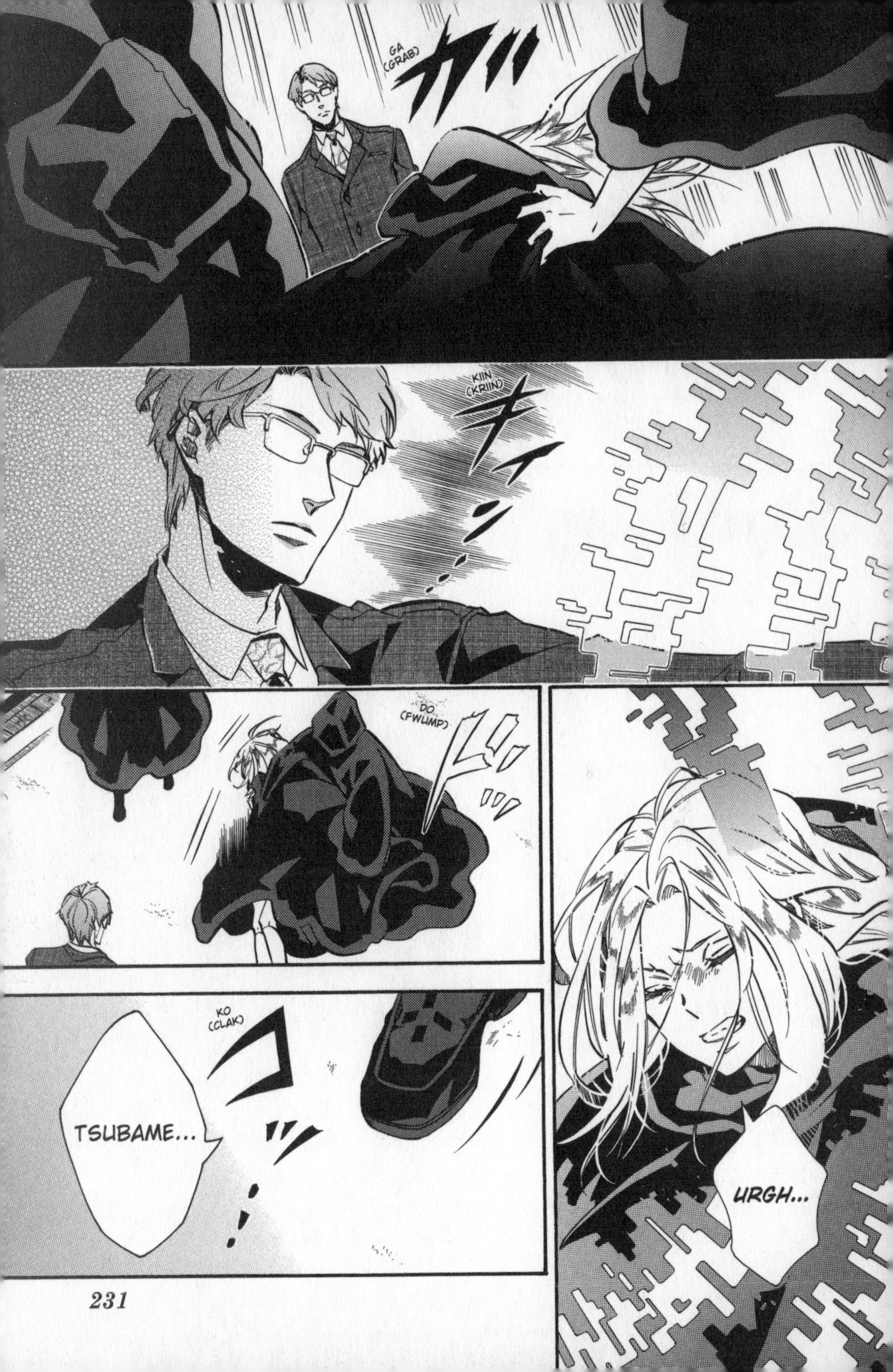
GA (GRAB)
KIIN (KRIIN)
URGH...
DO (FWUMP)
KO (CLAK)
TSUBAME...

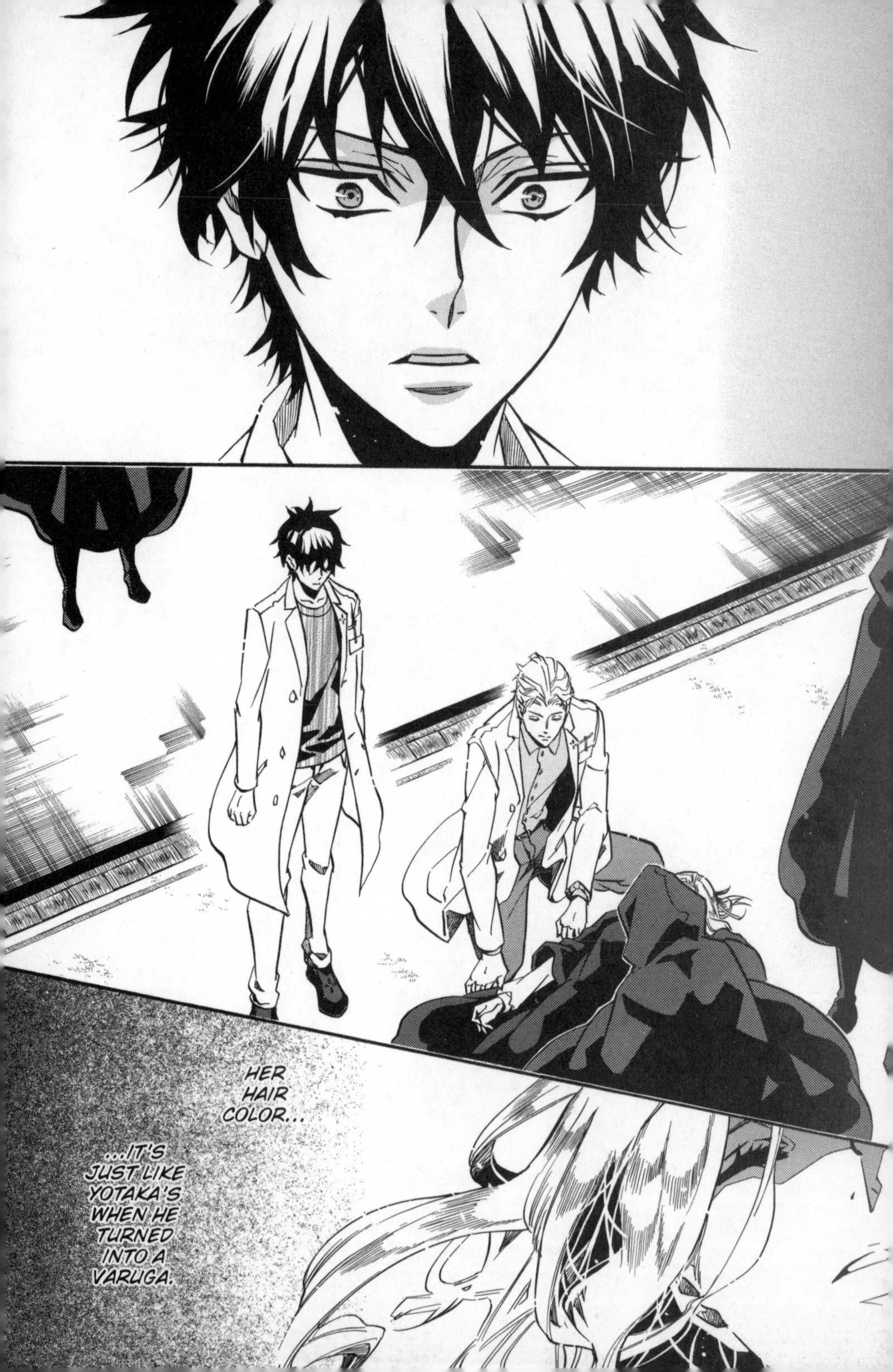
HER HAIR COLOR...
...IT'S JUST LIKE YOTAKA'S WHEN HE TURNED INTO A VARUGA.

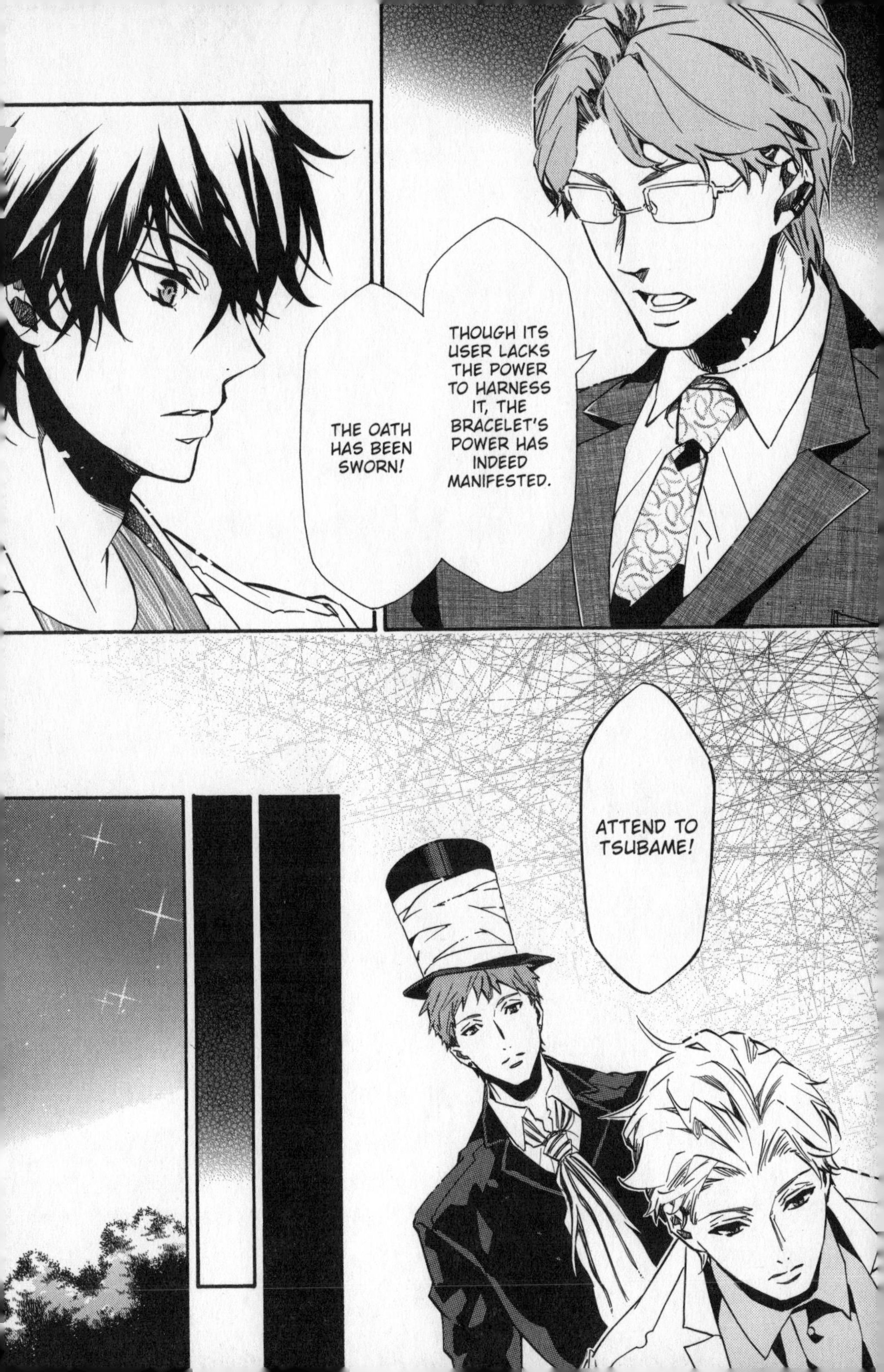
THOUGH ITS USER LACKS THE POWER TO HARNESS IT, THE BRACELET'S POWER HAS INDEED MANIFESTED.
THE OATH HAS BEEN SWORN!
ATTEND TO TSUBAME!

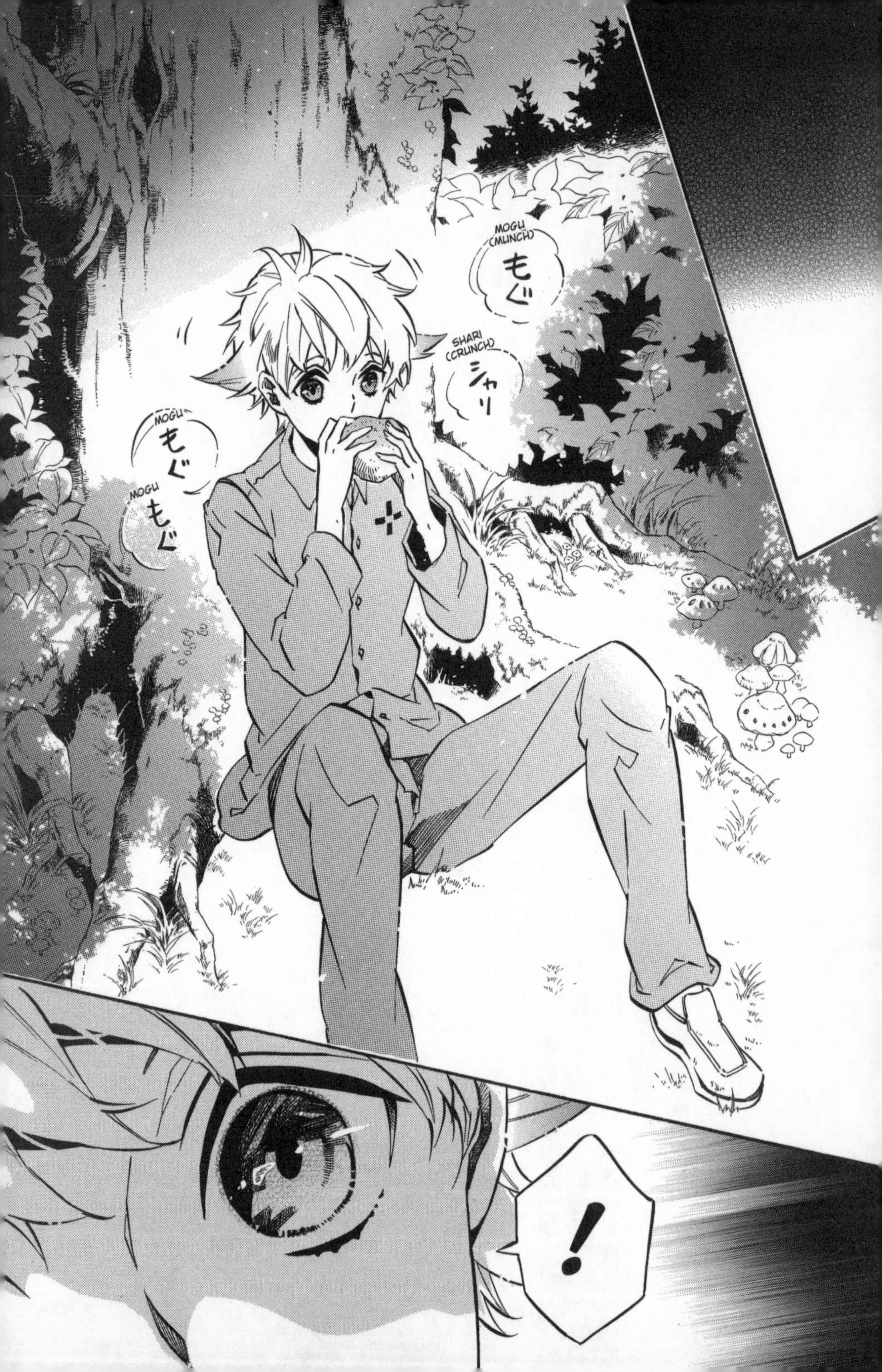
MOGU (MUNCH) もぐ
SHARI (CRUNCH) シャリ
MOGU もぐ
MOGU もぐ
!

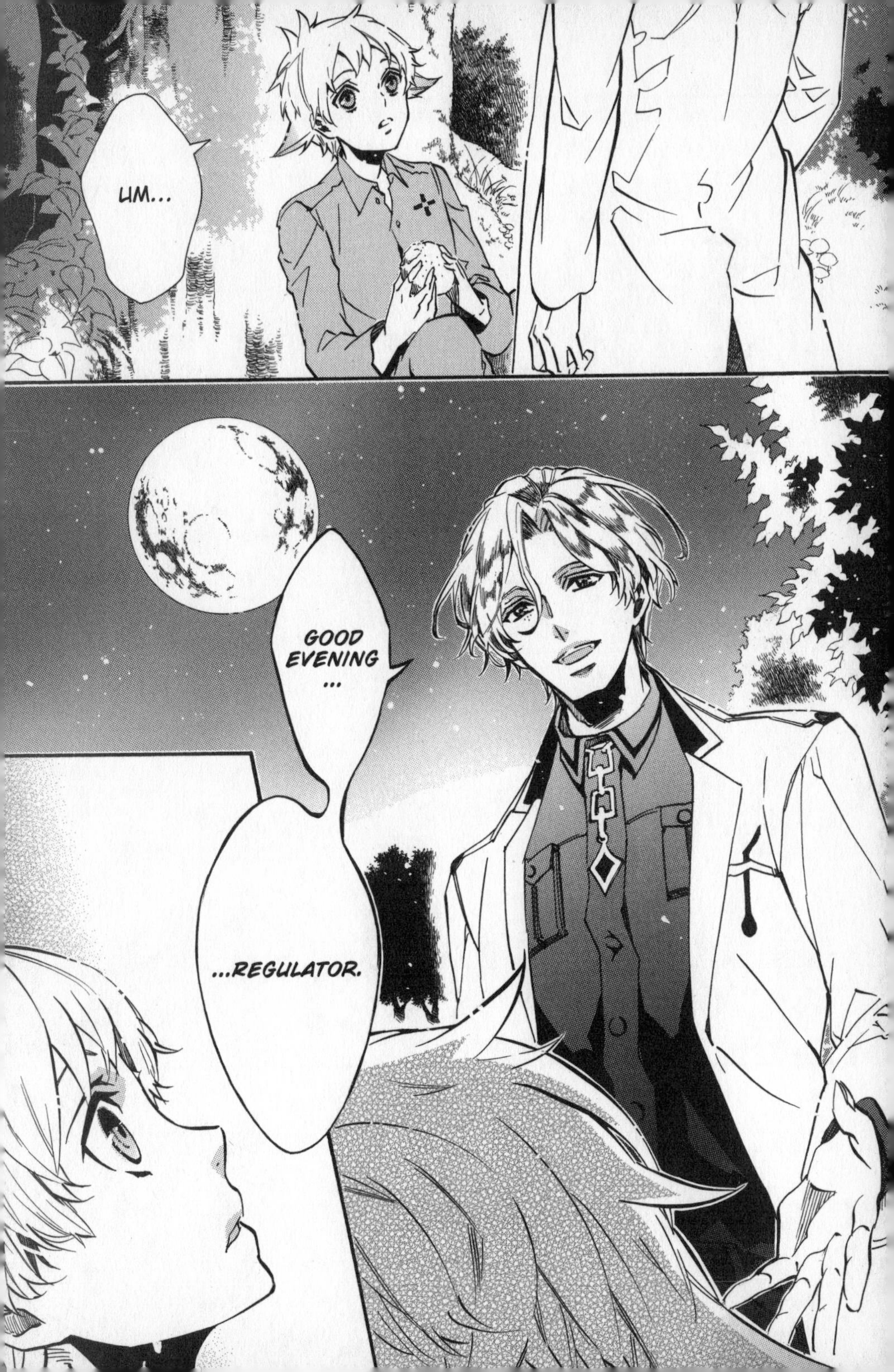
UM...
GOOD EVENING ...
...REGULATOR.

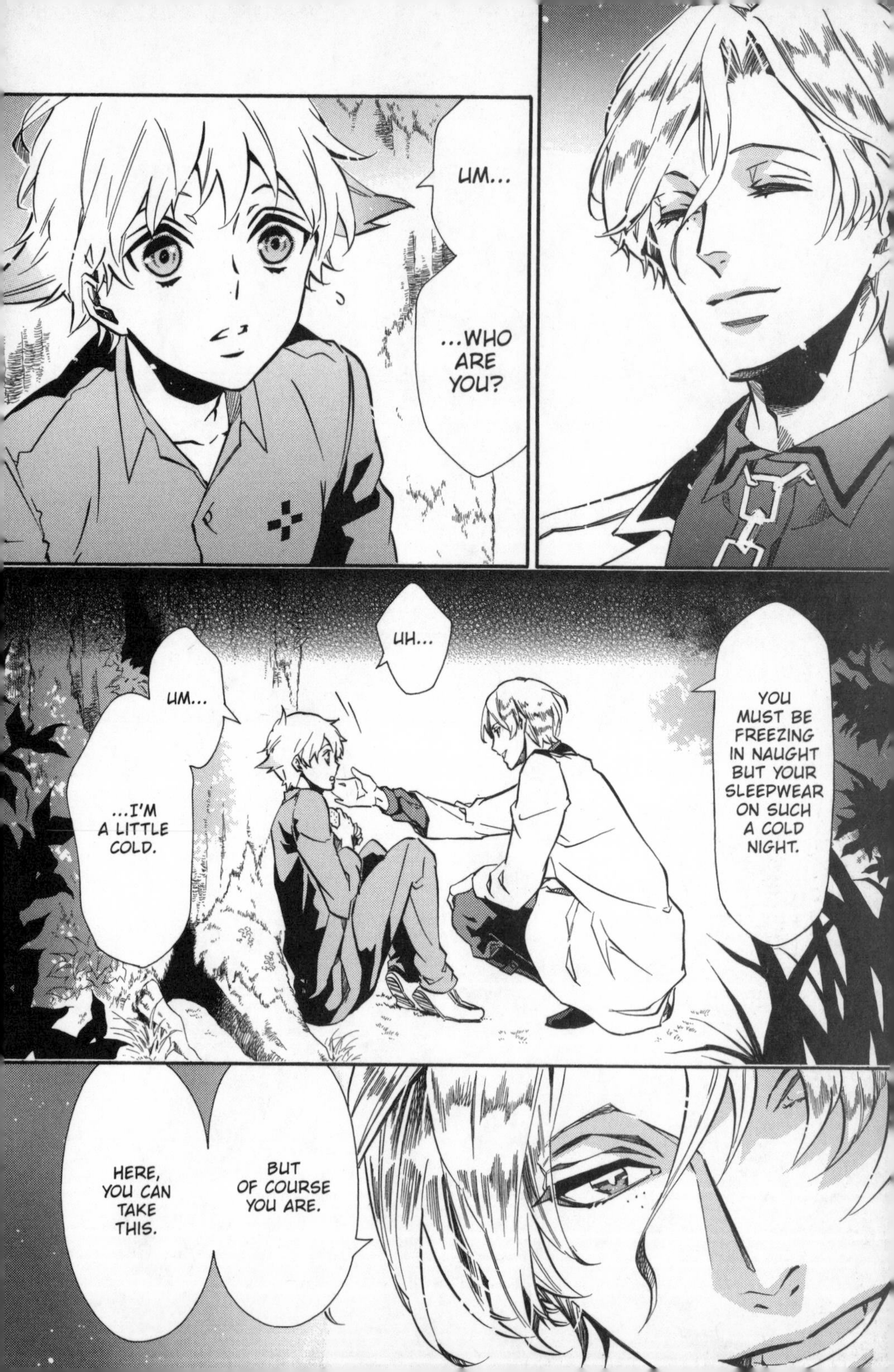
UM...
...WHO ARE YOU?
YOU MUST BE FREEZING IN NAUGHT BUT YOUR SLEEPWEAR ON SUCH A COLD NIGHT.
UH...
UM...
...I'M A LITTLE COLD.
BUT OF COURSE YOU ARE.
HERE, YOU CAN TAKE THIS.

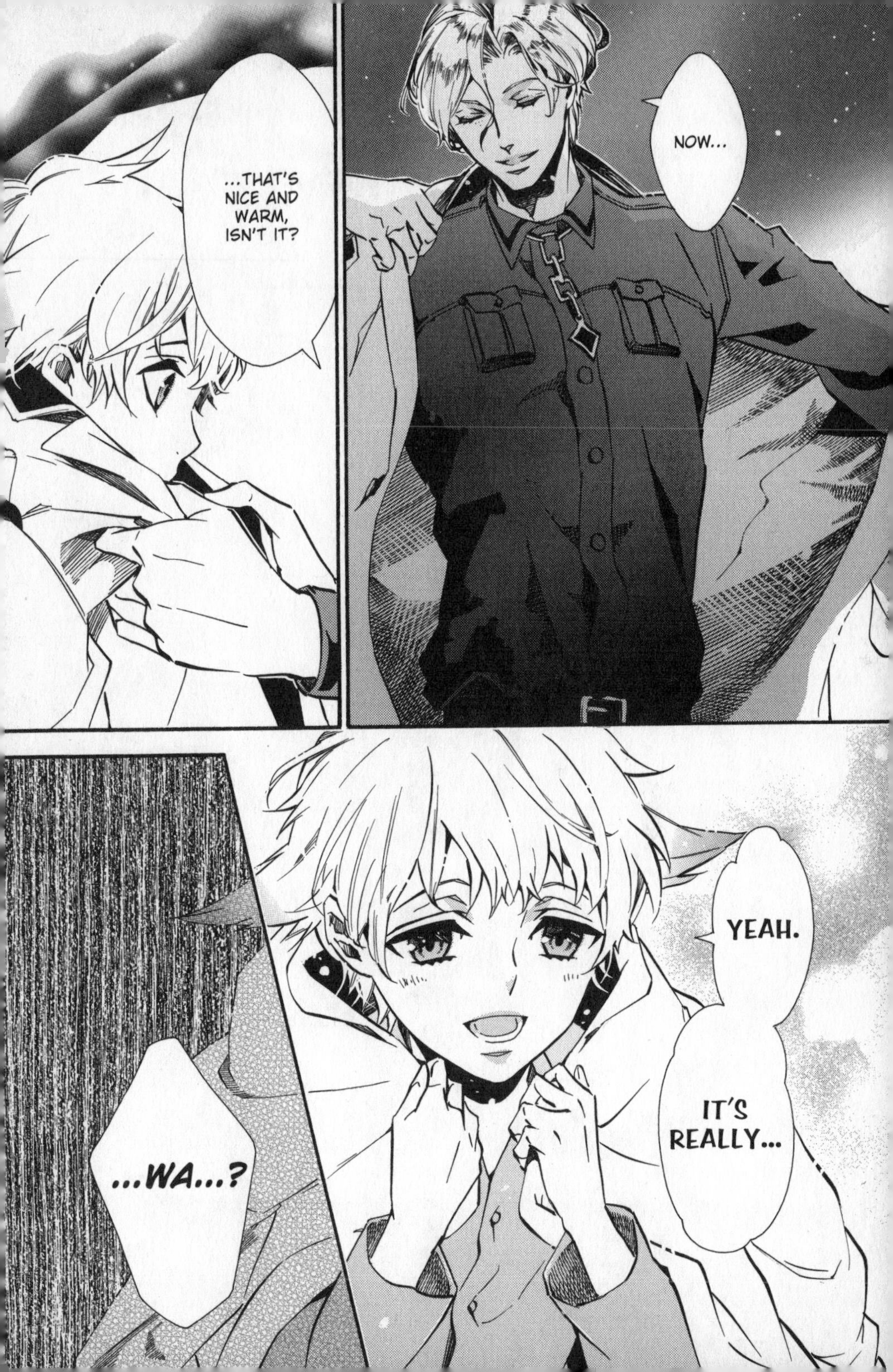
NOW...
...THAT'S NICE AND WARM, ISN'T IT?
YEAH.
IT'S REALLY...
...WA...?

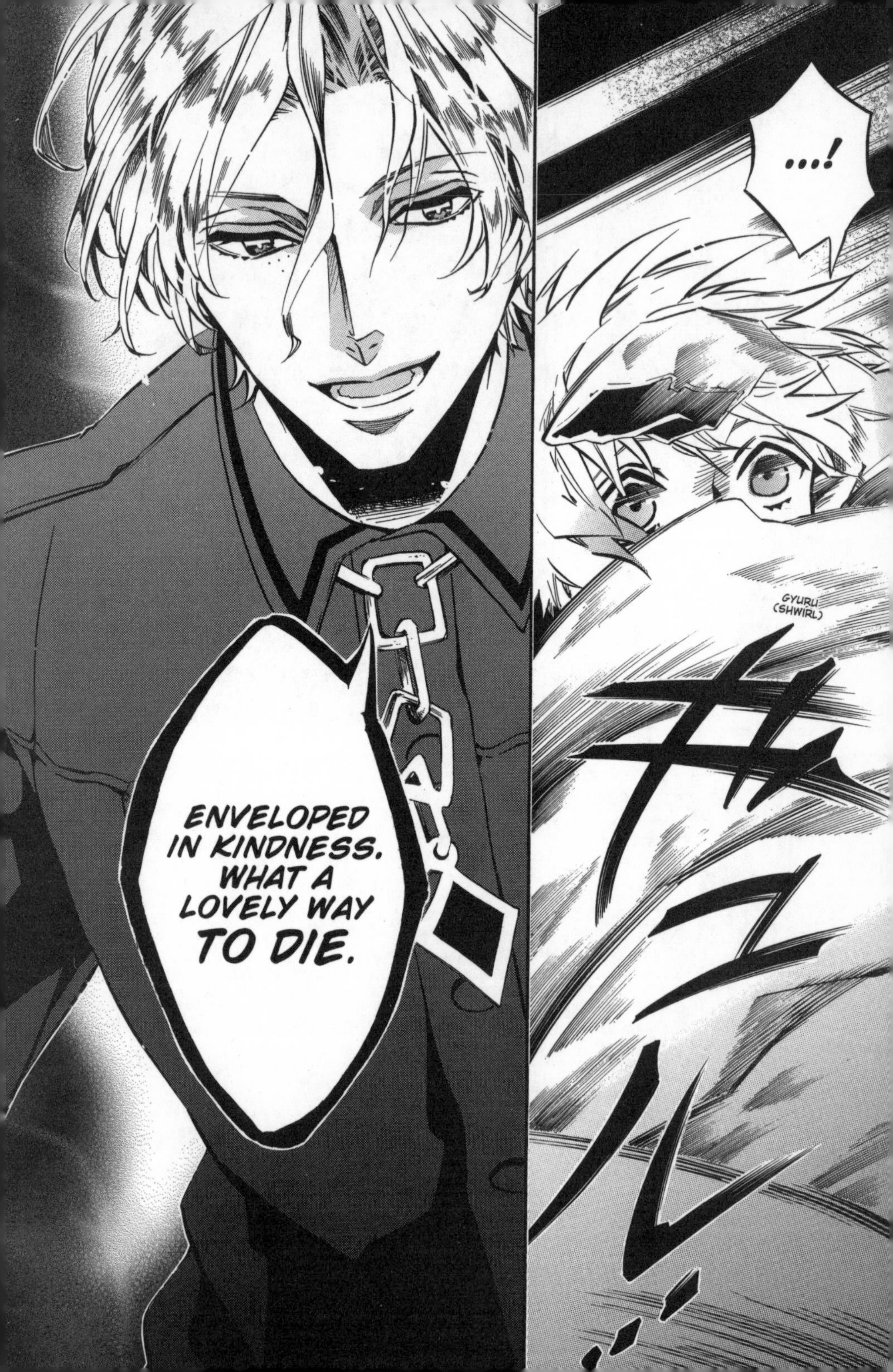
...!
GYURU (SHWIRL)
ENVELOPED IN KINDNESS. WHAT A LOVELY WAY TO DIE.

KARNEVAL

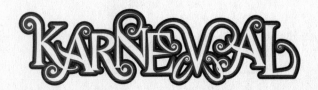

KARNEVAL

# Score 125: Unyielding Resolve

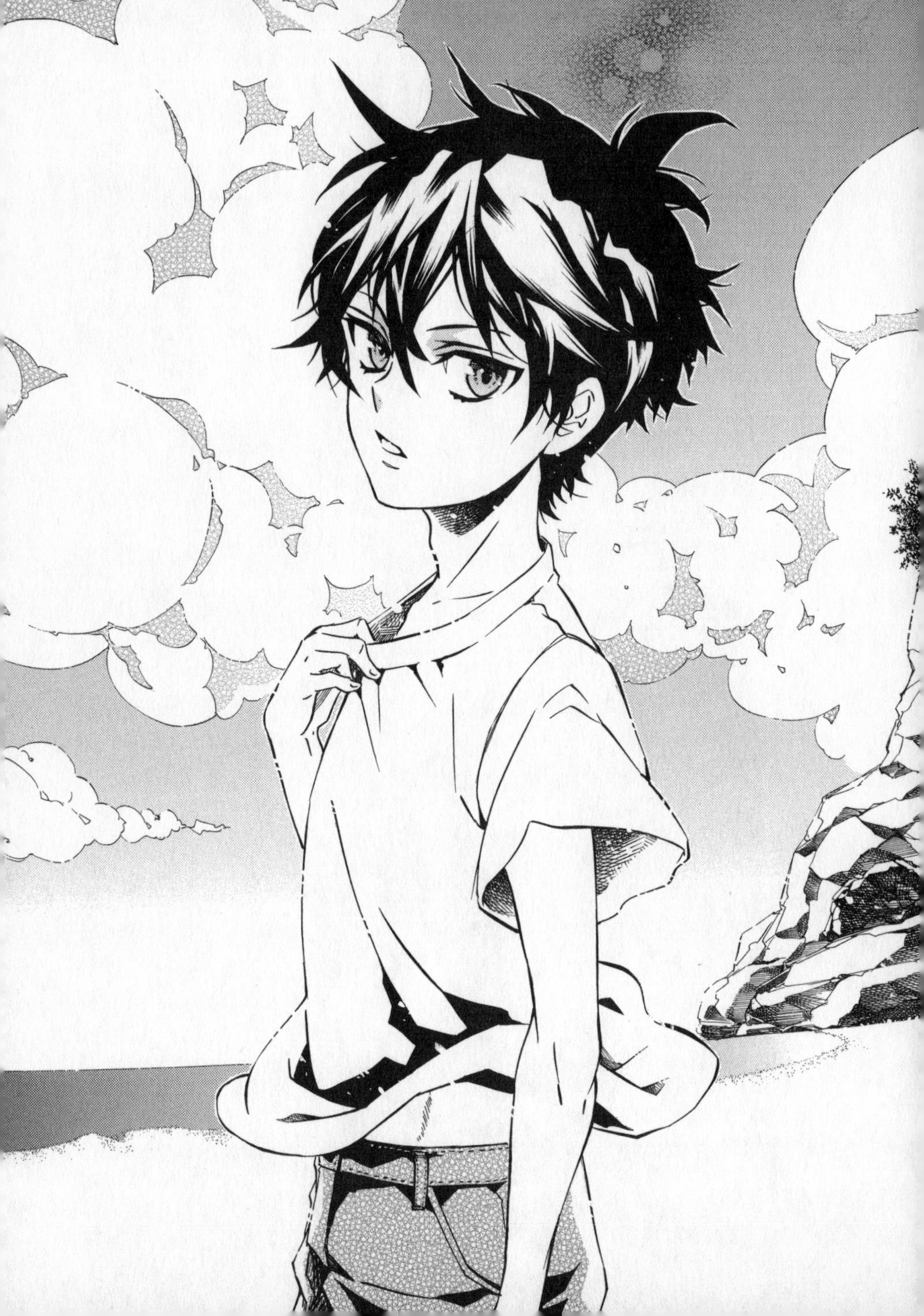

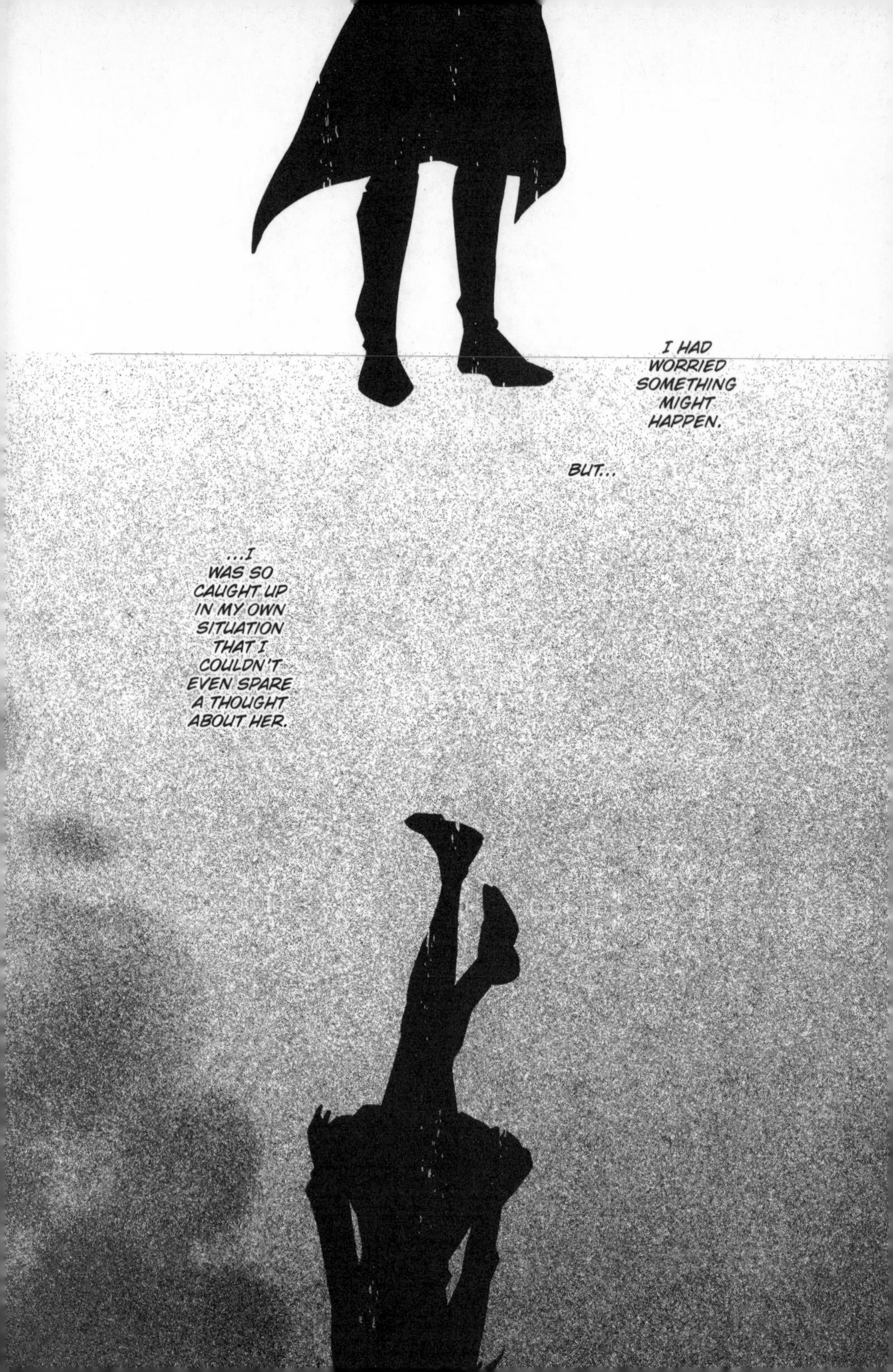
I HAD WORRIED SOMETHING MIGHT HAPPEN.
BUT...
...I WAS SO CAUGHT UP IN MY OWN SITUATION THAT I COULDN'T EVEN SPARE A THOUGHT ABOUT HER.

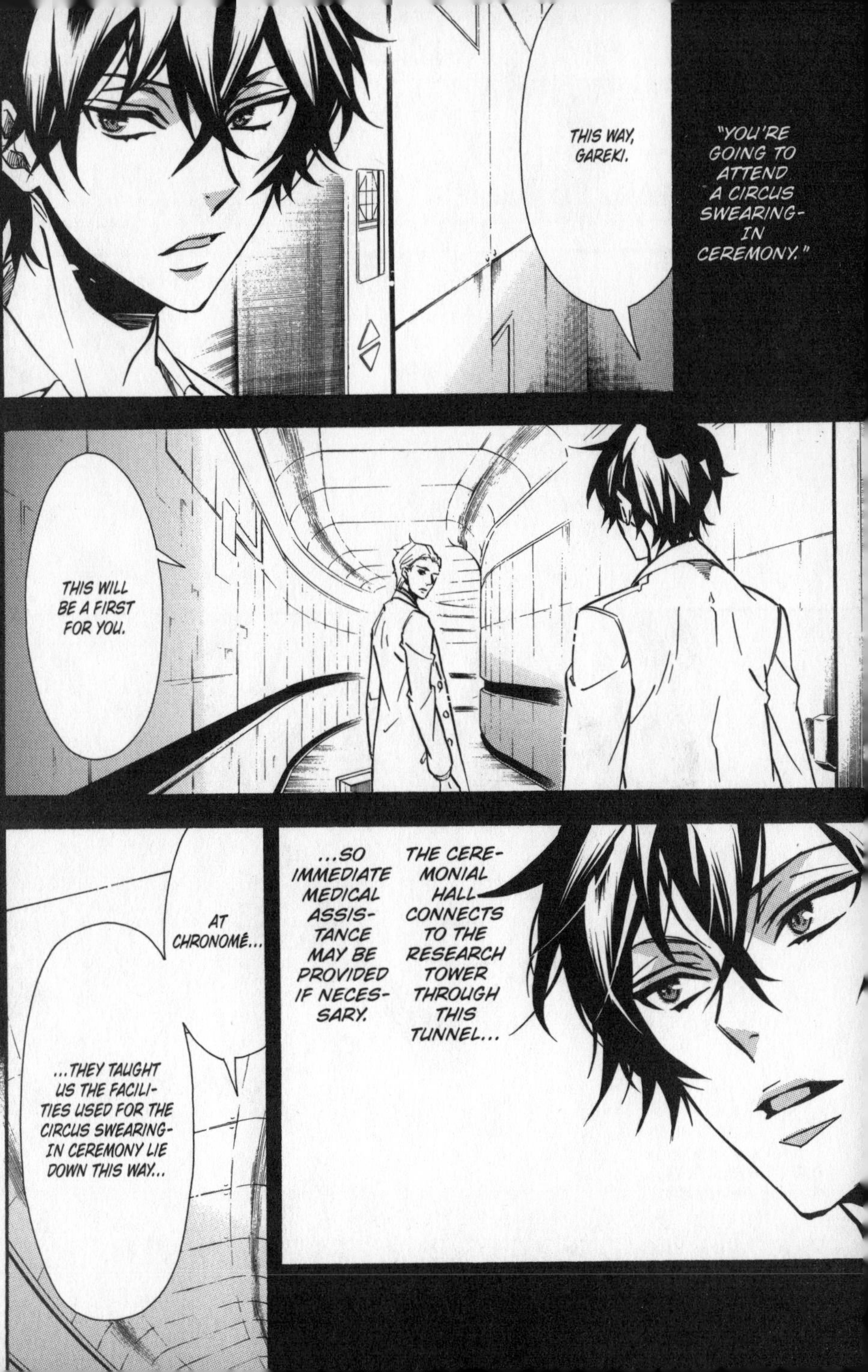
"YOU'RE GOING TO ATTEND A CIRCUS SWEARING-IN CEREMONY."
THIS WAY, GAREKI.
THIS WILL BE A FIRST FOR YOU.
THE CEREMONIAL HALL CONNECTS TO THE RESEARCH TOWER THROUGH THIS TUNNEL...
...SO IMMEDIATE MEDICAL ASSISTANCE MAY BE PROVIDED IF NECESSARY.
AT CHRONOMÉ...
...THEY TAUGHT US THE FACILITIES USED FOR THE CIRCUS SWEARING-IN CEREMONY LIE DOWN THIS WAY...

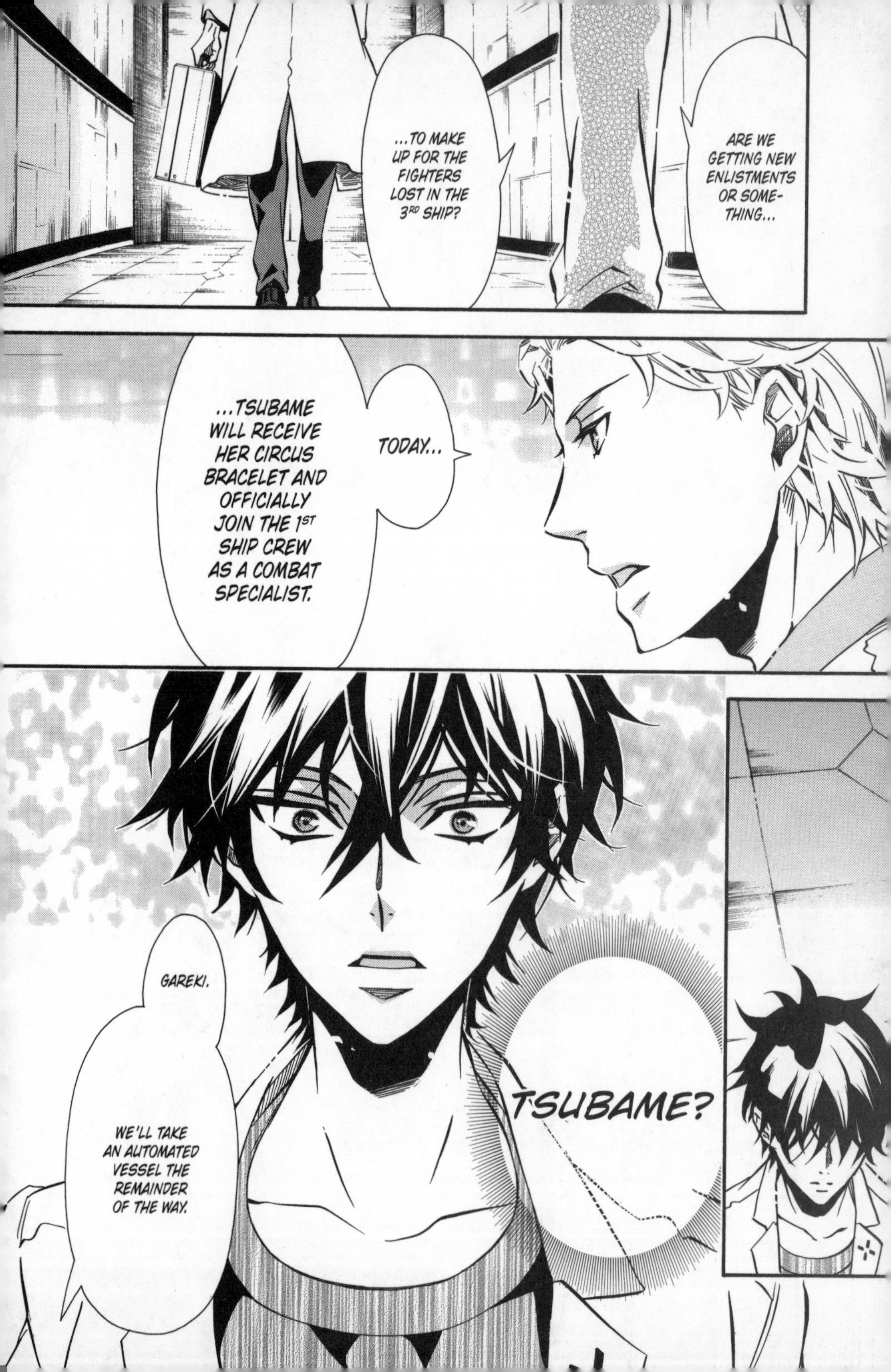

ARE WE GETTING NEW ENLISTMENTS OR SOMETHING...
...TO MAKE UP FOR THE FIGHTERS LOST IN THE 3RD SHIP?
TODAY...
...TSUBAME WILL RECEIVE HER CIRCUS BRACELET AND OFFICIALLY JOIN THE 1ST SHIP CREW AS A COMBAT SPECIALIST.
TSUBAME?
GAREKI.
WE'LL TAKE AN AUTOMATED VESSEL THE REMAINDER OF THE WAY.

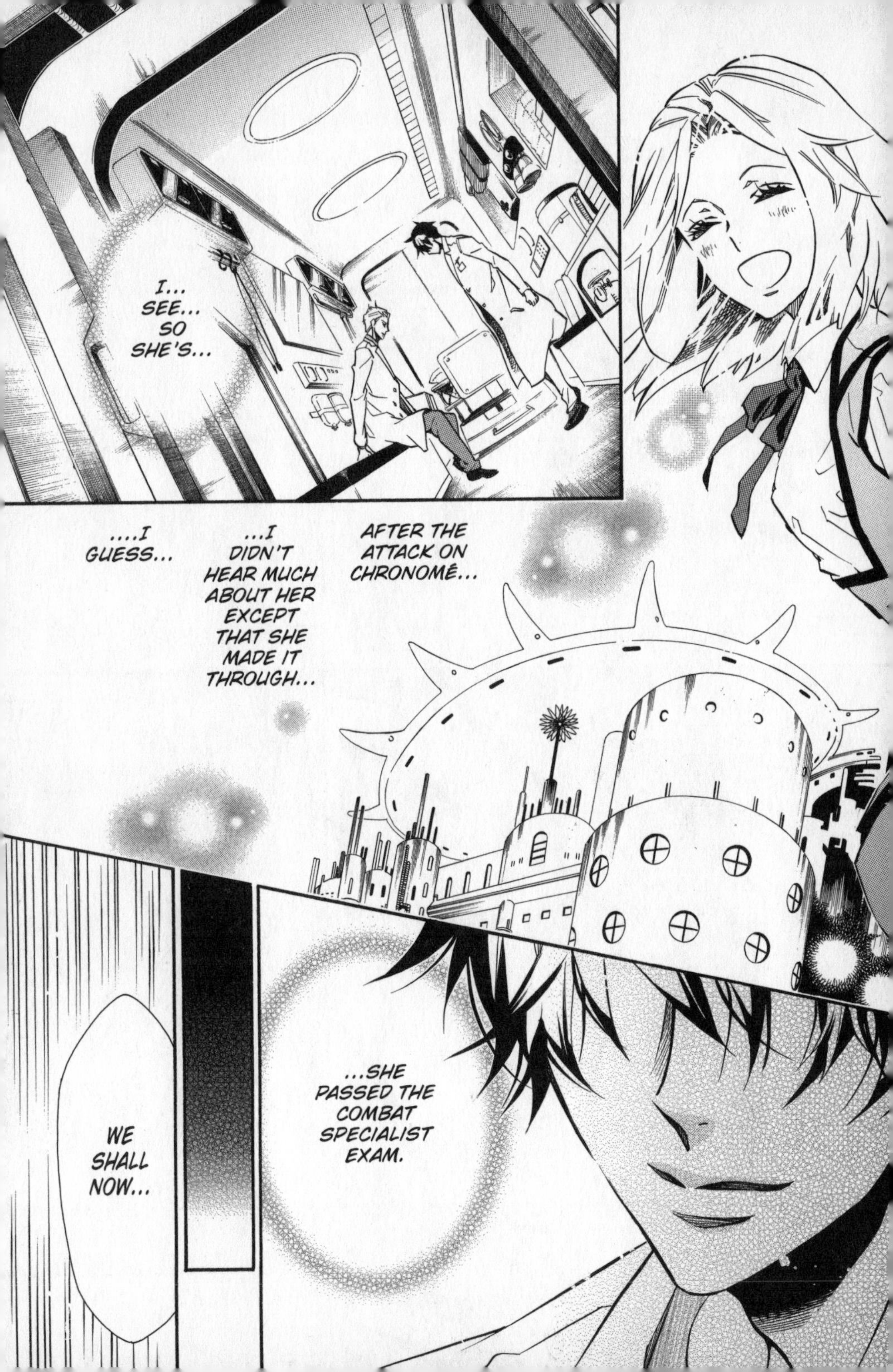
I... SEE... SO SHE'S...
AFTER THE ATTACK ON CHRONOMÉ...
...I DIDN'T HEAR MUCH ABOUT HER EXCEPT THAT SHE MADE IT THROUGH...
....I GUESS...
...SHE PASSED THE COMBAT SPECIALIST EXAM.
WE SHALL NOW...

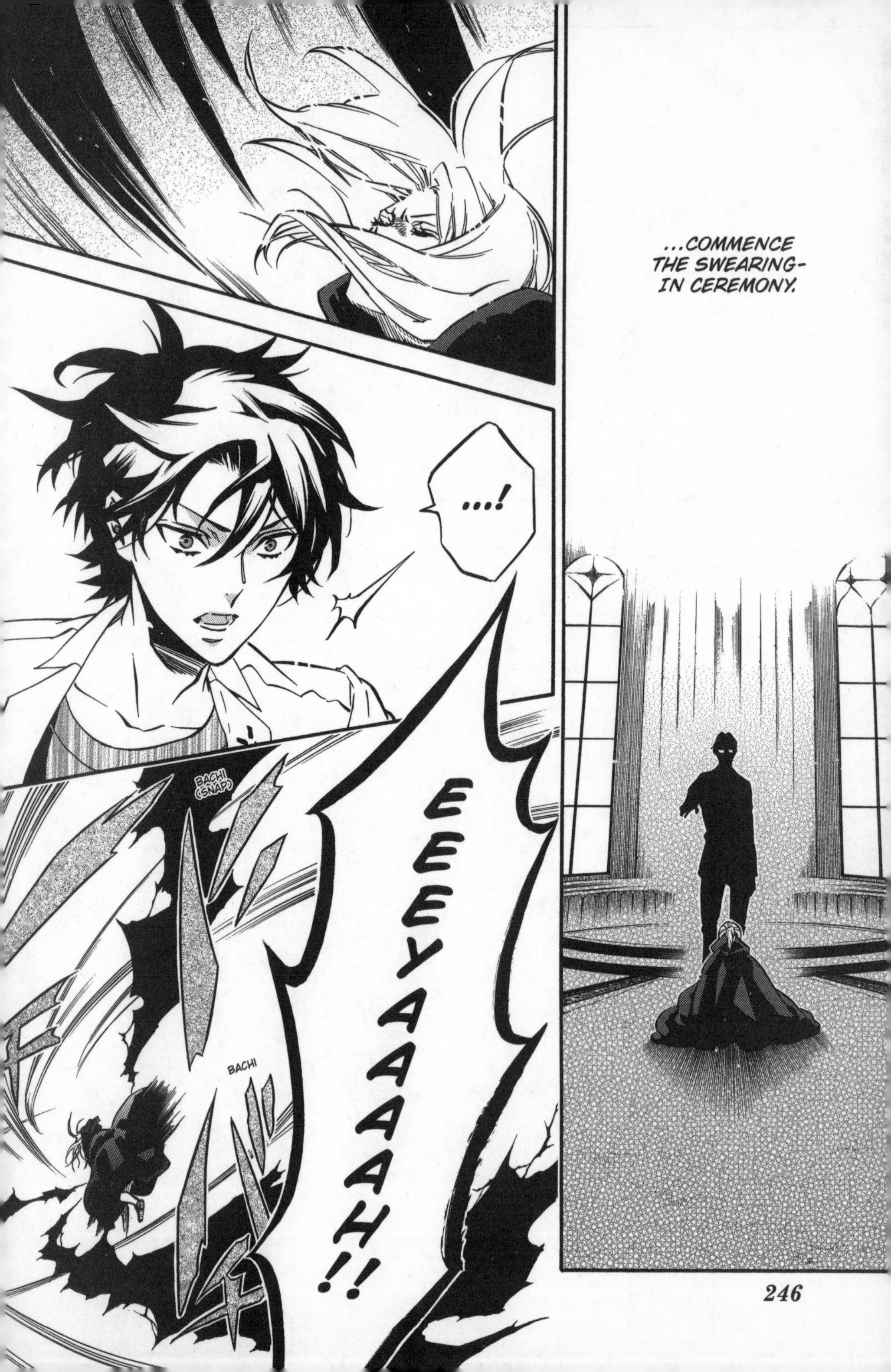
...COMMENCE THE SWEARING-IN CEREMONY.
...!
BACHI (SNAP)
EEEYAAAAAH!!
BACHI

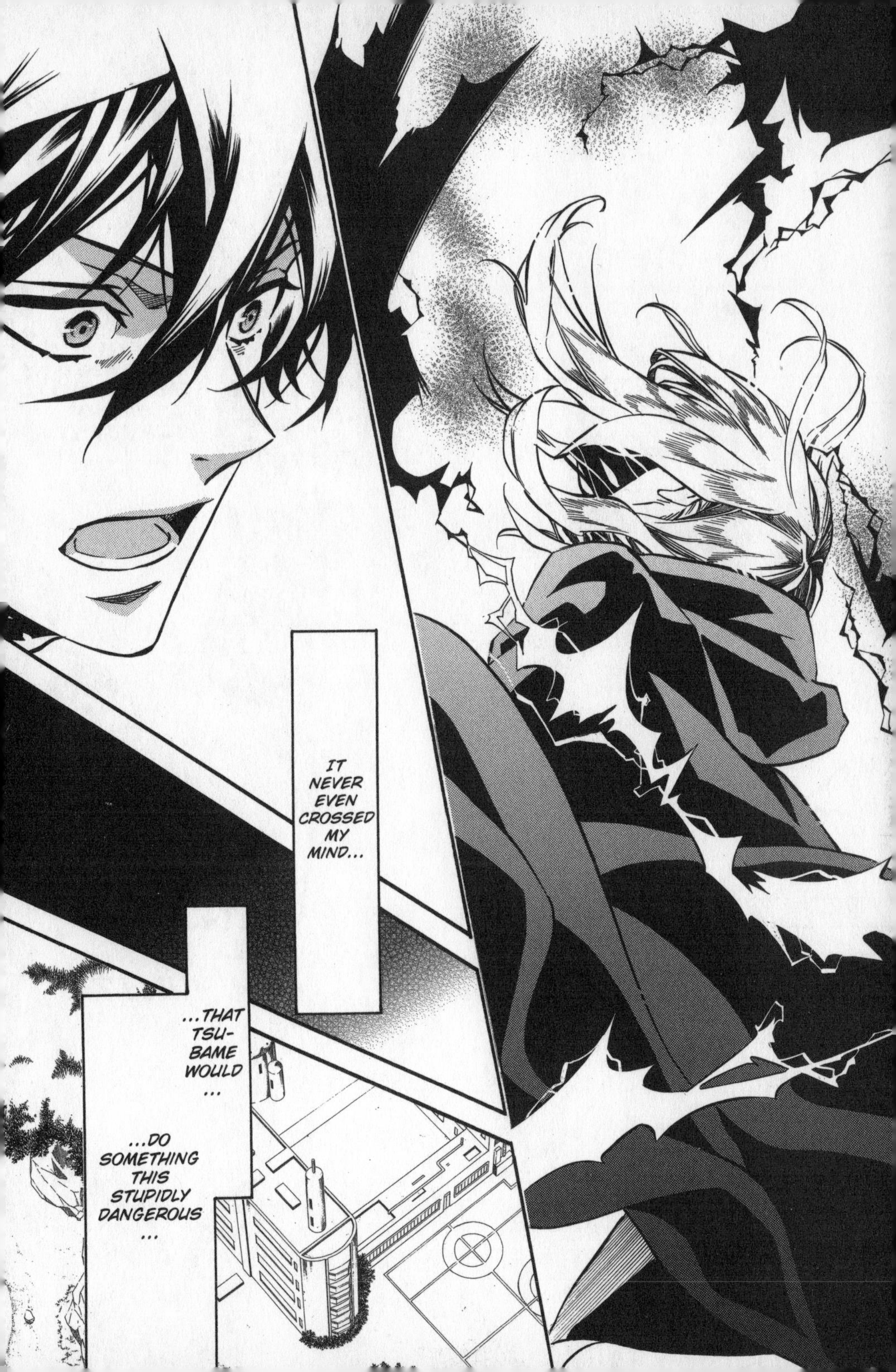

IT NEVER EVEN CROSSED MY MIND...
...THAT TSU-BAME WOULD...
...DO SOMETHING THIS STUPIDLY DANGEROUS...

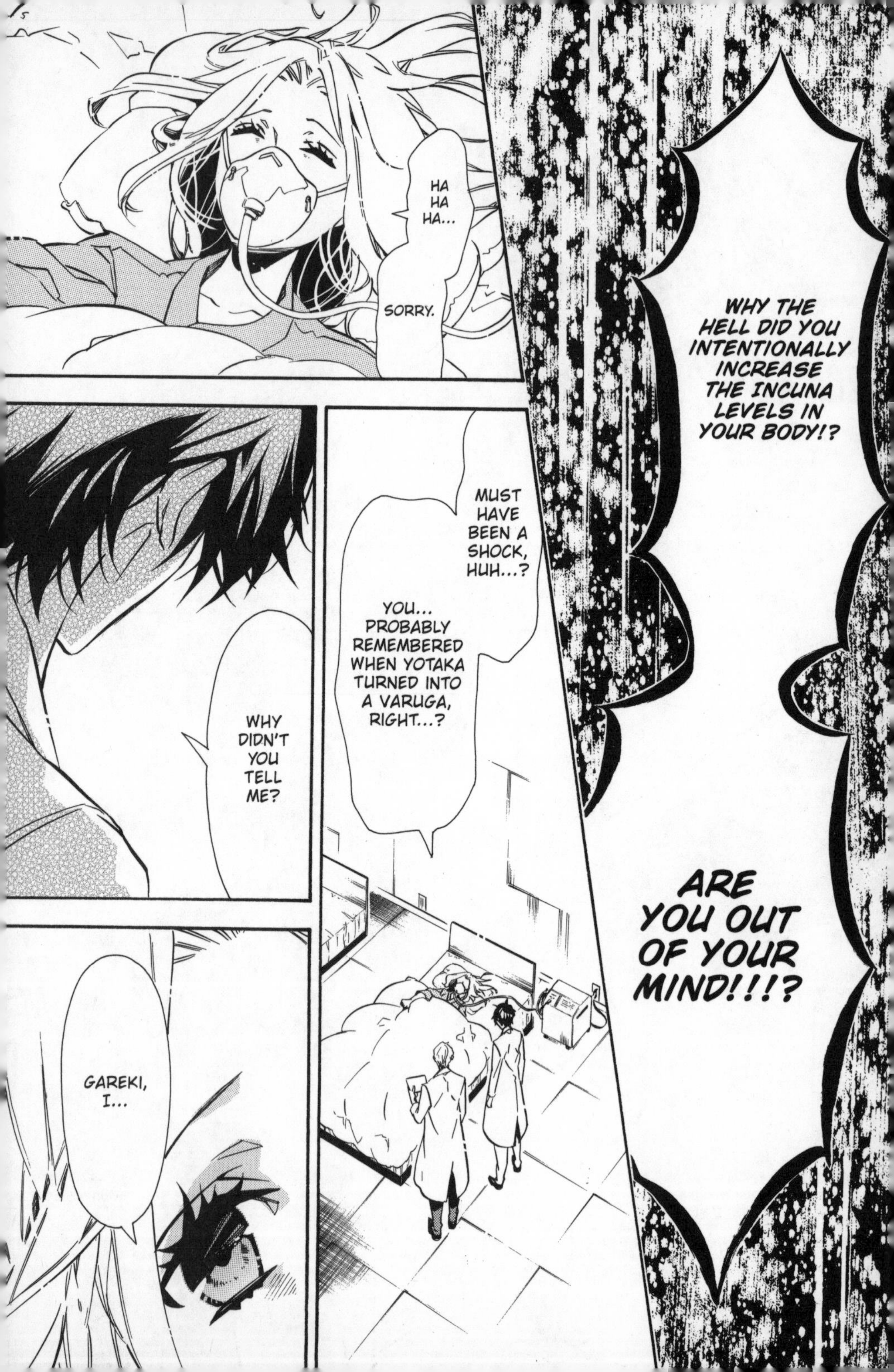
WHY THE HELL DID YOU INTENTIONALLY INCREASE THE INCUNA LEVELS IN YOUR BODY!?
ARE YOU OUT OF YOUR MIND!!!?
HA HA HA...
SORRY.
MUST HAVE BEEN A SHOCK, HUH...?
YOU... PROBABLY REMEMBERED WHEN YOTAKA TURNED INTO A VARUGA, RIGHT...?
WHY DIDN'T YOU TELL ME?
GAREKI, I...

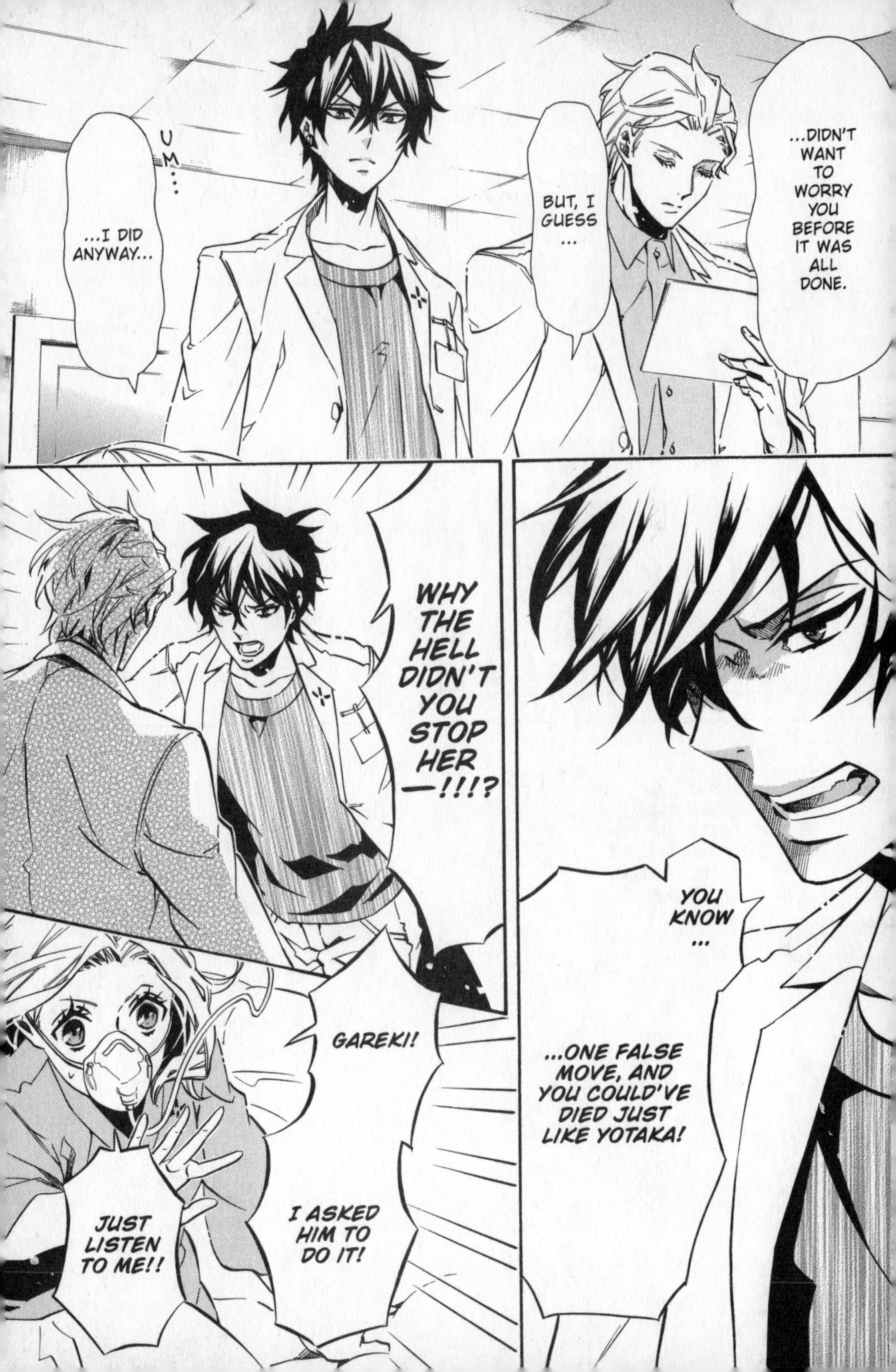
...DIDN'T WANT TO WORRY YOU BEFORE IT WAS ALL DONE.
BUT, I GUESS ...
UM...
...I DID ANYWAY...
YOU KNOW ...
...ONE FALSE MOVE, AND YOU COULD'VE DIED JUST LIKE YOTAKA!
WHY THE HELL DIDN'T YOU STOP HER—!!!?
GAREKI!
I ASKED HIM TO DO IT!
JUST LISTEN TO ME!!

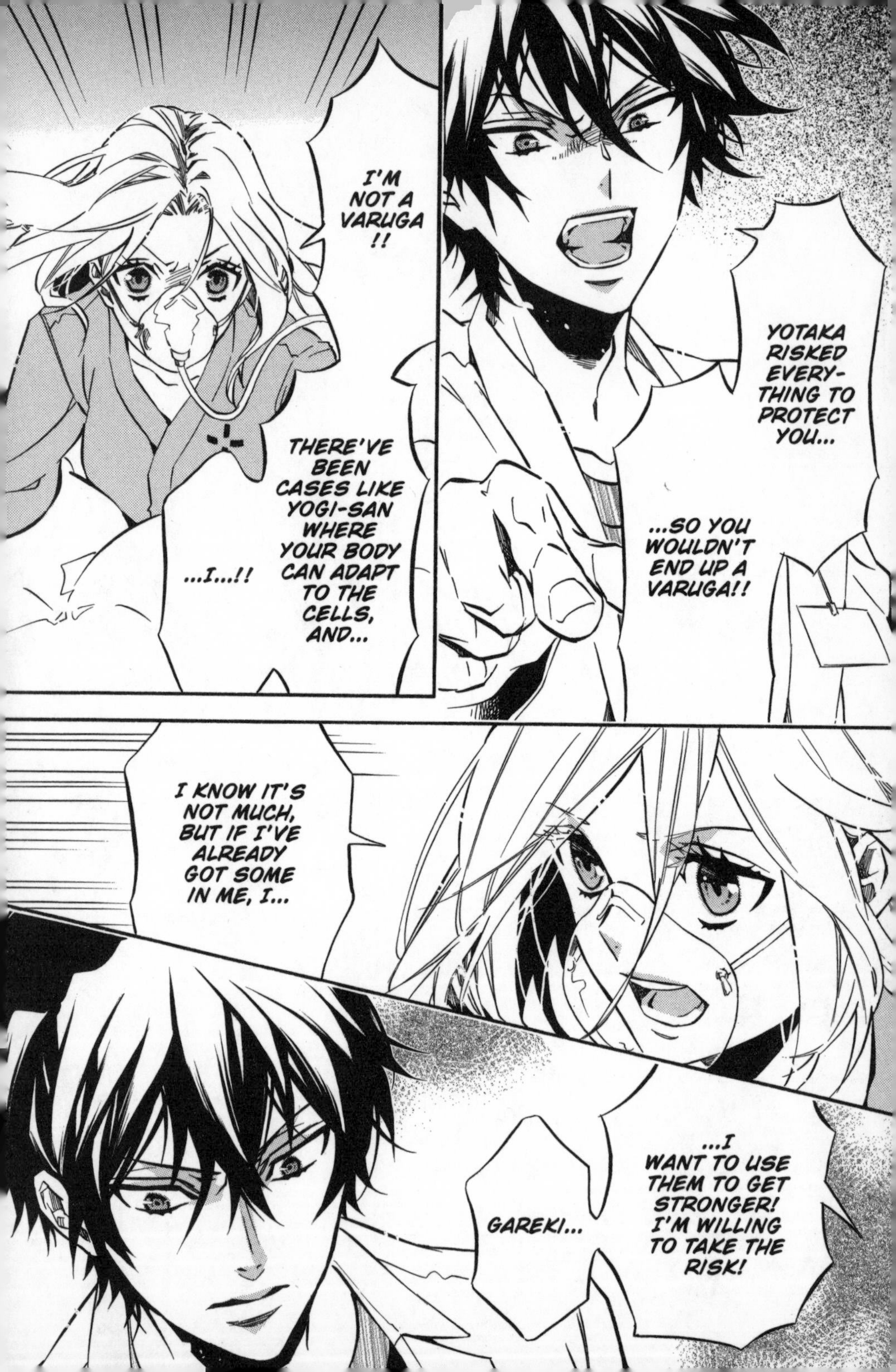
YOTAKA RISKED EVERY-THING TO PROTECT YOU...
...SO YOU WOULDN'T END UP A VARUGA!!
I'M NOT A VARUGA!!
THERE'VE BEEN CASES LIKE YOGI-SAN WHERE YOUR BODY CAN ADAPT TO THE CELLS, AND...
...I...!!
I KNOW IT'S NOT MUCH, BUT IF I'VE ALREADY GOT SOME IN ME, I...
...I WANT TO USE THEM TO GET STRONGER! I'M WILLING TO TAKE THE RISK!
GAREKI...

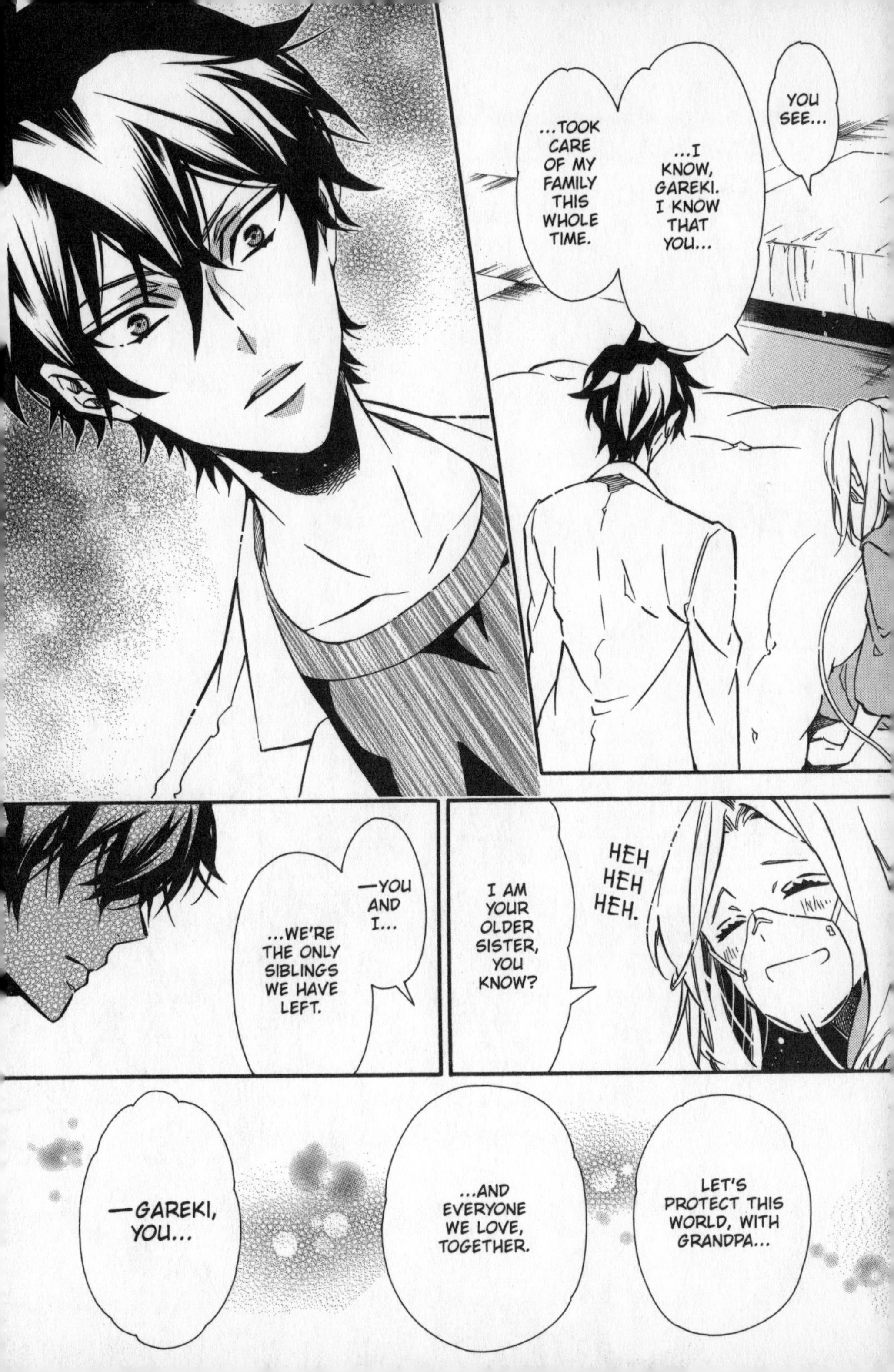
YOU SEE...
...I KNOW, GAREKI. I KNOW THAT YOU...
...TOOK CARE OF MY FAMILY THIS WHOLE TIME.
HEH HEH HEH.
I AM YOUR OLDER SISTER, YOU KNOW?
—YOU AND I...
...WE'RE THE ONLY SIBLINGS WE HAVE LEFT.
LET'S PROTECT THIS WORLD, WITH GRANDPA...
...AND EVERYONE WE LOVE, TOGETHER.
—GAREKI, YOU...

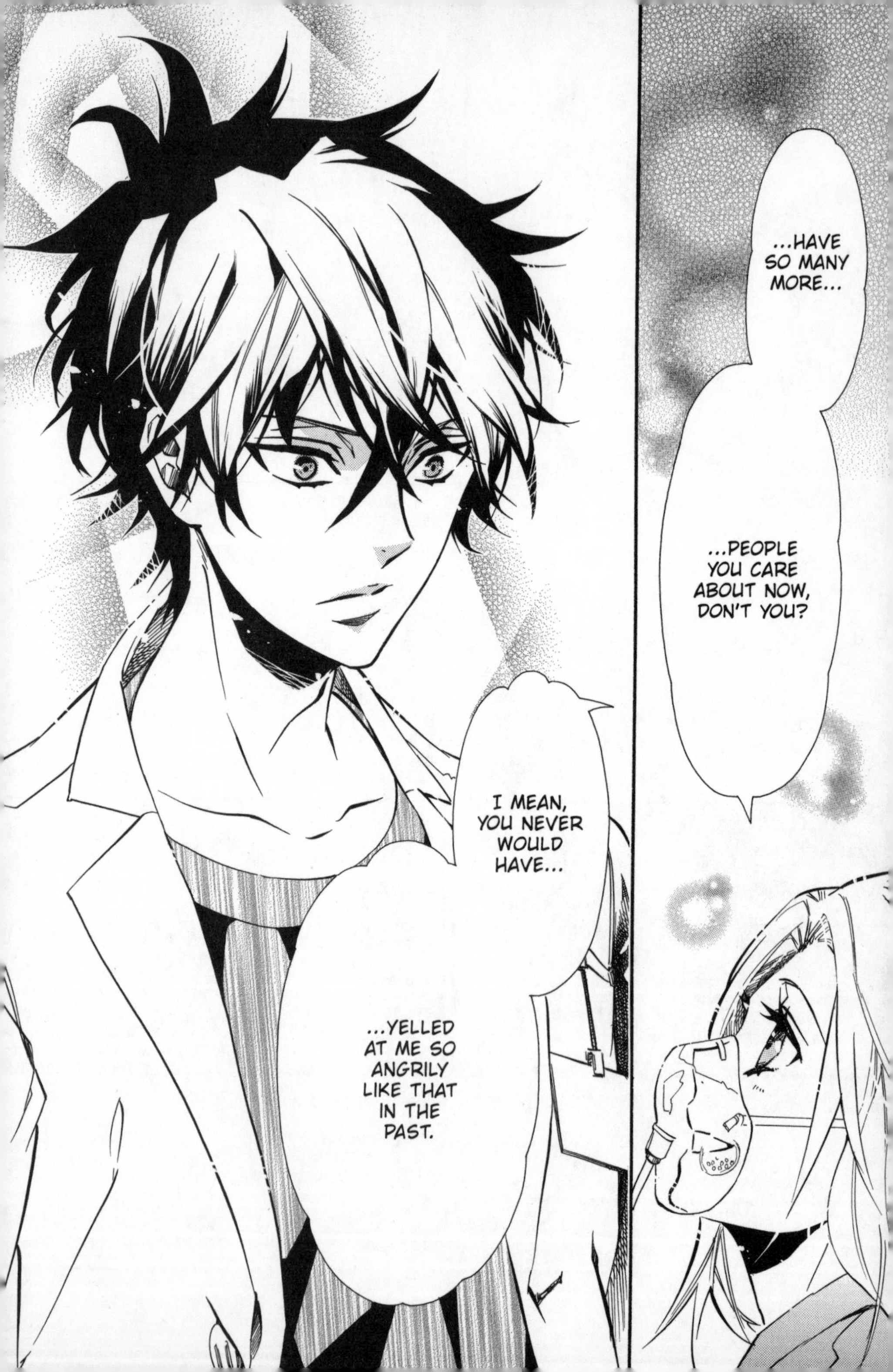
...HAVE SO MANY MORE...
...PEOPLE YOU CARE ABOUT NOW, DON'T YOU?
I MEAN, YOU NEVER WOULD HAVE...
...YELLED AT ME SO ANGRILY LIKE THAT IN THE PAST.

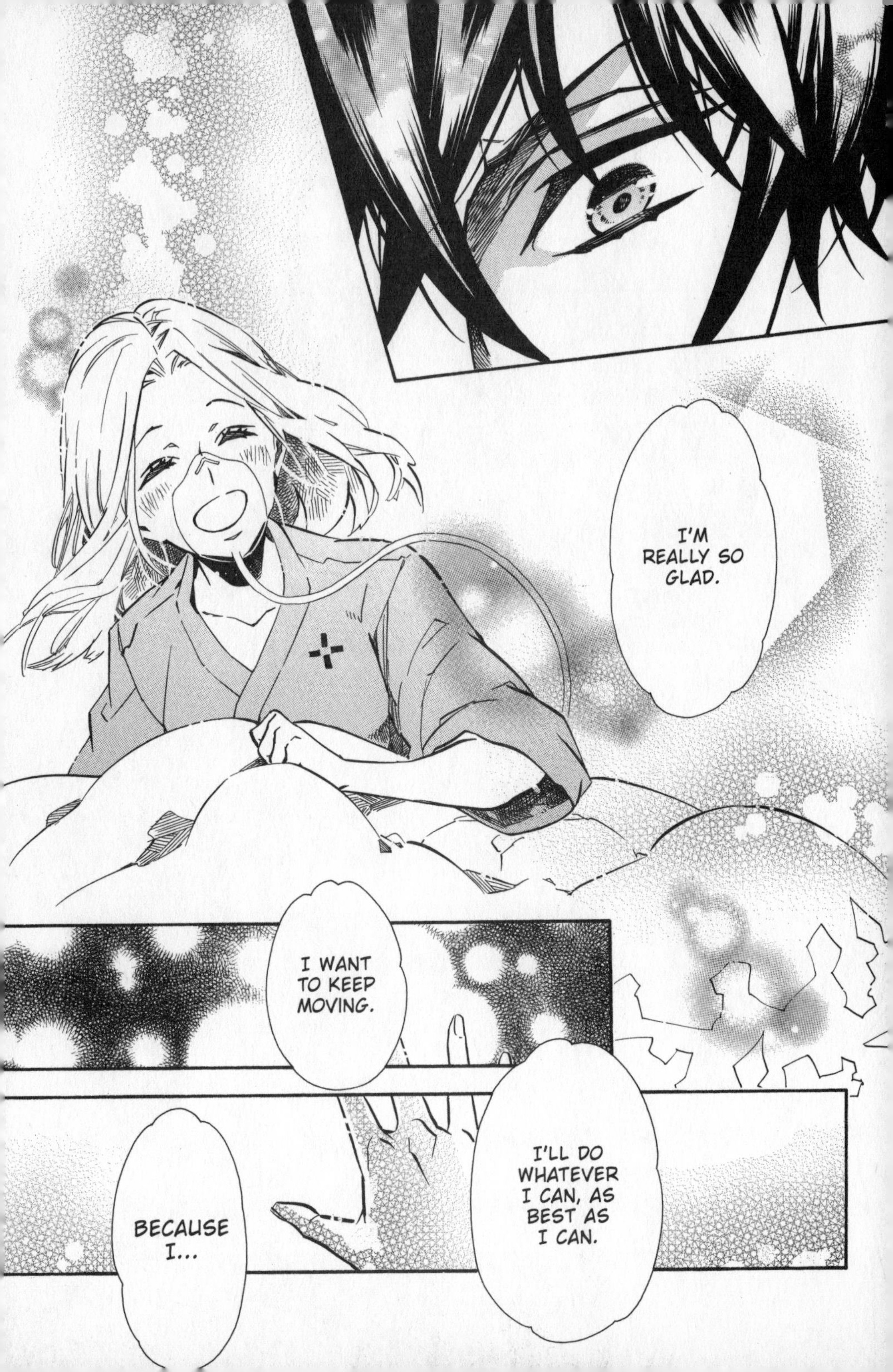
I'M REALLY SO GLAD.
I WANT TO KEEP MOVING.
I'LL DO WHATEVER I CAN, AS BEST AS I CAN.
BECAUSE I...

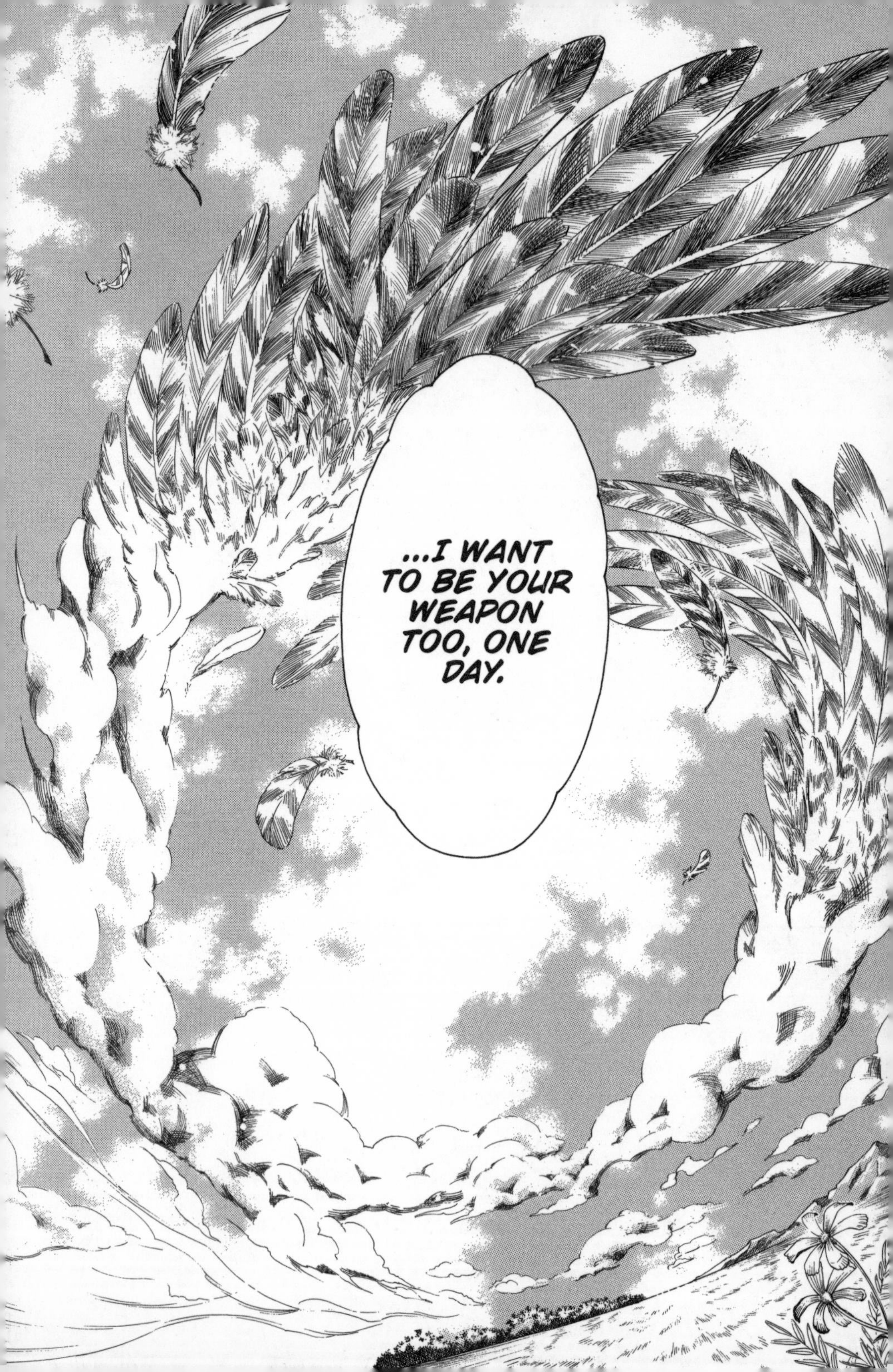
...I WANT TO BE YOUR WEAPON TOO, ONE DAY.

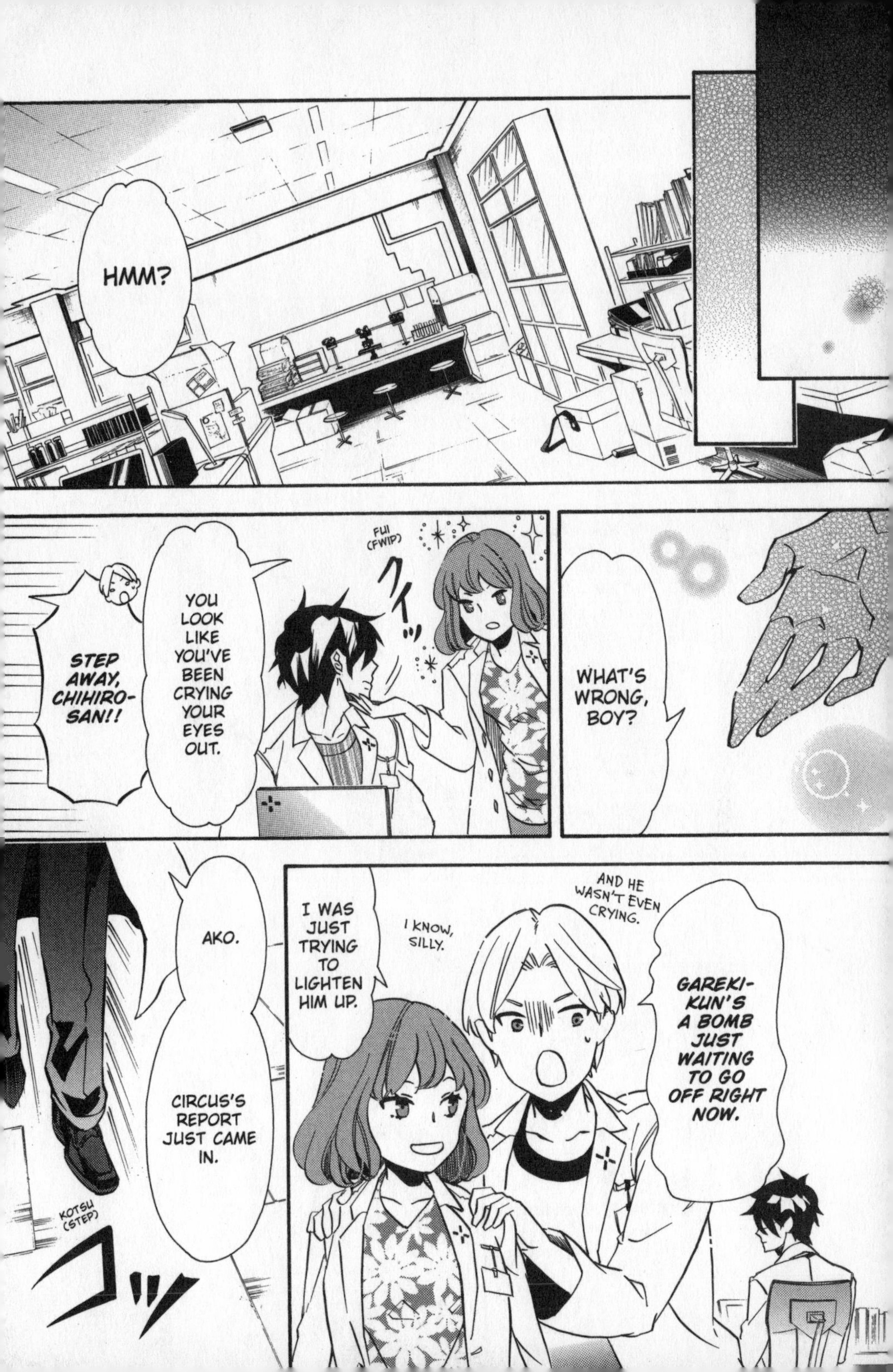
HMM?
WHAT'S WRONG, BOY?
FUI (FWIP)
YOU LOOK LIKE YOU'VE BEEN CRYING YOUR EYES OUT.
STEP AWAY, CHIHIRO-SAN!!
GAREKI-KUN'S A BOMB JUST WAITING TO GO OFF RIGHT NOW.
AND HE WASN'T EVEN CRYING.
I WAS JUST TRYING TO LIGHTEN HIM UP.
I KNOW, SILLY.
AKO.
CIRCUS'S REPORT JUST CAME IN.
KOTSU (STEP)

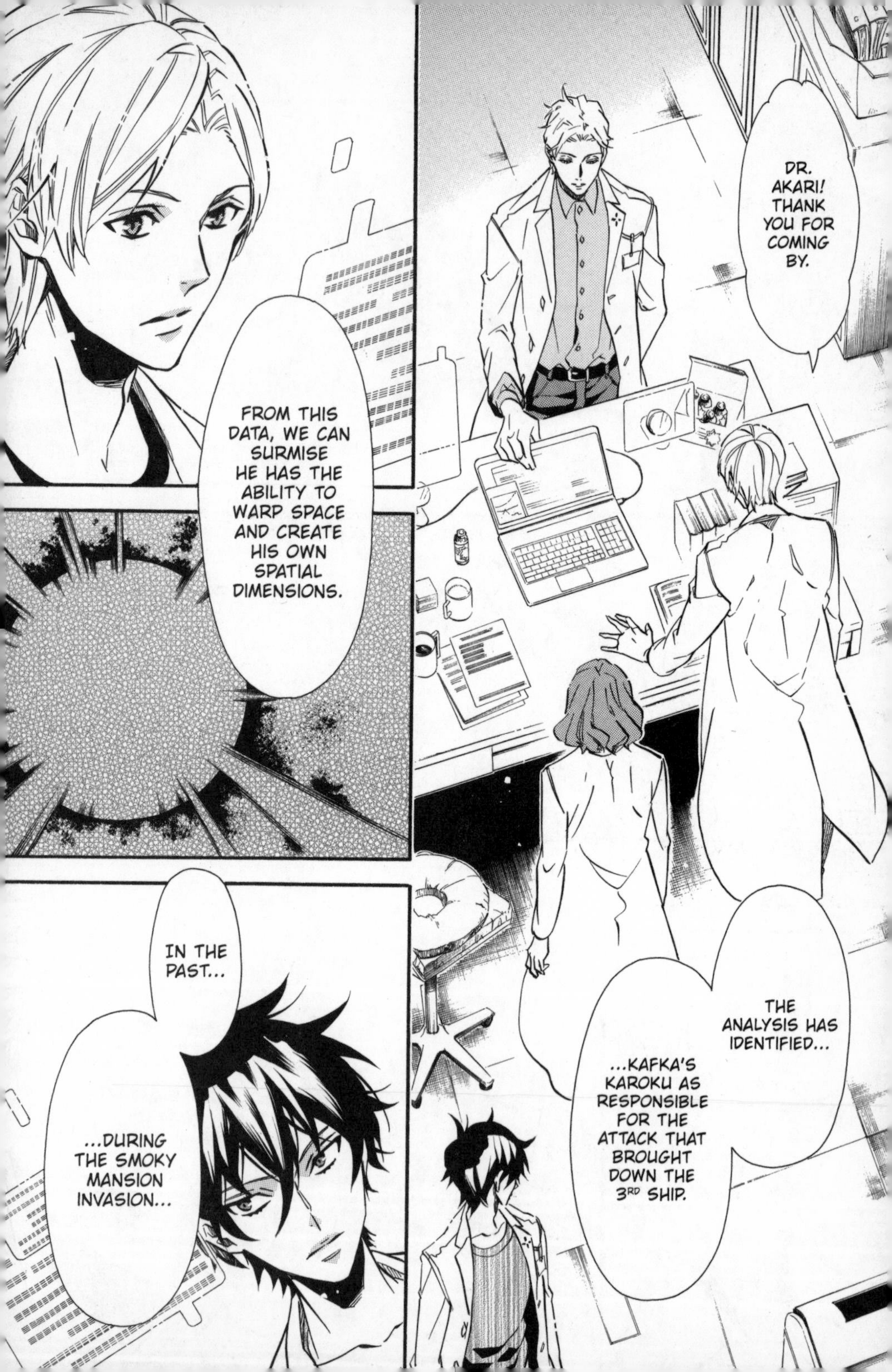
DR. AKARI! THANK YOU FOR COMING BY.
THE ANALYSIS HAS IDENTIFIED...
...KAFKA'S KAROKU AS RESPONSIBLE FOR THE ATTACK THAT BROUGHT DOWN THE 3RD SHIP.
FROM THIS DATA, WE CAN SURMISE HE HAS THE ABILITY TO WARP SPACE AND CREATE HIS OWN SPATIAL DIMENSIONS.
IN THE PAST...
...DURING THE SMOKY MANSION INVASION...

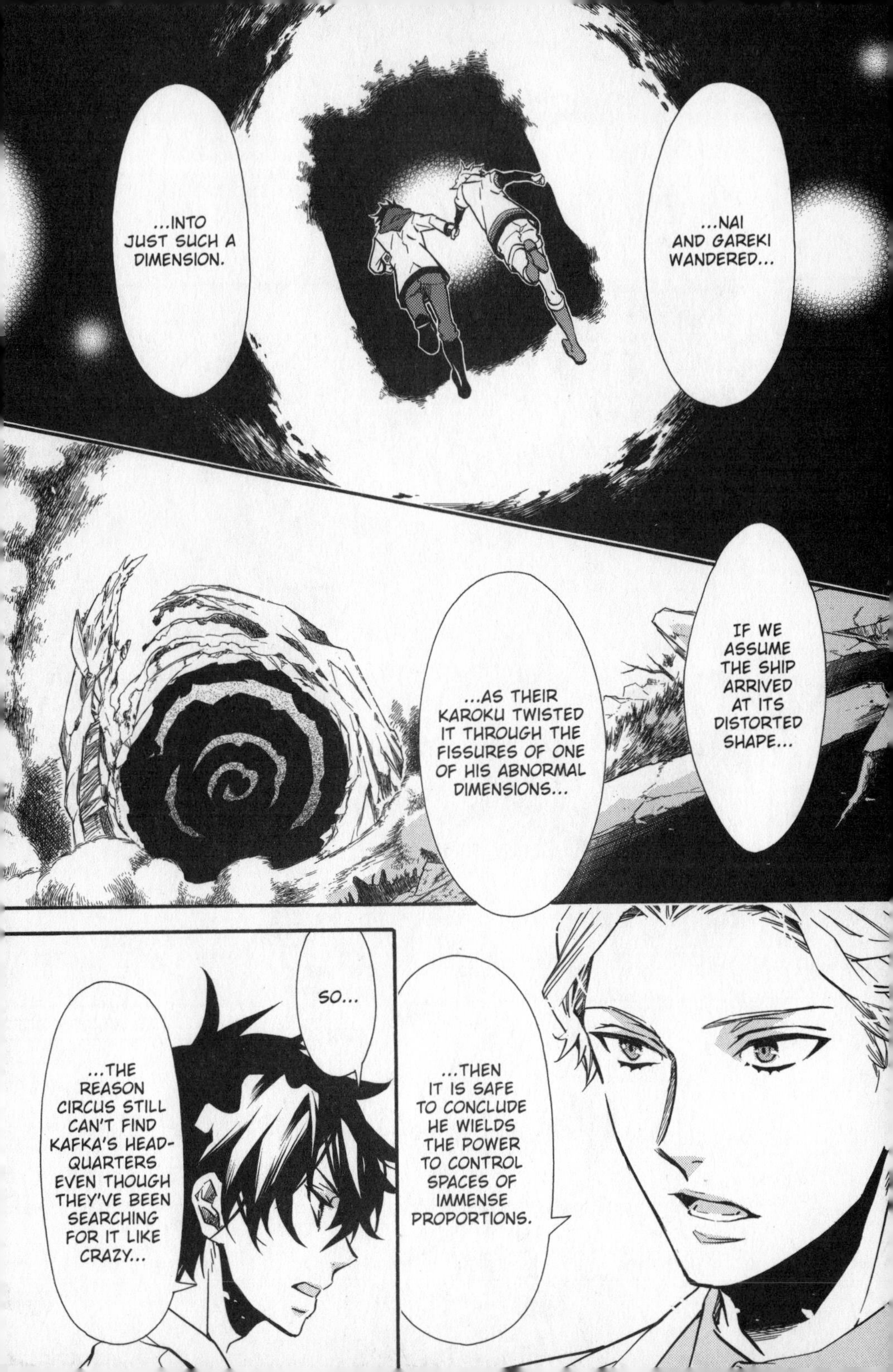
...NAI AND GAREKI WANDERED...
...INTO JUST SUCH A DIMENSION.
IF WE ASSUME THE SHIP ARRIVED AT ITS DISTORTED SHAPE...
...AS THEIR KAROKU TWISTED IT THROUGH THE FISSURES OF ONE OF HIS ABNORMAL DIMENSIONS...
...THEN IT IS SAFE TO CONCLUDE HE WIELDS THE POWER TO CONTROL SPACES OF IMMENSE PROPORTIONS.
SO...
...THE REASON CIRCUS STILL CAN'T FIND KAFKA'S HEAD-QUARTERS EVEN THOUGH THEY'VE BEEN SEARCHING FOR IT LIKE CRAZY...

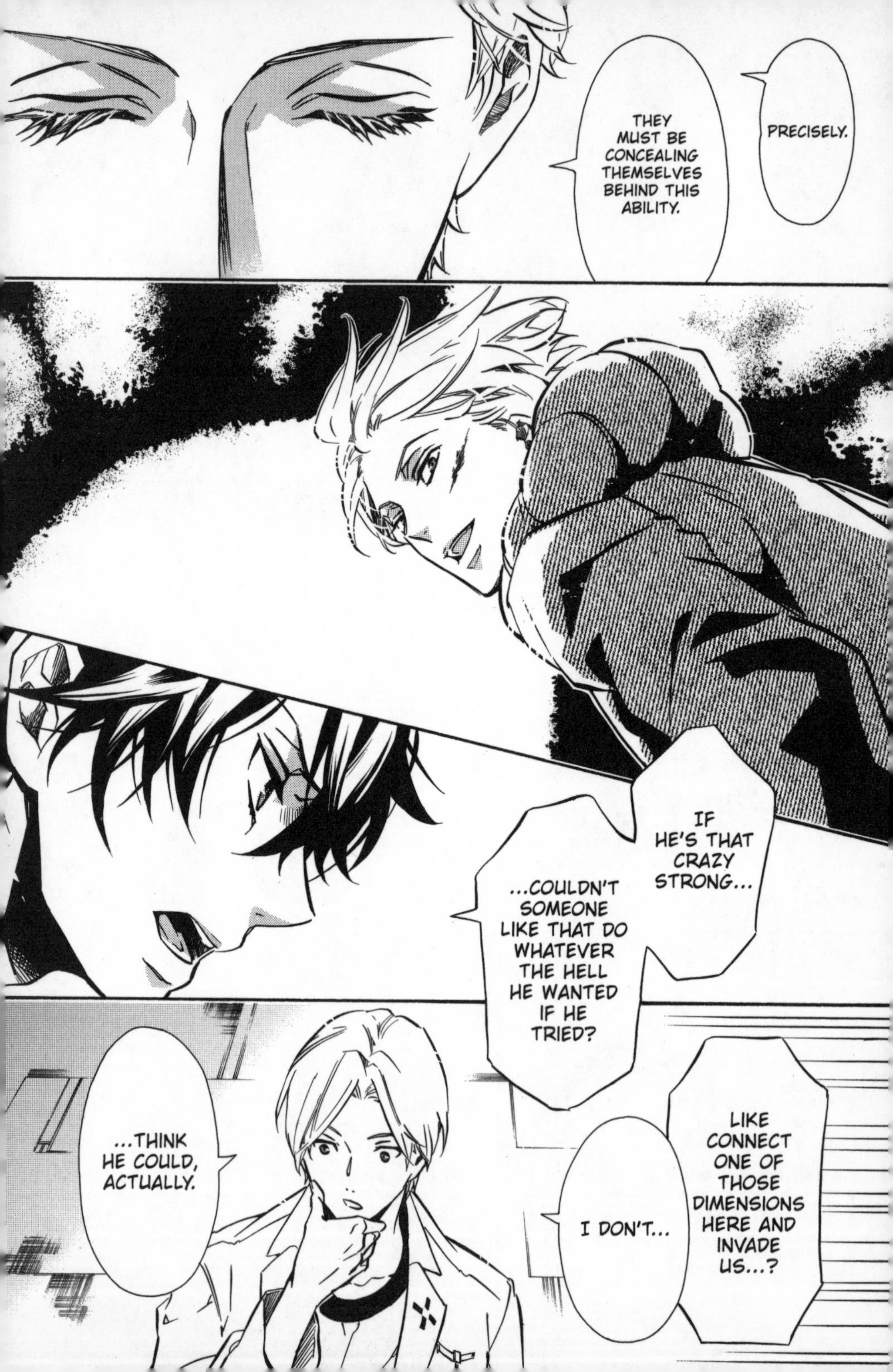
PRECISELY.
THEY MUST BE CONCEALING THEMSELVES BEHIND THIS ABILITY.
IF HE'S THAT CRAZY STRONG...
...COULDN'T SOMEONE LIKE THAT DO WHATEVER THE HELL HE WANTED IF HE TRIED?
LIKE CONNECT ONE OF THOSE DIMENSIONS HERE AND INVADE US...?
I DON'T...
...THINK HE COULD, ACTUALLY.

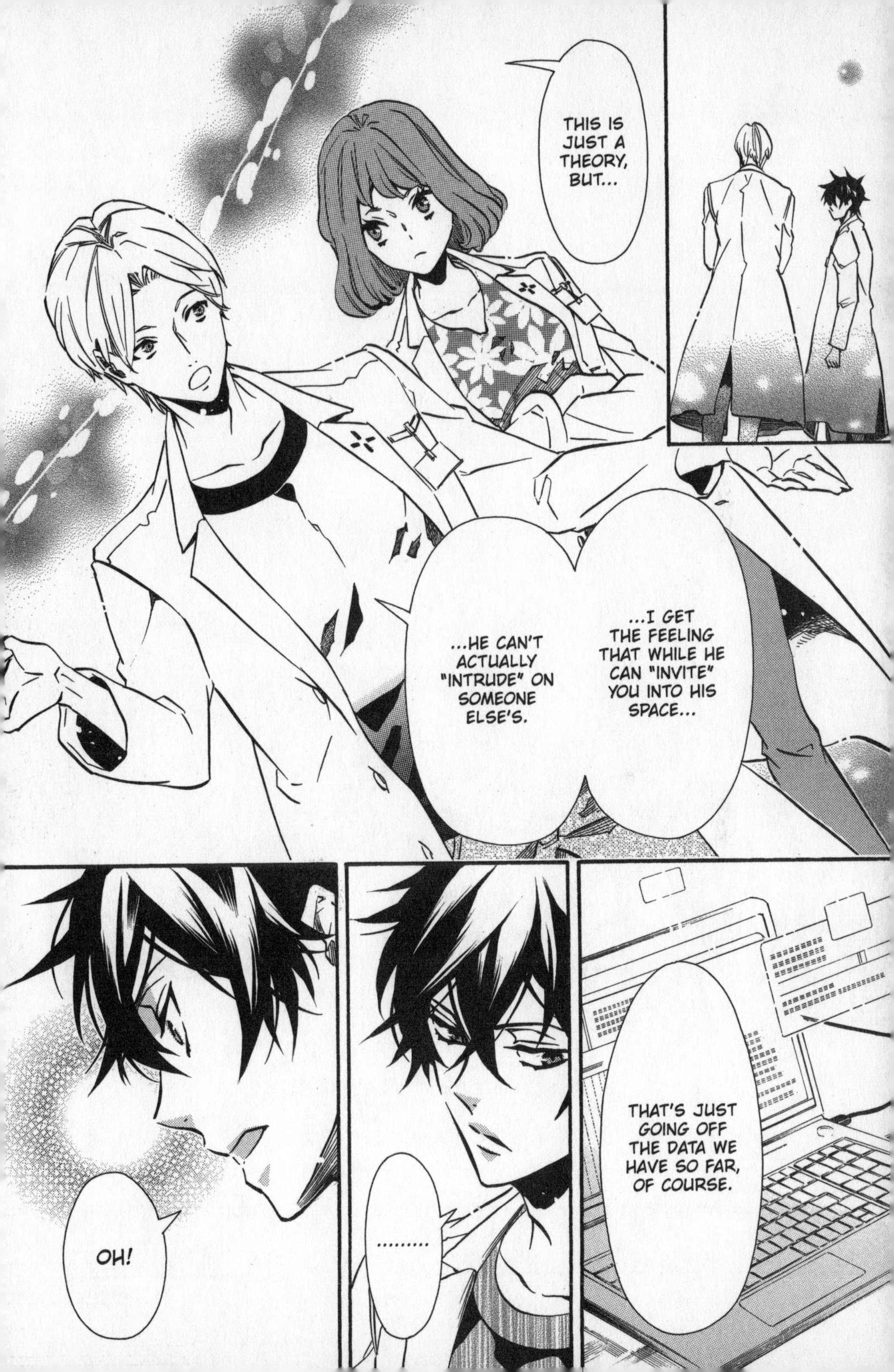
THIS IS JUST A THEORY, BUT...
...I GET THE FEELING THAT WHILE HE CAN "INVITE" YOU INTO HIS SPACE...
...HE CAN'T ACTUALLY "INTRUDE" ON SOMEONE ELSE'S.
THAT'S JUST GOING OFF THE DATA WE HAVE SO FAR, OF COURSE.
.........
OH!

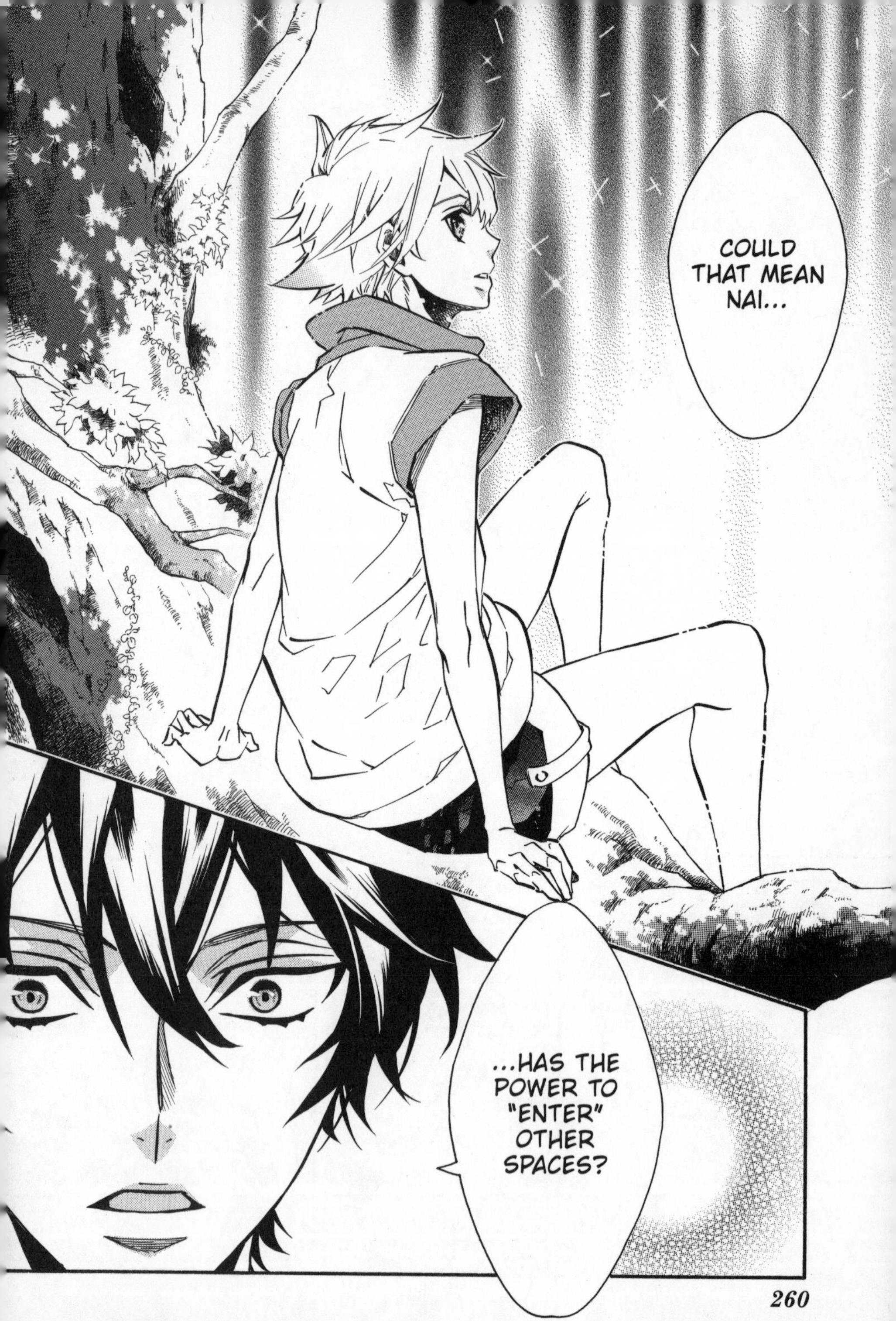
COULD THAT MEAN NAI...
...HAS THE POWER TO "ENTER" OTHER SPACES?

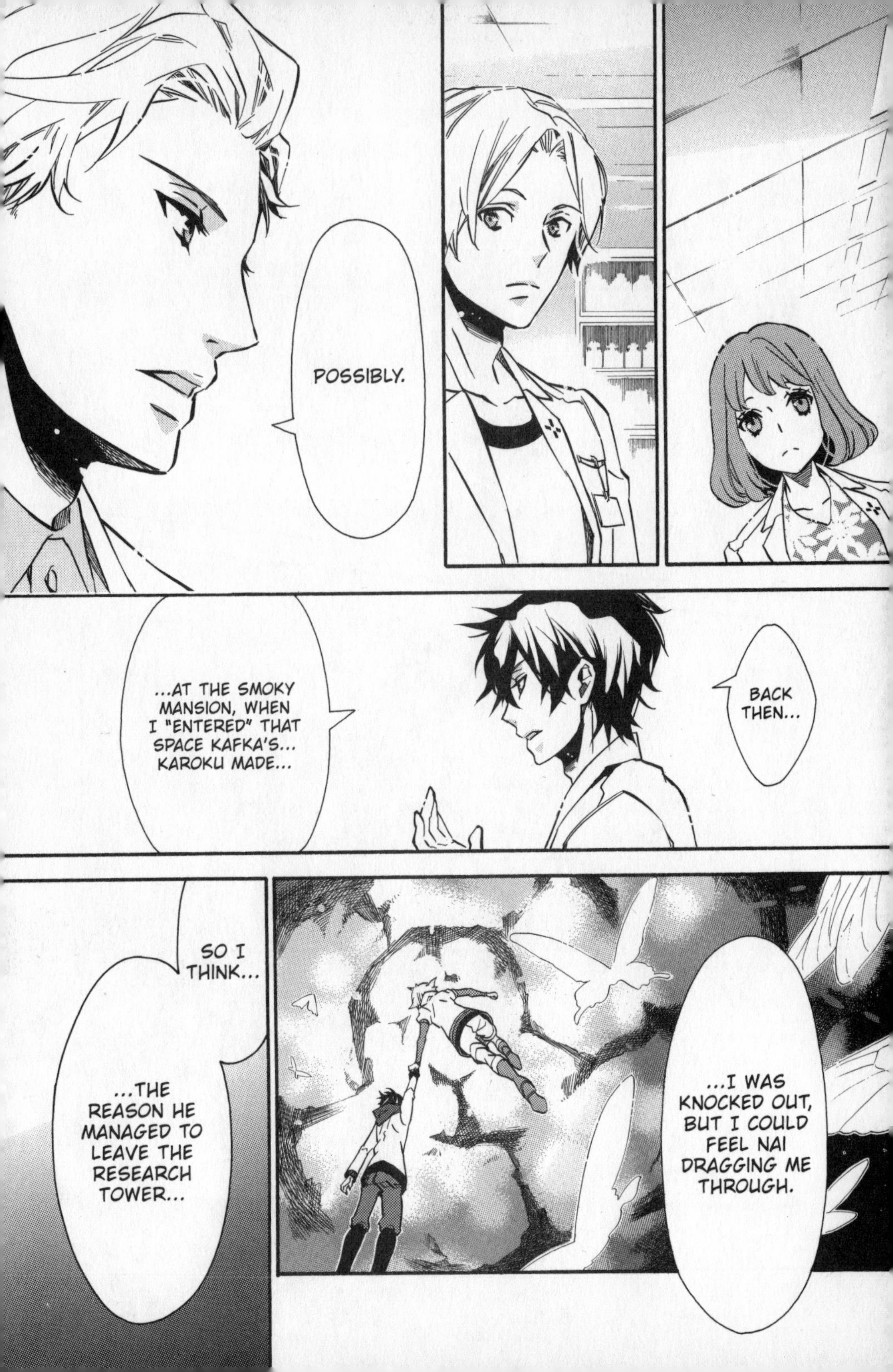
POSSIBLY.
BACK THEN...
...AT THE SMOKY MANSION, WHEN I "ENTERED" THAT SPACE KAFKA'S... KAROKU MADE...
...I WAS KNOCKED OUT, BUT I COULD FEEL NAI DRAGGING ME THROUGH.
SO I THINK...
...THE REASON HE MANAGED TO LEAVE THE RESEARCH TOWER...

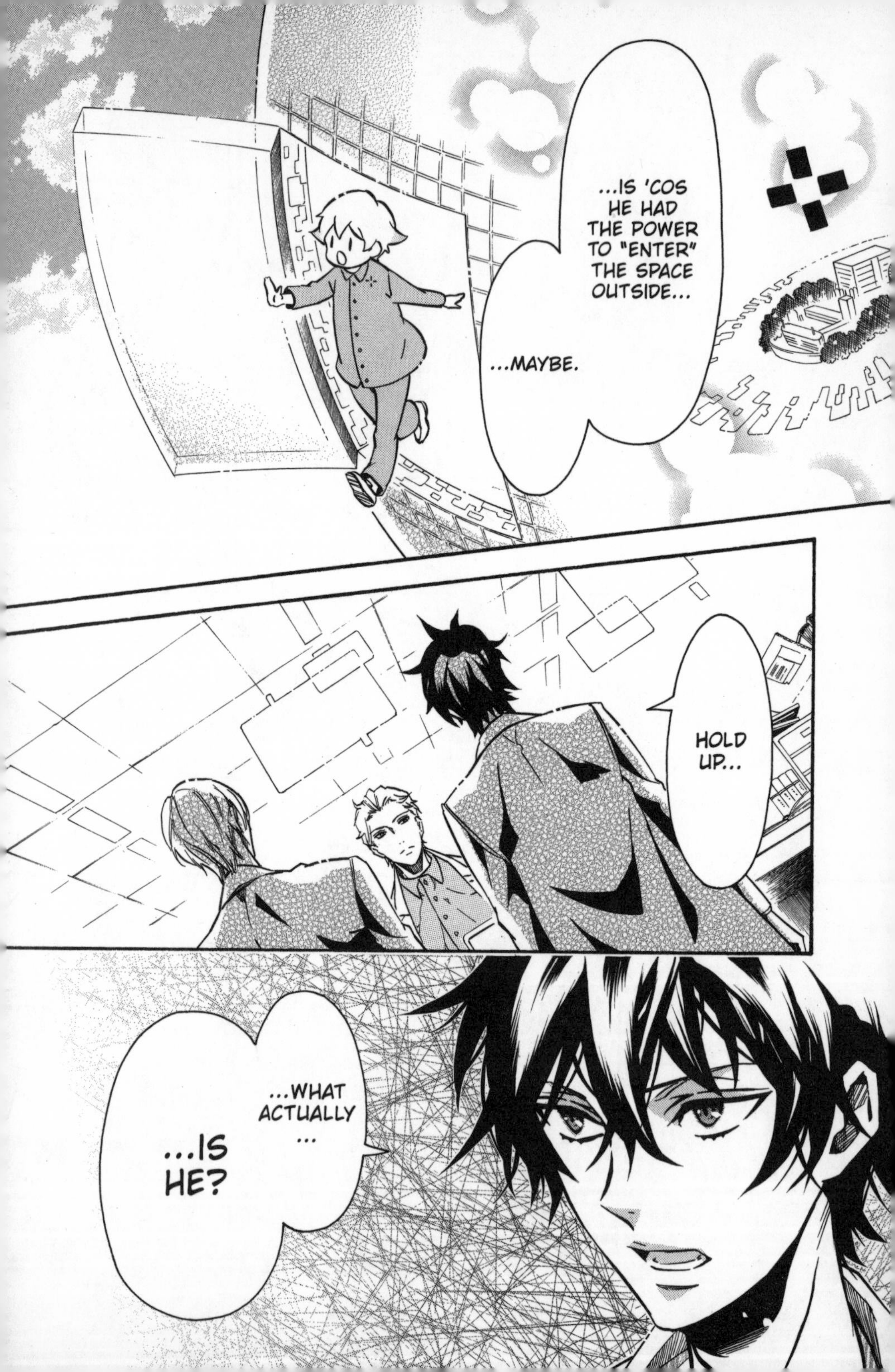
...IS 'COS HE HAD THE POWER TO "ENTER" THE SPACE OUTSIDE...
...MAYBE.
HOLD UP...
...WHAT ACTUALLY ...
...IS HE?

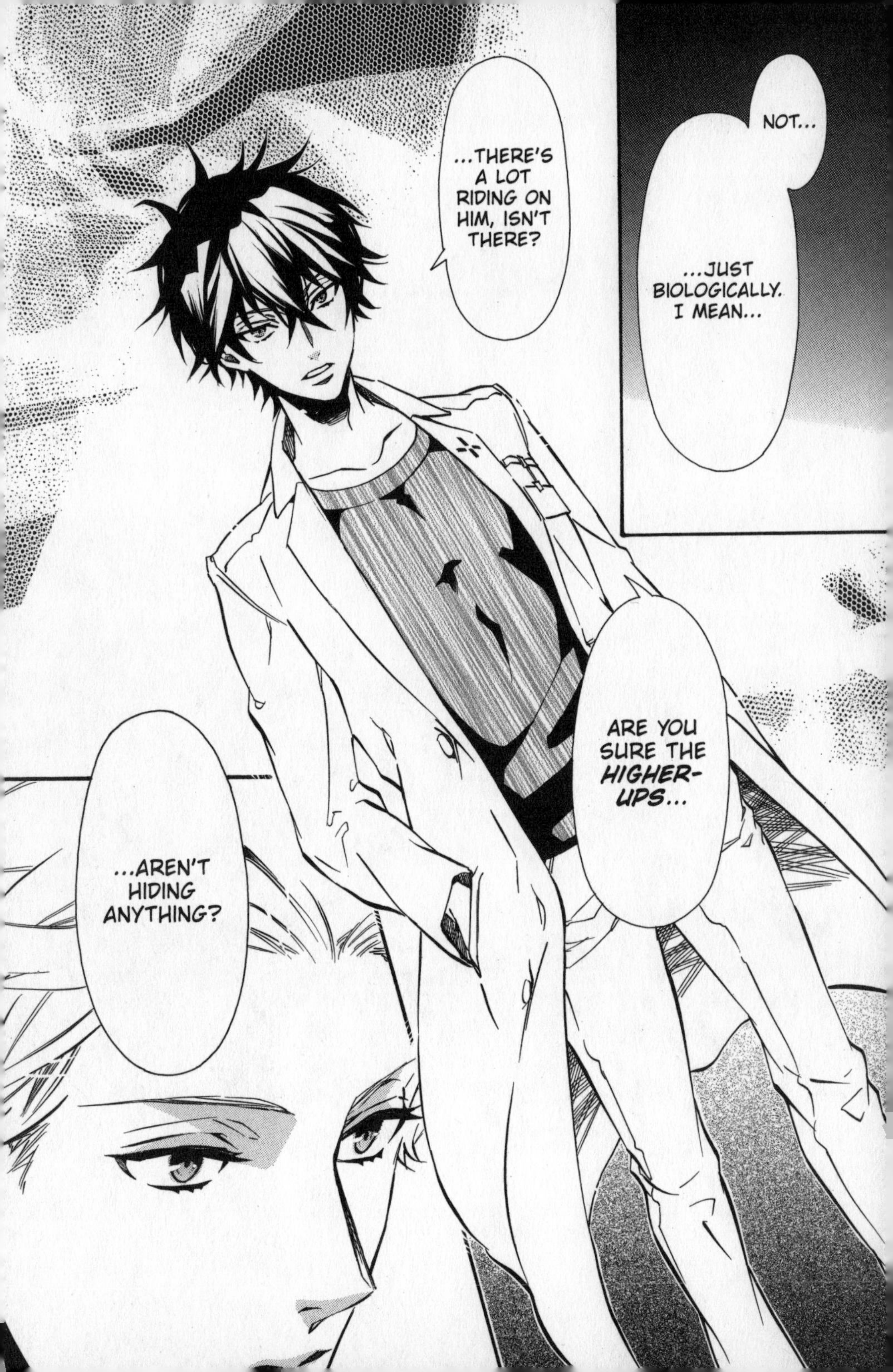
NOT...
...JUST BIOLOGICALLY. I MEAN...
...THERE'S A LOT RIDING ON HIM, ISN'T THERE?
ARE YOU SURE THE *HIGHER-UPS*...
...AREN'T HIDING ANYTHING?

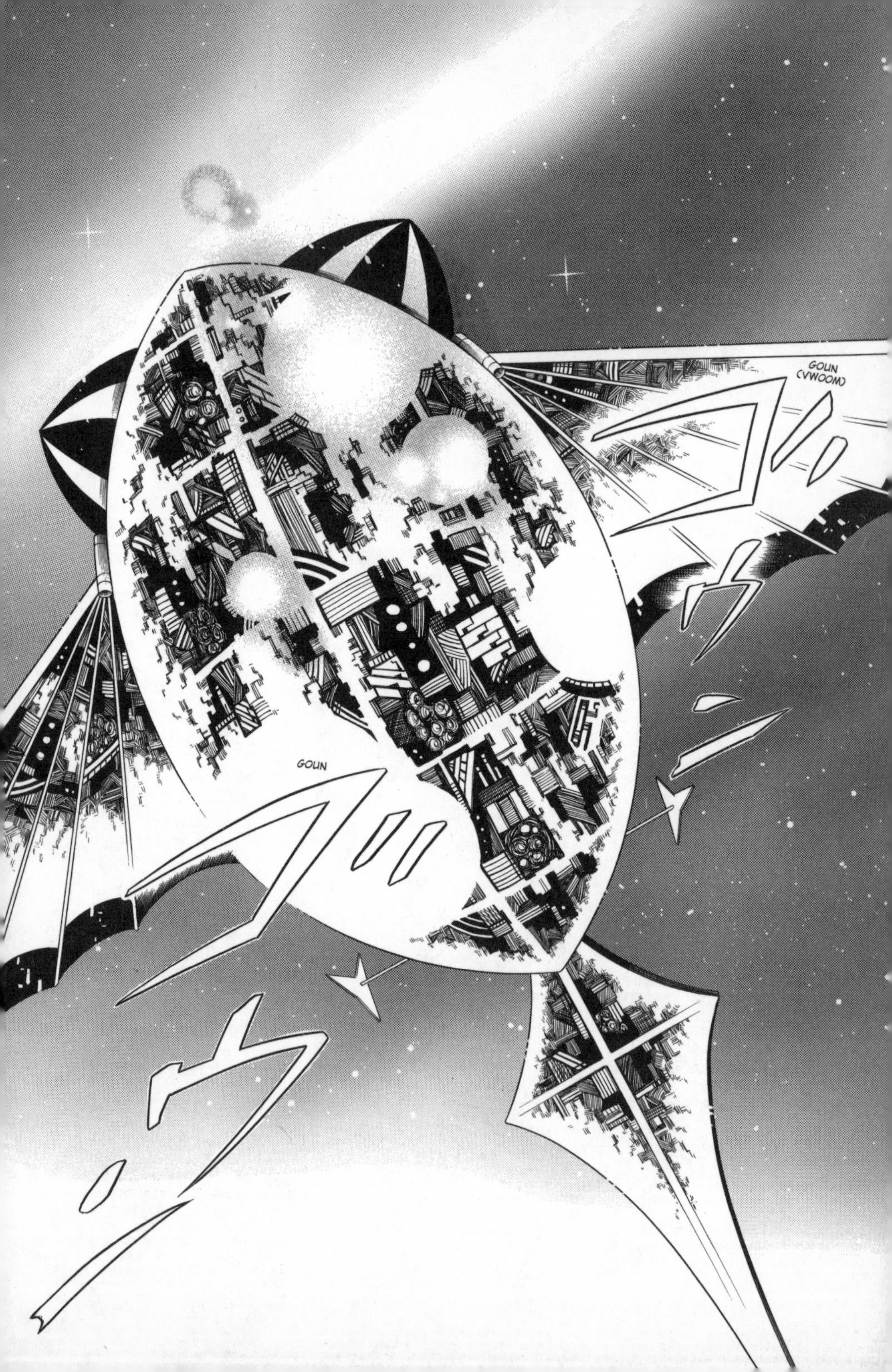
GOUN
(VWOOM)
GOUN

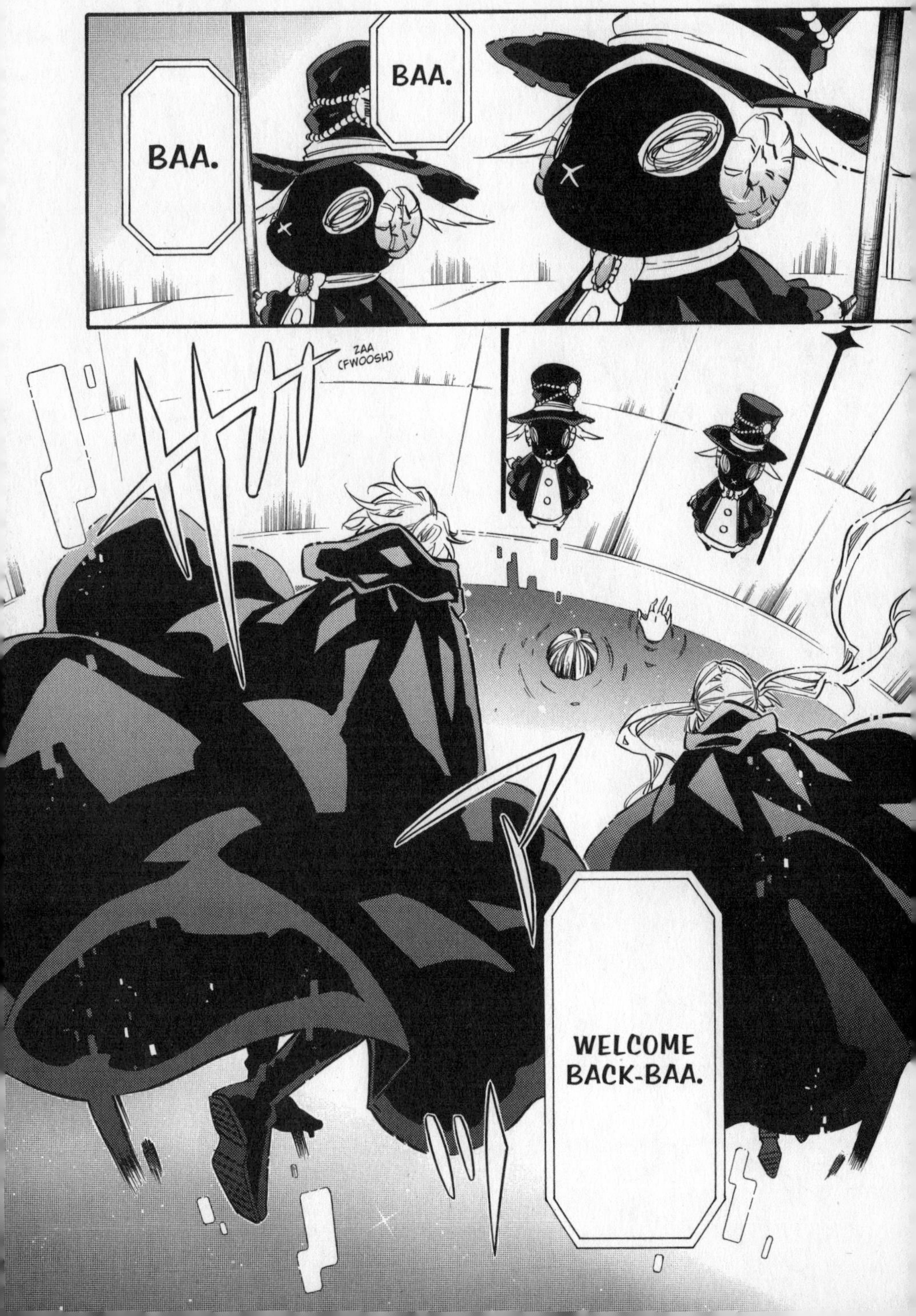
BAA.
BAA.
ZAA (FWOOSH)
WELCOME BACK-BAA.

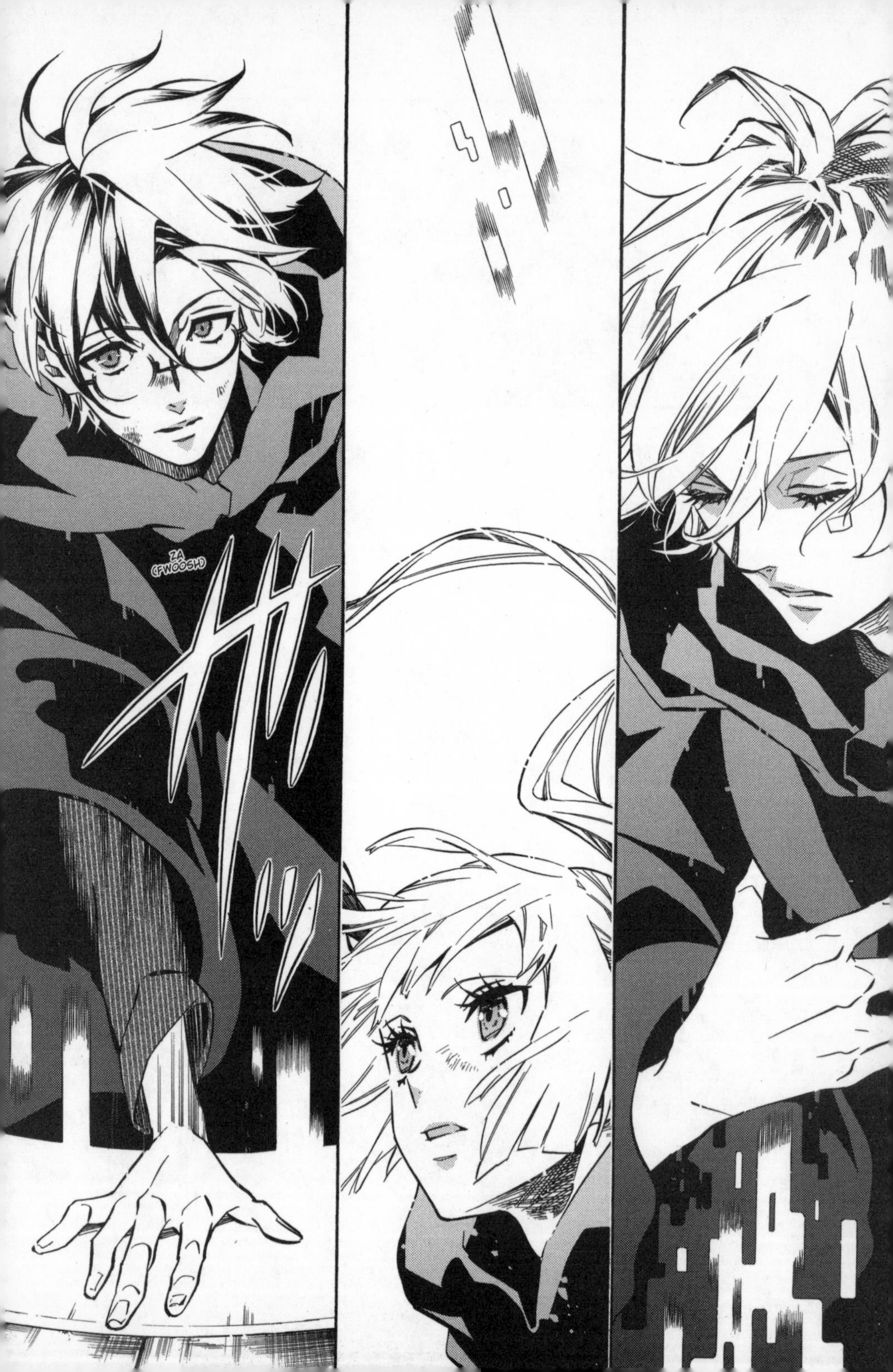
ZA
(FWOOSH)

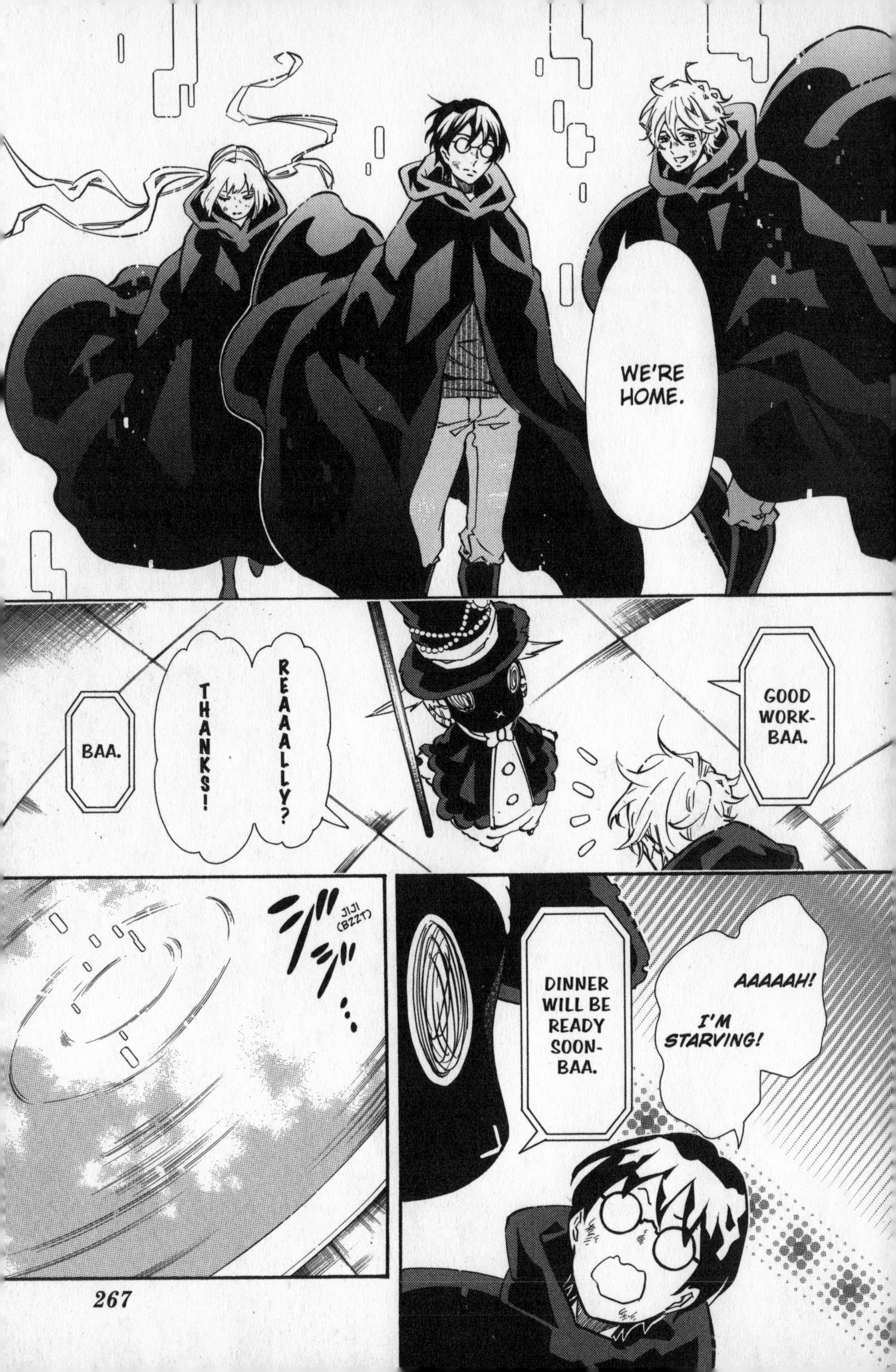
WE'RE HOME.
GOOD WORK-BAA.
REAAAALLY? THANKS!
BAA.
AAAAAH! I'M STARVING!
DINNER WILL BE READY SOON-BAA.
JIJI (BZZT)

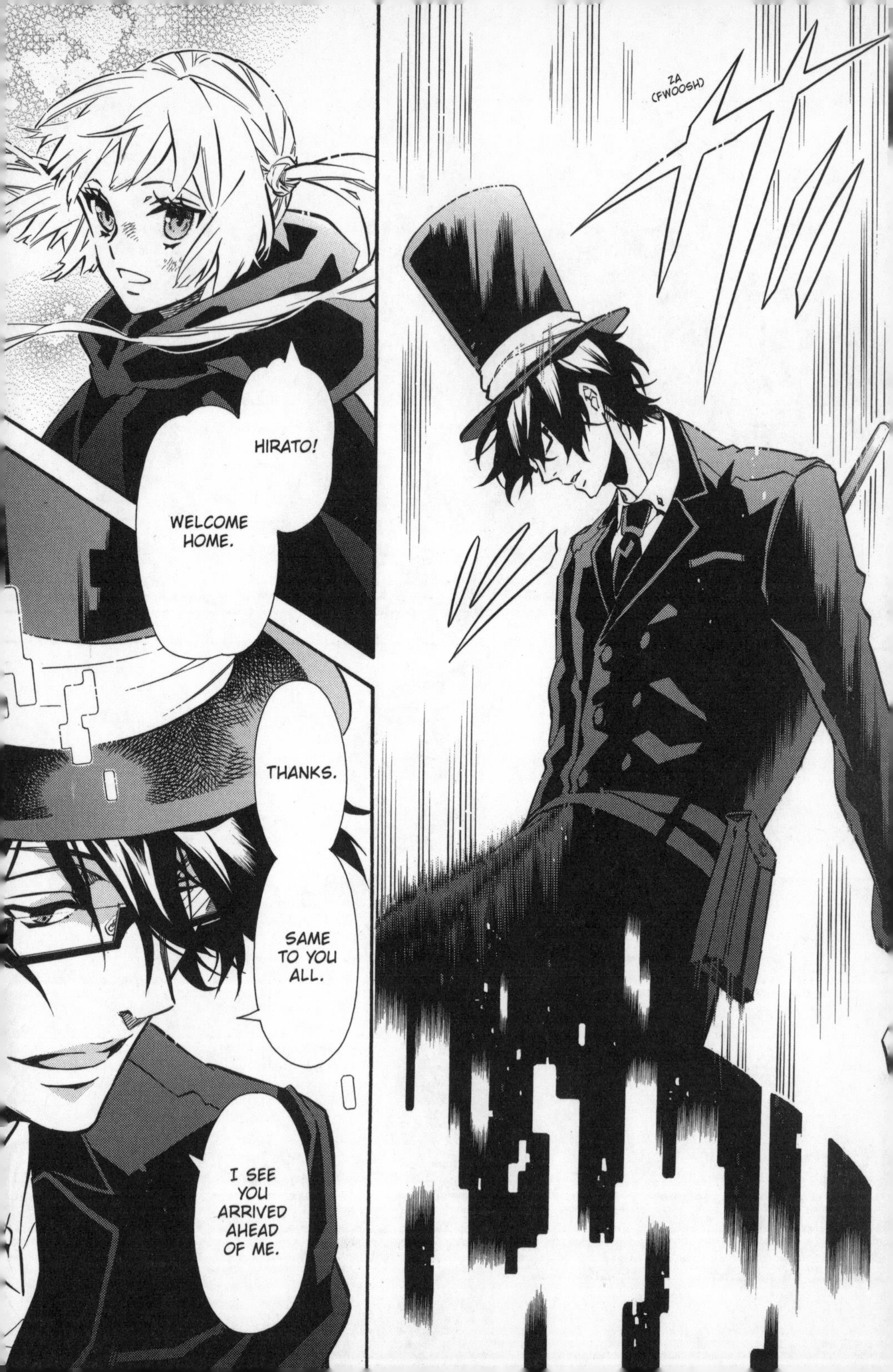
ZA (FWOOSH)
HIRATO!
WELCOME HOME.
THANKS.
SAME TO YOU ALL.
I SEE YOU ARRIVED AHEAD OF ME.

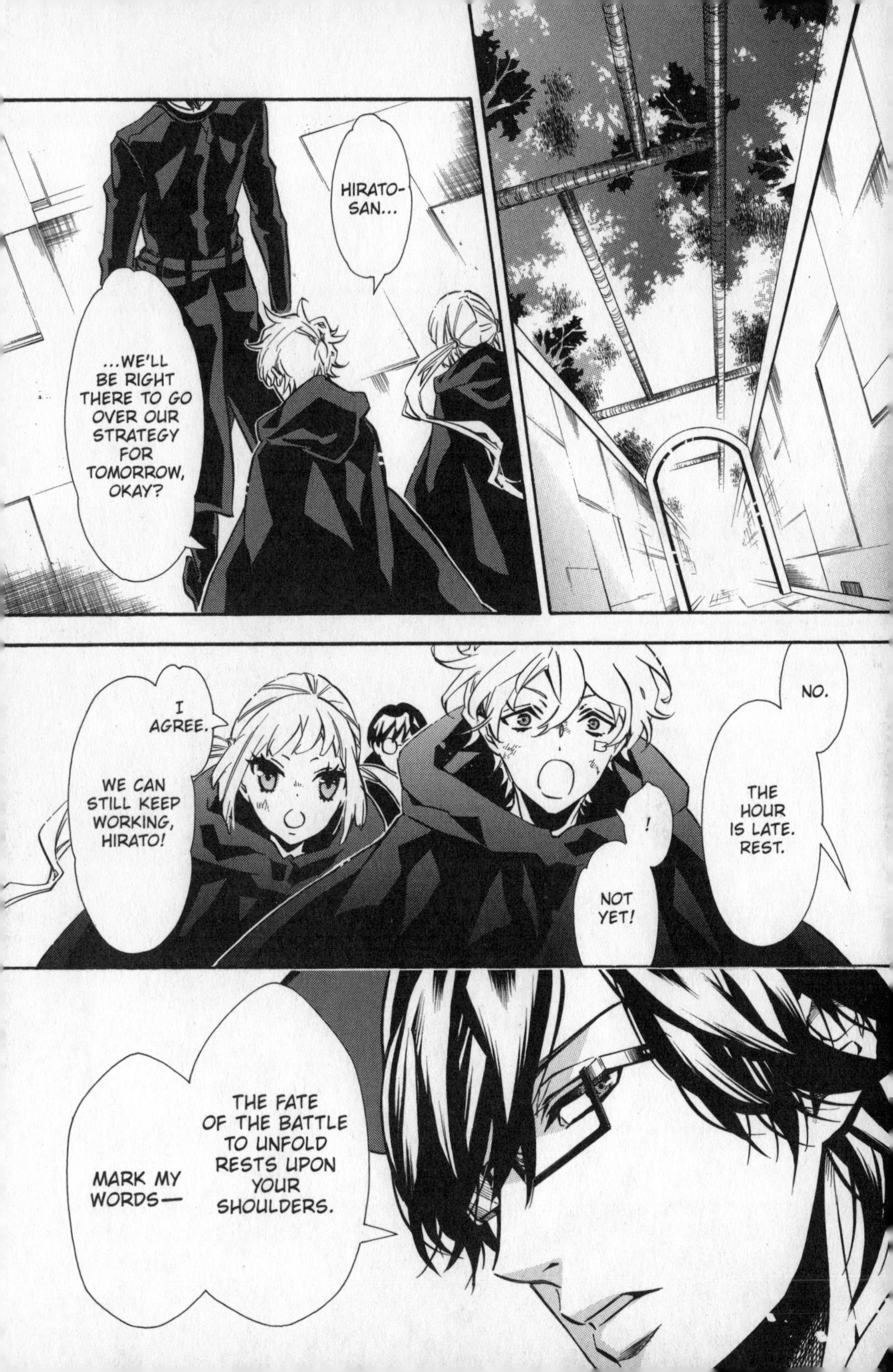
HIRATO-SAN...
...WE'LL BE RIGHT THERE TO GO OVER OUR STRATEGY FOR TOMORROW, OKAY?
NO.
THE HOUR IS LATE. REST.
!
NOT YET!
I AGREE.
WE CAN STILL KEEP WORKING, HIRATO!
MARK MY WORDS—
THE FATE OF THE BATTLE TO UNFOLD RESTS UPON YOUR SHOULDERS.

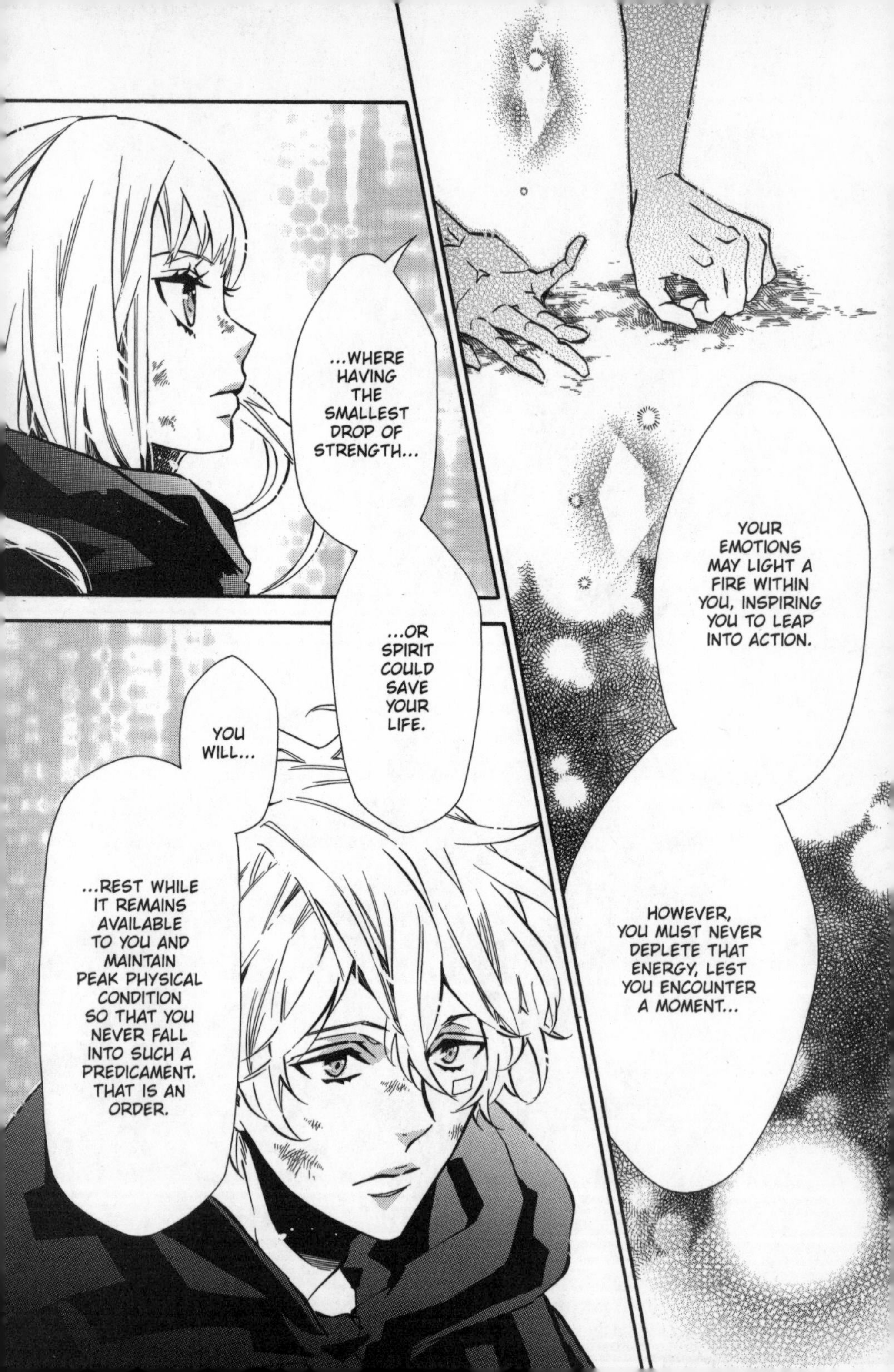
YOUR EMOTIONS MAY LIGHT A FIRE WITHIN YOU, INSPIRING YOU TO LEAP INTO ACTION.
HOWEVER, YOU MUST NEVER DEPLETE THAT ENERGY, LEST YOU ENCOUNTER A MOMENT...
...WHERE HAVING THE SMALLEST DROP OF STRENGTH...
...OR SPIRIT COULD SAVE YOUR LIFE.
YOU WILL...
...REST WHILE IT REMAINS AVAILABLE TO YOU AND MAINTAIN PEAK PHYSICAL CONDITION SO THAT YOU NEVER FALL INTO SUCH A PREDICAMENT. THAT IS AN ORDER.

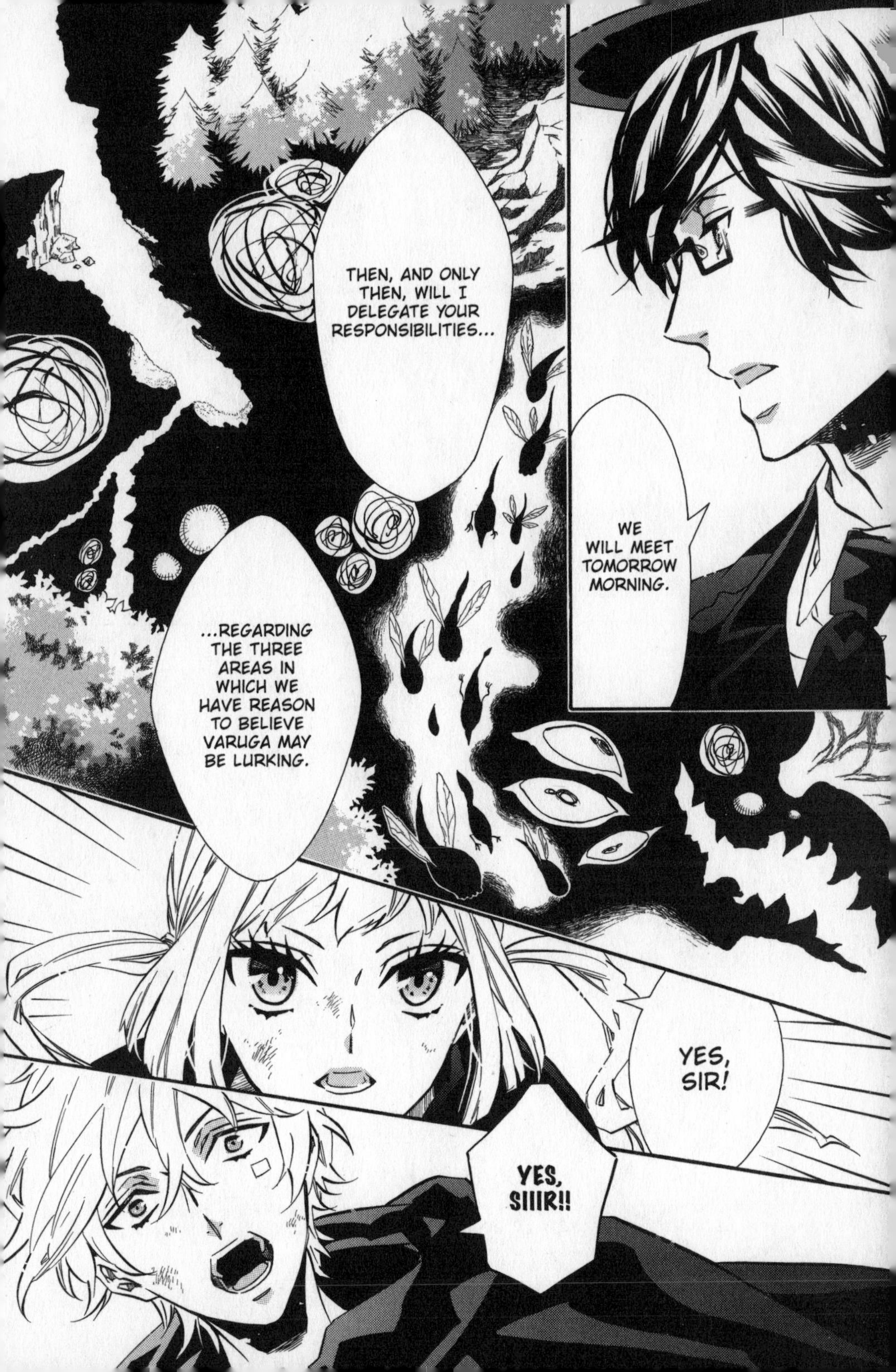
WE WILL MEET TOMORROW MORNING.
THEN, AND ONLY THEN, WILL I DELEGATE YOUR RESPONSIBILITIES...
...REGARDING THE THREE AREAS IN WHICH WE HAVE REASON TO BELIEVE VARUGA MAY BE LURKING.
YES, SIR!
YES, SIIIR!!

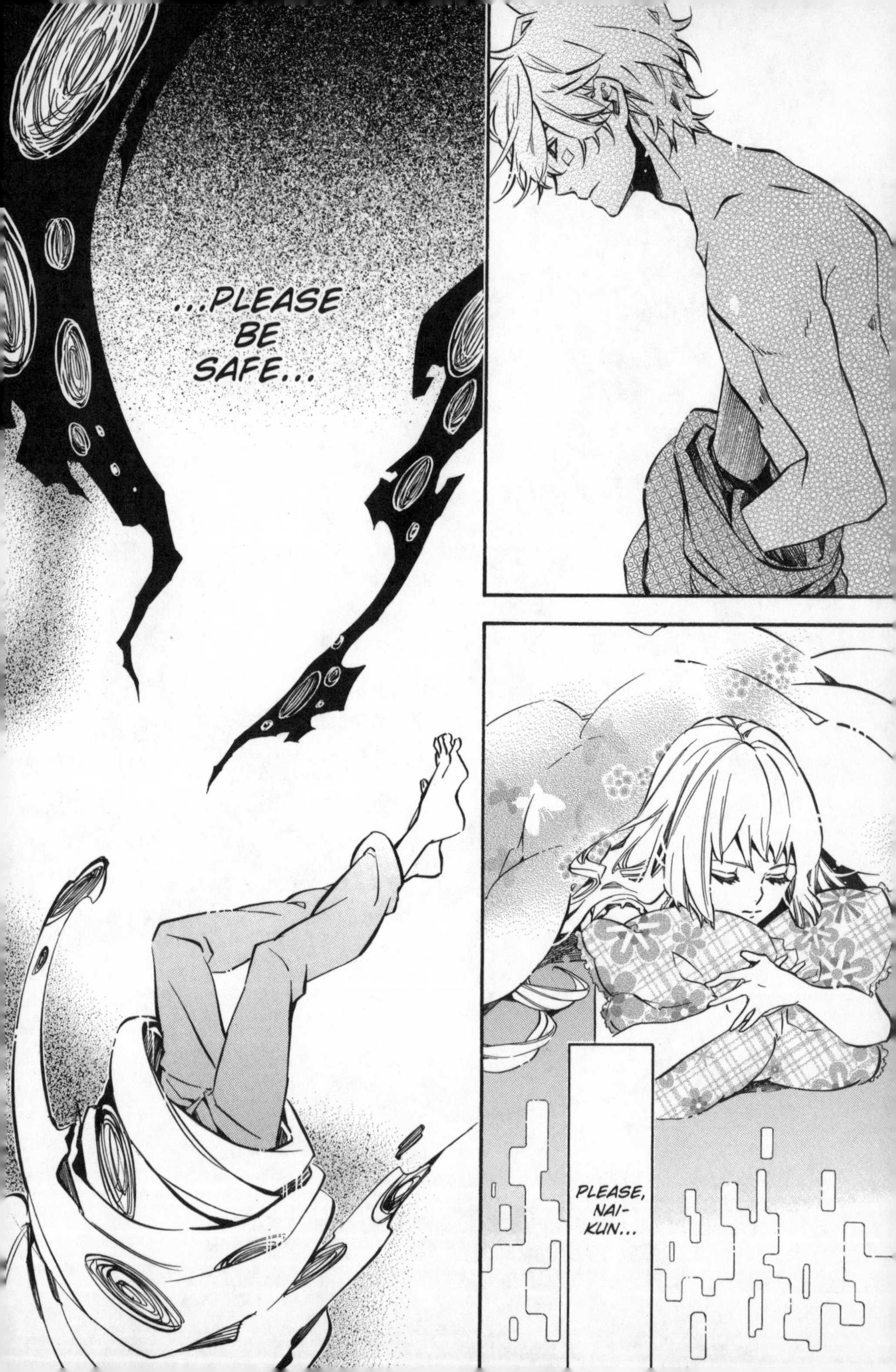
PLEASE, NAI-KUN...
...PLEASE BE SAFE...

KARNEVAL

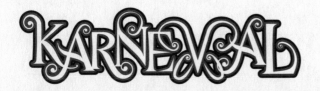

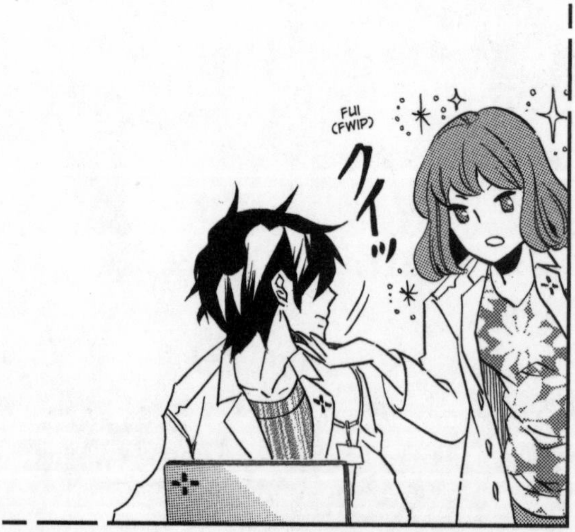
FUI
(FWIP)
クイッ

KARNEVAL

# Score 126: Scars

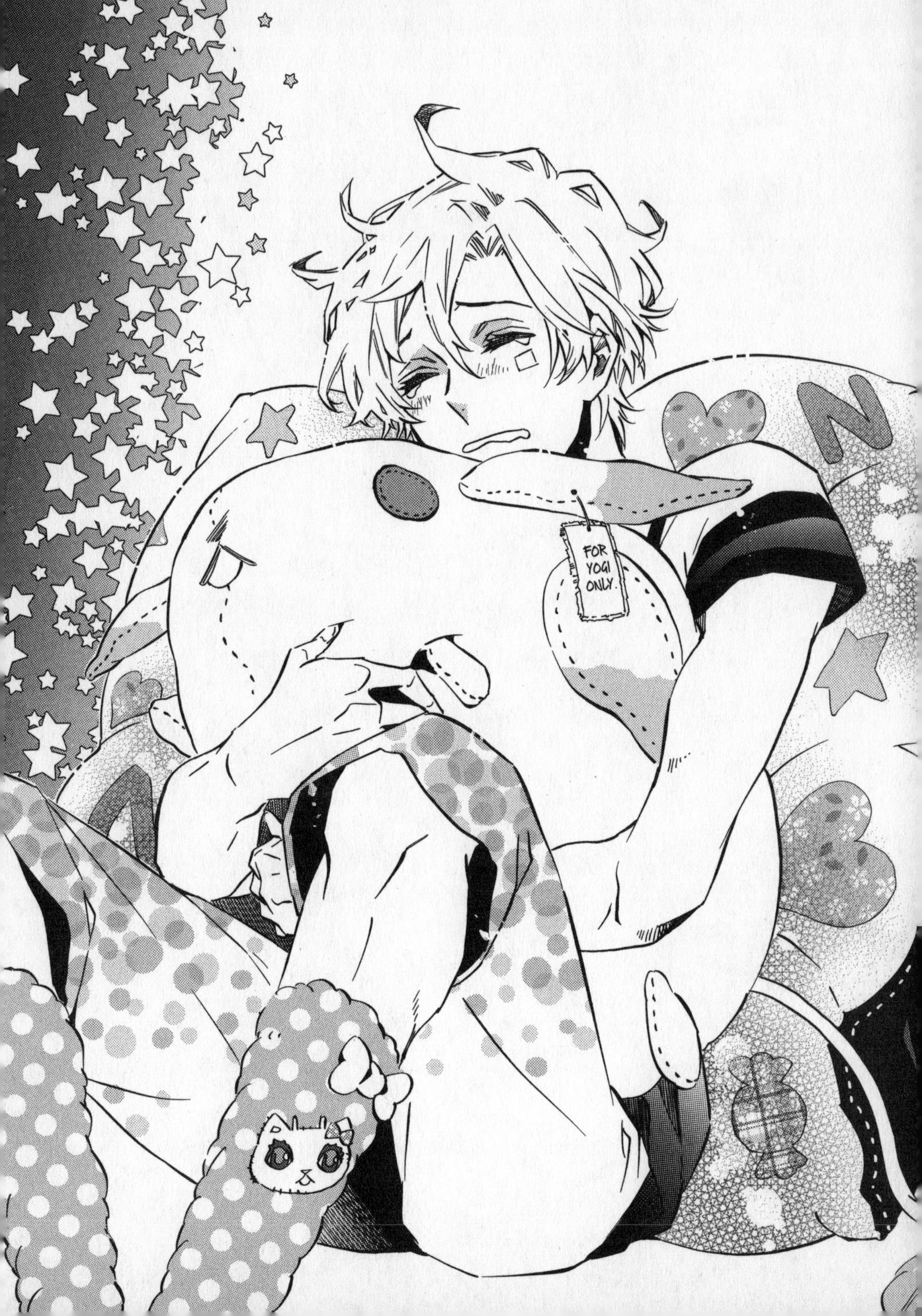

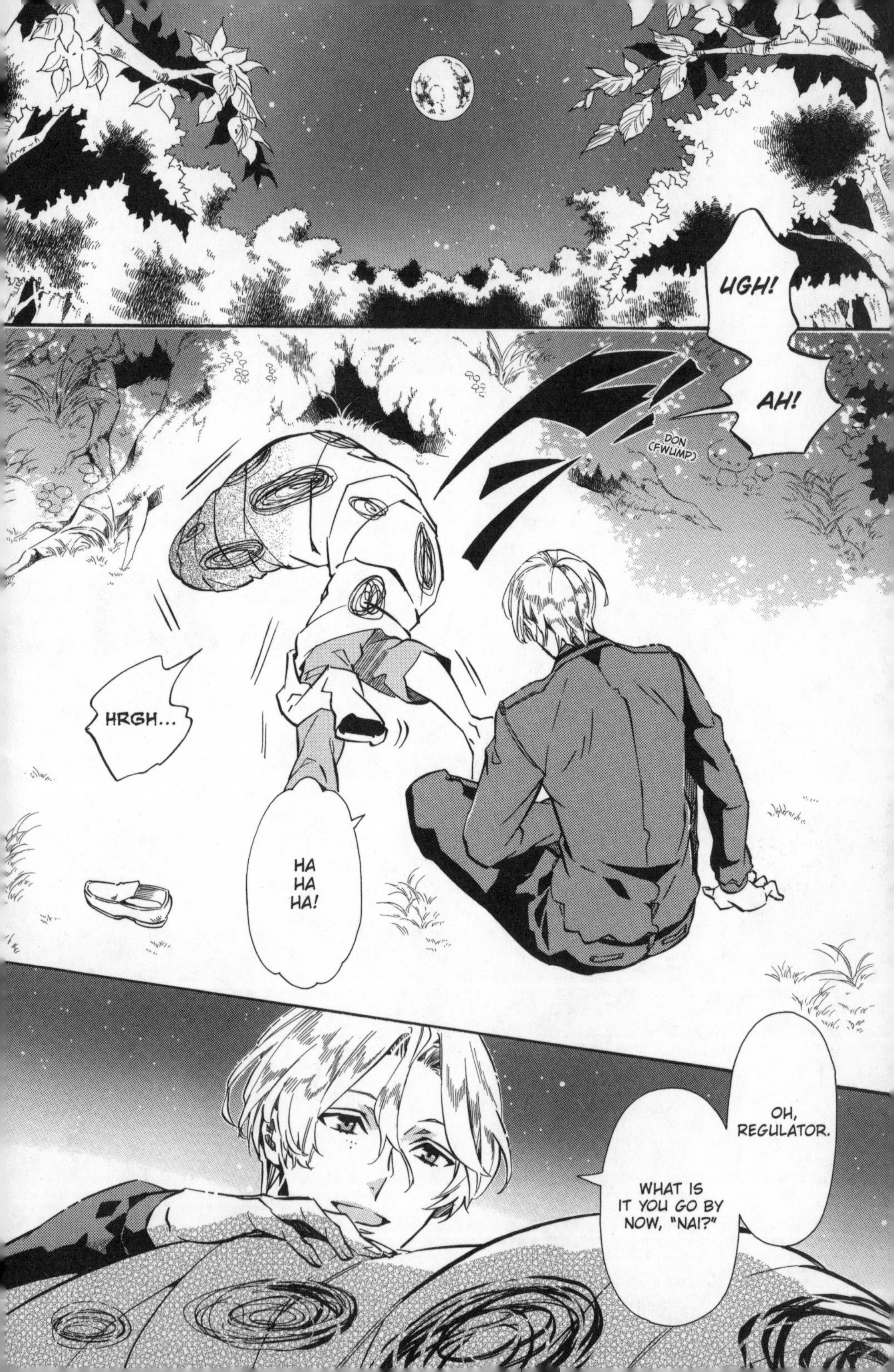
UGH!
AH!
DON (FWUMP)
HRGH...
HA HA HA!
OH, REGULATOR.
WHAT IS IT YOU GO BY NOW, "NAI?"

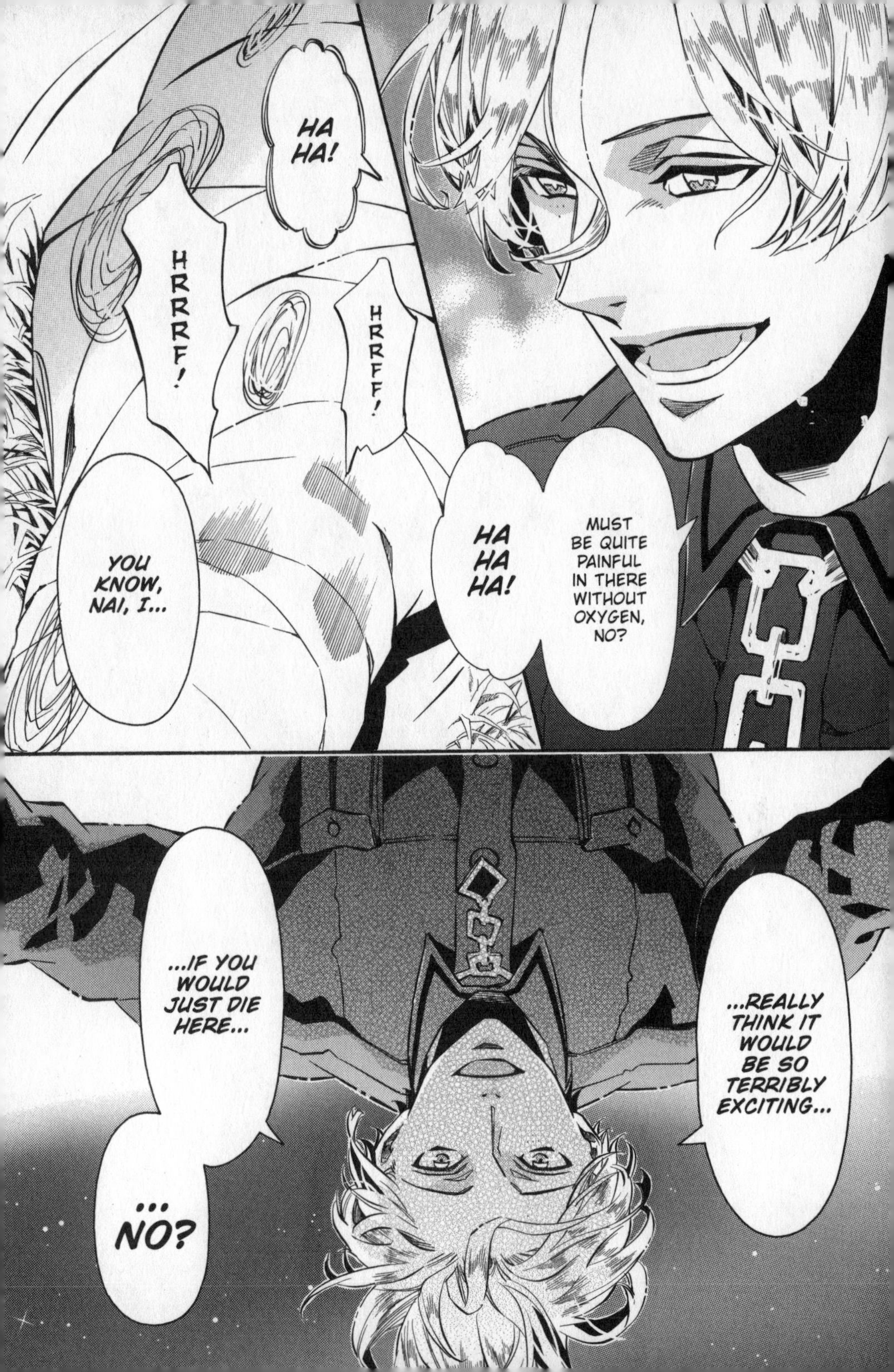
HA HA!
MUST BE QUITE PAINFUL IN THERE WITHOUT OXYGEN, NO?
HA HA HA!
HRRFF!
HRRRF!
YOU KNOW, NAI, I...
...REALLY THINK IT WOULD BE SO TERRIBLY EXCITING...
...IF YOU WOULD JUST DIE HERE...
... NO?

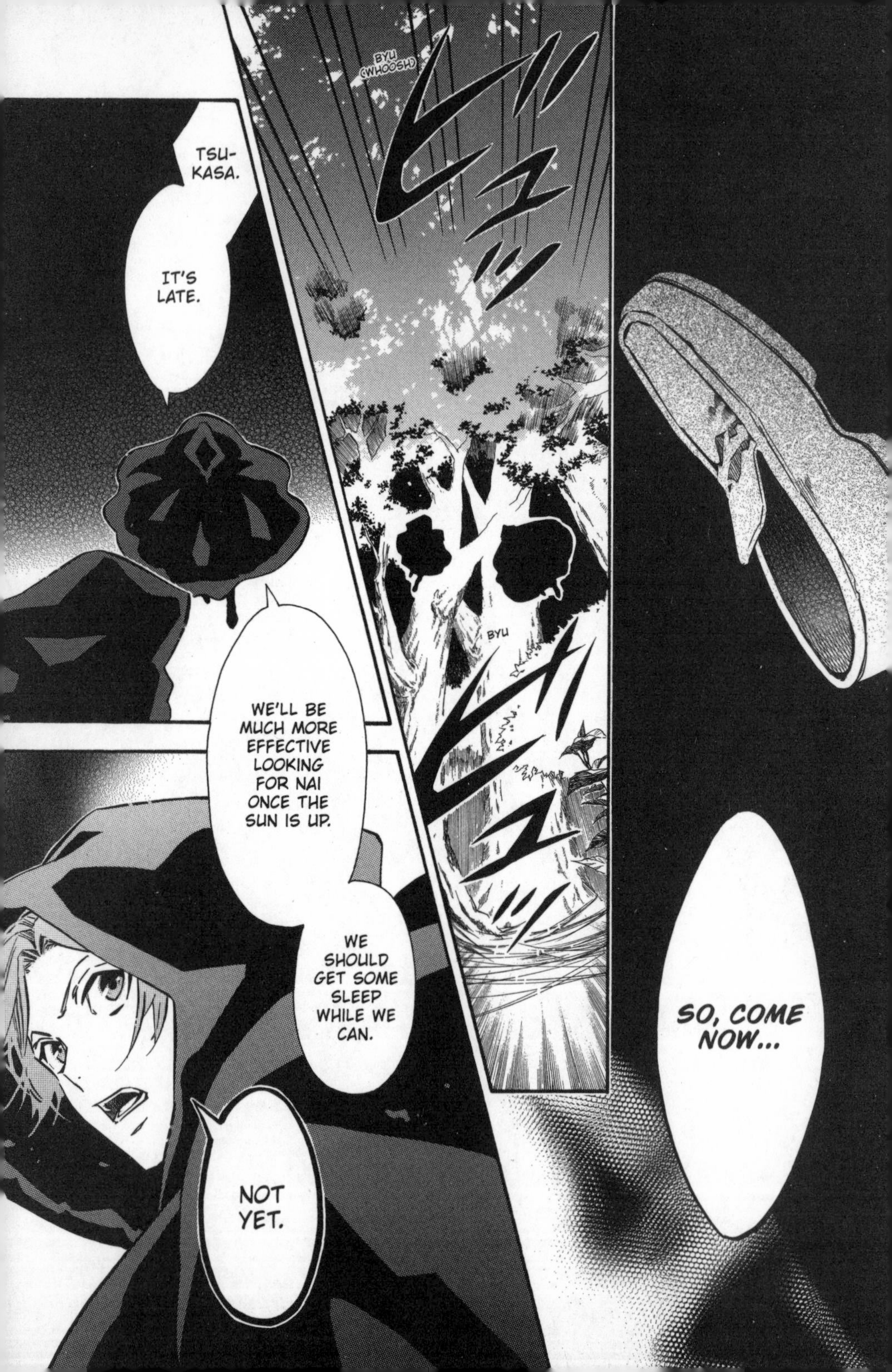
SO, COME NOW...
BYU (WHOOSH)
BYU
TSU-KASA.
IT'S LATE.
WE'LL BE MUCH MORE EFFECTIVE LOOKING FOR NAI ONCE THE SUN IS UP.
WE SHOULD GET SOME SLEEP WHILE WE CAN.
NOT YET.

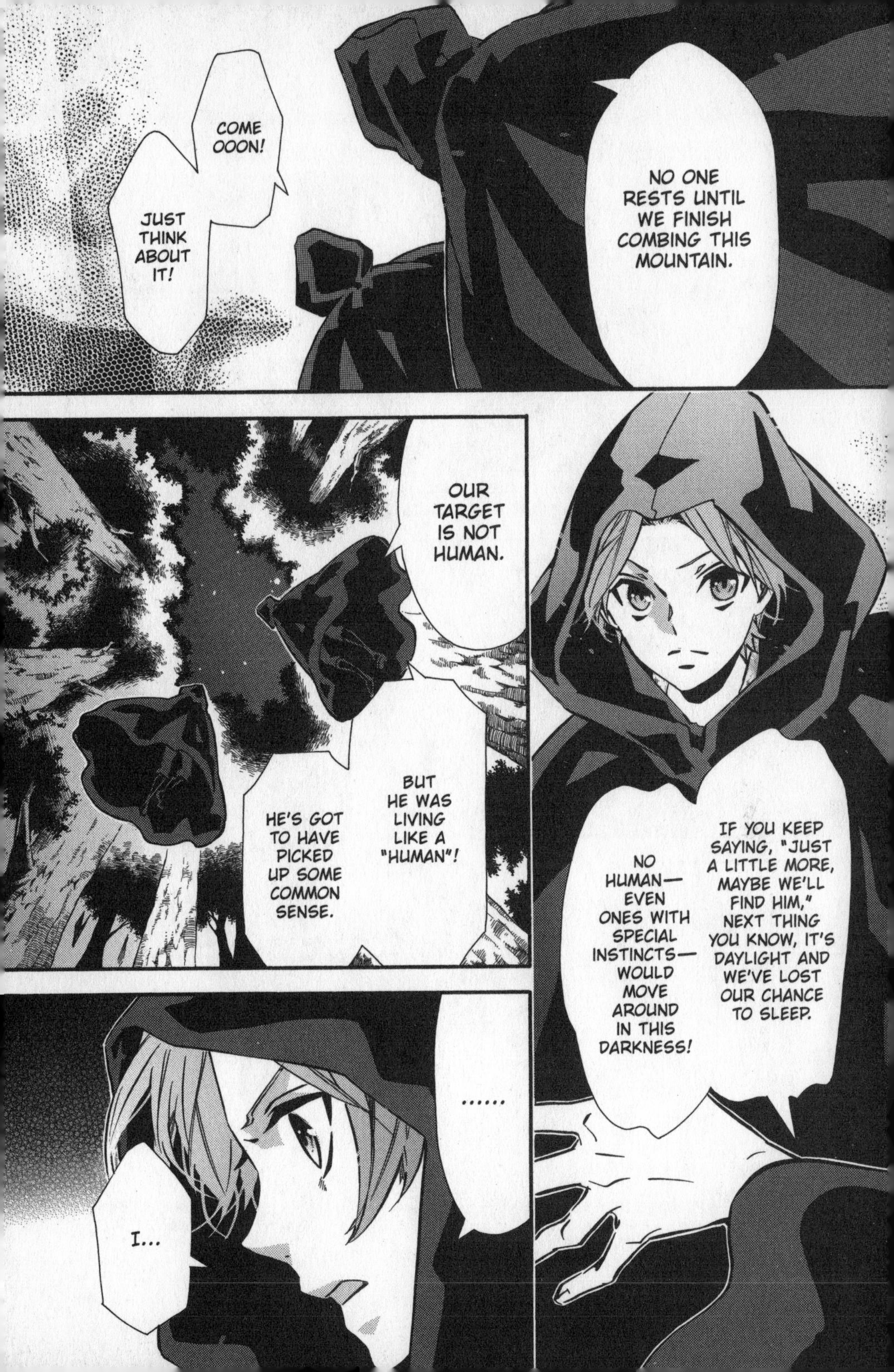
NO ONE RESTS UNTIL WE FINISH COMBING THIS MOUNTAIN.
COME OOON!
JUST THINK ABOUT IT!
IF YOU KEEP SAYING, "JUST A LITTLE MORE, MAYBE WE'LL FIND HIM," NEXT THING YOU KNOW, IT'S DAYLIGHT AND WE'VE LOST OUR CHANCE TO SLEEP.
NO HUMAN—EVEN ONES WITH SPECIAL INSTINCTS—WOULD MOVE AROUND IN THIS DARKNESS!
OUR TARGET IS NOT HUMAN.
BUT HE WAS LIVING LIKE A "HUMAN"!
HE'S GOT TO HAVE PICKED UP SOME COMMON SENSE.
......
I...

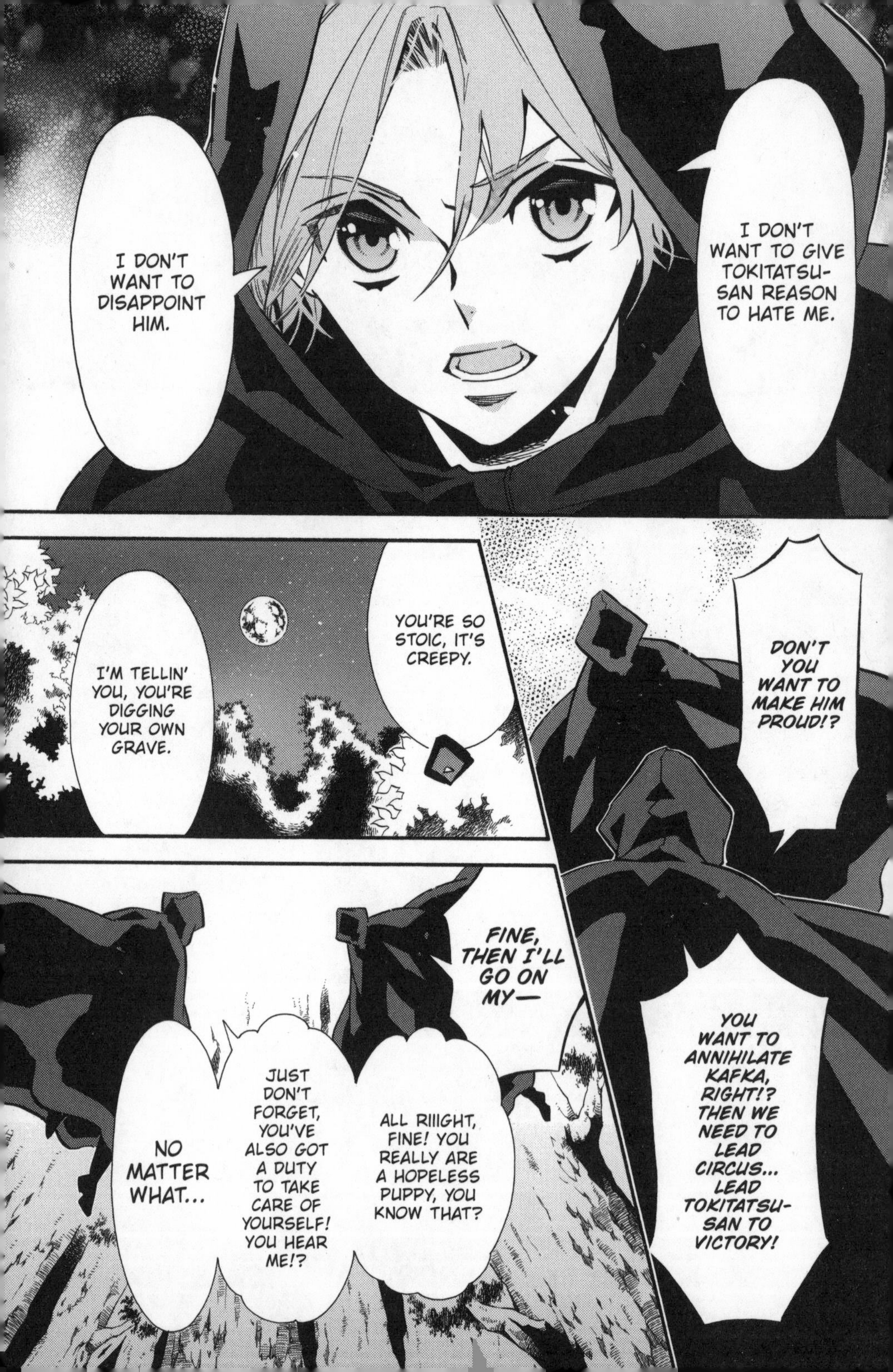
I DON'T WANT TO GIVE TOKITATSU-SAN REASON TO HATE ME.
I DON'T WANT TO DISAPPOINT HIM.
DON'T YOU WANT TO MAKE HIM PROUD!?
YOU WANT TO ANNIHILATE KAFKA, RIGHT!? THEN WE NEED TO LEAD CIRCUS... LEAD TOKITATSU-SAN TO VICTORY!
YOU'RE SO STOIC, IT'S CREEPY.
I'M TELLIN' YOU, YOU'RE DIGGING YOUR OWN GRAVE.
FINE, THEN I'LL GO ON MY—
ALL RIIIGHT, FINE! YOU REALLY ARE A HOPELESS PUPPY, YOU KNOW THAT?
JUST DON'T FORGET, YOU'VE ALSO GOT A DUTY TO TAKE CARE OF YOURSELF! YOU HEAR ME!?
NO MATTER WHAT...

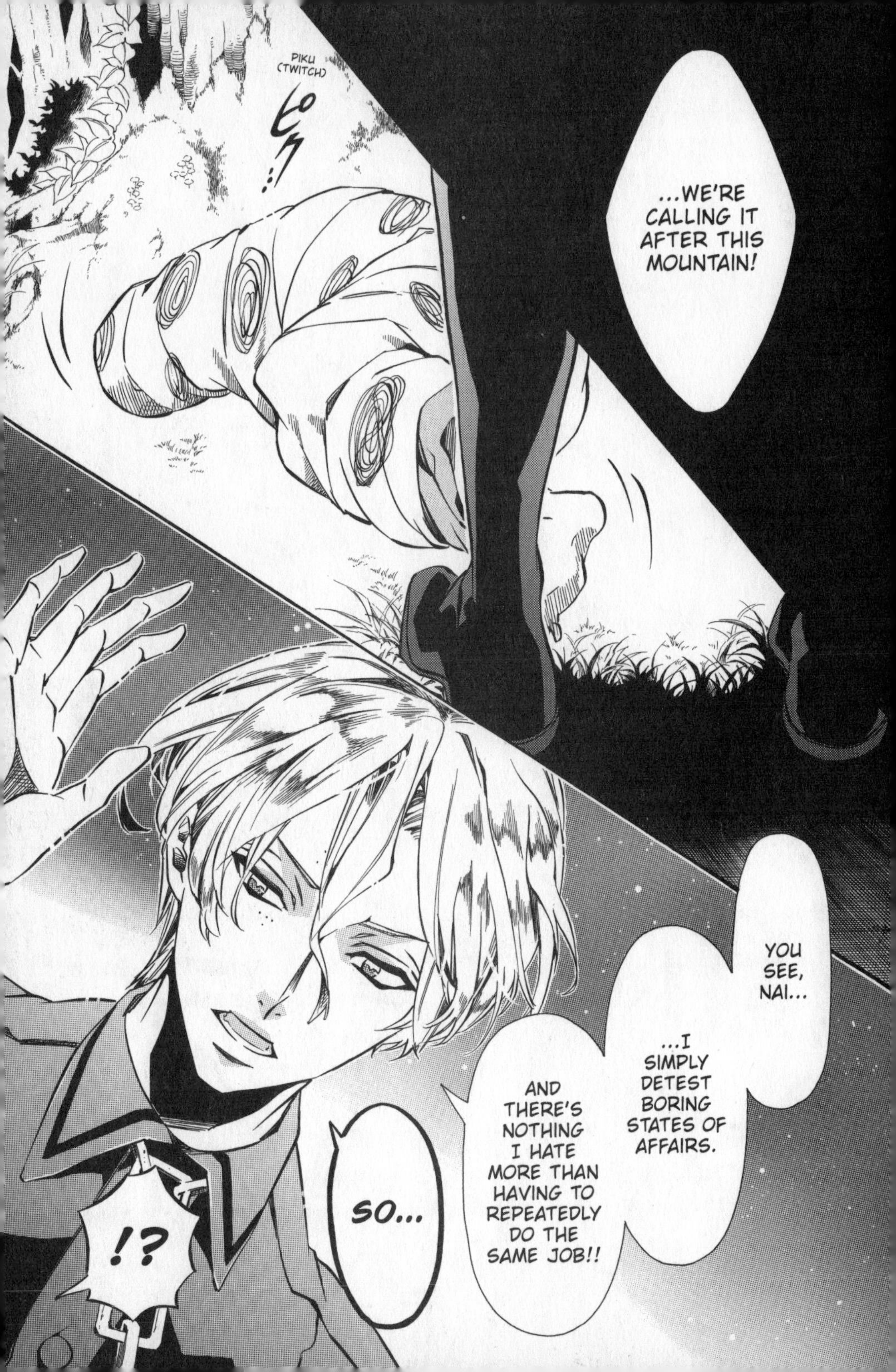
...WE'RE CALLING IT AFTER THIS MOUNTAIN!
PIKU (TWITCH)
YOU SEE, NAI...
...I SIMPLY DETEST BORING STATES OF AFFAIRS.
AND THERE'S NOTHING I HATE MORE THAN HAVING TO REPEATEDLY DO THE SAME JOB!!
SO...
!?

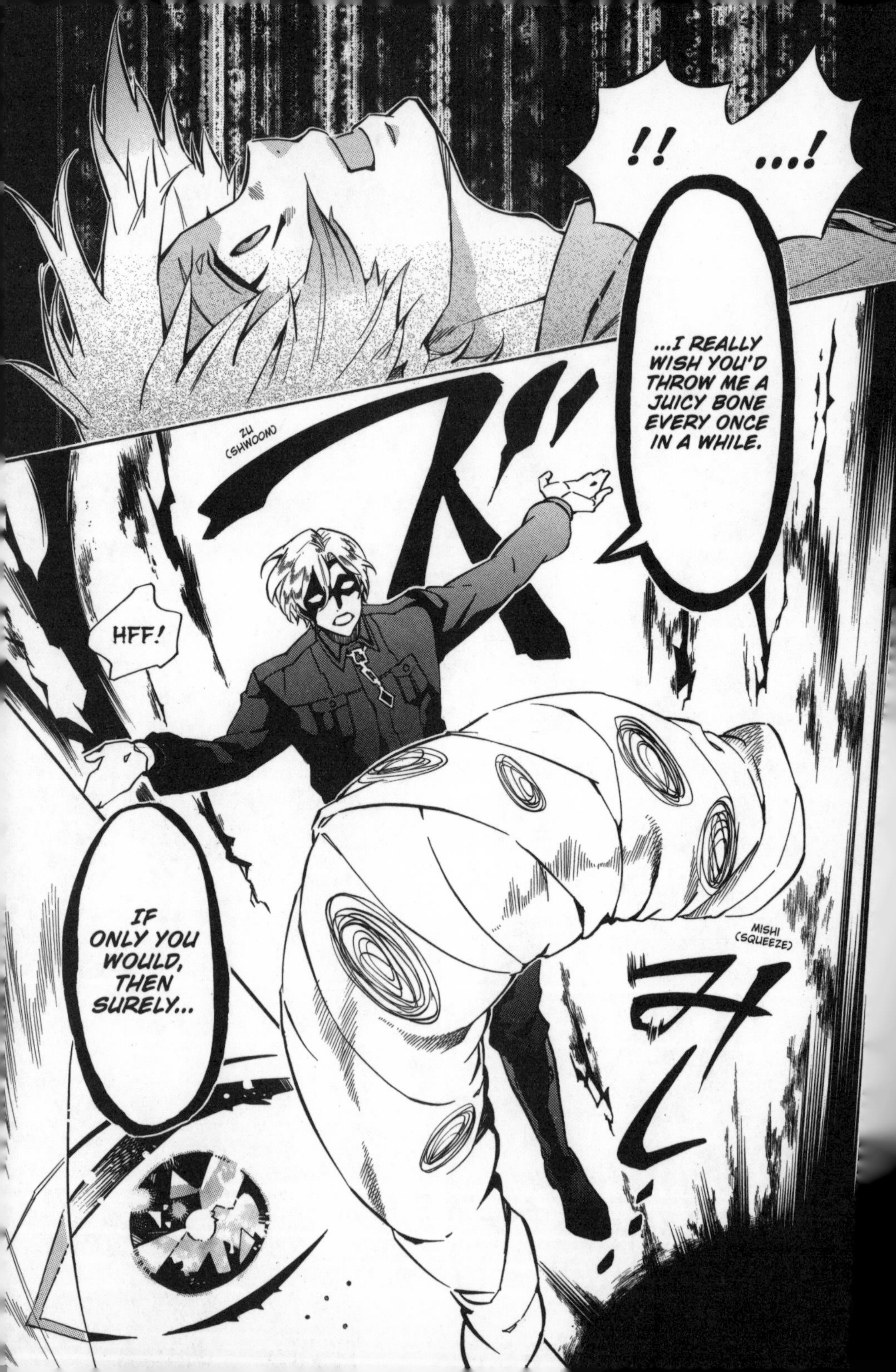
!! ...!
...I REALLY WISH YOU'D THROW ME A JUICY BONE EVERY ONCE IN A WHILE.
ZU (SHWOOM)
HFF!
IF ONLY YOU WOULD, THEN SURELY...
MISHI (SQUEEZE)

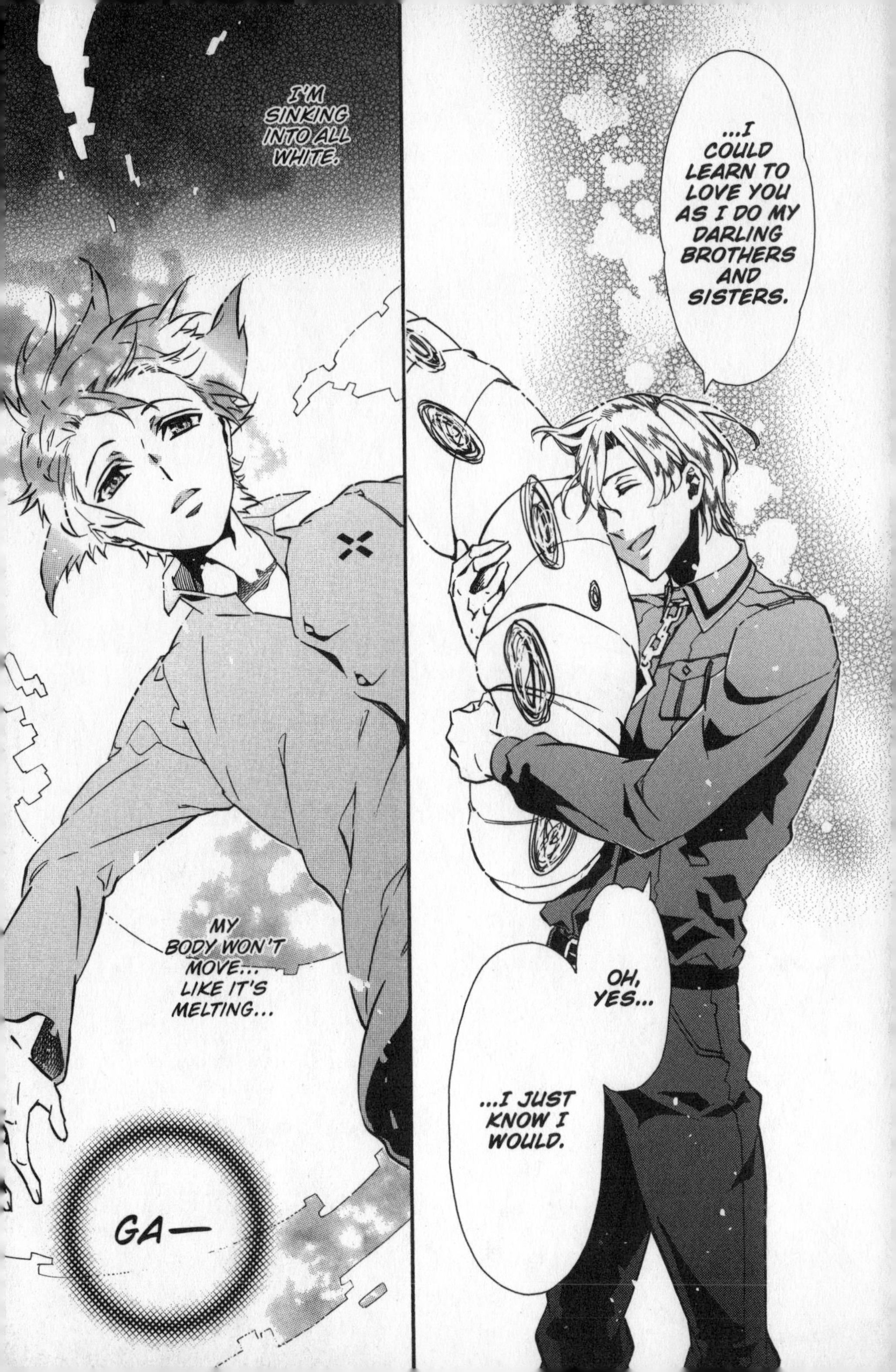
...I COULD LEARN TO LOVE YOU AS I DO MY DARLING BROTHERS AND SISTERS.
OH, YES...
...I JUST KNOW I WOULD.
I'M SINKING INTO ALL WHITE.
MY BODY WON'T MOVE... LIKE IT'S MELTING...
GA—

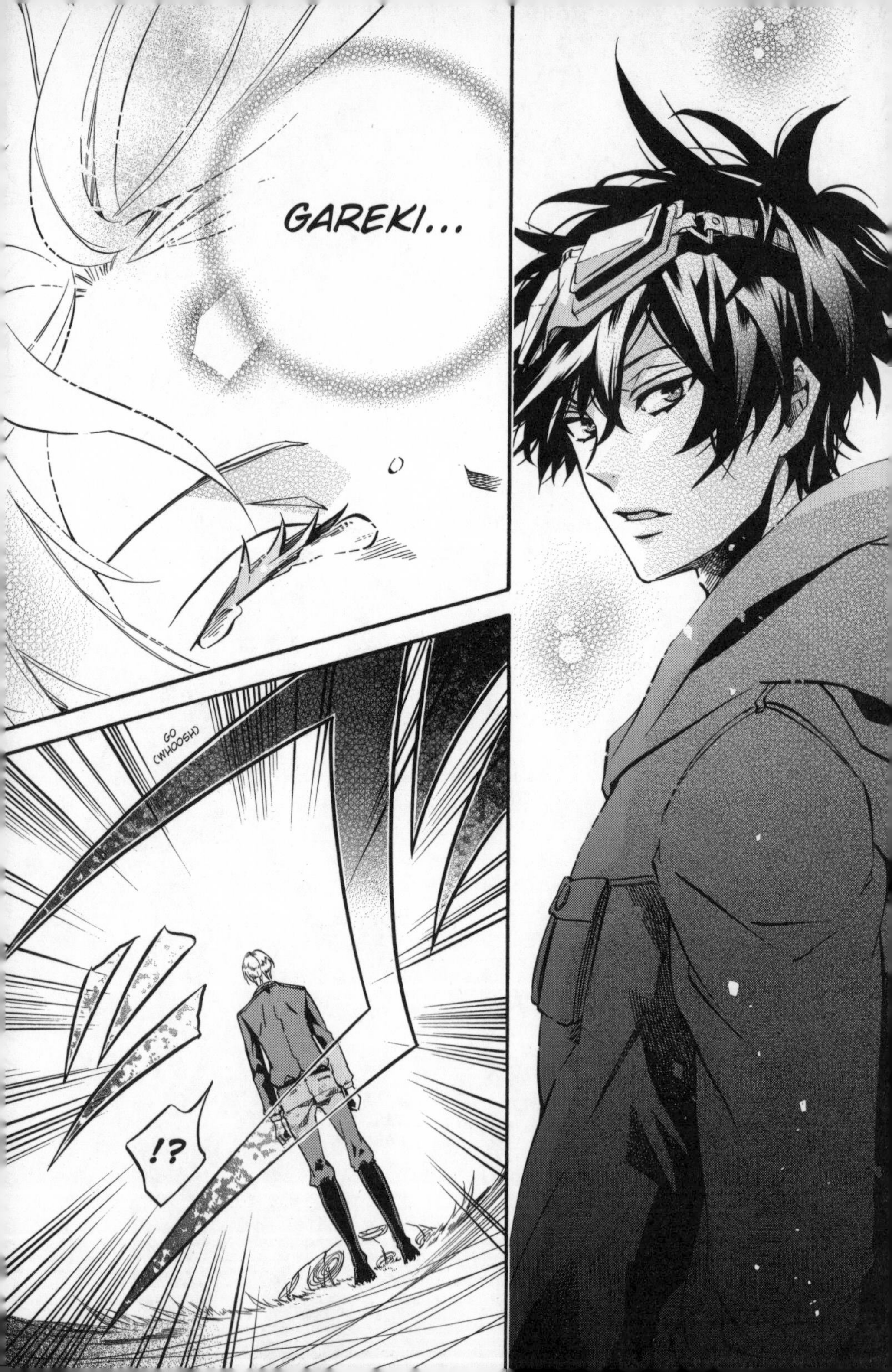
GAREKI...
GO (WHOOSH)
!?

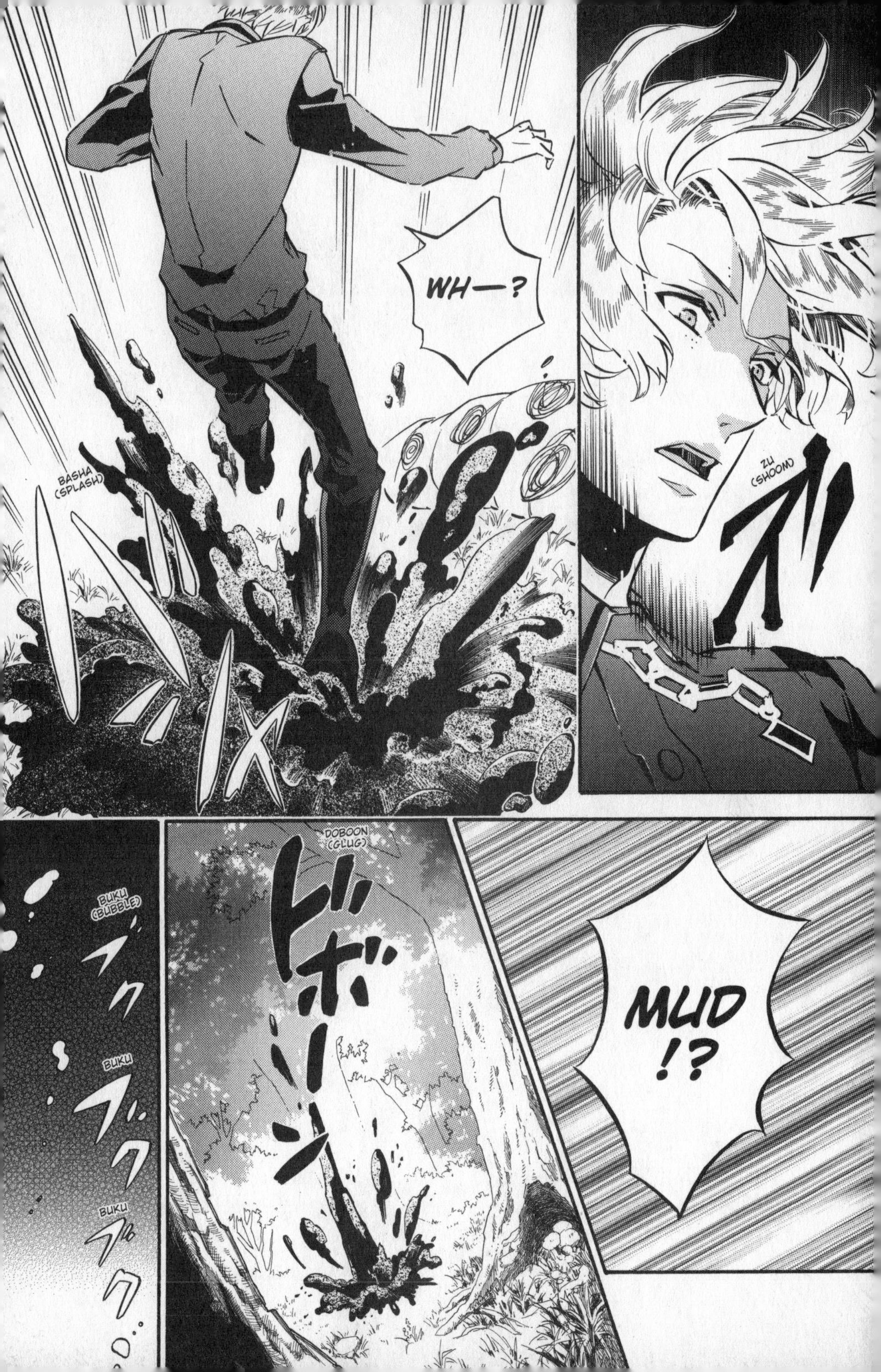
ZU
(SHOOM)
WH—?
BASHA
(SPLASH)
MUD
!?
DOBOON
(GLUG)
BUKU
(BUBBLE)
BUKU
BUKU

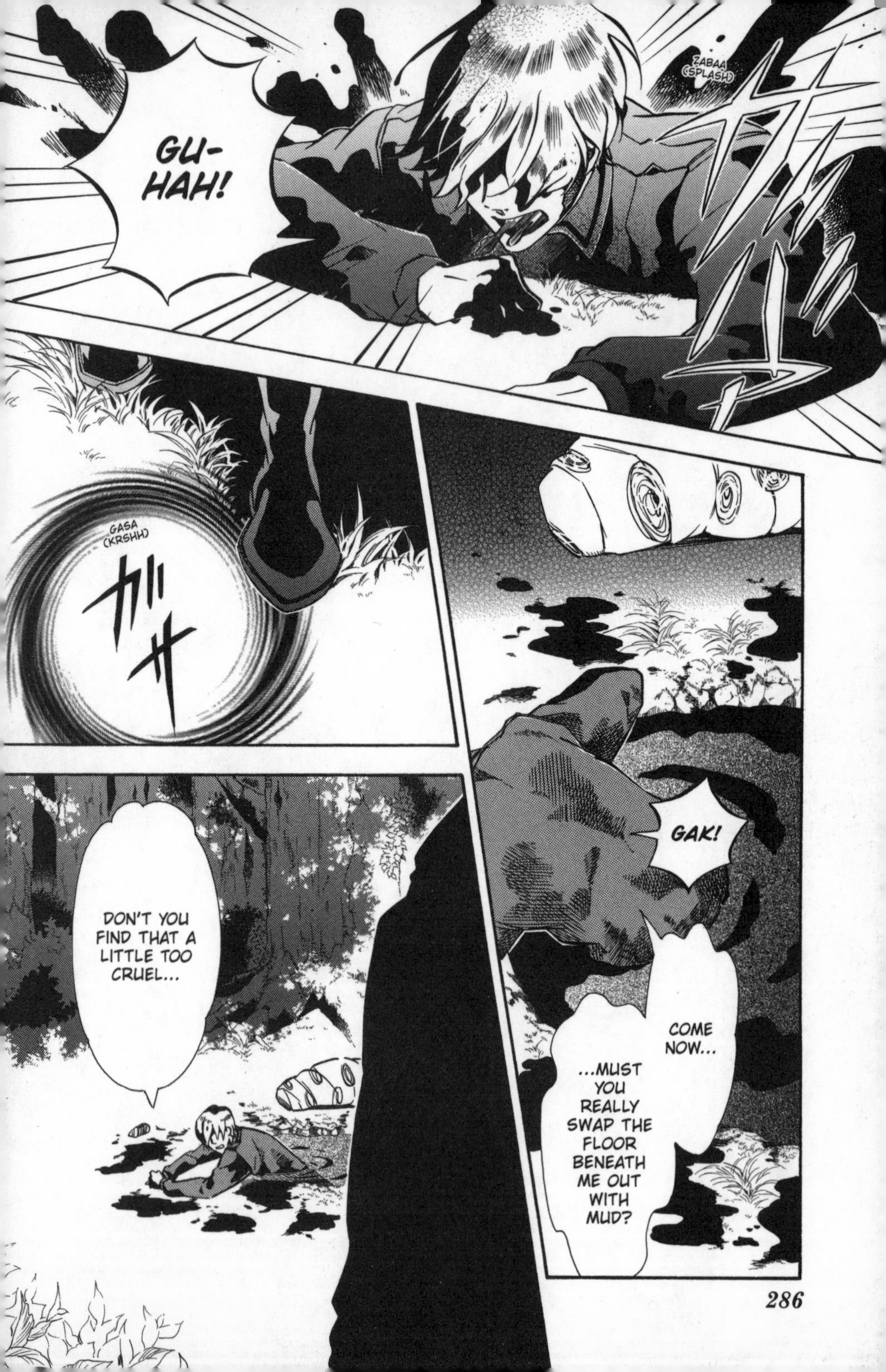
ZABAA (SPLASH)
GU-HAH!
GAK!
COME NOW...
...MUST YOU REALLY SWAP THE FLOOR BENEATH ME OUT WITH MUD?
GASA (KRSHH)
DON'T YOU FIND THAT A LITTLE TOO CRUEL...

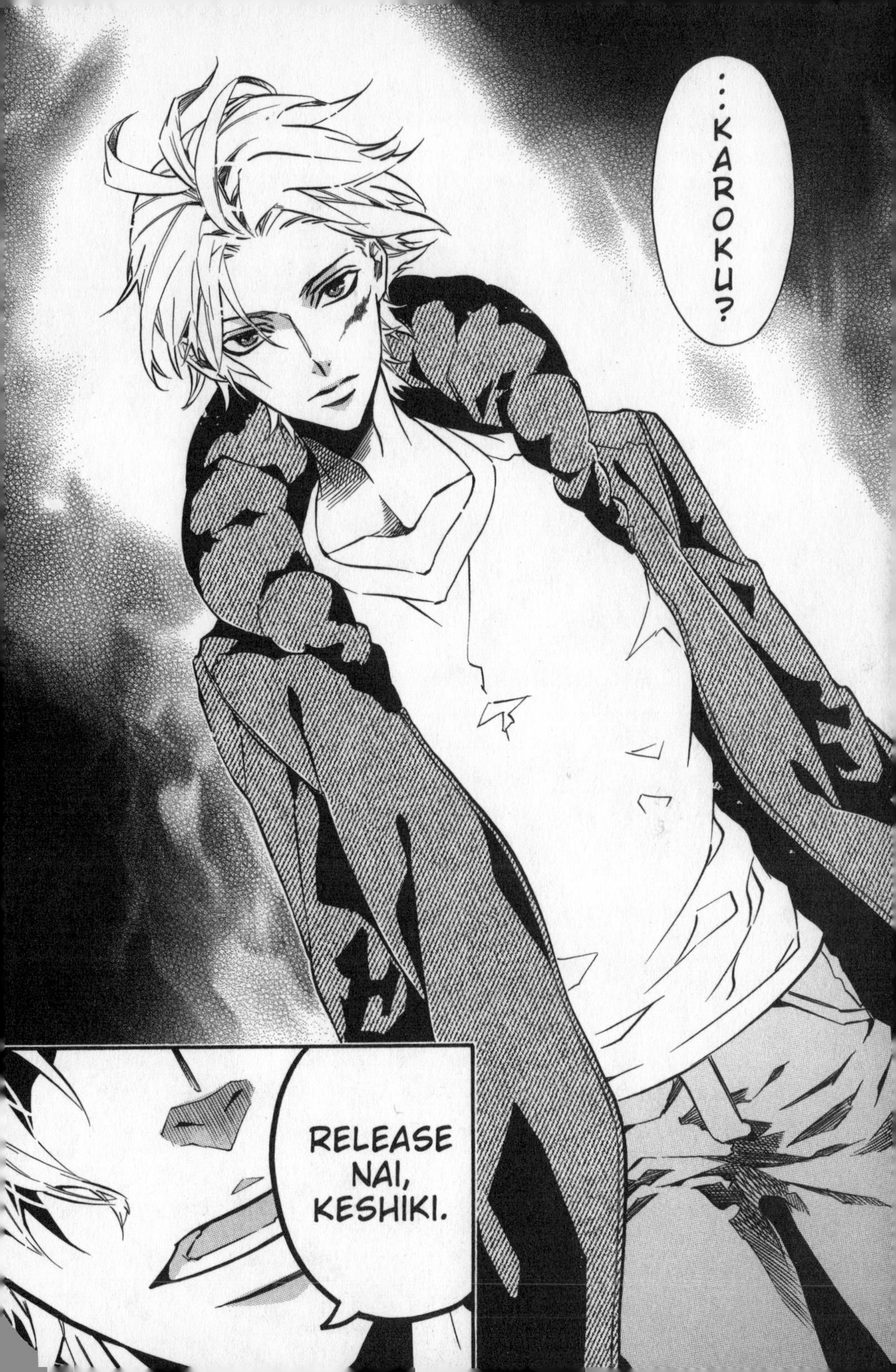
...KAROKU?
RELEASE NAI, KESHIKI.

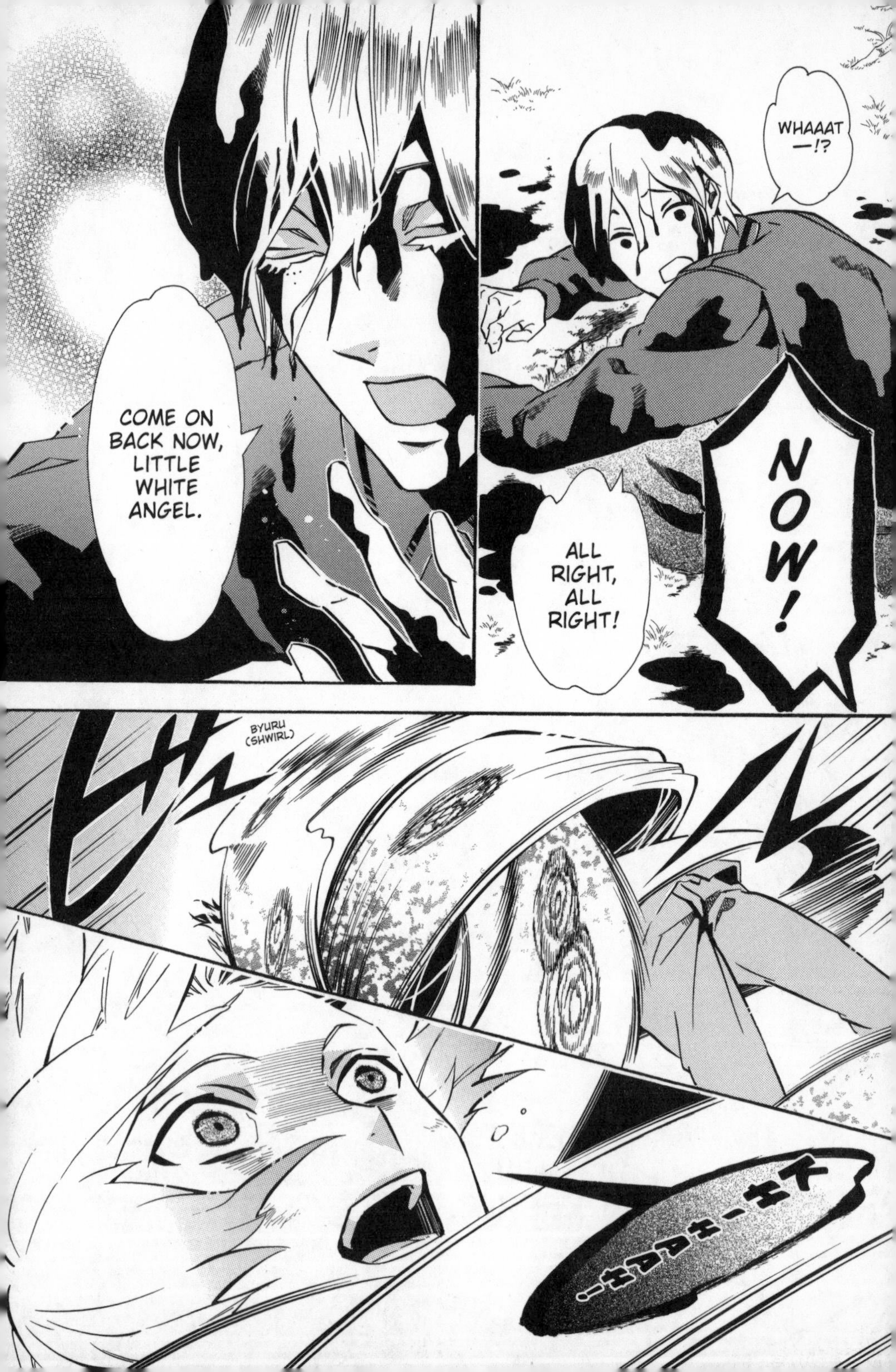
WHAAAT—!?
NOW!
ALL RIGHT, ALL RIGHT!
COME ON BACK NOW, LITTLE WHITE ANGEL.
BYURU (SHWIRL)
KH-H-HAAH-!

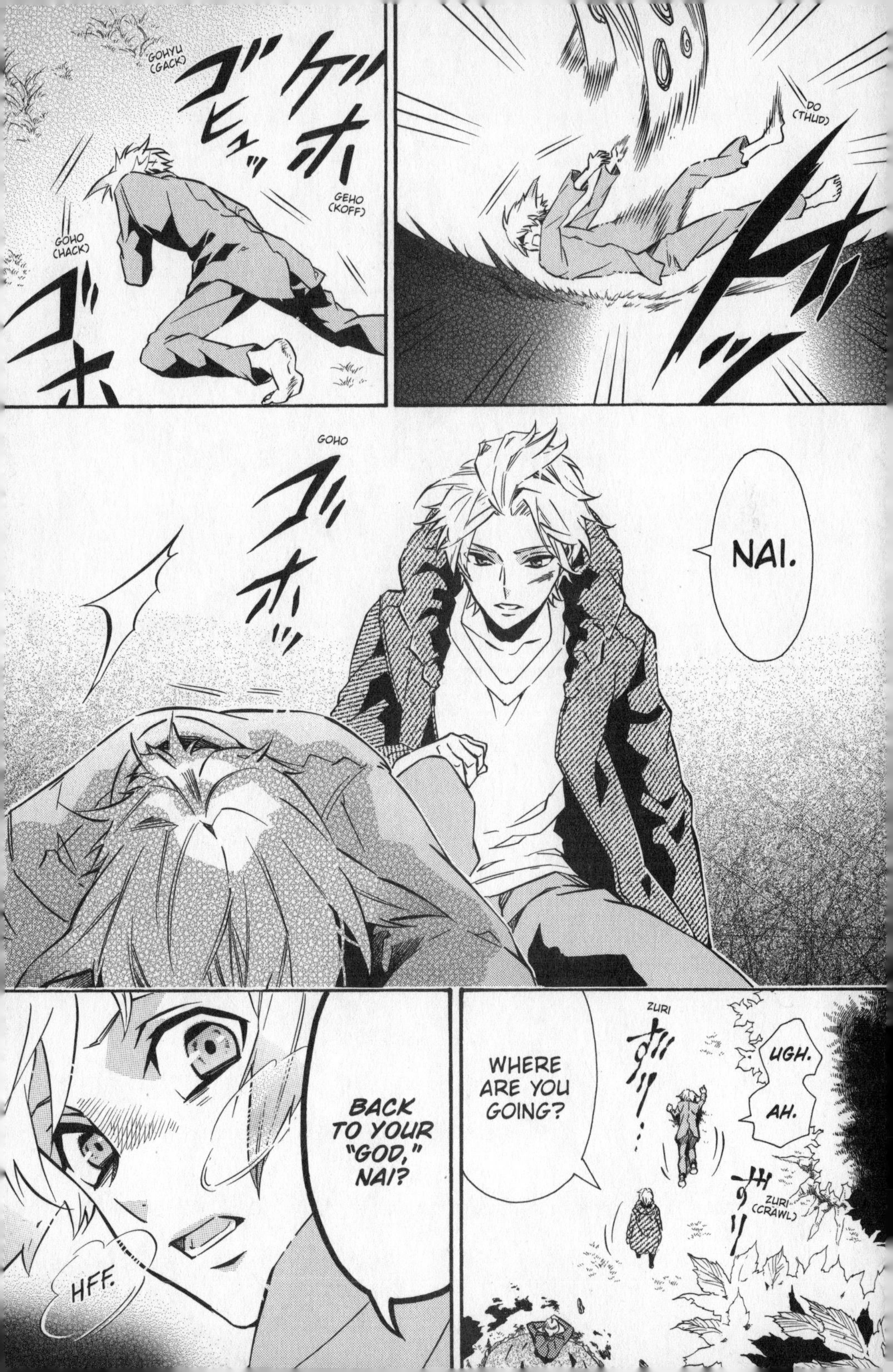
ドッ
DO
(THUD)
ゲホ
GEHO
(KOFF)
ゴヒュッ
GOHYU
(GACK)
ゴホ
GOHO
(HACK)
GOHO
ゴホッ
NAI.
UGH.
AH.
ZURI
ずり…
ずり
ZURI
(CRAWL)
WHERE ARE YOU GOING?
BACK TO YOUR "GOD," NAI?
HFF.

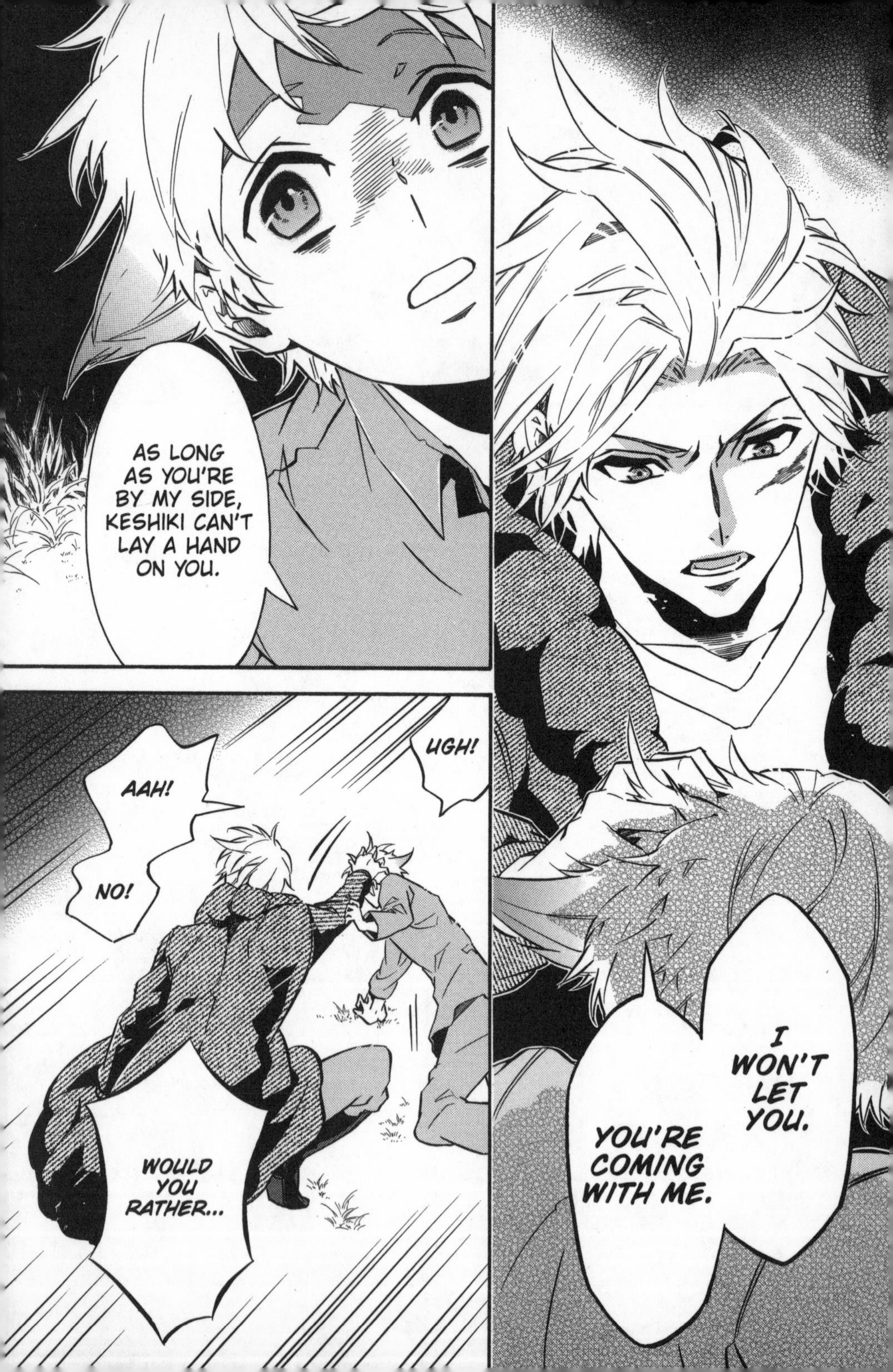
I WON'T LET YOU.
YOU'RE COMING WITH ME.
AS LONG AS YOU'RE BY MY SIDE, KESHIKI CAN'T LAY A HAND ON YOU.
UGH!
AAH!
NO!
WOULD YOU RATHER...

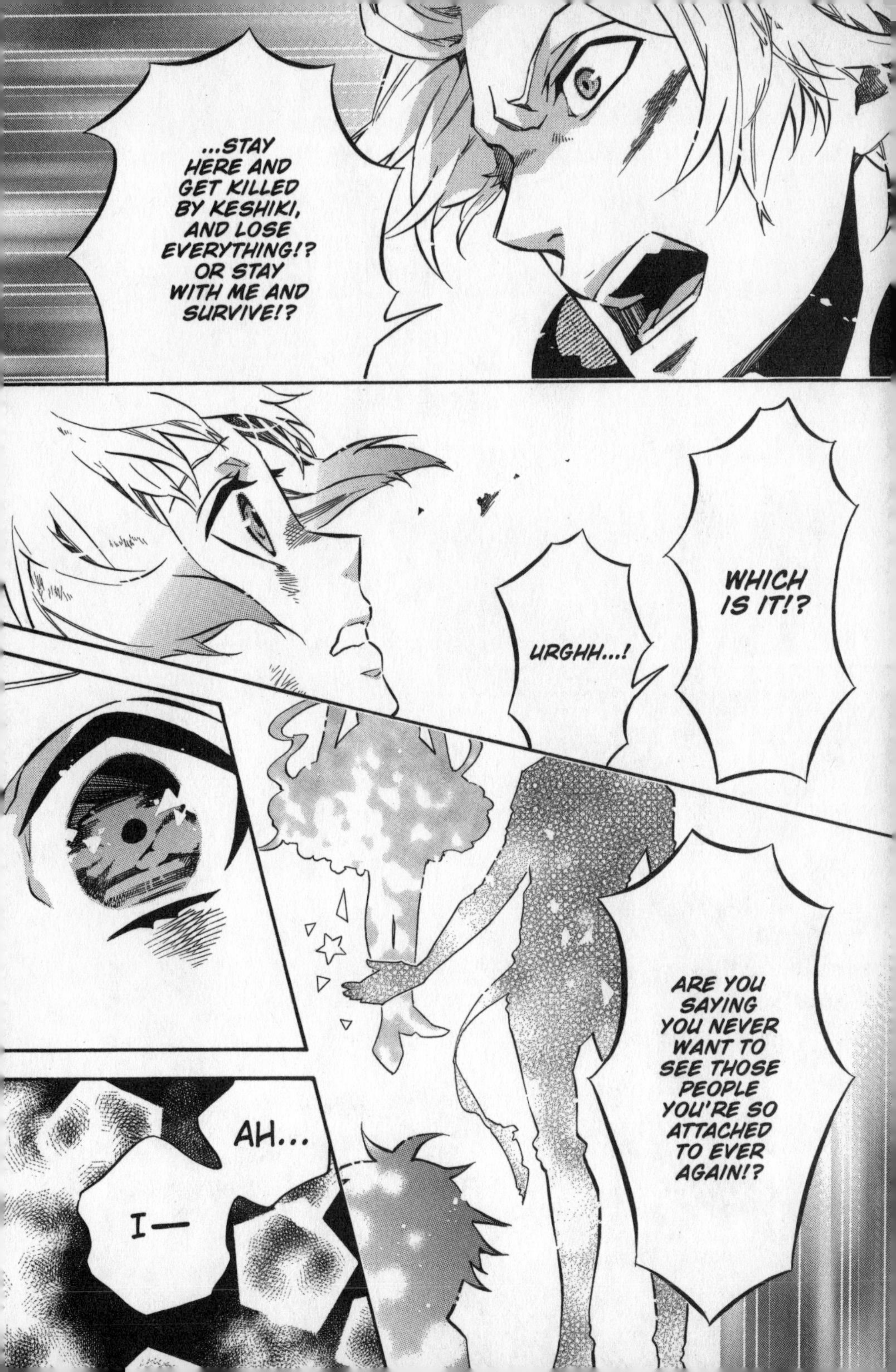
...STAY HERE AND GET KILLED BY KESHIKI, AND LOSE EVERYTHING!? OR STAY WITH ME AND SURVIVE!?
WHICH IS IT!?
URGHH...!
ARE YOU SAYING YOU NEVER WANT TO SEE THOSE PEOPLE YOU'RE SO ATTACHED TO EVER AGAIN!?
AH...
I—

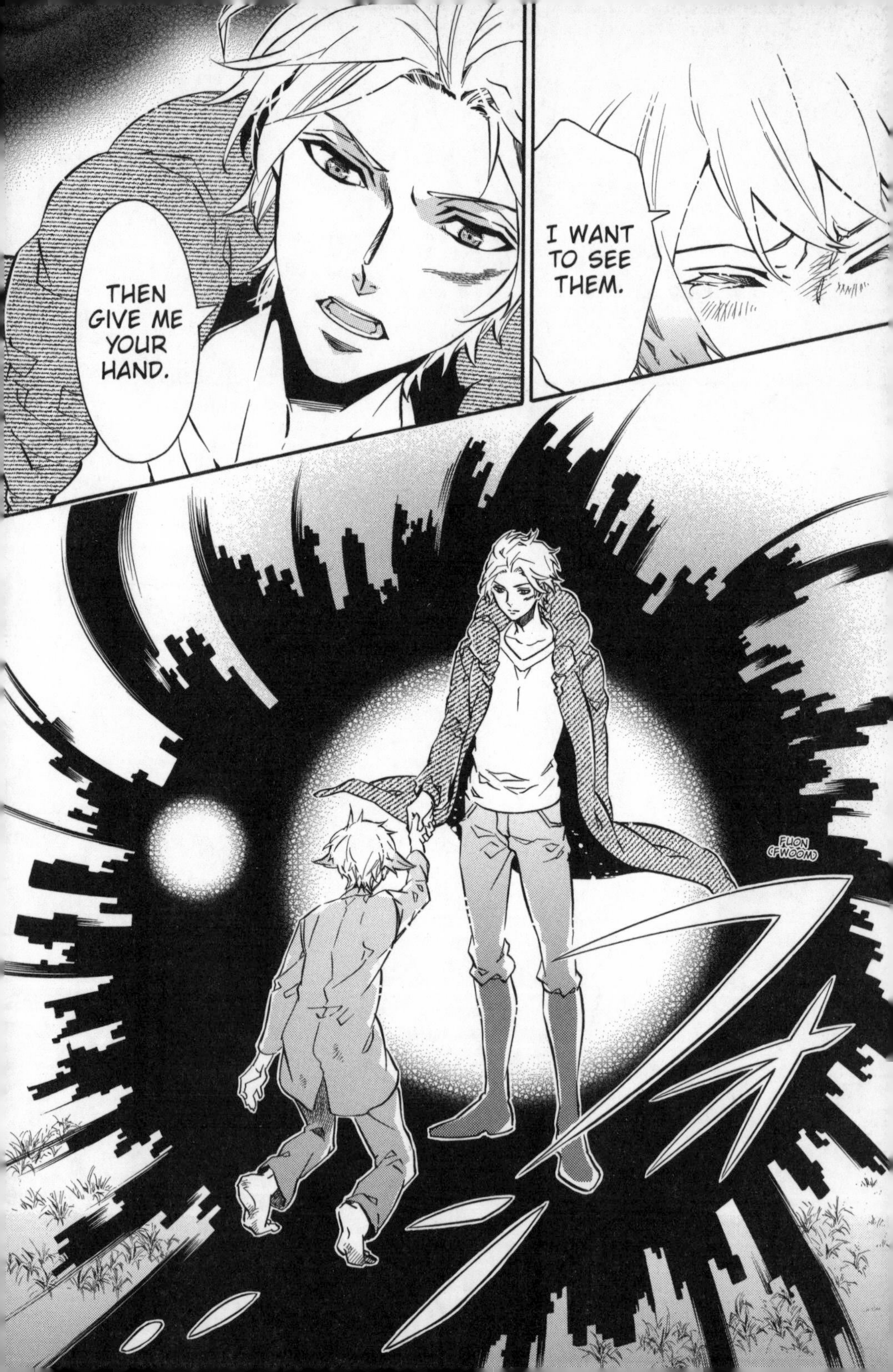
I WANT TO SEE THEM.
THEN GIVE ME YOUR HAND.
FUON (FWOOM)

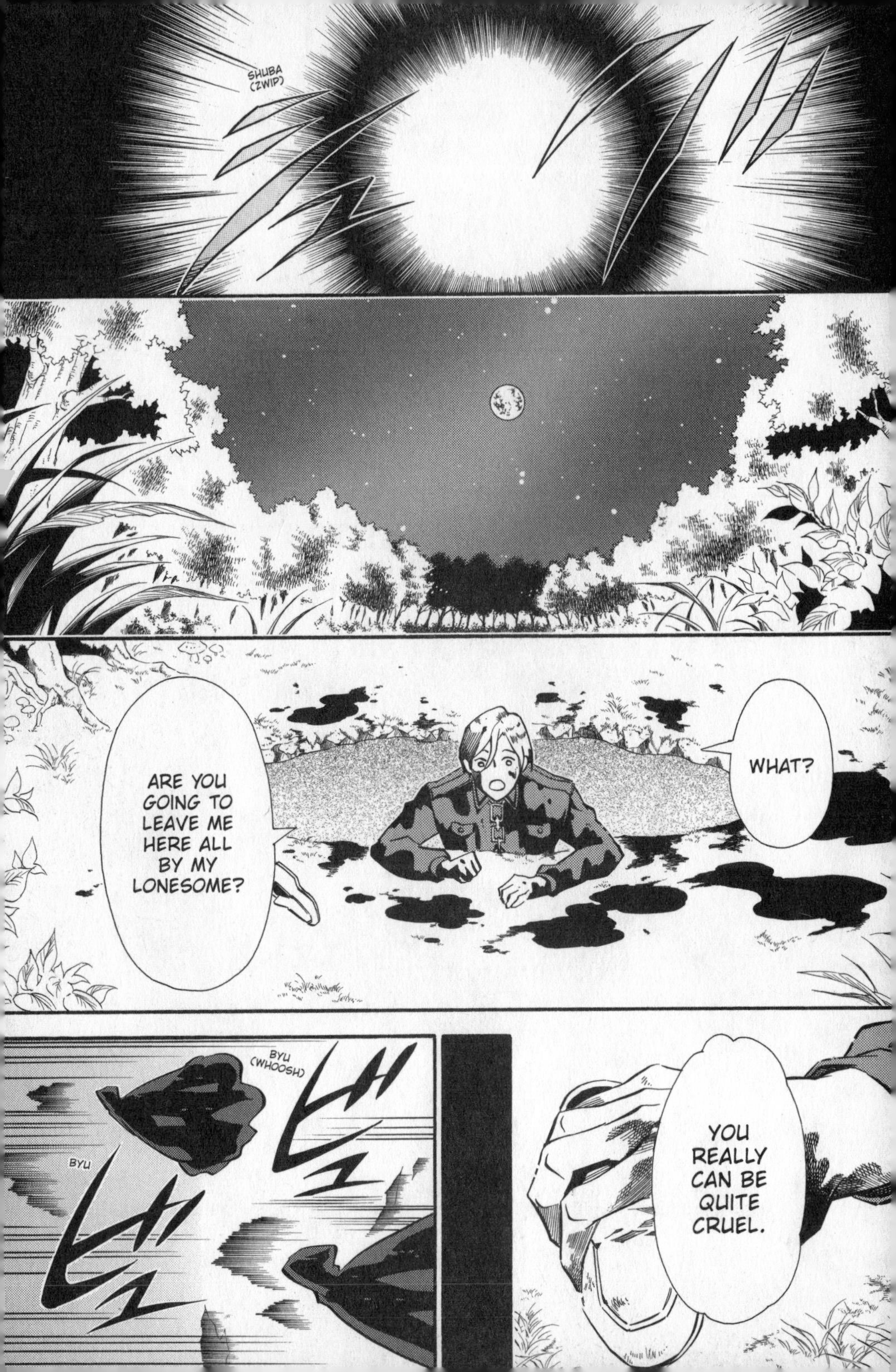
SHUBA (ZWIP)
WHAT?
ARE YOU GOING TO LEAVE ME HERE ALL BY MY LONESOME?
YOU REALLY CAN BE QUITE CRUEL.
BYU (WHOOSH)
BYU

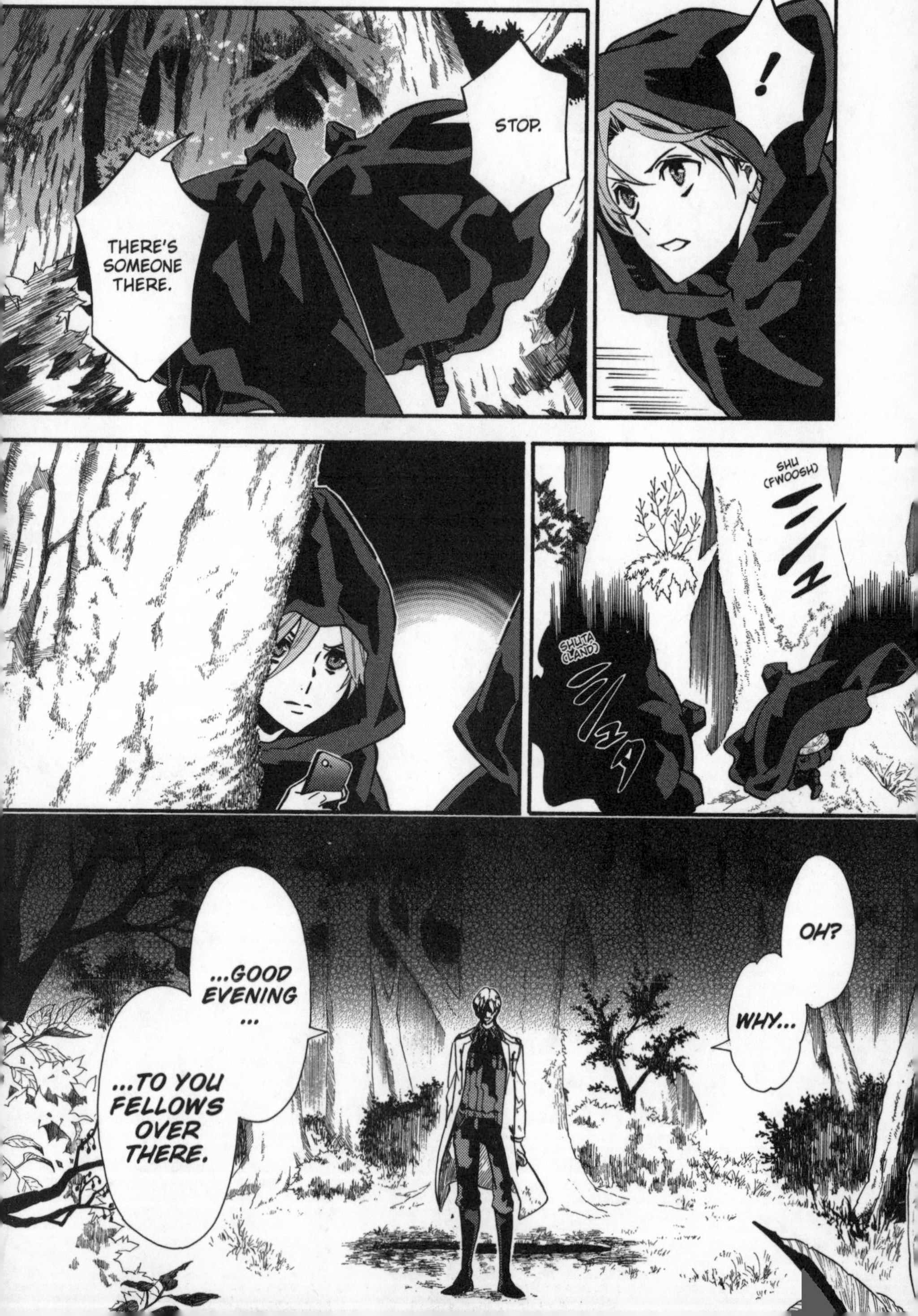
!
STOP.
THERE'S SOMEONE THERE.
SHU (FWOOSH)
SHUTA (LAND)
OH?
WHY...
...GOOD EVENING ...
...TO YOU FELLOWS OVER THERE.

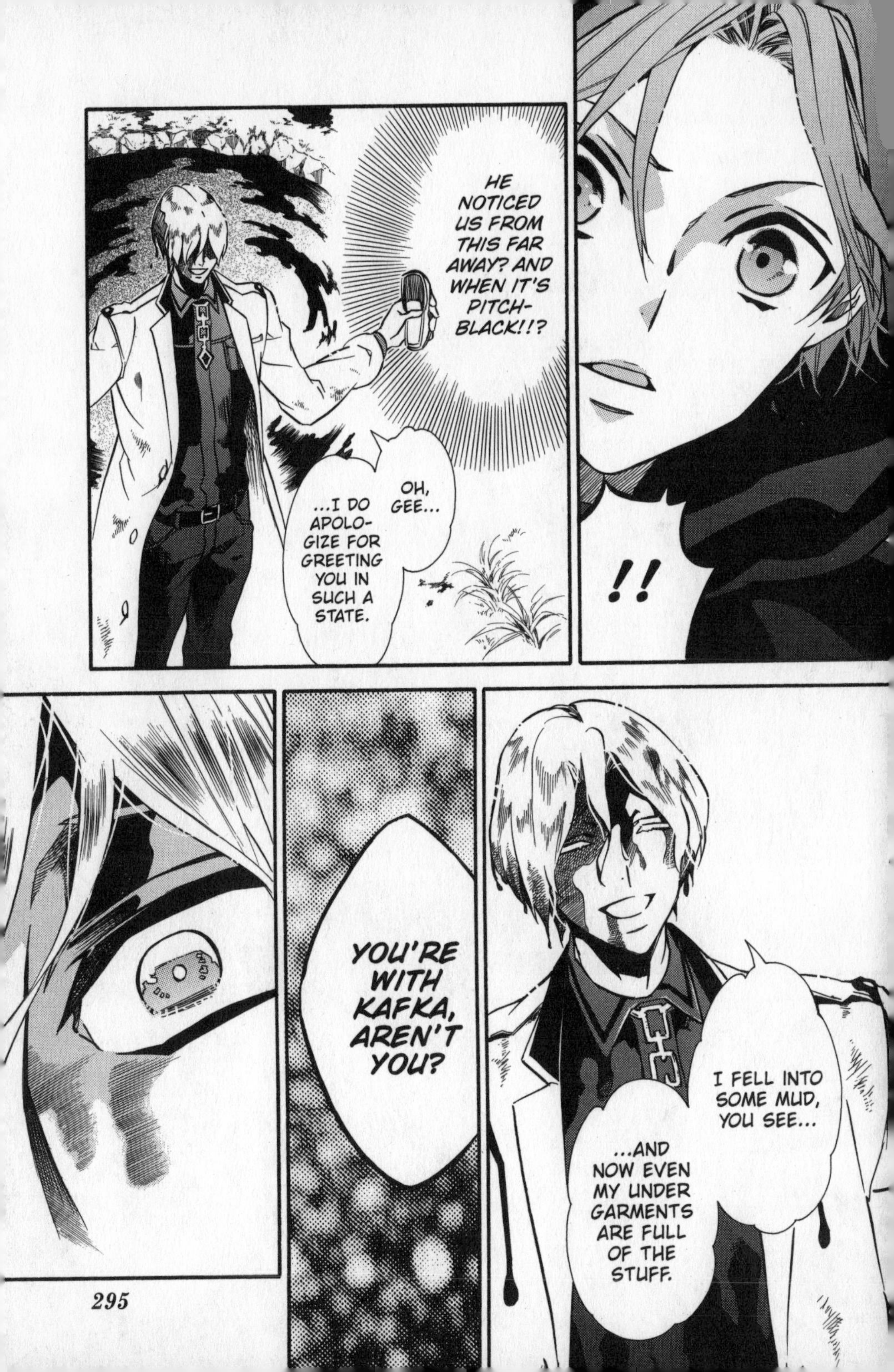
!!
HE NOTICED US FROM THIS FAR AWAY? AND WHEN IT'S PITCH-BLACK!!?
OH, GEE...
...I DO APOLOGIZE FOR GREETING YOU IN SUCH A STATE.
I FELL INTO SOME MUD, YOU SEE...
...AND NOW EVEN MY UNDER GARMENTS ARE FULL OF THE STUFF.
YOU'RE WITH KAFKA, AREN'T YOU?

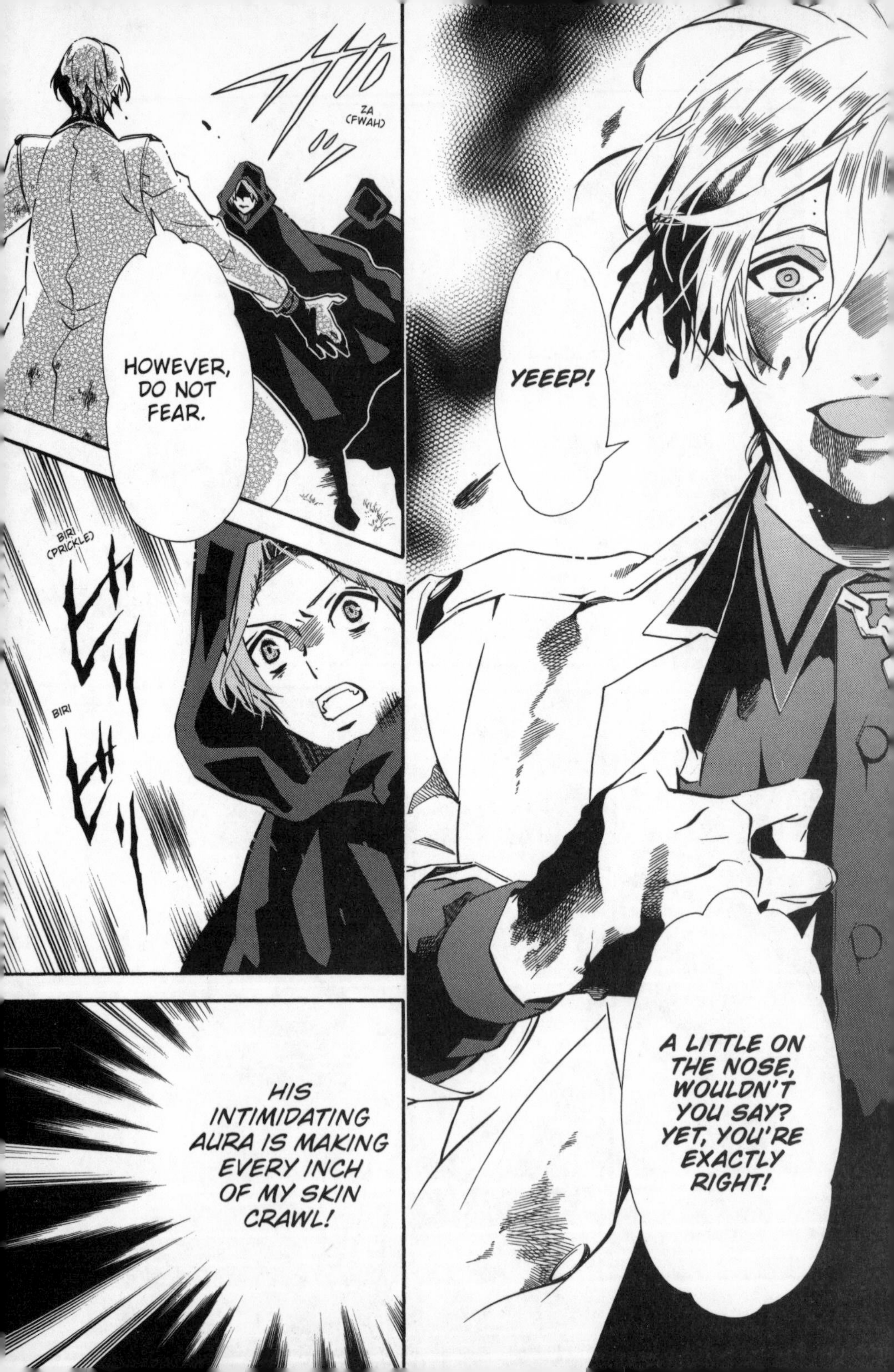
YEEEP!
A LITTLE ON THE NOSE, WOULDN'T YOU SAY? YET, YOU'RE EXACTLY RIGHT!
ZA (FWAH)
HOWEVER, DO NOT FEAR.
BIRI (PRICKLE)
BIRI
HIS INTIMIDATING AURA IS MAKING EVERY INCH OF MY SKIN CRAWL!

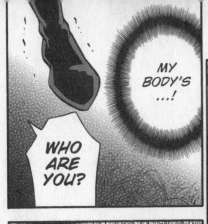

MY BODY'S ...!

WHO ARE YOU?

I'M NOT ONE TO TEASE MY BELOVED BROTHERS AND SISTERS WITHOUT CAUSE.

I BELIEVE I ALREADY TOLD YOU, *DEAREST BRETHREN*.

I AM YOUR "OLDER BROTHER."

OH, I KNOW!

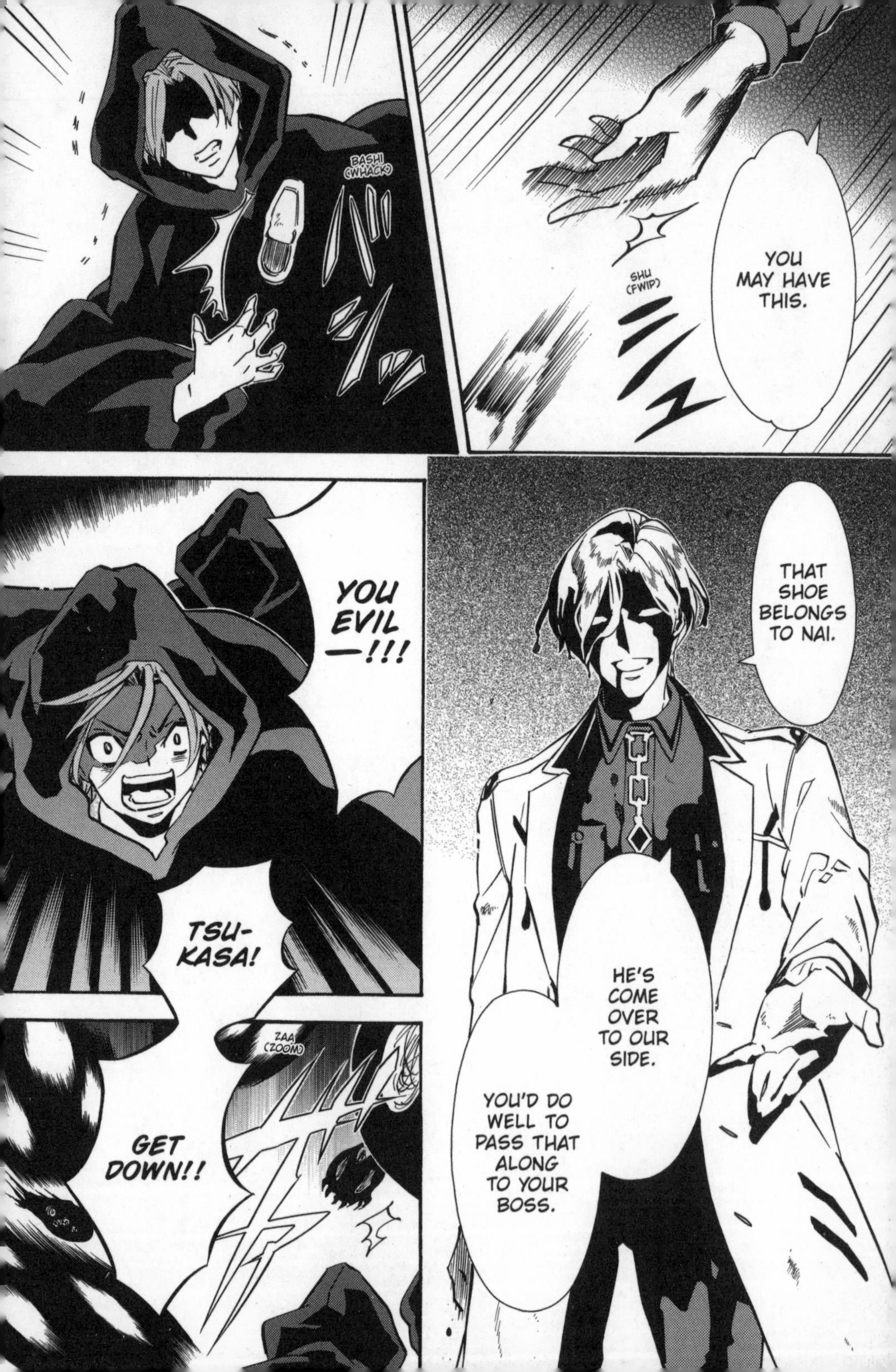
YOU MAY HAVE THIS.
SHU (FWIP)
BASHI (WHACK)
THAT SHOE BELONGS TO NAI.
HE'S COME OVER TO OUR SIDE.
YOU'D DO WELL TO PASS THAT ALONG TO YOUR BOSS.
YOU EVIL—!!!
TSU-KASA!
ZAA (ZOOM)
GET DOWN!!

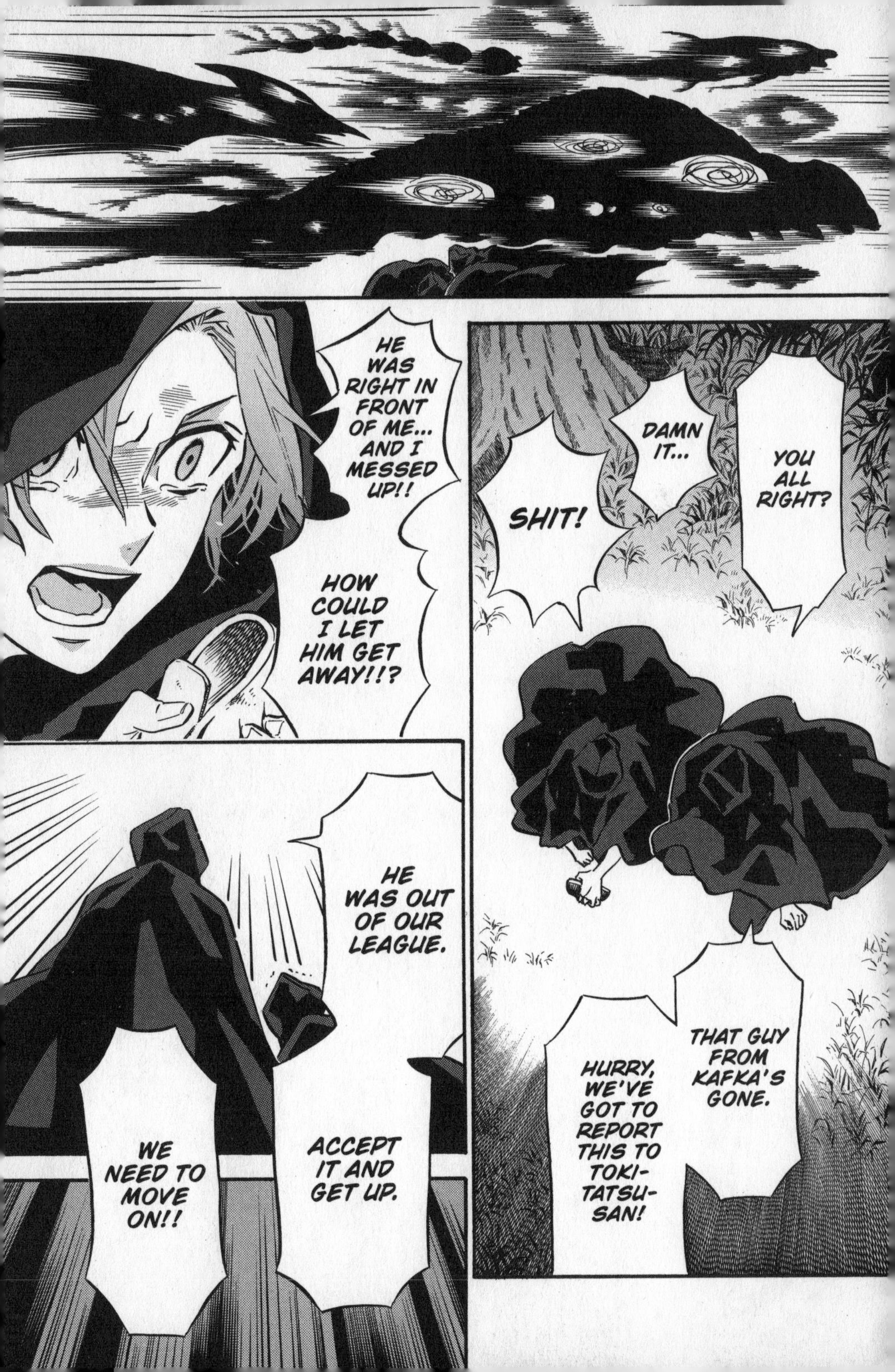
YOU ALL RIGHT?
DAMN IT...
SHIT!
THAT GUY FROM KAFKA'S GONE.
HURRY, WE'VE GOT TO REPORT THIS TO TOKI-TATSU-SAN!
HE WAS RIGHT IN FRONT OF ME... AND I MESSED UP!!
HOW COULD I LET HIM GET AWAY!!?
HE WAS OUT OF OUR LEAGUE.
ACCEPT IT AND GET UP.
WE NEED TO MOVE ON!!

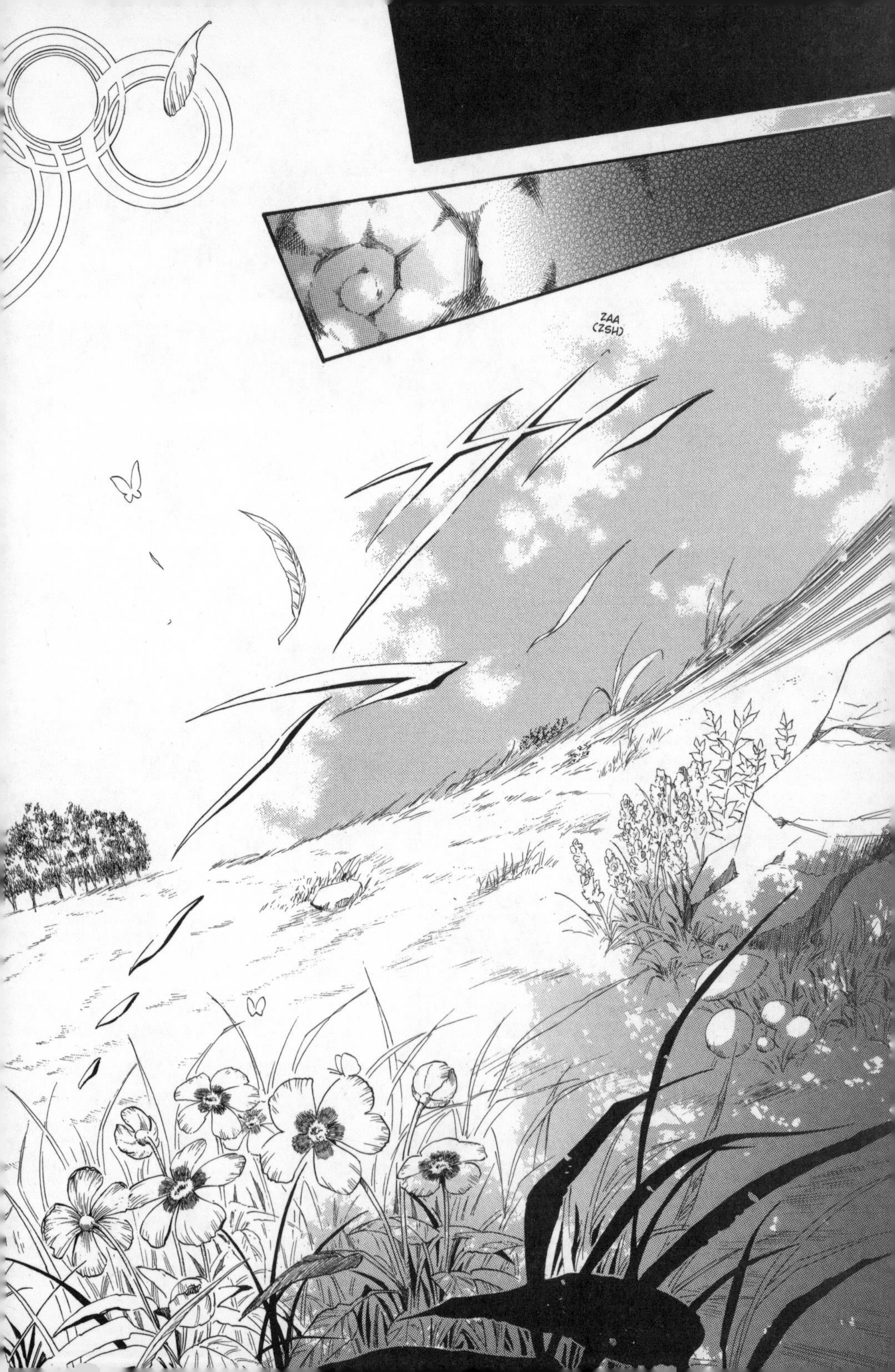
ZAA
(ZSH)

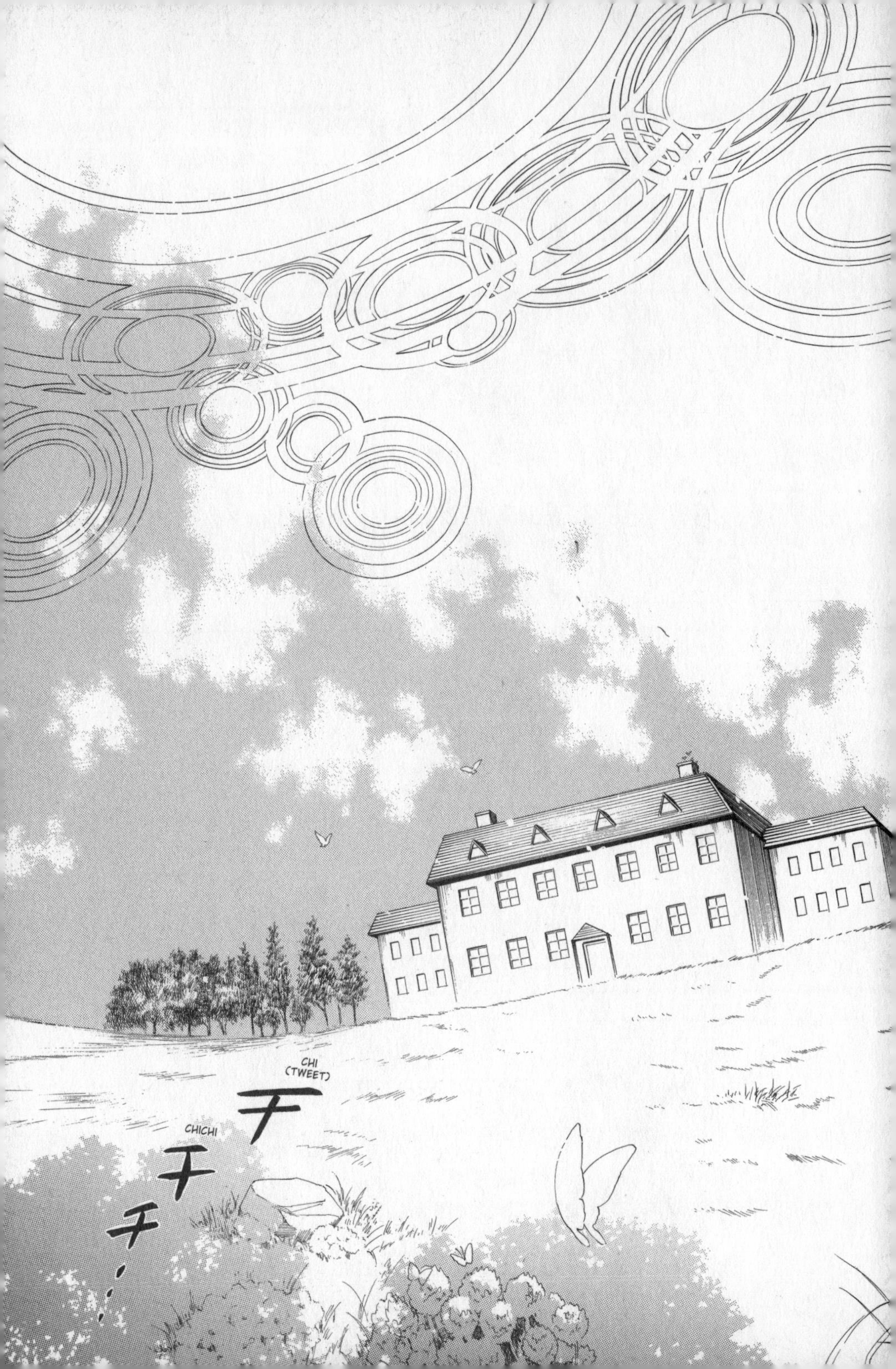
CHI
(TWEET)
チ
CHICHI
チ
チ…

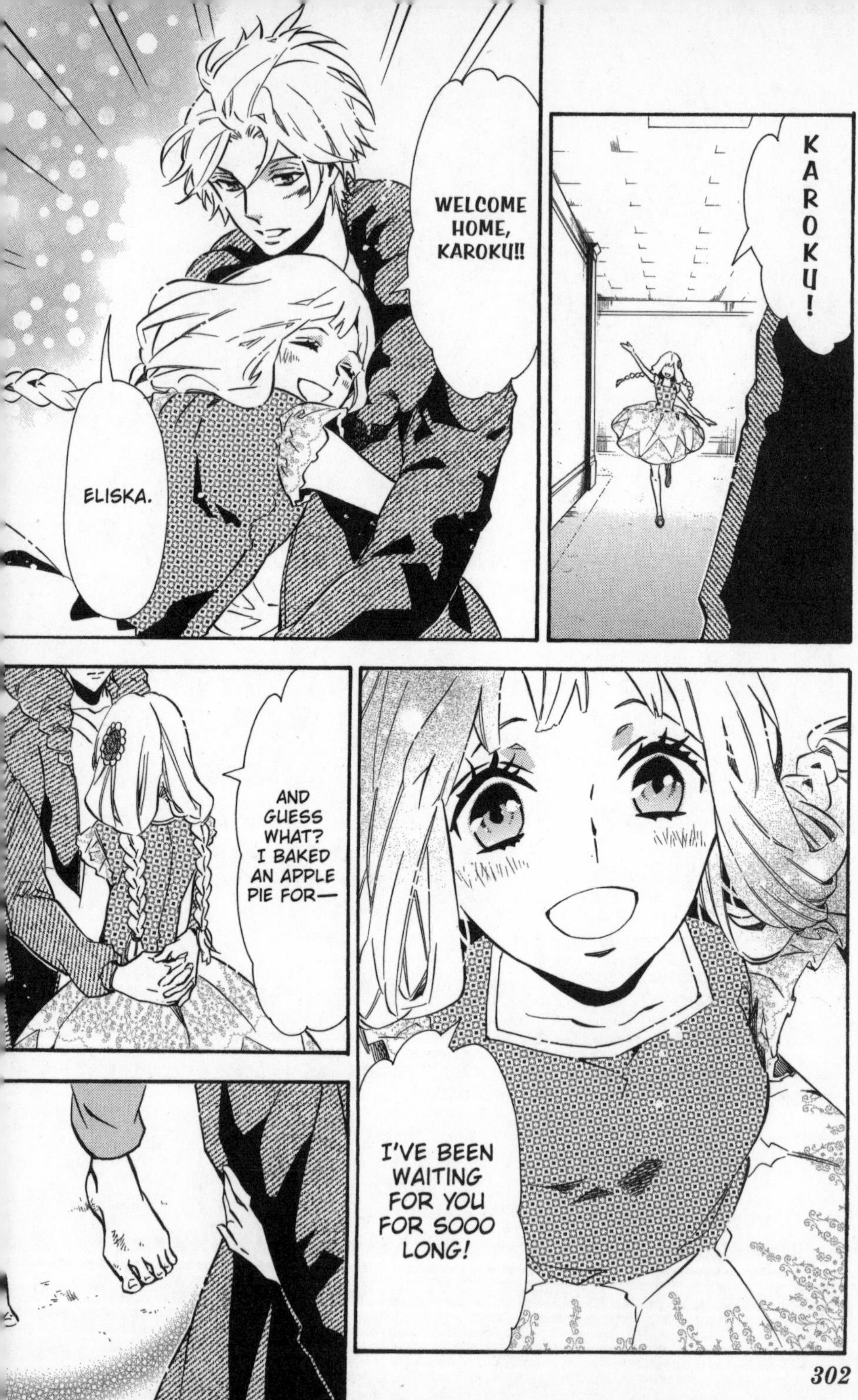
KAROKU!
WELCOME HOME, KAROKU!!
ELISKA.
I'VE BEEN WAITING FOR YOU FOR SOOO LONG!
AND GUESS WHAT? I BAKED AN APPLE PIE FOR—

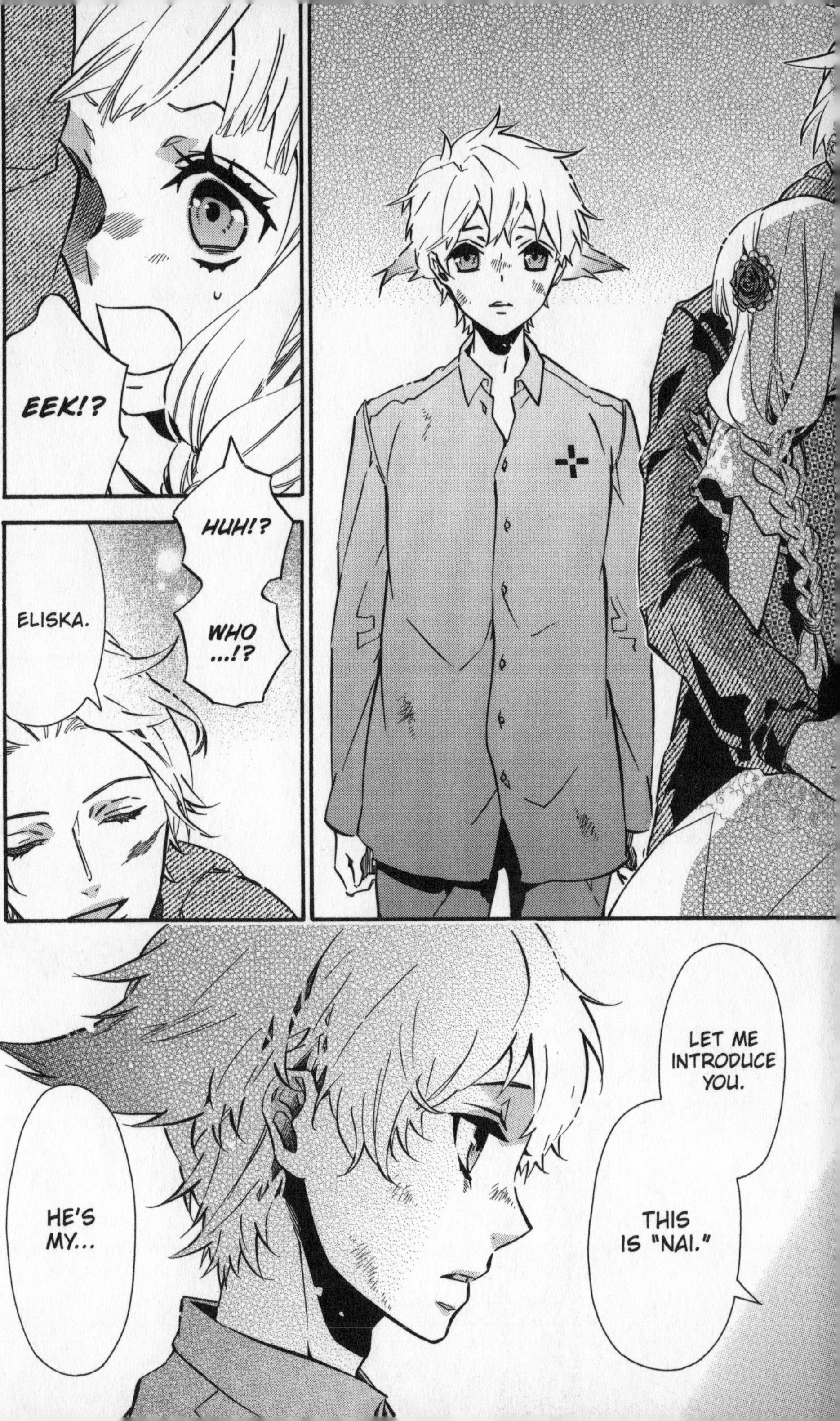
EEK!?
HUH!?
WHO ...!?
ELISKA.
LET ME INTRODUCE YOU.
THIS IS "NAI."
HE'S MY...

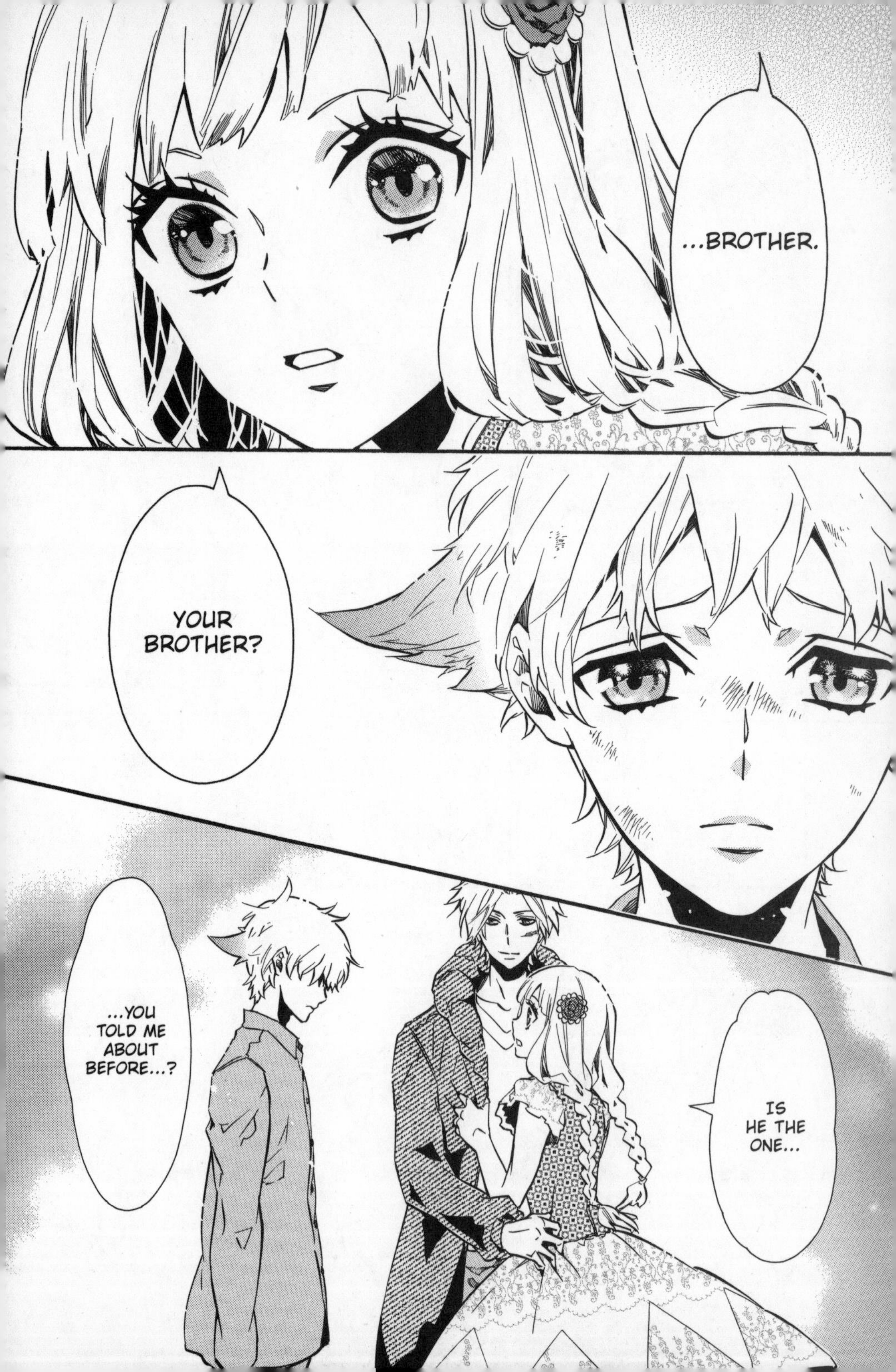
...BROTHER.
YOUR BROTHER?
IS HE THE ONE...
...YOU TOLD ME ABOUT BEFORE...?

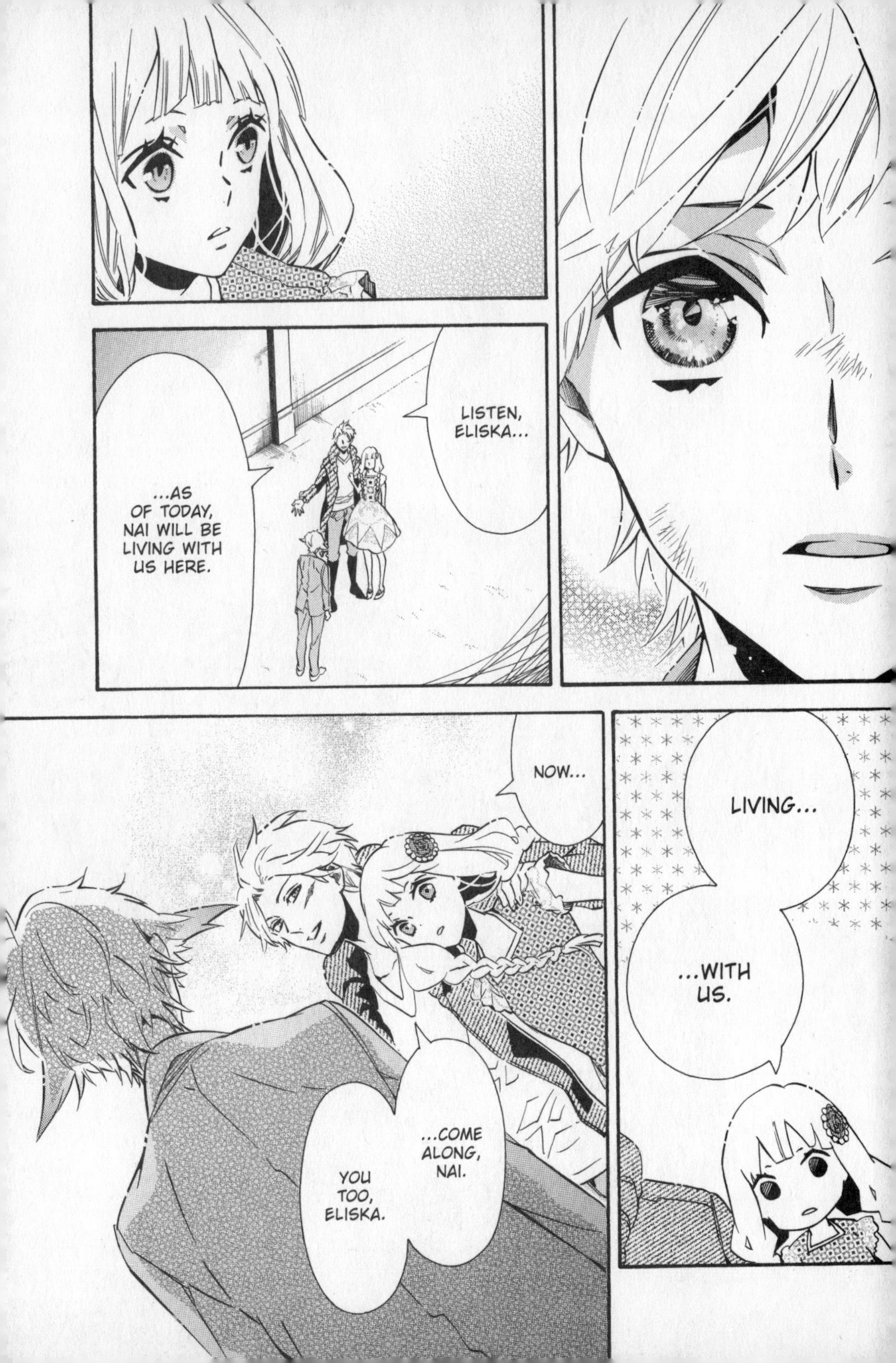
LISTEN, ELISKA...
...AS OF TODAY, NAI WILL BE LIVING WITH US HERE.
LIVING...
...WITH US.
NOW...
...COME ALONG, NAI.
YOU TOO, ELISKA.

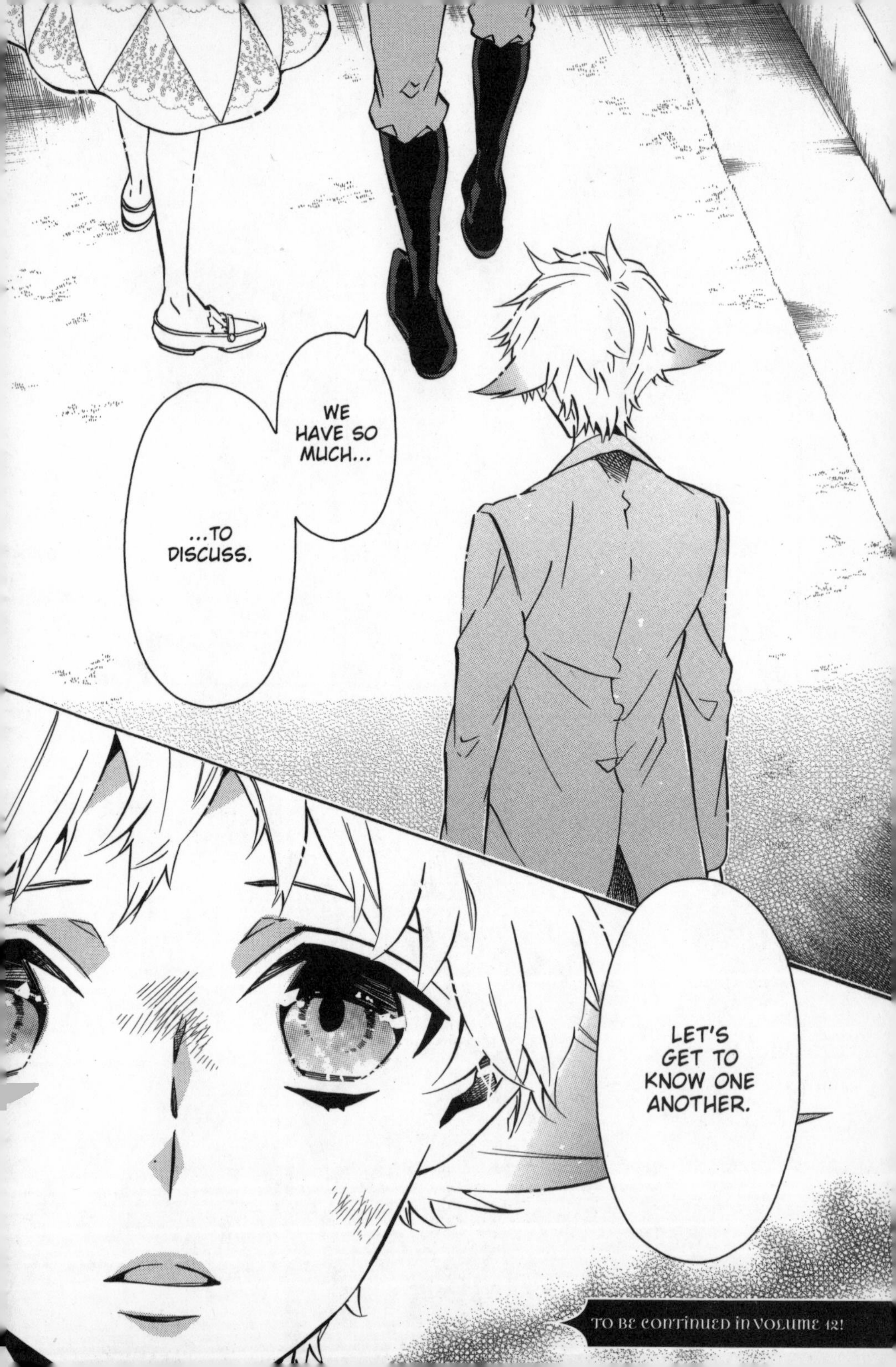
WE HAVE SO MUCH...
...TO DISCUSS.
LET'S GET TO KNOW ONE ANOTHER.
TO BE CONTINUED IN VOLUME 12!

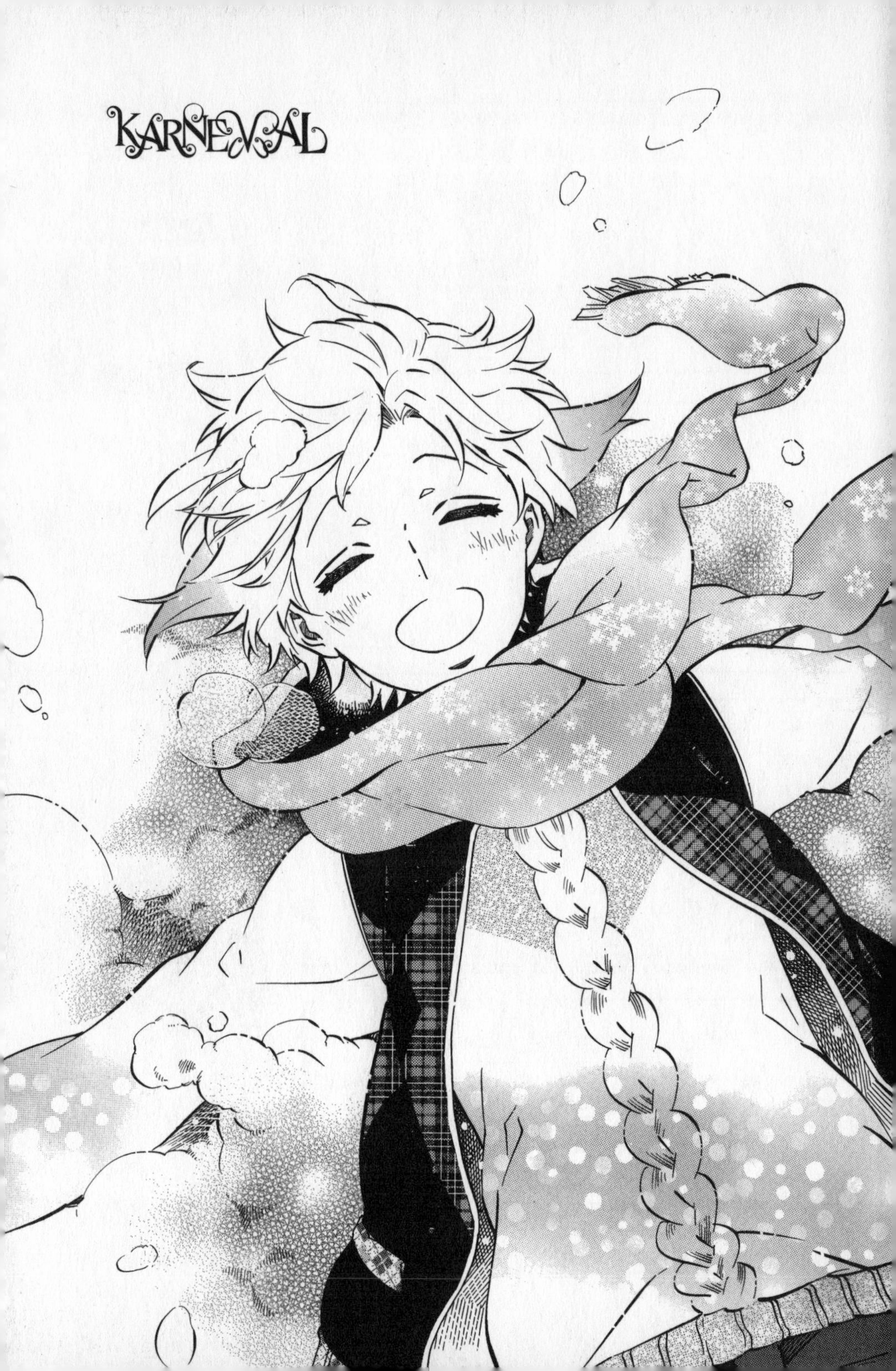
KARNEVAL

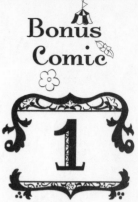

# Bonus Comic 1

## Shall We Chat?

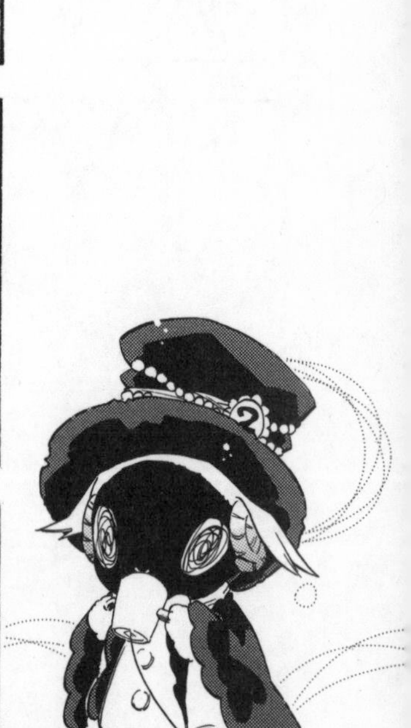

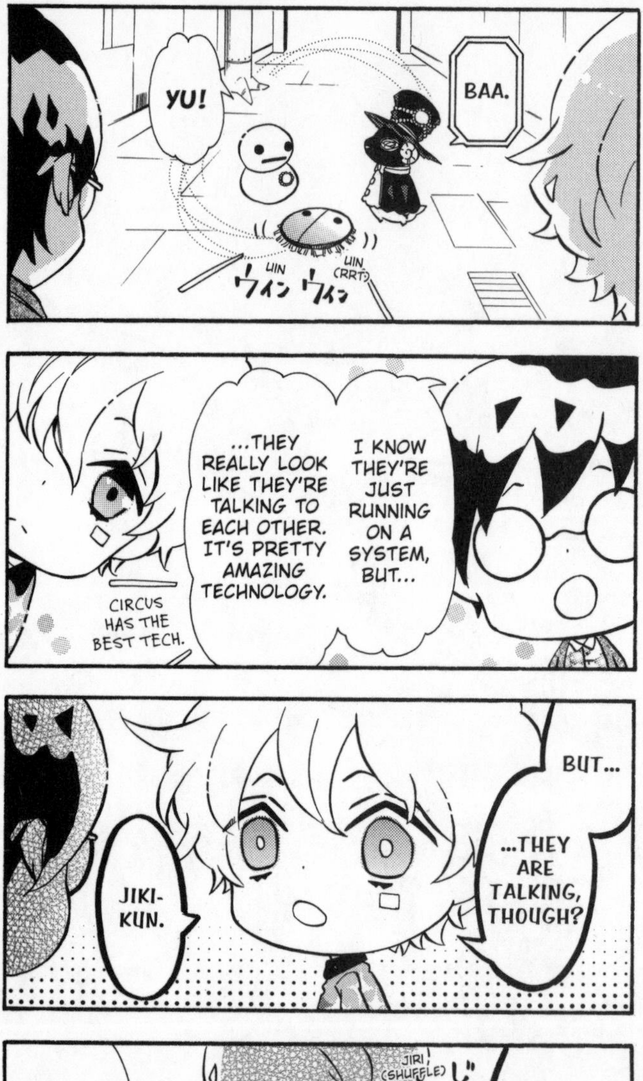
BAA.
YU!
UIN UIN (RRT)
ウィン ウィン
I KNOW THEY'RE JUST RUNNING ON A SYSTEM, BUT...
...THEY REALLY LOOK LIKE THEY'RE TALKING TO EACH OTHER. IT'S PRETTY AMAZING TECHNOLOGY.
CIRCUS HAS THE BEST TECH.
BUT...
...THEY ARE TALKING, THOUGH?
JIKI-KUN.
JIRI (SHUFFLE)
じり…
EVERY SHEEP HAS A MIND OF ITS OWN.
I FEEL LIKE SOMETIMES YOU AND I DON'T SPEAK THE SAME LANGUAGE.

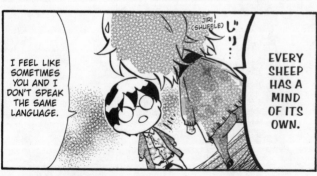

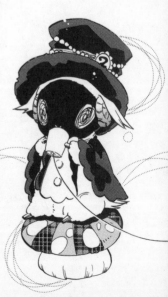

# Bonus Comic 2

## The Whites in Your Eyes

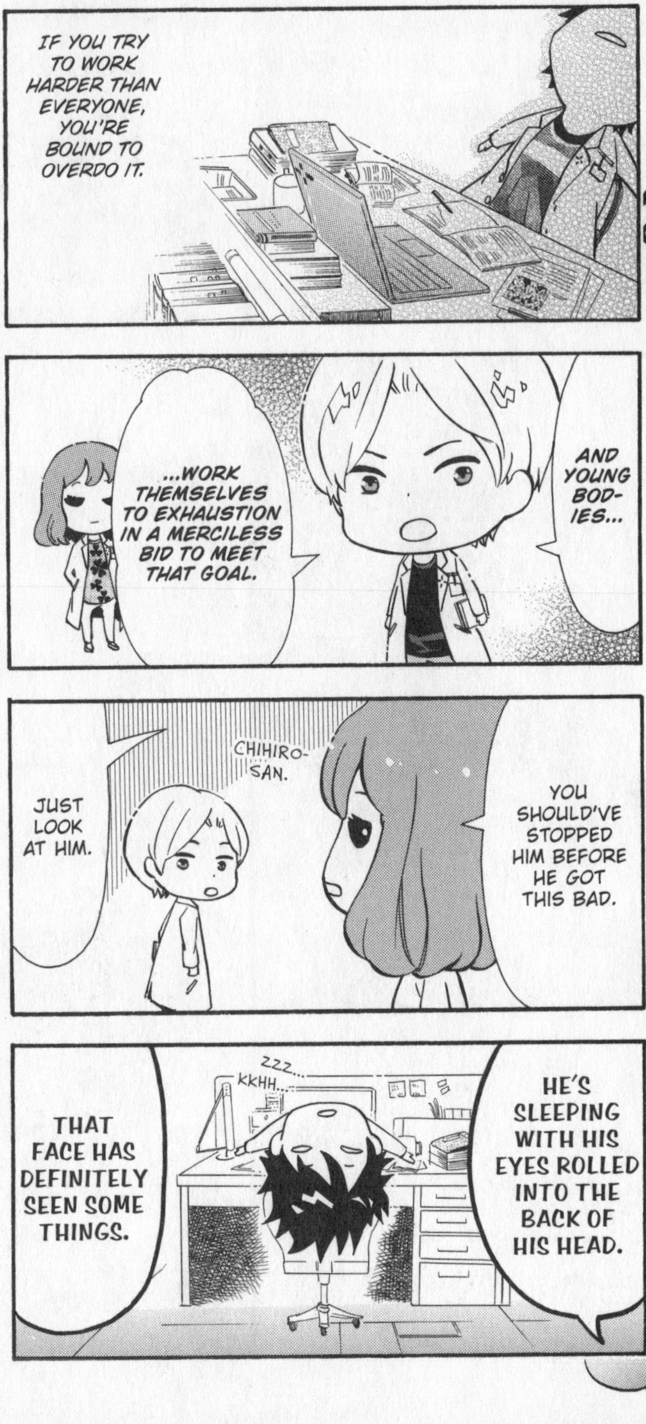
IF YOU TRY TO WORK HARDER THAN EVERYONE, YOU'RE BOUND TO OVERDO IT.
AND YOUNG BODIES...
...WORK THEMSELVES TO EXHAUSTION IN A MERCILESS BID TO MEET THAT GOAL.
YOU SHOULD'VE STOPPED HIM BEFORE HE GOT THIS BAD.
CHIHIRO-SAN.
JUST LOOK AT HIM.
HE'S SLEEPING WITH HIS EYES ROLLED INTO THE BACK OF HIS HEAD.
ZZZ...
KKHH...
THAT FACE HAS DEFINITELY SEEN SOME THINGS.

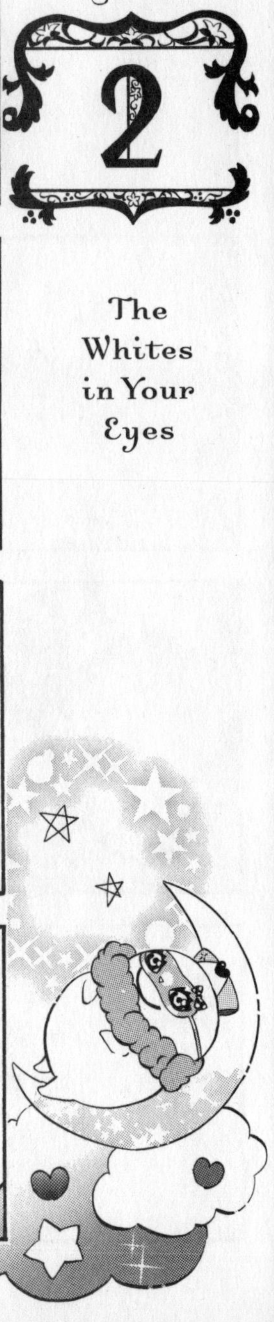

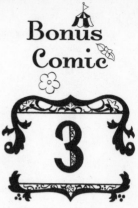

# Bonus Comic 3

## As We Fly Through the Starry Sky

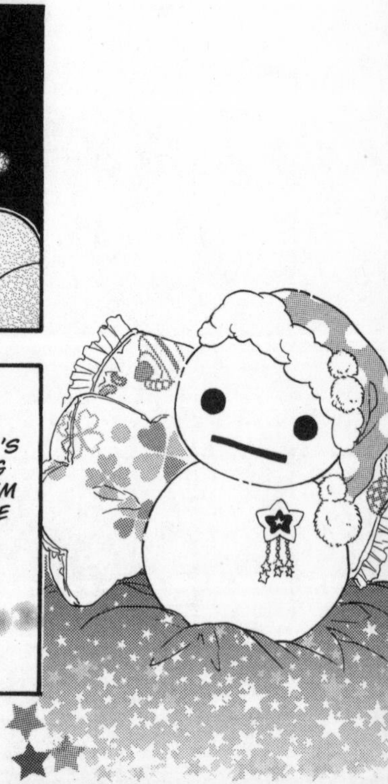

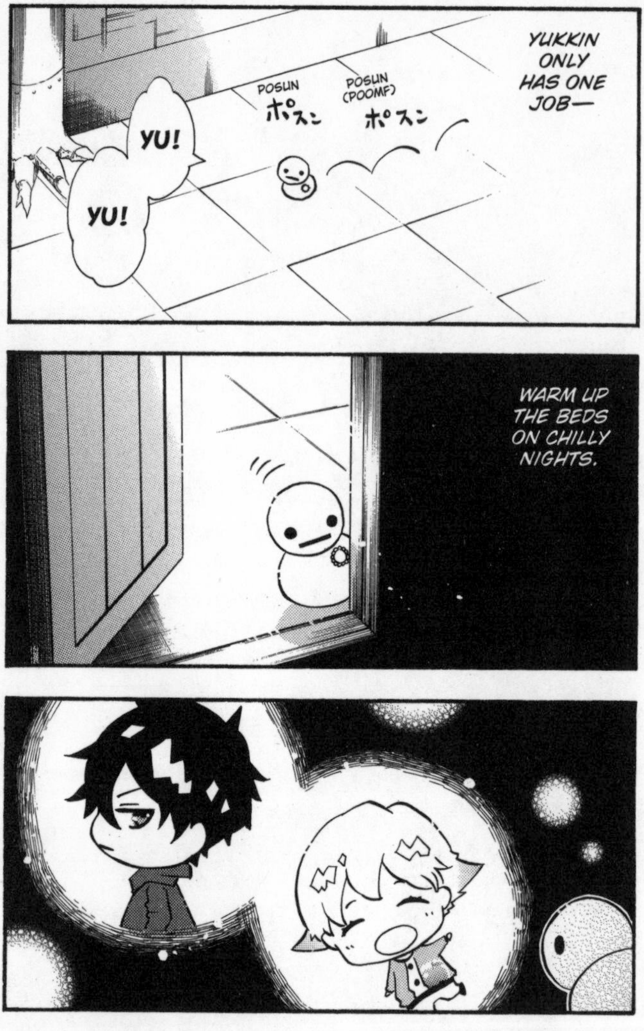

YUKKIN ONLY HAS ONE JOB—
POSUN (POOMF) ポスン
POSUN ポスン
YU!
YU!
WARM UP THE BEDS ON CHILLY NIGHTS.
RIGHT NOW, HE'S WAITING FOR THEM TO COME HOME.
SUYA (ZZZ) スヤ
SUYA スヤ

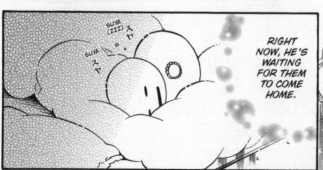

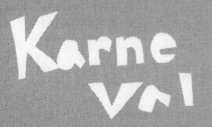

# Karneval

HAVE FUN DRAWING IN FACES!


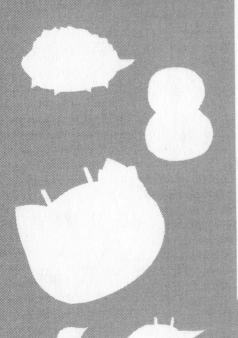

THANK YOU FOR READING VOLUME 11 OF KARNEVAL. I HOPE YOU ENJOYED IT. I ALWAYS LOVE READING THE LETTERS YOU SEND ME.

ON SEPTEMBER 28, THE ORIGINAL KARNEVAL KEYCHAINS AND MERCH MADE IN COLLABORATION WITH PRINCESS CAFÉ WENT ON SALE. I WAS SO HAPPY TO SEE HOW CUTE THEM CAME OUT!

MY STUDIO IS DECORATED WITH A LOT OF MERCH AND GIFTS THAT READERS KINDLY MADE SINCE WE STARTED KARNEVAL. THEY REALLY GIVE ME STRENGTH AS I WORK!

Touya Mikanagi


## Special Thanks

MOTSU-SAN SUAMA-SAN SAN

MY EDITOR, OOHASHI-SAN EVERYONE AT ICHIJINSHA PUBLISHING

ALL THE COLLABORATORS AND EVERYONE AT OUR AFFILIATED COMPANIES WHO'VE TAKEN CARE OF ME
MY FRIENDS AND FAMILY

AND TO YOU!!

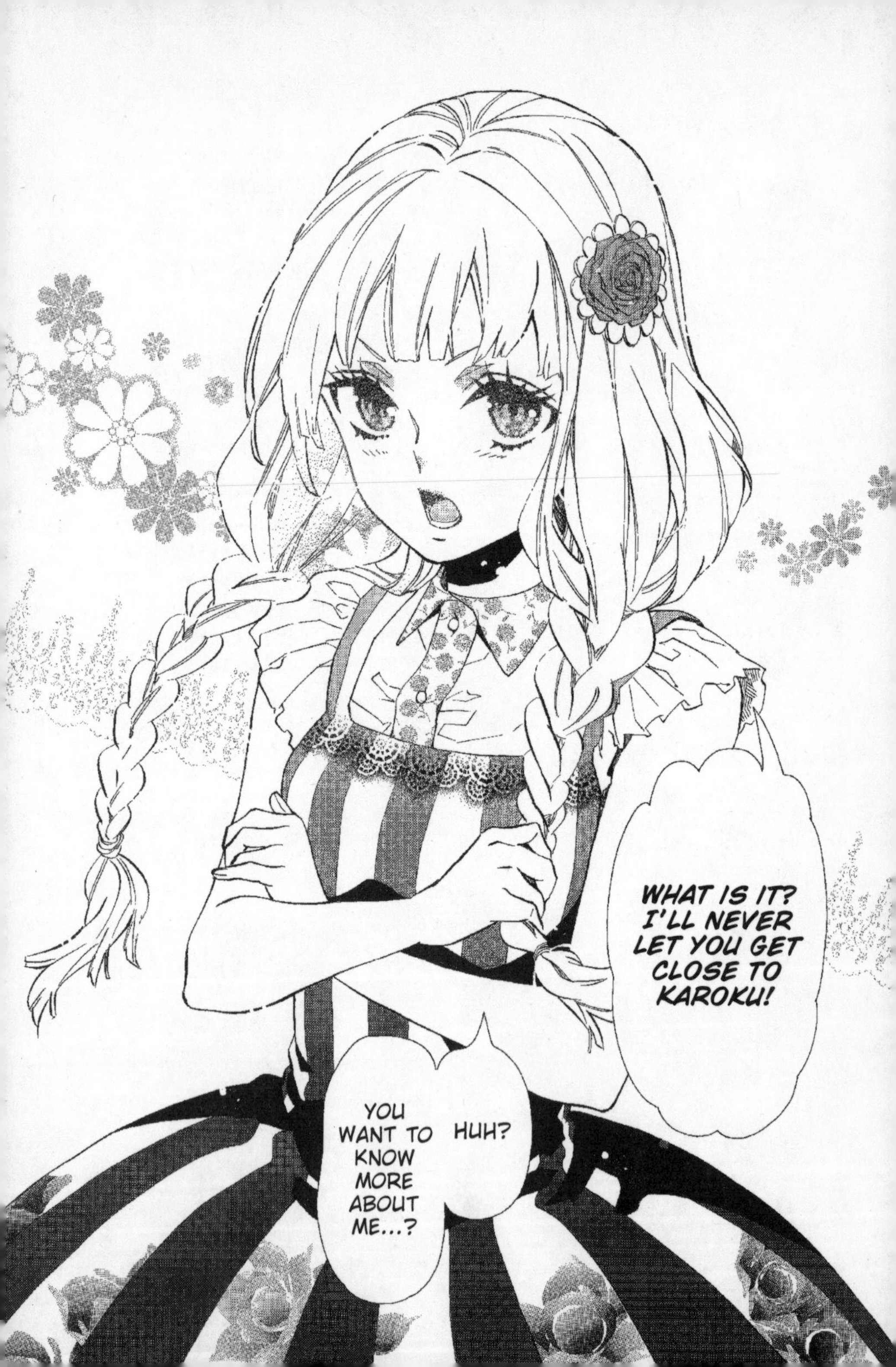
WHAT IS IT? I'LL NEVER LET YOU GET CLOSE TO KAROKU!
HUH? YOU WANT TO KNOW MORE ABOUT ME...?

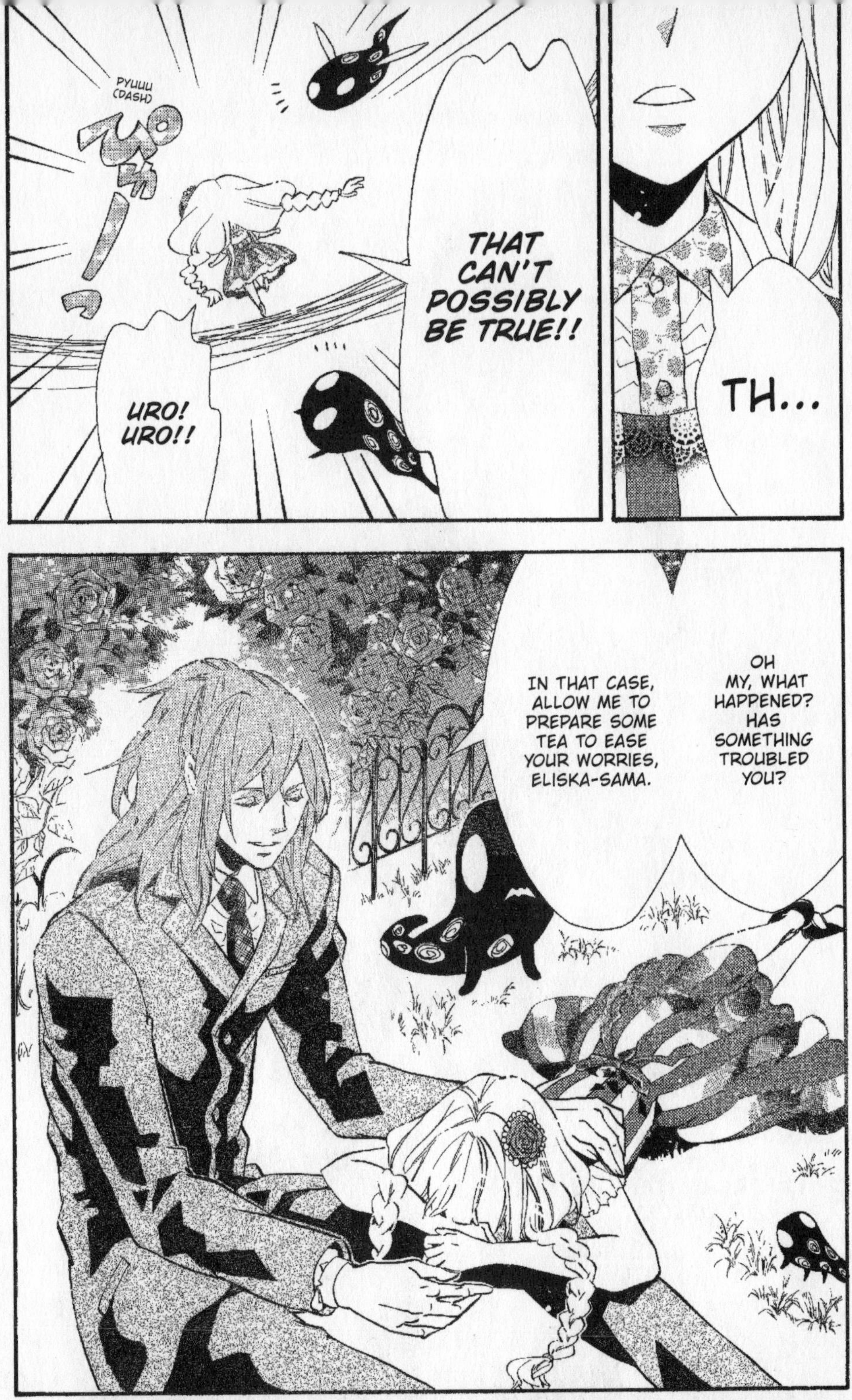
TH...
THAT CAN'T POSSIBLY BE TRUE!!
PYUUU (DASH)
URO! URO!!
OH MY, WHAT HAPPENED? HAS SOMETHING TROUBLED YOU?
IN THAT CASE, ALLOW ME TO PREPARE SOME TEA TO EASE YOUR WORRIES, ELISKA-SAMA.

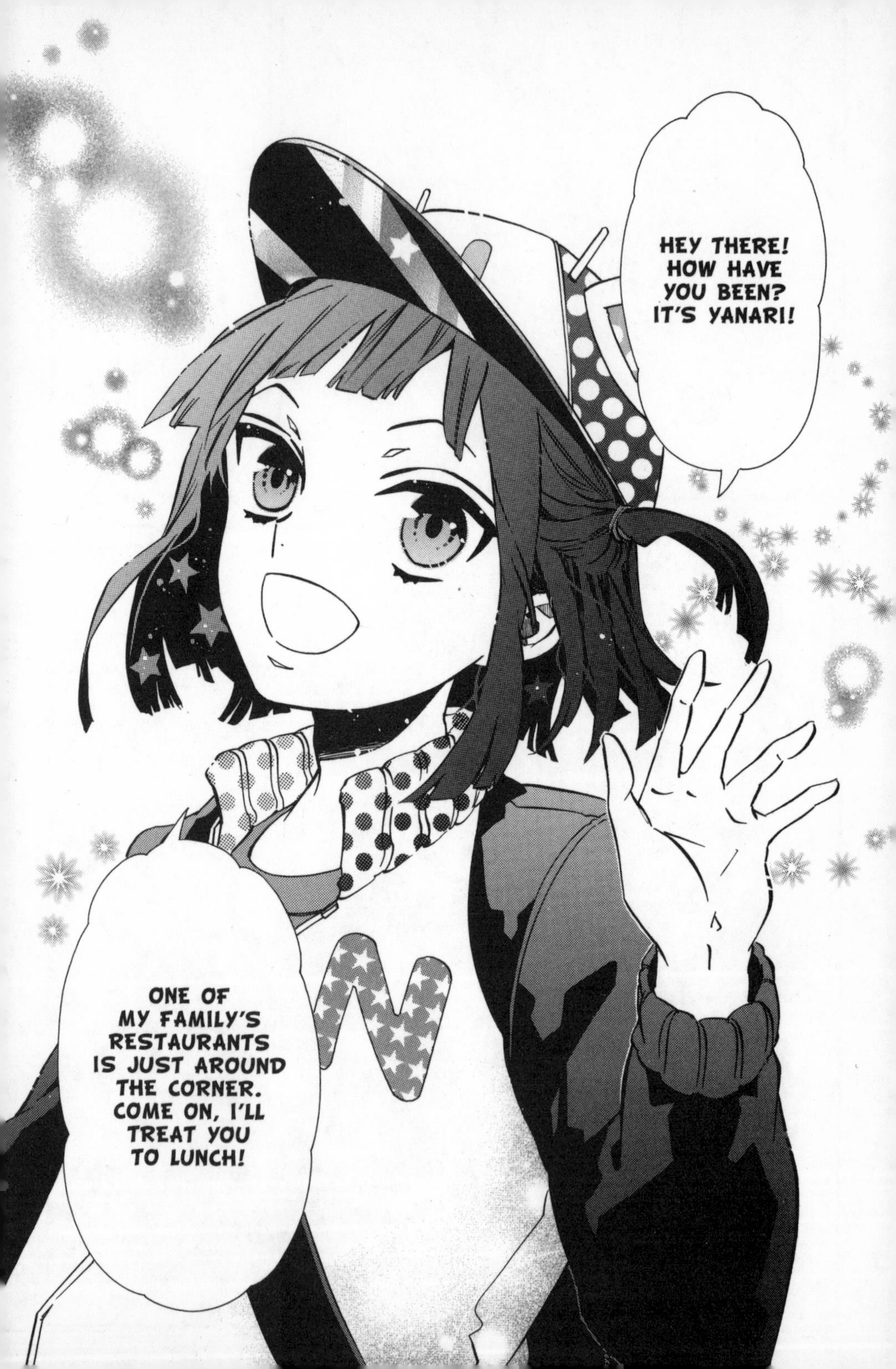
HEY THERE! HOW HAVE YOU BEEN? IT'S YANARI!
ONE OF MY FAMILY'S RESTAURANTS IS JUST AROUND THE CORNER. COME ON, I'LL TREAT YOU TO LUNCH!

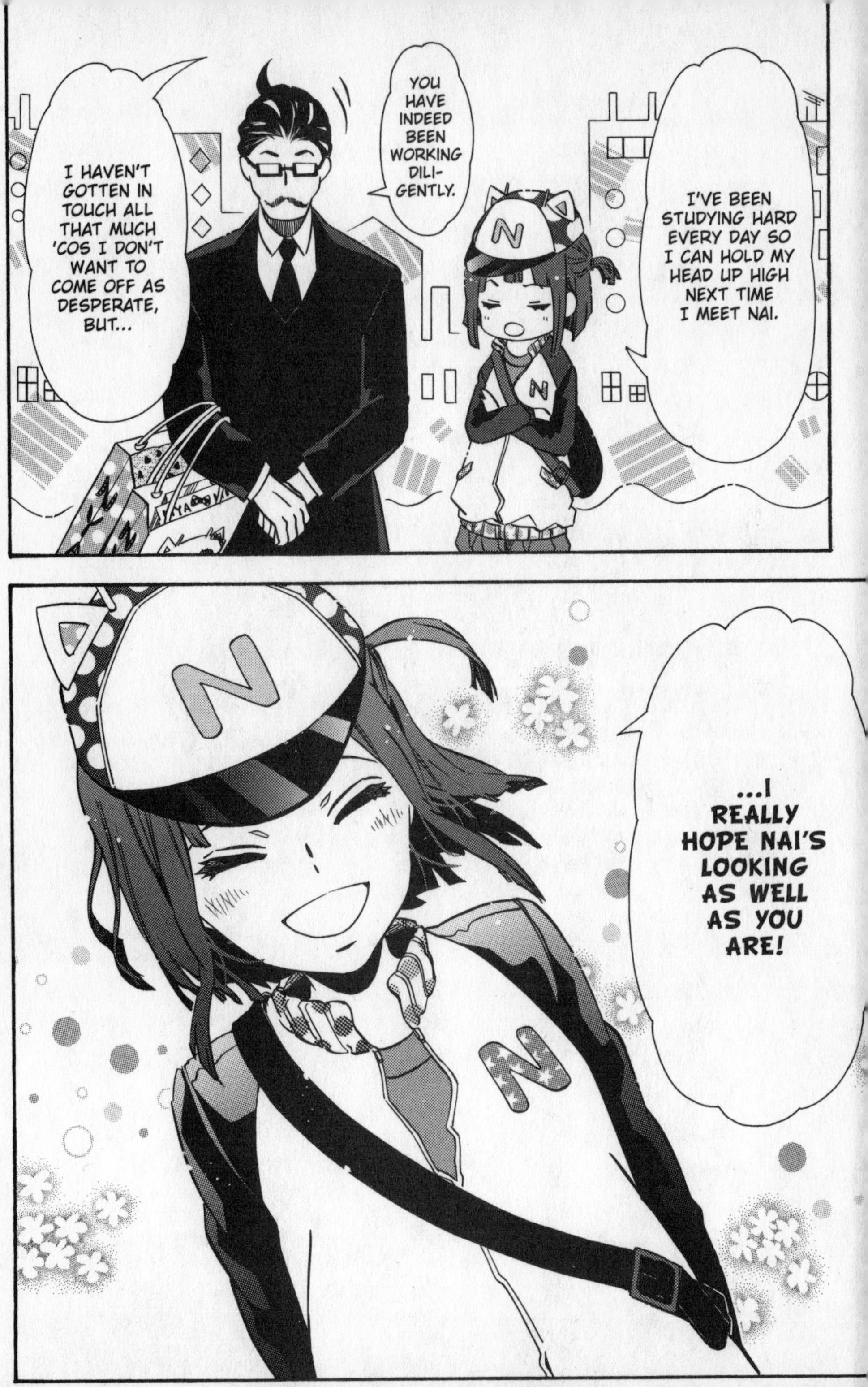
I'VE BEEN STUDYING HARD EVERY DAY SO I CAN HOLD MY HEAD UP HIGH NEXT TIME I MEET NAI.
YOU HAVE INDEED BEEN WORKING DILI-GENTLY.
I HAVEN'T GOTTEN IN TOUCH ALL THAT MUCH 'COS I DON'T WANT TO COME OFF AS DESPERATE, BUT...
...I REALLY HOPE NAI'S LOOKING AS WELL AS YOU ARE!

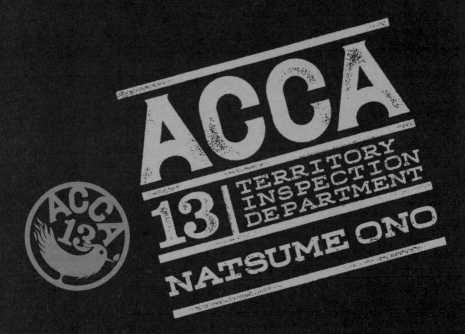

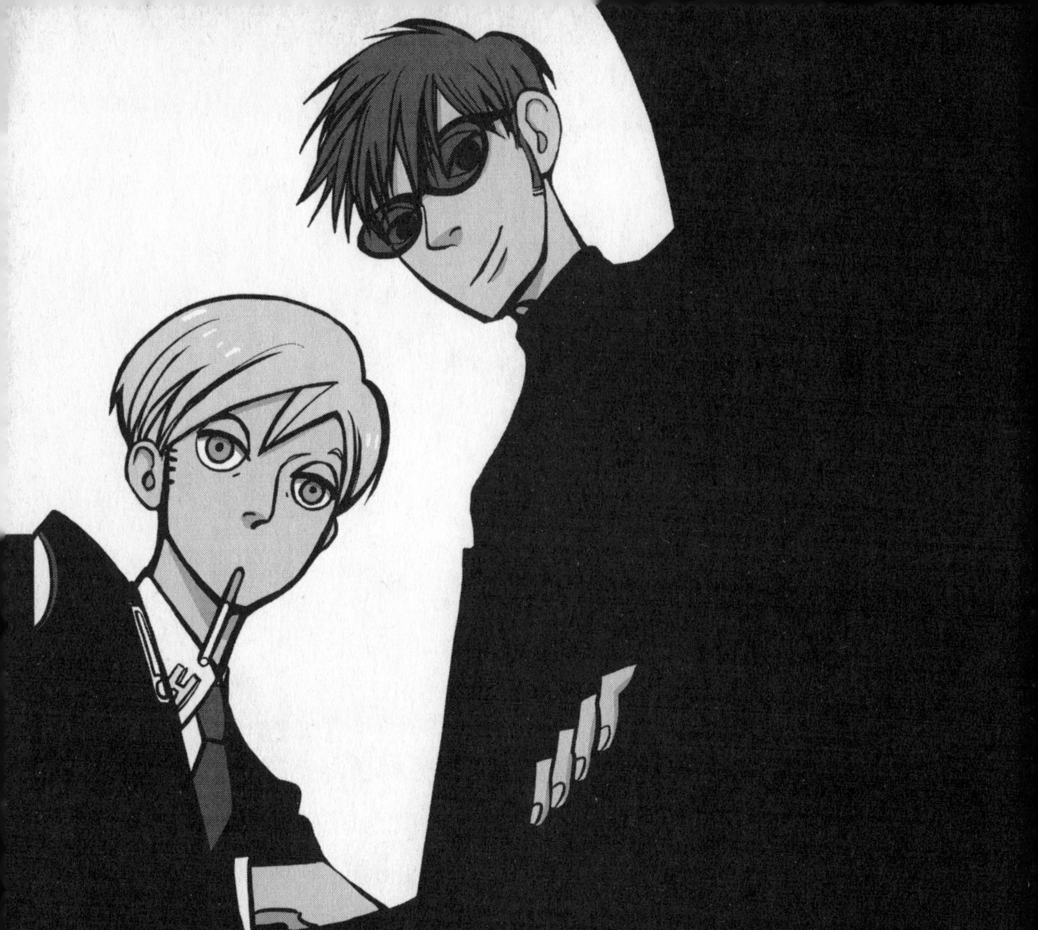

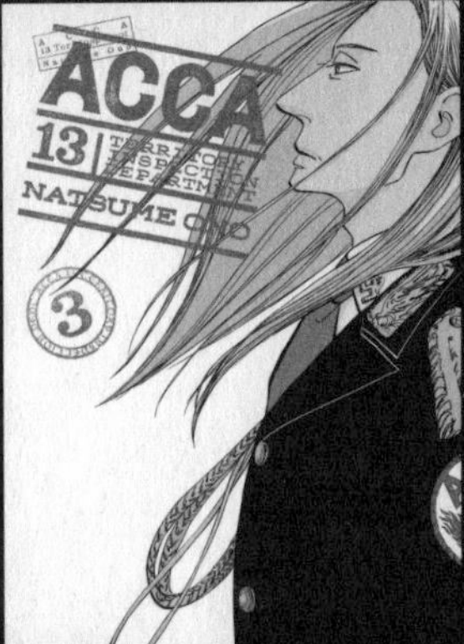
ACCA
13 TERRITORY INSPECTION DEPARTMENT
NATSUME ONO
3

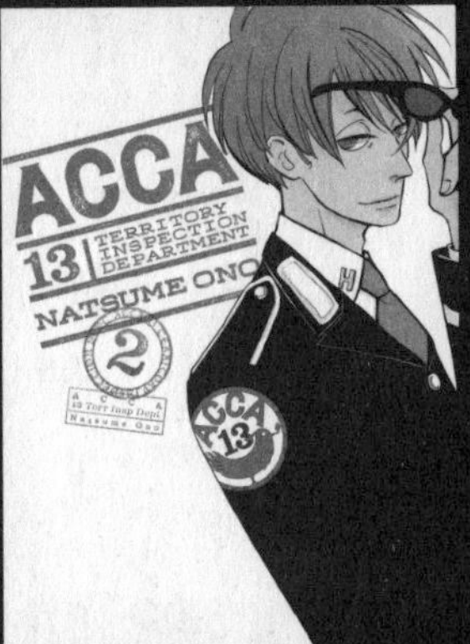
ACCA
13 TERRITORY INSPECTION DEPARTMENT
NATSUME ONO
2

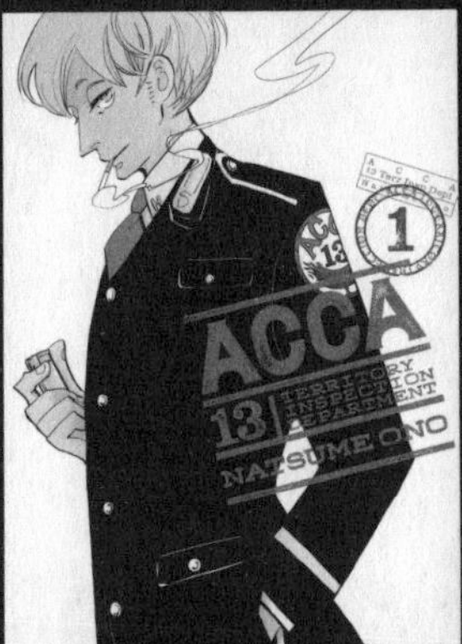
1
ACCA
13 TERRITORY INSPECTION DEPARTMENT
NATSUME ONO

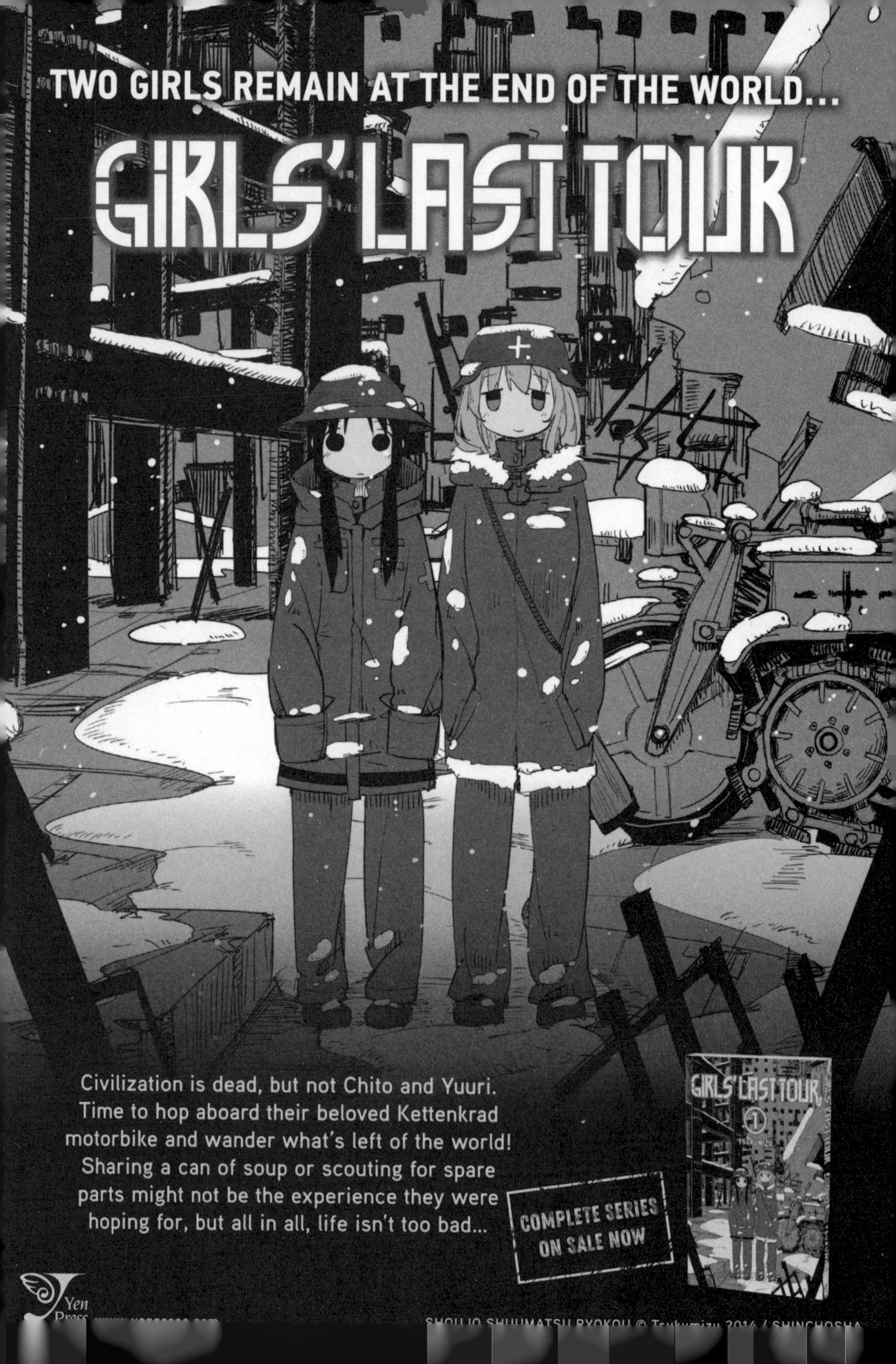
TWO GIRLS REMAIN AT THE END OF THE WORLD...
GIRLS' LAST TOUR
Civilization is dead, but not Chito and Yuuri. Time to hop aboard their beloved Kettenkrad motorbike and wander what's left of the world! Sharing a can of soup or scouting for spare parts might not be the experience they were hoping for, but all in all, life isn't too bad...
COMPLETE SERIES ON SALE NOW
GIRLS' LAST TOUR
1
TSUKUMIZU
Yen Press
SHOUJO SHUUMATSU RYOKOU © Tsukumizu 2014 / SHINCHOSHA

The legends foretold of six heroes awakening to save the world...

# BUT IT NEVER SPECIFIED WHAT TO DO WITH SEVEN!

The manga adaptation of the super-popular light novel series!

When the world is threatened with destruction, six chosen heroes will rise to save it. One of them is Adlet Meyer, who calls himself "the strongest man in the world." But when he answers the call to assemble with the other heroes and face the darkness, there are not six heroes but seven. Who is the traitor in their midst?

# ROKKA: Braves of the Six Flowers

©Aidalro/SQUARE ENIX

VOLUMES
1-8  IN STORES
NOW!

VOLUMES 1-13
AVAILABLE DIGITALLY!

# Toilet-bound Hanako-Kun

At Kamome Academy, rumors abound about the school's Seven Mysteries, one of which is Hanako-san. Said to occupy the third stall of the third floor girls' bathroom in the old school building, Hanako-san grants any wish when summoned. Nene Yashiro, an occult-loving high school girl who dreams of romance, ventures into this haunted bathroom...but the Hanako-san she meets there is nothing like she imagined! Kamome Academy's Hanako-san...is a boy!

Yen Press

For more information
visit www.yenpress.com

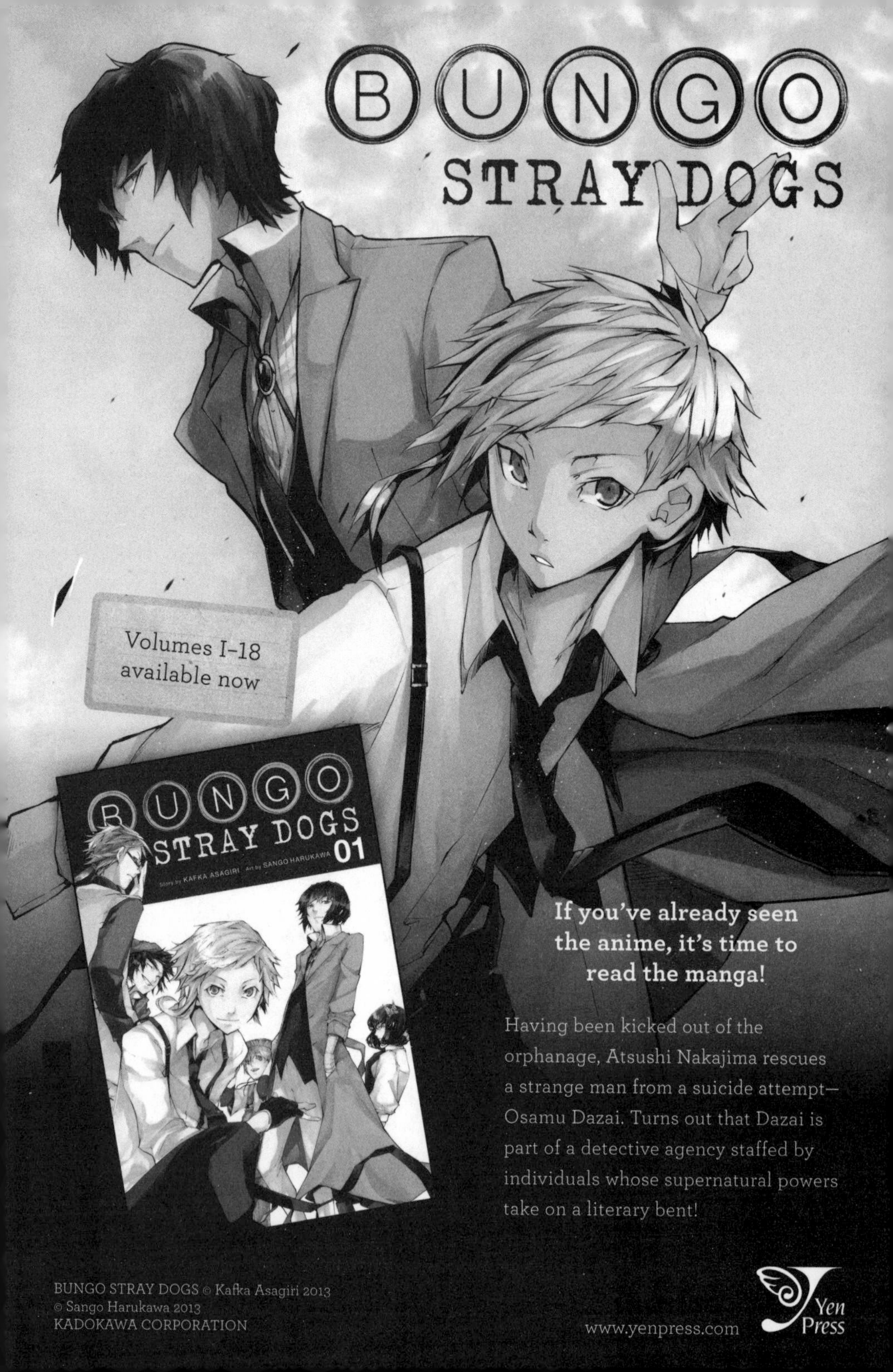
BUNGO
STRAY DOGS
Volumes 1–18
available now
BUNGO
STRAY DOGS
01
Story by KAFKA ASAGIRI Art by SANGO HARUKAWA
If you've already seen the anime, it's time to read the manga!
Having been kicked out of the orphanage, Atsushi Nakajima rescues a strange man from a suicide attempt—Osamu Dazai. Turns out that Dazai is part of a detective agency staffed by individuals whose supernatural powers take on a literary bent!
BUNGO STRAY DOGS © Kafka Asagiri 2013
© Sango Harukawa 2013
KADOKAWA CORPORATION
www.yenpress.com
Yen Press

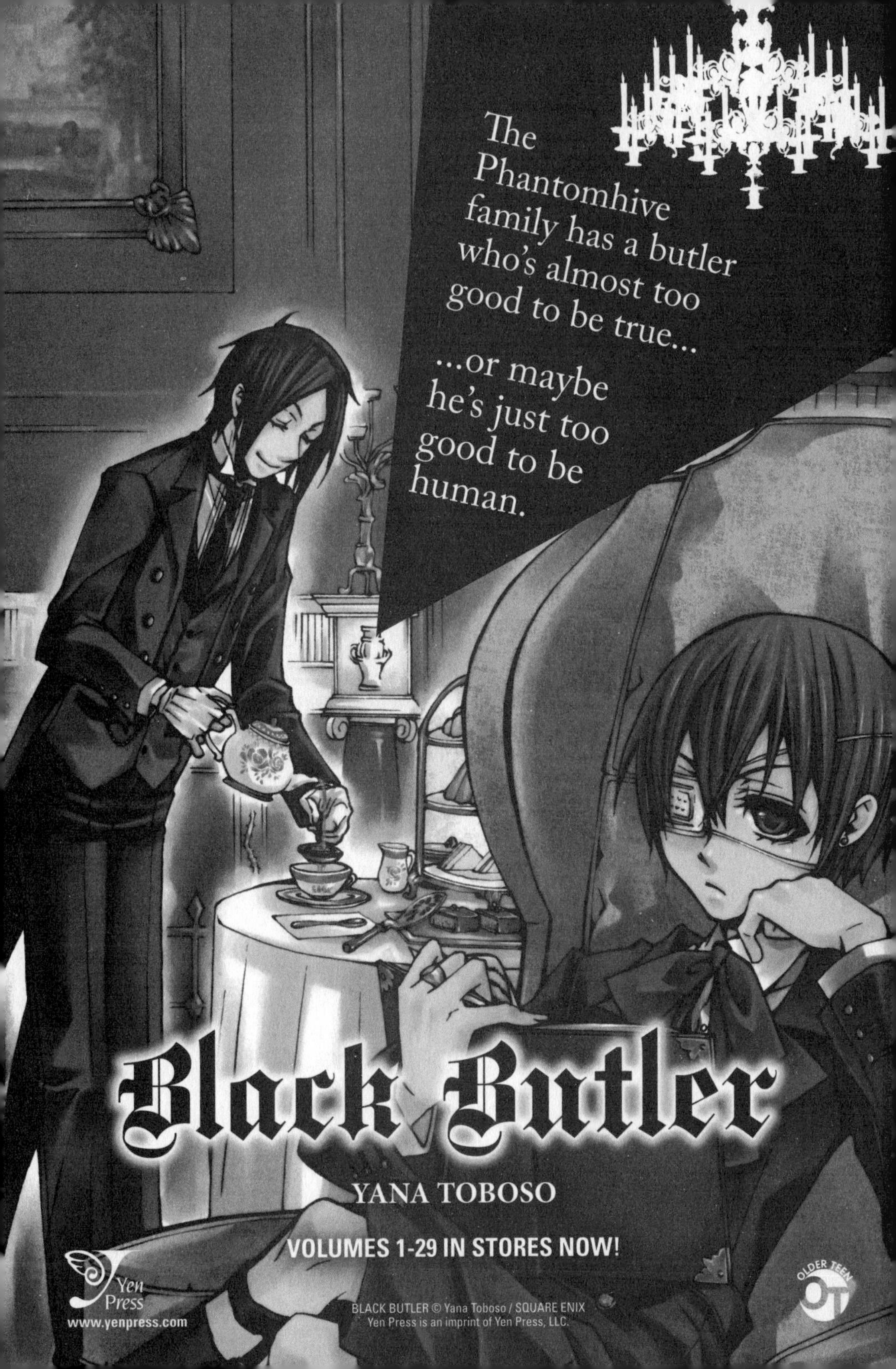
The Phantomhive family has a butler who's almost too good to be true...
...or maybe he's just too good to be human.
Black Butler
YANA TOBOSO
VOLUMES 1-29 IN STORES NOW!
Yen Press
www.yenpress.com
BLACK BUTLER © Yana Toboso / SQUARE ENIX
Yen Press is an imprint of Yen Press, LLC.
OLDER TEEN
OT

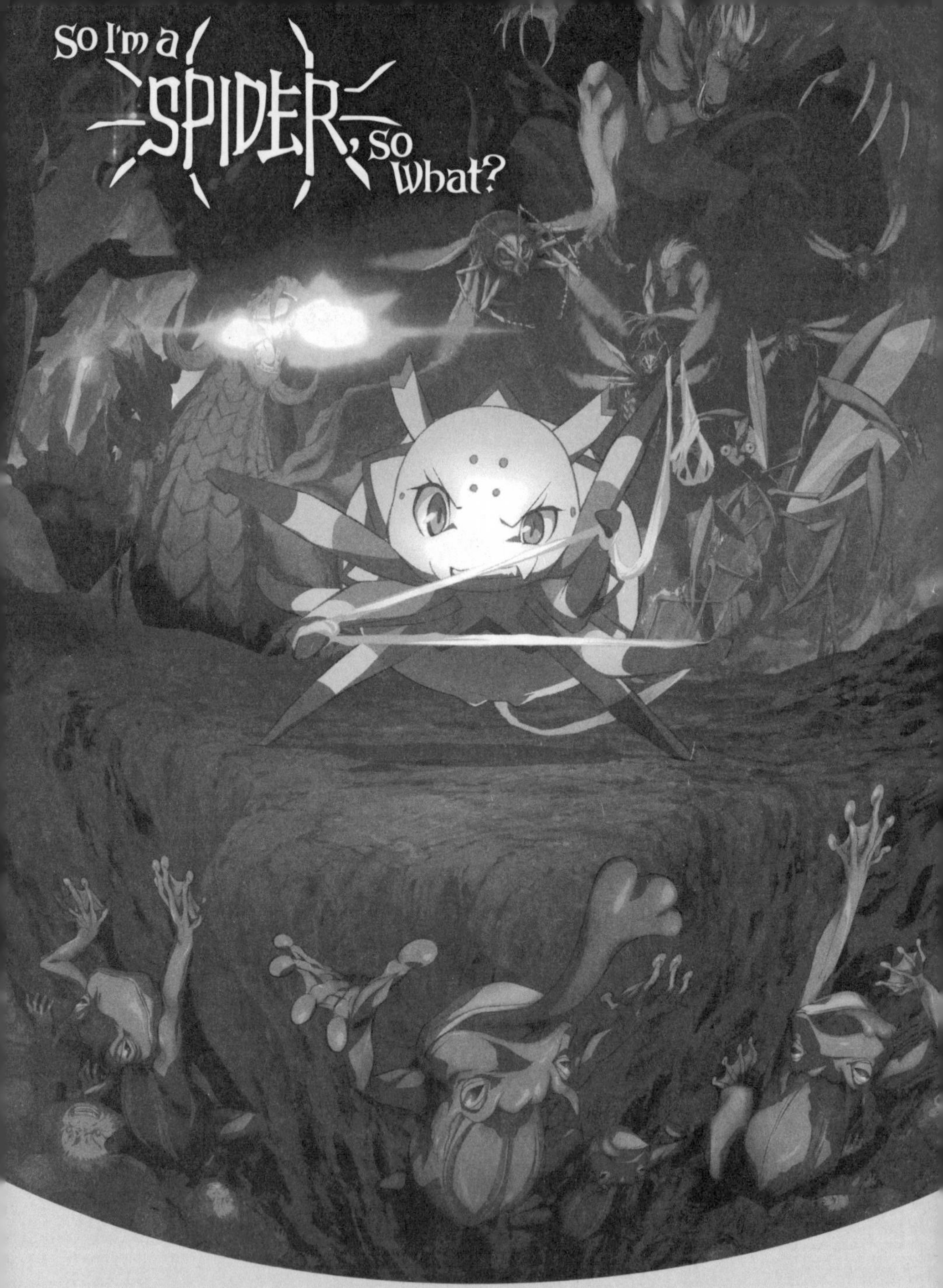
So I'm a SPIDER, so What?

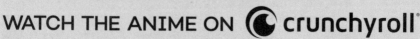

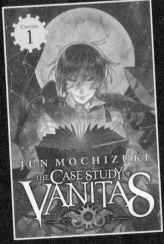

## KARNEVAL 11

### Touya Mikanagi

Translation: Alexandra McCullough-Garcia    Lettering: Phil Christie

Karneval vols. 21-22 © 2018 by Touya Mikanagi. All rights reserved. First published in Japan in 2018 by Ichijinsha Inc. Tokyo. Publication rights for this English edition arranged through Kodansha Ltd., Tokyo.

English translation © 2021 by Yen Press, LLC

Yen Press
150 West 30th Street, 19th Floor
New York, NY 10001

Visit us at yenpress.com • facebook.com/yenpress • twitter.com/yenpress • yenpress.tumblr.com • instagram.com/yenpress

First Yen Press Edition: March 2021

Yen Press is an imprint of Yen Press, LLC.
The Yen Press name and logo are trademarks of Yen Press, LLC.

The publisher is not responsible for websites (or their content) that are not owned by the publisher.

Library of Congress Control Number: 2016936531

ISBNs: 978-1-9753-1701-0 (paperback)
978-1-9753-2313-4 (ebook)

10 9 8 7 6 5 4 3 2 1

WOR

Printed in the United States of America